JOHN BETJEMAN

JOHN BETJEMAN
New Fame, New Love

BEVIS HILLIER

Item to John Betjeman (the most
Remarkable man of his time in any position)
We leave a Leander tie and Pugin's ghost
And a box of crackers and St Pancras Station
And the *Church of Ireland Gazette* and our confidence
That he will be master of every situation.

W.H. Auden and Louis MacNeice, 'Auden and MacNeice: Their Last Will
and Testament', *Letters from Iceland*, London 1937

JOHN MURRAY
Albemarle Street, London

First published in 2002
by John Murray (Publishers) Ltd.,
50 Albemarle Street, London W1S 4BD

Reprinted 2002

A catalogue record for this book is available from the British Library

ISBN 0-7195-5002 5

Typeset in 11.5/12.75 Monotype Sabon by Servis Filmsetting Ltd., Manchester

Printed and bound in Great Britain by Butler and Tanner Ltd., Frome and London

In affectionate memory of
Jock Murray,
publisher and friend

CONTENTS

ILLUSTRATIONS

The author and publishers would like to thank the following for permission to reproduce illustrations: Plate 1, BBC Photograph Library; 8, Michael Parkin Fine Art Ltd; 10, Mrs Sibyl Harton; 15, Noel Blakiston; 16, Christie's Images; 18, 20 and 21, Faringdon Estate; 27, Dallas Bower Esq; 28 and 29, *Weekly Illustrated*; 30, John Murray Archive; 37 and 38, Mrs Betty Packford; 44, National Buildings Record; 45, Mr Patrick Cullinan; 51, Douglas Glass/Sunday Times © News International; 53 and 54, Mrs Anne Dalgety; 55, Anthony Barnes Esq; 59, William Glenton; 63, Cincinnati Historical Society; 64 and 65, Mrs Van Meter Ames; 66, Mrs Elizabeth Bettman; 69, The Times © News International; 71, Doris Lurot Betjeman.

PREFACE

A recently published scientific book was described as 'long awaited, long despaired of' – a phrase which, in its neat trochaic cadence, might be the beginning of a Victorian hymn. In 1988, reviewing *Young Betjeman*, the first volume of this biographical trilogy, Professor John Carey was kind enough to write: 'It will be hard to wait patiently for Volume II.' I am afraid that he and others have had to wait. I have now devoted over twenty-five years of my life to the seventy-eight of John Betjeman's: if it did not seem disrespectful, not to say self-congratulatory, I might adapt the Kohima memorial epitaph, and claim: 'For your yesterday I gave my today.'

Because there has been such a gap between the two volumes, and because I cannot be sure that every reader of this book has read *Young Betjeman*, I am inclined to recapitulate some of the things I wrote in the preface to that volume. First, this is not a 'critical biography': I feel that that is a bastard art-form, yoking two disciplines that do not belong together – historical narrative and literary criticism. It is like the intrusion of a reporter's political views into a news story. However, the creative process and the editing, publishing and critical reception of a poet's work *are* part of his life, and are therefore included, as are chapters on his book-reviewing, his broadcasting and his *Spectator* column.

Those who would prefer a short, compact biography of Betjeman – 'A shilling life will give you all the facts' – should be advised that two such books exist: Derek Stanford's *John Betjeman* (1961) and Patrick Taylor-Martin's *John Betjeman: His Life and Work* (1983). And for those who find the written word itself too taxing, my own *John Betjeman: A Life in Pictures* (1984) tells the story in photographs and drawings, with the minimum of verbiage.

Taylor-Martin modestly begins his book: 'This is not the last word on John Betjeman.' My book will not be the last word either, but I have set out to create a more fully fleshed portrait. At the same time, I am not an admirer of the vacuum-cleaner school of biography. It has also been called the Nennian method, after the medieval Welsh historian Nennius. 'Coacervavi', he coolly admitted, 'omne quod inveni' – 'I have made a heap of all that I have found.' Yet in one sense I feel kinship with Nennius, and with his predecessor Bede: we are not only biographers: we are, willy-nilly, 'sources', too, chroniclers with direct

access to some of the people in our chronicles. I have had advantages
which no future biographer of Betjeman can have: friendship and long
talks with him and his wife Penelope, and interviews with many of his
friends and associates.

There are two ways of writing a biography. One is the strictly
chronological, in which one simply sets down the events in a person's
life in the exact order in which they happened. The other is the 'tectonic' method – a series of overlapping plates like those on an
armadillo's back. The chronological system has its virtues: as in a train
going through stations, you always know just where you are. But a
biographer is only as good as his sources; we do not have a precisely
detailed 'time-map' of most people's lives. And even if I knew what
John Betjeman was doing on every day of his life, I would still prefer
the tectonic method. Like the armadillo's back, it is flexible. While
living in Uffington, Berkshire, Betjeman became film critic of the
Evening Standard, worked as a publicist for Shell and began editing the
Shell county guides, sired a son, made friends with John and Myfanwy
Piper, published two books of poetry and a book on Oxford, edited a
magazine called *Decoration*, made radio and television broadcasts,
and served in the Observer Corps and in the Ministry of Information
before leaving for a post in Ireland, with his family, in 1941.

To attempt to draw together all these strands in a day-by-day calendar would be a recipe for muddle. Also, some of these aspects of
Betjeman's life need supporting explanation. For example, in covering
his film criticisms, one needs to know the stage that film-making had
reached in America and Britain; who his fellow critics were; how a 'documentary' movement was developing; and how the 'purity campaign'
enforced by the Hays' Office Code affected the movie industry. This
material would seem out of place if it suddenly irrupted into a day-by-
day account; but it fits in well if Betjeman's film-reviewing (1934–35) is
treated as one of the parterres into which his life naturally divides. The
time-frame of this volume is 1934 to 1958, but sometimes I have trespassed beyond it. I have reached back, in a chapter on Betjeman as conservationist, to show the spring – and springs – of his taste, and again
in a chapter on his early broadcasting, which began in 1932.

Elsewhere, I have tracked forward a little, to round off an episode.
Betjeman's reviewing for the *Daily Telegraph*, though it began in the
1950s, lasted into the Sixties and will be covered in the third volume,
as will his 'Men and Buildings' column in that newspaper. Also,
although he co-founded the Victorian Society in 1957, most of its campaigns were fought in later years; so they, too, will be treated in the
final volume, together with Betjeman's long-running feud with
Nikolaus Pevsner.

In the years that have intervened between *Young Betjeman* and this volume, Betjeman's daughter, Candida Lycett Green, has made a masterly job of editing his letters. Not only has she been indefatigable in corralling letters from all periods of his life; her introductions to each section are written with a chip-off-the-old-block vividness, elegance and sensitivity. The passages about the years in which she knew him are, of course, specially illuminating. Naturally I have drawn on her two volumes – as she drew on my first volume in her first – and I acknowledge the debt with much gratitude.

John Betjeman authorized this biography in 1976. 'Authorized' does not mean 'bowdlerized' or 'censored'. He created his own myth through his writings and his television stardom. The myth was nearer reality than most myths are: in general, he was as likable as he seemed. There may be some for whom the revealing of any flaw in him will seem the desecration of a national monument; but I have no training as a hagiographer. I have tried only to discover the truth and to tell it. For myself, I can say of my subject what his contemporary A.J.P. Taylor wrote in the preface to a life of Betjeman's sometime employer Lord Beaverbrook: 'I loved the man.'

Perhaps I should add, in view of the hiatus between this volume and the last, that the third (and final) volume – nearly completed – will be published in about a year's time. It will contain a bibliography.

THE STORY SO FAR

John Betjeman is born in north London on 28 August 1906, the only child of Ernest Betjemann (thus spelt) and his wife Bess. The Betjeman(n) family is probably of German origin but in the anti-German frenzy of the First World War it claims to be Dutch. Ernest is the third generation to run a London cabinet-making firm. Its products include smart dressing-tables, games boxes and tantaluses sold at Asprey's, sometimes to maharajahs. Ernest fervently hopes John will follow him into the firm as 'the fourth generation', but as a child John shows himself hopelessly unhandy with a chisel. At an early age he is convinced that he will be a poet. A lonely child, he treats his teddy-bear, Archibald Ormsby-Gore ('Archie'), as an intimate – a make-believe sustained all his life and borrowed by his friend Evelyn Waugh for the character of Lord Sebastian in *Brideshead Revisited*.

John first attends Byron House, a Highgate nursery school, where he falls in love with a girl called Peggy Purey-Cust. Then he moves to Highgate Junior School where the young T.S. Eliot is a master. John presents him with *The Best Poems of Betjeman* but Eliot tactfully makes no comment. John goes on to the Dragon School, Oxford, where Hugh Gaitskell, the future Labour leader, is a fellow pupil and friend. John shines in acting and has poems published in the school magazine. Already he is exploring and learning about architecture. While he is at the Dragon School the Betjeman family moves to Church Street, Chelsea. Holidays are in north Cornwall, where Ernest builds a house. Later, Cornwall becomes John's second home.

From 1922 to 1925 he is at Marlborough College – then more like a concentration camp than a school – with the poets Louis MacNeice and Bernard Spencer, the art historians Anthony Blunt and Ellis Waterhouse, the future film stars James Mason and James Robertson Justice, the historian John Bowle, and Graham Shepard, son of the illustrator of the Pooh Bear books. John is regarded as a clown and a bit of a dunce (he loathes the sarcastic classics master A.R. Gidney) but wins a poetry prize, is acclaimed as an actor and co-founds *The Heretick*, a rival to the school magazine. He falls in love with another boy, Donovan Chance.

John scrapes into Magdalen College, Oxford, in 1925 and reads English. Here he blooms and makes such friends for life as Maurice Bowra, Osbert Lancaster, John Sparrow and Kenneth Clark. He is something of a tuft-hunter, seeking the friendship of Irish aristocrats in whose country houses he stays – the Marquess of Dufferin and Ava, Edward, Earl of Longford, Lord Clonmore and Pierce Synnott – and of the millionaire Edward James. Patrick Balfour (later Lord Kinross) is also a close friend. John acts in the Oxford University Dramatic Society and edits *The Cherwell*, the University magazine. But again he does not excel academically; he hates his tutor, C.S. Lewis. He fails a divinity examination ('Divvers'), in spite of his lifelong interest in, and devotion to, religion and the Church, and leaves without a degree.

He takes two prep-school teaching jobs, an unorthodox but inspiring master; becomes private secretary to the Irish statesman Sir Horace Plunkett; and joins the staff of *The Architectural Review*, where he is expected to champion the Modern Movement. Following the example of his friend the architectural writer P. Morton Shand, he claims as pioneers of the Modern Movement architects and designers he really admires – Voysey, Ashbee and Lutyens. His first book of poems, *Mount Zion*, is published by Edward James in 1931; his book on architecture and style, *Ghastly Good Taste*, in 1933.

From the late 1920s on, he pursues aristocratic 'gels' – Camilla Russell, Lady Mary St Clair Erskine, Pamela Mitford and Penelope Chetwode, daughter of Sir Philip (later Lord) Chetwode, Commander-in-Chief of the Army in India. The Chetwodes regard him as a scruffy and penniless journalist and would prefer Penelope to find 'somebody with a pheasant shoot'. Penelope herself is torn between love for John and a desire to become an Indologist. The courtship is stormy. Penelope, in her torturing indecision, takes refuge with an aunt in the south of France. At the urging of Nancy Mitford, John follows her there and they agree to marry. There is a backsliding by John when, during Penelope's absence in India, he becomes engaged to one of her best friends, Wilhelmine (Billa) Cresswell (later Lady Harrod), but Penelope wins him back and the three remain great friends. John and Penelope marry clandestinely at Edmonton in 1933. In the autumn of that year, Penelope breaks the news to her dismayed parents. The couple live first in a little flat near the British Museum, next in St John's Wood, then in a street off the Strand.

1

UFFINGTON

Stuart, I sit here in a grateful haze
Recalling those spontaneous Berkshire days
In straw-thatched,
        chalk-built,
                pre-war
                        Uffington
Before the March of Progress had begun,
When all the world seemed waiting to be won,
When evening air with mignonette was scented,
And 'picture-windows' had not been invented,
When shooting foxes still was thought unsporting,
And White Horse Hill was still the place for courting,
When church was still the usual place for marriages
And carriage-lamps were only used for carriages . . .

John Betjeman, in *To Illustrate the Monuments: Essays on Archaeology
Presented to Stuart Piggott*, ed. J.V.S. Megaw, London 1976

In 1934 Neville Chamberlain, then Chancellor of the Exchequer, announced that the country had finished the story of *Bleak House* and could now sit down to enjoy the first chapter of *Great Expectations*.[1] The allusion would have been widely understood if only because, in the newspaper war of 1932–3, the *Daily Express* and the *Daily Herald* had vied with each other in giving their registered readers free sets of Dickens;[2] but the remark did not hold good for everyone. This was a year of mass unemployment and hunger marches.[3]

To John Betjeman, however, Chamberlain's comment might have seemed apt. The year 1934 brought three great changes in his life. In January he was appointed film critic of the London *Evening Standard* at a salary of over £800 a year – at that time, a high income for a man of twenty-seven.* (A year later, when the *Morning Post* sent the young William Deedes to cover Italy's war against Abyssinia – an episode embalmed in Evelyn Waugh's novel *Scoop* – Deedes thought his £15 a

---

* See Chapter 2, 'Film Critic'.

week 'good money'.)[4] The staff post marked the beginning of John's public fame. His first book of poems, *Mount Zion* (1931), and his light-hearted book about architecture, *Ghastly Good Taste* (1933), had won him a small following; but now he was writing for a leading London paper and his verdicts on films were placarded outside the capital's cinemas.

In February, John and Penelope moved to the village of Uffington, Berkshire.[5] For the first time they had a house, not just a flat. Up to then, apart from his Oxford years and his holidays in Cornwall and Ireland, John had been essentially a 'townie'. His tastes were metro-politan; most of his friends and interests were in London. Now he had suddenly to adapt to country life – though, as his job took him to London, he was still to be seen at the Café Royal and Boulestin's[6] and in the cocktail bars of the Dorchester and the Savoy.

In June John's father died. In 1927 when Ernest Betjemann's heart trouble had been diagnosed, John's anticipation of his death had been distasteful, almost vulturine.[7] But now the sense of release he felt at the eclipse of a figure who had seemed to him unsympathetic and domineering was gradually overtaken by feelings of guilt – not only regret at having failed to love or honour his father, but guilt at letting down the workers at G. Betjemann & Sons. For this was the time when, if he had been the 'handy-andy' son his father might have pre-ferred,[8] John would have taken over the running of the family firm as 'the fourth generation'.[9]

Christian Barman ('Barmy') of *The Architectural Review*, who lived in Uffington, had found a house there for John and Penelope, a modest building in the high street called Garrards Farm. Late in 1933, John had gone to Uffington to make the house ready, while Penelope spent three months in Germany taking a course in German to enable her to study the leading works on Indian culture and archi-tecture in that language. Choosing between marriage to John and a career as an Indologist had been an acute dilemma for Penelope – one that their clandestine wedding in July 1933 had not resolved. She felt she could both be a wife to John and become a scholar. 'Filth [Penelope] is still culture crazy,' John wrote to his friend Bryan Guinness in September 1933;[10] the Betjemans' daughter Candida Lycett Green goes so far as to suggest that 'my mother did indeed prefer her Indian studies to JB's affections', adding that Penelope's sojourn in Berlin left John feeling 'desperately insecure', even though it had the blessing of the couple's 'listening-post', P. Morton Shand.[11]

If Penelope could desert the marriage for a spell, so could John. To help get the Uffington farmhouse straight, he employed a pretty girl with dark brown hair called Molly Higgins. He had an affair with her and at once admitted it to Penelope – perhaps in a spirit as much of tit-for-tat as of contrition.[12] Penelope wrote to him from Germany: 'I did not realise until I got yours this mornin' that you were actually in love with Molly H. I thought you might be but did not let myself think that you really were.'[13] She in turn confessed that she had been attracted by other people while in Berlin. She had resisted the temptations.[14] By the time Penelope came back to England in January 1934, John's affair with Molly Higgins was over. He was probably referring to it when he wrote to Bryan Guinness on 14 January:

I am still distressed about my apparently strange behaviour with Our Little Friend. I must state here in clear type that I am not in love with her although I am sure I should be very happy were I in such a state. No. I merely find her a companion of an almost male order of intelligence and sympathy and therefore take pleasure in her company. Her physical charms cannot rival those of Philth.[15]

On 20 January, a Saturday, John wrote to Guinness again, to say that Penelope was coming back from Germany on the Thursday. He asked if they might spend the weekend at Biddesden, Guinness's house in Hampshire. He added: 'I shall go, I think, to the Charing Cross Hotel for the coming week as I am very fond of it there and like the sense of an impending journey there is about an hotel on the railway.'[16] Penelope's attitude to the approaching reunion was curiously negligent. Considering that she was the wronged party, her next letter to John from Berlin was oddly submissive and propitiatory. 'Darling, I'm so relieved you say I can come back. I think you will find it will work alright, anyway on my side now.'[17] But she also wrote: 'I hope you'll be happy with me but if you aren't you can always go off with M.H. [Molly Higgins].'[18] In spite of the bantering tone, there is a snook-cocking casualness about this, an air of 'Take me or leave me'. When, in the middle of her engagement to John in 1933, he had suddenly written to say he was marrying 'Billa' Harrod instead, Penelope had sent him a frantic telegram from India: 'Do nothing until you hear from me. I know I can make you happy.'[19] The ardent note of that message was absent from this new one. As it turned out, Penelope made friends with Molly Higgins, who sometimes stayed at the farmhouse and was no longer a threat.[20] Somehow the assertion of independence by both John and Penelope seemed to have strengthened their marriage rather than exposed it as fragile – as it were, the aircraft could still fly on a single engine when the other failed, could glide when both engines were down.

The Betjemans went to Uffington early in February. One of the first

people to see them was Ken Freeman, who was eight years old. His
father was the village carrier and drove the couple's furniture in his
lorry from Uffington station to their new house. Ken had recently
fallen over on his way to school. He had hurt his knee and a lump had
come up in his groin. He was laid out on a chair-bed on the lawn in
front of his parents' house, Vale Cottage. John stopped outside with
his hand on the wall and asked how he was. John and Penelope chatted
away to the boy, and word went round the village that the newcomers
seemed pleasant.[21]

Uffington village, in the Vale of the White Horse, had changed little
since Thomas Hughes described it in *Tom Brown's Schooldays* (1857).
Although the railway had reached Uffington, it was a place of extreme
rurality; it still is. Above, on the Berkshire Downs, was the White
Horse carved through the turf into the chalk, the one genuinely
ancient white horse in Britain, predating by centuries the impostor of
Westbury that John had known in his Marlborough schooldays. The
periodic ceremony of scouring the horse, described by Hughes in
another book and illustrated by Dicky Doyle (the designer of *Punch*'s
cover), was still kept up.

The White Horse was an appropriate emblem for the terrain, since
Uffington was in the heart of 'horsey' country, within easy reach of the
trainers at Lambourne. It was the country of the Old Berkshire Hunt,
which in the nineteenth century had raced from Swindon to Hyde Park
Corner in London.[22] The Betjemans' years together were all to be
spent in Berkshire, first in Uffington, then in Farnborough and finally
in Wantage, the largest town in the district. Their being uprooted from
London and plunged into the centre of horse country did not benefit
the marriage. Penelope was 'mad on' horses and was in her element in
the world of hunts and gymkhanas. John was not only uninterested in
horses, he actively disliked them. When Penelope asked him to hold the
reins of a horse for a photograph, he scowled into the camera lens with
theatrical grumpiness. The couple's divergence of interests put strain
on the marriage from the outset. Thirty years later, when a Wantage
neighbour, Jessie Sharley, came to the Betjemans' house after church
one Sunday and Penelope was nowhere to be seen, John remarked after
a while, 'If we were horses, Jessie, we'd have had a cup of tea by now.'[23]
But the marriage's loss was poetry's gain. John's reluctant encounters
with horseflesh led to such masterpieces of hippophobic satire as
'Hunter Trials' and 'Winthrop Mackworth Redivivus' and the tragi-
comic lines inspired by a trainer's gravestone –

Leathery limbs of Upper Lambourne,
Leathery skin from sun and wind,

Leathery breeches, spreading stables,
Shining saddles left behind . . .[24]

Because Molly Higgins and John had not altogether concentrated their energies on getting Garrards Farm shipshape, a lot still needed to be done in the house before the Betjemans could move in. They stayed at the Craven Arms for a week while painting and cleaning were completed and Penelope supervised the arrangement of the furniture. The Earl of Craven for whose ancestor the inn was named owned large estates in and around Uffington, including Garrards Farm, let to Farmer John Wheeler, who sub-let it to John and Penelope. There were two local legends about the Craven family. One told of the Curse of the Cravens, which caused every male heir to die before the age of twenty-one. (That was an exaggeration, though several of the heirs did die young, one by drowning.) The other rumour was that the Earl received a token £5 a year from the tobacco company Carreras for the use of his name on packets of Craven 'A' cigarettes – the brand mentioned by John in his wartime poem 'Invasion Exercise on the Poultry Farm'.

Garrards Farm is a white clunch building with brick dressings round the casement windows. With it, in 1934, came a few acres of fields, some outbuildings and the stables where Penelope kept Moti, the Arab gelding her father had given her. The two main rooms of the farmhouse were on either side of the front door. Another room faced you as you entered the house, but Penelope requisitioned that as a harness room. Most of the rooms were decorated with William Morris wallpapers; 'My mother even had a dressing-gown made of the "bird and anemone" design,' Candida writes.[25] Some of the villagers were scandalized by a mural John painted above the dining-room chimneypiece. The subject, perhaps emblematic of the Dutch ancestry that he claimed, was 'a naked lady with *art nouveau*-ish tulips growing out of her'.[26] The dining-room table was by Betjemann & Sons; the rush-seated, ladderback chairs – a wedding-present from Mrs Dugdale of Sezincote – were designed by Ernest Gimson.[27] John did his writing in his dressing-room upstairs, where the curtains were by Voysey and he had to move the bed to get papers out of a cupboard.[28]

The house was lit only by oil lamps.[29] When Penelope's father, the field-marshal, visited the couple, he insisted on staying at the Fox and Hounds across the road because he could not stand 'those stinkin' lamps'.[30] There were other smells too. Penelope kept a goat in the yard, as somebody had told her that goats' milk was better for humans than cows'. Snowdrop the goat was allowed to come in and out of the house and it was not unusual to find chickens indoors too. 'Penelope

Title-pages of Thomas Hughes's The Scouring of the White Horse *(1859)*

invented "free range" long before anybody thought up the expression,'
said Osbert Lancaster. 'The place was an animal sanctuary – and it
stank.'[31]

John asked Ernie Evans, the landlord of the Craven Arms, if he
would let his bright teenage daughters, Gwen and Betty, come and
work at Garrards Farm. 'Dad was a bit Victorian,' Betty Evans (now
Mrs Packford) recalled. 'He said, "Boys can go out to work, girls
can't" – you know, he worked in the bar where, in those days, girls were
never seen. But mother persuaded him that it would be very nice for
us and would bring in some extra money.'[32] So Gwen became the
Betjemans' cook and Betty made the beds and waited at table. Later,
after the girls left, the Betjemans took on a German maidservant,
Paula Steinbrecher, who stayed for a year. When she arrived she spoke
no English. For a long time she thought John's name was 'Shutup', as
Penelope said that to him so often.[33]

Already, in the week John and Penelope had spent at the Craven
Arms, the locals had had the chance to size up the extraordinary pair
who had landed in their midst. The regulars in the bar found that John
was well able to match them in drinking; better still, he was lordly in
buying rounds. He joined in a game of darts and amused the other
players by throwing underarm. He was equally unorthodox in playing
bar billiards, as Betty Packford remembers: 'He never aimed for the
pots like anybody else. He always aimed for the black mushrooms
which you weren't supposed to knock down. He used to tickle 'em to
death, they'd roar with laughter.'[34] Ron Liddiard, the young son of a
farmer in nearby Baulking, concluded that 'Here were some people
the like of which we hadn't seen before.'[35]

The couple attended Uffington Church, 'the Cathedral of the
Vale' – a cruciform building which John considered 'the best and most
complete' Early English church in the county, even though the pinna-
cles of the south porch had been knocked off when the tower spire
crashed in the eighteenth century. He became people's warden.[36] The
vicar was the Rev. George Bridle, an elderly bachelor – '*very* unmarried', as somebody described him. 'The old Reverend Bridle, he wasn't
a ladies' man,' Ron Liddiard said.[37] Ken Freeman recalled: 'He
wouldn't have a lady in the house, not to live or work for him. When
he first came to Uffington he had a manservant, did his cooking and
played the organ. Then he had a couple of boys out of Uffington, sang
in the choir, they worked for him. One was Arthur Iles . . . the other
was Eric Ayres, a cousin of Pam Ayres's father.'[38] In the 1970s Pam
Ayres, the daughter of an Uffington man, was to become almost as
famous a 'television poet' as John Betjeman, reading her own verse in
the loamy Berkshire accent in which 'fire' becomes 'foire'.

Freeman was not allowed to sing in the choir at Uffington Church because the Rev. Mr Bridle said he grunted like a pig. He was given the job of ringing the bell before the service. 'After church, pretty well every Sunday morning,' Freeman remembered, 'I'd go round with John Betjeman and one or two of the boys in the choir . . . We'd go round to Garrards Farm and go up into his study, and he'd get his cigarette cards out. He was a chain smoker, if I remember rightly. We'd get these cigarette cards out on the table and we'd swap them.'[39] John did not exchange the cards in a patronizing way. He was as keen to make up sets of film stars and locomotives as the boys were. Self-confessedly a case of 'arrested development' ('arrested about the age of thirteen, I suppose'), he got on well with children by remaining, in some degree, a child.

George Packford, who later married Betty Evans, introduced John to bell-ringing. 'John wanted to know what was going on up in the belfry. So I said, "Well, come up and see." . . . "Ooh," he said. "That looks easy!" So I said, "Have a go." He got the rope round his neck, would have nearly hanged his blooming self in a minute or two. So I twisted it back quickly and got it off. He said, "I don't think much of that!" I said: "Well, if you do the same as we do you'll be all right." . . . He thought he'd have another go. So we stuck him on number one, but he got tangled up again.'[40] John did eventually master the art of bell-ringing, after a fashion. What he learned from the Uffington ringers enabled him to set out, in his poem 'Bristol', the precise changes of 'the mathematic pattern of a plain course on the bells'. The book in which that poem appeared was called *New Bats in Old Belfries* and he gave his verse autobiography the title *Summoned by Bells*. His poem 'Uffington' begins:

> Tonight we hear the muffled peal
> Hang on the village like a pall;
> It overwhelms the towering elms –
> That death-reminding dying fall . . .[41]

John and Penelope started an Uffington Parochial Youth Fellowship. John was listed as president on the printed events card, but Penelope did most of the organizing. 'I think the Betjemans did more good for Uffington than anybody else,' Freeman said. 'They brought the place alive. Pre-war, there was nothing going on. After the First World War there'd been a terrible agricultural depression. Even in 1939, a farm-worker's wage was thirty shillings. John and Penelope got things going, especially for us youngsters.'[42] There were talks (Penelope later realized some of them may have been above the heads of the young audience), concerts, plays, tennis tournaments and garden fêtes. Every year a concert was held in the village hall in February or March.

> One sticks out in my mind more than the others [Ken Freeman said]. They hired a pantomime horse costume from London. George Packford and Arthur Iles were shoved into that, and Mrs Betjeman came in as a fairy in a tutu, sat on the back of George Packford – he was the stronger of the two. In that one I was the ringmaster. I wore a top hat and a tail coat. I had a long whip to flick 'em round.[43]

John's histrionic skills were sometimes conscripted. Ron Liddiard recalled:

> We were rehearsing this sketch. Margaret Norton, an attractive blonde lass, was a star turn in it and I was a convict. Penelope was producing it . . . We weren't very good but we had a lot of fun trying. And in the end we were due on the next night for a dress rehearsal in the village hall, and Penelope said: 'Pathetic! Useless! I don't know what we're going to do,' she said. 'It'll never get by.'
> So we all felt a bit down . . . 'There's only one hope,' she said. 'John comes home from London at six o'clock this evening. If I can get him to have a go at you, then perhaps he might be able to do something with you lot.'
> And he took us over . . . and he gave us a different approach. He showed each of us how to say our words and put meaning into them – the men's parts *and* the women's parts. And we came out thinking he was Gerald du Maurier and Sybil Thorndike rolled into one. He just had that knack.[44]

John liked to bring famous people to the Uffington garden fêtes. These included the French dress designer Schiaparelli and Tom Driberg, who wrote up the fêtes in his 'William Hickey' column in the *Daily Express*. ('The villagers stood aghast at the decorations on Schiaparelli's wrist; she was clanking with charms.')[45]

As well as making life in Uffington more entertaining, John took some of his protégés on jaunts, by river or road. Ken Freeman recalled: 'In the summer evenings the message would come round when I got back from school, "John Betjeman will pick you up at six o'clock tonight." And two or three of us with John, we'd go down to Radcot and he'd hire a punt with the old pole, and we'd go up the river.'[46] Driving the boys to Radcot one day, John was reminded of an accident that had befallen his father-in-law. Ken Freeman remembered: 'The old Field-Marshal used to keep his horses at Garrards. When he stayed at the Fox and Hounds he'd sometimes go hunting. Just before you get to Radcot there is a little back bridge, a very hump bridge, just past

Boulter's Farm. John Betjeman took it one day a bit too fast in the old Ford Prefect; the springs went the same way as the axle – whoop! in the air we went. "I ought to remember that bridge," he said. "My father-in-law was going hunting the other day with his top hat on and he took the bridge too hard. He was jolted up against a branch and his top hat was squashed as flat as a pancake." I have to say, John didn't seem too upset by that accident.'[47]

The most memorable jaunt, for Freeman, took place on an August bank holiday.

On the Friday, I'd gone to bed. About ten o'clock there was a knock on the door. It was John Betjeman . . . I heard him say that he was going to Lyme Regis on the Saturday to judge a town criers' competition and he . . . wondered if I'd like to go with him . . . I said 'Oh, yes please.' So, right, I had to be round at Garrards Farm at half past eight in the morning. He had to be at Lyme Regis, half past two, I think it was.

Anyway, got round there with my little case, pyjamas and slippers; knocked on the door. The car was out in the front all ready to go.

'Ah, Ken,' he said, 'I've been having second thoughts. You'll be on your own all day. Have you got anybody you'd like to take with you?'

So I thought, well, yes, Bill Messenger. I had to run across a couple of fields to get Willie . . . Halfway, about Crewkerne, we stopped for lunch, a pub lunch . . . John had a beer and we had ginger beer – two little stone jars of it with bread roll and cheese and a bit of pickle . . . When we got to Lyme Regis he. . . said, 'Right, boys, what shall we say? – five o'clock?' . . . He put his hand in his pocket and gave us each a pound. A pound in those days was an awful lot of money. You felt you were a millionaire. He said, 'That'll buy your tea and an ice cream.' I think we spent a pound on the teas and split the other pound.

We got back at the time he stated and 'Right,' he said, 'now we'll go for a swim' . . . and he hired a boat. He got hold of the oars and rowed us out a hell of a way. The people on the beach were like little flies. I couldn't swim nor could old Bill. Then he pulled the oars in and . . . took his jacket off, then he took his trousers off. Underneath, he'd got a pair of swimming trunks.

. . . He said, 'Right, boys, see who gets back first.' Over he went. And we had to get back. Can you imagine a young boy, damn' great oars? We'd never rowed a boat before . . . I suppose we thought, well, we had to get there somehow; but the trouble was, to start with, we were going round in circles. Anyway he got back to the beach first, he was waiting for us . . . Coming back towards Dorchester, there was a bed-and-breakfast sign on a farm gate. We went down a track to this old Dorset farmhouse. And we had supper and a glass of cider. And Bill and I had to share a double bed and John Betjeman went in the other room in a single bed. Then, on the Sunday, we came back across country and every village we went through we had to stop and go into church. We went in and he'd say, 'Oh look, how marvellous!'[48]

While making new friends locally, John and Penelope did not lose touch with their old friends. In April 1934 they started a visitors' book. Those who visited them before the end of the year, often staying for a weekend, included Lionel Perry, Billy Clonmore, Noel Blakiston[49] and his wife Georgiana, Frank and Elizabeth Longford, Edward James and Evelyn Waugh. Waugh stayed from 5 to 7 November. Unfortunately there is a gap in his diaries from 18 July 1934 to 7 July 1936, no doubt depriving us of a more than objective description of the Betjeman ménage.

The Betjemans were friendly with the poet–artist–calligrapher David Jones, who was living at Pigotts, Buckinghamshire, with Eric and Mary Gill, their daughter Joan and her husband René Hague. Jones wrote to Hague on 22 November 1934: 'Penelope is coming for me on Saturday morning. I like being there – it's right against the White Horse where Alfred bollocked up the black heathen men – that old GK [Chesterton] carried on about.'[50] Goronwy Rees, the left-wing Fellow of All Souls, stayed the same weekend as Joan Eyres Monsell, 5–7 January 1935. Lady Chetwode was a guest several times that year. Waugh stayed again from 30 March to 1 April. Other visitors of 1935 included Bryan Guinness, Gerald Heard and his friend Christopher Wood, the artist, Osbert and Karen Lancaster, W.H. Auden and Nancy Mitford, who wrote to her sister Diana Guinness on 25 April 1935:

I saw the Betjemans a lot at Easter and dined twice with Gerald [Berners] who had Maimie [Lady Mary Lygon] and Hubert [Duggan] staying with him. The B's took me to see Ashdown and Coles Hill. They had the [Cyril] Connollys who made themselves very agreeable but looked strange in rural surroundings.[51]

On one of the Connollys' visits John and Penelope had a violent row in which they rampaged over the house yelling at each other, passing straight through the bathroom where the Connollys were taking a bath together.[52]

Osbert Lancaster gives a vignette of life with the Betjemans at this time, in their 'charming cottage, stone-walled and Morris-papered':

At that time Uffington was one of the least spoiled villages in Berkshire which on an autumn evening, when the blue smoke was rising gently above the orchards and the thatch and the willow leaves were drifting slowly down, conformed with uncanny exactness to the vision of Eleanor Fortescue Brickdale[53] and might well have been specially commissioned by Messrs Black. This appearance of tranquillity was, however, deceptive, as life for the inhabitants was now no longer the undeviating round of rustic chores to which for generations they had been accustomed; for Penelope combined a missionary zeal for widening the cultural horizons of her rural neighbours with an energy and force of character inherited from her mother, the formidable Marschallin, and under her direction the Uffington Women's Institute became a transforming influence and its ceaseless activities demanded the full co-operation of all her friends. Its members were tirelessly lectured on Nepalese architecture and Indian religions, instructed in the preparation of mayonnaise (which, as none of them ever ate salad, they were rather puzzled to know what to do with) and firmly encouraged to keep and milk goats – animals they quite rightly detested and which regularly chewed up all their chrysanthemums.[54]

In November 1934 *The Sketch*, a *Tatler*-ish glossy magazine, ran a picture feature on the 'Uffington set'. One photograph was captioned 'MR JOHN BETJEMAN, who is definitely one of the Intelligentsia, is the author of "Ghastly Good Taste" and other books. He owns a Teddy bear, "Archie", which he is showing to LADY MARY PAKEN-HAM.' Another picture was of Penelope taking Peter Quennell and his future wife, Marcelle Rothe, for a drive in 'her old-world phaeton', drawn by Moti. In a third photograph, 'VISCOUNTESS HASTINGS is . . . posed with a charming little kitten.' Lady Hastings, the former Cristina Casati, was the wife of the future Earl of Huntingdon. He later married the writer Margaret Lane, who had been a friend of John's at Oxford.

Along with all the Bright Young People from London, one local name appears in the Betjemans' visitors' book: Stuart Piggott the archaeologist, a learned and likeable man who became one of their best friends in Uffington. Piggott, who was twenty-four (the same age as Penelope) in 1934, came of Uffington stock. His grandfather, at the age of ten, had been taken to one of the traditional festive scourings of the White Horse in 1857 by Thomas Hughes.[55] Stuart Piggott's parents moved to Hampshire but he spent many of his school holidays in Uffington with his grandparents and maiden aunts. He was a child prodigy of archaeology. At seventeen he made his first contribution to O.G.S. Crawford's magazine *Antiquity*. In 1931, still only twenty-one, he published an article on the White Horse of Uffington. In 1934, at a dig, Piggott told Reggie Ross Williamson, a friend, that he was going to visit his maiden aunts in Uffington.

And Reggie, who knew John Betjeman from *The Architectural Review*, said, 'You must go and introduce yourself to the Betjemans.' And so I did. I went along to their house about tea time . . . and John came to the door and I introduced myself. But I said, 'Look, I'm sorry, you've obviously got somebody to tea, I'll go off and come back another day.' He said: 'No, for God's sake come in. We've got the prime minister of Nepal here. It's absolute hell. Come and help us out.' This was a wonderful beginning . . . And after that I used to see them fairly often. I'd see the maiden aunts as a duty, and the Betjemans for pleasure.[56]

John and Piggott talked a lot about architecture. 'He got me excited about eighteenth-century buildings. It was the time of the formation of the Georgian Group.'[57] There were lighter-hearted exchanges about poetry, too. John tried out on Piggott – in an exaggerated Scottish accent – a ludicrous parody he had written of Hugh MacDiarmid, the fanatically Scottish poet whom both men thought a pretentious bore. John introduced Piggott to the works of the 'Uranian' poet the Rev. E.E. Bradford.

Both of us knew several of his poems by heart [Piggott recalled in 1989]. I still do. I was enchanted, of course. One of our favourites was:

> Edgar, Edgar, everywhere,
> Carolled out the blackbirds,
> Edgar, Edgar, Edgar, Ed,
> In and out and backwards.
>
> Once a whim for Willy White
> Made me fond of Willy;
> Now seem name and boy alike
> Frivolous and silly.

Bradford was published by some terribly reputable publisher, Longman's or somebody like that. And John found that they still had a lot of unsold stock. So I bought it up. And those copies have got, in the manner of books printed at that period, reviews printed at the end – 'Virile and manly verse' – *Times Literary Supplement*. That pleased John and me very much.[58]

Piggott became Penelope's friend as much as John's. Like her, he was interested in Indian archaeology. They went together to the Royal Academy Indian Exhibition in 1935. At the show, various Indian Army colonels and proconsular figures came up to Penelope and greeted her.

'Congratulations on your marriage, Penelope,' one of them said. 'This your husband?'

'Yes, isn't he *sweet*?' Penelope replied. Afterwards she told Piggott, 'You'd better be John for the afternoon. It'll save a lot of trouble.'[59]

Osbert Lancaster's dictum, that wherever the Betjemans lived they got to know the nobs and cobs, could not be applied to Uffington. Cobs there were aplenty, but no one in Uffington occupied the position of squire. The nearest to a squire were the Misses Butler of the Lodge in Woolstone – 'two good old spinsters', Ron Liddiard said.[60] They reminded John of the Misses Legge who had taught him at Byron House, in that Miss Molly Butler was redoubtable, while Miss Edmée was quiet and gentle and painted watercolours. Candida remembers:

> The formidable Miss Molly who was the more determined of the two had a face like a boot, a huge bulbous nose and stood with her feet at a quarter to three, while Miss Edmée was retiring, thin and wiry and looked like a shrew.[61]

Ron Liddiard said: 'You didn't plant potatoes in your front garden if Miss Molly wanted them in the back.'[62] The Misses Butler punctually collected the rents from their cottages, which ranged from 5s 6d down to 3s 6d for an old widow.[63] Both John and Penelope could do lifelike imitations of the Butlers. Miss Molly had an exaggerated respect for the memory of their late father, a tyrannical Captain Butler. John would mimic her constant cry of 'Father always told us to do this . . . Father always said we had to do that.'[64] In the introduction Penelope contributed to *The White Horse Recipe Book* (1979), she recalled:

> Our greatest culinary treat in those days was to lunch or dine with Miss Molly and Miss Edmée Butler at Woolstone Lodge. Miss Edmée was a superlative cook in the old English country house tradition and her spliced shoulder of lamb was a masterpiece: it took four days to make. She also used to train local girls, and on one occasion a new recruit waited on us at luncheon and held the dish of delicious garden peas (no nasty freezing in those far-off days) well above Miss Edmée's head, who pulled it down to table level while a lot of frantic whispering went on.
>
> On another occasion we were asked to dinner to meet the Misses Butlers' cousin from Camberley.
>
> 'Would you like John to change?' I asked Miss Molly on the telephone.
>
> 'Oh no, he need not bother.'
>
> 'Will your cousin be wearing a dinner jacket?'
>
> 'Oh yes, but he's used to it.'[65]

John greatly took to Ronald and Rachel Bennett of Kingston Warren. 'Ronald Bennett was a racehorse trainer,' Penelope said, 'but he was one of the few people in the "horsey" world that John really liked.'[66] The Betjemans often dined at the Bennetts' house. Sometimes John provided the entertainment at these dinners, by getting local girls to recite Berkshire dialect poems. One girl conscripted for this task was Marcella Ayres (later Mrs Seymour), the daughter of an Uffington farmer. John nicknamed her 'Caramella', perhaps from the sweets she received as a reward for reciting. He trained her to recite the poem 'The Berkshire Pig', which begins:

> Vathers' mothers, mothers' zuns,
> You as loves your little ones,
> Appy piegs among the stubble,
> Listen to a tale of trouble:
> Listen piegs in yard and sty
> How they Berkshire chaps zarde I [treated me].

When Marcella first recited the poem, she pronounced the word 'ones' in a BBC accent, not 'wons', the Berkshire way. 'Mr Betjeman stopped me dead. He made me recite the beginning until I got it right.' There was also trouble with the line 'Till some men with cursèd spite'. That seemed like swearing to Marcella, so she altered 'cursèd' to 'awful'. 'Mr Betjeman wouldn't let me get away with that. I had to say "cursèd".'[67] The routine was that, when dinner at the Bennetts' was over, John would pick up Marcella, she would recite a poem or two, then he would drive her home. 'One morning he came to book me for the evening performance, but I was ramping mad with toothache. He said to my mother, "Give her some Genasprins." My mother had never heard of Genasprins, but I was sent out to get some; and I did recite that evening, and received a small bar of chocolate from Mr Betjeman.'[68] As Anthony Powell once wrote, John had 'a whim of iron'. Mrs Seymour says: 'I had great affection for John Betjeman. There was not much money about and not much joy, in plain English. He would buy toffees and *fling* them on the grass outside the school – then we all scrambled for them.'[69]

At Pusey House, near Faringdon, lived Michael Hornby, heir to the W.H. Smith newsagent and bookstall empire, and his wife Nicolette, a young couple who had married two years before the Betjemans. Penelope had been at school with Nicolette, whom John nicknamed 'Knee Coal'. 'Nicole could be very pompous,' a mutual friend recalled. 'And Penelope would prick any balloon. I remember once

Nicole was being particularly pompous and Penelope said in her frightful cockney voice, "Oh, Ni-cole, do *shut up*! I remember when you put cream buns in your knickers." '[70]

The grandest house in Faringdon, and that which the Betjemans visited most often, was Faringdon House, built about 1780 by one of Britain's more lamentable poets laureate, Benjamin Pye. It was now the home of Gerald Tyrwhitt-Wilson, fourteenth Baron Berners, who had been a diplomat in Constantinople and Rome before inheriting his uncle's title just after the First World War. Berners, an ill-favoured man in his early fifties, lived with a handsome young protégé, Robert Heber Percy, who was known in the Berners circle as 'The Mad Boy'. Heber Percy wore clothes of parakeet brilliance and was given to outbursts of rage. More than once he attempted suicide.[71]

Lord Berners was something more than a dilettante of the arts. He had studied music with Stravinsky and is still well regarded as a Waltonesque composer. In 1934 his first volume of autobiography appeared, *First Childhood*: when John wrote the entry for Berners in the *Dictionary of National Biography*, he referred to the book's 'delightful and deceptively simple style'. Berners also painted, in a manner which those well disposed to him agreed was like Corot's; his limpid oil works included a sketch of Penelope galloping, adapted from a still from a Gaumont-British film. All of Berners's varied works had a tendency towards pastiche and parody. Nancy Mitford, who portrayed him as 'Lord Merlin' in *The Pursuit of Love*, wrote: 'As he was a famous practical joker, it was sometimes difficult to know where jokes ended and culture began. I think he was not always perfectly certain himself.'[72]

Berners's jokes had a strong flavour of camp. He dyed the fantail pigeons at Faringdon saffron yellow, shocking pink and turquoise blue. He had a clavichord in the back of his Rolls-Royce. He drew moustaches on photographs of royalty and played the piano with his bottom. Robert Heber Percy recalled in 1976:

> Gerald used to do this thing on the piano. Walter de la Mare's ' "Is there anybody there?" said the Traveller.' [*Lifelike imitation of Penelope:*] 'Yes, *me*! Penelope Betjeman! 'Ave you ever been 'ere before?' and he used to turn round and sit on the piano with a great thump of discord. He also used to do it with Chopin's Funeral March – Dah, dah de *dah* – the *dah* being a large range of chords played *a posteriori*. That used to make John laugh a bit. Used to make John scream.[73]

One of Berners's jokes was to announce his engagement to the lesbian Violet Trefusis. When a denial was insisted on, he said he would put a notice in *The Times*: 'Lord Berners has left Lesbos for the Isle of Man.'[74]

In 1934–35 Berners built, in the best tradition of eccentric peers, a folly tower. It was designed by the architect Lord Gerald Wellesley (later Duke of Wellington). Berners liked the Gothic style but while he was away in Rome Wellesley built a tall classical tower. On his return, Berners was furious and insisted that a Gothic 'topknot' should be added.[75] It was, and John and Penelope attended the grand opening in 1935. Edward James, John's first publisher, remembered:

> My mother knew Penelope's mother, 'Star' Chetwode [Lady Chetwode], very well. She would say, 'I must ask Star Chetwode's advice about that' – just as she would write in the margin of a poem of mine, 'Very morbid. Must ask Florrie Bridges' – the niece by marriage of Robert Bridges. Lord Berners held a party to celebrate the new folly, and Star arrived, still thinking it deplorable that her daughter had married this 'little Dutchman', John Betjeman. And at the party John got on tremendously with Gerald Wellesley. So Lady Chetwode went round saying, grudgingly, 'Well, I must say, Gerry Wellesley quite likes him.' It was an eye-opener to her, that John was so accepted in that *galère*.[76]

The folly caused the hoped-for outrage in the surrounding country. Miss Lobb, who lived at Kelmscott Manor with William Morris's daughter, May Morris, had campaigned to stop Berners building the tower, as it was (she alleged) going to have a siren and a searchlight on the top which would disturb the patients in the Radcliffe Infirmary – seventeen miles away. Berners, who knew her, wrote to a local paper: 'It would be better if Mr Lobb had ascertained the facts before writing a letter which sounded as though it had emanated from the brain of a crazy spinster.'[77] Miss Lobb had also argued, 'People might commit suicide from it.' So at the bottom of the tower Berners put a notice: 'All persons wishing to commit suicide do so at their own risk.'[78]

In her fictional portrait of Berners, Nancy Mitford noted how surprisingly tolerant were the local gentry of his exotic ways, and even of the folly: 'Though they were puzzled beyond words by the aestheticism and the teases, they accepted him without question as one of themselves. Their families had always known his family . . . He was no upstart . . . simply a sport of all that was most normal in English country life. Indeed, the very folly itself, while considered absolutely hideous, was welcomed as a landmark by those lost on their way home from hunting.'[79]

John wrote an ode on the folly in the manner of Thomas Moore:

> Oh fair be the tower that Lord Berners is rearing
> And fair be the light that illumines its walls
> But fairer to me are the trees in the clearing
> And the firs on the hill top are fairest of all.[80]

A later stanza describes the folly as 'surveying the seats of the baron and serf' – perhaps a *double entendre*?

Berners was delighted to have the Betjemans as neighbours. They were often invited to dinner. Heber Percy noticed that 'Penelope seemed overpowering when John was there, because she really didn't let him get a word in edgeways. John would be telling you about something very interesting when in would come Penelope and tell you a very funny story about what was happening among the chickens or cows; and then John used to subside. Equally, Penelope was tremendous company when *John* wasn't there.'[81]

Heber Percy remembered that, at one dinner-party, John claimed that Sir Walter Scott was a most erotic novelist:

> Gerald said he didn't believe it. So after dinner a volume of Scott was produced and John began reading. After he had been reading for quite a while – innocuous passages about knights and turrets and so on – something perfectly disgusting came out. And then John went on reading again, more tame stuff, when another passage of pure pornography was read out – all of course invented on the spot by John. John completely straight-faced and reading in a soporific voice.[82]

Berners invited the Betjemans to lunches with Aldous Huxley, H.G. Wells and Wells's mistress Baroness Moura Budberg ('Baroness Bedbug', as John called her) and Penelope was deputed to take these celebrities for jaunts in her phaeton. One day Berners invited Penelope to bring Moti into the great hall at Faringdon, with its neo-classical chimneypieces at either end, so that he could paint the horse's portrait with her standing beside it. This diversion was repeated to amuse or shock visitors: a photograph shows Evelyn Waugh sitting beside Moti on the drawing-room carpet, while Penelope and Heber Percy look on.[83]

At Faringdon John and Penelope met the surrealist painter Salvador Dali and his wife Gala. 'Gosh, she was an attractive woman,' Penelope commented. 'Never stopped talking about fur-lined wombs.'[84] Dali had Berners's grand piano placed in the shallow pool on the lawn and chocolate éclairs laid on the black notes.[85] (Berners offered to play 'Eclair de Lune'.)[86] John was much more interested to meet Max Beerbohm. He later wrote:

Most writers, when you meet them in the flesh, are either a disappointment or nothing like what you expect. Max Beerbohm was neither. Round
eyes, round head, neat and careful clothes, slow movements, slow, considered speech, always unruffled and gentle, he was the embodiment of his
exquisite prose and draughtsmanship. I once spent a whole day with him
at Faringdon House, Berkshire, when he was the guest of Lord Berners,
and it was one of the most fulfilled days of my life. I had prepared a lot of
questions about forgotten poets of the Nineties who interest me. He knew
about them all, delicious, revealing personal details, which subsequent
research proved to be quite correct: 'Let me see; ——, didn't he take to
drugs in order to shine at Aubrey Beardsley's parties? I think that was after
he had been rediscovered by Henry Harland and put in *The Yellow Book*.'
'Oh yes, ——. I doubt if he had a Christian name. I know he never wore
a tie.'[87]

John and Max kept in touch: in 1949 the venerable aesthete sent John
a letter about the publisher Leonard Smithers and Theodore
Wratislaw, who figures in John's poem 'On Seeing an Old Poet in the
Café Royal'.[88]

In 1936 John reported to Penelope a unique event in Berners's life,
a speech. It was at the opening of the cinema in Faringdon. Berners,
who was extremely shy in public, prepared it carefully and rehearsed,
pointing out to John a 'pause for laughter from the more expensive
seats'. In the event, he lost his nerve. When introduced by the manager,
he just stood to attention and said, 'I declare this cinema open,' and
they watched Gary Cooper in *The Lives of a Bengal Lancer*.[89]
Berners's party, which besides John and Heber Percy included Loelia,
Duchess of Westminster, and Lady Mary Lygon, was photographed
for *The Tatler*.[90]

The Betjemans were encouraged to bring their friends to Faringdon;
but when they brought John Sparrow Berners became jealous and
anxious. John's letter about the cinema-opening continues: 'Gerald is
very concerned about Robert and Hanbury [one of Sparrow's middle
names] and hopes Hanbury will not snitch Robert away or always be
ringing him up. I said I thought this unlikely.'[91] Penelope had written
to John of their meeting:

> John Sparrow staying here last week. On Thursday Robert came to dinner
> and got on nohow with JS. Robert then repaired to his car and JS said he
> would stay in his sitting-room and work for an hour or so. The motor left
> and we found the pink room empty. Next morning JS was very unforth-
> coming but admitted that Robert was extremely affectionate. JS is penni-
> less and I really believe that, owing to your beneficial influence, Robert

genuinely prefers the gifts of the intellect to the gifts of the pocket in
return for his friendship. Henceforth there will be no more Daimlers with
Vauxhall engines and gold cigarette cases but priceless treasures of the
mind.[92]

Heber Percy did not desert Berners for Sparrow.

Sometimes Berners took his guests to visit the Betjemans at
Garrards Farm. This happened when Gertrude Stein and her friend
Alice B. Toklas stayed at Faringdon to discuss the chorus that Stein
was to write for Berners's ballet *A Wedding Bouquet*. Stuart Piggott
was roped in to help entertain the daunting pair.

> A touring company going round at that time [he recalled] was playing *East
> Lynne*[93] – straight. They were going to produce it in the village hall at
> Uffington . . . an old British Legion hut. And John told me that Gerald
> Berners had got Gertrude Stein and Alice B. Toklas staying with him and
> they proposed to . . . attend this, and could they look in at the Betjemans
> for a drink beforehand? So John said, 'Come on, you must come along and
> help me out on this . . . Have you ever met the old thing?' I said, 'No, I
> never have.'
>
> 'Nor have I,' he said, 'and I've never read a word of hers; that's the
> trouble.' He said, 'I've found a quotation and it doesn't say what it's from,
> but it is Gertrude Stein.' . . . He said, 'I think it would be a good idea if I
> produced that, don't you?' . . .
>
> So then the party arrived. 'Oh, Miss Stein, it's wonderful to see you. You
> know, knowing that you were coming, the whole day a line of yours has
> been running through my head, and I can't think where it's from. I wonder
> if you can tell me?' And he produced it. And Gertrude Stein sat there
> firmly and squarely – as she was – and said, 'Well, no, Mr Betjeman, I can't
> quite think where that is from. Alice, do you know?' And Alice paused for
> a moment, then said, 'No, I don't know either.'
>
> So Gertrude Stein said, 'Well, you may rest assured, Mr Betjeman, it's
> not from one of my *major* works.'
>
> And after that, of course, it became a phrase with John and myself –
> 'It's not from one of my *major* works.'[94]

In personality, John and Berners had much in common. Each had
been a lonely, only child, closer to his mother than his father. Each,
when in his early fifties, wrote an account of his early years but never
added a sequel. Berners's biographer has written: 'Gerald's music was
immediately interesting, original, witty, with an obvious jokiness
often signalled by the titles; beyond that there is a melancholy.'[95] The
words would hold true of John's poetry. One difference between the

two men was that no one had thought of sending Berners to university where, like John, he might have bloomed and made friends. But what Oxford was to John, Rome – to which he had been sent in a junior diplomatic post in 1912 – had been to Berners.[96] In 1928 he bought a house there, 3 Foro Romano.[97] Its balcony commanded a fine view of the Forum. The artist Rex Whistler, who stayed there in 1929, wrote to his mother that he could see the wonderful view while lying in his bath. A postcard of his bedroom notes: 'Isn't it delightful? The walls are dirty parchment colour and the bed, curtains etc. are crimson damask. The head of the bed is carved and gilt.'[98] Berners took on a cook–housekeeper, Tito Mannini, who came to regard the house as his own. Edward James, who was meant to be staying indefinitely, found Mannini so rude and unbearable that he left after a month and alleged that he was using the front part of the house as an antique shop.[99] Diana Mosley was more taken with him, especially with his cooking.[100] In 1936 John, never one for foreign travel, was lured out to stay there with Penelope. Tito was, Penelope thought, 'rather out of sorts';[101] but John wrote to Berners: 'This is the first night in your house and I must write at once to thank you for lending it to us. It really is a bit of all right with that view of all those ruins and the charming Tito to whom I speak French, Italian, Deutsch or English very clumsily.'[102]

Berners put John and Penelope, scarcely disguised, into two of his novels, *The Camel* (1936) and *Far from the Madding War* (1941). The central characters of *The Camel*, which was dedicated to the Betjemans, are a vicar and his wife who 'as a girl had always been strangely attracted to the Orient'. Stravinsky wrote to Berners, 'La lecture de vôtre "The Camel" me ravit,'[103] and Dali always said it was one of his favourite books.[104] Penelope sent a mild protest to Berners about the portrayal of her (with 'an unmistakable voice') as Lady Caroline Paltry in *Far from the Madding War*,[105] though she was not nearly as annoyed as was Harold Nicolson to find himself depicted as the journalist-MP Mr Lollipop Jenkins.[106] Berners confirmed to Lady Chetwode that Penelope was satirized in the book, but to Penelope he wrote, with soothing humour:

> I can't imagine how you can have supposed that you in any way figured in my recent work on Oxford in wartime. Your mother wrote to me about it and, reading between the lines, I think I detected a slightly malicious pleasure at the idea of her daughter being held up to obloquy. I assured her of course that she had been mistaken, quoting lines from the well-known poem 'Can a mother's tender care cease towards the child she-bear?'[107]

Though John could take a tease in good part and had a gift for getting on with people whom others found 'difficult' (Tito Mannini is an example), he was never content to be surrounded only by friends and figures well disposed towards him. As a good story needs a villain, so his variegated nature demanded the ennui-dispelling stimulus of a bugbear. In Farmer John Wheeler, his landlord in Uffington, he found a satisfying new hate-figure to succeed A.R. Gidney of Marlborough and C.S. Lewis of Oxford. Like them, Wheeler was to be pilloried in a Betjeman poem. John's dislike for Wheeler went beyond his usual rebellion against authority. 'If John saw Farmer Wheeler coming, he would hide behind a wall or start walking fast the other way,' a friend remembered. 'It was absurd, really, because although Wheeler was a bit rough, he wasn't an unpleasant man.'[108] Wheeler was Ron Liddiard's uncle. A stout man, he suffered from diabetes and was a tee-totaller. When he went to Liddiard's house after a shoot, and others were asking for 'a drop of whisky' or 'a drop of gin', he would ask for 'a drop of your water, moi boi', in the high-pitched voice which earned him the nickname 'Squeaky'.[109] (In his poem, John called him 'Farmer Whistle'.)

Wheeler was respected in the Uffington area, as much for his cur-mudgeonliness and sly tricks as despite them. He could be brusque. Once, when he was cutting and laying a hedge along the side of a road, another farmer stopped for a chat and then said, 'Well, I must get on or I shan't be at the meet. You know, you ought to be coming with me and enjoying yourself.' Farmer Wheeler dropped his billhook and said, 'Bugger, oi *be* enjoying moiself.'[110] This and other examples of his repartee were effective enough to be repeated in the Uffington pubs;[111] but, because he liked to get the better of people, most of the stories about him showed how others had got the better of him.[112] Most popular was the 'guinea-fowl' story.

Farmer John had a lot of guinea fowl in his own grounds [Ken Freeman recounted]. The egg supply started falling off quite a bit. So he said to one of the chaps who worked for him, 'The old guinea fowl aren't laying quoite as well as they did. We shall have to see what we can do. There's summat going on, oi don't know what it is, but we shall foind out. Now, moi man, you shall come with me and we shall sit and watch.' They sat there two or three nights and early mornings too, because he was a hell of a fellow, he used to get up about three o'clock in the morning and blow a hunting horn, didn't he? People who came to stay in Uffington would say, 'What was that terrible noise that woke me up last night?' It was Farmer John with his blessed horn. But on this occasion he couldn't understand why nobody came. So he said, 'Well, we shall have to give up and think about something

else.' Within two or three days the eggs started going again. The one who
was taking them was this fellow who was with him watching![113]

Wheeler was considered mean in money matters. Robert Heber
Percy remembered that in 1945, when Penelope was making a collection for the returning soldiers, she asked Wheeler for a contribution.
'He gave her half a crown. She threw it on the ground and showed him
the door.'[114] Money was the root of the ill-feeling between John and
Wheeler. John was nearly always late with his rent, though when he
brought it round Wheeler sometimes tried to sweeten the pill by offering him a 'Berkshire Special' – gin and ginger wine. Wheeler's daughter Peggy (now Mrs Phillips) took her father's view of John. 'Father
was down to earth,' she said. 'He'd got no time for airy-fairy nitwits.
We all thought he was that. Mrs wasn't, but he was. I was talking to
somebody the other day and they said, "What did he do during the
war, then?" And I said, "Oh good Lord! They wouldn't have had *him*!"
He was just a *laugh*, wasn't he? As a poet, I reckon he's about on a par
with Pam Ayres.'[115] She had not forgotten the 'dreadful state' of
Garrards Farm when the Betjemans left it. 'All the animals had been
inside. Father said they had to put it back in the same order as they'd
found it, and of course they didn't want to.'[116]

John found three ways of taking revenge on Farmer Wheeler. First,
at the invitation of a farm-worker known as 'Little Titch', who had
formerly worked for Wheeler, he became secretary of the Uffington
branch of the Farm Workers' Union. Little Titch's 'real name was
Oziah Johnson', Ron Liddiard said, 'and he claimed to be a relative of
the Red Dean of Canterbury, Hewlett Johnson. He was hardly tall
enough to cut a good cabbage, but he had plenty of "get up and go"
about him. He'd got a hump back, poor chap.'[117] John got to know
Little Titch because the farmhand often did jobbing work for
Penelope. John presided over the Union's meetings and sent out entertaining memoranda. It greatly amused him to be the Wat Tyler of
Uffington, encouraging the workers to ask Farmer Wheeler for higher
wages and more days off. John joked that when the socialist 'slave
state' arrived, he would be spared from immediate execution because
of his good work in Uffington.[118]

Another way in which he was able to 'get at' Wheeler was in his rôle
as people's warden of Uffington Church. The Vicar wrote to John:

Dear Mr Betjeman,
   I am writing to you as People's Warden to request you to take steps, in
conjunction with Captain Piggott, to prevent another incident such as
occurred on Sunday morning last at the eleven a.m. service.

When Mr Wheeler brought the collection to the chancel steps he deliberately jostled me with his shoulder and if I had not been fairly firm on
my feet I should have been knocked over. His manner in church is never
very reverent and has been commented on many times, but it must be
made clear to him that his action of last Sunday must not be repeated.[119]

To make amends for his irreverence, Wheeler gave some land to the
church so that the graveyard might be extended. (By a nice irony, he
was the first to be buried in it.)[120]

John also took revenge on Wheeler in verse. In a Christmas card
sent to Stuart Piggott he wrote:

> Uffington Workers from their sloth arise
> A light of Marxist frenzy in their eyes . . .
> Miss Butler's barns are blazing! Wheeler's ricks
> Crackle and sport: and see the bright flame licks
> The Vicarage! the Church! the School! the Pubs
> The Institute, the Fellowship, the Clubs . . .[121]

Less ephemeral was John's satire on Wheeler in his poem 'The Dear
Old Village':

> See that square house, late Georgian, and smart,
> Two fields away it proudly stands apart,
> Dutch barn and concrete cow-sheds have replaced
> The old thatched roofs which once the yard disgraced.
> Here wallows Farmer WHISTLE in his riches,
> His ample stomach heaved above his breeches.
> You'd never think that in such honest beef
> Lurk'd an adulterous braggart, liar and thief.[122]

Admittedly there is no evidence that Farmer Wheeler was 'adulterous' (or indeed a liar or thief): here John may have been visiting on him
the sin of which he accused his own father. But later in the poem John
reprobates the sale of farm land for council houses, and in that the
caricature of Farmer Whistle tallied with the reality of Farmer
Wheeler.

> No man more anxious on the R.D.C.*
> For better rural cottages than he,
> Especially when he had some land to sell

* Rural District Council.

Which, as a site, would suit the Council well.
So three times what he gave for it he got,
For one undrainable and useless plot
Where now the hideous Council houses stand.
Unworked on and unworkable their land,
The wind blows under each unseason'd door,
The floods pour over every kitchen floor,
And country wit, which likes to laugh at sin,
Christens the Council houses 'Whistle's Win'.[123]

The entry for 'Uffington' in *Murray's Berkshire Architectural Guide* (1949), edited by John Betjeman and John Piper, begins: 'Despite a hideous colony of council houses at its east end . . . this remains one of the loveliest villages in the Vale.'[124]

2

FILM CRITIC

Films were gradually turning me dotty. I used to come out of a Press showing and caress the bricks in the street, grateful that they were three-dimensional.

John Betjeman, 'Good-bye to Films', *Evening Standard*, 20 August 1935

In 1987 Christie's in London sold a silver inkstand. An engraved inscription recorded that the piece had once belonged to Sir Robert Bruce Lockhart, the diplomat, British agent and writer who had died in 1971. In covering the sale, the *Daily Telegraph*'s art sales correspondent suggested that Lloyd George had sent Bruce Lockhart to Russia in 1918 to kill Lenin and Trotsky. The report drew an indignant letter of denial from Lockhart's son Robin, himself the author of a book on another famous British agent, Sidney Reilly.

What Robert Bruce Lockhart admitted he had done was remarkable enough. In 1911 he had taken first place in the Consular Service examination – largely, he claimed, because a chat with two French prostitutes in Green Park just before his French oral test had given him unusual fluency in it. At twenty-seven, newly married, he was acting British Consul in Moscow. He was sent home shortly before the revolution of 1917, ostensibly on sick leave, in fact to extricate him from the scandal of an adulterous affair. After the revolution the War Office sent him back to Russia to try to persuade the Bolsheviks to come into the Great War on the allies' side against Germany.

When the Bolsheviks and the allies fell out, he was imprisoned in the Kremlin. It seemed more than likely that he would be shot. The Bolsheviks also jailed Lockhart's most recent lover, Baroness Budberg. He managed to obtain her release and the two remained friends long after she became H.G. Wells's mistress.[1] Lockhart himself was freed in exchange for Maxim Litvinov, whom the British had imprisoned in retaliation for Lockhart's arrest. 'Over my body,' Lockhart wrote, 'two world systems had wrangled.' In 1935, reviewing for the *Evening Standard* the film *British Agent*, based on Lockhart's book, John wrote: 'These days must have been more stirring than any film can make them.'[2]

In 1928 Lockhart joined the *Standard* as joint editor, with Harold Nicolson, of the 'Londoner's Diary'. In 1933 Nicolson, who had little taste or aptitude for gossip journalism, resigned. ('I have won fame and lost reputation,' he wrote to his wife.)[3] Lockhart was left as sole editor of the 'Diary'. It is likely that he obtained John the post of film critic. Lockhart was, with the columnist Lord Castlerosse, one of the inner court of the newspaper's owner, Lord Beaverbrook – Malcolm Muggeridge described them as 'the two wild ones, *avec peur et avec reproche*'.[4] Lockhart was by now the lover of the Countess of Rosslyn, mother of Lady Mary St Clair-Erskine to whom John had unsuccessfully proposed marriage.[5] Both Bruce Lockhart and Castlerosse were often at the Rosslyns' house, Hunger Hill, Coolham. John is first mentioned in Lockhart's private diary in 1931, as one of a gathering of socialites who included John de Forest,[6] William Astor, Lord Hinchingbrooke and a friend of Lady Castlerosse known as 'the belching baronet'.[7]

Osbert Lancaster said that what commended John to Beaverbrook was an article, 'Peers without Tears', which John contributed to the *Standard* in December 1933 – an essay on 'dim peers' such as Lord Trimlestown, whom he had hunted down in Ireland.[8] Among the obscure peers mentioned were Lord Harberton, author of *How to Lengthen our Ears*, the late Lord Sherard who had lived in western Australia as 'Mr Castle' and Lord Talbot de Malahide who, when a deputation of literary professors asked to see the Boswell manuscripts he owned, gave a reply which had been described to John as 'short and ambiguous'. ('It must have taken a good deal of hard thought to make such a reply as that,' John commented.)[9] It was probably Lockhart who helped 'place' the piece; he was also in a position to draw it to Beaverbrook's notice. The *Standard*'s editor, Percy Cudlipp, wrote to John on 15 January 1934 offering him a job on the editorial staff from 29 January at 16 guineas a week.[10]

Malcolm Muggeridge, who joined the newspaper while John was film critic, recalled that the *Standard* was produced in a single large room, 'the idea being that thereby the whole operation of bringing it out would be integrated and cooperative'.

Whether this aim was realised is doubtful, but at least the arrangement accustomed me to working in conditions of noise and disorder . . . The single department which resisted the process of *Gleichschaltung* was the Women's Page, which fought a last-ditch battle to maintain its seclusion, and obstinately went on functioning in what looked like a little hut amidst the encircling chaos. Inside it, two stern unbending ladies continued to deal magisterially with readers' queries about such matters as too large pores and the appearance of hair in untoward places. Their resistance was finally broken when one night, in their absence, their little hut was razed to the ground. Arriving the next morning and finding it gone, they had no recourse but to sit among us, which they surlily did.[11]

In the 'Londoner's Diary' corner, Bruce Lockhart reigned as 'a quasi-independent satrap'. He had a direct line to Beaverbrook; Muggeridge once heard him call the press lord 'Titch'[12] – 'but the word was pronounced so softly and respectfully that it might have been an honorific title like "Your Eminence" or "Your Grace"'.[13] Lockhart could treat Cudlipp, the editor, as more or less an equal. Even when not on the premises, Beaverbrook kept close control of how the *Standard* was run and what went into it. Muggeridge recalled seeing an 'ill-starred leader-writer' with 'the receiver glued to his ear, and a look of anguish on his face, desperately trying to grasp and stamp on his mind each word Beaverbrook uttered.'[14] The peer had no principled views, Muggeridge thought, 'only prejudices, moods, sudden likes and dislikes'.[15] Overnight, he might reverse a previously held position as a result of a conversation. John may have found it easier to accommodate Beaverbrook's whims than did the newsmen and leader-writers. He did not come to film-reviewing as a learned *cinéaste*, or with any deep feelings or preconceptions about film as an art form.

He arrived in late January 1934, and was given a desk near Bruce Lockhart's. Heralding *British Agent*, the film based on Bruce Lockhart's book, he wrote:

> I see Bruce Lockhart every day in this office. He sits in a blue mist of pipe-smoke and sometimes feels his way out of it to relax a moment and come and tell me a joke. I wonder what Warner Brothers have made of him?
>
> Leslie Howard, who has just finished his part as Bruce Lockhart in 'British Agent', the film version of the latter's book, 'The Memoirs of a British Agent', certainly doesn't look anything like him.
>
> In fact, Bruce Lockhart has been wondering whether the film version of his extraordinary adventures in Tsarist and Soviet Russia will be a rather too romantic statement of the facts. He is nervous of appearing as a pleasure-loving Don Juan lounging from café to café followed by a chorus of beautiful women.
>
> I was able to reassure him.[16]

John had other friends at the *Standard*. On the 'Londoner's Diary' were Randolph Churchill (who may have owed the job to his father's friendship with Beaverbrook) and Patrick Balfour, who had been trained as a gossip columnist and in 1933 had enjoyed some success with his book *Society Racket* – John had been caricatured in one of the illustrations. Muggeridge joined the team slightly later, as did Lady Mary Pakenham (now Lady Mary Clive), whom John had first met four years earlier in Ireland. Lady Mary writes:

> I remember on my first day in the room where the Londoner's Diary was produced and also the cultural articles, how surprised I was to discover JB who had never shown any interest in films. (He was equally surprised to see me.) The other public-school boys in my room were as far as I can remember Peter Fleming (my contact), Patrick Balfour (Lord Kinross), Hon. Anthony Winn (killed in the War) & Basil Murray, the raffish son of Gilbert Murray – he was killed in the Spanish Civil War. Howard Spring (book reviews) sat in a corner by himself looking lugubrious. Bruce Lockhart also sat by himself. He seemed very grown-up, dignified & awe-inspiring and I had no idea of his lurid private life until his diaries were published after his death.[17]

Muggeridge recalled that it was part of John's duties to contribute occasional paragraphs to the 'Londoner's Diary', helping out with 'architectural and ecclesiastical news, especially clerical appointments'. He liked John, yet felt 'a sense of mystery' about him.

> Never did I meet any of his relations, nor do I recall anyone who did. There was in him too a certain coolness or standing-offness in personal relationships which can even be read into the famous poem about Miss J. Hunter Dunn. He also had a predisposition to melancholy, which led him often into practical joking. One of the more serious instances of this occurred when he met the Liberal Foreign Secretary, Sir John Simon, a severe, stuffed-shirt sort of character, on a London street. John Betjeman fell down in front of him, feigning an epileptic fit, which left the politician helpless and at sea, wondering what to do. Who would have thought then that Betjeman would become Poet Laureate?[18]

Sir John Simon was Foreign Secretary from 1931 to 1935, so this incident must have taken place while John was on the *Standard*.[19]

The first film John had to review for the paper was *Catherine the Great*, starring the German actress Elisabeth Bergner, one of the foreign-accented stars who had successfully made the transition from silent films to 'talkies'. Because John was not a film-fan, he did not know that for the past few months the British trade press had been abuzz with speculation as to which would be bigger box-office, Bergner in United Artists' *Catherine the Great*, or Marlene Dietrich in Paramount's rival film on the same subject, *The Scarlet Empress*. By some impulse of the *Zeitgeist*, two movie moguls had had the same idea at the same time.

Catherine the Great excited trade interest for another reason, too. It was the first film produced by Alexander Korda as a partner of United Artists. In the late 1920s, when American film companies were overwhelming Britain and Europe, the British Government had established a quota system: a rising percentage of British-made films had to be screened as a balance to the American-made films. The Americans found ways of wriggling round this provision. They hired British companies to make short films known as 'quota quickies' and sometimes showed them to the charwomen in their cinema chains, in the mornings, running a full (American) programme in the afternoons and evenings. But in 1933 Douglas Fairbanks and the other United Artists partners were persuaded to admit to their ranks a British producer – Korda – who would make high-quality quota pictures.[20] Korda was 'hot': in 1933 he had had an immense commercial success with *The Private Life of Henry VIII*, starring Charles Laughton.

As soon as the documents were signed, Korda and UA jointly announced production plans for *Catherine the Great*, an adaptation of a French play. Bergner insisted that her husband, Paul Czinner, be the director. Flora Robson, a young British actress who, like Eleanor Roosevelt, made an asset of her shining plainness, was cast as the old and dying Empress Elizabeth. The veteran actor Sir Gerald du Maurier took the cameo part of the Czar's French valet. There was great competition for the rôle of the mad Czar Peter III. At first the Korda group considered Joseph Schildkraut the best choice, but both Bergner and Schildkraut spoke with German accents and it was decided that 'one Kraut was enough'.[21] The part went to Douglas Fairbanks jr, who was out to prove that no nepotism was involved (his father was on the UA board) and that he could do justice to a character lead, not just continue to ape his father's swashbuckling fantasies. Of all this simmering expectancy about the film, John seems to have been unaware. He knew nothing of the dramas there had been on set: how Paul Czinner, intimidated by his star wife and the calibre of the cast, had directed 'too gently and sympathetically', with the result that Korda had left his producer's office, stormed on to the set and taken over.[22]

In February 1934, *Catherine the Great* was given two big Hollywood-style premières, one in London and one in Paris. John's review of the film appeared on 10 February under the headline 'LITTLE CATHERINE *IS* GREAT'.

> The best film of the week is 'Catherine the Great', at the Leicester Square Theatre.

After all, most pictures that you go to see you regard as temporary relief from the misery of being alive. You visit them in the same spirit in which you get 'a novel' from the circulating library.

You don't demand more than a joke or two, a love interest and a sustained plot, and the book goes back to be read and forgotten by someone else, in the same way that you have read and forgotten it yourself.

But there are some books which you will want to buy and keep in your memory. So there are some scenes in films which one can never forget. I remember as I write, 'Poil de Carotte' hanging in the barn; Manuela being called on that bleak school staircase in 'Mädchen in Uniform'; I also remember a chandelier twinkling with glass and hanging from a dark painted ceiling. This last is from 'Catherine the Great'.

There is no enthralling love interest, and only one joke. What I chiefly remember is the most beautiful architectural scenery, the most correct eighteenth-century interiors, the most awe-inspiring Russian onion domes, the most colourful eighteenth-century dresses I have ever seen in any historical film or play.

Not even Elisabeth Bergner, the stately little Empress, transcends this impression. And that is perhaps the chief fault of the film. The scenery and dresses are too much. Doors open and more doors open and more doors still – an old trick on the films that still delights me – and not even Elizabeth of Russia (Flora Robson), tall and virile as she is, can stand out amid the richness that surrounds her.

In this first review, John set the tone of the articles that were to follow in the year-and-a-half he remained film critic. He gave praise freely; but there was enough adverse criticism to scotch any idea that he was merely a public relations auxiliary to the studios. His comment on the sets of *Catherine the Great* begins as praise and glissades into dispraise. He does his best to establish his credentials as a film critic, by dropping the names of the few films that have made any impression on him, such as *Mädchen in Uniform*, to which he had taken one of his prep-school pupils in 1931.[23] More convincingly, he is quickly establishing himself as a 'character', entertaining and quirkish. He treats his readers as intimates, allowing them to see the depressed state of his mind. Films are 'temporary relief from the misery of being alive'; *Catherine the Great* is 'an event in my gloomy existence'. These asides suggest something more than a comical glumness *à la* Buster Keaton. Perhaps the strains of marriage were beginning to tell. Perhaps he felt that in accepting a well-paid job as a journalist he was betraying his vocation as a poet. Or Muggeridge may have been right when he wrote of 'a predisposition to melancholy'.

Gradually John settled into the routine of the job. He would get up about seven in the morning. After breakfast Penelope would drive him to Uffington or Challow station and at about 7.30 he would catch a slow train to Didcot; after that, a fast one to London. He saw the films in the morning, wrote about them in the afternoon, then caught the train home. 'It was always a bit of a rush,' he told his granddaughter Endellion in 1977, adding, 'The slowest part of the journey was the underground railway from Paddington to Farringdon Street, the nearest underground station to the *Evening Standard* office [in Shoe Lane].'[24] It was while travelling to work on the Underground, on 26 June 1934, that John had an uncanny experience. In recalling it, for Endellion, in 1977, he described it as 'the only ghostly experience I had which can be witnessed'.

> One morning I was travelling down on the Inner Circle underground from Paddington to Farringdon Street when the train did a very unusual thing. It waited for a long time at King's Cross station. My father, your great-grandfather, had a factory, founded in 1820, on the Pentonville Road (it is still there and now owned by the Medici Society). King's Cross under-ground was the nearest station. I remember thinking as the train waited at King's Cross, 'Shall I go out and see my father?' A voice inside me seemed to say, 'Yes, do go and see him. It won't take you long and you won't be too late for the film.' The train went on waiting but I felt too lazy at that time of the morning to bother to get out and take a tram up the hill. Then we went on and with other film writers I saw an American musical film called *George White's Scandals*.[25]
>
> When I got back to Uffington that evening the telephone rang. It was my father's managing clerk, Mr H.V. Andrew, and he told me that my father had died that morning while talking to him. He was recalling a date. Do you think my father was trying to get through to me? Do you think he knew he was going to die so swiftly? I don't know. All I can tell you is that it happened and Gramelope [Penelope] will remember it.
>
> She offered me a strawberry that we had grown in our garden at Uffington when I heard the news and I remember being too upset to want to eat it.[26]

There was a further shock at Ernest's funeral, which took place in Chelsea Old Church. John's Oxford friend Alan Pryce-Jones recorded in his memoirs:

> John was an only child, and while he and his mother were waiting for the ceremony to begin a scene occurred like that in the second act of *Der Rosenkavalier*. A second, unknown, Mrs Betjeman suddenly irrupted with a second family, and it turned out that for many years Mr Betjeman [*sic* for Betjemann] had lived a second and hitherto secret life.[27]

Ernest was buried in Highgate Cemetery, where an obelisk marks his grave; and a slate tablet to his memory, designed by Frederick Etchells, was set in the wall of St Enodoc's Church in Cornwall.

Ernest had not cut John out of his will, as he had allegedly threatened to do in 1930.[28] He appointed as executors his wife Bess and Philip Asprey, of the famous Bond Street fancy-goods shop. His properties were to be sold to form a trust fund which would benefit Bess in her lifetime and, after her death, would be held 'in Trust for my Son John Betjemann absolutely'.[29] Only two further bequests were made. Ernest's sporting guns were left to his godson Hugh de Paula – John would have no use for them. And £300 went to Miss Norah [*sic* for Noreen] Kennedy of Kilrush, Co. Clare – perhaps his mistress.[30] Within ten years the business Ernest and his forebears had built up was liquidated. During those years, John did his best to help when asked – for example, writing, at Horace Andrew's request, some advertising copy to promote the company's 'Datoclock'. But there was never any question of his taking over. Some of the men who lost their jobs when the business failed were bitterly resentful. 'John Betjeman let a great business go to rack and ruin,' said William Hammond, one of Ernest's most skilled workmen.[31]

John seems to have displayed a conventional grief at his father's death. Later, Lord Clonmore wrote to Lionel Perry: 'You will remember the crocodile tears which were shed over Ernie, after all the abuse the poor man had to suffer when alive.'[32] John's writings suggest that only over many years did he come to feel he had misjudged his father and had failed to obey the Fifth Commandment, 'Honour thy father and thy mother . . .'[33] If there were tears, crocodile or genuine, they did not last long. Nerina Shute, film critic of the *Sunday Referee* in 1934–35, and now, in her nineties, the only surviving London film critic of that time, remembers John as anything but melancholic – always sunny, full of vivacity and mischief.

> He and I used to meet at every film show; and we had a feeling of rapport, because I couldn't take it seriously and neither could he. To us it seemed mad that we should be doing this, and that all this money should be spent on film shows. We had two or three film shows a day. We drank enormous amounts of gin and whisky provided by the publicity people. We had parties, we had huge meals at the Berkeley and the Ritz and the Savoy, with directors and stars. I couldn't believe this was happening to me and I don't think he could believe it was happening to him. Anyway, we used to giggle together.
>
> At 10.00 or 10.30 a.m. we joined the other critics at the Tivoli Cinema or the Carlton. If it was a comedy the critics seldom laughed. If it was a tragedy they sometimes laughed a good deal. After a hard morning of

passion or a weary morning of comedy we were offered drinks and sandwiches to revive us. Quite often another film was shown in the afternoon.
This meant a magnificent tea, including delicious chocolate cakes – and
more drinks for those who felt in need of them.

One day we were all going to a film show at the Carlton in Lower Regent
Street. A show in the afternoon, a big film. I got there on time and John
got there more or less on time. And he said: 'My wife is coming, and I can't
stand here waiting for her. Will you look out for her for me? You can't miss
her – she's hideously ugly. I'll draw a picture of her for you.' And he drew
a very funny picture of his wife, with a downturned mouth like a clown's.
He said: 'That's what she looks like. When you see her coming, go up to
her and tell her that I'm in here, and send her in.' Of course, when his wife
arrived, she wasn't ugly at all.[34]

When Nerina Shute began reviewing for the *Referee*, the queen of
the film critics was Iris Barry of the *Daily Mail*, a former girlfriend of
Ezra Pound,[35] who with stubborn bravado stuck to her conviction that
the talkies were just a passing phase and that silent films would return.
Shute, who was paid £5 a week by the *Referee*, was awed by Barry's
reputed salary of £1,000 a year.[36] But in 1930 Barry left England to join
the staff of the Museum of Modern Art in New York.[37] During John's
stint as a film critic, the most respected reviewer was C.A. (Caroline)
Lejeune of the *Observer*, quiet and dauntingly cerebral. Shute also
remembers the Australian Campbell Dixon, of the *Daily Telegraph*, who
was often accompanied by his embarrassingly alcoholic wife, Alice.[38]

In 1934, at twenty-three, Shute was the youngest film critic in Fleet
Street. Though four years younger than John, she had two advantages
over him. First, she had worked, before joining the *Referee*, as 'studio
correspondent' to one of the main British film-fan papers, *Film
Weekly*. Through that job, she had become a friend of leading figures
in the British film industry, such as the director Herbert Wilcox and
his protégée Anna Neagle, Madeleine Carroll, Ralph Lynn and Tom
Walls.[39] Second, Nerina Shute had lived in Hollywood in her teens.
She had gone there with her mother, the flighty Mrs Cameron Shute,
who was trying (in vain) to sell the film rights to her novel, *The
Unconscious Bigamist*. Nerina, too, had written a novel, published by
Grant Richards in 1931. Its title, *Another Man's Poison*, was an arch
reference to lesbianism. Rebecca West, reviewing the book, wrote:
'Miss Shute writes, not so much badly as barbarously, as if she had
never read anything but a magazine, never seen any picture but a
moving one, never heard any music except at restaurants. Yet she is full
of talent.'[40] The *Sunday Referee* promptly billed her as 'Nerina
Shute – the Girl with the Barbarous Pen'.[41] She did her best to live up

to the tag with mildly disobliging comments about Madeleine Carroll ('a ruthless Madonna') and Nelson Keys ('a Baby Austin lady-killer').[42] Like John's film-reviews, her articles were sparkling rather than analytic or profound.

Nerina Shute appealed to John's snobbery and to his taste for boyish girls. Her grandfather, Sir Cameron Shute, had been a major in the cavalry charge at Balaclava; the family property, Woldhurstlea, near Crawley, Sussex, a Victorian mansion surrounded by 200 acres of field and forest, was turned into a housing estate whose roads included – to the satirical glee of John and Nerina – Humpty Dumpty Lane. Nerina was strikingly good-looking: her dark, ambiguous beauty later caught the eye of Lord Beaverbrook, who paid her a backhanded compliment: 'You know, you're a beautiful woman. But very few men will realise it.'[43] (She later married the radio commentator Howard Marshall;[44] but she spent her later years with women lovers and in 1992 'came out' as a bisexual in her memoir *Passionate Friendships*.)[45]

John and Nerina were something of a 'twosome'. They sat next to each other in the cinemas and sometimes went on jaunts together to the British studios. The young film director Dallas Bower encountered them when making his first film in 1934. He recalled:

> I made a film at Riverside in 1934 called *The Path of Glory*. It was an adaptation of a very well-known radio play by a man called L. du Garde Peach. I was slightly apprehensive about the whole operation. It was my first film as a director and had a most distinguished cast. Felix Aylmer, no less, was the lead and it was Valerie Hobson's first film.
>
> One morning I found standing on the set, about noon, two figures . . . I asked my assistant Charles Jourdain who they were and he had no idea. And I think he sent *his* assistant to the door and . . . 'Oh yes, they've been sent from the London office.' The two individuals seemed rather oddly adjusted. The man was wearing a hat he'd obviously bought in Whipple's [the ecclesiastical outfitters], a flat hat of the kind you only see now in television adaptations of *Barchester Towers*; and the lady looked an odd companion for him. I thought: what are they doing here? And I became slightly irritated. Most directors don't like visitors unless they're told who they are. And in due course I discovered that the man in the hat was Mr John Betjeman and that the lady was Miss Nerina Shute. They had come to report on Riverside's first production.[46]

Bower welcomed them and gave them lunch.

> And then a very odd thing indeed happened. . . . I usually saw my rushes at lunchtime; but on this particular day I decided I would go back and get on with the afternoon's work, and I saw my rushes when we finished – half

past five, six – went down to the projection room, and for some reason or other the 'phone from the actual projection room itself to the box had broken down. I wanted to re-run my rushes, so I opened the door to the box – and there was Mr Betjeman standing in the box with the projectionist.

He said: 'Oh, I'm awfully sorry, old top.'

So I said, 'Well, *really*! May I ask what you're doing here?'

He said, 'Oh, I feel very embarrassed indeed.'

I said, 'Well, not a bit.' I *was* slightly irritated. But I said, 'Not a bit. But you know if you'd wanted to see the rushes, there's no reason whatever why you shouldn't have asked and I would have been delighted for you to have sat in with me.' . . . What I really wanted to do on this occasion was to choose takes; so I had old John come back – by this time looking very humble indeed, hat in his lap, I might say. Now, whether he had slipped a coin to the projectionist, I have no idea; more probably he said: 'I wonder if . . .' – you know, he had the most enormous charm which he could turn on at the biggest possible wavelength. He said to me: 'Well, I've enjoyed my day enormously.' I took to him but I was rather frightened of him – what he might write about us. He said: 'I want to do a piece.'

I said: 'Delighted. What do you intend to say?'

'Oh, the usual sort of stuff, you know.'

To the best of my knowledge, nothing ever appeared.[47]

The next time the two men saw each other was in 1940, when Dallas Bower was 'fished out of the army' to join the Films Division of the Ministry of Information, and found himself sharing an office with John.[48]*

Lady Mary Clive also accompanied John to a film studio. 'It was typical of JB that when I casually mentioned that I had never seen a film being made he at once offered to take me down to Elstree, although he was new to the job and precariously perched. We saw an insignificant Ruritanian film being made and were quite well treated, though of course it was nothing like the days when he was a telly star himself. (Years later he did one of our local churches in Herefordshire, and for two days the village was *en fête*.)'[49]

John had friends at court in the British International Pictures studios at Elstree. Walter Mycroft, the dwarfish hunchback whom Alfred Hitchcock appointed scenario editor there, had preceded John by a few years as film critic of the *Evening Standard*.[50] And Mycroft had found a job at Elstree for Sidney Gilliat – later a respected film director – the son of an editor of the *Standard*. At a rehearsal for one of Mycroft's films John spotted an old friend. On 12 August 1935 he wrote:

* See Chapter 11, 'Minnie'.

Ten years ago a tall and beautiful schoolgirl might have been seen bicycling about the quiet don-infested roads of North Oxford.

She wore a blue tunic dress, black cotton stockings and a blue straw hat with a dark blue ribbon and a little green crest on it.

Undergraduates stopped to look, and even dons put on their back-pedalling brakes as she glided past them at a more youthful pace.

She was boarded out in one of those Gothic, red-brick houses surrounded by laburnums and pink may, and a garden mostly composed of bicycle sheds.

This girl was Leonora Corbett.

History and English: Good. Mathematics: Very poor. Classics: Poor. Drawing: Excellent.

HEADMISTRESS'S REPORT: Leonora has tried hard this term, but there is room for improvement if only she would concentrate on her work instead of dreaming about the future.

And what did the future hold in store for this lovely schoolgirl? As soon as she left school she went to the Festival Theatre at Cambridge, there to delight the rival undergraduates with Shakespeare in Mexican dress and Toller's plays performed on cubes with remarkable lighting effects.

From here she went on tour; then came to the West End.

And now she is being made into a film star. You will see her in 'My Heart's Delight' with Richard Tauber quite soon . . .

Walter Mycroft, production chief of British International Pictures, is so pleased with her performance that he is going to put her opposite Otto Kruger . . .[52]

In these lines is seen the first budding of John's poem 'Myfanwy at Oxford', which is about a bicycling girl and begins, 'Pink may, double may, dead laburnum . . .'[53]

Apart from Mycroft and Leonora Corbett, John knew few people who could give him a direct entrée into the film world or feed him its secrets. Two of the British stars – Heather Angel and Evelyn Laye – happened to come from Faringdon, so he heard something of them on the village grapevine. Emlyn Williams, whom he had known in the Oxford University Dramatic Society,[54] acted in *My Song for You* and *Roadhouse* in 1934, as King Christian VII of Denmark in *The Affair of the Dictator* and in *City of Beautiful Nonsense* in 1935, among other films. John's Magdalen friend Gyles Isham went out to Hollywood to appear with Garbo in *Anna Karenina* and sent him useful gossip about her – for example, her ability to gobble up the entire top tray of a trolley of canapés in two minutes flat. Anthony Bushell, a friend of John and of Evelyn Waugh,[55] acted in British films and was good for a story or two. Robert Donat (pronounced 'doughnut', John told his readers) was a nephew of the architect C.F.A. Voysey, whom John had met when on *The Architectural Review*. But John had one contact who was in the vanguard of the British film industry – his old schoolfriend Arthur Elton. After experience in Gainsborough's script department and cutting-room and on the studio floor in England and Berlin, Elton had become a leading figure in the documentary-film movement.

The word 'documentary' was first used by John Grierson in a review written for the *New York Sun* in 1926. It was derived from *documentaire*, a term which the French applied to their travel films. Grierson used it to characterize Robert Flaherty's *Moana*, an account of the daily life of South Sea islanders. Later, Grierson defined this film genre as 'the creative treatment of actuality'. In 1927 Grierson, a Scot born in 1898, had called on (Sir) Stephen Tallents of the Empire Marketing Board (EMB) 'brimming with ideas'. Tallents had already won Rudyard Kipling's support for his plan to 'bring the Empire alive' in films. Grierson was appointed films officer of the EMB. The first documentary he made for it was *Drifters* (1929), about the North Sea herring fisheries – boats swinging out to sea from small grey harbours, nets flung wide, fishermen about their daily tasks. Grierson had studied the work of Russian directors and had helped prepare the version of Sergei Eisenstein's *The Battleship Potemkin* shown in America.

Grierson gathered round him at the EMB a group of young film-makers. Besides Arthur Elton, they included Basil Wright, Paul Rotha, Stuart Legg, Harry Watt, Edgar Anstey, Donald Taylor and John Taylor, all of whom preferred 'the dog-biscuits of EMB production to the flesh-pots of Elstree and Shepherd's Bush'. To school themselves in documentary techniques, they watched films by Eisenstein and screened Alberto Cavalcanti's *Rien que les heures* (1926), about the passing of a day in Paris. They were also impressed by the pioneer documentaries of the explorer Robert Flaherty: *Nanook of the North* (1920–25), the story of an Eskimo family; *Moana* (1926) on the Samoans; an experimental film about New York City (1927); *Tabu* (1929–31) on Tahitian legend; and *Man of Aran* (1933–34), about life on one of the Aran islands off the coast of Ireland.

Flaherty, fifty in 1934, was the oldest of the documentarians. When John began reviewing for the *Standard*, Flaherty was on a barnstorming tour of England to promote *Man of Aran*. He appeared at cinemas with Aran islanders in homespun and tam-o'-shanters. His life story was published in a Sunday newspaper and copies of it were handed out by usherettes dressed in fishermen's jerseys. In the Edgware Road, London, an excited crowd tried to cut locks of hair from Tiger King, the film's hero. Maggie Durante, the heroine, went on a tour of

Selfridge's store sponsored by the *Daily Express*, to discuss silk stockings and the modern woman. On 30 July 1934 John wrote: 'The most important general release this week is Bob Flaherty's "Man of Aran". Do not let it be said that I didn't warn you. If you are going to this film expecting to see a tale of smuggling off the Irish coast with a lot of colleens keening and calling out "Acushla, Machree" you will be disappointed.'

Flaherty became a drinking companion of John's. He was good company; Sir Stephen Tallents wrote of him that 'If he had been born an arab, he could have made his fortune as a story-teller in the bazaar.' Over the drinks, John heard about Flaherty's latest projects, and brought his readers news of them. 'The new Bob Flaherty film will have a "story",' he wrote on 23 January 1935. '"Man of Aran" had not a "story" in the accepted sense of the word. In three weeks Bob Flaherty will no longer be seen with his reverend white hair, red face and twinkling blue eyes in the Bohemian cafés of London. He will be on his way to India. The story of his new film has been written by Lajos Biro, who wrote the words of "The Private Life of Henry VIII" and of "The Scarlet Pimpernel". It is to be called "Elephant Boy".'

There was more advance trumpeting of the enterprise on 11 February, in an article headed 'Six People in Search of an Elephant'.

> In ten days there will be leaving for India Bob Flaherty, Fred Flaherty, Mrs Flaherty, two sound engineers, one assistant and a charm against snakebite and all.
>
> And when they get to India they don't know where they will go.
>
> It may be to Burma, or nearly two thousand miles away to Mysore, or a five days train journey up to the north. They have got to find elephants and friendly people who do not object to acting for the films.
>
> Then there will be nine months getting to know elephants well. Bob Flaherty has been reading about elephants for weeks. There is one incident which particularly strikes his fancy and which he hopes to use, but it won't be too easy to film.
>
> A *mahout* (elephant boy) was devil-dancing in Ceylon round a fire. He was wearing a terrifying mask. His elephant waited in the background. For fun the *mahout* danced round his elephant.
>
> Not recognizing him in the mask, the elephant raised its trunk, and killed him with a blow. The mask fell off and the elephant saw who he had killed. He picked up leaves with his trunk and laid them over the body. Then he charged through the watching group mad with grief and rushed about for two months, killing people, breaking down huts and trees, until he was captured.

The extraordinary communion between an elephant boy and his charge is to be the subject of Flaherty's film.

The Hollywood film-makers are just names in John's column; but through the introductions he gained from Arthur Elton he was able to present the documentary-makers as flesh and blood. Elton himself he had known too long to take quite seriously.

Talking of films without sex in them, let me introduce you to Arthur Elton, a director of sexless films. He is a peculiar figure in Wardour-street.

He has a yellow beard, dresses in rustic style, and lives in Bloomsbury. I remember that at school he always used to carry a peculiar umbrella in which he kept his books. It must have been made of some extra strong material.

Now he carries films in huge tins slung across his back in some string contrivance. He always was an ingenious man.[56]

Paul Rotha, 'young and bearded' (he was a year younger than John), 'used to write in those expensive magazines without any capital letters in them. Now he is making films for the millions.' Rotha was directing instructional films for Gaumont-British. John praised his *Rising Tide* (1934), about the building of the dry dock at Southampton, and contrasted it with the usual run of factual films. 'There is hardly any talking, not that irritating Children's Hour voice, "And here is the *dry dock* itself!" With the maddening jokes. "My! I expect it would like a drink! Here goes! 400,000 gallons of water!" '[57]

John Grierson – 'the wild-eyed director of the Post Office Film Unit' – was also praised for getting rid of inane commentary. On 1 July 1935 John reported:

John Grierson's latest experiment is to employ a poet to write a poem to a series of shots of collieries, most of them at a standstill. The poet is a tall, thin friend of mine, called Wystan Auden. He produces tall, thin volumes of verse that actually bring him in money. He is one of the few poets to achieve this.

The poem for the film is recited on the sound track and a choir sings specially composed music by Mr [Benjamin] Brittain [*sic*], a young composer.

Auden's celebrated soundtrack-lyric for *Night Mail* (directed by Harry Watt and Basil Wright) was composed in 1936, after John had left the *Standard* job.

Lord Beaverbrook, with his jingoist British Empire campaign, encouraged his journalists to favour British products, and the British studios were near at hand. Among the directors John met besides the documentarians were the 'nervous and aesthetic' Anthony Asquith, Basil Dean, Alexander Korda, Michael Powell, Sidney Bernstein and Alfred Hitchcock. Walter Mycroft introduced him to Hitchcock, who told him the origin of his film *The Man Who Knew Too Much*. But American movies dominated the British cinemas. The public wanted to see them, and John had to cover them; but he was determined not to be taken in by Hollywood hyperbole. He told his readers of a conversation between two American film executives about a film. 'No,' said one, 'it's not stupendous – only colossal.' At first John decided not to write about stars more than was necessary. 'I considered them as "pandering to the box office and to the lowest elements in a cinema audience",' he wrote in his farewell article of 1935. 'But now if I were to meet Greta Garbo in the street I would faint right away with excitement.'[58]

John overcame his distaste for the star system. He wrote rapturously about Fred Astaire's and Ginger Rogers's dancing in *Roberta*.[59] He had lunch with Charles Laughton 'where he always goes, and where I go too – a small restaurant in a small street in that part of London which looks like Paris, behind the Tottenham Court Road [perhaps Charlotte Street].' Laughton was about to appear in *Ruggles of Red Gap*. 'I can safely say', John wrote, 'that he is the only actor of renown I know who knows all about modern painting, literature, architecture and art. But don't be put off by that.'[60]

John had a soft spot for the actress Dolly Haas, whom he described as 'the Vesta Tilley of Berlin'. He first met her in June 1934 at Elstree Studios, where a stage hand was yelling: 'Miss Ass! Miss Ass! You're wanted.' John noted: 'Dolly, whose name rhymes with stars and the "h" is aspirated, is playing the lead in *Girls Will Be Boys*, a new comedy for which she has come over from the Continent specially to act.'[61] Her father, he revealed, was half English 'and her grandfather was a bookseller in the Strand and a friend of Sir Henry Wood'. In February 1935 John sat next to Dolly Haas at the first showing of *Girls Will Be Boys*. It was the first time she had seen it, too. 'You won't be able to sit next to her and hear what she says, like I did. Ha! Ha!' John gloated. 'When Cyril Maude appeared she blew a kiss to the screen. "I lof heem – a lofly man." '[62] John's favourite film star was Myrna Loy – 'my beloved freckled Myrna Loy, with auburn hair and blue-green eyes'. She visited London and he interviewed her for the *Standard*. When the conversation became slightly sticky, he asked, 'Do you mind if I say you like English Perpendicular?' Miss Loy said it was fine by her, honey; and the interesting insight into her taste in architecture was duly relayed to the British public.[63] Reviewing *Evelyn*

Prentice in 1935 he wrote: 'I am still in love with Myrna Loy, despite the hats she wears in her new film.' He was less enthusiastic about Joan Crawford. 'I think she is a splendid actress,' he wrote, 'but I am always a little repulsed by her shining lips, like balloon tyres in wet weather.'[64] In January 1935 he advised his readers: 'If you want to see Joan Crawford soundly beaten with a hair-brush by Clark Gable . . . go and see *Forsaking All Others* at the Empire.'[65] He had no luck when he tried to get an interview with Katharine Hepburn, though he forgave her in his review of her film *Spitfire* in June 1934:

I have every reason to be annoyed with Katharine Hepburn and to write rudely about her if I have the chance. I was one of those unlucky people who went down to Plymouth when she came to Europe recently on that mysterious trip.

I went there to bring back to my inestimable and countless readers an inestimable message from her lush and longing lips. Instead, I found her cabin door locked, and not the most intrepid reporter was able to catch a glimpse of her. She was one of my most notable social failures.

But I can't be rude about her as a person. *Spitfire* (Plaza) only confirms the general impression that she is Garbo's only really serious rival.[66]

Next to Walt Disney's 'silly symphonies' with Mickey Mouse and the rest, which he considered the best things on the screen,[67] John liked comedies. W.C. Fields was by far his favourite male star. 'A creative genius' he called him in December 1934. 'I have only to see his face to laugh.'[68] John did not think Bing Crosby mixed well with Fields on screen. He disliked all musicals, quoting in support of his view 'a Neasden correspondent'. He missed no opportunity of savaging Bing Crosby. He wrote of *We're Not Dressing* (1934):

The interminably crooning sailor is Bing Crosby: he croons when he is on board the yacht; he croons when he is nearly drowning in the vasty deep; he croons when the sun sets on the desert island; he croons when the moon rises, and of course he falls in love with Carole Lombard, the little rich girl who gets prettier and less useless as she settles down to desert island life. But why must we see so many close-ups of Bing Crosby? He has a nice innocuous face, but he is not a great actor.[69]

Eight months later, reviewing *Here Is My Heart*, John speculated, 'I suppose this is the swan-croon of Bing Crosby':[70] wishful thinking.

Another of John's dislikes was child stars. He gave grudging praise to the five-year-old Shirley Temple, who started the fashion for 'screen babies', and was impressed by the fourteen-year-old British actress

Nova Pilbeam and by Freddie Bartholomew's performance – opposite
W.C. Fields – in *David Copperfield*.[71] But in general, John wrote, he
was 'not touched by kiddie appeal'. He added: 'I have never been particularly keen on Baby Le Roy. But when I see a whole chorus of semi-
sophisticated two-year-olds, dolled up like the silly little mascots some
people have in the backs of their cars, and yelling out some nitwitted
love lyric, I have to get up and go out.'[72]

John's distaste for the 'screen-babies' may have had causes deeper
than hostility to the sentimental. In 1935 he was being taunted by
Maurice Bowra with his failure to get Penelope with child. But others
of the film critics shared John's views on child stars. Nerina Shute
thought them 'pretty gruesome'.[73] Graham Greene, who joined John
on the red plush seats in July 1935 as film critic of *The Spectator*, later
wrote a ribald article about Shirley Temple in the magazine *Night and
Day*, which provoked a successful libel action by suggesting that the
child star's act was calculated to appeal to an audience of slavering
'dirty old men'.[74]

The 'purity campaign' was an issue that all film critics had to
address in 1934–35. In 1934 the Hays production code, governing
movie morality, was imposed on the Hollywood studios, with severe
sanctions against transgressors.[75] Will H. Hays, president of the new
organization Motion Picture Producers and Distributors of America,
intended to do for the film industry what Judge Keneshaw Mountain
Landis, the 'czar of baseball', had done for that sport after gambling
interests had fixed the World Series in 1919: to put the house in order
from within before the demand for public regulation became irresistible. Much of the pressure for censorship came from Roman Catholic
activists, who formed a National League of Decency in the United
States. In 1930, what became known as the Hays Office Code, drafted
by two Midwestern Roman Catholics, Martin Quigley and the Rev.
Daniel Lord, SJ, was formally adopted; it was made mandatory in
1934. A fine of $25,000 was set for any company releasing a film
without a seal of approval. A list of twenty-eight prohibited words
included 'Gawd' and 'hot' (applied to a woman). White slavery, mis-
cegenation and sexual perversion, 'or any inference of it', were forbidden. When Anna Neagle starred in the British film *Nell Gwyn* (1934),
a potential American distributor told her, 'It would be okay if only
you would *marry* King Charles II.'[76]

As the Code took effect, a few naughtinesses slipped under its net,
such as Loretta Young's diaphanous underwear in *Born to Be Bad*
(1934) – a film dismissed by the *Los Angeles Times* in a two-word
review, 'It is.'[77] But in 1942 George Jean Nathan wrote that, after the
Code came in, 'most characters in their amorous reactions to each

other' were presented as 'practically indistinguishable from little children dressed up in their parents' clothes and playing house'.[78]

John knew where he stood on the censorship question. He disliked being told what to do; even more, he disliked being told what not to do – or see. In several of his reviews he hit out at the censors and would-be censors. On 27 October 1934 he complained:

The new purity campaign has had a deadening effect on many films. They were born spicy and the spice was taken out. This leaves them tame and dull.

I become nervous about where this cleanliness is going to stop. If crime films are to be messed up with the Puritan scrubbing brush, what will happen to many able but villainous actors?

For instance, what will happen to James Cagney? It will not do for him to appear too often in such films as 'He Was Her Man', now showing at the Regal. It is quite a good story, and there is nothing much wrong with the acting, but somehow it seems unreal to make Cagney play a part in a sweet old-world romance, set in an out-of-the-way fishing village.

On 24 November, reviewing *Belle of the Nineties*, he wrote:

Before I tell you about the film, I want to extend a vote of sympathy to Mae West. No wonder she sings a song in this film about people 'going round scandalizing her name'.

It is a scandal that purity pussyfoots should affix their pince-nez firmly to their noses, so soon as one of her films is made. It is a scandal, too, that our censors should whip out their scissors and ruin the continuity of the picture.

Her jokes have an honest quality about them that is infinitely less offensive than the necking and pawing that appears in many new purity films.

On 1 June 1935 John reviewed Mae West's *Goin' to Town* and Jean Harlow's *Reckless*. He began the article: 'Being a film critic nowadays is rather like being at school and watching a row going on. Someone has got to get into trouble. Who is going to get the stick? The schoolmistress has told us that Mae West and Jean Harlow are both in disgrace. The next piece of work they show up to her will decide her. The schoolmistress, I need hardly add, is Mrs Purity, who, though she is quite new to the school, is already a feared, if hardly popular figure.' Of *Reckless*, he wrote: 'I enjoyed only little bits of the film. It seemed to me that Jean Harlow herself had great cobras fascinating her, and she was unable to forget them and be her proper self. These cobras were the beetle-browed Puritan censors, watching every dress she wore and every remark and movement she made, waiting to strike.'

On 27 May 1935 he protested at the banning of the Claudette
Colbert film *Private Worlds*. 'What is a lunatic asylum? If I were asked,
I should say, many of those "musicals" where you see hundreds of legs
whirling in space and forming patterns like a Victorian kaleidoscope.
The British Censor – a charming, cultivated man, whose head may
often be seen through the plate-glass windows of his exclusive London
club – is not allowed to pass lunatic asylums for the English screen. He
passes the maddest musicals, but he is not allowed to pass " 'Private
Worlds', the film of Phyllis Bottome's book".'

American censors thought that British film-licensing standards
were far too liberal. John attacked two of Hays's men in his column
on 8 July 1935. The piece contains his first disparaging reference to
'executives' – a lasting antipathy, most pointedly expressed in his
caustic 1960s poem 'Executive'.

> I do not think there have ever been so many Hollywood stars in England
> as there are at present. But I wonder whether those mysterious people
> called executives are so keen?
>
> You will remember that Messrs Milliken and Quigley came over here to
> tell us about the American purity campaign. Their reception was cool. So
> cool, indeed, that Mr Martin Quigley, who does not seem to be gifted with
> much of a sense of humour, has just published an extraordinary attack on
> British films and film magnates, in an American film paper. He says (and
> I wonder what he means) *'Very filthy and objectionable things have been
> contained in British pictures sent to this market, objectionable even to
> Americans.'*

A phrase much bandied about in the censorship controversy was
'good taste'. The production code imposed in 1934, for example, stipulated that 'The treatment of bedrooms must be governed by good taste
and delicacy.' The subject, and of course its antithesis, 'bad taste',
were in the air. Here John, after the publication of *Ghastly Good Taste*
(1933), could be considered an authority. In the spring of 1935
Montagu Montagu-Nathan, a British expert on Russian music, and
Arnold Haskell, the ballet historian, organized 'An Evening of Bad
Taste' at the Garden Club in Curzon Street, London.[79] John may have
had a hand in the design of the printed programme. The front was decorated by irregular type and a drawing of a garden gnome; on the back
cover was a badly designed advertisement for Shell; and an inside page
promised 'CROONING', that pet hate of John's, and 'BUFFIT'. It
also promised that 'Mr John Betjeman, author of "GHASTLY
GOOD TASTE", will hold forth.'

Some idea of what else was in store for the partygoers was given in an anticipatory article by Cedric Belfrage, who twenty years later was to achieve notoriety when he was deported from the United States as an alleged Communist.[80] 'If London's latest quaint conceit doesn't arouse the interest of James Douglas,[81] and others who hold a thermometer under flaming modernity's tongue,' he wrote, 'I miss my guess.' He thought the party in prospect sounded like 'the very next thing to a night in a looney institute'. Bad-taste exhibits were to be on show, including 'views of Highland cattle and a rare number entitled "I's Taller Than You, Mummy"'. Bad taste in dress would be optional.[82]

Although the 'Bad Taste' programme billed John as one of the evening's star attractions, he was in fact unable to attend the party: he had to write his *Standard* column. Instead, he sent along a 78 r.p.m. gramophone record of his voice, to be played to the guests. The record survives.[83] On it can be heard the voice of the twenty-eight-year-old Betjeman, sounding slightly more affected than it was later in his days as a television celebrity.

Mr Chairman, art lovers and art haters –
    I can think of nothing in poorer taste than accepting an invitation and coming like this. When you know why I am here in such record form you will find me in poorer taste still. I am at the present moment, while you are sitting here, writing rubbish about what sort of throat pastilles Bing Crosby uses, what sort of lingerie Garbo wears, why Clark Gable always has a bath in melted butter. I am telling my thousands of eager readers all about Helen Vinson's little dog, the only Scotch terrier in Hollywood to have its nails painted with crimson enamel. You wouldn't prevent my writing this, would you? Especially when my exquisite prose is going to appear in the great and glorious evening paper. And yet, when I come to think of what I am writing, it seems to me to be in better taste than what I used to write. For what is bad taste? If you will forgive my saying so, it is what is usually called good taste. It is self-consciousness. It is refeenment. If someone says to me, 'Do you know Mrs So-and-So? She's such an artistic woman. Her house is in fearfully good taste,' I know what she must be like. I can see the good taste of that house. Mentally, I bark my shins against the unstained oak table and trip over the expensive steel furniture of that artistic woman's drawing-room. Good taste nowadays is an aping of mass-production, which sends up the price of what should be cheap. Good taste nowadays has come to be identified with the expensive; and so I thank God that I am poor.

John added that he had always disliked 'good taste'.

Church architecture, which has oddly enough been my study for many years, is ruined by good taste. How infinitely preferable are the garish

mid-Victorian stained-glass windows in Prussian blue and crimson lake to
those anaemic sham Burne-Jones creations in pale greens of the Nineties
that are still being made today. How very much lovelier are, let us say, the
Houses of Parliament, that masterpiece of early Victorian Perpendicular,
than . . . the Draughtsman's Gothic of the present Liverpool Cathedral;
and, in painting, how much more interesting is the work of Holman Hunt
than that of Sir Frank Brangwyn . . . Don't you find the tuppenies like *Peg's
Paper* – modern betting paper – much more fun than those in a class above
such as, well, *Home & Decoration*, *The Home Beautiful* . . . and the
Happy and the *Merry* and all those sort of things? And aren't *they* more
interesting in their turn than *Blackwood's* and the *London Mercury* in its
present state and the *Cornhill*? And aren't even they more interesting than,
say, the *New Criterion* and so on?

John went on to suggest that the film business was affected by 'this
craze for good taste'.

Historical films are, I suppose, efforts to be cultured and tasteful. And
how dull they are compared with good old gangster films and murder mys-
teries. The better the taste, the less interesting the article, or rather the
worse the article. And what, conversely, is so interesting as a remark in bad
taste in the company of well-bred people? I wish I'd been tasteful enough
to come tonight to be entertained by your programme of bad taste – I love
it. And perhaps a little later you will hold an Evening of Good Taste. I
suggest that you couldn't choose a better place for holding it than
Burlington House as it is at present. Thank you, art lovers – or possibly,
art haters like myself. You may take this record off. It is not double-sided.

'Montie' Montagu-Nathan wrote to John on 11 March 1935 to thank
him for his contribution to the evening. 'The thing "got over" with
complete success. And your proxy received such a greeting that instead
of wishing you were present on the platform I should like you to have
been in the audience.'[84]

Though John was playing for laughs, the pettishness in his recorded
voice as he describes his work for the *Standard* suggests how irksome
he was finding the job. As he became increasingly bored by reporting
on films and stars, he hit on an ingenious way of writing instead about
the London suburbs, which interested him far more – Wood Green,
Acton, Ealing, Stepney, Maida Vale, Kilburn, Hammersmith and
Streatham. He pretended to be doing 'field work', analysing what
kinds of film were most popular in each suburb. In reality he was por-
traying the character of the suburbs – as he was to do in his
'Metroland' film on television almost forty years on.

United Arts Society

EveninG of Bad Taste

⟨and perhaps some good⟩

&

Exhibition of Industry without Art

 The Garden Club

Thursday. 7th March, 1935

PROGRAMME

Price
6d.

Programme

CROONING

RECEPTION
Miss Cicely Hamilton
Will Register Pleasure
&
will make
SOME TASTY ANNOUNCEMENTS.

× × ×

CROONING

During
THE
Evening

RECITATION
by
Mr. Roger Wimbush
of some choice excerpts
from
"POETRY" & "PROSE"

Mr. EDWIN EVANS will ROLL UP

SOME BALLADS
will have full justice meted out to them
by
Miss Winifred Knight
— o —

Mr. John Betjeman
author of
"GHASTLY GOOD TASTE"
will hold forth.

(probably
b e f o r e
the
EATS)

then
BUFFIT

Ninety-nine years ago Wood Green became a place of retirement for Aged Fishmongers and Poulterers, who still have an institution there.

Now it is hardly a place for the noisiest fishmonger to retire to. It is busy making sweets, stockings and batteries. It resounds with trams, roars with buses, blazes with lights and squelches with shops. Long streets struggle up the hill to where, like a broody flamingo, the 'Ally Pally' reigns over all. She even broods over the Gaumont Palace, which is big enough, heaven knows.[85]

Or again:

On no account confuse Meeda Veel with Kilburn. Both banks of the valley will resent it. It is like confusing Streatham with Balham, or ginger ale with champagne, or the other way round, according to which district you live in.

Two memorable events in the history of Kilburn occurred on August the Fourth, 1914. One you know. The other was that on that day the first super cinema in England was opened – the Grange, Kilburn. Since then it has remained one of the biggest houses in London, for it seats close on four thousand.

And those who don't sit down, stand up. For the old days of double seats which made the Grange so popular are over. But the Grange is still as popular as the crowded Kilburn High-road – the second biggest shopping centre in London. The 1914 decoration wears well and the audience has a family flavour about it that in the past was not above indulging in a family row.

The manager, Mr Turnbull, can recollect having to turn out patrons who had a wrestling match on the floor during the showing of 'Hearts Adrift', featuring Mary Pickford, I think.

In fact, Mr Turnbull is Kilburn's kind uncle . . . 'Dear Sir,' writes one of his patrons, 'My friends think my boy of ten would be very good on the films. He can sing like a man and a lady, also he can dance and twist his body about anyway, and he can disguise himself. So if you could see your way to seeing him and sending him to Elstree, I should be much obliged.'[86]

Another diversion John allowed himself as a change from the drudgery of workaday film-reviewing, was to make up verses about the films and stars. Sometimes indulgent sub-editors let these through. It was irresistible for him to write a verse notice of the Universal film of Poe's *The Raven*, starring Boris Karloff and Bela Lugosi.

Here's to Universal Pictures, who gainsay the Censor's strictures
And present to teeming millions, films of horror by the score.
Torture chambers all created for the unsophisticated,
Hulking, mouthing Boris Karloff not much different from before.

Add a pair of lovers tearful and a doctor mad and fearful –
    Same old plot and nothing more.

Just to keep things far from rosy, Doctor 'Dracula' Lugosi
Supervises all the tortures in his old-world basement floor.
Edgar Allan Poe conceived them, somehow Hollywood achieved them
But not even I believed them, for they smacked of films of yore
So I hope that nothing worse'll come to us from Universal
    Than 'The Raven' – evermore.[87]

John again broke into verse – which anticipates his 1940s poem
'How to Get On in Society' – to comment on an American report that
Hollywood (because of the attack on it by the purity movement) 'has
its back to the wall and is breathing hard . . . It is fighting for its very
life.' He imagined Mae West, Marlene Dietrich and Jean Harlow
singing this dirge:

> I have had to give up my steam cruiser,
>   I have sent my tame elk to the zoo,
> And though used to a staff of two hundred
>   I am now contented with two.
>
> There is rust on my platinum bathroom,
>   And dust on my fine Louis Seize
> Which I ought to have sold to a dealer
>   Before all this chromium craze.
>
> The scent I am using this morning
>   Was once but a bath for my chow,
> But you'll see what an honour I've done you
>   – I use it for interviews now.
>
> I can offer you tea and a biscuit,
>   Will you please go and shout at the door,
> Over there at the end of the ballroom,
>   As the bell doesn't work any more?
>
> It's terrible, all this privation,
>   I can't understand what they mean,
> If we give up our platinum bathrooms
>   Well, how can we ever be clean?[88]

Occasionally the *Standard* would let John off the leash to write
feature articles on subjects other than films: 'How to Look at the
Map'; 'Museums Should Be More Attractive'; 'How Do the Clergy
Live?' and 'Why I Am Glad that We Are Negotiating with Ireland'.[89]

Stuart Piggott gave him help with a debunking piece headed 'The Druids Were Over-rated'.[90] The most vivid of the general articles were on afternoon teas and preparatory schools. In the teas article, he mocked the names of country tearooms – 'Dame Nature's Pantry', 'Primula's Kitchen', 'At Ye Signe of Ye Olde Spynnynge Wheele', and warned of what awaited people who braved teatime in country hotels.

> The afternoon is sleepy. The porter is having his nap. No one is about. 'Ring bell for waitress.' You ring. A long pause.
> 'May I have tea, please?'
> 'Will you have it in the lounge, or in the coffee room?'
> If you choose the coffee room, you will sit among the tables laid for dinner, looking at someone's special bottle of sauce and someone else's bottle of spa water, not quite finished, waiting for the next meal.
> If you choose the lounge, be it wicker chair and palm variety, or mahogany and stained glass, there will be out-of-date numbers of weekly periodicals to look at. Tea will be brought eventually, and you will be glad to step out into the open air.[91]

The article on prep schools was headed 'Little Hells Let Loose'.[92] Before launching into an attack, John was careful to state that the prep school to which he had been sent – the Dragon School – 'was one of the happiest places in the world, and made all subsequent education seem repulsive'. The piece detailed torments devised by both masters and boys. It drew a letter from Rex Graves of Ultra Film Productions, Wardour Street, London, asking whether John would like to help write 'a series of films on the lines of a modern *Tom Brown's Schooldays*, full of wholesome humour that will take the city man back to his schooldays'.[93]

John replied that he could not spare the time. As with Harold Nicolson, the *Standard* job was bringing him fame, if not reputation, and he received many requests to write articles, collaborate on 'projects' and make public appearances. One commission he accepted was to write for *Kinematograph Weekly* an article criticizing the architecture of London movie theatres. The piece appeared in the issue of 17 January 1935 under the headline 'Has England Any Artistic Kinemas?' Because this subject engaged John's interest, the article is more spirited – more Betjemanesque – than the general run of his *Standard* film critiques.

> When I write about kinemas as buildings, I cannot help thinking, without any disrespect, of churches. Kinemas are often the churches of to-day. In the provinces and in the suburbs whole families attend the kinema with

the weekly regularity that their grandparents attended church or chapel. They have their special seats, just as their forbears had their special pews.

But there is this difference. Churches, until a hundred years ago, led the way in architecture. Kinemas lag behind.

The new Gaumont Palace at Chelsea . . . is in a pseudo-Swedish style that is already out of date. In ten years that interior will be a curiosity like the echoing vaults of the St Pancras Hotel or the terra-cotta fastnesses of the Hotel Grand Central. It will cost a mint of money to bring it 'up to date'.

Again the knowledge that John was gaining was to be redeployed in television many years later. In a television film of 1967 about cinema buildings ('Think of all the emotion that must have gorn on in those seats!') he led the cameras into the Astoria, Finsbury Park, with its Spanish cloister, the Astoria, Brixton, with its hanging gardens, and the glories of the Tooting Granada. ('Sidney Bernstein wanted to produce a Spanish-Moorish-Gothic cathedral for the people of Tooting. And by Jove he did it.')[94] In the same film he walked slowly from the back of the New Victoria's auditorium towards the screen, making laboured breast-stroke motions with his arms as he passed the mural decorations of seashell sconces and painted mermaids. 'In the business,' he murmured, 'we used to call this "Macfisheries".'[95]

When leaving the *Standard* job in 1935, John wrote that he had been more a 'film informer' than a film critic.[96] As well as reviewing, he was expected to tell his readers facts and news about the stars. The readers learned that Boris Karloff, of Frankenstein fame, was in reality Billy Pratt, born in Dulwich and entitled to two public school ties – Dulwich College and Uppingham. Tullio Carminiati, star of *One Night of Love* (1934), was really Count Tullio Carminiati di Brambilla and had acted with Mussolini.

John was not a success as a newsman. Robert Bruce Lockhart wrote in his diary on 1 October 1934:

A quiet day with one customary annoyance. I brought back from Mary [Lady Mary St Clair Erskine] the whole inside story of Pempe Dudley Ward's engagement to play in the Bergner film of *Escape Me Never*. I was told to do it for Diary. Then I was told it was to be a news story and that Betjeman was to do it. I gave him my stuff. Not a word of it was used, and in the stuff that appeared there was a bad mistake – saying that she had left that day for Venice whereas she was not leaving till end of week . . .[97]

One story of John's hopelessness as a reporter became Fleet Street legend. As told to Simon Jenkins, who was a journalist on the *Evening*

Standard in the 1970s and became its editor in 1976, the story runs like this. John knocks at Percy Cudlipp's door. 'Come in. Oh, hello, Betjeman. What's the matter?'

'Please, sir, I think I've got one of those "scoop" things.'

'Oh, really? How do you know it's a scoop?'

'Well, I've rung the *Evening News*, and they haven't got it.'[98]

A genuine scoop of John's – one of only two pieces by him that made the front page of the *Standard* – was about Merle Oberon's breaking off her engagement to the movie mogul Joseph Schenck. According to Osbert Lancaster, Schenck 'made such a stink' about the story that Beaverbrook ordered Cudlipp to fire John; but (Lancaster said) the British film industry advertisers protested strongly about the sacking – threatening to withdraw their advertising – and John was reinstated.[99]

John's other front-page scoop was that Lady Caroline Paget, eldest daughter of the Marquess of Anglesey, was to star in a film.[100] John had good reason to know the inside story on that, since he himself took a small part in the film, as a clergyman. The film was made at Ashcombe, Cecil Beaton's Georgian house in Wiltshire. Beaton's and John's friend John Sutro,[101] who was a director of London Film Productions, had often wondered why even the smallest movie should cost such a lot of money. Would it not be possible to produce something worthwhile for only a few hundred pounds? Sutro and Beaton decided to attempt at Ashcombe an amateur film of David Garnett's story *The Sailor's Return*, about a Victorian sailor who brings back to his village from overseas a black wife named Tulip, a small dark daughter and a parrot. The cast was to consist of friends, neighbours, farmhands and the family of Betteridge, the Ashcombe gamekeeper. From Denham Studios came make-up men, electricians and photographers with their arc-lights. The studio became a dormitory and the dining-room a canteen. The costumes were run up in a day.

Beaton played the sailor who returns with his black bride, Tulip (Lady Caroline Paget), to be innkeeper in his native village. He falls victim to village prejudice and religious difficulties and is eventually killed. Meanwhile Tulip has to escape home to avoid the village clergyman (John), who wants to make her son 'as white as snow'. John Sutro played Tom, the life and soul of the pub. Beaton recalled the filming in his book *Ashcombe* (1949):

We were blessed with a stretch of ten cloudless days. In a hearteningly short time we managed to shoot a splendid portion of the story, but on the Saturday evening disaster almost overtook us, for the coloured child, indispensable to the plot, who had been dispatched from Denham Studios

Casting Office with her negress mother and caged parrot, had disappeared
without trace. Telephone calls to all the neighbouring railway stations
were made in vain; yet, curious as it now seems, we were supplied by the
Sunday night with another coloured mother and daughter, though a
Daimler had to be sent many miles to pick up another caged parrot.

The experiment at picture-making far surpassed our expectations . . .
John Betjeman was the parson, and so realistic was John Sutro's appearance as the yokel that, while leaning against a five-barred gate on location,
in between acts he was joined for a country chat by a genuine rustic. The
make-up of Caroline Paget as Tulip was exaggeratedly 'Black Sambo', and
belonged more to the realm of ballet, and my own performance as the
Sailor was painfully self-conscious. However, a few weeks after the film
was shot, I was rather proud to learn that one of the local farm-boys was
suing me for severe damage done to his jaw during the fight-scene, which
was staged most realistically in a neighbouring hayfield.[102]

Beaton's near-neighbour and friend Edith Olivier took a bit part as
a villager. She wrote in her diary for 14 July 1935:

[*Ashcombe*] . . . a very hot exhausting crowded time wasting sort of day . . .
18 people in the house – and they wanted me to stay! The producer is only just
down from Oxford and is quite inexperienced but the many photographers
and make-up men seemed capable. Caroline Paget exquisite as Tulip –
though her black kept coming off and it is cruel to deprive her of that rich
magnolia skin of hers – a little professional negress child played Sambo.
Very sophisticated and also very childlike. Quite calm and businesslike
when performing and then rollicking about with the cook's child who
adored her! John Betjeman was admirable as the clergyman. Cecil like the
sailor in *Matelot* – very stylized and good at it, and so kind and considerate to all his guests. Lots of yokels . . . The whole day spent in waiting about
in violent heat and then doing a disjointed episode, always cut off. There
is no acting in film-acting. It is only *joining up bits of photographs*. The
picture is made *after* the episodes have been shot. In spite of Cecil's hospitable objection I got away at midnight . . . bringing John Betjeman for
the night. There is a terrific row with the Angleseys about Caroline being
in this because Cecil couldn't resist having it in all the papers, so now she
is in high disgrace. It is odd that she should do these outré things and get
her reputation, for she has that lovely dreaming, aloof character, always
seeming apart from whatever is going on, and without enthusiasm or
ardour.[103]

Edith Olivier had first met John in July 1932 when Penelope had
brought him to stay at her house in Wilton for a weekend. 'He is . . .

cleaner than I expected,' she wrote in her diary then – she had been given a scathing report on him by Penelope's mother.[104] A day later she had decided: 'His instincts are all right. He does not jar. *If* they stick to each other, I don't think Lady Chetwode need feel Penelope is more likely to be unhappy than in any other marriage . . .'[105] In October 1933, after John and Penelope had married, the painter Henry Lamb came to tea with Edith Olivier, who noted: 'He thinks John [Betjeman] less critical and cynical than I do . . .'[106] Now, as film critic of the *Evening Standard*, John was a figure of influence and could be useful to her. By having him to stay for the night, she hoped to persuade him to write some letters of introduction to Fleet Street for her. In April, when she had stayed with John and Penelope in Uffington,[107] he had offered to see what he could do. He seemed unwilling to put her in touch with a Fleet Street editor but suggested instead that she should prepare a gazetteer for Robert Byron's *Shell Guide to Wiltshire* – as, indeed, she did.

The Sailor's Return was never completed. 'As with many amateur enterprises,' Beaton wrote, 'there was no enthusiasm left to supply the dreary but essential finishing touches, and the film was never finally cut or the sound-track added.'[108] If John had intended to remain a professional film critic, the experience of helping to make a film – however amateurish – might have been of value to him. But a month after taking part in the Ashcombe film, he was writing an acerbic farewell article in the *Standard*, 'Good-bye to Films'. Nerina Shute's recollection was that he was fired, this time without reprieve. 'Someone had arrived from Hollywood, I can't remember who, but some very well-known star; and it was a *news* story – you had to go and meet this person and interview them and it was very important. And he just didn't go. He couldn't bear to go to Southampton or wherever it was to meet a film star. And the editor said, "Why didn't you go?" and he said "Well, I didn't feel like it." That was the end of John Betjeman on the *Standard*. I remember his telling me about it and laughing. He thought it was terribly funny, and so did I; because anybody in Fleet Street, as I'm sure you know, thinks that the most important thing in the world is a news story – it's the Holy Grail.'[109]

As when leaving *The Architectural Review*, it seems likely that he precipitated his own downfall at the *Standard* when sick of the job. In the farewell article he spared no one's feelings.

Yesterday I wrote my last article as film critic in this paper. When I started off, a pale green bogus-intellectual, a year and a half ago, what a different man was I.

A visit or two to some Continental films, a sarcastic sneer to any people who told me they were in love with Greta Garbo, and that was the sum of my cinematic experience. The word 'montage' was on my lips, 'art' was written in poker work across my heart, 'prose style' was embroidered with raffia on the reverse side of it.

I was as typical a middlebrow as ever thought he was highbrow and tried to write poetry in Hampstead.

And now what would you see, were these lines of type to fly about and form themselves into a portrait of the author, as in some French surréaliste short film? You would see a bald elderly man, still pale green, but with a tough expression, grim business-like lips and a pair of unscrupulous eyes gleaming behind recently acquired horn-rimmed spectacles. In fact, you would see a typical member of the film business.

For the film business does not want any rot about art. Those garish offices in Wardour-street are not temples of the drama, they are shops with very clever men behind the counter who sell the products of Hollywood, Elstree and other film factories to exhibitors.

Every product of the factory is advertised as 'colossal', 'stupendous', 'poignant', 'the sensation of the century', just as fruit on a street stall is labelled 'choice', 'grand-eating', 'luscious', too often regardless of its merit.[110]

John summed up what he had liked in the cinema and what he had disliked:

A murder story held me spellbound. A fast moving comedy in almost incomprehensible American made me hit the critic sitting next to me on the head with excitement.

Then I wondered why I was entertained, and I couldn't find out. I only knew that if a film was pretentious I was bored. Historical films, singing in old Vienna, crooners against a picture postcard background of Monte Carlo or Haiti bored me to distraction.[111]

In sarcastic reference to the cause of his dismissal, John asserted that many of the stars were 'ordinary shy people who don't want to be bothered by a lot of fatuous questions'. Of those he had met, some stood out in his memory as 'really good company' – Jean Parker, Helen Vinson, Gracie Fields, George Arliss, Robert Montgomery, Loretta Young, Paul Graetz and Dolly Haas. John thanked heaven for the stars he had met. 'I also thank heaven for those I have not met. They have still all the glamour for me that they had for my readers. And now good-bye to them all.'[112]

The farewell article appeared in the *Standard* eight days before John's twenty-ninth birthday. He still had the resilience of youth. Even when venting his exasperation with film-reviewing, he kept his sense of humour.

> Films were gradually turning me dotty. I used to come out of a Press showing and caress the bricks in the street, grateful that they were three-dimensional. If I saw a thuggish-looking man with his hat pulled down over his face, I expected to be shot in the back.
>
> Worse still, I was becoming unable to think. Thinking was being done for me on the screen and not very hard thinking, either. I was beginning to become historical in my style. 'Jean Arthur, whom you will remember in "Passport to Fame", and who before that was in so-and-so, and so-and-so, is now in so-and-so.' Paralysis was creeping over me.[113]

John considered he had done well to stick at such a mind-numbing job for a year and a half. 'The old old story seven times a week is . . . more than enough for the most willing ears after a year.'[114] And brief as his reviewing stint was, it made him – in 1930s Britain with its cult of the gentleman amateur – a 'films expert'. When, in 1938, Charles Davy edited a book titled *Footnotes to the Film*, John was one of the contributors, alongside Alfred Hitchcock, Robert Donat, Graham Greene, Alberto Cavalcanti, John Grierson, Alexander Korda and Sidney Bernstein.[115] And during the Second World War, when a medical board pronounced John unfit for any war service, his reputation as a films expert enabled Kenneth Clark to find him a job in the films division of the Ministry of Information.*

* See Chapter 11, 'Minnie'.

THE DIARIST

V depressed. P[enelope] depressed too. Imminence of war. Damned if I will
fight: Rescue work, yes, but not killing. Dread death.

John Betjeman, diary entry, 12 October 1935[1]

After resigning from the *Standard*, John had time on his hands. He
used some of it to keep a diary, intermittently, during the second half
of 1935 and the first few months of 1936. As far as we know, it was the
only journal he ever kept. Parts of it are gossip, and there are jottings
on architecture, but the diary also gives a view of him in his late twenties more intimate than any of his printed writings, where his frank-
ness about his appearance and his melancholia conceal as much as
they reveal. In the diary his preoccupations and fears are naked, not
dressed up for public consumption. There is no sense that he is writing
with an eye on posterity.

It was a meeting with George Bernard Shaw and his wife Charlotte,
at Lord Berners's house, that inspired him to begin it, in August 1935.
Shaw was a direct link with one of John's heroes, William Morris.[2]

August 17th GB Shaw and M[rs] a charming old thing, Irish gt admirer of
'GBS' at lunch with Gerald. I said 'You ought to see the tithe barn at G[t]
Coxwell.'[3] GBS replied: 'I remember Morris took me there.'[4] Morris
pulled hairs out of his moustache when he was angry. Very painful for
onlookers. Said how he filled up sentences in Intelligent Woman's Guide
to Socialism[5] costing £300 in corrections. Likes close printing as Morris
did. Went to Folly & to White Horse. GBS had a wish on the eye &
climbed down the back to Dragon Hill. Aetat 80.

On 18 August John heard the Rev. Lord de Mauley,[6] who was in his
ninetieth year, take matins at Little Faringdon and deliver an eloquent
sermon on 'Let everyone that crieth . . .' 'Cross between Voysey & Dr
Pusey to look at,' John wrote. 'Elegant frail old voice.' John had tea
that day with Frederick Etchells.[7] On 21 August he and Etchells went

on a three-day church-crawl. At Gayhurst there were high pews, 'probably Wren'; at Thornton, 'perfect 1800–40 fittings' and nuns sewing in
the garden. The two men spent the first night at Kimbolton: 'Best
small town I've seen. D[uke] of Manchester. Etchells pleased he was
mistaken for him. Hunts [Huntingdonshire] churches disappointing.
Mostly no plaster on the walls.' In Northamptonshire he dismissed
the famous Saxon church of Earls Barton as 'hideous' – 'Tower looks
half-timbered. Saxons weren't architects only decorators & artists.
Pleasantly incongruous setting of red brick industrial villas.' At
Wellingborough, a 'good heartily ugly Midland town', they visited the
'exquisite' St Mary's Church: 'Enriched Perp . . . [Ninian] Comper will
spoil it if he puts on any more colour . . . C is a first class architect.'
John thought the interior detail 'pleasingly effeminate' but the stained
glass 'execrable'. At Great Houghton there was a 'perfect steeple' but
a 'wrecked interior'; at Melchbourne, 'a fine row of cottages'; at
Ravenstone church, 'a good monument to some dim peer Earl of
Nottingham – figure reclining on a cushion under curtained canopy.
Black and white.'

John was back in Uffington by 24 August. Percy Cudlipp and his
wife were meant to visit the Betjemans but let them down. The next
day, however, 'Dean Inge, M^{rs} & Richard a plodding but pleasant son
came to lunch.' John found the 'gloomy Dean' of St Paul's, who was
a prolific newspaper columnist at the time, 'very difficult – a Victorian
Lazarus to my Dives'. This was a case of the biter bit. Only two years
before, reviewing a coal miner's book about his experiences at Oxford,
John had commented on the miner's failure to engage Inge in conversation at a New College lunch party: 'That is not the way to get on in
Society,[8] Mr Dataller. Even the broadest-minded of us observe social
conventions. The Warden won't ask you again.'[9] Now he, too, was
finding that small-talk was not the Dean's forte. John and Penelope
took the party to Faringdon, where Inge was introduced to Robert
Heber Percy. 'Robert asked him something. Getting no reply he asked
again. "Yes, I heard," said Dr I. "I was thinking."'

After a long gap the diary is resumed on 5 October, at which time
Penelope was in Rome, attending a Conference of Orientalists. John
dined with Berners, Diana Guinness (later Lady Mosley) and W.H.
Auden.

We all went to W[ystan Auden]'s play 'Dance of Death' well produced
& impressive satire,[10] wish there had not been the clumsy attempt at
realism at the end. D[iana] thought Mosley bits excellent & pro-fascist,
clapped. Hissed when red flag appeared . . . Diana took us back to Eaton
Square & played the leader's speech & Hitler's on gramophone. W[ystan]

unimpressed. As Gerald says 'I feel I may have a row with Diana any minute.' W finds Gerald a v sympathetic character.

On 6 October John lunched with Auden at Curtain's restaurant. 'No talk about literature thank God,' he wrote. 'Find him refreshingly unchanged. Said I wished he'd kept D[ance] of D[eath] satire all through. "You forget my views, my dear." Saw his piece [a boy Auden admired at the Downs School, where he had been teaching until recently] accompanied by master arrive at Waterloo. W dashed back to say, "What do you think?" "Not bad." Big ears.'
Six days later John wrote:

Oct. 12 whether it is convalescence from this flu or what I don't know. V depressed. P[enelope] depressed too. Imminence of war. Damned if I will fight: Rescue work yes, but not killing. Dread death. Thoughts of Ernie [his father] all alone in that waste of marble at Highgate. How he must hate it if he knows.[11] Bess [his mother] in Matlock leaving no address. How I shall miss Archie & [illegible] & Uffington when I go to get gassed by progress. The Captain [Raleigh] brought in his book Chronicles of Slyme Court. Do not know what to say . . .

After another hiatus in the diary, John wrote up a visit to E.E. Bradford, the 'Uranian' poet whose verse made him and Stuart Piggott scream with laughter.[12] However comic John found the verse, he was sympathetic to the poet.

December 9th Yesterday I had the inestimable privilege of spending Sunday afternoon and evening with the Reverend EE Bradford DD, author of 'Passing the Love of Women' & many other volumes of verse. He has been vicar of Nordelph, Downham Market since 1917 & is now 75.
    Nordelph is miles away in the Norfolk fens, a village of 2-storey houses most of them sloping on unsafe foundations strung about with telegraph poles & electric light poles. Church 1865 red brick decorated after Butterfield, no tower or aisles. Vicarage brick Gothic & flimsy. Dangerous and it is shored up.[13] No answer for some time. No garden, goats & grass & trees (only trees for miles in . . . wonderful December sunset over rivers, eaux, fields & rows of cabbages & heaps of parsnips).
    Vicarage hall dark, grim black line . . . Terribly poor. Bradford hurried out of room in dressing gown. 'Quite safe in here, only other side of house is falling. I'm not bothered.' High voice, like Cottam's,[14] talks a lot & v fast. Sit on hard kitchen chairs. I sat by fire in arm chair. Large American Organ 2 manual plays Bach. Likes conversing in French. Not up to it, me. Various reproductions of Tuke[15] and Millais's 'Princes in the Tower'.[16]

Pictures everywhere. All very neatly docketed: press cuttings & articles. V scholarly like Anthony [Blunt].

Funny bald head flat on top & pearshaped. Blue eyes. Poor old man obviously cataract coming on. Won't admit he is failing. Knocked over firescreen & broke it. Quiet hurried little movements. Frail sweet little person. Walks 16 miles on some days. No car, walks everywhere. Thrilled at sight of motor. Ran 3 miles 2 years ago when late for a funeral. Found he was not tired afterwards. Believes in helping young.

V interested in Eddington,[17] Jeans[18] &c. A modernist but likes ritual. Last boy friend called Edmund [?Edward] Monson. Not had a boy friend for 30 years. V happy with Nordelph. A saint & thinks laws against sexuality wicked cruel & out of date. Thinks Cottam no poet & going mad.

Said the Queen asked him for an autograph of one of his books. Obviously a joke played on him poor old thing. 'I wonder why she wanted it. Perhaps for the Prince of Wales [later King Edward VIII and Duke of Windsor]. I have often thought he may be a Platonist.' Platonists mentioned a good bit.[19] Read Freud, doesn't believe him.

Said he had a dream the other day that a big boy asked him to go to a house . . . at Torre where he lived as a child. Knew he was to go there for a bad purpose. Saw house. Experienced nothing – felt as though he was a boy of eight again. Got his DD for proving St Paul contradicts himself on the subject of Free Will. Advocates birth control and says that logically Onan[20] is a must, ∴ [should] be permitted in public schools.

Service fairly well attended . . . Children get a penny for coming, kept in little boxes in a drawer of his desk. Plays organ himself. Candles on red altar, black cloths. All candles lighted. Plays organ v well. Handsome little fellow pumps. Sermon v abstruse & clever on certainty of existence of God. Talked of Julian Huxley[21] . . . Cold supper in vicarage . . . Felt the better for seeing such a sweet & saintly little man . . . Surely never did a bad thing in his life.

That night, John stayed with his old Marlborough friend Anthony Blunt at Trinity College, Cambridge.

Meeting W.H. Auden again had made John want to see more of him. On 16 December he wrote:

Wystan Auden stayed. P[enelope] in London to see her father Sat night so W & I got tight or at least mellow & went through the whole of Evensong (broad to high). More fun later. Sunday went to hear Cottam preach. Ch v empty. Terrific attack on the people of Wootton he knew of no parish which helped its clergyman so little. As W says he is obviously going mad. His eyes roll & he never looks at one but out of the corners of them – persecution mania. W thinks he will have to be taken away soon.

The F[ield] M[arshal] [Penelope's father] came to lunch. In a letter Monday . . . he says 'Why do poets always look as though they were rams which had been dragged backwards through a thorn bush. Yours had not brushed his hair for a week.' I saw W actually run a pocket comb through his hair before lunch – a hangover from prep school. I like W much more than I thought I would after all this time. His energy & enthusiasm are terrific. Invert [?] at Fyfield told us funny story of Cottam. He didn't get on with his organist & was always trying to get rid of him. Finally he put a dead hedgehog in the organist's hat. This hat trick worked. The organist is now at Kingston Bagpuize. Dinner with Gerald [Berners] in the evening. P[enelope] there. P made W write some of his Hansel & Gretel dialogue for the infants.

W an avowed Communist. 'I feel it is my duty to make notes & report on the bourgeoisie.'

Ten days later, two former schoolfellows of John's came to Uffington. One was Graham Shepard, son of the illustrator Ernest H. Shepard, who was a particular friend and had probably introduced John to Osbert Lancaster when the three of them were at Oxford.[22] The other was Louis MacNeice, with whom John was never on easy terms.[23]

Dec. 26th . . . Graham H. Shepard & his wife & Louis MacNeice came to lunch – ½ an hour late. MacN an hour late. P[enelope] very cold, like the lunch. I found MacN as gauche & literary & irritating as ever. I was obviously expected to mention his poetry but abstained from doing so. It seems to me to be Twilight Blunden. He brought a Borzoi with him. His wife has left him for a Jew – Reverted to type?[24] Seemed unmoved by it. Mrs GHS had a frightful dog which didn't like the indoor fireworks. A dismal party. Tea with Etchells refreshing.

Other links with Marlborough were renewed on 27 December when John met Clifford Canning,[25] who had been a housemaster at the school, and Cyril Norwood,[26] who had been Master and – after a spell as headmaster of Harrow – was now President of St John's College, Oxford.

Dec 27th Went to tea with Canning & Dr & Mrs Norwood at St John's. The great man unbent so much as to imitate Gidney[27] to us telling Anthony Richardson[28] to write no more books. He showed me round the College. Library Laud's vestments.[29] Chapel early 19th Gothic. Lodge long panelled passages. Nice talk & a big tea for schoolboys. What a nice man Dr N is. He was in P[lus] 4's which look odd on him. Had been for a walk in the Parks with the Chaplain of Harrow – a man like Birley[30] but with the new clergy decisiveness of diction.

The diary then jumps to 7 February 1936, for an entry about Uffington villagers.

> To-day poor old Mrs Townsend died getting out of bed. 'I heard the death rattle last night,' said T[ownsend] '& then this morning she said the bottle was cold & I thought, "that's funny" for it was warm enough to wash up the tea things. So I brought her another & then found her all in a heap on the floor.' He changed into his Sunday clothes at once & went off on his old bicycle. Old Mrs Norton died in the Radcliffe at 2 a.m.

The entry shows John's Pinter-like ear for the colloquial ('that's funny' . . . 'all in a heap'), his sympathy, his preoccupation with death and sense of its mundaneness. (Not for nothing is there an echo of the early poem 'Death in Leamington' – 'Nurse came in with the tea-things . . .')[31] Both his compassion and an eye for significant detail are revealed in the words 'He changed into his Sunday clothes' – which could well be a line in a Betjeman poem.

The final entry in the diary, on 9 April 1936, briefly records that Sir Ralph Glyn and his wife came to tea. Glyn was MP for Abingdon, and John wanted to show him ten condemned cottages in the village. 'Hope we shall get something done. Demolition order suspended. Craven Estate to be approached.'

The diary of 1935–36 is fragmented and truncated; but it gives us a direct conduit into John's thinking at the age of twenty-nine. One strand in it is the peculiarly eager interest in literary homosexuals, not to say paedophiles. The visits – almost pilgrimages – to S.E. Cottam and E.E. Bradford have later analogies in his seeking out the Uranian novelist and art historian Forrest Reid, in Belfast,[32] and in his suggestion to Siegfried Sassoon, in the 1950s, that they should call on Sidney Mavor, the last surviving boyfriend of Oscar Wilde. (It turned out that he had just died.)[33] Too much should not be read into John's renewed friendship with Auden and his light-hearted appraisal of Auden's 'piece'. Much more significant are the entries which show that John was anti-fascist, convinced that a war was coming and determined not to fight in it. At that time he was still formally a Quaker:[34] that fact, as well as his admitted fear of death, may have been a motive for wishing to avoid the battlefield – fighting shy of it, one might say. Most of the Oxford undergraduates who in 1933 caused national outrage, when they voted that they would not fight for King and Country in a future war,[35] served in the armed forces when war broke out. John's outlook was also to change completely by 1939. Then, it was the armed forces that rejected him, not he them.

'THAT'S SHELL – THAT WAS!'

Pray forgive my extremely confidential and frank letter. Perhaps you are a little disgusted at my exposure of all these facts . . .

John Betjeman, letter to Jack Beddington, 17 August 1933

In 1964, when John had been editing the Shell Guides to English counties for over thirty years, he was infuriated by an attempt by Shell to alter James Lees-Milne's guide to Worcester without consulting him. He wrote a long letter to the artist John Piper, who had worked with him on the guides since the 1930s. It began: 'Owing to difficulties with the present arrangements between us and Shell . . . I find myself so discouraged and insecure that I do not want to go on with the guides.'[1] The real purpose of the letter was not to apprise Piper of the situation, which he knew only too well, but to have a copy placed in front of the Shell 'executives', to make them aware of John's anger and his threat to resign.[2] In the letter, John went into the history of his association with Shell: how he had started the guides in 1933, conceiving them; doing the writing, the make-up and production of the first two himself; after that, collaborating with Piper and other authors.

> The guides, in those days, were not expected to pay. They were prestige advertising, subsidized by Shell. There were no publishers' contracts and the whole thing was done on a personal basis, because Beddioleman [Jack Beddington] and subsequently William Scudamore Mitchell and I and the printers all knew each other. No-one made much money out of the guides, unless it were the publishers, printers, block makers and binders. I got a salary of £800 a year from Shell for editing and doing the make-up and writing the guides.[3]

John had been introduced to Jack Beddington, the dynamic publicity manager of Shell, in his (John's) days on *The Architectural Review*.

Beddington (1893–1959) was a son of one of seven brothers called Cohen who were all members of the London Stock Exchange in the 1890s. All seven changed their name, on the same day, to Beddington – the name of a Surrey village. Newly named, they arrived for work one morning to find a banner across the main hall of the Stock Exchange: 'And the Lord said unto Moses – Good Morning Mr Beddington!'[4] (John wrote to Beddington in 1939: 'Have you read "The Stockbroker's Clerk" by Conan Doyle – one of the Sherlock Holmes stories? – the villain in it is called Beddington.')[5] John and his friends called Beddington 'Beddioleman' because an American called Grimaldi, on leaving the publicity manager's office, had said: 'Well, hi, Beddy ol' man!'[6] Like his father, Beddington was one of several brothers. 'John called them Beddioleman, Beddimiddleman, Beddiyoungestman and so on,' John Piper said. 'One of them – Beddioldestman – went into Wildenstein's, the art dealers.' Jack Beddington was known as 'Beddi' for short.[7]

A Balliol man, he had served in the First World War. He had been appointed publicity manager of Shell in 1928. In 1932 Shell and British Petroleum amalgamated their publicity and trading operations in the United Kingdom in a separate company, Shell-Mex BP. It moved into Shell-Mex House, the monolithic, much reviled new building by Francis Cashmore which replaced the old Hotel Cecil on the Victoria Embankment of the Thames. Beddington became publicity manager of this new company.

To Kenneth Clark, Beddington was like 'a Levantine pirate who had tactfully removed his earrings';[8] to John Piper, he was 'a great jolly bouncing man';[9] to John's daughter, Candida, 'uproariously funny';[10] to the artist Richard Guyatt, 'a suave and worldly wizard'. Guyatt also wrote of Beddington's 'clubman chic' – the brushed-up moustache, bowler hat and rolled umbrella: 'He was a bit of a dandy/boulevardier.'[11] Harry Blacker, a young graphic artist who worked for Shell in the early 1930s, also thought him 'very dapper', adding: 'He was extremely friendly; he never talked down to anybody, and he would listen to you, which was something very new for me.'[12]

Beddington was an inspired patron of artists, many of them young and untried. Among them, besides Piper, Guyatt and Blacker, were Graham Sutherland, Ben Nicholson, Duncan Grant, Rex Whistler (who caricatured him), E. McKnight Kauffer, Edward Bawden, Edward Ardizzone and Mary Kessell, who became Kenneth Clark's lover.[13] Beddington commissioned several of them to contribute to a great poster campaign. Instead of getting safe academic poster artists to paint landscapes of local beauty spots, as the railway companies were doing, Beddington relied on the humorous approach. The poster

that caught on best was the 'double-headed man' designed by John
Reynolds, son of a *Punch* art editor: the idea was that the man's head
was swivelling violently from one side to the other as a car full of Shell
petrol roared past in a blur of dust. The slogan was 'CRIKEY!
THAT'S SHELL – THAT WAS!'

A long-running series presented the types of people who used Shell
petrol: 'Theatre-goers Use Shell' (John Armstrong); 'Tourists Prefer
Shell' (Tristram Hillier); 'Guardsmen Use Shell' (Ben Nicholson) and
'Film Stars Use Shell' (Cathleen Mann). John Piper was asked to
design 'Clergymen Prefer Shell', but the poster was banned as disrespectful to the Cloth. The photographer Maurice Beck produced a
series of distorted photographic heads to illustrate 'People We Do Not
Cater For'. The sparky, facetious mood of the campaign was caught
in another photographic poster which showed Beddington himself
doing up (undoing, John alleged) the buttons of his wife's dress. The
'I say, I say' music-hall caption was:

Do you read the Shell advertisements?
Yes, but I still use the petrol.

One of Beddington's great attractions for indigent artists was that
he paid cash. On taking over publicity he had arranged for designers'
fees to be paid direct from his own department. 'In this way,'
McKnight Kauffer's biographer writes, 'payments did not have to be
churned through an elaborate and lengthy accounting procedure . . .'[14]
Ruari McLean took a less charitable view: 'He kept a fund of cash in
his desk and paid artists on the nail, thereby getting their works of art
much cheaper than if they had invoiced and waited.'[15] But both
Blacker and Guyatt recalled with affection how Beddington had given
them much-needed pocket-money by commissioning work he did not
require.

Beddington gave work to writers as well as artists. Evelyn Waugh and
Peter Quennell both contributed. Early in 1933 John suggested to
Beddington the idea of the Shell Guides – a series of guidebooks to
British counties that would display the individuality of the writer as well
as of the county. John was to be general editor. At first he did the work
at weekends and on holidays but after he stormed out of *The Architectural
Review* in 1935,[16] he was able to devote much more time to the project.
This was perhaps the first paid work he had undertaken – apart from
writing poetry – which promised to be really congenial.

As a youth he had sated himself with guidebooks and he knew what
he did not want in his series. A manifesto was later printed:

The fuzzy 'camera study' view is never included; Georgian architecture is noticed; as a newspaper has said, 'everything an intelligent tourist could want to know is touched upon.'

No writer of a Shell Guide is allowed to use those worn out words 'picturesque', 'fine', 'beautiful', 'quaint'.

The writers are selected for their powers of observation and their ability with prose. There is no guide-bookese in a Shell Guide, no cracking up of E.E. piscinae . . .[17]

On 8 February 1933 Beddington's secretary wrote to John to confirm that he would be paid up to £20 for making up a dummy for 'the proposed Shell Guide Book'.[18] It was agreed that the Architectural Press, which published *The Architectural Review*, would produce the books for Shell. But on 17 August John wrote Beddington a panicky letter from Frederick Etchells's office–flat in Davies Street, where he was temporarily cuckoo-nesting. It began:

Dear Beddioleman,

I hate to disturb you during your chickenpoxed holiday but as I am far from a holiday myself and very righteously indignant at being put upon, I must beg you in the name of Lansdown Road, in the name of John Armstrong[19] and all you hold sacred to help me in an almost unbelievable position.[20]

The letter continued with a long tirade against Maurice Regan, part-owner of the Architectural Press. (John was still editor of *The Architectural Review* 'in all but name'.) Regan was, John claimed, 'a good simple soul with a mind for figures' but 'a person of no aesthetic susceptibility whatever'.[21]

If you saw his little home and his cousins uncles father and other relations who predominate in the architectural press you would realise why it is that the archie rev never goes quite the whole hog . . . and why the book department here is a complete flop. I have been co-opted on to the books and my salary raised from three to four hundred a year . . . I do not wish to be unpleasant about the Regans, but they are not our sort. They all live in Wimbledon, have closed saloons, see no one but each other and are not interested in anything but getting money which they do not know how to spend.[22]

The one person of whom the Regans were afraid, John added, was 'the Chief' – Percy Hastings, who on his visits to the office left them shaking.

But here is the iniquity that I am bursting to tell you . . . Maurice Regan
has told the 'chief' all about the Shell Guides and the 'chief' is delighted.
He has not mentioned however that the idea was mine, the make up was
mine and that I saw you first and started the whole thing . . .[23]

John went on to say that he did not think Maurice Regan was trying
to do him down; Regan simply wanted to prevent John 'being "too
mad" as he would say' and being given authority to arrange the make-
up. John thought the guides would be a failure if Regan had anything
to do with the aesthetic side of them. He foresaw that, if they were a
success, Percy Hastings would give all the credit to Regan for preventing John from going too far.

John emphasized that he was not asking Beddington for money. But
there were two things he could do for him – 'or at least one of them,
which will shew the bloody Regans that in the outside world I am
thought a little more of than in the Architectural Press'.[24] Beddington,
he pointed out, had not yet signed the contract. John wanted him to
insert two clauses. The first would stipulate that all questions of make-
up, illustrations, maps and letterpress were to be in the hands of Mr J.
Betjeman. (As an aside, John wrote that his own make-up, on which
costs had already been calculated, was not going to be more expensive
than anything Regan might devise – 'It may be cheaper.') The other
clause John wanted Beddington to insert was that 'you reserve the right
to discontinue the guides if you wish it at the settling up of the Cornish
Guide and also that you can take them elsewhere if you want to continue
them again . . . or rather that, *in the event of their success, you insist
upon my remaining their author and I can then dictate my own terms*'.[25]

The morose, somewhat paranoid letter reveals John's depressed
state of mind at that time. But it also shows the political skill with
which he could always urge his case when he wanted something. First,
there is the background summary of the situation at the Architectural
Press, with just enough malice and piquant detail to hold Beddington's
interest as the long moan continues. There is the frankly snobbish confidence that the Regans are 'not our sort', with their closed saloons
and Wimbledon homes. And then comes the clear staking-out of the
two things John wanted Beddington to do for him. *En passant*,
although he has damned the Regans as penny-pinching, John is
careful – as he is writing to a businessman – to present his proposals
as economical. Like a good civil servant briefing a minister, he feeds
Beddington with drafts of telling arguments to put to the Regans on
his behalf. The naked candour of the letter may flatter Beddington,
though John has the nous to assure him he will not denigrate him to
others as he is denigrating the Regans to him –

Pray forgive my extremely confidential and frank letter. Perhaps you are a little disgusted at my exposure of all these facts and think I might treat you in the same way. Believe me I would not and it is only an accumulation of examples such as this last of my misrepresentation to the 'chief' and lack of appreciation from the Regans that has made me write this letter.

You see I have become a little disgusted too.

I bear the poor dears little ill will . . .[26]

The sub-text of the letter is: 'I would like to leave *The Architectural Review* and come and work for you at Shell.' This plea is implicit throughout and John comes close to making it explicit:

There is one more thing . . . with which you could save my bacon. If the guide is a success and [the Regans] continue to pay me four hundred a year and make me do the rest of the guides and edit the Archie Rev as well I will not only be underpaid but overworked. These guides interest me far more than anything else because I hate urban life and am really cut out for archaeology, make up and photography, and know England pretty well. But it is useless to undertake work like this as a side issue where one is cramped and crabbed by the narrowness of the Regans and I would very much like to have the opportunity of getting away from my present unappreciated position and doing the guides on my own with some other publisher . . .[27]

He had chosen Cornwall first, he wrote, because he knew it well. 'With other counties it might not be so easy to do it in a half time way.' If Shell would only take him on, he would demand 'no more than a living wage . . . less than I get now because I should be doing something I liked . . . and [would] work solely for Shell.' However, he realized that any decision Beddington made would depend on whether or not the Cornwall guide were 'a roaring success'.[28]

Jack Beddington picked up every nuance of the letter and knew what he could promise and what, at this stage, he should not promise. On 19 August he wrote John a soothing letter, beginning, 'My dear John, You do want a holiday – what a cri de coeur!'[29] He could and would insist that John was to be responsible for the whole make-up and was to get the credit for the entire job. He could also promise the same for future guides, though he did not think he would be able to issue them without the aid of the Architectural Press. On John's ambition to join Shell he put a damper: he could see little chance of that happening and was convinced that 'it would be a great mistake for you at the moment to try to do such a thing'.[30] But he told him not to despair and asked him to come to lunch after he (Beddington) returned from his holiday, in September.

Beddington added: '*Private*. Secretly between you and me personally for my part I rather liked Regan (as I believe that privately for your part personally you do too) . . .'[31]

In fact, John continued to feel resentment towards Maurice Regan and his family. His satirical poem 'Kegans', first published in *Uncollected Poems* (1982) but written years before – probably in the 1930s – was originally entitled 'Regans'. The last two stanzas run:

> And bridge and golf and golf and bridge
> And travels in the car,
> A large saloon with all aswoon
> From Reginald's [Maurice's] cigar;
> From three to four an A.A. tour
> And then the cinema.
>
> We've left our hearts in Wimbledon
> Our feet are in the waves,
> And when the rain comes down again
> We'll shelter in the caves,
> And if we see impurity,
> Remember 'Jesus saves'.[32]

John wrote the first Shell Guide, on Cornwall. Published in 1934 at 2s 6d, it had a title-page of fantastical typography, reminiscent of the covers of *Mount Zion* and *Ghastly Good Taste*; but the new cover was a simple photograph with the title in austere sans-serif lettering. The endpapers were photographs of shells and the book had a spiral wire binding – very Modern Movement. Besides topographical and architectural details and photographs, *Cornwall* contained a recipe for Cornish pasties and an article on fishing in Cornwall, contributed by Ernest Betjemann. In the acknowledgements John thanked his father for the article and added: 'If an Editor is allowed to dedicate a book, he would like to dedicate this one to him. His father first taught him to love Cornwall.' This, in the last year of Ernest's life, was as near as John came to a gesture of reconciliation.

The Cornwall guide included a section by John on the Scilly Isles. Peter Temple, who was a junior clerk in Beddington's department, recalled:

> When I read what John Betjeman said about the Scilly Isles, I thought that would be a nice place to go, and I took the girl who was eventually my wife. When we arrived, I looked around for a guide-book. Reading it, I

thought, 'This seems familiar.' And it was – because when John Betjeman wrote that section in the Cornwall guide, he had never been to the Scillies; he had bought the same guide as us, and had made generous use of what it said. But when he read that guide, he had the same idea – 'This sounds a nice place' – so by the time we went to the Scillies, he had been there, and he gave us the name of the people he had stayed with on Bryer – Mr and Mrs Charlie Jenkins. Charlie was a fisherman. He said, 'What a funny man that John Betjeman is. He didn't like his photograph being taken. He would only be taken standing behind a wall with just the top of his head showing' – Charlie showed us the picture.[33]

The Cornwall guide was very successful and Beddington asked John to plan guides for other counties. In January 1935 John sent him a progress report. The Northumberland guide was under way, but John wanted Beddington's permission to offer W.H. Auden money to contribute a general article on the county. Paul Nash's *Dorset* was in final page form at the printer's and Peter Quennell's *Somerset* was 'on the way'. John himself had been working all January on Devon – 'a wonderful feat of the imagination composing a gazetteer of every village in the county'; it would also contain an article by John on 'the Face of Devon' and one on Devon county families by Roger Fulford. 'The text will be interspersed with spells & curses – Devon is still great on witchcraft, I find.'[34]

John was often described – in his later years especially – as 'bumbling'; but this letter to Beddington again shows how businesslike he could be when he chose. He is aware that Beddington wants to know what has been done, what is being done, what difficulties may arise, when he can expect results – and what it is all costing. ('The setting up of the type [of the Northumberland guide] has cost £12, we have spent another £88 in blocks & maps . . .')[35]

John's second guide, *Devon*, appeared in 1936. It contained advice on 'How to Charm an Adder' and an article on 'Sailing' by Lord Stanley of Alderley. John's instinct for conservation is expressed in the captions – 'Barnefield Crescent, EXETER (1798–1800), ingeniously ruined by modern villa'. Other guides followed in quick, efficient succession. 'John farmed out the Shell Guide commissions to all his cronies,' said Sir James Richards. '*Kent*, I remember, was edited by a slightly dissolute peer.'[36] The dissolute peer was Lord Clonmore, whose account of Canterbury Cathedral began: 'To travel in Kent without visiting Canterbury is rather like eating plum pudding without brandy butter.' Like the Cornwall guide, *Kent* had auxiliary contributors – the Dean of Rochester on Rochester Cathedral, Miles Sargent (a Marlborough master) on hop-pickers ('The Invasion of Kent') and Arthur Waugh on Charles Dickens and Kent.[37] Robert

Byron edited *Wiltshire* (1935), for which Lord Berners designed an extraordinary collage cover. Edith Olivier, with her intimate knowledge of the county, wrote the gazetteer section of the Wiltshire book. It has been plausibly suggested that the elegantly compressed style of her entries influenced John's later topographical writing.[38] Christopher Hobhouse edited *Derbyshire*, with several pages on the Cavendish family. Other guides were masterminded by H.G. Wells's son Anthony West, the town-planner Thomas Sharp, Freddy Birkenhead's sister Lady Juliet Smith and John Piper, who was to become John's favourite collaborator.* Piper and Paul Nash both paid tribute to John in their acknowledgements. Piper thought that John's *Devon* should be the model for all the guides. Nash wrote in *Dorset* (1936): 'I have based the guide throughout upon the first and, to my mind, the best of the series – *Cornwall* by John Betjeman. That is to say I have, in the main, examined and admired the way he had treated each section, and then done something as different as possible. This is because I recognize Mr Betjeman as highly ingenious but inimitable . . .'

The success of the Shell Guides and the fun of working with John finally persuaded Jack Beddington to take him on to the staff at Shell as a copywriter. John was given a desk in a large office at Shell-Mex House, near the company's Church of England chapel which he called 'St Mary Mex'.[39] He shared the office with Beddington's other aide-de-camp William Scudamore Mitchell, a gentle, good-humoured man whom John and his friends called 'Scudamore' to tease him about his kinship with the Lords Scudamore whose Baroque tombs were illustrated in the Shell Guide to *Wiltshire*.[40] Like Philip Harding at Marlborough, Mitchell was a quiet, sympathetic figure who played stooge to John's fizzing vivacity. John tried out new poems on him. Mitchell was given a manuscript of 'Holy Trinity, Sloane Street', headed in John's best Arts and Crafts lettering embellished with Voysey hearts.[41] He also kept a rhyme John sent him on a postcard –

> Ere church bell panged on Hintock Green,
> Full many a curious thing he did:
> He sprinkled his hair with Beddioline
> And went for a walk with a caryatid.[42]

John and Mitchell exchanged libellous limericks about the imagined sex-life of Beddington's secretary. (Over twenty years later, Harry Blacker met John at an ABC Television luncheon in London;

---

* See Chapter 6, 'The Pipers'.

Blacker was now reviewing for *The Stage*. 'I hadn't seen him in all those years. We had both aged a bit since the early 1930s. I stood in front of him and said, "Hello, John." And I could see his filing system clicking away, and then he said, "I'm sorry, I don't remember your name – but whatever happened to that lovely tall girl in the office?" and I immediately knew he did remember me – Jack Beddington had a super secretary, and all the boys used to make passes at her, including John.')[43]

John and Mitchell were joined in their office by a third assistant. Mitchell recalled:

One day Jack called me in – then John – to ask if we would mind having a third person, a German Jewish refugee called Jacobsohn,[44] in the office. Of course, John and I did not demur – thought he *might* be funny. In the event he was. Small, bespectacled and unhandsome,[45] he spoke very little English, but was keen to learn more. This was right up my street and John's and we decided to use in his hearing certain words which were quite ridiculous. We would comment to each other unsmiling that it seemed to be raining 'pell smell'. He bought a notebook and keenly entered this and other grotesque expressions. In the end John burst out laughing, as did I: we did not want to be cruel.[46]

Apart from Beddington, 'Scudamore' and Jacobsohn, the person John saw most at Shell was the photographer Maurice Beck. He knew him already through Beck's photographs for *The Architectural Review*. For Shell, Beck worked both on poster campaigns and on the Shell Guides, often accompanying John on his fieldwork for the guides. He had met Beddington when both of them were living in China. Harry Blacker remembered the two men 'discussing their night attire. They wore those things that Dorothy Lamour used to wear – *sarongs*, they slept in sarongs – and they were discussing the silks that they had just bought.'[47] To William Mitchell, there was something 'Far Eastern' in Beck's appearance.

Himself portly and short, he looked very much like Buddha, of whom he had a large effigy in his office. He was baldish and usually dressed in a smock and pumps. He was a great raconteur. He was of a good family, the Adams Becks, who had long since disowned him as a black sheep . . . He had been a very successful society photographer in London and then when his business declined Jack took him on. He had a flat in Cecil Chambers, a relic of the Hotel Cecil with a frontage on the Strand. He had a devoted assistant, Miss Fewtrell, whom John B. and I used to say was his mistress, which I am sure she was *not*.[48]

John called Maurice Beck 'the Old Filthy', because he had won prizes for photographs of nude women. (Today, some of these pictures are in the photographic collection of the National Portrait Gallery.) 'John used to go photographing with the Old Filthy before I knew them,' John Piper said.

> They used to go on these jags. John took Old Filthy to Cornwall. And Old Filthy used to get his own back. He talked with a funny sort of accent, Old Filthy, but he'd been somewhere like Eton, so he used to get his own back on John. John bossed him around when they went on the photographic expeditions. John would say, 'Oh, look here, old man, can you get this clump of primroses in?' And then one day they were in a Devon lane somewhere and Old Filthy found an unusual flint and he shouted up the road to John, 'Here you are, John, here's something you'd like, with your *double brain*!'[49]

The writer Roald Dahl, who at twenty was a management trainee at Shell in 1935, remembered the strictness of the regime. 'If you signed on 10 seconds late your name was sent up to the directors and there was a black mark against you.'[50] Beddington's junior clerk, Peter Temple, confirms that the rules were strict, but had the impression that John was exempt from them.

> He didn't acknowledge the existence of rules. He was not there all the time – he seemed to come and go as he pleased. But he was liked very much by everybody, because he was such a comical man. Very untidy and dusty. He pretended he had a fixation on the telephone-exchange girl. He chased her down the corridor. He didn't seem to mind that we *saw* him chasing her.
>   When he went up to the chief clerk's desk to put in his expenses, he did not take a seat. The chief clerk never offered anybody a chair. So John just knelt down. It was putting the chief clerk in his place – but that man was too thick to realise it.[51]

Part of John's job was to think up slogans for the poster campaign. He was especially adept at the punning topographical slogan – 'Ashby-de-la-Zouch but SHELL sur la route'; 'Stow-on-the Wold but SHELL on the Road"; 'Chorlton-cum-Hardy but Winter SHELL come Monday'; 'Lanteglos-by-Fowey but Motorists Buy SHELL'. The cartoonist Nicolas Bentley rendered 'Wormwood Scrubs but . . .', 'Gerrards Cross but . . .' and 'Mother Shipton's Well but . . .' John thought he should be sent to Le Mans to draw 'Bentleys of Bentleys'. Edward Bawden designed the Freudian nightmare of 'Stonehenge Wilts but SHELL goes on for ever' – the giant stones actually drooping. Other puns were still more extravagant. 'JUBILEEVE IN SHELL?' celebrated the silver jubilee of George V and Queen Mary in 1935. John may have suggested subjects for the straight topographical posters, such as 'Hadlow Castle, Kent' by Denton Welch. Certainly one suspects his influence behind Lord Berners's poster design of the Faringdon folly.

E. McKnight Kauffer (1890–54) was the finest poster artist employed by Shell.[52] He made typography an integral part of his designs, not just an added label. Like John – and often with him – 'Ted' Kauffer and his girlfriend Marion Dorn enjoyed the *bon vivant* entertainment that Beddington offered his friends at the Café Royal and the Gargoyle Club in London. Kauffer and Dorn became John's friends. He visited them in their successive ultra-modern flats, furnished in beige, dove-grey and aluminium, with modernist rugs by both of the couple. Kauffer designed a surreal jacket for John's collection of poems *Continual Dew* (1937). At the time the artist was strongly influenced by the work of the French posterist A.M. Cassandre; it was perhaps the resulting European look that caused the volume to be reviewed, by one English paper, as *Continental Dew*. As well as writing copy himself at Shell, John was able to exercise some limited patronage. Ruari McLean called on him in 1936, hoping that his having been at the Dragon School might persuade John, another Old Dragon, to help him find a job.

> As I remember it [McLean wrote], he worked in a large room full of other people & he had a desk in a corner; above it was a piece of ecclesiastical architecture in wood, filched from somewhere, with a lady's silk stocking hanging over it.
>
> He then and there typed out a letter of introduction for me headed 'To whom it may concern' – announcing my skills in the most glowing and absurd terms (of course he didn't know anything about me – I was about nineteen) – and round the typed page he wrote in his own hand 'And the words on that tin mean go in and sin – Ta-ra-ra-boom-de-ay.' [This was a familiar schoolboy corruption of 'go in and win', the stirring words in the Dragon School song about the school's dragon weathercock.][53]

McLean never used the letter. He did not see John again until long after the war.

Anthony Powell, whom John had known slightly at Oxford, but now knew much better through Powell's marriage into the Pakenham family,[54] was encouraged to try his hand at slogans for the old-and-new 'Times Change . . .' advertising campaign. John wrote the following letter to him in 1937:

Telephone:
Temple Bar 1254

Telegrams:
Shelbeepee,
Telex. London

SHELL-MEX AND B.P. LTD

Distributors for the Shell and Anglo-Iranian Oil Groups

P.O. BOX·NO. 148 · SHELL-MEX HOUSE
VICTORIA EMBANKMENT · LONDON · W.C.2

Your Reference ....   *Our Department* .... Publicity JXB/KSM

Date October 19th, 1937.

Anthony D. Powell, Esq.,
1, Chester Gate,
Regents Park,
London N. W. 1.

Dear Tony,

    Thank you very much for the suggestions
which I have shown to Beddioleman. He says they
are very good but ones that always occur to people
when they first think of Shell and B.P. advertising.
That means to say that he cannot use them. The
doodles one has apparently been done by someone
or other before.

    What he does like very much is the suggestions
for Times Change and three of them he is having
experiments made with. I am sending back the others.

    Roland Young has said that he cannot let us
know until tomorrow morning whether he can lunch or
not, but anyhow you and I will lunch and let's hope
that Roland Young will come too. Meeting here at
1 o'clock.

    I am glad Christine's play was such a success
Love to old Violet. *(What a nice, formal, letter this
is)*

        Yours,

       John Betjeman

JOHN
BETJEMAN

ENCLOSURE
No 457

...ffers subject to acceptance by return of post unless otherwise stated

Powell commented in a letter of 1988:

Shell did indeed use at least two of my suggestions for Old & New; so far as I can remember, an Old Time Sergeant saying 'Fall in, defaulters', New Type, 'Fall in, Trigonometry candidates' and Old Time actor, 'I trod the boards with Irving', New type, 'Noël's practically offered me a part', but Shell never sent me a halfpenny for using them which I thought pretty shabby as a couple of guineas would have been most acceptable at that moment.[55]

In recounting this episode – in almost identical words – in his journal (31 October 1988), Powell added: 'I always thought that rather discreditable on Betjeman's part.'[56] Since John was Powell's contact at Shell, it was perhaps natural for Powell to bear him a grudge over the non-payment; but as Beddington held the purse-strings at Shell he was probably more to blame than John. The publicity manager was not universally popular. The film director Dallas Bower, who in the early 1940s shared a room with John in the films division of the Ministry of Information – a division headed by Beddington – left the Ministry because he 'could not bear him'.[57] Another film-maker, Sidney Gilliat, thought Beddington was just out for himself, just dressing his own shop window for the benefit of the Minister.[58] Ruari McLean heard that Beddington had got his job at Shell through one of his brothers, who was a senior executive of the company – 'and when the executive-director brother left, Jack Beddington was *finished* – the other management people didn't like him'.[59] But, to John, Beddington was one of his guardian angels, one of the people who could do no wrong for him, while Gidney, C.S. Lewis, the Regans and Pevsner could do no right. When Beddington died in 1959 John wrote to *The Times* to recall how his late friend had not only started the Shell Guides but had also, after the war, introduced him to Peter Mills, the director and producer of motor-racing films. 'He thought the unlikely combination would bear fruit,' John wrote; the twenty two-and-a-half-minute films on British scenery and buildings which Mills made with John for commercial television were the real beginning of John's fame as a 'television personality'. With his characteristic trick of mystifying a public readership with an impenetrable private joke, John ended the letter: 'I hate to think I shall no longer be pulling his leg by calling him "Beddioleman", a name singularly unsuited to this bi-lingual and jovial exquisite.'[60]

'To Mr And Mrs John Betjeman, A Son'

Look at the Egg. If we sit here long enough, it may say something.

John Betjeman on his son Paul, in conversation with Alan Pryce-Jones,
late 1930s

At first the villagers of Uffington viewed the Betjemans as strangers and Bohemians, exempt from the rules by which they themselves lived. Gradually this attitude changed. The newcomers' warmth and sincerity established a rapport with all but a few of the local people. Even so, there were limits to the pleasure John and Penelope could derive from conversations about the price of bran or about the macabre agricultural accidents which are part of folklore.

Three men who took houses in the Uffington area in the 1930s became friends of the Betjemans: Adrian Bishop, Christopher Blunt and Arthur MacKenzie. Bishop was a friend of Maurice Bowra. He had come to Uffington to recover from a bout of *encephalitis lethargica* (sleepy sickness) from which he had almost died. His baptismal name was Herbert Frank Bishop and he came from Dublin, where his father was maltster in the Jameson distillery.[1] Called Frank at home, he was known as Adrian at Eton and Cambridge, and as such the Bowra circle referred to him. Bowra had first met him in 1921 when he visited Oxford, and was not sure that he liked him. 'He was tall and heavy and dark, with slightly curly hair, a receding forehead and noticeably bad teeth. He was used to dominating any group in which he mixed, and in this, as in other ways, he resembled Oscar Wilde, who came from the same layer of Dublin society.'[2] This was Bowra's way of indicating that Bishop was homosexual; as Penelope put it, 'I'm afraid he liked the gentlemen.'[3] Bowra respected Bishop as a classical scholar. He relished his 'overpowering vitality, his gift for juggling with words, and his quick, satirical wit'. Bishop transformed any gathering at which he was present: 'Everyone became more responsive and more agreeable when his genius turned their most casual remarks into fantastic and fanciful shapes.'[4]

Between meeting Bowra in 1921 and appearing in Uffington in 1935, Bishop had spent some time in Vienna – an episode fictionally recorded by Alan Pryce-Jones in his pseudonymous novel of 1939, *Pink Danube*.[5] In 1926 he had become a colleague of Anthony Blunt's brother Wilfrid as an assistant master at Haileybury. ('I admit', Blunt wrote, 'that even I was surprised when he said to me one day, "My dear Wilfrid, I want you to come to tea this afternoon. I have invited the six most *beautiful* boys in the school to meet you." I should have guessed that what I would find were the six plainest boys of his acquaintance.')[6] After Haileybury, Bishop had taken an educational post with the Anglo-Persian Oil Company. Bowra glosses over his dismissal by the company, but Blunt reveals that it was 'the result of extra-curricular instruction given to some of his more attractive older pupils'. Bishop could not return to Dublin, 'where because of an earlier indiscretion he was liable to immediate arrest'.[7] He wandered around southern Europe, spent a year in the Aegean on the yacht of a total stranger into whose ken he had literally swum off Corfu; and settled for a time in Berlin, where he introduced Bowra (though the don was too discreet to say so in his memoirs) to the male brothels celebrated in Isherwood's novels.

In 1936, when Bowra was lecturing at Harvard, he received a letter from Bishop saying that, no doubt as a result of his brush with death, he had been brought to God. 'His hostility to religion and his derisive jokes about it', Bowra wrote, 'indicated that it played a larger part in his mind than if he had been merely indifferent.' Bishop's letter 'was in his usual comical vein and did not state anything clearly, but there was no doubt that something transcendent had happened'.[8]

To John Betjeman, the combination in Bishop of wit, homosexuality, religious conversion and a recommendation from Maurice Bowra made the Irishman an interesting neighbour. Bishop was invited to dinners, introduced to the Berners circus and dragooned into Penelope's village entertainments. Osbert Lancaster recalled – and drew – one of these:

For their industry and perseverance [the Uffington villagers] were from time to time rewarded by musical evenings in which all [Penelope's] guests, even if tone-deaf, were expected to take part. On the most memorable of these, which coincided with the annual prize-giving for the best home-made wine, the principal item on the programme was a performance of 'Summer is icumen in' sung by Adrian Bishop, Maurice Bowra, my wife

Caricature by Osbert Lancaster: 'Summer is icumen in' performed at Uffington in the 1930s by (left to right) Lord Berners (at the piano), Adrian Bishop (at the back), Maurice Bowra, Karen Lancaster, John Betjeman, Osbert Lancaster and Penelope Betjeman (strumming a guitar)

and the poet himself, accompanied on the piano by Lord Berners and by Penelope on a strange instrument resembling a zither. My own contribution to the ensemble took the form of a flute *obbligato*. So powerful was the effect that all remained rooted to their seats even when, as happened from time to time, a home-made wine bottle exploded, showering those unfortunates in the immediate vicinity with broken glass and elderberry juice. But the enjoyment of the audience was as nothing to that of the performers and I cannot recall in all the years that have since elapsed, ever having spent an evening of such continuous and unalloyed pleasure.[9]

Christopher Blunt, the brother of Anthony and Wilfrid, lived with his wife Anne at Woolstone, the village next to Uffington. Two years younger than John, he had been at Marlborough with him. A merchant banker by profession, he was also the leading expert on Anglo-Saxon coinage. Wilfrid considered Christopher 'by far the best of the Blunts', though he added that 'both Anthony and I thought him a shade pompous . . .'.[10] John too thought Christopher 'a bit of an old stuffy', but went over to Woolstone when Anthony visited his brother. Anthony was still on good terms with John, though according to Wilfrid 'his close friendship in early days with John Betjeman later fell apart because he felt that John, who had the makings of a scholar, elected – as Anthony saw it – to prostitute his talents by popularizing what he could have directed into serious study'.[11] Wilfrid had three good reasons to come to Woolstone: his brother, Adrian Bishop and the Betjemans. In 1935, when still art master at Haileybury (three years later he moved on to Eton) he visited Christopher and Anne. Adrian Bishop, Penelope Betjeman and Lord Alfred Douglas, who was staying with John and Penelope, joined the Blunts to judge the local baby show. 'Owing to some confusion over the numbering of the babies,' Blunt wrote, 'the prize did not go, as had been intended, to the deserving infant of the local milkman, and for many weeks afterwards milk was very hard to come by. Penelope had ridden over, and while the judging was in progress her horse had seized the opportunity to roll in a dungheap. Lord Alfred and I were therefore ordered to scrub the animal down.'[12] In his memoirs, Blunt published a photograph of the bottle-nosed old man whom Wilde had once described as a 'slim, gilt soul', holding Moti while Blunt scrubbed manure off the horse's flank with a besom.[13]

Arthur and Eileen MacKenzie lived just down the road from John and Penelope. The archaeologist Seton Lloyd recalled in 1989, at the age of eighty-seven, 'They lived in a rather disorganized house in Uffington, the wife bringing up five sons on practically no money at all while he worked assiduously and continuously in the hothouses

producing innumerable incomprehensible sculptures, which nobody,
at that time, bought.'[14] John procured MacKenzie a job as art master
at Oundle,[15] where he created many more sculptures. (Eventually he
was given a one-man show in London under the pseudonym George
Kennethson, and sold about half a dozen.) Arthur's parents lived in
Beaulieu and in 1945, recovering from an operation, John would go to
stay with them, and write 'Youth and Age on Beaulieu River, Hants'.[16]

In August 1936 a chance encounter on a train brought the Betjemans
two new friends: the Rev. Francis Harton, Vicar of Baulking, four
miles from Uffington, and his wife Sibyl. In her nineties, Mrs Harton
recalled her first meeting with John and Penelope. She was in a train
on the little line that ran under White Horse Hill. Her husband had
become vicar three weeks before. In the railway carriage, besides
herself, were a young couple and an elderly woman – 'very much a
countrywoman, and in those days they were very poorly clad'. The
young couple attracted Sibyl Harton's attention at once because they
were bickering. 'They were glaring at each other. I hadn't met that
kind of thing before. They were quite oblivious of being in public.'
Sibyl Harton did her best to concentrate on a book.

> But about the second station the old lady was preparing to get out. And,
> this is what was so noticeable and so typical of John. At once he was up
> opening the door, handing her out her old country parcels, without any
> self-consciousness and without a great deal of attention to her person-
> ally – but just doing it. It struck me very much. He would do just the same,
> in the same sort of way, for anybody. That's what I always noticed about
> John: he had this innate kindness which was more than ordinary, and it
> would be the same whether you were in rags or in a crown.[17]

When the train arrived at Sibyl Harton's station, her husband was
on the platform to meet her. 'I flung myself out of the carriage without
having anything to be done for me, and I noticed that the young couple
looked at each other, they just gave a glance at each other.'[18] The next
Sunday, the young man (she had not yet found out who he was) was in
Baulking church, with another man. After the service, the two introduced themselves as John Betjeman and Adrian Bishop.

Both became devoted disciples of Father Harton, as he liked to be
known. John read his book *Elements of the Spiritual Life*, on a
holiday in Rome with Penelope and Joan Eyres Monsell in 1937, and
felt his faith renewed by it.[19] Maurice Bowra, who also became a great
friend of the Hartons, commented that it must be the first time
anybody had been converted to Protestantism by a journey to Rome.[20]
John often attended church at Baulking, rather than Uffington, and

Father Harton became his confessor. Harton encouraged John to bring to church a list of his sins. Once John dropped the list on the path to the church and there was a frantic search for it in the moonlight.[21] Penelope also went to Father Harton for confession. Sibyl Harton recalled: 'After her first confession she went off to the Uffington village hall, where she bumped into Mrs McIver, who was married to the Earl of Craven's agent. And she told me, "Even Mrs McIver looked beautiful after I had confessed all my sins." We didn't like Mrs McIver very much. She was a person who would always try to sell you something. One time Lord Berners visited her house, and said out of devilry, "Oh, Mrs McIver, I do admire that vase!" "It's yours, my lord, for £5." '[22]

Francis Harton was something of a marriage guidance counsellor to the Betjemans, too: Sibyl Harton remembered 'a lovely letter to him from Penelope which said, "Thank you for making our marriage so happy again." '[23] Harton took seriously Adrian Bishop's 'vision' and urged him to think of entering the religious life. Eventually Bishop became an Anglican novice at Nashdom Abbey. 'At times his ebullience was a little too much for his fellows,' Bowra wrote. 'When Penelope visited him on Corpus Christi Day, she was delighted to hear him using his fine baritone voice to some effect as he walked in procession. She made complimentary remarks on him to one of the monks, who answered, "Yes, it would be all right if he did not drown all the rest of us." ' Bowra noticed that after his conversion Bishop seemed to be free of the black moods and acerbities from which he had sometimes suffered.[24]

Father Harton was one of the few people capable of putting Penelope in her place. She was renowned for her dislike of cocktail parties. She drank only ginger beer and did not enjoy trivial chat. At a party given by her cousin Lord Methuen at Corsham Court near Bath, she spent some time ostentatiously darning two pairs of John's socks. Sibyl Harton remembered a party at Baulking Vicarage. 'We had four or five people in. She came in, wasn't interested in them or didn't like them, and promptly – I can see her – went up to the bookshelves and turned her back on us all and browsed. When our guests had left, my husband said to her, "Penelope, you're *the rudest woman in Berkshire*." '[25]

For a time Penelope played the harmonium for evensong at Baulking. 'Her playing', Bowra wrote, 'was unusual, even in a country parish, since her improvised voluntaries were often based on secular works like German folk-songs or Offenbach's *Goddesses three to Ida went*.' A day came when Father Harton decided he had had as much as he could take. He sat down and wrote Penelope a letter which has become celebrated in the annals of plain speaking. 'One dark morning', as Bowra records, she received these lines:

Baulking Vicarage

My dear Penelope,

I have been thinking over the question of the playing of the harmonium on Sunday evenings here and have reached the conclusion that I must now take it over myself.

I am very grateful to you for doing it for so long and hate to have to ask you to give it up, but, to put it plainly, your playing has got worse and worse and the disaccord between the harmonium and the congregation is becoming destructive of devotion. People are not very sensitive here, but even some of them have begun to complain, and they are not usually given to doing that. I do not like writing this, but I think you will understand that it is my business to see that divine worship is as perfect as it can be made. Perhaps the crankiness of the instrument has something to do with the trouble. I think it does require a careful and experienced player to deal with it.

Thank you ever so much for stepping so generously into the breach when Sibyl was ill; it was the greatest possible help to me and your results were noticeably better then than now.

Yours ever

F.P. Harton.[26]

'Penelope accepted the decision', Bowra wrote, 'with the utmost grace and good temper, remained on excellent terms with the Hartons, and was delighted to receive a copy of H.V. Morton's *In the Footsteps of the Master*, inscribed, "With grateful thanks from the Vicar and Churchwardens of Baulking".'[27] In fact, Penelope screamed with laughter when she read the letter. Father Harton's spirituality was more strongly developed than his sense of humour.

The Betjemans loved and respected the Hartons, but that did not stop them making fun of them behind their backs. Harton they dubbed 'Father Folky', while Sibyl was 'the Abbess'. The folky-ness really belonged to Sibyl, who was apt to offer her guests Blue Vinney cheese and raspberry cordial. She was the author of several books with somewhat twee titles, such as *Once Upon a Bedtime, Being 52 Delectable Stories from the Bible for the Want-to-Be-Read-tos* (SPCK, 1937). A later book, *Stars Appearing: Lives of 68 Saints of the Anglican Calendar* (1954), she dedicated 'To John Betjeman, a good friend'. She radiated goodness; one's own character seemed shoddy by comparison. A neighbour described her as 'scraped pure'. But there was an edge of intolerance and censoriousness to her saintliness.

What gave piquancy to the Betjemans' light-hearted mocking of this holy and slightly fey woman was that her own life was touched with . . . hardly scandal, but an apostasy inspired by romance. Like John, Sibyl (whose maiden name was Robin) was brought up in north London. Her father had a wholesale-leather warehouse at Crouch End. She entered the convent in Wantage, intending to become a nun. 'I had never thought of anything else, really. But I didn't get as far as being a novice. My [future] husband was coaching me in Greek and Old Testament, because I was working for a theological degree; he'd been coaching me for some time. And when we came to say goodbye – I suppose he realised it more than I did, but anyway we both realised it the moment we were separated: we were in love. So I came home very quickly – to the horror of my family, relations and friends. They were horrified that I could change so quickly.'[28]

The Hartons were hospitable. Sibyl was a good cook and the Betjemans were often invited to dinner, the food accompanied by elderflower wine, parsley brandy and other home-made liquors. Maurice Bowra was often of the party.

> He and Francis liked each other very much [Sibyl Harton said]. He respected Francis's classical side and he got him to give a Latin sermon. Once a year in St Mary's Church in Oxford there has to be this Latin sermon. I suppose it still goes on, it's an endowed thing. But it was getting very difficult to find anyone who could do it. Not many people attended – I went, of course. And Francis made just one slight mistake – plural noun and singular verb or something – and they all tittered. You could see, they were so pleased to have caught him out in something.
>
> I remember Bowra coming to dinner with us one night at Baulking – John and Penelope were there. I had a cheese soufflé, and cheese soufflé does not wait for anybody. I timed it just right; but they didn't come and they didn't come. A friend from Oxford was driving him. At last they arrived. The man who was driving had lost his way in the country lane and he said that Bowra spent the whole time, as they were meandering about, translating some very third-rate modern novel into Latin. It was just absurd. But he was a very good guest when he did arrive.[29]

Bowra's companion was in fact John Sparrow, who recalled that 'The dinner proceeded in frigid silence.'[30]

More frequently, the Betjemans played host at Garrards Farm. In 1934 Penelope had taken on a German maid, Paula Steinbrecher, who was dressed in a white cap and apron and took over from Betty Packford the task of serving at meals.[31] Maurice Bowra describes how

after Sunday supper Penelope would play the piano and lead hymns
with a fine *bel canto*, while the rest joined in. The hymns 'were largely
chosen for their emotional richness, and the Reverend John Bacchus
Dykes was a favourite composer. When the German maid, Paula, burst
in to clear the remains of the meal, Penelope would dismiss her
abruptly, "*Aber, Paula, Sie können nicht einkommen. Wir haben
Gottesdienst.*" ("Paula, you can't come in. We are having a religious
service.")'[32]

Because John was so often in London writing film reviews or
working for Shell, Penelope was better known and better liked in
Uffington than he was. To some of the villagers she became a kind of
white witch or shaman.

> She saved my baby's life, you know [said Farmer Wheeler's daughter,
> Peggy Phillips]. Well, I always say she did. Because the poor child was very
> ill. She had colitis . . . The poor baby was getting, oh worse and worse. I
> met Mrs Betjeman in the village one day and she said, 'Hello, how's the
> baby?'
>   'Oh,' I said, 'she is *so* ill.'
>   'What's the matter with her?'
>   I told her.
>   'Oh, that's nothing,' she said. 'That's nothing. Go home,' she says,
> 'grate a bit of green apple, put glucose on it and give it to her. She'll be all
> right at the end of the day.'
>   I thought, 'Well, fancy giving a poor child grated green apple who hasn't
> eaten anything for a month! It'll kill her.' But the child was in such a dread-
> ful state and almost gone to a bag of bones, I couldn't care less. I thought,
> well, if it kills her, I'll go to prison. That won't matter. The baby will be
> out. But within half an hour that child went to sleep. Next day she was
> quite all right. The child ate as if she was starved.
>   She had a touch of colitis again in twelve months' time and I gave her
> the apple again just the same and she was quite all right. I swear she would
> have died, I swear she would.[33]

Penelope was best known in Uffington as a brilliant horsewoman.
The country people acknowledged her skill, but they knew she was
not a countrywoman born and bred. It was the one occasion when she
came spectacularly to grief through her lack of country lore that had
most currency in farmhouse and public-house gossip. Ken Freeman
tells the story:

> Penelope used to come round to the shop at Uffington, to Mrs Norton, the
> shopkeeper. And when she rode Moti he'd go up on the pavement, Mrs

Norton would unlock the door, he'd go inside and she'd give him a sweet. That was all right when you were in riding tackle, but one night she came round with him in the four-wheeler. He put his head in for his sweet; and Penelope took the bridle off, with the blinkers. He turned his head into Mrs Norton's to get his sweet, and of course the wheel went backwards and he saw it in the corner of his eye, because the blinkers were off – and away he went. He went down to the road, got to the church and couldn't turn the bend at the bottom. He jumped a little gate, smashed the cart to pieces. There were two walnut trees in there and he got lodged between them and that held him. He was all right, but the cart was a write-off. I don't think there was anything left of it.[34]

The other popular story about Penelope and horses was her encounter with General Higgins[35] on the hunting field. The general, a crusty old gentleman in a tall hat, known locally as 'General Buggins', pulled up his horse beside Moti. The following conversation took place.

'Well, my girl, where did you get that Arab?'
'Injer.'
'And what were *you* doing in India?'
'My father was out there.'
'And what was he? A sergeant?'
'Commander-in-Chief.'[36]

John was so tickled by this story that he made a watercolour cartoon of the scene.[37]

Penelope had not yet despaired of turning John into an enthusiastic horseman. She paid Joy Bassett, a Berkshire horsewoman of great repute, to give him a course of riding lessons. 'I never made him a horse-lover,' Miss Bassett said. 'He wanted just to be able to trot. What he used to do, he used to play at being a bird taking off when he was sitting on the horse and he was trying to, what he called, "catch his bumps" – with his toes stuck downwards and flapping his elbows like wings. The only thing he was really keen about, in talking horses, was if he could bring in the port fetlocks. That was the only part of the horse he really knew – well, I don't think he *really* knew it, but he knew it as a phrase.'[38] When Penelope had paid Joy Bassett for the lessons, she took John out for a ride. She was full of happy anticipation. 'It turned out that he was completely useless,' she recalled. 'So then I said to Joy Bassett, "Well, what the *hell* have you been doing? You haven't taught my husband a *thing*." And Joy Bassett said "Well, he was such an interesting conversationalist, we just used to go for walks." '[39]

The Uffington stories told about John were less about his mishaps on horseback than about his tribulations in getting off to London in the mornings. Ken Freeman again:

John used to tear off to Challow station in his Ford Prefect to catch the 8.5 or whatever it was, and it was always by the skin of his teeth. And there was the odd time or two when he missed out. On one occasion . . . Fred Shorey was groom, handyman and general factotum at Garrards, he'd previously been cowman for a family called Reid at Baulking, and this was a step up for him, to have clean shoes for a bit. He was a likable old boy but a real old countryman, steady as a rock, big strong fellow – spit and polish on the harness. On this occasion John went out about eight o'clock to catch the five past eight at Challow, with everything agin him. It was a coldish morning. Pressed the button: nothing happened, you see. *Rrrrr. Rrrrrr.* So, oh dear, oh dear, he's in a terrible fret. He shouts out: 'Fred! Fred! Where are you?' So Fred comes sauntering round the corner with all the time in the world. 'What's up, then?'

'Oh, it won't start,' he said. 'Do something, Fred, don't just stand and look.'

So Fred said, 'Where's that handle?' – the cranking handle.

'I don't know where the handle is,' he says. 'What handle?'

And Fred says, 'Well, there's a thing that goes in the front.'

Anyway, they found it under the seat and hoicked this handle out. So Fred puts it in the front of the car, it used to go through a little hole in the bumper, and it was very wobbly. And he was a big strong fellow, so *Whirrrrrrr!* The car nearly went round the handle like a football rattle. He tried two or three times but the carburettor was full of vapour, you see, and it gave a colossal backfire. It shook the village. And John shouted: 'You've broken the bloody thing, Fred!'[40]

Another time John missed the train was recalled by Sammy Loader, Pam Ayres's uncle, who was porter at Challow station. 'He used to tell a story about John tearing down the platform with the train moving and John hanging on to the door handle,' Freeman said. 'On one occasion . . . you know how the old platforms used to dip away? John was like somebody paddling in water and getting out of his depth. He couldn't get hold of anything. He ran to the best of his ability but the train disappeared. And he threw down his hat on the ground and jumped up and down on it, shouting, "I'm *ruined*! I'm *ruined*!" '[41]

In 1937 both John and Penelope were asked to help organize the Uffington and Woolstone celebrations for the Coronation of King George VI. John was on the committee, which was chaired by Captain Hilary Raleigh of Johnings, Woolstone. A son of the literary historian and critic Professor Sir Walter Raleigh, who had himself written a book in Uffington in 1904, Raleigh was the author of jocose novels and short stories. His books included *Excess Baggage* (1932), *Chronicles of Slyme Court* (1935), *The Merry Mug* (1936) and *Sheikh Stuff* (1937). His style was a lumbering blend of Dickens and Wodehouse. His characters had names like Blenkinsop and Higginbotham, and the chapters titles like 'A Geologist Loses His Trousers' or 'Ghastly Predicament of an AA Scout'. A man with that sense of humour was natural chairman-of-committee material. He was also genial and enthusiastic and got everybody to join in. The celebrations were well rehearsed and ready in time.

On 8 May 1937, four days before the Coronation, *Weekly Illustrated* magazine devoted a double-page spread of its Coronation Programme and Guide to Uffington's and Woolstone's preparations. One photograph showed Captain Raleigh chairing a meeting in Uffington village hall; John's balding head could be seen in the centre of the back row. Other pictures showed a party of women dragging the Earl of Craven's 1831 fire-engine;[42] Ken Freeman in fancy dress as a Belisha Beacon;[43] and the Rev. George Bridle looking particularly crabby above the caption 'Vicar Writes Coronation Sermon: The Vicar is no shirker . . .' In another picture, Moti, escorted by two besmocked farmers – Gaffer Reynolds and Gaffer Breakspear – was seen pulling a cartload of children.

John and Penelope wrote words for the village 'King' and 'Queen' to declaim, and rehearsed them in their speeches. Both parts, curiously, were taken by girls, Pearl Pearce and Joyce Bowlly, and another girl, Jean Packer, performed the crowning ceremony, wearing a top hat. The involvement of John and Penelope (and Moti) in the 1937 celebrations integrated them more securely into Uffington life. They were no longer regarded as strangers, 'Lunnon people'.

Four years into their marriage, the couple had still had no children. The field-marshal began to think that another of his suspicions about John might be well founded. Maurice Bowra wrote a long humorous poem in which the philoprogenitive Frank and Elizabeth Pakenham (later Earl and Countess of Longford) point out to the Betjemans a stallion serving a mare in a field and suggest they should take heed of this practical sex education.*[44] Penelope stood on the White Horse's eye and prayed to the pagan gods for fertility.[45] In 1937 she became pregnant. 'I wish it could be a little horse,' she said to Sibyl Harton.[46] Paul Betjeman was born on 26 November 1937, with wispy blond hair. Penelope had had an agonizing time, with three days of labour followed by a Caesarean.

* For Bowra's poem, see Appendix.

When it was known that Penelope was expecting a baby, the Betjemans paid for Betty Evans to take a six weeks' training course at the Truby King School for nannies in London. A very experienced nanny from the School came to Uffington for the first fortnight after Paul's birth; then Betty took over. When she was asked in 1989 what Paul had been like as a baby, her husband George chipped in: 'A little ruffian!' She corrected him: 'No, he was quite sweet. Yes, he was a little bit on the wild side as he got older, rather strong-willed; he was nearly five when I left him. But he was a very good baby. His dad used to call him "Egghead" because he had a very oval head and very little hair, to start with. They always used to say, "Oh, come on, Egghead!" '47

Betty Packford recalled some of the hazards of life with the Betjemans at Garrards Farm:

> The getting-up routine, with John Betjeman, was pretty awful, because he nearly always went off with either odd socks or odd shoes and he walked around with his Bible while he was dressing – reading a chapter of the Bible. You all had to keep well out of the way, because he never looked where he was going. The Bible-reading took him an awful long time. He was very slow in getting down to breakfast.
>
> Quite often, I took him to Didcot station, it just depended on the routine of the day . . . So if I drove Mr Betjeman to Didcot, Mrs Betjeman would have Paul and play with him for a while before I came back to bath him and feed him. I remember one particular morning there was a bit of an argument because Mr Betjeman wanted some papers taken into Faringdon and Mrs Betjeman said, 'Betty won't have time: she's got to come back and see to Paul.' It was a frosty morning. So when we got in the car, he said, 'Well, it's not going to take you very long to go straight through from Challow to Faringdon, is it?' He said, 'I'd like these papers delivered.' Well, of course, I skidded, didn't I? Turned the car upside down! So I not only got into trouble when I got back, but I was bruised and had to go to bed.48

Betty remembered other quarrels. 'Oh dear, yes. There was always arguments. They used to shout at one another. He'd be upstairs and she'd be shouting downstairs, or the other way round. And also the bathroom was never vacant when she wanted it because he took such a long time. And he could never find his hat; he could never find the right shoes. There were lots of arguments, but they were nice ones – they didn't come to fighting.'49

At eight weeks old, Betty remembered, Paul was put 'straight on the back of a horse'.50 The moment was photographed for the album Penelope had given her with 'Betty' in gold paint on the front. Later

Penelope bought a goat cart, like that in which Queen Victoria's children were tugged about the grounds of Balmoral. Paul was sat in the cart and Betty had to walk in front of Snowdrop with a carrot. Betty also had to milk the goat twice a day, as Paul was brought up on goat's milk.

Betty Packford's opinion was that 'John Betjeman was not what you'd call a good father. He very rarely came up to the nursery. John Sparrow, who used to come for weekends, liked to come up to the nursery. We used to call him "Tweet tweet", he was ever so nice. And John Piper used to come up, he was interested in Paul. Osbert Lancaster came sometimes, and Graham Sutherland[51] quite often. But we didn't see much of Mr Betjeman in the nursery.'[52] It was not, Betty thought, just a matter of John's being too involved in his work: 'I don't think he was fond of children anyway.'[53] This lack of sympathy for children is suggested in such poems as 'Sun and Fun' and 'Original Sin on the Sussex Coast'. One might have expected John, after his unhappy relations with his own father, to have lavished special affection on his son. Rather, his behaviour towards him seemed to recreate his own miseries. In the same way the oppressed chimney-sweep Tom, in *The Water Babies*, when asked what he wants to be when he grows up, says he wants to be like Mr Grimes, and to have apprentices to beat. John might have agreed with Philip Larkin, who wrote: 'The realization that it was not people I disliked but children was for me one of those celebrated moments of revelation, comparable to reading Haeckel or Ingersoll in the last century.'[54]

Most of John's friends were agreed that he was a failure as a father. Alan Pryce-Jones said: 'Of all the fathers I have known, not excepting myself, he was the worst. I think he liked the *idea* of being a father – the notion of the Victorian *paterfamilias* presiding over the roast beef at Sunday luncheon. But he found that being a father was no fun at all. He was actually cruel to Paul. I have been there when he said, "Look at the Egg. If we sit here long enough, it may say something." A child doesn't like being exposed to that, in mixed company.'[55] In later years John and Penelope more commonly referred to Paul as 'The Powlie', a corruption of his name that fitted into the semi-Irish, semi-Cockney dialect they used in private. The teasing and taunting continued well after infancy. Sibyl Harton remembered travelling to London in the train 'with John teasing Paul until he said, very quietly, "If you don't stop it, I'll get out."'[56]

Paul's two main playmates as a child were Sheila Matthews and Roy Weaver. Sheila was born the same year as Paul. It was very convenient for her mother Mary Matthews that Penelope let her leave Sheila with Paul in Betty Packford's care. In return, Mary allowed

Penelope to use her cheese room to run an infants' school for local children. Penelope taught scripture and French. 'The only word that Sheila remembered when she was tiny', Mary Matthews recalled, 'was *derrière*.' Sheila and Paul remained friends until he went off to the Dragon School.[57]

His other Uffington friend, Roy Weaver, lived next door to Garrards Farm. He was the son of Queenie Weaver, Ken Freeman's 'Auntie Queen'.[58] Mrs Weaver said:

> Paul and my boy got into a lot of mischief. I remember once Mrs Betjeman came round and she said, 'You're not to let Roy come down to play with Paul for a week, because they're getting in so much mischief.' Well, partly it was her fault; because she used to take up the carpet in the hall of their house and let them go racing up and down. One day they got a saw and sawed a leg off a little chair. So I said, 'All right, I'll keep Roy home. He shan't come up to play with Paul.' I kept him home two days and she was down and said, 'Let Paul come and play with Roy. He gets into more mischief without him.'[59]

Another friend of the Betjemans who thought John deficient as a father was Jean Kellie (now Mrs Rome). She came to Stanford-in-the-Vale, near Uffington, in 1939 as the young bride of Captain Geoffrey Kellie, who had been comptroller to Sir Philip Chetwode in India.[60] As a daughter of Colonel Frederick Robertson, a sapper, she had herself been out in India with Penelope, when they were both seventeen. At that time Jean thought 'only of the next dance' and was intimidated by Penelope's cleverness. But on returning to England Jean had 'changed completely' and become an artist. The two couples got on well and Geoffrey Kellie was a specially welcome guest when Penelope's father was staying in Uffington. Jean's impression of John's behaviour towards Paul was that 'He blew hot and cold. He'd find him amusing for a bit, and then he wanted to get rid of him.' Penelope was more conscientious but Paul was 'terribly spoilt – he was odious as a small boy'.[61]

Both Paul's waywardness and Penelope's sublime tactlessness are illustrated by a story told by Robert Heber Percy. When Paul was a small boy, Penelope brought him to tea with Lord Berners at Faringdon House. Paul was throwing a golf ball about in the grand salon, and to Penelope's horror smashed a fine rococo looking-glass. With great courtesy, Berners made light of the accident, assuring Penelope that he could easily find a replacement for the mirror in the Portobello Road market. After tea he saw them into their car. Penelope told Paul to wave goodbye and began to drive off. Suddenly there was a screeching of brakes and a grinding of gears as she reversed up the drive. Arriving outside the house again, she stuck her head out of the window and shouted to Berners:

'I'm awfully sorry, but we've forgotten our golf ball!'[62]

THE PIPERS

If a Mephistopheles were to say to me, 'You can have your life over again; but you must make a choice. You can either give up creating all your works of art, or you can give up all the jokes you have enjoyed with John Betjeman' – unhesitatingly, I would give up the works of art.

John Piper, *Piper at 80*, BBC Television, 1983

In 1936 John Piper contributed some abstract paintings to an exhibition mounted by the Artists' International Exhibition (AIE), a left-wing organization which had been founded to help the Soviet Union and refugees from Nazi Germany. The show's organizer was Peggy Angus, the first wife of J.M. Richards, who had been John's junior colleague on *The Architectural Review*. 'She was responsible for hanging my pictures rather well,' Piper said.[1]

Richards came to the private view. He and Piper had known each other for some time. Richards had been encouraging Piper to contribute to the *Review*. At the private view he broached another idea: possibly Piper might write the Shell Guide to Oxfordshire, in the new series of which John Betjeman had already written *Cornwall* and *Devon*. Not long afterwards, Piper received a letter from John: 'Dear Artist, Marx Richards tells me that you are good at writing guidebooks. Would you like to do Oxfordshire?'[2] Piper went along to the Shell offices to meet John and be introduced to Jack Beddington.

Piper was thirty-three – three years older than John. Like Bertrand Russell, he looked older than his years when young, but then changed so little in fifty years that he seemed youthful when old, except in the mental impairment of his last years. A description of him at eighty by his namesake (but not relation) David Piper needs no adaptation to convey an image of the man who entered Shell-Mex House in 1936.

The person is spare – yielding to the art historian's weakness for attribution, I would define it as transitional between late romanesque and early gothic . . . The expression, in repose, is austere, even severe. The smile, however, when it comes is astonishing as spring sunshine, and the atmospherics are those of modesty informed by an unconscious but real authority, of a gentleness and a courtesy that nevertheless sheath a purpose of steel. Flexible tempered steel, certainly not rigid iron, though also, I suspect, susceptible to some arrogance despite the modesty.[3]

Piper was shown into an office where John Betjeman and William Scudamore Mitchell were amusing themselves by writing limericks about the Shell secretaries. 'Some of them were fairly indecent,' Piper said. 'And I thought the atmosphere in the office was more amusing than anything I'd seen, because I had never been in an office before.'[4] John showed Piper a book by Basil Fulford Lowther Clarke – presumably *St Mary's Church, Monmouth*, which was published that year. 'Clarke was "obscure", as John would say, a curate at that time,' Piper remembered. 'He wrote *Church Builders of the Nineteenth Century*, which became a classic. And he became a great pal of all of us, and later on he wrote a book with John called *English Parish Churches*.'[5] Inspection of the Clarke book led naturally to talk of churches. John and Piper found that they had given themselves the same kind of training, bicycling round the countryside looking at church architecture.

Neither man yet knew it, but there was another link between Piper and the Betjemans: Myfanwy Evans, then his girlfriend and soon to be his second wife, had been at school with Penelope at Queen's College, London, during the First World War. 'I remember Armistice Day,' Myfanwy said. 'We were in a singing lesson. The Second Mistress came in and said, "I've got a very important announcement: the Armistice has just been signed." None of us knew what to say, but Penelope blurted: "Ow! Now we shall go to France!" '[6] And Myfanwy independently knew Jack Beddington, because she was involved in the Group Theatre's meetings in Great Newport Street, London, which he chaired.

John Piper and Myfanwy had been together since they were introduced by the painter Ivon Hitchens in 1934; Piper's first wife, Eileen Holding, had gone off to France. Piper was still an almost exclusively abstract artist. But he was also a photographer.[7] It was through his photography that he had built up a reputation as a topographer and architectural historian. He and Myfanwy had been driving round England in a 1920 Lancia which he had bought for £15, photographing Romanesque font-carvings. They had shown the photographs to Thomas Kendrick,[8] then Keeper of British and Mediaeval Antiquities at the British Museum, who became their friend. Kendrick reported to them that A.E. Clapham (later Sir Alfred),[9] author of *English Romanesque Architecture after the Conquest* and secretary of the Historic Monuments Commission for England, had asked him, 'Who

are these two young people who I hear are going round England
photographing those awful *golliwogs*?'[10] Kendrick had been mystified
by the question, as he did not know that Clapham called the
Romanesque carvings golliwogs. Piper and Myfanwy were amused
but mildly indignant.

> We were trying to say that these carvings were like Henry Moores or
> Barbara Hepworths [Piper recalled]. We went round solemnly and I made
> a map of England showing where all the golliwogs were. We had very little
> else to do: no children at that stage. I always remember the wonderful
> waking up in the pouring rain on the top of some very high Yorkshire
> moors, miles from anywhere – rather despairing about packing the tent up
> and getting it back in the bag. There were a lot of Yorkshire golliwogs, a
> lot of crosses and things. The Oxford University Press considered them
> and then they said, 'No, we couldn't do anything on these lines unless it
> were a *corpus*' – meaning, unless we spent our life on it and got every little
> bit of cross that could be found, they weren't going to be interested. It was
> a pity. It would have been a lovely book. Jim Richards was very keen that
> it should be published.[11]

Though the 'golliwogs' portfolio never became a book, it showed
Richards that Piper had application as well as talent. He told John
Betjeman he was sure that Piper, if commissioned to prepare the
Oxfordshire guide, would deliver the goods. At the Shell-Mex House
meeting, Piper was given the commission. John Betjeman suggested
that the guide should be called simply *Oxon* – and so it was. 'John just
let us get on with Oxford,' Piper said. 'He didn't exercise editorial
control. He was amazed by the production that he got; he thought that
everything was absolutely super. He got funny pictures of signposts at
Salford and articles by Myfanwy about Deserted Places. He was shat-
tered by the manuscript he got, and he didn't alter one sausage of it.
The only intervention he made was to write the most frightfully funny
captions – including the celebrated "tree of knowledge" one [John's
description of a multi-flanged signpost].'[12]

   In 1937 Myfanwy became pregnant and she and John Piper decided
that they ought to get married; he was by then divorced. In the same
year Piper's mother bought them a farmhouse at Fawley Bottom,
Henley-on-Thames ('Fawley Bum', as the Pipers and Betjemans called
it in their correspondence) and the Pipers had water put in, though,
like Garrards Farm, the house was still without electricity. It was to be
their home for the rest of their lives. Jack Beddington lived just up the
road at Turville Heath; and Osbert Lancaster and his wife Karen also
became neighbours, in Henley.

Piper was to be John's dearest and most compatible friend. His modesty was a foil to John's exhibitionism. His gifts as an artist and photographer complemented, and did not challenge, John's as a writer. As Richard Ingrams has pointed out, the two had a great deal in common.[13] They were both children of the middle class. Both had rebelled against fathers who wanted them to take over the family business: after Epsom College, Piper had become an articled clerk in his father's firm of solicitors, but on his father's death in 1928 had at once given up the law to become an artist, studying first at the Richmond School of Art, then at the Royal College of Art. Above all, the two men shared a sense of humour. Late in life, Piper said on a television programme: 'If a Mephistopheles were to say to me, "You can have your life over again; but you must make a choice. You can either give up creating all your works of art, or you can give up all the jokes you have enjoyed with John Betjeman" – unhesitatingly, I would give up the works of art.'[14]

And then there was Myfanwy. She was to be one of John's muses, the inspiration of two poems. The 'golden Myfanwy' of Arthur Machen's *The Secret Glory* was an almost mystical harbinger of his meeting her.[15] He loved her. She had the 'schoolgirl' look that always appealed to him; but also there was something austerely mystical about her, something of the Celtic enchantress, of witchcraft, medievalism, Pre-Raphaelitism and the young Edith Sitwell. He called her 'Goldilocks' – sometimes 'Goldilegs'.[16] In the poems 'Myfanwy' and 'Myfanwy at Oxford' (both written in the late 1930s and published in *Old Lights for New Chancels*, 1940) he fantasized about her schooldays and her life as an Oxford undergraduate, teasingly implying in both poems that she might be the object of lesbian longings.

From 'Myfanwy':

> Were you a prefect and head of your dormit'ry?
> Were you a hockey girl, tennis or gym?
> Who was your favourite? Who had a crush on you?
> Which were the baths where they taught you to swim?[17]

From 'Myfanwy at Oxford':

> Gleam of gas upon Oxford station,
> Gleam of gas on her straight gold hair,
> Hair flung back with an ostentation,
> Waiting alone for a girl friend there.
> Second in Mods and a Third in Theology
> Come to breathe again Oxford air.

> *Her* Myfanwy as in Cadena days,
>   *Her* Myfanwy, a schoolgirl voice,
> Tentative brush of a cheek in a cocoa crush,
>   Coffee and Ulysses, Tennyson, Joyce,
> Alpha-minded and other dimensional,
>   Freud or Calvary? Take your choice.
>
> *Her* Myfanwy? *My* Myfanwy.
>   Bicycle bells in a Boar's Hill Pine,
> Stedman Triple from All Saints' steeple,
>   Tom and his hundred and one at nine,
> Bells of Butterfield, caught in Keble,
>   Sally and backstroke answer '*Mine!*'[18]

John referred to these poems in a letter to Myfanwy ('My darling prefect') of 28 January 1938:

I have made the Oxford poem more sophisticated, less spontaneous, sexy in a sexless way. The quotations come, most of them, from the *Cherwell* . . . Goronwy Rees of the *Spectator* told me that a *lot* of people think you beautiful.

  I like to think that you were at St Hilda's and had a senior girl keen on you who got a Second in Mods and Third in Theology, like the girl in the verses.

  I am so glad you liked the verses. It is most odd how you have undone an unpublishable gush of verse in me . . .

  I can't be grateful enough to old Karl Marx [J.M. Richards] for introducing me to John Piper, the best photographer and topographer I have ever met. Nor can I thank J.E.C.P. [enough] for bringing you into my life . . .

  Ever your adoring fag,
                 JB[19]

On 11 March 1938 the Pipers drove over to Uffington for lunch.[20]

I was pregnant with Edward [Myfanwy remembered] and John Betjeman was in a very traumatic state because Penelope had just had Paul, and she had a very difficult birth and suffered from insomnia afterwards. I was frightfully impressed with Uffington. We arrived at Garrards Farm and John opened the door. And as he opened the door, Penelope called out: 'They can't have sherry. Lunch is ready!' But, as you can imagine, John took no notice at all and gave us sherry. And then we had lunch. It was a most delicious lunch.[21] Penelope was then a kind of queen of village life.

She had these two girls from local families whom she taught to cook.
[Betty and Gwen Evans, who had come back to help after Paula left.] So
she could provide delicious lunches at the drop of a hat. One of the girls
John used to go and read Blake to. Lovely library. Photographs of Penelope
everywhere, by Moholy-Nagy. She was beautiful then – absolutely ravish-
ing to look at.[22]

So now there was a friendship, not just between the two men, but
between the two couples. When John was at a loss how to entertain Sir
Philip and Lady Chetwode, he drove them over to Fawley Bottom for
lunch in the Pipers' kitchen, with its scrubbed-pinewood shelves and
mocha-ware pottery. Myfanwy had met the Chetwodes twenty years
before, when as Penelope's schoolfriend she went to tea in St John's
Wood. The Henley visit was a success, though at first conversation
with the field-marshal was somewhat sticky. 'We had a custard marrow
on the table,' Myfanwy recalled. 'He said, "What's that?" and I said,
"It's a custard marrow." And he said, "Were you ever in Kashmir?" '[23]
  John and Myfanwy Piper were introduced to the Betjemans' circle
of friends. Piper credited John with having converted himself and
Myfanwy to Christianity. John modestly denied this: 'It was probably
looking at all those Norman fonts,' he said.[24] The Pipers were introduced to Father Harton. 'We were baptized by Father Harton,' Piper
said, 'and then we were confirmed by the Bishop of Oxford, which was
fairly frightening, with hundreds of kiddies in Uffington Church. We
were put at the right-hand end to take Communion first and then
married later. Neither of us had been baptized before.'[25] Piper thought
Harton was 'a pompous old trout'. He added: 'We never knew what
to say to him. He was lazy, never did much. What could one converse
about? He wasn't interested in music especially, or painting, so there
wasn't anything to say. I'm a talkative type; but with old Harton you
had to form sentences that demanded an answer, or you didn't get
one.'[26] The Pipers did not take to Adrian Bishop much, either.
  An introduction to Osbert Lancaster was much more successful.
'Osbert was sent to Fawley Bottom by John,' Piper said. 'He arrived
on his bicycle one day and said, "I'm Osbert Lancaster" and I said,
"Well, anybody could see you were." And we got on like a house on
fire. He was then living in a cottage with Derek Verschoyle, the literary editor of The Spectator, who was married to Osbert's future wife
Anne Scott-James.'[27] Lancaster and his first wife Karen became such
great friends of the Pipers that they moved to Leicester House, Henley,
to be near them; and in 1951 Piper and Lancaster together designed
the Grand Vista for the Festival of Britain's Pleasure Gardens at
Battersea.[28]

Piper also met Cyril Connolly, and later designed the collage jacket of his *Palinurus: The Unquiet Grave*. There were visits to John Dugdale at Sezincote and Piper was also introduced to John's mentors, Frederick Etchells and P. Morton Shand. He met Stuart Piggott at Garrards Farm. Piggott recalled the meeting in an eightieth-birthday tribute to Piper:

> When, in 1950, Sir Thomas Kendrick published his study of early anti-quarianism, *British Antiquity*, he gave it a characteristic dedication in Latin – *Ad Jo. Piperum necnon et Jo Betjehominem, Lelandi discipulos*, John Leland (1503–52) being the great antiquary-topographer of Tudor England. It was appropriate that I first met John Piper in the 1930s in the Betjemans' house in Uffington ... I was a young archaeologist with a taste for architectural history, the Picturesque and the Romantic Revival (and a friend of Tom Kendrick), and immediately found in John P. a most congenial fellow-explorer in these delectable by-ways of antiquarianism.[29]

The Pipers met Kenneth Clark – who was to find work for both Betjeman and Piper in the war – independently of John. Myfanwy edited a magazine called *Axis*, a running manifesto of abstract art. (John Piper designed the lay-out.) 'I wrote to K. [Clark],' she recalled, 'not to ask him to contribute, just to ask him to subscribe; then he invited us round to his house in Portland Place. I remember bullying him, being awfully schoolgirlish and brash about the whole thing.'[30] When the American 'mobile' sculptor Alexander Calder was staying with the Clarks, they invited the Pipers to tea with him and his wife. Then the Calders spent three weeks with the Pipers at Fawley Bottom while Calder made the works for his first London show. 'Sandy did his circus during those three weeks with us,' said Myfanwy. 'He made a toy circus about which a book has now been published. The circus was a marvellous thing.'[31] John Betjeman drove over to meet Calder, but there was no rapport. 'John did not care for that kind of art,' Piper said, 'and Sandy Calder wasn't verbally very skilful.'[32]

Piper, who had not been to university, felt a little excluded from the intimacy of the Oxford circle, the disciples of Maurice Bowra. 'It was an indissoluble ring which I was outside. I knew I would never be as close to K. Clark as John Sparrow was. One day Clark said to Sparrow: "I'm sure you are going to be very surprised and probably rather worried, but I'm going to be married." And this was a kind of ghastly traumatic experience for Sparrow. But he did get on well with Jane.'[33]

One of the introductions John made to Piper was, in Piper's view, the making of his own career as an artist. The introduction was to

Lord Alfred Douglas, who wrote a foreword to Piper's *Brighton Aquatints* (1939). John had interested Piper in eighteenth-century guide-books illustrated with aquatints. The best known were those of the Rev. William Gilpin who travelled round Britain on horseback and published a series of *Tours*. Before the war, John and Piper went together to Dublin, where such books could be bought for a few pounds. Piper was inspired by the aquatint illustrations and decided to take a ten-guinea course in the technique at the engraving department of the Royal College of Art, then housed in the Victoria & Albert Museum. He began making a series of sensitive aquatints of Brighton. John suggested that they should be published as a book, and that Lord Alfred Douglas should be asked to contribute a preface. 'John got Bosie to come up from Brighton,' Piper remembered. 'We all had lunch – Myfanwy, John, Bosie and I – at Overton's outside Victoria station, so that Bosie could get back to Brighton where he could see up the little girls' skirts from his basement flat as they went over the iron railings – his tastes had changed.'[34]

Brighton Aquatints was published in two editions, one of them limited to fifty copies in which the prints were coloured by hand. One of these, 'Brighton from the Station Yard', was hand-painted in all fifty copies by John Betjeman.[35] Piper always claimed that it was *Brighton Aquatints*, and in particular Douglas's foreword, that 'put him on the map'. He thought it was probably the Douglas foreword that had attracted Osbert Sitwell to write a full-page review of the book (with an illustration) in *The Listener*. Sitwell wrote that Piper's drawings manifested 'all the quality, the ease and speed, of beautiful handwriting'.[36] Piper said: 'After that I became one of the boys.' The article was immediately followed by an exhibition at the Leicester Galleries, which sold out.

The aquatints book brought a new and eccentric figure into the Betjemans' and Pipers' lives: Mervyn Horder, then chairman of Duckworth who published the book. 'He was the son of Lord Horder, the King's doctor,' Piper said in 1978, 'and he had two sisters. He said he spent his childhood under the table in the dining room which had tassels; it was the only place he could get away from women. But he is rather like that: he has spent half his life, as it were, under a stone not being seen.'[37] Horder lived in solitary squalor in St John's Wood, London. His reclusiveness was intruded upon by the press in the 1960s when he was twice convicted of sending homosexual pornography through the post.[38] A talented composer, he was to set some of John's poems to music; and after John's death he became president of the Betjeman Society.

John Summerson took to Piper, as he did not to all of John

Betjeman's friends. 'I knew Summerson very well,' Piper said. 'Admired him. He was always an aloof, stately character. I remember Griggers [Geoffrey Grigson] and us discussing which of our friends would become a knight first, and without one hesitation we all said: "John Summerson!" And of course we were right. He was a jolly good pianist – little-known fact. And of course he was brilliant at the paper games.'[39]

All the Pipers' friends took part in the paper games after dinner at Fawley Bottom. Stuart Piggott has written:

> I particularly recall the paper games the Pipers had devised, with joint contributions in the manner of the still familiar Victorian 'Consequences': one (drawn) The Church Game, the other (written) The Guide Book Game. In the first the players drew, from west to east, the south elevation of a church, in sections in which the only clues to continuity were roof and ground lines; the aim was to embody as many architectural eccentricities and grotesqueries as possible. I could just get by with my amateur draughtsmanship, but what could you do with the west end of a nave, knowing that John Piper on the hidden fold had just drawn a stunning western tower, and Osbert Lancaster, eyes rolling and looking like Canon Fontwater, was waiting to pounce with an egregious transept or outrageous chancel? The porch was one's main hope, with help from crazy stove-pipes or derelict guttering if all else failed. Or if the paper hadn't run out east of the chancel there was an extra chance for a Mausoleum, perhaps in the Normano-Chinese manner.
>
> The Guide Book Game was more flexible, and depended on a loving acquaintance with the phraseology and attitudes of the writers of dim county guide-books round about the beginning of the century (the Methuen *Little Guides* were our favourites), in which all architecture after the Middle Ages was 'graceless', 'modern', or 'debased'. Worthy authors all – and there were exceptions such as John Meade Falkner on Oxfordshire – but asking for parody. The players compiled a parish entry, with place-name, location, church, manor, local families, and so on, and here Myfanwy was the acknowledged expert on Local Customs, where under the flat prose dark hints of unimaginable rustic obscenities could be glimpsed. Good games for Leland's disciples.[40]

In addition to these two games which involved drawing and prose-writing, there was a third game, called 'Church Consequences', which required the players to write verse. Piper recalled: 'Summerson was very good at it; John B. was of course supreme. Osbert could never get the rhyming right. Mervyn Horder, he was really rather good at it, he had that Wykehamist literary jib. But John regulated everything, altered other people's lines when necessary so that they scanned.'[41]

Mervyn Horder (later Lord Horder) told Richard Ingrams in 1983:

I have the most agreeable memories of evenings spent at Fawley at the end of . . . early topographical expeditions. The preparation of Myfanwy's incomparable supper usually took place to the sound of American musical comedy numbers and Mozart's piano concertos; John [Piper] played both by ear with enormous élan occasionally rescued and redirected by me with the music at a second piano. The music carried on after supper, with the addition of solo hymn-singing by Myfanwy, till the end of the day when we gathered on sofas round a huge log fire and settled into half an hour of Church Consequences, a game of unknown origin which I have never played anywhere else.

Each player writes down a single line about a church – as it might be – *Poor old Terrington St Clements, sinking in the marshes fast* – his neighbour then adds a rhyming line plus a line of his own which *his* neighbour has to amplify in the same way, and so on . . . The topics ranged as widely as possible over every likely and unlikely aspect of British church life: churches, churchyards, incumbents, curates, organists, cleaners, diocesan authorities, liturgy, heating and lighting systems, children's corners; to say nothing of the private lives, marital affairs and inmost thoughts of all concerned . . . I have often since wished I had quietly picked up and stowed away the best of these sheets of instant doggerel . . .[42]

The Pipers recalled one complete 'Consequence':

When they called in Sir Gilbert at Reading St Chad's,
He took the whole building away,
And erected instead, which was one of his fads,
A marquee which was blessed the next day.
When the weather was wet it was empty of course,
But when it was fine it was thronged,
And the smell of the grass made the worshippers hoarse,
And liturgical rights were all wronged.[43]

John Betjeman remembered only a fragment referring to the parish of Milbrook, Bedfordshire.

Believe me, Canon Cotton,
The acoustics here are rotten.[44]

The two Johns agreed to write the Shell Guide to Shropshire together. (Although written in 1939, the book was not published until after the war.) It was a county neither knew well, though John had read the book on Shrewsbury by W.H. Auden's father and had been to Apley Park, a Berners property. They drove up to Shrewsbury in Piper's car – by now the 1920 Lancia had been replaced by a Citroën Light 15 – and made their headquarters at the Prince Rupert Hotel, conveniently near St Mary's Church where John Betjeman attended Communion each day. 'It was marvellous going with Mr Piper for the first time,' John told Richard Ingrams. 'It was like going to Brazil or somewhere.'[45] In all, the two men made about five separate journeys to Shropshire, sometimes accompanied by Myfanwy. Piper took photographs and made sketches. 'He drew absolutely certainly with a quill pen,' John recalled, 'and you could tell at once from the line whether it was decayed or Victorian . . . I don't think I've ever felt so confident as I did with Mr Piper. I remember once in Salop I suddenly lost my temper and then I felt I had wounded a tame animal.'[46] Ingrams suggests that this loss of temper may have been caused by Piper's unremitting energy. Piper recalled John's complaining, 'I can't do more than ten churches a day, old boy.'[47] In defence of John, whose appetite for 'church-crawling' was usually insatiable, he was suffering badly from piles on the Shropshire excursions. He may also have had the 'flu, as the gazetteer entry for Ludford reads: 'On the occasion of our visit in May 1939 the sacred well of St Julian (under a lead cover by the churchyard well) proved efficacious in a case of influenza.'[48] John's maladies may account for a distinct testiness in some of his entries. 'It is surprising,' the gazetteer notes, 'how many prominent but indifferent architects of the last seventy years have been employed in the town of Ellesmere.'[49] One critic noted this asperity, referring to the two men as 'a waspish pair, consisting of a writer of funny verses and odds and ends, and an austere, would-be latter-day Cotman'.[50]

In a biography of Piper (1979), Anthony West, the son of Rebecca West by H.G. Wells, persuasively suggested that there was a cross-pollination of talent on the journeys John and Piper made together for the Shell Guides. Piper 'gained a great deal from this intimate working association with a poet who, whatever his carefully maintained public persona and his lighter verse may suggest to the contrary, combines a profound seriousness with a refined sensibility'; while 'The poet's eye fed on what was valued by the painter's . . .'

> Both men benefited from the collaboration; it was not only refreshing to their daily selves as very good fun, it also contributed to their aesthetic maturation. It had a great deal to do with the deepening seriousness of Betjeman's poetic as opposed to public performances, and to the stabiliza-tion of their hierarchies of values. While working together the two men

learned more than they were aware of at the time about what was of fundamental importance to them . . . Both were interested in the literary prece-
dents for the kind of work in which they were involved, and both, having
first become collectors of early nineteenth-century guidebooks and travellers' vademecums, went on to investigate the literature of the picturesque which had burgeoned from the developing consciousness of the
beauties of natural landscape in aesthetic circles in the seventeenth and
eighteenth centuries.[51]

However, light-heartedness was in the ascendant on the topographical jaunts. Piper told Richard Ingrams that it was at Much Wenlock,
on the Shropshire trip, that he got his Betjeman nickname of 'Mr
Piper' (or, as John usually wrote it, 'Mr Pahper'). They called at a
hotel for tea and were told to sit in a waiting-room. Finally a waitress
came in and said in a strong North Country accent, 'Will you two men
come forward, please?' When they sat down, John started talking in a
similar accent, pretending to be a businessman and addressing his colleague as 'Mr Pahper'.[52] Stuart Piggott recalled that when he first met
John Piper, 'he and John Betjeman were just back from a tour in con-
nexion with the Shell Guides . . . and kept up conversations in a comic
Shropshire accent, full of flat vowels and hard "g's" – "swimmingg"
and "singgingg" . . .'[53]

The joke was prolonged in John's poem 'A Shropshire Lad', about
the exploits of Captain Webb, who swam the Channel. A direction at
the beginning of the poem urges: 'N.B. – *This should be recited with
a Midland accent*. Captain Webb, the swimmer and a relation of Mary
Webb by marriage, was born at Dawley in an industrial district in
Salop.' The Captain Webb poem was published, with the two
Myfanwy poems, in *Old Lights for New Chancels* (1940). Like
Captain Webb, Myfanwy was a champion swimmer. In the study of
Piper which he contributed to the Penguin Modern Painters series in
1948, John wrote: 'Mr Piper's wife, Myfanwy, used to travel with us.
She very much appeals to me with her wide-apart blue eyes and soft
peach-like skin and athletic figure. She had been a swimming blue at
Oxford.'[54]

On 28 March 1939 John took Myfanwy to the Sir John Soane
Museum in London. He wrote this verse in the front of the museum
catalogue:

> Sir John has blessed our union
> Myfanwy, my own,
> Here in his grey communion
> Of plaster cast and stone.

Green to the skilful skylight
Sir John has made the walls;
How chaste and mild the highlight
On child or cherub falls.[55]

Myfanwy loved John too; but it was not an uncritical love. Five months after his death in 1984, when the exhibition 'John Betjeman – A Celebration' opened at the National Theatre, London, she wrote in *The Times* that it was 'hard . . . not to feel a little jealous of an old friendship with someone whose store of acute perceptions and eccentricities has, as it were, gone public'.[56] John, she suggested, had approached all human relationships by way of an idea of character or an invented situation. ' "Approached" is perhaps the wrong expression: "staved off" is more like it. When I first met him, nearly fifty years ago, the game had to be played; the invented character and ambience discovered, then accepted with a good grace and then exploited to mutual satisfaction and many jokes. All the people accepted and loved by him had to put up with it, even and especially his own family.'[57] Myfanwy added:

It was when he carried the game beyond affectation and into social comment and alien territory that 'long-suffering' was an appropriate term. There was an occasion in an apparently empty bar at the Mytton and Mermaid near Shrewsbury when the Shropshire guide was being written. He suddenly spied, in a corner, a commercial traveller writing up his notes. We were then treated to a long imaginary sales talk about a whistling kettle in a persistent, boring Midland undertone. It was very funny and we were appalled: hopeless tears of laughter were mixed with tears of embarrassment – could what was going on be heard, or guessed at?

When the victim did not participate and was not intended to, there was ruthlessness, even cruelty, in the performance just as there was in his constant references, in public and in private, to his few implacable hatreds. But these were a matter of conviction. The people or opinions that he hated were those that could destroy the things he loved, things that were, until he brought them into the fold of his appreciation, orphaned by fashionable taste, or by academic judgments. Like Blake he feared both pretension and learning (as opposed to knowledge), seeing them both as destructive of feeling, as substitutes for the eye, the ear and the heart.[58]

7

CONTINUAL DEW AND AN OXFORD UNIVERSITY CHEST

It would not have been fun to come out uniform with Stephen Spender.

John Betjeman, letter to Edward James, 2 November 1937

John's first collection of poems, *Mount Zion*, published by his rich Oxford friend Edward James in 1931,[1] had been something of a private joke – as it were, an amusing literary party held for friends. Five years later, he began looking around for a 'proper' publisher to present his poetry to the world. The book would contain the best poems from *Mount Zion*, with others written since. T.S. Eliot, John's old prep-school master, courted him in 1936 as a possible Faber author;[2] but he was too late. By then, John had agreed to be published by his friend John ('Jock') Murray. The book, *Continual Dew*, appeared in 1937.

After Eton, Jock Murray had been at Magdalen, Oxford, from 1927 to 1930, and had thus overlapped with John for one year. He recalled John's terror that the college 'hearties' would smash up his rooms, like the philistine 'undergrads' in his poem 'The 'Varsity Students' Rag'.[3] In those days Jock's name was Arnaud Robin Grey. He changed it to John Murray when he joined the family firm in 1930 as 'chief slave and bottle-washer'. His mother, Dorothy, was a sister of the firm's chairman, Sir John Murray, whose ancestor, John Murray II, had published Byron's poems from the building the firm still occupied – and occupies – No. 50 Albemarle Street, London. (On the door is a brass plate engraved, in copperplate script, 'Mr Murray N° 50' – John Betjeman used to imitate this on his envelopes to Jock. In the grate of the main salon upstairs, the second John Murray had burned Byron's memoirs – at the insistence of Byron's family – to prevent further scandal.)

Jock's father, Thomas Grey, also worked for the firm, and Jock had lived at Albemarle Street in his youth. He had met Sir Arthur Conan Doyle and Aldous Huxley's father. Now, because his uncle was childless, he was the heir apparent – John Murray VI. As part of his training in the business he learned typesetting with Eric Gill, who insisted that he should work, like himself, in the nude;[4] became assistant editor first of the *Cornhill Magazine* in 1931 and then, in 1933, of the *Quarterly Review*, each of them a famous Murray periodical.

John and Jock kept up their friendship after Oxford, and the care with which Jock Murray preserved John's early letters suggests that he had some inkling of his future fame. (Murray had shown his sure publishing instinct as early as 1929, when it was he who saw the potential of Axel Münthe's *The Story of San Michele*.) John inscribed a copy of *Mount Zion* 'To Jock Grey (Murray), quite a clever chap, from that very clever chap, John Betjeman.'[5] On 13 March 1931 he wrote to him from *The Architectural Review*:

> Dear Jock,
>   A thousand thanks for the book. Do you mean that I shall keep it? . . .
>   I can scarcely express in simple words, which are all that we have in our old English language, the emotion and delight with which I received the news that you have discovered again the Inigo Jones notebook and the Flaxman sketchbook.[6] With what trepidation upon goloshed feet I, and perhaps if you will permit it, my editor, will call at 50 Albemarle Street on Monday next at 5.30 . . .
>   Tinkety-tonk,
>   Your devoted slave,
>   J. Betjeman,
>   Sub Editor.[7]

Murray remembered driving 'round and round' in a taxi with John while his friend tried to make up his mind whether or not to marry Camilla Russell.[8] In December 1931 John wrote from Edward James's house in Culross Street, which he was sharing with Randolph Churchill, apologizing for failing to keep an appointment with Murray – 'I was told in a dilatory manner by my bloody servants that you had called in vain.'[9] (John was giving himself airs: they were Edward James's servants.) The letter ended: 'When oh when shall we meet again again, meet again, meet meeet & while there is life there is Anthony Hope keep on hoping, Yours devotedly James Joyce.'[10] In May 1932 John wrote regretting that he had felt obliged to attack a Murray book in *The Spectator*. 'I have a bee in my bonnet about the production of school books & do not mean to attack your excellent firm personally. Pray God I have not got an old & valued friend into hot water.'[11]

Jock Murray sometimes sent John review copies. In September 1932 John wrote to him from Frederick Etchells's office in Davies Street:

My dear Jock,

Thank you so much for chronic constipation which has made me so nervous about my inside as a result of reading merely the first chapter, that not only am I convinced of the excellence of the writer, but also of the necessity of consulting the Docor [sic] at once. Clifton Chapel is healthy antidote.

Have you got my Priest & the Acolyte?[12] You might let me know as I cannot remember & if it is with you it will be safe, if with the police, it will not.

Yours in the sure & certain hope of a speedy resurrection . . .[13]

Jock was 'in the know' about John's engagement to Penelope in 1933. On 5 May of that year, three months before the marriage, John wrote to him, 'I am so sorry I could not come to your pretty little party last night but Philth [Penelope] was coming to see me, & although I should have had no qualms in bringing her, she came too late to make it polite for me to come . . .'[14] In October of the same year, John wrote:

Dear Jock,

Thanks, old boy, for the congratters. They were topping. Penelope goes to Germany for three months on Sunday while I have to look for a house in the country but within easy reach of London. This will not be bad fun provided P comes back faithful and not a Nazi. I have a lot of funny things to tell you.

Would you care to reprint Mount Zion with considerable additions?

I will be in London Monday for the rest of my life . . .[15]

This was John's first tentative overture to Murray, but no further move was made until 1936, and by then there were three serious obstacles to a Betjeman–Murray collaboration. First, Sir John Murray was very dubious about the poems as a commercial proposition. Second, it was uncertain whether Edward James held the copyright in the *Mount Zion* poems and, if he did, whether he would allow them to be reprinted. Worst of all, John, with his usual inclination to say 'yes' rather than disappoint, had told a young publisher called Reginald Hutchings that he might issue a selection of his new poems; and Hutchings had actually had a number set in type.

Jock Murray solved the first difficulty. When his uncle said to him,

'My dear young fellow, we can't start publishing that sort of thing,' Jock was so sure that the poems would catch on that he offered to guarantee them with 100 shares of Bovril that his grandfather had given him on his eighteenth birthday. 'He agreed – and I never had to sell the Bovril shares,' Jock recalled.[16]

John knew how difficult and cantankerous Edward James could be; but luckily there was something James wanted from him, and in return he was prepared to let the *Mount Zion* poems be reissued. James wanted poems and essays by John for *Minotaure*, a new review in which he had a financial interest; he also wanted John to use his influence with his literary friends to get them to contribute. Perhaps Lord Berners would 'allow us to print those of his very funny verses that are not improper for publication – such as the poem about Red Roses and Red Noses which describes how that whereas "red roses blow only from May until September, as regards to red noses, one can blow all the year"'. James wrote to John from the Waldorf-Astoria, New York, on 18 December 1936:

> Now that John Murray is bringing out your new verses as a book, you must ask him whether if in return for my consent to poems from 'Mount Zion' being reprinted in your new book he would allow in the 'Minotaure' one or two of the new poems to appear, provided that the 'Minotaure' is issued either simultaneously with your book or slightly afterwards . . . Without taking away from the freshness and virginity of your new book, it will be a valuable, active, and really a very useful piece of publicity for the book – entirely free.[17]

James did not pass up the chance to tell John how shabbily he thought he had behaved in not letting *him* publish the new poems. James had lost money on *Mount Zion*, he complained, because John had given away 55 per cent of the copies. John had definitely promised him first refusal on any new poems, and there had been a plan for Mark Ogilvie-Grant to draw illustrations. 'You are such an elusive and difficult fellow to catch or to tie down to anything that I let things drift . . .'[18]

Meanwhile, John had managed to slide out of his agreement with Hutchings. Although he had no formal contract with the young man, John felt, he told Jock Murray, 'a fearful shit'.[19] In the same letter of 28 September, he listed the poems from *Mount Zion* which he thought could be omitted from the new collection '& any others you like to remove' – 'Varsity Students' Rag', 'A Seventeenth-Century Love Lyric', 'Mother and I', 'For Nineteenth-Century Burials', 'Competition', 'School Song', 'Camberley', 'Arts and Crafts' and 'St Aloysius Church, Oxford'. Jock Murray wrote 'Keep' beside 'A Seventeenth-Century

Love Lyric', but it was not kept. However, John was persuaded to leave in 'For Nineteenth-Century Burials', 'Competition' and 'Camberley'.

In February 1937 he sent Jock Murray a new poem for the collection, the famous 'Slough' ('Come, friendly bombs, and fall on Slough!/It isn't fit for humans now . . .'). Murray had sent him specimen proofs of Antique type, which he liked. He commented, with his usual nice judgement on such matters, 'The 14 pt is better but there must be the same depth of text on each page, so as to balance. The rest should be entirely decorative.'[20] He thought the ornaments on the proof were too pale, small and finicky, and drew for Murray a curly and more solid *art nouveau* leaf which he thought preferable, though eventually it was not used. He asked that Murray should include in the contract, or in a letter, the author's veto on copies being sent to the *London Mercury*, *New Verse*, *Contemporary Poetry and Prose*, the *Morning Post*, the *New Statesman* and if possible the *Times Literary Supplement*. The request shows how morbidly sensitive he was to adverse criticism.

The new book was to be almost as striking and eccentric in appearance as *Mount Zion*. John thought some of the designs could be adapted from Victorian and Edwardian books. He wrote to Jock Murray on 15 July 1937:

> Here is an old Temple Macbeth. The title pages have a different design from the new Temple Classics. I suggest that if we use the enclosed design Shakespeare's face should be removed on the left and the title on the right and the blank spaces filled with my verse. Perhaps I am wrong in calling them Temple Classics. I notice they are called King's Treasures of Literature. Each has a different and more horrible title page than the last.[21]

John went to Dent's, who published the King's Treasures series, to obtain permission to use their design and came away convinced he had obtained it; but this blithe assumption led to trouble, as an angry letter to Murray of 29 July reveals.

> My dear Jock,
> Dent's have done the dirty on us. 'As Mr Hadfield[22] understands it' is not as it actually happened. I telephoned to Dent's & they said I could look over the King's Treasures file. When I called to look over said file, a man came down from the inner recesses & I explained to him what the border was wanted for, showed him the proofs of Osbert's drawings & the poems . . . He said that would be quite all right & there would be a nominal fee. The business of the nominal fee was echoed by the elderly woman assistant also in the shop. I said Murray's would write confirming this.

I think you should point this out to Dent's & say you have had the block made. They have no right to try to shove the blame on to me & to ignore what was actually spoken in their shop.

Supposing all this fails I send by this post a volume of the *Dome* containing a design by GM Ellwood (still alive, see *Who's Who*).[23] If he would give us permission to reproduce his design, we might get him to write out the Exeter poem in the appropriate lettering so that the gel effect would be like this [drawing]. Very nice, I fancy. I will write to him if Dent's refuse to give in.

Ellwood is a member of the Guild and I doubt not that I could point out to him tactfully the sort of thing I want and get him to do it. No Guild man costs very much. This would really be better than anything up to now but I do feel sorry for the way you have been treated by Dent's. I never said *I* would write to them, I said you would.

> Yours,
> John B.[24]

This letter shows John's boiling rage when he thought somebody was doing him down, slighting him or accusing him of untruthfulness. It also reveals his talent for lateral thinking, his ability to make contingency plans when it seemed as if things might go awry. And it displays another of his traits, an acute awareness of what the other person may be feeling. As with his dealings with Jack Beddington at Shell, he knows that Murray, as a businessman, will be worried about the cost of his fancy schemes, and does his best to reassure him. In the end, John found, living in Uffington, an Edwardian artist called Gabriel Pippet, who was paid three guineas to draw the border for the poem 'Exeter' – a sensuous, if somewhat clodhopping, *art nouveau* design of water-lilies.

Osbert Lancaster designed arborescent lettering and mock hinges to be stamped in gold on the cover. For the title-page and the jacket, John had more avant-garde plans. The book's title was of course taken from *The Book of Common Prayer*; to absolve himself of maudlin religious sentiment, or perhaps just to shock, he proposed a diagram of a dripping tap for the title-page. He wrote to Murray on 20 July 1937:

Here is the tap and tracing with the way to draw the drops of water. You might make a test and see whether they fall from the outside rim of the tap. Certainly not the middle.

Leave in 'plunger', 'washer', 'rim of valve' – they add poignance. Put a rule round and reduce to a suitable width. I should thing [*sic* for think] the deeper the better for the drips . . .

I think it ought to look very nice indeed. Perhaps you will let Ted Kauffer know of this. He might incorporate it in his dust jacket.[25]

Edward McKnight Kauffer, with whom John had worked on Shell posters, did not use the tap on the jacket. He drew a surreal design of a severed hand, the wrist sprouting into fleshy leaves, with heavy dew falling from fluffy white clouds. John received an early copy of the book in October. He wrote to Jock Murray:

Thank you so much for the book with which I am delighted. Ted's cover is magnificent. Most appealing & an agreeable contrast with the lovely black & gold inside. The gilt edges are lovely. So is the grey paper. Loveliest of all is the prayer-book paper [used for Pippet's 'Exeter' design].

'If the amount of trouble & money that has been expended on the production of this undergraduate persiflage had instead been spent on some of our young poets, the publishers at least could be congratulated.' Anticipated letter from *New Statesman and Nation*

You might put that on to the cards you intend to send out.

My dear Jock, I feel it unlikely that you will sell more than a dozen copies and I do appreciate the charity, for I can only call it that, which has made you publish the verse in so exquisite a style. You and Lord Gorell [editor of the *Cornhill Magazine*] will get your reward in heaven . . .[26]

Jock Murray indeed deserves credit for persuading his traditional-minded firm to publish the book with such lavishness and eccentricity. He may have thought it as well to humour John, to keep him as an author. He may also have recognized the publicity advantages of the flamboyant production. Or he may just have enjoyed entering the spirit of the enterprise. There were disadvantages too, however. Had T.S. Eliot not been pipped at the post by Murray, John's poems would probably have appeared in the normal chaste Faber format with elegant letterpress but with no decorations, dripping taps, dendriform lettering, leaf-sprouting hands or prayer-book paper. The reviewers might then have taken John more seriously, as one of the 'Thirties Poets', along with W.H. Auden, a Faber author – though, as John wrote to Edward James, 'It would not have been fun to come out uniform with Stephen Spender.'[27] Eliot might not have allowed John his facetious sub-title, 'A Little Book of Bourgeois Verse'. John may have hoped that the sub-title would disarm criticism by forestalling it, but it did not work. His aggressive flippancy was a red rag to some critics. An English master, reviewing the book for the Dragon School magazine, *The Draconian* (in which Betjeman verse had first appeared in print), accused him of preciosity, unkindness, snobbishness and affectation, and advised him to confine his humorous writing to subjects in better taste. (Pillorying this critic in the preface to his next book, John noted, 'He has translated Homer into Esperanto.')

Evelyn Waugh, however, writing in *Night and Day*, gave bantering praise to the book's originality and modernity. 'Mr Betjeman's poetry is not meant to be read, but recited – and recited with almost epileptic animation; only thus can the apostrophic syntax, the black-bottom rhythms, the Delphic climaxes, the panting ineptitude of the transitions be seen in their true values.'[28] Maurice Bowra's review in *The Spectator* was kindly but pedestrian (it was said of him that 'His talk was brilliant, but it died on the page'). He credited John with 'the true historian's passion for the thoughts and tastes of a lost generation': 'From the relics of Victorianism he has built a world which lives in its own right and has the sturdy independence of a real creation. But though he is a learned historian, he is a historian with a bias. He selects from the past what appeals most intimately to his own tastes, and what draws him most strongly to the Victorians is their solid churchmanship.' The *Daily Express* said of the poems, 'Blimps won't understand them, tho' they satirize bourgeois civilization mercilessly.'

In spite of John's injunction that no copy should be sent to the *New Statesman* (he had sour memories of what its critic had said about *Mount Zion*, and a left-wing magazine was hardly likely to welcome a book of confessedly 'bourgeois' verse), Peter Quennell reviewed it for that magazine. The heading under which the review appeared, 'Flowers of Mediocrity', must have prepared John for the worst; but it referred to the subject-matter, not the poetry: 'a dark, limitless suburb – street after street of little houses, now stiffening into prospects of dismal down-at-heel respectability, with old newspapers littered beneath the laurel bushes of innumerable front gardens, now flaring into the watery brightness of Saturday shopping thoroughfares, with their fried-fish shops, wireless stores and cut-price tobacconists'. On the poetry, Quennell (a friend of the Betjemans) was complimentary.

> He is a writer of very remarkable wit and facility; but he is something more – a passionate observer of the second-rate who (just as a physician might become positively enamoured of the various morbid phenomena he has selected for clinical examination) is now almost attached to the life he condemns . . . After all, there *is* a strange poetry in the very mindlessness, in the deep essential vulgarity, of modern industrial civilisation. Why sentimentalise about the passing of the manor house – that elegant façade badly needs repainting: the poor old colonel was obliged to lay off another

gardener last week – when we can rattle a walking-stick along the dusty cast-iron railings of Palmers Green, explore the derelict factory buildings that diversify Slough, or visit a Milk Bar in Cricklewood's humming high street?[29]

Quennell thought that *Continual Dew* was illustrated with 'the tasteful tastelessness that the subject demands'. Another friend, J.B. Morton ('Beachcomber' of the *Daily Express*), whom John used to meet in John Squire's circle at the Temple Bar Restaurant in the Strand, also gave the book a largely favourable notice in *The Listener*.

He has something to say, and says it in a manner which is a blend of the early Sitwells and an intelligent Oxford don (if such be not a contradiction in terms). But he has a vigour of his own, and a trick of sudden contrast, of a swing-over from earnestness to mockery which will make those who love Cheltenham think that *he* loves Cheltenham, and those who hate Tunbridge Wells think that *he* hates Tunbridge Wells. He is never serious for long; at least not for long enough to enable the reader to see into his mind. He hears the bells of Westgate-on-Sea, and appears to be about to regret the heart-breaking beauty of the eighteen-nineties. But no sooner has he seen his vision of the past than he dislikes it intensely. He begins a poem called 'Croydon', and you prepare to laugh. But the joke is deferred, and many a Croydon exile in lands beyond the waves, reading these lines, will see, through a mist of tears, the dear old gasworks, the goods-yard and the public library . . . The author's obsession with garden cities and queer sects is redeemed by a hatred of Calvinism which is quite unusual today, and a sign of robust mental health. But he . . . seems to me to be painfully self-conscious – possibly because Mr W.H. Auden has begun to imitate him.[30]

Continual Dew, dedicated to Gerald Berners, was published on 2 November 1937 – three weeks before Paul was born. On 5 November, John wrote to tell Jock Murray that Auden (it was he who had suggested to Eliot that Faber should publish a Betjeman collection) had asked if he might include two of the poems in his *Oxford Book of Light Verse*. 'Very flattering, I'm sure,' John wrote. 'I don't want a copyright fee. Are you entitled to one?'[31] Auden's anthology was published in 1938.[32] In the same year appeared John's book *An Oxford University Chest*, a companion volume to Mary Benedetta's *Street Markets of London* (1936) and *Eton Portrait* (1937) by a young Black Watch subaltern, Bernard Fergusson (later Lord Ballantrae), who, when commissioned to write the book, was ADC to the poetical general Archibald Wavell.[33] The publisher, John Miles of Amen

Corner, London EC4, was a newly established subsidiary of Simpkin
Marshall, a large firm of wholesale booksellers. It was intended that
Miles should launch out initially in a small way, with a short list of
high-quality books.[34] Those by Benedetta, Fergusson and John were
all to be illustrated with photographs by the Hungarian-born László
Moholy-Nagy, a member of the Bauhaus.[35]

With his taste for the obscure, John had always been attracted by
the lesser-known Edwardian publishers. The *Chats* series by Arthur
Hayden, a Highgate friend of his father,[36] had been published by T.
Fisher Unwin – '*Chats on Old Clocks, Chats on Old Chafing Dishes,
Chats* on anything,' as John satirically wrote of the series. Spaciously
printed memoirs by doctors, lawyers, politicians and explorers were
published by Eveleigh, Nash & Grayson. Regimental uniforms and
pond life were specialities of Seely Service & Co. It had always been
John's ambition to appear under an obscure imprint of that sort,
perhaps Rivington's, 'originally High Church and later wholly educational'.[37]

One of the most mysterious of the publishers [he wrote in 1977] was John
Miles. Whether he had a moustache or pince-nez I cannot be sure, and
how he got on with . . . Simpkin Marshall, I do not know . . . So, when a
letter came from John Miles . . . I could not resist the temptation offered
me by its signatory, Mr Harry Paroissien,[38] to write a book about Oxford,
packed with illustrations. It was the illustrations which tempted me, for
Harry had a gift for layout, and the look and feel of a book, and so, I
thought, did I.[39]

The photographs were to be on shiny art paper, the text on rough
paper. There could be wide margins and in the headings 'black letter
type such as might have pleased Caxton' was allowed.[40] Osbert
Lancaster drew some caricatures of Oxford characters – lady dons on
bicycles, swells in the Bullingdon Club and scarfed rowing men. Line
drawings from *The Adventures of Mr Verdant Green* (1853) by the
Rev. Edward Bradley mixed in well with Lancaster's. But the main
illustrations were the magnificent photographs by Moholy-Nagy.
John later wrote of him:

He was a huge man with a constant smile and shaped like a large, oval
water beetle which suddenly comes to the surface and dives out of sight.
Moholy (Mowli-Wogie, as my wife called him) had a Leica and rushed
about frenziedly photographing everything he saw. At Encaenia, when
honorary degrees were given to distinguished persons, my father-in-law
being one, he became particularly excited. The result of Moholy's clickings

was hundreds of little prints measuring about one square inch, and from these he selected those which were to be enlarged.

That was where his genius lay. He knew just which to choose, showing the beauty of crumbling stone, the crispness of carved eighteenth-century urns, and members of the public who were quite unconscious that they were being photographed: undergraduettes scratching their spots; the master of Balliol waiting to post a letter; ladies flat on punts; people browsing in Blackwell's; and everywhere bicycles.[41]

In the same recollection of 1977, John wrote that his text was designed to be 'entertaining reading only, and useless in the examination industry'. It was an odd mish-mash, combining a furious polemic on the way the colleges had allowed their estates round Oxford to be developed; an architectural tour; observations on undergraduates, dons and scouts; and deeper thoughts about 'the three Oxfords' – the old city, or 'Christminster', the university and what he called 'Motopolis', the hateful creation of 'William Morris the Second' (Lord Nuffield). The reviewers took the book more seriously than he did. *The Listener* judged:

> Mr Betjeman's book is funny but not frivolous; he is not facetious or whimsical and does not patronize his subject . . . He is not behind the times, yet he seems to wish he could be. He disarms attack by admitting that he is an 'escapist': certainly he is a very self-conscious and subtle one . . . He is at best when he describes North Oxford: he should write a whole book about it. Norham Gardens, Bardwell Road, North Parade, Park Crescent – these names inspire him as the names of medieval knights inspired the early Victorians. It is 'escape' country . . . It is very rarely that such an entertaining and original book is published.[42]

John did not write a book about North Oxford; but that Gothic Revival district, where he had lived as a prep-school boy, inspired one of his best-known poems.[43]

The Spectator sent the book to Graham Greene, who wrote a page full of praise.

> Nobody can catch atmosphere better than Mr Betjeman – whether he is describing the little shops poked away in St Ebbe's with their 'painted fire-screens, writhing vases, cumbersome clocks such as might deck the parlour of some small farm among the elms ten or twenty miles away', the 'purple mouldering quality of Oxford stone', or the literary society ('a lot of chuckling between the pipe-sucks as to who has got the unexpurgated edition and who has not'). He can distinguish with the exactness of an anthropologist between the different college and inter-college sets . . .[44]

He fervently agreed with John about 'the monstrous new Bodleian which is rising in Broad Street with the apparent purpose of balancing Baker's, the big store at the other end'.

The *London Mercury* described the book as 'mordant'.[45] *The Times* reported John's view that Oxford was 'no longer a provincial town but a replica of London' and noted that 'Mr Betjeman likes [the scouts] better than most dons whom he has met.'[46] (In acknowledgements, John thanked not only Harry Paroissien, whom in letters he addressed as 'Parishioner', but the Magdalen butler J.W. Gynes for his inside information on the underworld of scouts.)[47] The only hostile notice appeared in *The Architectural Review*. It was by the editor's brother, Maurice Hastings, a man John and his friends regarded as a philistine of philistines – it was his shooting the genitalia off the statues at Rousham that had outraged James Lees-Milne and impelled him on his career as a conserver of the English heritage.[48] Hastings began approvingly enough, writing of 'Mr Betjeman's great powers of heart' and complimenting him for 'at last' giving the eighteenth century 'precedence over the crumbling Gothic'; but then he became severe. 'Alas, much though we may admire the brilliance of the prosecution, we are bound to admit the weakness of Mr Betjeman's case.'[49] He took issue with John's maledictions on specialist dons. John had, Hastings thought, no idea of the proper function of a university.

> He implies continually [Hastings complained] that Oxford offers her children a stone for bread, that for Culture is substituted pedantry. He remarks that the English School is really Anglo-Saxon, Northumbrian, and tedious medieval poems. He draws a sad picture of Miss Angle extending her few wits over Gutnish[50] in the Bodleian . . .
>
> Scholarship is only dry as dust to the non-scholar, and the University must cater for the highest, not the lowest, standard of scholarship. There is no law to compel people to take academic courses, and if you don't like Gutnish, or think it a waste of time, don't do it. But what would be really serious would be an inability to obtain all the Gutnish there is and the very best brand of it from the University, if you did want it.[51]

Fair comment; but when John criticized the Oxford English School he was not concerned to be fair. He was sustaining his relentless vendetta against C.S. Lewis (that enthusiast for Nordic languages).

DECORATION

The last two years of the 1930s were not a happy time for John. In
the surviving letters of his friends we find variations on 'I am sorry you
are so depressed.' His *Angst* went beyond the gloom that most
Englishmen felt as the 'low, dishonest decade'[1] drew to its close and
war with Germany began to seem inevitable. It is hard to account for
the degree of his misery. Ostensibly he was a success. He was newly a
proud father. *Continual Dew* had appeared in 1937. *An Oxford
University Chest* and *Sir John Piers* followed in 1938,* and the
Hogarth Press pamphlet *Antiquarian Prejudice* in 1939.†[2] He was
making a name as a radio broadcaster and book reviewer. In January
1939 his old boss de Cronin Hastings wrote to him:

I am following your career (?) with a good deal of interest – at a distance
naturally – it seems to me you are doing rather nicely, sitting well down,
and taking your fences without hurrying 'em – by gad – You know we sold
a book in thousands as a result of your review in the S[unday] Times.
Much to Arthur [Doyle]'s[3] astonishment – He now has an almost unlimited admiration for you.[4]

But by 1939 John's state of mind was such that Penelope insisted he
see a psychoanalyst 'to get rid of his persecution mania'.[5]

Much of his anxiety could be traced to money troubles. He had
flounced out of *The Architectural Review* and had lost his job as film
critic of the *Evening Standard*. His work at Shell was only part-time

---

* See Chapter 7, '*Continual Dew* and *An Oxford University Chest*'.
† See Chapter 23, 'A Preservationist in the Making'.

and ended in 1939 when it became clear that the Shell Guides would have to be 'held over' until after the war. Like most freelances, he missed the assurance of a regular pay-packet. Farmer Wheeler pursued him for his rent. The baby was a new expense. John ate humble pie and begged to be restored to his job on the 'Archie Rev'. Much as de Cronin Hastings liked and admired him, he was not able to oblige him in this. 'The board is damned,' he wrote, 'if it is going to switch everything round again to please you. It admits that you leave a gap. Already you have fulfilled the prophecies of those who shall be nameless, who in their wisdom laughed and said, "In six weeks he'll be wanting to come back." I said: "Nonsense. You've lost a genius. In six months you will be wondering why you were so mad as to let him go . . ." '[6]

John flailed around, trying to find ways of making extra money. His old friends in journalism were of some help. He sent in paragraphs for the *Evening Standard*'s 'Londoner's Diary'. Percy Cudlipp, who had left the *Standard* and was now with the *Daily Herald*, asked him for ideas. Geoffrey Grigson – never quite a friend but now an editor at Harrap's – agreed to look at a synopsis of a proposed book on the Isle of Man, while hinting to John that it was unlikely to be a runaway bestseller.[7] Raymond Mortimer took reviews and poems for the *New Statesman*. Allen Lane asked John to write a book on churches for Penguin. John accepted a £50 advance from Hamish Hamilton to edit the 'decadent' letters of Graham Robertson[8] – in the end he had to pay back this sum. Harold Nicolson, who had got caught up in Oswald Mosley's fascistic New Party, inveigled John into sending an article on housing to the British Union's *Quarterly*, though the lukewarm response to the piece by the editor, A. Raven Thomson ('A Ravin' Lunatic', as John called him), and his holding it over for a later issue, displeased John and in June 1938 he wrote to tell Thomson that *The Times* had asked for something 'on the same lines' and he was sending the article to that newspaper. It is clear from Thomson's letters to him (John's half of the correspondence has not survived) that John was expressing sharp reservations about the movement.[9]

John's best journalistic contacts were with the *Daily Express*. His Oxford friend Tom Driberg was writing the 'William Hickey' gossip column. Osbert Lancaster began drawing his 'pocket cartoons' for the paper in 1939. The features editor, John Rayner, married another of John's friends, Joan Eyres Monsell, who had earlier been engaged, briefly, to Alan Pryce-Jones and was later to marry Patrick Leigh Fermor. Rayner won – what was never easy to obtain – the whole-hearted approval of Lancaster, who later wrote: 'Whatever modest success the [pocket cartoons] series may have enjoyed was for me of far less importance than the friendship with John Rayner which sprang from it. This distinguished bibliophile and pillar of the Foreign Office was then the youngest, and by far the best, Features Editor in Fleet Street; an erudite typographer, he had recently transformed the whole appearance of the *Express* by his energy and that of most of the other dailies by his example.'[10]

Rayner liked to set writers challenges at odds with their characters. A dog-hater would be invited to write up a poodle parlour, a butterfingers to extol the joys of village cricket. The resulting friction, he thought, would strike sparks. For John he found the most perfectly unsuitable of commissions: to write a regular column of household handyman hints entitled 'Man about the House'. John, who hardly knew how to change a fuse, was expected to tell his readers How to Unblock That Sink or What to Do with That Cupboard Under the Stairs. 'All he used to do', Penelope remembered, 'was to go straight along to Bill Packer, the Uffington blacksmith, with each problem. Bill would tell him what he needed to say; John would put it in his own words and send off an article to John Rayner.'[11] For a sub-series on 'Furnishing the Perfect House', John received further tips, with scale drawings, from his Oxford friend the architect Michael Dugdale. If anything could be less congenial to John than writing the household hints articles, it was answering readers' letters about their domestic problems. At least he got paid for writing the articles. In compensation, one reader's letter was a source of unending hilarity to John and his friends. (He recalled it yet again in conversation with Jonathan Stedall in the 1982 television series 'Time with Betjeman'.) It was from a desperate man who wrote: 'Dear Sir, The man in the flat next to mine has an enormous frig that makes a terrible noise all night long. What can I do about it?'[12]

Few of the *Express* readers' enquiries yielded this kind of entertainment. More typical was a letter from Mrs Dorothy Grimes of Gloucester Place, London, who was about to take over a basement flat from 'a gentleman who is being called up'. She had therefore found John's article 'How to make a dark room light' of great help, but sought further enlightenment:

First of all, can one buy distemper in pots all ready to use, or does it have first to be watered down? Also, can you recommend any particular distemper, and what is the price? Most of the walls at the moment are a very uninteresting buff-yellow, and I should like if possible to make them cream. Is this possible, or can one not put a paler distemper over a darker? One room in the flat has been used for lumber, and I want to convert it into a bedroom. It has a stone floor, and I am wondering if it is all right to put linoleum down first and then a carpet, or if wood should be put down first . . . [More questions followed.][13]

Another enquiry was relayed to John by M. Nettleton of the *Express* features department.

> Dear Mr Betjeman,
>   A reader telephoned me the other day complaining that she had 'worms in her furniture'.
>   I wonder if you would be kind enough to help her with this problem. The name is Mrs Scanes, 4, Kennard Road, London N.11.[14]

Acknowledging his reply to another query, Lucy Milner, the women's page editor of the *Express,* wrote to John on 19 August 1938, 'Thank you for your charming letter and the answer to the futile woman.'[15] By that date the deluge of readers' problems had become such a nuisance that John asked Rayner if he could be paid for his answers. Somewhat to his surprise, he was told he could be. Lucy Milner further bolstered the Betjeman family exchequer by commissioning a long-running cookery series from Penelope, who wrote the articles under her two middle names, Hester Valentine. Like John, she sometimes took advice from the Uffington villagers. 'She came up to my mother once,' George Packford remembered, 'and said, could she think of anything appertaining to rabbit? So of course mother told her how to make a pie. When Penelope wrote it up, she called the recipe "Rabbit Packford".'[16] But Penelope needed little help from anybody on what to write: she was, when she had a mind to be, a wonderful cook. John praised her culinary and journalistic skills to others, though once or twice he reflected wryly on the disparity between the mouth-watering dishes she described in the *Express* and the more humdrum fare she commonly served at home. When John unexpectedly brought Cyril Connolly home to dinner, Penelope squawked from the kitchen: 'I'm going out in ten minutes. I'm sorry, you can only have hard-boiled eggs.' John took Connolly to the well-stocked wine cellar and said, with an air of solemn rumination and fastidious connoisseurship, 'Now, Cyril, I wonder what goes best with *hard-boiled eggs.*'[17]

Connolly asked John for poems for the early numbers of *Horizon,* the arts-and-letters magazine launched in 1939.[18] Another editor who commissioned work from John was T.S. Eliot of *The Criterion,* of which the last issue appeared in January 1939. The two men had met again, after a gap of over twenty years, in 1937. As we have seen, Eliot courted John as a possible Faber author. John Murray beat him to the poems, but Faber's did end up publishing the Shell Guides for a time.[19]

Eliot and John became friends, drawn together by old acquaintance and by their allegiance to the Church of England, their interest in English topography and their similar senses of humour. They lunched and dined together. Eliot came to stay at Uffington.[20] John persuaded him to open an exhibition of original Shell advertising drawings at Shell-Mex House. The opening was attended by Sir Philip Chetwode, who asked John who 'the young feller' was who made the speech. On being told that the speaker was Mr Eliot, the famous poet, Chetwode demanded, 'What's he written?' The only words John could remember on the spur of the moment were, 'The moon shone bright on Mrs Porter . . .'[21] John also got to know Eliot's invalid friend John Hayward, the bibliophile and critic, crippled by muscular dystrophy. Eliot and John attended dinner-parties at Hayward's flat in Bina Gardens, London, and John and Hayward corresponded; Hayward's letters arrived at Uffington in elaborately decorated envelopes.

Several publishers besides Faber's suggested to John ideas for books. One of the more intriguing came from Michael Sadleir of Constable.[22] The suggestion was to have a series of chapters representing famous biographies inverted – Johnson's *Life of Boswell*, Nelson's *Life of Southey*, Gladstone's *Life of Morley* and so on. Would John be prepared to undertake Dr Arnold's *Life of Stanley*? John Hayward had refused to contribute, deciding that 'he was not a parodist'. John Sparrow had 'responded with his usual charming eagerness, but could not think of anything but Christ's Life of S. John which I felt would be hardly suitable'. John expressed interest, but no contribution from him ever arrived.

Early in 1938 he was discussing with James Shand of the Shenval Press and the designer Robert Harling the possibility of starting a weekly magazine called *The Christian*. It was to be of the same format as *The Spectator* and John was to be the general editor at a starting salary of £400 a year. At about the same time, Father Bernard Clements OSB of All Saints', Margaret Street, London – the Butterfield building that was among John's favourite churches – wrote to ask whether John would help form a Guild of Catholic Writers ('Catholic' in the sense in which that word is used in the Church of England). This was to be an evangelistic group, working through an 'apostolate of the laity'. John was misinformed of the date of the first meeting – actually 4 May 1938 – so did not attend, but in his absence he was elected to the committee, on which Tom Driberg and Dorothy L. Sayers, the writer of detective fiction, were also to serve.

The scheme for *The Christian* fell through, but later in 1938 Shand approached John with a new idea: would he like to take over from a man called Smitthels the editorship of the quarterly magazine *Decoration*, which was in the Shenval Press stable? John accepted the offer.

PUBLISHED BY THE SHENVAL PRESS

DECORATION A QUARTERLY

56 BLOOMSBURY STREET LONDON WC1 PHONE MUSEUM 6015

Again Harling was to be the art editor – 'a dapper, urbane figure with a stake in a number of diverse projects',[23] among them an advertising agency in Park Street, London, which promoted the furniture shop Heal's and Boot's the Chemist.[24] John's deputy editor was Hugh Casson, the future president of the Royal Academy. Later on, when Casson's practice as a very 'modern' architect expanded, he and John did not always see eye to eye; but, looking back, he saw a likeness between John and himself in the Thirties.

He was very amusing, which shows, as a rule, that you're not confident, I think. You're hiding your shyness or unease under a constant lightning of sparklers and hoping people won't notice you aren't as interesting as you think you are. I think John was unconfident and not entirely happy all the time, until his last years when he enjoyed being a telly star. Rather like me.[25]

Meetings were held, mainly in the Café Royal, and on 26 May 1938 Harling sent John a summary of the contents of the first two issues, each of which was to contain forty-eight pages of editorial matter. In the September issue would appear the first of a series, 'Architects at Home', perhaps by Casson, 'Scandinavian Pottery', to be written under Harling's direction, 'Church Art', for which John was the obvious author, 'Wall Coverings' and 'Fireplaces'. The December issue would offer another article in the 'Architects at Home' series, 'Room and Music', possibly by Lord Berners, 'Theatre Interiors', 'Timber Houses in England', 'Carpets' and 'Flowers in the House'.

There was a lot of architectural content in these outlines. De Cronin Hastings might well have felt that John was poaching on his preserve; and indeed John may have had some mischievous idea of bringing home to the board of the 'Archie Rev' what a star performer they had lost in him. In sending the outlines, Robert Harling added:

> One or two things strike me in reviewing these notes.
>
> First: One more article could be included in the first number. What about one on Lighting or Beds or an Interior of a Hospital, or something fairly serious for 6 pages?
>
> Second: In the December issue which will come out at Christmas-time, there should be an article on Christmas in the home. One or two very pleasant Victorian touches could be introduced into this. TIMBER HOUSES could be reduced to 8pp.
>
> Third: In our original discussion we talked of having a survey of fire-places and wall coverings in the one issue. I don't think this is wise. Other articles which can be brought forward or interchanged are ROOM AND BOOK, or PICTURES IN THE HOME.[26]

These were not bad ideas, but there was a tone of bossiness about them that did not bode well for the relationship between John and Harling. The young designer was very talented in several arts – he became a novelist and half a century later wrote the play on which the film *Steel Magnolias* (1989) was based. But John did not like having the law laid down to him by anybody, and in this case he might reasonably have thought, 'If I am editor, I am going to edit, without inter-ference.' The innuendo of Harling's 'something fairly serious' would not have been lost on him. James Shand was usually more tactful, but as proprietor he also wanted to stick his oar in. He wrote to John on 10 June:

Dear Betjeman,

   Harling has sent me a copy of your letter of May 29th.

   The 'wall objects' article is a good suggestion, but we have already had
an article by Paul Nash on 'Surrealism in Interior Decoration'. As an
author he is a bit academic and not thorough enough in his reporting . . .[27]

By the end of June, Harling was already beginning to chivvy John in
an affable way: 'This is a note to remind you that you are getting in
touch with Lord Berners for the Room and Music article for the first
issue under your editorship.'[28]

A month later, John had a letter from his and Penelope's old friend
and temporal confessor, P. Morton Shand (no relation of James
Shand), who was now head of Fortecon (Foreign Technical
Concessionaires), the family textiles firm. He had heard from Paul
Nash that John was now editor of *Decoration*. 'This is really good
news, though it is amusing to think of you as a Shand employee, as I
think that if you can resist the temptation to be too amusing you have
a real chance of knocking out that horrible rag "Studio". But what has
happened to Smitthels?' He added: 'Fortecon is getting under way
slowly, and we are now concentrating more particularly on textiles,
pottery, electric light fittings, and other things which are more directly
up your street . . . From our point of view "Decoration" might be quite
the right sort of paper for us to start advertising in.'[29]

As with *The Architectural Review*, advertising was important for
the survival of the magazine. The need to procure advertisements was
always on the proprietor's mind, and John was expected to help. On
18 October 1938 James Shand wrote to him:

Dear Betjeman,

   I hate to inflict unnecessary viewing on you, but the enclosed invitation
for Pilkington Brothers' new showrooms is important to us insofar as
Pilkington [big glass manufacturers] are important advertisers. John
Gloag[30] handles Pilkington's account and placed with us a year ago a contract for ten colour pages which unfortunately has not since been renewed.

   If you could find it possible to drop in for say just two minutes, bump
accidentally into the corpulent Gloag, either from front or behind,
murmur something about DECORATION and then disappear rapidly,
you will be doing us a world of advertising good . . .[31]

John made a more wily and subtle approach to Gloag. In November
he wrote to ask him if he knew anybody who might be prepared to
take over the floundering firm of Betjemann & Sons.[32] Gloag replied

that he did not think Sir Ambrose Heal would be interested (as John had thought he might be) as he was primarily a retailer, not a manufacturer. But Gloag would himself write to the great furniture craftsman Gordon Russell.[33] A few days later, Gloag sent John a copy of his letter to Russell. 'Dear Gordon, I don't know whether you know that John Betjeman is connected with a very old family business which makes a lot of rather lovely and exciting things, not always well designed, but produced with superb craftsmanship? He has got there a team of craftsmen that would make your mouth water! . . . That particular business has got to a stage when it might interest somebody like you.'[34]

Russell said he did not feel able to take on Betjemann's. But he did write to John on 20 December 1938: 'I felt I would like to write and tell you what a good job I think you have made of "DECORATION". If this policy of showing reasonably well-designed things can be maintained it should do quite a lot of good. It seems to me there is often far too much attempt made to show purely stunt stuff in this sort of paper.'[35] A by-product of the Betjeman–Gloag–Russell correspondence was that John managed to persuade Gloag to place more Pilkington advertising with *Decoration*.

So far, so good; but trouble was brewing. On 2 February 1939, P. Morton Shand wrote from Fortecon, with all the comic irony that John had picked up from him, to complain about Harling's behaviour towards him.

My dear John,

What an odd young man your Mr Robert Harling seems to be! A month or two ago he wrote and asked me for an article on Aalto.[36] No waste of time about did I think Aalto would make a good subject for Dickory-Dec, or anything like that. Just wanted an article on him.

So I thought I'd better do it. Duty to poor old Aalto to save him from a Grim-Carolingian interpretation of his non-existent ideology, and all that. And regard for editors' requirements being second nature with me, I managed to do the thing from a 'decorative' angle, sending it in with all the Aalto photos that could possibly be said to have a 'decorative angle'.

Mr Harling made no fuss about the article, which was very polite of him, but he soon rang me up to say he found these photos 'very austere' and would like some of Aalto's interiors. I pointed out gently that, looked at from one point of view, or even most, Aalto's work certainly was rather 'austere', and that this was all he need have expected to find it. Also that, as I had said in the text, the only 'interior' Aalto has ever carried out is his own house, which he declares is still unfinished and won't let anyone photograph . . .

Regularly once a week now Mr Harling rings me up to ask for some Aalto 'interiors' and something 'Less austere', and every time I have to give him the same answer. Can he have perhaps mixed up Aalto with Heppy or Mrs D'Arcy Bradell of naughtier bathrooms fame? Anyhow you might have a gentle talk to Mr Harling about Aalto when, if ever, you see him . . .[37]

Two weeks later, Morton Shand wrote again to John, sending him 'the dope on Fortecon fabrics predigested for copy-writer's use'. He confided in him his own dire financial plight. The advertisement Fortecon were taking in the March *Decoration* was their 'last shot' at reviving their fabrics.[38]

The antagonism developing between John and Robert Harling came into the open in March 1939, when Harling wrote to James Shand about 'the problems involved in the editorial direction and details of production of DECORATION'. He wrote: 'Obviously Betjeman is in disagreement with the way I have gone ahead with certain things on the editorial side of the magazine. I think it would be a good idea, therefore, if at this stage (which allows a reasonable time for the production of the next issue) we were to decide exactly what the respective jobs of Betjeman and myself are to be.'[39] He proposed that John should be responsible for planning contents, writing leaders, commissioning articles, dealing with contributors and supervising the collection of material for those articles, including photographs and captions. As art editor Harling was to be responsible for planning the make-up, layout of articles and photographs and all details of production prior to printing. He would also commission any photographs or drawings John requested. In his last paragraph he commented tartly:

I feel that it would simplify things from Betjeman's point of view if he would spend one afternoon a week at the Bloomsbury Street office, dealing with such matters as correspondence from contributors and so on. I find, for example, that in the production of the present issue something like forty-five letters concerning editorial matters have been dealt with at this office.[40]

Harling sent a copy of this letter to John.

Morton Shand's financial difficulties caused more trouble in April. Possibly encouraged by John, he sent in a large bill for photographic expenses on the Aalto article. James Shand, signing himself 'Hamish MacTavish' (presumably to indicate Scottish penny-wisdom), protested to John:

I think P. Morton Shand's bill is much too much of a good thing, especially when we borrowed four of the blocks from Finmar, another one from the Mars catalogue and bought another couple of them from the Arch-Rev. And yet he has the temerity to charge a reproduction fee of 10/6d on every illustration that appears in his article.[41]

When these arguments were relayed to Morton Shand, he cunningly replied that he would accept whatever Mr John Betjeman thought it was fair to pay him – no doubt thinking that John, as an old friend, would be generous.[42]

Robert Harling, who may or may not have been aware of John's and Morton Shand's conspiratorial manoeuvres behind his back, was becoming increasingly exasperated by John's lackadaisical attitude to his job. He wrote to him very directly on 12 July 1939, in reply to an apparently contrite letter.

Nothing would please me better than to be rid of these editorial duties of DECORATION in which I have become involved. TYPOGRAPHY [another Shenval magazine] keeps me far more pleasantly busy. This situation would never have arisen, however, if you had acted as an editor of DECORATION from the beginning. As far as I can see you have taken your editorial duties very lightly indeed, and somebody had to write captions and the rest of the gubbins. Calling (and breaking up) occasional meetings to fit in with the GWR [Great Western Railway] time-table seems to me an odd way of editing a magazine; and that an editor should need gentle reminders concerning the necessity for a leader is, of course, almost incredible, but it happened. I am happy to find, therefore, that you have had this sudden awakening of your editorial conscience . . .

I suggest that you put your new-found principles into practice by revising [A.J.A.] Symons' article as you wish.[43] You can make fresh blocks from the illustrations, which you say you have, to the sizes shown on my layout.[44]

Five days later, Harling sent an irritable chaser to Pakenham Hall, County Westmeath, where John was staying with the Longfords.[45]

You forgot to send Symons' page proofs to me. It is, therefore, holding us up no end. Is there any way of getting hold of these? I presume they are at Uffington.

Nothing seems to have been done about the page layouts which I sent to Symons concerning the overmatter. It is most unfortunate that things should have been left in this state.[46]

John spent most of his holidays of the late 1930s at Pakenham Hall, seldom accompanied by Penelope. He was there early in 1938 when he designed the sets for a play Christine Longford was producing at the Gate Theatre, Dublin, her own adaptation of Maria Edgeworth's *The Absentee*. She was thrilled with the 'gorgeous designs . . . The Gothic library is peculiarly lovely.'[47] Cathleen Delaney, the 'Colleen',[48] played the heroine, Clare Nugent. It is clear from a letter she wrote John in February 1938 that she had developed a *tendresse* for him.

John, dear

I don't believe that even in prison the time could pass so slowly as these few days have done. I can't even bear to think of the week-end after you had gone. We went over to Insany [Dunsany Castle][49] on the Saturday, but there again they all started talking about you, until I nearly went mad . . .

I'm afraid I sound full of self pity which is not true. I am very happy really, and you mustn't think I'm not. It's only your leaving was such a wrench. It made me feel so dreadfully alone. It's such an awful thought, that in spite of feeling about you the way I do, I haven't the slightest claim on you, not the very least in the world. The man you buy your cigarettes from, or even the merry villagers you loath [sic] so much – they at least can see you every day, or ask how you are feeling. But I can't. If your name comes up when I'm in the room I've got to put on a fairly detached air, and look appropriately disinterested. I can't tell anyone in the world how I really feel about it, or ask anyone all the things I long to know about you, things I shall never have time to learn, because we'll never be alone together – and yet, I love you, John, though I have no right to do that either . . .

I was very well received on my return [from a tour of Ireland with *The Absentee*]. I had got so fat that John [O'Dea, her husband, the Eigenherr] was too pleased to pick on me for not writing or anything. His attitude towards me is rather that of the witch towards Hanzel [sic] & Gretel. When the bones are unduly prominent I've got to watch my step. But when I'm fattening up I can get away with murder . . .

John, nothing in this world could please me more than to think I've in any way helped you to write poetry. If I can help you at all darling, I'll understand why all this happened. It must be for some good, because neither of us are going to hurt the other in any way, therefore we must have been brought together to bring each other something we needed. I suppose each of us lacked something that only the other could give and so long as we only take that something, and not what belongs to other people, well then I think we can thank God for each other.

Good bye, dear. God bless you
All my love
Cathleen.[50]

Cathleen Delaney's mention of having helped John to write poems – perhaps meaning that she had inspired some of them – leads one to look at John's verse of 1938 for a poem referring to a 'colleen'. Just such a poem is found in *Sir John Piers*, the verse sequence published as a pamphlet by a newspaper at Mullingar, near Pakenham Hall, late in 1938. The second poem in the sequence, 'The Attempt', begins:

> I love your brown curls, | black in rain, my colleen,
>   I love your grey eyes, | by this verdant shore
> Two Derravaraghs | to plunge into and drown me,
>   Hold not those lakes of | light so near me more.[51]

Some of the romantic afflatus may have gone from this relationship by January 1939, when Cathleen Delaney wrote to John: 'I think you flatter yourself a great deal when you make up your mind that the village suspects you of fathering your maid's child. A Don Juan is the last thing I would credit you with being. Odd, if you like, but not amorous.'[52] Or perhaps the taunt was intended to kindle or revive his ardour.

Cathleen Delaney's presence in Ireland is unlikely to have been the reason John began looking for a house there in 1938. He may have had some idea of saving his family from bombs if war broke out. What weighed with him more was his feeling that Ireland had not been 'ruined', as in his opinion England was being ruined. In July 1938, when Robert Harling berated him about the missing Symons proofs, John wrote to T.S. Eliot from Pakenham Hall:

> In the silence here – a silence so deep one hardly dares speak in it and where there is no sound over the hills except at evening when you can hear the turf carts rumbling over the bog two miles away – I will be able to get it all in the right perspective. London seems like some mad dream in all this green, wet civilisation.
>
> > In the city dusty
> > Is the old lock rusty
> > That opens rasping
> > On the place of graves.
>
> Do you know Oireland? It is what England was like in the time of Rowlandson with Roman Catholicism thrown in. I can't think why we don't live here. If I had any competence of my own I would.
>   There aren't any aeroplanes.
>   The roads are too small for many motors.
>   The Church of Ireland is 1835 Gothic and 1835 Protestant . . .[53]

Later in the year Edward Longford wrote to John, 'We are ever so pleased you want to settle here. It ought to be possible to provide quite a decent place for two thousand pounds . . . I should fancy Tipperary would suit you.'[54] John wrote to his mother: '. . . I really think I stand by my original idea of going to Ireland and buying a small property there. I can get a decent sized house and demesne for about twelve hundred pounds. I shall spend eight hundred on repairs. That is two thousand. I shall borrow the money on a reversion. Won't want to do it with P[enelope]'s money, because the Chetwodes would kick up a fuss, as they hate Ireland and the Irish. How I am going to afford to live in Ireland, I neither know nor care. All I do know is that away from aeroplanes and motor cars I at once expand. I have written all that I have written which was worth writing in Ireland, and I regard it as salvation. I think it possible that should Europe collapse, Ireland will become what it was in the seventh century, the last house of civilisation in the Dark Ages. P likes horses and the country and religion. She will get all three.'[55] He added that he would like Paul to be brought up in beautiful country, as he himself had been. 'Ireland is like what Cornwall *was*.' John corresponded with estate agents in Waterford and Clonmel. He was tempted by Belline House, Piltdown, Co. Kilkenny, 'about eleven miles from Waterford and close to the late Lord Bessborough's estate', but money seems to have been the sticking point. He may also have paid some heed to the wise advice of Constantia Maxwell, a distinguished historian at Trinity College, Dublin, who had first written to him for help with her book *Country and Town in Ireland under the Georges*, eventually published in 1940. When, in his reply, he mentioned that he was looking for a house in Ireland, she wrote: 'You would enjoy Ireland for 6 months, then you would begin to get melancholy, & long for English intellectual society & the comforts of your own country.'[56] For somebody who had never met John, this was a remarkably accurate prophecy of what actually happened when he became a diplomat in Dublin during the Second World War.

Robert Harling was outraged to discover that not only was John staying at Pakenham Hall, blithely uninterested in the fate of proofs, but that he was also going straight on to Swanwick, Derbyshire, to lecture at a Student Christian Movement summer camp. It was T.S. Eliot who had let John in for this experience. Eliot was friendly with Mary Trevelyan, the warden of Student Movement House in London,[57] and with Brother George Every of the Society of the Sacred Mission, Kelham, Nottinghamshire, who was also a leading organizer of the summer camps. Eliot first asked John to lecture at the camp in 1938:

Respected Betje,

Soft you, a word or two before you go: I have done the Shell some service, and I know't. Now is the chance for your good deed . . . So listen. By none but me may the tale be told, the butcher of Rouen, Big Berold.

> Betjeman must betake himself to Swanwick
> To prattle about Art and Architectonic.

The good Bro. George Every, S.S.M. of Kelham, a charming and saintly young man whom you ought to know, has arranged a set of informal lectures for the summer course of the S.C.M. at Swanwick . . . He only wants the best: Michael Roberts[58] is doing one of his talks. He had Porteus[59] for Art, but Porteus has fallen down, I think he funks speaking in public, and you can't get anything at Swanwick to cheer you up. It is supposed to be a talk on Modern Art, but you could quickly divert it to the Bressey Report, 18th century box pews, or anything else you like, embellished from your inexhaustible fund of wit & humour. He wants you, YOU, and has probably written, and this is to back him up. You will deliver your talk either Saturday *next* or the following Monday: preferably Saturday in order to draw the crowd away from the rival attraction on that morning, C.E.M. Joad.[60] I am sure that your public spirit will compel you to accept.[61]

John replied that he could not accept, because he was due to stay at Pakenham Hall on those dates. He was approached again in 1939, this time agreeing to lecture just after his visit to Pakenham. He gave a comic account of the ordeal – with illustrations – in his thank-you letter of 31 July to Edward and Christine Longford.

> On the Midland Railway
> but as from Garrards Farm
> Uffington
> Berkshire

Dear Edward and Tine,

The journey was terrible: the crossing rough in the extreme, but I had managed to get some seasick remedy in Dublin which saved me from being sick, but my stomach is only right this morning and my head didn't cease to ache until yesterday (Sunday) morning.

You may guess how much I enjoyed myself at the Swanwick SCM camp from the fact that here on this train back to London at an hour when no one else is awake, I am *pleased* to be going to Shell-Mex House. It was the ideal antidote to Ireland. Because even after Ireland, London seems pleasant, as a result of sandwiching the Swanwick in between the experiences.

I must give you some details, as our prophecies were nearly all right. After a cross country journey lasting from eight twenty-five till three p.m. and mostly sitting four a side in third class smokers with children's buckets and spades scraping my face, I arrived at Derby. A typical young man in a tiny battered car met me, with spectacles, long nose, khaki shorts and a dull, respectful manner. He was not able to find his way out of the town. The interesting thing about Swanwick, where 'The Hayes' (the Mansion converted into a conference place) is situated, is that although it is twelve miles from Derby, there are houses down every road, coal tips on every hill and mineral lines down every valley. We all wore labels, little round discs of various colours (because mine was pink people called me 'Sir') with our names written on. The young man who took me, had 'JACK BRIGGS Home Student, Newcastle University' or something like that written on his disc. When I got to the camp it had been arranged that I should sleep in a tent – round about forty in a tent. I set on the excuse of a rough cross-ing, and managed to get into 'the hostel' where I was given a cell with a window which wouldn't open.

The food was very, very plain and in the camp, one had bits of last meal's butter on our knife and some cabbage on the spoon for tinned apricots. Then all the spoons would be beaten on the table and the students would shout, 'We want a story from JIM DOWSER.' Up would stand old Jim and tell us a funny anecdote about the Archbishop of York or a verse from the *Bab Ballads*.

'Art and Values in the Conservatory' were a complete failure. I was too doped to notice many of the questions. But I remember one, 'Will Mr. Betjeman explain his theory systematically?' I could not remember what my theory had been. On the spur of the moment I had decided to judge architecture by the criterion of the Seven Deadly Sins. It seemed as good as anything else, though Lust was a bit difficult.

After the International Sing Song there was some humorous entertain-ment and a woman with a foghorn voice conducted singing of 'Green Grow the Rushes Oh' and I could not help noticing the blacks singing 'Three-three, the lilywhite boys, clothed all in green-oh'. At the beginning of meals in the hostel, all the women burst into singing 'Let us with a glad-some mind' and then sat down to corned beef and little bits of potato which had dropped into each glass.

What it was all about I never discovered. The girls fell in love with the Kelham students in their black habits. The services were very broad and inter-denominational. Presbyterians and Baptists and Central Church-manship predominated. There were about six Anglos. [C.S.] Lewis I saw, who was most effusive, but I managed to avoid him.[62] He dazzled pipe-smoking chaplains and embryo missioners with High Table jinks. Miss Eleanora Iredale, as Tine supposed, was from the Sorbonne and had

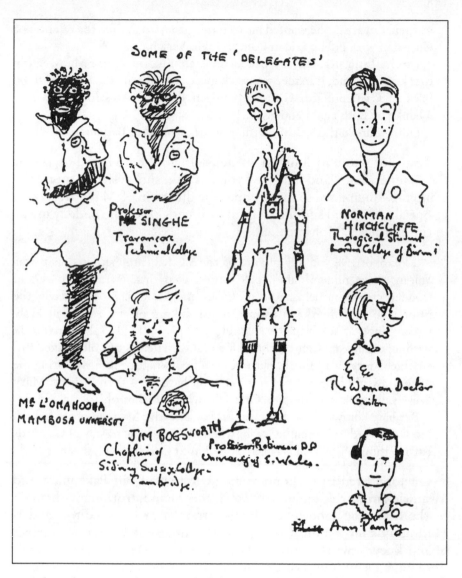

John's drawings of Swanwick delegates in his letter of 31 July 1939 to Edward and Christine Longford

written a treatise. She wanted me to join a group to discuss the relation of
Christian with Public Life in Caxton Hall. Very nice.

I feel a little sick and my headache is coming on again. Many, many
thanks for Ireland. It made Swanwick more awful than ever. Oh God to be
back in Castlepollard. Give the Colleen Peter Powell's love from me.
Thank you both again and again.

From yours in the S.C.M. (Uffington Branch), Jack Betjeman.[63]

T.S. Eliot wrote to John on 8 August 1939, 'I have heard of you at
the summer camp, and imagined you in khaki shorts sitting round the
camp fire, singing sea shanties under the direction of Mary Trevelyan.
I hope also that you supplied a fund of limericks for the midday meals
in the marquee.'[64] John replied:

> . . . I cannot give you any picture of the S.C.M. camp situated as it was
> among those mineral lines, bus routes, coal tips, terraced villas and
> trodden grey-grim fields. And the jokes and Mr C.S. Bloody Lewis, the
> tutor who sent me down from Oxford, hiking off to a Central Holy
> Communion at seven in the morning and plying High Table small talk
> with pipe-smoking Central churchmen all with hearts of gold. I liked Bro
> George [Every] very much, but not even my liking for him will bring me
> to that awful place again. I dare say you have been there. I liked Mary
> Trevelyan immensely, despite 'Green Grow the Rushes-oh'.
>
> But have I drawn these delegates for you already? My memory is failing.
> I look forward to September 16th [when Eliot was due to stay at Garrards
> Farm – though this visit was postponed until October]. That is fine . . .[65]

On John's return to London and Uffington from Pakenham and
Swanwick in July 1939, he wrote to James Shand, frothing with anger
at the hectoring tone of Harling's letters. 'Am I not editor, and is
Harling not my subordinate?' was the burden of his *cri de coeur*.[66]
Shand knew how to soothe John. He wrote: 'Dear Betjeman. O.K.
Toots! Let us meet and discuss these large issues. I will come to Shell
Mex House at 3 o'clock on Wednesday, unless you command to the
contrary.'[67] But, as it turned out, the outcome of the Betjeman–Harling
spat was of academic interest. A greater conflict supervened. On 26
September 1939, James Shand wrote to John, after Britain's declar-
ation of war on Germany:

> O'Shaughnessy and I have tried to get some advertising for the tentative
> issue of DECORATION, but we cannot get any response even from some
> of our oldest advertisers. Very, very reluctantly we have come to the con-
> clusion that there is no use doing any more about DECORATION until
> the war is over.

It is a nasty blow, but might be worse. TYPOGRAPHY too will have to await the resumption of the peace.

Thank you for your offer about your salary, which I am accepting, as soon as I can send you a cheque for £25. We are a bit short at the moment, but there are some advertising accounts to come in which we expect to get within the next few days.[68]

With the end of *Decoration* and the temporary end of the Shell Guides, John was once again badly in need of a source of income. A lifeline came from Richard de la Mare (the poet's son) of Faber's on 30 September: 'I wonder if, now that you are temporarily free from Shell, you are thinking of writing a book of a rather more topical nature than the architectural one that we suggested to you, that would amuse or edify or both, in these miserable times?' He asked John to think of a subject, but six days later suggested one himself: to relieve the solemn atmosphere in which the war was being conducted, would John like to write a book called something like *Information of Use to the Enemy*? It might, perhaps, contain a chapter based on the opportunity which might never come again for the destruction of unsightly public buildings. Göring's pilots could be given a definite route to follow on their raids, naming particular streets to be bombed, the Regency crescents to be spared. Other chapters he tentatively suggested were 'How to Get into the Ministry of Information and What to Do When You Get There' and 'The Englishman's Breakfast'.[69] John eagerly took up the offer, promising that the book would be in 'refreshingly bad taste';[70] but, sadly, it was never delivered.

OBSERVER CORPS

I am here in a silly thing called the Observer Corps...

John Betjeman, letter to [Sir] Ninian Comper, 12 October 1939

John had not waited until the outbreak of war to 'do his bit' to oppose Nazism. In 1938 he had joined the Observer Corps (later styled the Royal Observer Corps), the volunteer force responsible for tracking and recording the movements of aircraft over Britain. The Corps had its origins in the the First World War, and in the Twenties.[1] Networks covering first Kent and Sussex, then Hampshire and the eastern counties, were established, with Observer centres linked to air defence headquarters. All personnel were unpaid special constables. On a gridded operations room table, aircraft positions were plotted with coloured counters. On 26 September 1938 the Corps was called out for the first time as a fully fledged organization, and on 24 August 1939, while holiday makers sunned themselves and one newspaper proclaimed there would be no war, it manned its posts and centres and began a watch on the skies which was to continue for six years.[2]

Derek Wood and Derek Dempster, who in their book *The Narrow Margin* have given the clearest description of how the Corps operated, write: 'It was like a large club with an intimate atmosphere and a marked dislike for the more unpleasant features of military discipline.'[3] That aspect of the Corps, at least, would have appealed to John.

Observers at the posts [Wood and Dempster record] were provided with an instrument which consisted of a flat circular map table, spindly tripod legs and on top what appeared to be a pantograph stood on end. This plotting apparatus, produced by the War Office at minimum cost, became familiarly known as 'Heath Robinson'...[4]

There was little to show the existence of an Observer post except for a pair of telegraph wires ending, for no apparent reason, in some out-of-the-way spot, and the last telegraph pole having a small wooden box on it usually filled with earwigs.

When the RAF required the services of its 'eyes and ears', a man would arrive with a bulky box. From this he produced a length of cable and inserted one end into the box on the pole. The tripod was then set up and an extraordinary assortment of men in plus fours, gumboots or perhaps spats proceeded to gaze skywards. One turned the upended pantograph hopefully in the direction of a passing aircraft, another spoke into an antiquated army head and breast telephone set. The Observer Corps was a source of bewilderment to the passing public and high amusement to inquisitive small boys, but it worked.[5]

Post X2, which John helped to man, was in Parrot's Field, Uffington, and was connected to Oxford, Wantage and Sutton Courtenay. Among those who served with him were Bill Packer (the head of the post), Ron Liddiard, Edmund Weaver, Bernard Lee, Charlie Field, an old tailor called Lovegrove, the station master Mr Westcott, Farmer Wheeler's son-in-law Edmund Phillips and Harold Long, head gardener at Kingston Lisle. They wore Air Force-blue battledress blouses, armbands with the Observer Corps badge and berets with the badge. The men had a hut to protect them from bad weather. The 'Heath Robinson' instrument, about twenty yards from the hut, was surrounded by a makeshift shelter of corrugated iron which John called 'the urinal'.

'If there was a 'plane coming in fast', Liddiard recalled, 'someone would shout, "Look out, chaps!" and John, who was usually reading a book or writing something, would yell, "Out to the urinal!"'[6] The corrugated iron was to protect the operators from blast, if there was a bomb. 'One day John got halfway to the urinal and got entangled in the wire – fell arse over tip before he got there, shouting, "We're going to lose the war!" He spoke to Oxford on the walkie-talkie set while rolling about on the ground trying to free himself.'[7] One essential for the job was that the men should be able to recognize aircraft and distinguish friend from foe. Each was given a set of aircraft silhouettes; but John found equally helpful a set of cigarette cards of aircraft that he acquired from Ken Freeman in one of the Sunday-morning after-church 'swap' sessions.

Ron Liddiard wrote a comic poem about the group, an 'Ode to X2'. He remembered some of the lines, including:

> P is for Packer, the head of our post;
> Of the worrying entailed, he gets the most.[8]

Westcott, the station master, was teased about his size. 'He was a tremendous fellow,' Liddiard said, 'about 6 ft wide and 4ft 6 tall.'

W is for Westcott, Westcott our friend . . .
Without him we should not be complete;
But a little piece of advice, boy – be careful when you sit on a seat.

'And I wrote truer than I knew,' Liddiard added. 'We had one of these
El-San things.' He sat on it and the whole thing collapsed.' Bernard
Lee was famous for having got lost on his way to the post one night.
The lines about him in the Ode were:

L is for Lee, 'twas a bit of a lark,
Late for night duty, he got lost in the dark.

Edmund Weaver, Queenie's husband ('W is for Weaver, our one
familee/George, Edmund and Tom, a total of three'), told Liddiard
that when John was up at the hut he would rather clean shoes or do
any chores other than watch for aeroplanes. It was John's failure at one
of these chores that won him a mention in the Ode. Liddiard recalled:

About twice a week, for want of something better to do, we used to scrub
the hut out. Charlie Field was the great scrubber. He happened to be on
duty with John Betjeman on one occasion, it was an eight-hour shift. And
John said, oh, *he'd* scrub the hut out, yes, he'd *like* to do it . . . John fixed
himself up with a bucket of water. Charlie said, you never saw such a performance. John got buckets of water, he sloshed it about – he loved having
a go and he was really enjoying it. He made a hell of a mess, and of course
old Charlie was laughing at him. Charlie was a bricklayer. John Betjeman
to him was out of this world, he'd never seen anything like him . . . So I
wrote in the Ode:

B is for Betjeman, of charring he's fond;
The floor when he's at it is like a gert pond.[10]

In 1971, when Ron Liddiard's father Cyril was killed in a tractor
accident, John wrote his old friend a warmly sympathetic letter. In it
he mentioned 'the laughs we used to have in the Observer Corps before
the war and that very serious man Mr Long always looking out for
enemy aeroplanes, and you ringing up and saying it was Hitler speaking . . .'.[11] Back in 1939, John was less enthusiastic about the Corps.
He wrote to the architect Ninian Comper on 12 October: 'I am here
in a silly thing called the Observer Corps, and hope to get into the
RAF. But only if I can persuade myself it is right to fight at all. At
present fighting in a war seems to me to be committing a new sin in
defence of an old one.'[12]

The letter to Comper illustrates John's ambivalence about the war. As we have seen, he had written in his short-lived diary in 1935: 'Imminence of war. Damned if I will fight. Rescue work, yes, but not killing. Dread death.'[13] Those words were written in low spirits and may have been partly inspired by the pacific Quakerism which he still formally professed until 1937. As he acknowledged, he was not a man of eminent physical courage.* He may have been slightly influenced, too, by his friendship with Diana and Oswald Mosley, to whom the idea of war with Hitler (who had attended their wedding reception) was abhorrent. Pulling him in the opposite direction was his patriotism and his detestation of cruelty; perhaps, too, there was some fear of being left on the sidelines – even handed white feathers by women in the street – while his friends acquired Sam Browne belts and shoulder pips. His willingness to take on uncongenial duties in the Observer Corps suggests a degree of pure public-spiritedness. As early as September 1938 he had written to the Home Office to offer his services in the national interest in the event of an emergency. His letter was forwarded to the Ministry of Labour, which sent him a form to complete, and in April 1939 registered his name as somebody ready 'to accept appropriate employment in the event of war'.[14]

Despite his views in 1935, in 1939 John pulled all the strings he could to try to get into the armed forces. A friend in the RAF, Air Commodore W.F. MacNeece Foster, recommended him to the Air Ministry to help obtain him an RAF Volunteer Reserve commission (it never entered John's head to join any service as an 'other rank'), but there was a snag; the Ministry of Labour had screened John because, as an editor, he came under the heading of 'reserved occupations'. Before the RAF would consider commissioning him, it required evidence that the Ministry of Labour was prepared to make an exception for him.

Luckily, John had an ally at the Ministry of Labour – the high-ranking and picturesque civil servant Humbert Wolfe, a very successful poetaster whom W.H. Auden snidely called 'the typists' poet'.[15] In November 1939 Wolfe promised to enquire into the position and by the beginning of December was able to tell him that the 'reserved occupation' restriction would be waived in his case.[16] John thanked Wolfe warmly and promised him a copy of his next book of verse.[17] John now applied for an Intelligence post with the RAF. About this time, Sibyl Harton, 'the Abbess', wrote him a reflective and cautionary letter.

---

* But see Chapter 29, 'Cloth Fair and Rotherhithe', for a daring roof-top exploit of his.

Dear John,

I wonder if you have yet made a move? I hope not. I have intended each day to write to you, but laziness & being-outness have prevented. I thought of you so much after your last visit & then had many things to say: the chief was to beg you to do nothing in a hurry; nothing could be lost by waiting a little & much might be gained. Anyone can count revs. a second, but surely your writing & your knowledge of what is beautiful are things that cannot be learnt & used by anyone, & equally surely there must be some unique use for them now. There must be a way in which they can be of positive & constructive value even in the present state of things. They might have a place for you in the Ministry of Information. I expect a stupid Civil Service degree is necessary for a lot of the posts you could usefully fill. Better to do something with the young, whose future counts more than ours, than with aeroplanes. What impresses me is the need for using & not wasting yourself, & there must be a way. But perhaps by now you are nearer a solution.[18]

Characteristically, she suggested that 'a day or two's retreat next week at Cowley would, without necessarily showing you a way, certainly provide you with peace & patience to await one . . .'[19]

In January 1940 John was turned down by the RAF on medical grounds. In later years, his encounter with the medical board became the subject of one of his set-piece anecdotes: he claimed he had been rejected because the interview exposed his terror of spiders. A more plausible explanation was offered by H. Beauchamp, a Roman Catholic staff chaplain who was an acquaintance of John's. John called him 'Padre Beauchamp' – he may have been a part model for the Church of England priest in John's pre-war poem beginning 'Our padre is an old sky pilot . . .', though no doubt there was an echo of the poem by 'Woodbine Willie' (G.A. Studdert Kennedy), the famous First World War chaplain, which begins

> Our Padre were a solemn bloke,
>   we called 'im dismal Jim.
> It fairly gave ye t'bloomin' creeps,
>   To sit and 'ark at 'im . . .

Beauchamp wrote: 'I am afraid it is impossible to make an appeal or find out why you were disqualified. From my knowledge of medical examinations, it was probably caused by your casual remark that you had once been treated therapeutically.'[20] John next applied to join the Royal Marines, which had commissioned his Marlborough and Oxford friend Philip Harding. Again he was turned down. He had one last, powerful string to pull. He persuaded his father-in-law, the field-marshal, to write on his behalf to contacts in Government and the forces. But privately Chetwode – who must have had many reservations about John's suitability for a commission – was urging him to take a job offered by Sir Kenneth Clark. 'Get a written offer of the film job [in the Ministry of Information] and *accept it at once.*'[21]

Since John had first met Clark in Maurice Bowra's salon at Oxford, the young art historian's rise had been meteoric. At twenty-nine, in 1933, he had become the youngest ever director of the National Gallery. A popular legend about his appointment as head of the Films Division of the MoI was that Churchill had growled, '*He* knows about pictures, doesn't he?'[22] On paper, John had a strong qualification to be Clark's assistant in the Division: he had been film critic of the *Evening Standard*. But that was not why Clark chose him. 'I wanted his flexibility and originality of mind,' he said, 'and also his charm – because, essentially, ours was a public relations rôle.'[23] So John moved into a third-floor office in the University of London's Senate House, an Art Deco ziggurat of Portland stone by Charles Holden which had been completed in 1938.[24] By 1940 the Ministry of Information needed all the charm and flexibility of mind it could get. The war was going badly for Britain; the Ministry was in chaos; the press were antagonistic, the film-makers disgruntled.

TAKING TO THE AIR

He immediately saw what fun it could be, and, by Jove, what fun it *was*!

Lance Sieveking on John Betjeman's first radio broadcast, in *The Eye of the Beholder*, London 1957

By the late 1930s John was already well known as a radio broadcaster. His BBC programmes were reaching far more people than his poems. He had become a minor celebrity; and this had not happened by accident. He was ambitious, avid for fame. Without appearing to be scheming or pushy, he had used his contacts to get work in this relatively new medium, in spite of some early rebuffs which would have discouraged anyone less determined.

The origins of his roundabout route to the airwaves can be traced back to January 1929 when he obtained his post as private secretary to Sir Horace Plunkett through the Irish statesman's right-hand man, Gerald Heard.[1] When John Bowle, who succeeded John as Plunkett's secretary, was asked in 1976 how John knew Heard, he replied, with a snort of laughter, 'Through the Homintern!'[2] – the network of left-wing homosexuals which was believed to exercise a disproportionate power in the arts.

The influence of homosexuals was particularly strong at the BBC. Not only was the Corporation run by Sir John Reith, who, though married and capable of sacking staff for homosexuality, had marked homosexual inclinations;[3] it also employed, during John's early years as a broadcaster, Guy Burgess (later a Soviet spy), who had been at Cambridge with John's Marlborough friend Anthony Blunt;[4] Lionel Fielden, one of the set around E.M. Forster, who lived near Plunkett's Surrey house; and J.R. Ackerley, later literary editor of *The Listener*. Fielden and Ackerley both 'came out' (Ackerley posthumously) in frank autobiographies published in the 1960s.[5] Ackerley was a friend of Gerald Heard; in his memoirs he described Heard's appearance at the Ackerley family's dinner-table in purple suede shoes and a leather jacket with a leopardskin collar.[6]

With such attire, Heard could scarcely be called a grey eminence; but it was again his networking behind the scenes that procured John an introduction to the BBC. On 9 January 1929, the day before Sir Horace Plunkett recorded in his diary how pleased he was that Heard had found him John, 'a new secretary who will be able to do literary work',[7] John wrote to Malcolm Brereton, a talks producer at the BBC: 'Gerald Heard told me of an idea that I should talk on Architecture for the BBC and that he had spoken to you on the subject. I should be delighted to give a talk on early nineteenth-century styles should you desire it.'[8]

In the letter John addressed Brereton as 'Dear Sir', but in a later letter he asked, 'Are you my old friend C.S.M. Brereton?'[9] Indeed he was. John had known him at Oxford. Brereton, like John Bowle, had taken up a Brackenbury Scholarship at Balliol College in 1924.[10] His full, grandiloquent name was Cloudesley Shovell Malcolm Brereton;[11] he was a descendant of Admiral Sir Cloudesley Shovell, murdered in the Scilly Isles in 1707 for his emerald ring. John with his penchant for giving people embarrassing nicknames, later called Brereton 'Cloudesley Shovell', no double calculating that he had jettisoned his first two names as too high-falutin – though John might have argued that he was only calling a spade a spade. On 10 January Brereton replied to John: 'I think that Gerald Heard misunderstood me. I had to find a speaker at rather short notice to take the place of Mr Christian Barman and that has already been arranged. At the moment there is no space available for a talk such as you suggest.'[12] But, he wrote, he would bear John's suggestions in mind.

John's first radio broadcast was produced in 1932, not by Brereton, but by Lance Sieveking, another BBC official who pruned the floridity of his full name – Lancelot de Giberne Sieveking. Lionel Fielden, who had shared an office with Sieveking on Savoy Hill before the BBC moved into Broadcasting House in 1931, wrote: 'Lance lived somewhere among the rolling clouds of his vivid and sometimes erratic imagination, and occasionally from these clouds there fell a shower of brilliant ideas. His impact on broadcasting . . . was considerable. He was in the forefront of all experiments and afraid of nothing.'[13]

Here was somebody who could appreciate the wilder flights of John's jokiness. And John was fascinated by Sieveking's poetic and religious background. His mother was a first cousin of Gerard Manley Hopkins.[14] His grandfather, Judge George de Giberne, had taken up photography in 1849 and had photographed Hopkins when the poet was a boy.[15] And Sieveking's great-aunt, Maria Rosina de Giberne (Sister Maria Pia), had fallen in love with Cardinal Newman and trailed around Europe after him, a religious 'groupie'. In a pamphlet entitled *John Betjeman and Dorset* (1963), Sieveking recalled what he claimed was John's first broadcast.

> I remember so well, a little over thirty years ago, when Betjeman was assistant editor of the *Architectural Review* and I was, not a Christian slave, but one of the small and lucky band of producers at the BBC who were allowed to put on the air anything they thought of – or practically anything . . . I put a sort of variety show into the microphone in which was a turn billed as 'Betjeman major, the Highbrow of the Upper Fifth'.[16]

Sieveking remembered 'the spontaneous enthusiasm with which the young Betjeman threw himself into the job of preparing to appear in public disguised as a sort of mockery of himself . . . a sort of gentle satire on one side of himself, yet with the other side, the romantic, showing through'.[17] When Sieveking asked John to take part in the programme, 'he immediately saw what fun it could be, and, by Jove, what fun it *was*!' Sieveking quoted chunks of the script John had given him:

> I'm going to recite poetry with action (*bicycle bell*). You won't be able to see the action, but, my hat, you'll hear it all right (*Rifle report and thunder*).
>
> So allow me to trespass upon your senses for an hour or so. I and some other fairly talented people in the school want you to join with us in a little literary venture . . . We're going to found a magazine which will be an outlet for . . . er . . . as it were, our inner consciousnesses . . . and I thought of getting hold of Ramsay MacDonald or Winston Churchill or some other fairly intelligent and talented person to write an article for it so as to ensure its circulation in the school.
>
> The thing I've written is fairly intelligent and Kittiwake,[18] who is sub-editor with me, says it's as talented as anything Coward has done. It's about Westgate-on-Sea where my people took a bungalow so as to be near the vegetarian restaurant. It's the first thing I've done since my Beardsley period. I was at a preparatory school at Westgate, you know, just near our bungalow. It was – for those who know Westgate – that uneven red brick and tiled building with a spire at one end and a tower at the other joined together by a rather clever imitation of a Swiss chalet between. Bells, please.[19]

In his 1963 pamphlet Sieveking noted that the second verse of 'Westgate-on-Sea' which John read in the broadcast was not included in the poem as published in his *Collected Poems* of 1958. Other verses in the programme which were not reprinted in 1958 were those of 'The

Most Popular Girl in the School', which John said were by his sister, Miss Jessie Betjeman. Sieveking quoted two stanzas.

> It isn't the same at St Winifred's now Monica's left the school –
> She was so calm and collected, cultivated and cool;
> I shall never forget the example she set to a girl like me
> By the way she carried her rifle in St Winifred's OTC.[20]

> Gosh, I was fond of Monica! She was a regular sport,
> It was rotten for her her complexion seemed to fall rather short
> Of what is expected of schoolgirls, but I think it's a filthy disgrace
> To say that a girl looks ugly just 'cos she's spots on her face.[21]

John's broadcast ended with a recital of his poem 'Dorset' – the pretext for Sieveking's somewhat arbitrary choice of title for his pamphlet. This is how John introduced the poem:

> I am now going to conclude with a rural poem about Dorset. (*Two bells ring.*) Those are the bells of Puddletrenthide [*sic*, for Piddletrenthide][22] Church. I couldn't bring Puddletrenthide into my poem, but I have brought in as many oddly named Dorset villages as I could. And mixed up with them modern names like Gerald Heard – only not him – to make the poem the more curious. Here is the highbrow result. (*The two bells cease.*)[23]

The mention of Heard, whose name was probably not known even to 1 per cent of the listeners, was characteristic of John. He expected people to accept his world without explanation and its *dramatis personae* without introduction: Myfanwy and Miss J. Hunter Dunn must be as real to them as to him. He was also paying an oblique compliment to the man who had given him his entrée to the BBC.

Though John was always prepared to have fun on the radio, he also realized, early on, its potential as an instrument of propaganda. The first script of a Betjeman talk which survives in the BBC archives is 'Waterloo Bridge Is Falling Down', broadcast on 17 February 1932. In its original, unedited form it began:

> I have in my hand today's paper. The headings read 'Old Waterloo Bridge Doomed – To be pulled down this summer – LCC [London County Council] Decision'. Eight years ago the cracks in Waterloo Bridge were noticed by the *Architects' Journal*, and the agitation started. Mr Herbert Morrison, a late Minister of Transport, said that before the agitation started ninety-nine people out of every hundred had not noticed the

beauty of the bridge, which is a 'debatable' point. (Meaning the beauty of
the bridge is a debatable point.) I will not contradict him, although it was
Canova, the great sculptor, who said that it was the finest bridge in
Europe. I shall leave Mr Herbert Morrison to quarrel with Canova.[24]

John was twenty-five when, with this mixture of humour and anger,
he told Government ministers and the rest of the population why Old
Waterloo Bridge should not be replaced. Eight months later he wrote
to Ackerley (by now 'My dear Joseph') asking if he might give a radio
talk on 'the cause of British architecture'.[25] Ackerley sent the letter
through to Lionel Fielden, asking, 'What do I reply?' Fielden
answered: 'I don't know! I should tell JB that we had a whole thump-
ing series on architecture from every point of view and it bored listeners excessively. And we can't just boost architects because they're out
of work.'[26]

John returned to the charge in 1933. He wrote Ackerley an earnest,
long-winded letter suggesting that a row about Carlton House Terrace
should be used as a lever to campaign for an amendment to the Town
and Country Planning Act. He was not necessarily putting himself
forward to make the broadcast; he proposed that it might be made by
Howard Marshall, the broadcaster who later married Nerina Shute,
John's friend in his film-reviewing days.[27] Again Ackerley sent John's
screed through to Fielden. John was already on 'Dear Lionel' terms
with Fielden. In 1932 the two had a joshing correspondence. When
John was due to have a conversation on the air with Sir Daniel Hall,
an expert on agriculture and horticulture,[28] Fielden sent him Hall's
laborious draft of the proposed dialogue, writing, 'No doubt you will
be messing it about in your own way.'[29] Fielden, who had his own line
in camp badinage, enjoyed John's wit; but he was not prepared to let
him ride his architectural hobby-horse and risk boring the listeners.
The grandson of John Fielden who had carried the Ten Hours Bill
through the House of Commons, he had a short way with people who
took themselves too seriously.[30] Replying to Ackerley, Fielden scrawled
across John's letter about Carlton House Terrace, 'What *is* all this
bilge?'[31]

In March 1934, only two months after he became film critic of the
Evening Standard, John tried to persuade Fielden to appoint him film
critic of the BBC.[32] John's long, axe-grinding letter to Ackerley may
have made Fielden wary of him. He sent a sniffy reply: '. . . I doubt
very much whether you are "a master of the microphone". I think your
writing is admirable, but that's quite a different thing, and particularly
in the case of film criticism, where we want someone who will ring the
bell every time.'[33] In any case, Fielden wrote, the pay – only ten

guineas a fortnight – was unlikely to tempt John away from the *Standard*.

Nevertheless, John was increasingly in demand as a broadcaster. He was a natural choice for any programme that required some erudition and wit. In July 1934 Ackerley wrote to ask whether he would take part in a new series of talks being planned, 'Speeches that Never Happened' – for example,

> The armament manufacturer who admitted that the best policy was to supply both sides.
> The press magnate who admitted that the sales of his paper were falling.
> The motorist who admitted that pedestrians were fair game.[34]

In June 1935 Malcolm Brereton told John of a scheme 'to evolve a technique of a short story especially adapted to the microphone'.[35] John replied that he was fascinated by the idea.[36] A month later, G.N. Pocock of the BBC wrote a memo to Brereton:

> I had a talk with Betjeman this afternoon, and he read to me his story beginning, 'Just a minute, sir' over the microphone, though of course we had no effects. His idea is not simply to have a story with effects, but effects worked into the plot and taking the place of essential description. This seems to me to be extremely interesting and probably sound. Anyhow, it is well worth looking into and experimenting with. I recommend you to get some of these records – there must be a train, for instance, and probably noises of feet scrunching – and to try out this story. In the meantime I have asked him to do another one on similar lines and we might do them both in the same period, with real effects.[37]

In the event, only one was broadcast, ten years later.

In May 1936 John received twenty-five guineas for a programme called 'May Games'. The fee included his expenses in visiting Helston, Padstow and Minehead with the BBC recording van, to record pagan festivities – the Helston Furry Dance, the Padstow Hobby Horse and the Minehead Hobby Horse.[38] John's expenses became the subject of a voluminous correspondence between him and Ronald Boswell, a long-suffering and good-humoured BBC official who usually made allowance for the poet's train fares and meals. 'Dear Mr Boswell, Here are some sickening details . . .' one letter began. It continued:

> I enclose a railway voucher which I was unable to use. I have a season ticket from Paddington to Uffington. I got in a fast train to Bristol at Paddington which did not stop at Uffington. The Ticket Collector would not take my

voucher and my season ticket which together completed the journey, so I had to pay the excess from Uffington to Bristol. Could you give me the price of this voucher on my next cheque?[39]

Just occasionally John managed to present an itemized expense sheet, which gives an idea of the topographical commando-course he was prepared to undergo.

Expenses, Weston and Clevedon 14 April 1938

Uffington to Swindon	1s	6d
Breakfast in "	2s	1d
Swindon to Weston (return)	7s	11d
Luncheon in Weston-super-Mare	2s	6d
Ward Locker's [*sic*] Guide to Weston	2s	6d
Local Weston papers		5d
Weston to Clevedon (W.E. & P.R.)		9½d
Clevedon to Yatton		6½d
Bristol to Broadway	7s	11d
Tea		9d
Bus fares in Weston		7d
Admission fees in Weston to private waxworks		8d
	£1 7s	8d[40]

(To add to Boswell's problems, John's total was wrong.)

Guy Burgess, now a BBC talks producer, who already knew John through Anthony Blunt, wrote to him in July 1937: 'Dear John, We are having a series of talks called "Eccentrics", and I said to myself who more suitable than you to talk about one of the others?'[41] He added: 'When are we going to meet again? The last meeting was a great success at least from my point of view, as you will remember.' It might be carrying speculation too far to discern a sexual undercurrent in this, though Burgess's promiscuity and indiscretion were notorious. (John's reply ended: 'I hope your evening meeting continued as successfully as it started';[42] and Burgess wrote in his next letter, 'I had a very nice evening yesterday.')[43] Burgess suggested that John might choose the troglodyte Duke of Portland as his eccentric; but John wrote that he would prefer to talk on Nollekens, the sculptor, and possibly also on the architect Sir John Soane, 'who was more cracked than eccentric'.[44] In the end he spoke on Adolphus Cooke, the nineteenth-century neighbour of the Pakenham family in Ireland who feared that he might be turned into a screech-owl after his death, or into a fox that would be hunted down by the then Lord Longford.[45] 'He beats anything I have heard of,' John wrote to Burgess in August 1937.[46] In the same month, Burgess had to chivvy him about a programme on 'What Is Wrong with the Cinema?' in which John was to question John Grierson, Alfred Hitchcock and Rose Macaulay. Burgess wanted to know in advance what lines John's questions might take. 'The thing is to work like a snowball,' Burgess wrote, 'and there is no snow yet.'[47] The programme was broadcast on 4 September. Hitchcock had dropped out and was replaced by Sidney Bernstein.

Although in 1934 Lionel Fielden doubted that John was 'a master of the microphone', in 1946 Ronald Boswell wrote to the Talks Booking Manager, 'As Mr Betjeman is a speaker of great reputation and experience, I am wondering whether we could not consider putting his standard fee for a fifteen minute talk up from 10 guineas to 12 guineas.'[48] The increase was agreed. In the intervening twelve years, John had gradually improved his broadcasting technique. In the early days, he was amusing, but mannered and a little toilsome. In April 1937 he talked about Bristol in a series called 'Town Tour'.

I feel a bit of an insult, coming here as a non-Bristolian to talk about the good and bad of Bristol. What right have I, a green-faced, bald-headed semi-intellectual, to say something that will make a city father wince or cause some kind-hearted housewife sitting in the ugliest villa between here and Weston, listening in to a wireless set whose fret-work case looks like a cross between a bonded warehouse and the Taj Mahal – what right have I to criticize? The idea of this talk and of the subsequent ones I hope to give on West Country towns is to help you to look about you when you are in a town. If people took as much trouble to preserve decent simple houses in towns as they do to preserve views and downs and woods in the country, if people were as anxious to have abolished vulgar buildings covered with beams and whatnots in various repulsive shades of red brick, if people were as anxious to abolish these as they are anxious to preserve the blue-bell and the lesser stitchwort – England might even yet have a chance of being as beautiful as it was before the [First World] war.[49]

However, he was developing a more conversational style, less laboured and less patronizing. On Plymouth (1937): 'You know what an idiot you would feel if you turned up for a tennis tournament in plus fours: well, that's just how you feel if you turn up as a landlubber in Plymouth.'[50] On the Plymouth style of architecture, from the same talk: 'The exterior plumbing hangs about it like ribbon from a pair of pince-nez.'[51] On Swindon (1937): 'People who do not live in Swindon consider it a blot on the earth . . . Swindon is full of good hearts and ugly houses – and it's the ugly houses I am going to talk about.'[52] After this programme 'A Swindonian' wrote: 'Well, Mr John Betjeman, I hope the next time I hear you broadcast it will be to boost a place not to ridicule it';[53] but May Morris, William Morris's daughter, wrote from Kelmscott Manor, 'I am glad to hear that you said nasty things about the town of Swindon . . . The town is a disgrace . . .'[54]

In John's two talks entitled 'Seaview' (April 1938) the pontifical aesthete of the Bristol talk had given place to someone familiar with the practicalities of ordinary people's lives. There is still a garnish of humour.

'SEAVIEW' – 1

'Visitors'

'Come away, Henry, from those common little children: they're only visitors.'

'Don't have anything to do with those people, Bertie – they think they own the place.'

Who of us does not know that eternal struggle between Residents and Visitors which goes on from year to year round our wave-washed shores? I have arranged the first two of these talks like a boxing match. Round one, which I propose to describe now, is going to be a victory for the visitors. I'm going to show you that the poor visitors have a good deal to complain of.

While you were all thinking how cold it was this Easter, I was mooning about from watering place to watering place, being a visitor.

The first thing that the visitor complains of is high prices. High rents, for instance . . . 'To Let Furnished, 63 shillings a week'. Now if this bungalow were lived in all the year round, if the things in it worked, if the rooms didn't smell of damp, mice and stale biscuits, if the garden were bright with flowers, forty-two shillings would be expensive but just reasonable. But it isn't lived in. It was bought by a man in, let us say, Bristol, for £500 fifteen years ago. Since then he has let it to successive tenants during the holiday seasons at three guineas a week. No tenant has ever been there twice. The furniture consists of not enough plates, two aluminium teaspoons, four hard beds, some torn matting, a back number of a magazine left by a former tenant, a broken lawn mower, and a cake of washing soap which has stuck in the waste-pipe of the sink . . .[55]

In the second 'Seaview' programme, John invented a resident, Colonel Cabbage, who keeps a diary.

August 17th A little rain last night, so I went into the lower field to look at the rain-gauge. Found a couple of bell-tents there and a sickly socialist-lookin' fellow shavin' his pimply face, actually usin' the water in the gauge to shave with. 'Who the devil gave you leave to pitch camp here, sir?' I said. 'No one,' he replied, 'the people have a right to their own country.'[56]

This invention of spoof characters (Colonel Cabbage, with his dropped 'g's, perhaps owed something to Penelope's father) was a frequent ploy in John's broadcasts. His gift for mimicry brought them to life.

At times John's levity and insouciance worried the BBC mandarins, who as the leaders of a comparatively new institution were concerned about 'standards'. In February 1939, when John gave a talk on Parson Hawker of Morwenstow in a series on 'Western Worthies', his producer, C. Pennethorne Hughes, sent the script through to the Corporation's religious adviser, who wrote back: 'I don't think any of this "unwise", but Hawker's first interest was as a parish priest – in his people *and in religion.*' He felt that John's anecdotes exaggerated the eccentric side of Hawker 'and make the sketch rather one-sided – it is almost the picture of a pagan clown!'[57] Pennethorne Hughes replied: 'I had already impressed upon Betjeman that we were anxious that Hawker should not be presented as a figure of fun, so that I am sure he will agree to alter the emphasis of the two paragraphs you suggest.'[58] John was fond of Pennethorne Hughes, a descendant of Sir James Pennethorne who had designed the Geological Museum in Jermyn Street where John had inserted conkers in a showcase with a spoof label.[59] He readily agreed to tone down the Hawker talk.

Two months later, he was in trouble again. On the first page of the script of a series called 'Built to Last', he had written: 'I regard this series as something far more important, in a way, than crises or foreign politics, because it's about England and how we can keep it worth living in.'[60] Pennethorne Hughes received a frosty memo about this from his superior, R. Maconachie (a man best remembered for refusing to allow the MP Josiah Wedgwood to air his anti-fascist views on the radio). Maconachie wrote: 'Doesn't this exceed the limits of admissible extravagance and give good ground for charging Betjeman with being a "crank", which he denies?'[61] Again John gave in gracefully, but in January 1940 he got into a scrape from which it was a lot harder to extricate him.

In a talk on the poet Sir Henry Newbolt, whom he much admired, he said that Newbolt's only son had been killed in the Great War. Unfortunately, Captain Newbolt was very much alive, and 'hopping mad'. John said he had been misled by a phrase in Major R. Furse's preface to Sir Henry Newbolt's *A Perpetual Memory* (1937), which even Sir Henry's widow later agreed was ambiguous.[62] But Captain Newbolt was not to be easily appeased. Through his literary agent, A.P. Watt, he demanded to be sent a copy of the talk, so that he could correct it before it was published in *The Listener*.

This I did [reported M.T. Candhi of BBC Programme Copyright] and this afternoon had another telephone call from W.P. Watt [of A.P. Watt]. He stated that the whole talk was full of inaccuracies from beginning to end, that Captain Newbolt had started to correct it, but found it was impossible. Even facts regarding personal details were wrong. Captain Newbolt is naturally annoyed that such a broadcast should have been given, and I understand that his mother is also distressed about it.[63]

A stiff letter shortly arrived from Captain Newbolt himself. 'Let me say at once', he wrote, 'that I recognize that [the talk] was written in a spirit of appreciation, not to say admiration.' But John had referred to Sir Henry's cigars ('He was a non-smoker all his life,' Captain Newbolt expostulated), to his motor cars ('He never possessed one') and to the loss of his only son ('who now has the unpleasant task of writing this letter').[64] On 1 February 1940, Pennethorne Hughes visited John at Uffington, to try to sort the matter out. In an internal BBC memo, he defended him vigorously:

Of course, what is *really* so infuriating is that we should have been lucky enough to discover anyone who would talk about Newbolt without laughing at him, and then through his making this one silly mistake should have it implied that there are other admirers who could have done better. Particularly as, apart from this, the talk seems to have been a very successful one.[65]

Captain Newbolt was now demanding that the BBC should commission a second, more accurate, talk about his father by Sir Henry's friend Walter de la Mare. Eventually a compromise was reached: a reading of Newbolt's poetry was to be broadcast on 23 March, with a short introduction by de la Mare. George Barnes, head of the Third Programme, wrote to Pennethorne Hughes: 'The (dead) son and the son-in-law and the widow are all in on it. You will be glad to hear that my patience is almost exhausted.'[66] The new programme was not exactly scheduled for a peak listening time: it ended at midnight.

Three weeks after his visit to Uffington, Pennethorne Hughes suggested to Barnes that John be allowed to give a talk on the return to railway travel. 'Humbled by Newbolt,' he wrote, 'he should not do anything dangerous . . .'[67] John had other ideas. Maddened by the demand of the Inland Revenue that he produce the grubby receipts that he always found so hard to save for Mr Boswell, John wanted to give a mischievous talk on 'What to Tax Next'. Pennethorne Hughes was very nervous about this idea. 'Obviously,' he wrote to Barnes, 'he cannot be allowed to give the impression that he is making considered representations about taxation policy, but on the other hand it is certainly desirable, as you say, that he should not be flippant.'[68] Barnes scribbled across this memorandum:

> Spoke to Pennethorne Hughes 27th. He is getting in touch with Betjeman at once
> (a) to keep him off anything waggish about taxation
> (b) to get his script early.
>   I said that we must try to keep B. in the space, if necessary asking him to say at the beginning of his script, 'Taxation's too grim, so I am going to talk about the upholstery of railway carriages.'[69]

The Taxation talk, scheduled for 8 June 1940, was cancelled at the last moment by John, 'as he was unable to fulfil his engagement'.[70] Instead, he presented a series of 'Comments in Wartime'. Recommending to Barnes that the second of these should be commissioned, Pennethorne Hughes wrote: 'It seems to me . . . that it should be the sort of thing which people will like. His last talk was very popular and there were about 20 letters of appreciation about it.'[71] With admiring allies at the BBC and compliments coming in from listeners, John seemed set for a more prominent broadcasting rôle. In the early 1940s he might have become a radio star to rival J.B. Priestley; but war service supervened.

'Minnie'

John Betjeman wandered along the corridors of the Senate House with that half-quizzical, half-bewildered expression that since became familiar to millions on television. He was just one of scores if not hundreds of people trying to do something useful but finding it very difficult.

Michael Bonavia, *London Before I Forget*, Upton-upon-Severn, Worcs., 1990

My dear fellow, I am a bore – but it's all for the Mother Country.

John Betjeman, letter to Sidney Gilliat, 5 December 1940

On 7 February 1940, Bess Betjeman wrote from the Hotel Regina in Bath to her husband's old friend Philip Asprey, who was now her business adviser. As so often, the first paragraph was about her health, but in the next she relayed good news about her son. 'John has just written me he has got a job at the Ministry of Information. He is living with Lady Chetwode and going home for week ends, £700 a year. I feel so relieved.'[1]

As early as July 1935 a subcommittee had been set up to consider how best to control and issue news if war were declared. A report of 1936 recommended the setting up of a Ministry of Information. In 1938, as the crisis over Czechoslovakia deepened, Michael Bonavia, assistant clerk of the University of London Court – which managed the University's finances, property and maintenance – was told that, if war broke out, a ministry would be set up in the Senate House; the University departments would move out.[2] Bonavia was called back from his summer holiday at the end of August 1939 to find the University staff already beginning to move to Royal Holloway College, Egham. Paper notices and telephone cables appeared in every room of the Senate House. War was war, but Bonavia was sad to see Charles Holden's beautiful brand-new building 'vandalized by crude improvisations and the scruffiness that seems to prevail in all minor Government offices'.[3]

In September 1939 the Labour MP Ellen Wilkinson wrote to the film impresario Sidney Bernstein, who was wondering whether to apply for a post in the Ministry: 'The Ministry of Information is in chaos . . . The place is stuffed (rather than staffed) by Everyone's relations . . .'[4] Tommy Handley's ITMA (It's That Man Again) radio programme called the department 'the Ministry of Aggravation'.

The Ministry's prime duty on the home front was to sustain civilian morale and produce long, detailed weekly reports on public opinion and public spirits.[5] To begin with, it had four other broad functions: the release of official news; security censorship of the press, films and the BBC; the conduct of publicity campaigns for other departments; and the dissemination of propaganda to enemy, neutral, allied and Empire countries.[6] By April 1940 the Ministry's responsibility for censorship and news had been lost to the newly created Press and Censorship Bureau.[7] It was quickly clear that the MoI was going to be a Cinderella among wartime Government departments. The service departments issued their own communiqués. The Foreign Office insisted that it alone controlled propaganda to enemy countries. The censors were amateurs whose blue-pencillings often infuriated journalists. And, as Bonavia observed, 'the "creative" rôle of the Ministry was supposed to be executed by a hastily recruited collection of novelists, dons, poets, film-script writers and artists, given little guidance on policy and often virtually nothing to do'.[8]

Lord Reith, the Minister, was riled at not being a member of the war cabinet. He also resented the growing influence of Churchill – 'a horrid fellow', he noted in his diary.[9] The feeling was mutual. Churchill, who called Reith 'Wuthering Heights', had never forgiven him for refusing to let the Government use the BBC as its mouthpiece during the General Strike of 1926. At least Reith was an experienced media man. To that extent the film-makers welcomed his appointment. So far, they had been dismayed at the Government's wartime treatment of the film industry. Its first action, on the outbreak of war, had been to close down places of entertainment. It was perhaps a reasonable step, considering that bombs and poison gas were expected at any moment; but the leading film director Sidney Gilliat thought it 'panicky . . . a craven measure'.[10] Visiting London in September 1939 he saw a notice outside the old Coronet Cinema, Notting Hill: 'NEAREST CINEMA, ABERYSTWYTH. 239 MILES'.[11] The ban on cinema attendance was soon rescinded, but film production was severely disrupted. Two-thirds of all technicians were called up and over half of studio space was requisitioned by the Government. The film producer Ted Black told Gilliat, 'They're putting sugar in

Denham Studios and the Mint at Pinewood and they want to take over Islington, shut it down. It's absurd – the British public will have no British films.'[12] The Board of Trade was reluctantly persuaded that no more space should be taken away.

Because those who planned the Ministry of Information had worked on the assumption that cinemas would be closed, film was given a low priority in their calculations about wartime propaganda. Lord Macmillan, briefly and unhappily Reith's predecessor, had not improved matters by appointing as head of the Films Division Sir Joseph Ball, who had made his name as a film propagandist for the Conservative Party. The tactless choice inevitably provoked attacks by the Labour Party.[13] Ball followed the policy laid down by Sir William Jury during the First World War: that the best way of handling film was not to set up a specialist team inside the Ministry, but to go outside it to commercial producers. The results of Ball's methods are described in Caroline Moorehead's biography of Sidney Bernstein (1984):

> The first films to emerge from Ball's Division in the autumn of 1939 showed only too clearly the dangers of using undirected advertising, commercial or newsreel companies. Some of the films were withdrawn without ever being shown; others had to be drastically re-edited. In the newspapers, particularly the left-wing literary magazines, critics deplored what they saw to be a wasteful combination of cliché and vulgarity, beneficial to no one, patronizing and contemptible. In Germany, on the other hand, the film side of propaganda had got off to a magnificent start, and at one point British audiences were reduced to seeing the early days of the war on German footage, bought from the neutral countries.[14]

There was one exception to this dismal record. Before the start of hostilities, Alexander Korda, a friend of Churchill, tried to show him how important it was for the war effort to save the film industry. As the director Michael Powell recalled it, 'over two large brandies [Korda] said, "Winston, I want you to promise me one thing. When the 1914 war broke out, the British film industry, as I understand it, just vanished. I don't want that to happen again. If I turn over the whole of the technicians in the studio who are now making *The Thief of Bagdad* into making a huge propaganda film, we'll deliver that film to you in a month's time. You can send it all round the world. It may just hold Hitler back."'[15] The result of this proposal was *The Lion has Wings* (1939), produced by Korda, co-directed by Powell and starring Merle Oberon and Ralph Richardson. It was the first full-length propaganda film of the war. Its purpose was to reassure the British public and a doubting world that the Royal Air Force was ready for the German bombers. The critics panned it but the public flocked to it. The film was not financed by the Government. Initially the MoI indicated its approval of the project, but its civil servants had second thoughts when they had had time to think about the 'disjointedness' caused by the haste with which it was finished.

Kenneth Clark was brought in by Reith to replace Sir Joseph Ball. In his Senate House office, Clark surrounded himself with fragments of the civilization that was under threat. Harold Nicolson, who was working at the MoI on the home morale campaign, wrote in 1940:

> I go into KC's room for something and there lying on his pillow with eyes upstaring is the most beautiful marble head. For the moment I assume that it is Greek until I look at the hair and lips which are clearly Canova. It is a bust of the Duc de Reichstadt which K had picked up in a junk shop. A tragic and lovely thing. I feel cheered by this. I do so admire K's infinite variety. He does not like being here really and wld be far happier going back to the Nat-Gallery and vaguely doing high-brow war service. Yet he works like a nigger here because he loathes Hitler so much.[16]

Clark sent John to Sidney Bernstein's office in Golden Square to ask his advice. 'What', John asked Bernstein, 'should the Government be doing about film and propaganda?' As Caroline Moorehead records, it was a satisfying moment for the chairman of the Granada cinema chain. 'He reached down, opened a drawer in his desk and drew out a prepared typed document: "British Film Production and Propaganda by Film". He had occupied some of the days before war by mapping out his thoughts on how films could be used in case of war.'[17] Bernstein's main contention was that propaganda must be completely concealed behind a screen of entertainment. However, he also emphasized that newsreel was essential and that for its distribution, as for the distribution of all films, good relations with the big American film companies were crucial. 'Sidney now passed the document over to Betjeman, who was gratifyingly astonished.'[18] Not long afterwards, Clark invited Bernstein to join the Ministry, but by this time Bernstein had decided that he did not want to join while Chamberlain, the appeaser of fascists, was in power.[19]

As at Oxford, Clark enjoyed John's company. His biographer, Meryle Secrest, writes that 'He sometimes went to a nearby restaurant with John Betjeman or Arthur Waley, but one had to dine at seven sharp as the raids began at 8.15 and even he, with his love of spectacle, did not fancy the trip back through a hail of shrapnel, not to mention bombs.'[20] The traitor William Joyce, 'Lord Haw-Haw', in one of his radio broadcasts (which always began 'Jairmany calling') predicted that the Senate House would be an early target for German bombers, and for once he spoke the truth. Five bombs fell within the Senate House's curtilage in 1940–41. None of them was large but a big bomb fell next door, almost demolishing College Hall, a former hall of residence for women students that was being used as a temporary hostel for Canadian troops. 'After the bomb,' Bonavia writes, 'walking wounded or stretcher-borne soldiers in pyjamas, grotesquely covered in plaster dust, were brought across the road into Senate House.'[21] Goebbels called the Ministry of Information *die grosse Lügenfabrik* – the great Lie Factory – and wanted it destroyed.[22]

The Films Division had considerable power. It regulated supplies and rawstock[23] and ruled over exemption from military service. Every script had to be passed. If film-makers wanted 'facilities' from any Government department, including the service departments, they had to go through the MoI for their contacts and permits. John's main work was to commission films and to read the scripts as they came in. Many of the films were 'five-minuters' on such subjects as 'Careless Talk Costs Lives' (the slogan of a famous series of posters by Fougasse),[24] the uses of dried egg, economizing on bath water, the need for blackout at night, and 'Dig for Victory'. This last was an encouragement to grow vegetables, with a doggerel commentary beginning 'Dig, dig, dig, Feel your muscles getting big; Keep on pushing in the spade.' A short film on fuel economy had the unfortunate slogan 'Let's switch off and go together'. (This meant 'go to the cinema together' – because people sitting in cinemas used up less fuel per person than when they were at home.)

Sidney Gilliat, whose career in films had begun with British International Pictures at Elstree in 1928, was asked to call on John at the Ministry. 'All I knew about him', Gilliat recalls, 'was that he had been film critic of the *Standard*, that he was a poet and that he had some interest in architecture.'[25] Gilliat had imagined that John would be 'rather a quiet, withdrawn person'. Instead he found 'this extraordinarily extrovert man – or maybe he was *acting* the extrovert, I don't know'.

> He didn't start by saying what he wanted. He said, 'My dear fellow, come into this refined gentlemen's lavatory. Take no notice of the carpet. As a temporary civil servant, largely unpaid, I'm not entitled to a carpet, so this is my own carpet.[26] The lamp and lampshade, the same. I'm not entitled to a lamp or lampshade of this description.'
>
> And then, before we could get on to anything, the 'phone would ring and he'd say, 'No, no; this is not Mr Findlay, or in fact Mr Findlay's office.

Mr Findlay has for six weeks been occupied for the Ministry in – I forget whether it's Rio or Buenos Aires, but he's not been here. I have told them on the exchange. Please try somewhere else or get back to the exchange.' Then he put the 'phone down and said, '*The fucking lot of cunts.*' And of course in those days you didn't use language as freely as we do today; I certainly didn't expect it from the Films Officer of the Ministry of Information. And this went on all the time. Each time it was a call for Findlay – whom I happened to know, he was a Hugh Findlay, had been a PRO at Gaumont. And this went on all the afternoon. Each time Betjeman would get more icily polite on the telephone and more foul-mouthed when he put the 'phone down.

Then there was a tap on the door and a man came in with a paint-pot and a piece of rag and overalls and a cloth cap.

'Oh,' he said, 'I'm sorry, sir.'

Betjeman said: 'I don't blame you for mistaking this for a gentlemen's urinal; but what can I do for you?'

So he said: 'Oh, it's all right, sir. I only wanted to wet my rag, sir.'

He said: 'My dear fellow, if you must wet your rag, there is the tap, there is your rag, pray go across and wet it. Pay no attention to us; we're merely supernumeraries in this tiled palace.'

And the poor wretched man, trembling, wet his rag under the tap – 'Thank you, sir' – and went out. And of course Betjeman then exploded again.[27]

Eventually John explained to Gilliat, with clarity, what he wanted – a film on the Empire. 'Come and see Professor Harlow,' he said, 'and he'll tell you what the Empire's all about and will tell you what to do.' Vincent Harlow, the colonial historian from Oxford, was in another room at the Senate House. Gilliat did not find his comments very helpful. Next John suggested that Gilliat should telephone Leslie Howard, who was to be the star of the Empire film. Howard invited Gilliat to dinner in a house on Farnham Common that he was sharing with the film-maker (Sir) Anthony Havelock-Allan. Gilliat spent a night there, during which an air raid took place. 'Leslie Howard and I were supposed to discuss this Empire film,' he recalls. 'I found him charming. I suppose that by origin he was Jewish-Romanian; but in manner he was very English. There were eight or nine people at dinner, including Roland Pertwee, and we all washed up and dried the dishes, Howard included. And then he sat down at the piano and played – rather badly but spiritedly – old music hall songs, and we all sang them. It was a most surprising evening to me. I don't think we ever discussed the Empire film – but it was made. It was called *From the Four Corners*.'[28]

Clive Coultass writes of this film in *Images for Battle: British Film and the Second World War, 1939–1945* (1989):

> . . . Howard had helped to work out for the MoI an idea for a short film in which he encounters in Trafalgar Square three servicemen from the Commonwealth: an Australian, a New Zealander and a Canadian. They have responded politely to the gushing compliments of an upper-class lady on how they have come of their own free will from the Empire to help the motherland, and Howard tries to redress the balance with what he believes to be his own less patronizing version of what they all are fighting for. Nevertheless, it is still England that is the birthplace of the values they have in common, as he explains in some detail. New Zealand is complimented on bringing English equality to the Maoris, Canada on respecting the rights of French Canadians, and even South Africa is mentioned in the same breath, although its particular internal contribution to the democratic ideal is not specified. [The film] promoted the Leslie Howard persona as the champion of British liberalism but fell on stony ground as a statement of war aims.[29]

One day in 1940, John arrived in his office to find that a second desk had been moved in. The man sitting at it, with sleek black hair and spectacles, looked slightly familiar.

'Hello! How extraordinary we should be together!' said the newcomer.

'I'm sorry,' John said, '– I feel I know you, but I can't quite put two and two together.'

'*The Path of Glory* – remember?'

John did not.

'You came down with Nerina Shute and hid in the projection booth.'[30]

It was Dallas Bower, whom he had last met in 1934. Since then, Bower had moved out of films into television. In 1936 he had become one of two drama directors at the newly opened BBC television station at Alexandra Palace. Reith, who thought television was a gimmick that would not last, called Bower and his colleagues 'the Fools on the Hill'; Churchill, in rare agreement with Reith, described television as 'a tuppence coloured Punch and Judy show'.[31] In 1939 Bower had produced Pirandello's *Henry IV* for the small screen. It was the last play on BBC television before the service closed down 'on that ghastly evening when we were told simply to pull the breakers . . . Everything went totally off the air . . . just prior to the declaration of war.'[32] Bower joined the army – he was the first BBC man in uniform – and became 'a not very effective Signals officer' at Whitby.

Kenneth Clark brought Bower into the Films Division, as he was recommended to him by their mutual friend, the composer William Walton. Bower's brief was to bring some professionalism into the Division; and, having invaded John's office, he lost no time in letting him know how things were going to be from now on – even though the two had the same rank of Films Officer, and John had seniority of tenure.

I said [Bower recalled] 'Well, we're rather pressed, because this is going to be my production office. I'm afraid the telephone is going to ring continuously.' And John said, 'Oh well, never mind, old top, I don't suppose it'll be too awful. What I'm here for is to read scripts.' We went off to have some lunch together and I discovered that he wasn't really very happy there. I soon found that he had established himself as something of an eccentric. There were people who found him a little bit too much to take. John Sutro[33] would arrive, because he always had some project or other that he wanted to get under way. And John Sutro and John together were a music-hall act. They would never hesitate to talk at the top of their voices in the corridors of power at the Senate House.

There were two civil servants at the MoI called Forbes and Hieatt. They were dour Scotsmen and they were pretty difficult chaps to cope with, frankly. I think Forbes was John's chief dislike. He was an odd bird, and the other man, Hieatt, was very dour indeed and the Post Office must have been only too delighted to have got rid of him into the MoI. John took the most awful scunner against both of them. He was always putting the needle into one or the other of them . . .

Forbes was prone to work into the long hours and the early morning, drafting contracts and so on. And it was discovered that he looked after himself rather well. He had whisky and tinned food and had set up a little camp bed in his office. Well John, in one of his rambles in Camden Town, looking for some Presbyterian chapel, discovered an undertaker's shop with a notice in the window saying 'BED TO LET' – there was a room above the shop. He went in and managed to persuade the undertakers to sell him the notice. When he came back to the office he said, 'I've found the most wonderful treasure. Look at this!' I said, 'It looks as if it came from a boarding-house in Bexhill.' He said, 'Yes, that's it!' When Forbes was out, John stuck it up over the camp bed in his office. Anybody else would have laughed, but not Forbes. There was hell to pay. The most terrible commotion. Nobody knew who'd done it, and of course I wasn't telling.[34]

Even with Bower added to the team, the Films Division was still badly understaffed. Bower found his workload gruelling. 'John said,

"You're getting very overwrought, old top, very overwrought indeed. It won't do. Come along, now, we're going across to the Bedford. We'll have a nice sandwich and a lager, then I'll take you up to Islington and show you a beautiful altar screen." And that's exactly what we did. We came back about three o'clock and I must say I was jolly pleased to have seen the altar screen. It completely relaxed me – I was fussed, something had gone wrong, we had to re-make.'[35]

Just occasionally, John was less sympathetic and added to Bower's burden, turning the tables on him perhaps in mild retaliation for his overbearing 'This is my production office' line. Bower wanted to commission a 'five-minuter' for the Ministry of Food, starring Alastair Sim. No director was immediately available, so he decided to trust the direction to an experienced cameraman called Desmond Dickinson.

I had every confidence that he would be able to direct [Bower recalled]. John was dubious about it. But Dickinson did take it on. And John and I were both present when there came up on screen – thank God in rush, not in any kind of cut – a staircase that went nowhere. John made the most tremendous fuss about this, although it didn't really matter a damn. He said, 'I think it's quite dreadful. Somebody like you should know better.'
I said, 'All right, John, all *right*!'
'Well, how much is it going to cost to redo that long shot?'
I said, 'Well, it's going to cost whatever it costs.'
He was so insistent – and he wasn't my boss, we were neck-and-neck.[36]

The 'production office' became still more crowded when a desk was brought in for Graham Greene, who was working on some scripts. He was not with the Division for long, but while he was there Penelope came up to fetch John for lunch. 'Apparently Graham Greene had never met Penelope,' Bower said. 'Poor Penelope, there she was, and John – "Oh!" he said, "well now, you don't know old Graham, do you? This is my wife Propeller. She's *hipposexual*." '[37]

John usually had a beer-and-sandwiches lunch at the Rising Sun public house in Tottenham Court Road, often with his old school-friend Arthur Elton. But sometimes he went to the Ministry's canteen. There he chatted to MoI personnel outside the Films Division, including Dame Rachel Crowdy, who had been head of the VAD (Voluntary Aid Detachment) in the First World War, a gnome-like man called Bock, who had been brought in as an expert on South America, and Henry Maxwell, who was a Regional Information Officer – one of the people who, if the Germans landed, were to be the core of the Resistance and set up a communications system.

John Betjeman came up to me in the canteen [Maxwell recalled] and said how much he liked my father's and grandmother's novels. My grandmother was M.E. Braddon (Mrs John Maxwell) who wrote *Lady Audley's Secret* and other three-decker best-sellers; and my father was W.B. Maxwell who wrote *The Devil's Garden*, which was also a best-seller and which was followed by an even bigger success, *The Guarded Flame*. How John knew this, I don't know – he had a genius for finding out people's background.[38]

The next time I met him was a week or so later, a glorious afternoon when a man came to demonstrate a bombard to the Home Guard, and he did this in the big Chancellor's Hall, the largest room in the Ministry where all big meetings were held. John and I were among those asked along to witness the demonstration. The man was very apologetic that owing to the shortage of arms he could only show us a dummy one made of wood instead of the proper materials. We all gathered round. He put the thing together and then – again with many apologies – he put in a wooden projectile and pulled the string. And there was the most shattering detonation you ever heard in your life, and a large piece of the wall was blown away – to everyone's joy, except those who were in its immediate path. It passed over their heads, singeing them. John, of course, was ecstatic about this.[39]

Maxwell also met John at meetings in the Duty Room at which Osbert Lancaster came from the Foreign Office to tell the MoI any news he could. 'It was a very coveted assignment,' Maxwell said. 'The service ministries and the Foreign Office sent people along, and you did hear one or two things there – we were so much in the dark.'[40] Lancaster often joined John for a drink or a meal at the Hotel Russell. 'On one occasion,' Lancaster said, 'we returned to the Senate House after lunch and the armed guard on duty at the entrance asked John if he might see his pass. "No you can't," John said. "I'm a German spy." '[41]

When the bombing was bad, Lancaster sometimes spent the night at the Senate House. 'One night,' Bonavia writes, 'there was a particularly loud bang nearby and, getting up to investigate, I encountered in the corridor Osbert Lancaster – black moustache, eyebrows and all – gorgeous in a superb plum-coloured silk dressing gown, looking exactly like the villain of some Victorian melodrama. The same thought struck a ribald Press censor, who fell on his knees in front of this apparition crying, "Spare my daughter, Sir Jasper!" '[42]

Henry Maxwell remembered the time when Kenneth Clark's loyalty to John was put to its severest test.

As well as a Minister, we had these directors-general, and their deputies. We were always having people brought in from outside, often senior civil

servants who were supposed to pull us together, because most of these
little departments were staffed by amateurs who were a perpetual pain in
the neck to the established civil servants, so despairing efforts were made
to impose some sort of discipline. And they brought in, as deputy
director-general, this man called Colonel Scorgie. He was sent to us from
the Stationery Office; although he was moving from one civilian ministry
to another, he insisted on calling himself 'Colonel'. He had a reputation
as an efficient, no-nonsense man. With a flourish of trumpets he was to
bring order out of chaos. We were told that this fire-eater was coming,
who would see to it that we conformed and behaved. And he hadn't been
in the Ministry a week before he issued a letter to all staff, very much the
sort of naïve pi-jaw the headmaster of a prep school would give to the
school if he thought they were being 'slack' – to 'pull up our socks' and
'put our backs into it' and 'all pull together'. It was rather resented, I must
say, by people many of whom were eminent in various walks of life, and
were not accustomed at their age to be addressed in that way – but there
it was. Anyway, two days later, John found himself in the same lift as
Scorgie, whom he recognized. And turning to the lift-man, an old catch-
'em-aliveo from the '14–'18 war with one arm and practically stone deaf,
John said, 'I say, have you seen anything of this fellow *Scroggie*? They tell
me he's not really *pulling his weight*.' It was all round the Ministry by
lunch-time. It was the beginning of the end for Scorgie.[43]

Clark remembered the Scorgie episode. 'Colonel Scorgie said to me,
"That fellow Betjeman will have to go. He's half-baked." I replied:
"John Betjeman has one idea a month that is better than all the other
ideas of my Division put together. You must, with respect, keep
him." '[44] But even Clark found John's prankishness tiresome at times.
Nicolas Bentley, the cartoonist, remembered Clark's pausing in the
middle of an address to his staff to say, 'Betjeman, I shall be obliged if
you will remove those bicycle clips from your ears.'[45]
    On 10 May 1940, Chamberlain resigned and Churchill became Prime
Minister. In June, Reith was replaced by Duff Cooper. Both he and Lady
Diana Cooper were friends of John's. Lady Diana had the eccentric idea
that she would like to live 'over the shop' in the Senate House, but was
told in a frosty interview with Michael Bonavia that the structure of the
building made that impossible.[46] Duff Cooper was a Churchill man, but
he too became disenchanted with the Ministry, which he later called 'a
misbegotten freak'. In the year he was at the Senate House he had little
but bad news to communicate. 'When I appealed for support to the
Prime Minister,' he wrote in his memoirs, 'I seldom got it. He was not
interested in the subject. He knew that propaganda was not going to
win the war. Looking back, I think he was right . . .'[47]

With Chamberlain gone, there was now nothing to stop Sidney Bernstein joining the Films Division – or so it seemed. Duff Cooper offered him the job of Films Adviser. However, MI5 raised objections: Bernstein, they told Cooper, was a member of the Communist Party and was known to visit the Russian Embassy every week. (Bernstein disputed both allegations.)[48] During the investigation into Bernstein, a colonel from MI5 came in to question Dallas Bower. 'He said [Bower recalled], "I was hoping we'd be alone, Mr Bower." So John got up and said, "You will be. You will be. If you want me, Dallas, you'll find me in Dame Felicity's loo." There was no Dame Felicity: he just invented her.'[49]

Duff Cooper stood up to MI5. Caroline Moorehead records: 'Duff Cooper, with his little moustache and rather petulant drawl, stated flatly: "Bernstein is in."'[50] The cinema mogul arrived with his own antique desk and high bookcase, and threw out the Government-issue furniture. He hung his pictures on the walls. His job was honorary – unlike John's, which was on the civil service establishment – so his décor was left undisturbed while John's rug was banished. The civil servants, Moorehead writes, 'did not find him cosy. He was grander, richer, busier and more detached than most of them, in his perfect dark-blue suit, his white shirts, his navy overcoat slung nonchalantly over his arms [sic] as he dashed down the corridors, heading for another appointment, another Ministry. He didn't often join the "boys from Mini" as they set off on their lunchtime expeditions to the Rising Sun in Tottenham Court Road . . .'[51]

Bernstein's main value to the MoI during John's time there was that he had the contacts, the clout and the diplomatic skill to get the often reluctant film industry to put on the films the Government wanted screened. He also got feedback from his Granada cinema managers – weekly reports on audience reaction to the propaganda 'shorts', which ranged from 'Well received' to 'Received with derisive laughter'.[52] Bernstein was frustrated by the Ministry's inability to make fast decisions. To a friend who was training to be a bomber pilot, he wrote: 'the atmosphere is now a cross between a daily lecture by a school master, a revivalist meeting in Bloomsbury and the Burning of the Cross . . . I have seen Ministers, Directors, Generals and Deputy Directors and all, but we don't seem to get much forwarder, or perhaps we do, but not fast enough to me.'[53]

By now, Kenneth Clark had 'moved upstairs' at the Ministry, and Jack Beddington – another old friend of John's – had succeeded him as head of the Films Division. Opinions about Beddington at the MoI were mixed. Michael Balcon thought him 'the ideal man for the job', a 'real expert salesman', and found him easy to deal with.[54] But Sidney

Bernstein did not like him and Dallas Bower could not stand him. 'He was aggressive in a way John Betjeman could never be aggressive,' Bower said. 'And there was something rather flash about him.'[55] Sidney Gilliat gave Beddington credit for setting up, on his suggestion, an 'ideas committee', but thought he had an ulterior motive. 'He saw his job as a shop window for himself; and if he could bring important people together in an ideas committee, that was a bigger and better shop window.'[56] John served on the committee, but was disdainful, calling it 'Beddi's Brain Box'. Among the Betjeman papers at Victoria, British Columbia, are two drafts of a playlet which John wrote while at the Ministry, satirizing meetings of the ideas committee. In both he represents himself as a put-upon underling, patronized and sneered at by some of his colleagues – particularly Helen de Moulpied (who in 1948 married [Sir] Denis Forman, the future chairman of Granada Television), the prolific author Arthur Calder-Marshall,[57] and Montagu Slater ('Monty'), who later wrote the libretto of Britten's *Peter Grimes*. Though John may have overemphasized his insignificance in the Ministry pecking-order, the two drafts probably give, in parodic form, a fair impression of the meetings. The more finished version, entitled 'BEDDI'S BRAIN BOX or a meeting of the JOINT PLANNING COMMITTEE of the FILMS DIVISION of the M. of I.', runs:

> *Dame de Mouilpied* [*sic*] 'I want to make a film on a fair wage in the tin plate industry and public relations to Beveridge, P.I.D., P.E.P. & P.W.E. I am sure it would interest the D.A.K. My R.I.O.'s are clamouring for it.'
>
> *Arthur Calder-Marshall* 'As a matter of fact we are making something on the same lines for Yugo Slavia. But ours is pretty strong meat.'
>
> *J. Betjeman* 'Are you sure the subject is likely to be of general interest in English villages? or that it will make a film at all? Of course, I don't know about foreign distribution. I hate abroad.'
>
> > Jarrow is rising in Montagu Slater's pipesmoke. He is not going to answer yet. He is thinking it out dialectically, squaring it with the party. All eyes are turned on him, almond eyes of Dame de Mouilpied, blue eyes of Calder-Marshall. He is a monument of silent power. The power of the party.
>
> *Arthur Calder-Marshall* challenged, insulted. His ideals have been questioned. What are his ideals? He is not quite sure. At any rate they are not those of that irresponsible little fascist reactionary, J.B. But he won't be too hard on him. He may come in useful. He could use him to play off the Inter-Allied Films Committee against the P.R.O. of U.N.N.R.A. in one of his intrigues. He must both ignore J.B.'s remarks yet score off him & give an answer to shew Montagu Slater that he is toeing the party line too.

'The whole social structure needs blowing up and this is a way of doing it. But to be any good it must be dynamite.'

Dame de Mouilpied's eyes flash. 'Yes dynamite – that's the word.' How splendid to be holding her own on equal terms with these men! To be giving them ideas! Didn't someone say she had a brain like a man? She senses the feeling of the room. Left's in. Johnny's out. Amusing no doubt. But superficial. Didn't Beddi say he was quite a good minor poet, but no use in the films division?

Montagu Slater 'Of course this is fundamental. If we can get it past Gates.'

Dame de Mouilpied Fundamental! There the serious man speaks. The Dame sees herself with a blue sash on her bosom marked 'Dame of the British Soviet'. She is going to a dinner where her fellow Guest is Sir Montagu Slater. No Monty Slater CBE. Titles will have been abolished. Arthur C-M is to report at the dinner for the Daily Worker. But, dreams apart, left is right, isn't it? Left stands for clinics, civics, the clover leaf for ever, community cocoa centres, uninhibited children on municipal swings in constant sunlight – we will have controlled the weather by then. Everything getting better & better & better.

Arthur C-M (sarcastic) 'Of course we can introduce some *religion* into it for Johnny.'

J.B. 'Thanks awfully for the offer old boy. But no thanks all the same.'

Dame de Mouilpied 'Who will we get to write it?' Rex Warner?[58] James Fisher?[59] Christopher Hawkes?[60]

M. Slater enjoying his power & slowly sucking at his pipe. All eyes on him. 'I agree we make it. I think I could get Palme Dutt[61] for the script.'

Dame de M 'Could you really get Palme Dutt? But how are we to get it past Beddi?'

Arthur C-M 'Oh just give it a catchy title – what about 'Tinketty-tonk'?'[62]

M. Slater 'A bit dated isn't it?'

Arthur C-M 'So's Beddi.'

M. Slater 'I've got to go to Ag & Fish [the Ministry of Agriculture and Fisheries]. See you at the Production Conference this afternoon.'

Production Conference

Beddi 'Well Ladies & Gentlemen. I'm sure we're all pleased to welcome Mr Godfrey Wynn [*sic*].[63] There's no need for me to introduce him. But he may need to know the kind of chaps we are. And I think our daily business chat first – if you don't mind, Godfrey – will help him to do so. The first item is *Tinketty-Tonk*. Well, it's a jolly good title. What's it about, Helen?'

Dame de M 'You explain, Monty.'

M. *Slater* 'To shew the fundamental (suck & puff) basis of wage earning & its aspect in the tin plate industry. It's a bit revolutionary.'

Beddi 'Do you think it's a good idea, Monty?'

M.S. Nods his head & smokes.

Beddi 'Fine. Go ahead then. Into production at once. That'll make 'em sit up.'

Carried nem.con.

Why did John go to the trouble of writing two drafts of this playlet, one rough, the other an amended fair copy? The piece had no conceivable market value, though words and ideas in it are echoed in later poems.[64] It was not the first time he had written a playlet. He had done so in an Oxford magazine in 1927, in *The Artsenkrafts*, a savage pasquinade against his father.[65] Perhaps in the new piece he was once again just releasing frustration and anger – much as he later did in his television play about road development, *Pity about the Abbey*.[66] But surely one draft would be enough to achieve that catharsis? Possibly John intended to show the skit to somebody like Kenneth Clark, to demonstrate the futility of his own rôle at the Ministry and angle for a different job, more rewarding and prestigious. The fair copy is a toned-down version of the first draft. In the original playlet, entitled 'DOING BEDDI'S THINKING FOR HIM', Helen de Moulpied tartly comments, 'But, Johnny, you don't know what it is not to have a living wage'; and her plans for a soviet future include 'Browning for all; Auden for all; really deep, fundamental things like that'. After she has outlined her plans, she sits back with satisfaction. 'She has ousted Johnny. She is above him.'[67]

The two drafts might indicate that John had plenty of time to kill in the office; but on the back of the fair copy he made nine detailed notes for the revision of a film script about education. The first note began: 'Cut out swishing [flogging]: bad human [illegible] not to be harped on.' A letter that he sent to Geoffrey Grigson in July 1940 shows that John wrote at least one film script himself.

My dear Geoffrey . . .

Have you ever tried your hand at writing a short incident for the cinema? The M of Inf. is doing five-minute films on various subjects prescribed by other ministries. All that is needed is a visual sense which you have. You do not write it as a film script, but just as though you were writing a story for the *Evening Standard*. It must have a bit of a climax or point the moral required.

If you feel you would like to try, do let me know and I will send you a

subject to be turned into a film. It really is most exciting work, especially
when you see what you have devised on the screen. I've done one and it is
quite a success. I am most surprised.[68]

After Beddington's arrival at the MoI, the four main executives of
the Films Division all had surnames beginning with 'B'. John wrote a
poem about 'The Four B's' which, as Caroline Moorehead writes,
'conjured up the spirit of the place, with its camaraderie, its touch of
whimsy and its absolute exclusion of all things bureaucratic':[69]

> I wish I were – I often think –
> Another Maurice Maeterlinck
> So I could write a play with ease
> About four little busy B's
> Who fly about and buzz and buzz
> And stay exactly as they wuzz
> And buzz about and fly and fly
> About the spacious MoI
> Then settle in the glittering sun
> Content with having nothing done.
> Sing,
> Beddington, Bernstein, Betjeman, Bower
> Sing,
> Winken, Blinken and Nod
> Sing,
> Shell, Granada, sing Norman Tower
> Make a five minute treatment of God.
>
> Take down this letter, dear Miss Broom,
> And send it – to you know whom
> Say that we've got a peculiar feeling
> There *was* an idea received from Ealing
> Last month – or was it the month before –
> We've lost it – but couldn't he send some more
> Say that we're glad to have anything new, Sir
> Make it amusing – write dear Producer.
> There's the letter – now go and compile it
> Get a reply and forget to file it –
> Sing,
> Beddington, Bernstein, Betjeman, Bower
> Sing,
> Ho! for the Treasure-ee
> Sing,

Hey! for a Conference once an hour,
Sing,
Ho! for Victor-ee.[70]

Almost forty years later, in 1989, Sidney Gilliat took part in *Filming for Victory*, a television programme about wartime films, presented by Professor Christopher Frayling. Later he said: 'I noticed that in the film there was a tendency to write Betjeman off as an eccentric who had a brief, hilarious and unproductive spell at the Ministry; but I think that in many ways, given the difference in their areas of operation, he was a lot more effective than Jack Beddington, because Beddington used the Films Division to promote himself, whereas Betjeman didn't appear to give a damn about what happened to him so long as he got something going . . . Also, John was very approachable. You could say to him, "I think that's a bloody silly idea," and he'd listen; you wouldn't dream of saying that to Kenneth Clark or Beddington.'[71]

Gilliat did have one complaint about John. He thought that because of John's schooldays with Arthur Elton (whose services were much used by the Ministry, and whom Beddington eventually appointed to the Films Division)[72] and his friendship with Bob Flaherty when film critic of the *Evening Standard*, John was prejudiced in favour of the documentary film-makers and against makers of commercial feature films of the kind made by himself and his business partner Frank Launder. 'Elton was a splendid fellow,' Gilliat said, 'and Paul Rotha was good too. But Grierson I always thought was more a cult figure and more a "Godfather" than a particularly brilliant documentarian.'[73] In *Filming for Victory*, Gilliat added: 'The documentarians had the moral advantage of being much more approved . . . and publicized by critics, from [C.A.] Lejeune onwards. They always got a good press. But when it came to pushing those people into war propaganda with a considerable output, there just wasn't the talent to do good work in sufficient quantity. So you got the best, like Humphrey Jennings, doing very well; but down the line some of the results were deplorable.'[74]

At one of the first meetings of Beddington's ideas committee, about twenty of the 115 documentaries that had been made so far were shown.

You couldn't stomach more [Gilliat said]. You didn't ever want to see any more, they were dreadful. The documentary film-makers had this notion that 'real people' should be used, not actors. In other words, a billeting officer should be played by a billeting officer, to make the thing more realistic. He's coming home to lunch when these calls come on the telephone for billeting, and the poor chap has literally got a hot potato in his mouth, and is trying to remember lines that he hasn't been taught how to speak. The result was, it was like no one in God's earth, really.[75]

Gilliat may have been overestimating John's reliance on the documentarians. As he himself conceded, 'The documentarians felt they were a lowlier species with higher ideas; and we were a higher species with lower ideas. Something roughly like that. Each side had a chip of a different kind on their shoulder.'[76] Michael Balcon, of Ealing and not a documentarian, had however no complaint about the volume of work he got from the Ministry. In 1940 Ealing turned out several information, propaganda and instructional short films for the Films Division. Three of the films were on the theme of 'Careless Talk Costs Lives'. A directive had come through to the Ministry that this subject was to be given top priority. Dallas Bower said to John: 'The first thing to do is to make quite sure that we've got proper distribution facilities for these films.'[77] Sam Eckman, the European representative of MGM, was invited to the Senate House. He agreed to take on the three 'Careless Talk' films and eventually managed to have them shown in 4,300 cinemas.[78] Bower recommended John Paddy Carstairs as scriptwriter. John asked Carstairs to make the scripts 'as light as possible but with a thrust at the final fade-out'.

> One of the 'Careless Talk' films [Bower remembered] had a very effective scene of a rather suspicious barmaid gossiping stupidly. She was doing the normal kind of work that a barmaid does including the washing-up. And a plate is put in the basin and it very slowly sinks to the bottom of the basin – and that was fade-out.[79]

The Boulting twins, still in their twenties, also got work from the Films Division. John Boulting was in the RAF, Roy in the Royal Artillery. John Betjeman first met Roy, who was in his army captain's uniform, in the brasserie of the Café Royal in 1940. They drank some bottles of 1924 Cheval Blanc, a fine claret which the restaurant served as a table wine until supplies ran out. They had a conversation about films. The next time John Betjeman saw what he took to be Roy, he continued the conversation; the thread was picked up very quickly. He wondered why Roy was now wearing RAF uniform, and assumed he must be in some high-up Intelligence unit which required him to dress up in different uniforms. After a while the young man said, 'You think I'm Roy Boulting, don't you? Well, I'm not. I'm his twin brother.'[80] The Boultings had reason to be grateful to John when he defended them at a preview of their MoI film *Dawn Guard*. Clive Coultass writes:

Dawn Guard, which was finally released in January 1941, is an unusual film for that period because it was not content only to emphasize the need to stand up to Hitler, but also took a reformist view of the social outlook for postwar Britain. Its medium of achieving this, in the form of a dialogue between two Home Guards standing by a country windmill, may appear to be somewhat halting. One of them was played by Bernard Miles, who participated with the writer Anna Reiner in the planning of the film. According to Roy Boulting's account, the MoI's Films Division knew nothing of the content of the film until it was previewed. He also recalled that its official reception was cool, the only MoI officer to make brief favourable comment being John Betjeman, although the left-wing aspirations of the script surely sound too mild for serious objection.[81]

Sidney Gilliat was himself commissioned by John to make a film called *Partners in Crime*, equating the purchase of what was known to be black market meat with theft.

It began with a woman in bed [Gilliat remembered] and a burglar came in and stole some Treasury notes from a drawer; and then that had some line of parallel with black market meat being smuggled into the butcher's shop, carcases carried in. Robert Morley played the judge in the case and we equated the guiltiness of Mrs Wilson buying the meat, with the burglar. (Robert Morley, in his judge's wig, had to sit for quite a long time under very hot lamps. He said to me, 'If I'd known, I'd have brought my early tomatoes with me to ripen them.') But the funny thing was that there was a little scene in the pawnbroker's and a scene in the butcher's – and all these people objected. Questions were asked in the House. The Pawnbrokers' Association objected because one of their members was shown receiving stolen goods. The Master Butchers' Association had a question asked in the House. And, to cap it all, two CID men appeared on the doorstep of Edward Black, who was the producer. They said, 'We believe you have been involved in forging Treasury notes.'
   So Black said, 'What do you mean?'
   And they said, 'Well, we don't know the full details, Mr Black, but we understand that you have photographed Treasury notes, and that is technically an offence.'
   And Black said, 'Where was that?' He found it hard to remember: it was, in fact, when the burglar opened the drawer. We used genuine pound notes. And so Ted, with a brilliant flash of improvisation when he saw these chaps were going to be completely literal-minded about it, said, 'Well, you know, you've come to the wrong person, complaining to me. These are Treasury notes; the Treasury financed the picture; go to the Treasury.' They then departed and were heard of no more.[82]

1. John in one of his earliest BBC Television programmes, *How to Make a Guide-Book* (1937). The producer, Mary Adams, wrote: '[The programme] Opens on Betjeman sitting on bench with large basket . . . Various objects will be withdrawn from the basket and shown. On two occasions Mr Betjeman will rise and draw on a blackboard near him.' The sketch on the blackboard was intended as a caricature of a typical antiquarian

2. Penelope on her gelding Moti in front of Garrards Farm, Uffington, which the Betjemans rented from 1934 (when this photograph was taken) until 1945

3. John expressing with a scowl his dislike of horses

4. John's caricature of Penelope on the hunting field. This exchange actually took place as described

5. Farmer Wheeler, the Betjemans' landlord, was a bugbear of John, who put him in his poem 'The Dear Old Village' as 'Farmer Whistle'

6. In John Sutro's *The Sailor's Return*, Cecil Beaton played the sailor and John a clergyman. *The Bystander* called it 'The film with a Mayfair cast'

7. Penelope with Lady Caroline Paget, who played Tulip, Princess Dahomey

8. and 9. *Treason's Bargain*: John was once more a clergyman, Cecil Beaton this time a dowager, and Lord Berners made his début as king

WELL - KNOWNS FANCY - DRESSED
FOR A PRIVATE FILM AND A PREMIÈRE.

10. Father Harton, John's confessor, whom he both liked and mocked

11. Adrian Bishop, a raffish figure who later became a monk

12. Evelyn Waugh, who after Penelope's conversion in 1948, tried to bully John into becoming a Roman Catholic too

13. Osbert Lancaster, a friend from Oxford days

14. John in 1934 with Marcelle Rothe, who later married Peter Quennell

15. John holding his bear Archibald Ormsby-Gore

16. T.S. Eliot, painted by Sir Gerald Kelly. John's former schoolmaster tried to procure his poems for Faber, but was pipped at the post by Jock Murray

17. Stuart Piggott, the young archaeologist who helped John out when the Prime Minister of Nepal came to tea

18. Faringdon House, the home of John's friend Lord Berners. Berners was the inspiration for Nancy Mitford's Lord Merlin

19. Tea at Faringdon. *Left to right*: Diana Heber Percy ('Bubbles'), sister-in-law of Robert Heber Percy, Moti, Penelope, Robert Heber Percy and Lord Berners

20. Lord Berners with Gertrude
Stein, whom John entertained at
Uffington

21. The opening of the Faringdon
Picture Theatre in 1935: John sits
in the back row with Penelope to
his right; in the front row Lord
Berners 'exchanges a joke' with
Mrs MacDougal; to his left is the
film star Stewart Rome

22. Jack Beddington, 'Beddioleman', by Rex Whistler. He was Shell's publicity manager at the time of the Shell Guides to English counties, edited (and in some cases written) by John

23. The title-page of John's *Shell Guide* to *Devon* (1936)

24. Field-Marshal Sir Philip (later Lord) Chetwode with his grandson Paul Betjeman

25. Penelope with Paul, his nanny Betty Evans (now Packford) and Snowdrop the goat

26. Myrna Loy. When John was film critic of the *Evening Standard* he had to interview her. 'Do you mind if I say you like English Perpendicular?' he asked. 'It's fine by me, honey.'

27. The film director Dallas Bower, whom John met when on the *Standard*, and later at the Ministry of Information and in Ireland

28. Captain H.M. Raleigh, the novelist, chairs a meeting in Uffington Village Hall. John can be seen near the centre, at the back

29. Moti in the Carnival. Ken Freeman is the small boy next to the black–faced rider. He went as a Belisha beacon. The 30 m.p.h. limit had just come in

30. John Piper by Osbert Lancaster

31. Myfanwy Piper. She was a muse of John's; he put her in two poems and nicknamed her 'Goldilegs'

32. E. McKnight Kauffer's surreal design for the jacket of *Continual Dew*

33. From *Continual Dew*, the page design by Osbert Lancaster for 'Our Padre'

34. Miss Joan Hunter Dunn

35. Sidney Gilliat (at the typewriter). When John was at the Ministry of Information, he commissioned films from Gilliat

John also asked Gilliat to write the script for a short film about blackout precautions, called *Mr Proudfoot Shows a Light*. John's letters to him, which Gilliat kept, give an insight into the nature of John's work at the MoI. Most of them were addressed to Gilliat at his house in Hilcott, near Marlborough. John knew that district from his schooldays, and in the letters mentions several of the local villages and their churches. The first letter, of 8 November 1940, shows the tact he could deploy when he had unwelcome news to break.

Dear Author,

I am very, very depressed to tell you that the black-out subject has shifted its focal point from night to early morning, and the Ministry of Home Security yesterday told us that they wanted a film on black-out in the early morning, which is quite another thing, and I do not see that your present excellent script can possibly be adapted to this. I feel criminal myself in having caused you – one of our best script writers – to waste your time, but believe me this was unwitting and but another example of that collaboration between Government Departments!!

I will not ask you, after this reverse, to think out another story on black-out in the early morning, but I would very much like to know how you are getting on with that Empire script.[83]

Gilliat thought that resetting the blackout film in the early morning was 'a silly idea'. The script he had submitted to John was about an evening billiards game – 'and of course you couldn't re-jig it to have a billiards game going on at seven o'clock in the morning; it would have meant an entirely new script'.[84]

John wrote Gilliat very businesslike letters about payment for films, but sweetened them with touches of whimsy. On 5 December 1940:

Dear Author,

Here's a pretty mess. Minnie is now mad keen to make your blackout script. D & P [Denham and Pinewood Studios] have budgeted for £1300: this is double at least what we have been paying for other five-minute films. Therefore, we must wash out D & P.

Can you answer us these questions, from the leafy lanes of Wilts.: go into that nice Norm. Interior at Manningford Bruce (or is it Bohun?) and think, and then let me have the answers.

(1) How much do you envisage it costing?
(2) Would it be possible for a promising young man at G.B. [Gaumont British] to direct it under Carole [*sic*] Reed in between the big moments of the feature films?

(3) If the answer to (2) is 'No', have you a director in mind for it who has sensibility, humour and skill enough to make it at a nice dim little studio with Butcher's? We have found that a director–producer can do so well with Butcher's that it might easily be the G.P.O. Film Unit.

(4) How would you like to direct it yourself? And if so, where?

My dear fellow, I am a bore – but it's all for the Mother Country.
    Yours,
        John Betjeman[85]

When, in December 1940, Gilliat suggested that a pool of script-writers should be formed, John poured cold water on the idea. Most war topics, he told him, were best dealt with as on-the-spot documentary, not in a studio. Only about one film in four was a studio subject *in toto*. 'Therefore, it would be raising false hopes in the breasts of many first-class screen writers to suggest that we could give them much work. Also, how are we going to prevent the duds getting in, if we are going to take any official action?'[86] This letter struck a raw nerve with Gilliat, who already felt the documentarians were being over-favoured. He wrote a forceful reply, which drew from John a placatory letter, with Christmassy illustrations, on 20 December.

John was still in a conciliatory mood when he wrote to Gilliat again ten days later. 'Are you feeling OK about it all? If in any way offended, sore, angry, hurt, diddled, please write to me & quote reference number above [F/149/66].'[87] Changing the subject, he added: 'I have fallen in love with a girl in the catering department here who is a doctor's daughter from Aldershot. She was lacrosse captain & tennis champion at Queen Anne's Caversham.'[88]

The girl in the catering department was Miss Joan Hunter Dunn, the subject of John's best-known poem, 'A Subaltern's Love-song' –

> Miss J. Hunter Dunn, Miss J. Hunter Dunn,
> Furnish'd and burnish'd by Aldershot sun,
> What strenuous singles we played after tea,
> We in the tournament – you against me!
>
> Love–thirty, love–forty, oh! weakness of joy,
> The speed of a swallow, the grace of a boy,
> With carefullest carelessness, gaily you won,
> I am weak from your loveliness, Joan Hunter Dunn . . .

In a radio programme of 1976, John remembered how he had first encountered Joan Hunter Dunn. 'I was walking down a corridor at the

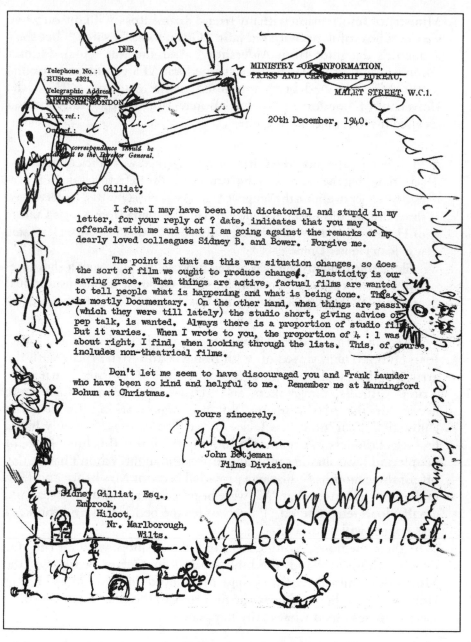

Telephone No.:
EUSton 4321.
Telegraphic Address:
"MINIFORM, LONDON"

Your ref.:

Our ref.:

All correspondence should be addressed to the Director General.

MINISTRY OF INFORMATION,
PRESS AND CENSORSHIP BUREAU,

MALET STREET, W.C.1.

20th December, 1940.

Dear Gilliat,

I fear I may have been both dictatorial and stupid in my letter, for your reply of ? date, indicates that you may be offended with me and that I am going against the remarks of my dearly loved colleagues Sidney B. and Bower. Forgive me.

The point is that as this war situation changes, so does the sort of film we ought to produce change. Elasticity is our saving grace. When things are active, factual films are wanted to tell people what is happening and what is being done. This is mostly Documentary. On the other hand, when things are passive (which they were till lately) the studio short, giving advice or pep talk, is wanted. Always there is a proportion of studio film. But it varies. When I wrote to you, the proportion of 4 : 1 was about right, I find, when looking through the lists. This, of course, includes non-theatrical films.

Don't let me seem to have discouraged you and Frank Launder who have been so kind and helpful to me. Remember me at Manningford Bohun at Christmas.

Yours sincerely,

John Betjeman
Films Division.

Sidney Gilliat, Esq.,
Embrook,
Hilcot,
Nr. Marlborough,
Wilts.

A Merry Christmas
Noel: Noel: Noel.

A letter that John sent to the film-maker Sidney Gilliat from the Ministry of Information on 20 December 1940

Ministry of Information with my friend Reggie Ross Williamson when
we saw a beautiful girl with red hair. "Gosh, look!" I said, "I bet she's
a doctor's daughter from Aldershot." And she was.' Joan Hunter
Dunn was not, as Dallas Bower assumed, an ATS volunteer seconded
to the MoI. She had been appointed to the catering staff of the
University of London by Michael Bonavia before the war. Bonavia
recalled his first meeting with her.

Mrs [Winifred] Bruce, the Catering Manageress, was efficient and conscientious, but the increase in the turnover of the Refectories made it necessary for her to obtain the support of an Assistant. One day, I interviewed
three girls for this position. One girl had a diploma from King's College
of Household and Social Science, and had a vivid personality. Her name
was Joan Hunter Dunn.

She seemed slightly amused by the proceedings and wore a short eye-
veil. I asked her, rather pompously, what she knew about institutional
catering. 'Nothing at all,' she replied, and laughed. She got the job.[89]

When war came, and the University moved out of the Senate House,
Joan Hunter Dunn stayed on with Bonavia and Mrs Bruce. With the
arrival of the MoI and the constant stream of visiting journalists,
writers, officers, film-makers and artists, life became much more
hectic for the two women. 'When I was working for London
University,' Joan (now Mrs Jackson) recalled in 1995, 'we only had a
few select dinners to organize. Suddenly there was this huge surge of
people and I was on duty morning, noon and night. I didn't have a day
off for three months.'[90] Bonavia provided beds for Mrs Bruce and Joan
in the Senate House cellar. 'We were bombed every night for a year and
a half,' Joan remembered. 'I'd get under the bedclothes and think, "I
just hope it will be quick."'[91]

In their memoirs, Lord Clark and the fashion writer Ernestine
Carter (whose husband, the bibliophile John Carter, worked at the
MoI) both claimed that they had introduced John to Joan Hunter
Dunn and that they had been the first to read the celebrated poem. In
1995 Joan described what really happened.

Michael Bonavia summoned me into his room. 'I've got someone here who
would like to meet you,' he said. Inside was John Betjeman, who went
down on his knees. I just burst out laughing. My first impression was one
of extreme humour. I thought anybody who got down on his knees to say
'How d'ye do' to me must be mad. He asked Mr Bonavia if he could take
me out to lunch. 'Certainly,' he said.[92]

In a *Sunday Times* interview of 1965 she told what happened next.

In the taxi on the way to the restaurant he put a copy of *Horizon* magazine into my hand and said, 'I hope you don't mind, but I've written a poem about you.' I must say I was absolutely overwhelmed. It was such a marvellous break from the monotony of the war. It really was remarkable the way he imagined it all. Actually, all that about the subaltern, and the engagement is sheer fantasy, but my life was very like the poem.[93]

John told the same interviewer: 'When I showed her the poem she told me she lived in Farnborough, Hampshire, but I considered that near enough Aldershot to count.'[94]

Joan married a MoI civil servant, H. Wycliffe Jackson, in January 1945.[95] John was invited but sent a telegram to say he was unable to attend. 'I never got to know John well at the Ministry,' Joan said, 'but when I did get to know him was in 1963, when my husband suddenly died, of a coronary, in Rhodesia. Our three sons were at school in England, one of them at Winchester, the two youngest at prep school. John wrote to me and was so, so kind. He took each of the boys out to lunch, separately, and helped to make arrangements for the rest of their education.'[96] In the *Sunday Times* article two years later, John recalled Joan in the war. 'When the bombs fell she bound up our wounds unperturbed. She was so marvellous at first-aid – I used to wish desperately for a small wound from a bomb so that she would minister to me.'[97]

OLD LIGHTS FOR NEW CHANCELS

He ought to be erected in Piccadilly Circus as a monument to the English middle classes. Eros is an obvious misfit. I'd open a subscription any day to buy Betjeman for the nation.

Geoffrey Grigson, letter to John G. Murray, 21 February 1940

In October 1939 John wrote to tell Jock Murray that John Miles, the publisher of *An Oxford University Chest*, wanted to publish twenty-two new poems of his. 'As you took the risk of publishing *Continual Dew*, I don't want to do anything without first getting your permission.'[1] Murray sent the no doubt hoped-for reply that he would like to publish the collection himself. On 20 October John wrote to him: 'The poems are being typed & when they are ready I will send them. A cheap, unillustrated edition like a Victorian hymn book would be nice.'[2] John sent the poems on 20 October, including the set of Irish lyrics that had been issued as a pamphlet printed by the *Mullingar Examiner* in 1938 as 'Sir John Piers', under the pseudonym 'Epsilon'.[3] Most of the new poems had never appeared in print.

If you do publish them [John wrote], I should like to write a short preface pointing out that they are not satirical. I had enough encouragement from reviews last time to do this, & it might save me from being reviewed by professional humorists. I would say some funny things about people's reactions to my verse, backed by quotations . . .

I have a feeling that 'The Heart of Thomas Hardy' is below standard, also 'A Drunk Scottish Nationalist Looks at Cleopatra's Needle' is pure parody & might do better elsewhere. [This was the parody of Hugh MacDiarmid that John had shown to Stuart Piggott.] I hope you will like them & not find them too indecent.[4]

In his reply Jock Murray agreed that the Thomas Hardy and Cleopatra's Needle poems were 'better away' and asked whether there were any others that could take their place. He added, 'We are going into ways and means and I shall write to you again in a day or two.' On the copy of this letter, Murray filed a memo in handwriting for himself and perhaps for other staff members of Murray's: 'The new collection has not, I think, quite so wide an appeal as *Continual Dew*.'[5]

With England now at war, there was no question of making the book a lavish production like *Continual Dew*. John understood that, but as usual was full of ideas for the book's 'physique' – 'As to production, I should like to see a small, chaste octavo printed very simply in exact imitation of William Pickering's books of the late [18]30s or of the Aldine Poets. Binding, dark blue cloth. Paper creamy brown. White label on spine. A sort of pocket book. No illustrations beyond a Pickering tailpiece at the end of the preface. Very wide margins. 8 or 6 pt Modern Face or Baskerville. But you may not want to publish them.'[6] His first suggestions for a title were 'The Negligent Incumbent' or 'Poems Amatory and Topographical'.[7]

On 1 November Jock Murray wrote to John that his firm would certainly like to publish the new volume, on the same terms as before. 'Your suggested style of production seems most apposite . . . As you suggest, we would use one or two of the designs from Pickering's publication.'[8] Murray, who once he had made a decision did not let the grass grow under his feet, enclosed with this letter a specimen page set in Plantin type. John replied on 2 November that, though he was delighted Murray would publish the book, he hated Plantin. 'Do you remember how they printed Robert Bridges's *New Poems*? The type there seemed absolutely right for poetry. Plantin is too heavy & looks like the Shropshire Lad.'[9] He enclosed a book of Henry Lyte's poems, which struck him as 'the ideal way of printing poetry'. He also thought the binding of the Lyte book 'very pretty': 'I would like this book bound in the serviceable school book manner. The cover of early copies of *North & Hillard* [Latin primers] comes to my mind.' As for poems to replace the two that had been discarded, 'Blackfriars' was about to appear in Cyril Connolly's new magazine *Horizon*, and John was writing a poem on 'Sunday Morning in Swindon' which he hoped to have ready in the next few days.

As before, Jock Murray showed himself ready to indulge John in almost all his whims. He said he would try to get the text nearer to that of the Lyte book, and offered one idea of his own: 'By the way, Pickering used on some of his books that most elegant chaplet of leaves and acorns. I think we might introduce that into the book somewhere.

What do you think?'[10] On 7 November John came up with a new notion: 'What would you say to a silhouette of me for a frontispiece? Cheap to reproduce & would look nice – wearing a smoking cap & by a Colza oil lamp with the signature underneath.'[11] Murray gave enthusiastic approval to this, too; on 20 November he wrote, 'I look forward to the silhouette with enormous curiosity!'[12] With the silhouette frontispiece, John was reinforcing the 'personality cult' that always meshed with his literary reputation. It was arranged that John Piper would draw the silhouette by projecting John's profile on a wall at Garrards Farm like a children's entertainer bunching his fist into a bunny-rabbit head for a shadow-pictures show. John wanted the words 'Frontispiece by John Piper' to go on the title-page (a further plume for his own reputation), but Piper refused as it was 'only a tracing'. He continued to refuse even when Murray telephoned to try to cajole him, on John's insistence.[13] But John did find a way of bringing Piper's name into the book, by dedicating it to him and Myfanwy in amusing dog-Latin, corrected by John Sparrow:

AD

M. ET J. PIPER

FELICES ET DULCES

APUD

VILLAM FAWLIENSEM PROFUNDAM

HENLEY

HIC LIBER

CUM

GRATIIS ET FIDELITATE*

On 11 November 1939 John wrote that he was delighted with the new specimen pages which Butler & Tanner of Frome had printed for Murray, basing them on the Lyte book.[14] On 23 November he suggested that the book's paper should have 'a faintly bluish tinge like an old-fashioned banker's draught [sic] or a letter from a firm of country solicitors'.[15] The title was still giving trouble. John was fecund with suggestions.

An Old Clergyman & Other Poems? There is no poem called An Old Clergyman, which would make it interesting. Or The Negligent Incumbent?* Or Sir John Piers or Topographical & Amatory Verses? or Nave & Chancel*? Or The Baptistery? Stained Glass Windows? Or Squint & Squinch? Decay? Damp Rot? Or Death Watch Beetles? Or Cemetery Gates? Or From Holloway to Mullingar? Or Holloway to Multifarnham?*

* To M. and J. Piper, happy and sweet, of Fawley Bottom House, Henley, this book with gratitude and fidelity.

Or Upper Holloway*? The Tortoise Stove*? Heating Apparatus? Oil &
Gas? or New Lights for Old Chancels? or Old Lights for New Chancels?**
Or By Southern Electric & Great Southern? The Parish Room**?

I favour those marked with a star. Perhaps you can think of others.
Second title should be Topographical & Amatory Verses . . .[16]

With this letter John enclosed his preface to the book. He also sent 'my
compliments & love to your wife, whom I have not yet seen'. Jock
Murray had just married Diana Ramsden James.

The preface was John's bid to throw off the irksome label of
'satirist' and to be recognized by the critics, if not as a serious poet, at
least as a sincere one. After sketching in his literary ancestry – Crabbe,
Clare, Hardy, Tennyson – he mounted a pugnacious self-defence.

I see no harm in trying to describe overbuilt Surrey in verse. But when I do
so I am not being satirical but topographical. No doubt many of the lines
of Tennyson I have quoted have been quoted by those who have other ideas
about poetry, as examples of bathos. The suburbs, thanks to *Punch* which
caters for them, are now considered 'funny'. Some people still think
Victorian industrial scenery is only fit for invective. Churches are always
'funny' unless they are written about by a devotional writer. Gaslight is
funny, Pont Street is funny, all sorts of places and things are funny if only
the funny writers are funny about them. I love suburbs and gaslights and
Pont Street and Gothic Revival churches and mineral railways, provincial
towns and Garden cities. They are, many of them, part of my background. From them I try to create an atmosphere which will be remembered by those who have had a similar background, when England is all
council houses and trunk roads and steel and glass factory blocks in the
New Europe of after the War.[17]

This was disingenuous: clearly John intended to poke fun at, for
example, Pont Street (also satirized by Osbert Lancaster as 'Pont
Street Dutch'). But in the closing words of the preface, John begged:

my old Esperanto friend whose disgust I aroused with my last volume [the
schoolmaster who had reviewed *Continual Dew* in *The Draconian*] to
accept that though this may be 'minor' poetry, its author is
　his *sincerely*,
　　JOHN BETJEMAN

Jock Murray told John that he found the preface 'most moving': 'It is
a most important addition to the book and, therefore, there are no complaints to make about its length! I am rather uncertain about the unwis-
dom of using caps and smaller caps for the names. However, unless you

send immediate instructions to the contrary they shall go into the proof
and you will see what they are like.'[18] John got his way over this. At the
time, the convention of putting names in capitals was preserved in
Times leaders; by adopting it, John may have hoped to give more of an
ex cathedra air to the preface. But though Murray was still humouring
John – he had even agreed that one of the poems could appear in Welsh
translation opposite the English original – he could not resist adding: 'I
am just wondering how far the joke under your silhouette is quite in
keeping with your introduction. However, we can think that out in a
quiet hour.'[19] What the joke was is not clear, but it must have been pretty
extreme, considering the toned-down version John proposed in a letter
of 26 November 1939: 'I feel that if we just put "Apollo" under the silhouette & excise "Betjeman" from the signature, the difficulty will then
be met. Those who know me will understand, those who don't may
think it is Apollo.'[20] That was how the silhouette eventually appeared.

Murray had asked John to summarize the book in a 'blurb' of one
hundred words. John wrote:

Mr Betjeman's verse arouses either dislike and contempt or else admiration. In this volume he includes two satires and other poems devoted to
topographical subjects such as London, Bristol, Shropshire, Berkshire,
Ireland, Oxford, Cheltenham, Cornwall, Surrey. For the first time he
comes into the open with a preface explaining what he is doing in poetry
and a plea to be taken not purely as a satirist and humorist.[21]

However, John suggested to Murray that instead of using this blurb,
he should print on the jacket a few extracts from the more favourable
reviews of *Continual Dew*, including Waugh's and Quennell's. With
some relief, Murray agreed to that plan.

John had left it up to Murray what to call the book. The publisher chose *Old Lights for New Chancels*. In early December John was still uneasy about this title, which he thought 'a bit of a mouthful'. He was pressing again for 'The Negligent Incumbent'. He added: 'Perhaps "Old Lights for New Chancels" is rather nice, but "Old Lights for Restored Chancels" would be more true.'[22] He returned to the subject a month later: 'The title page is a great improvement but I honestly do not like the title. I would much prefer "Cheltenham & Clifton" or merely the sub-title. I feel the present title is too humorous and cancels out my preface. I hope that it is not too late to alter it . . . "First Edition" is a bit like counting your chickens before they are hatched . . .'[23]

Jock Murray replied that there was a great deal to be said for counting chickens before they were hatched. 'The title is a very different matter. Your suggestion of "Cheltenham and Clifton" is horrible, and to call the book by its sub-title is to put a weight against success. I do not really feel that "Old Lights for New Chancels" is any more contrary to your preface than is the frontispiece. One of the points of the book seems to me to be that humour and a serious purpose are not incompatible.'[24] John, who usually had such a feel for the popular pulse, was curiously uncertain of touch in his choices of titles. Here his genuine eccentricity skewed the composition. Murray's strong objection to 'Cheltenham and Clifton' was all the more forceful because of his normal compliance with John's wishes – it was as if a vicar swore. It would have been easy enough for him to tell John that it was now too late to make any changes; but with his usual scrupulousness he wrote, 'As a matter of fact, it would just be possible to change the title, though it is really rather late to do so in view of the fact that the book has already been subscribed in many parts of the country under its present title. Even though it is just possible, I hope you may make a final decision to let it stand. I happened to mention the problem to Osbert [Lancaster] , and he was in favour of keeping it, whatever weight his opinion may have in your mind. Whose opinion have you taken?'[25] He offered a concession: if John wished, a note could be published in the 'prelims' saying that the publisher was responsible for the title. A day later, Murray wrote again to John, to say that 'Hobby' (Christopher Hobhouse)[26] had been staying with him: 'He tells me to write and say that he is highly distressed at the idea of altering the title from "Old Lights for New Chancels".'[26] When Murray wanted something, he could be as obstinate as John.

John was still not convinced. He wrote on 14 December: 'Would A Three Decker Pulpit be a possible title? It has some meaning in this instance, but if you must stick to "New Lights &c" [*sic*], you must. The Pipers think it is a bit too funny. Old Osbert, on the other hand, must be taken into consideration. Has he read the verses? But don't let me put you to too much inconvenience. I do rather favour A Three Decker Pulpit, though. It's short & to the point & churchy.'[27] Two days later: 'All right, then, stick to this title, but what about "Box Pews"? Three deckers are very serious to me. Fountain pen running out . . .'[28] John deferred to Murray's judgement on the title, but he stuck to his guns over the word 'panters' in the poem 'Group Life: Letchworth' ('Wouldn't it be jolly now,/To take our Aertex panters off . . .?') – '"Panters" is OK. "Panters" an affectionate diminutive of "pants".'[29]

Meanwhile, the bibliophile John Carter, who had been at Eton with Jock Murray and was now the London representative of the American publisher Scribner's, was helping with the jacket design. He lent a rare Pickering book of 1844 in printed boards. 'Please don't let anybody breathe on the volume, whose pristine condition is infinitely precious.'[30] During this period Murray, who had joined the Royal Artillery, was often away on manoeuvres. On 23 January 1940 Sir John Murray wrote to John, 'I have opened yours to Jock as he is away in Oxford and you will be pleased that he has become a father and a daughter was born yesterday. Both Diana and the baby are doing very well.'[31] John wrote Jock a letter of congratulation. 'I hope the waiting was not agonizing and that your poor wife had only a few hours' hell. Propeller had three days of it & a Caesarian at the end. I hope the daughter will turn out as clever as Maria Edgeworth, as lovely as Jane & Anne Taylor [sic][33] . . . Was she born at Oxford? If so, where, and who was the doctor? Please let me know.'[32]

By February, Jock Murray was back in the office and sent out proof copies of Old Lights – to L.A.G. Strong, John Hayward, J.R. Ackerley of The Listener, William Plomer, John Sparrow, the President of Magdalen, Edmund Blunden and Geoffrey Grigson. Strong replied, 'The sample which I have looked at tells me I shall read it with great delight.'[33] Plomer answered in his beautiful handwriting that he was enjoying the poems very much indeed and was going to review them for The Listener.[34] Sparrow thought the poems 'quite the best collection he has yet published, and delightfully produced. They have cheered me a great deal during 36 hours' leave which I am now enjoying. They are trying – much against my will – to turn me into an officer . . . I hate Aldershot and was much happier in the ranks than I am among embryo second lieutenants.'[35]

The President of Magdalen, George Gordon, himself a poet and a former Professor of English Literature at Oxford, wrote: 'You shower favours on me. John Betjeman is a ONE. His verses are most attractive and have cheered me up a lot. I feel sometimes that I'm not getting *all* the points but I get enough for camaraderie.'[36] Murray passed on this comment to John. Edmund Blunden, whose poetry John had admired since his undergraduate days, and who was glowingly mentioned in the preface to *Old Lights*, wrote, 'The proof of the Aldine (and Wreath!) edition of Mr Betjeman's poems delights me and will help me through the remains of an unpoetical illness. He speaks of individual poets – all I can say is that *his* work will command future devotees by its particular emotion & detail. It is of the kind which makes the question of major and minor poets seem quite academic, at least while one reads and responds.'[37] Grigson, who was politically unsympathetic to John, and whose sharpened 'billhook' was always at the ready, replied as graciously as he knew how.

Thank you for the proof of Betjeman's new poems. They are some of the best he has done, I think, and I hope they go as well as they deserve to.

Originality isn't necessarily a virtue, but they are original and they are civilized and colloquial in a way that makes APH [A.P. Herbert] and the other light versifiers very light indeed. But that's because Betjeman's a true poet and a snob who knows all about snobbishness and because he's in love with the things he makes fun of and the things he celebrates. He ought to be erected in Piccadilly Circus as a monument to the English middle classes. Eros is an obvious misfit. I'd open a subscription any day to buy Betjeman for the nation.[38]

The book was published on 14 March 1940 – an ordinary edition at 5s and a special edition of only twenty-nine copies on blue-laid paper, 'outrageously bound and signed by the author' (Murray wrote to a friend) at 10s 6d. Murray had turned down John's last-minute suggestion that a band should be put round the dust-jacket reading 'NOT RECOMMENDED BY THE BOOK SOCIETY'; this, he told John, would be 'rather facetious in a way which might again bewilder your poor reader, who reads your introduction'.[39] On publication day Murray treated John to a celebration lunch, inviting several of his friends, including Father Harton. John later wrote:

Dear Jock,

It was most awfully nice of you to ask all those chaps to lunch. I *did* enjoy myself. It was very nice to see so many kind people. I was overwhelmed. As Father H said to me this evening about John Murray's, 'It's so nice to be dealing with *gents*.' He was thrilled by the intellectual life he saw at the lunch & when he went on to see John Piper at his exhibition, he could not see the pictures for the dazzle he was in from the lunch.

Your select edition arrived at the Woadery[40] this morning. Woad [Sir

Philip Chetwode] opened it by mistake. 'Hello, someone's sent me a present. A book of poems. How curious.' I said, 'Oh, I think that must be meant for me.' 'By Jove, yes.' Then he went up to tell Mrs Woad of the odd happening. He was very puzzled.

William Plomer has done me proud in the Listener. This kindness is too great. I cannot believe it & certainly do not deserve it . . .'[41]

Plomer's review said about John exactly what John wanted to hear: 'He still produces more or less violent reactions and gets called precious, snobbish, reactionary, bourgeois, anti-Christian, and so on and so forth. He naturally causes alarm by being clever, observant, and sometimes satirical, and it seems that to be good-humoured is to be mistaken by solemn persons for a fribble.'[42] Plomer, three years older than John, was perhaps the contemporary poet who had most in common with him, sharing his taste for Victoriana, sinister Gothicism ('The Dorking Thigh') and jokes. His D'Arcy Honeybunn, 'A rose-red sissy half as old as time' has passed into the dictionaries of quotations, with Peter Sellers's Balham, 'A rose-red city half as Golders Green'. A homosexual – what John would have called 'a hundred percenter' – Plomer found the 'Uranian' poets as diverting as did John; in his *Listener* review of *Old Lights* he made an 'in' joke about the then still living Dr E.E. Bradford, whose ludicrous paedophilic poems were a running joke between Stuart Piggott and John.

[John Betjeman] likes legends of the obscure and all that is *local* [Plomer wrote]; forgotten minor poets and bouncing sports girls, old men and children; and all the various, curious atmosphere of the backwaters and byways of England, with a church of some sort generally visible in the background. He will often take us into a church, and it is then perhaps that he runs the greatest risk of being misunderstood, for there is something playfully affectionate about his interest in the variations of Anglican architecture, furniture, ritual and worship. It cannot be said of him, as of Dr E.E. Bradford's Digby Neville:

> He found all wrong.
> He did not like the chancel screen.
> He thought the light was far too strong.
> He hated choral evensong.

His trenchant satires on those who use religion as a cloak for self-interest, and the sympathy that he is not ashamed to show for the unfortunate, make it plain that he is on the side of the angels . . .

Twenty years ago people who had accustomed themselves to conventional poeticisms and reach-me-down imagery were upset by the early poems of

T.S. Eliot and now a generation which is used to verse garnished with pylons and bombers and Arms for Spain and anti-Nazism and Hampstead surrealism will perhaps be shocked by a poet who alludes to pink may, laburnum, tinned peas, cigar ends, church bells, gym shoes, devilled whitebait, hockey girls, picnics, racing stables, and old City dining-rooms; a poet who, in a piece called 'Sudden Illness at the Bus-Stop', chooses to evoke a whole lifetime of genteel poverty in a university town. It would, however, be a cold and narrow mind that failed to be entertained at least by what may be called the music-hall aspect of Mr Betjeman's talent . . .[43]

John wrote to Plomer on 17 March 1940:

My dear fellow,
    It was most awfully good of you to have written so eloquently and kindly of my verse in dear poor Joe's[44] paper. I don't care what other criticism I get now. I know that the whole point of my writing is understood by someone for whom I have deep admiration . . .
    I still laugh when I see that bit of Dr Bradford – and what a choice bit. I hope the old boy sees it. He is just the man to subscribe to a press cutting agency. It is awfully good to have got him in quite seriously, as though he were as well known and respectable as Proust or Brooke or Eliot or Auden. What *will* people think? I hope they buy his books as a result. Digby Neville is in *The True Aristocracy*[45] isn't he? I have the whole set at home here. *The New Chivalry*[46] is the most outspoken.[47]

John can have been scarcely less happy with the review by 'Senex' of the *New Statesman*.

Historians and psychologists of a future age, picking their puzzled way through the present century, will find in Mr John Betjeman a curious problem. Here is a writer (they will note) who, during a period that has brought forth a superabundance of bad poetry, is content to produce exceedingly accomplished verse and enters the Muses' shrine as it were by the back-door, whither he has gone under a pretence that he admires the plumbing. Unlike most contemporaries he has not forgotten that verse should be readable. His productions always benefit by being read aloud: and in that respect he might be compared to William [*sic*] Mackworth Praed – he has the same wit, the same versatility, the same rhythmical readiness – were the subjects he chooses and the colouring he gives them less idiosyncratic. By severe critics he has been accused of preciosity. It is true that he shares some of his chief foibles with amateurs of the amusingly second-rate: but what in Mr Betjeman looks like dilettantism turns out to be something far more interesting – a real passion, a kind of lucid

monomania. Is it a clue to his temperament to say that he is in love with
the past, and that the suburban landscape which is for many of us the
background of childhood – the bright smelly shops, oozing railway arches
and dusty privet hedges – has a romantic quality that he has never quite
outgrown? Childhood associations abound in his verse, either conveyed
directly, as in *Trebetherick* – one of his most successful metrical experiments – or imaginatively, as in the first of the three *Amatory Poems*, with
its memorable evocation of the black-stockinged bicyclist tinkling her way
home towards school-room tea . . . *Myfanwy* – Beatrice to Mr Betjeman's
Dante – supplies the starting point of yet another journey in pursuit of the
past – this time to the dim paradise of Oxford women's colleges, cocoa
parties, reading circles and girlish enthusiasms . . .[48]

'Senex' noted that nostalgia – 'the love-hatred of a born Romantic' – was an important element in John's style; but this reviewer
thought that 'when he merely satirizes (as he does in *Bristol and
Clifton* and *In Westminster Abbey*) his verse loses much of its interest
and half its pungency'. He added:

> Except by quotation (which is itself a poor substitute for recitation) one
> finds it hard to illustrate the qualities of this remarkable book. One can
> only recommend that every reader who appreciates verse (which may or
> may not include poetry – *Upper Lambourne* undoubtedly crosses the
> border-line) should take *Old Lights for New Chancels* to bed with him
> several nights running. Whatever his immediate response may be – whether
> he is shocked or amused or mildly diverted – and whatever his taste in
> Anglo-Catholic architecture, Nonconformist places of worship, braw
> games-playing, biking, hiking school-girls, decrepit Irish peers and Surrey
> tennis courts, certain phrases and certain rhythms will stick in his memory
> till little by little an entire poem has been got by heart and he has begun to
> regard the world with a slightly different and a more romantic eye. Not all
> Mr Betjeman's exercises in neo-romanticism reach the same level of tech-
> nical accomplishment – there are one or two weak lines and some poor
> concluding stanzas; but his new book is a decided advance on *Continual
> Dew*, while his range of interests is becoming gradually more extensive. It
> is to be hoped, however, that his devotional preoccupations (which it would
> be irreverent to regard as yet another engaging oddity) are not permitted to
> dilute or adulterate his poetic style. Those occasional delicate suggestions
> of a pensive lubricity and just-audible invocations to the rebellious flesh
> could not be purged without real damage to the poet's character.[49]

Goronwy Rees, a friend of the Betjemans, reviewed the book for
The Spectator. 'Mr Betjeman is both a traditionalist and an innova-

tor,' he wrote, 'one of the most original poets now writing. His originality springs most of all from the ambivalence of his feelings towards the subject matter of his poetry . . . The trouble is that Mr Betjeman writes for an extremely sophisticated audience, which cannot really believe that his passion for Butterfield, for Myfanwy, for the "Anglo-Jackson shade" is serious, above all that his religious ecstasy is serious; and this lack of trust in turn affects Mr Betjeman, who becomes even more devious in his devious approach to the heart. This is by no means unfortunate; for no doubt his extreme technical felicity, both old-fashioned and experimental, is the fruit of his effort to make his experience palatable and credible to himself and to others.'[50] He thought that 'Mr Betjeman, if not quite a saint, is certainly a mystic.' Of the three religious poems in the book, he considered two were failures, but the third, 'Olney Hymns', seemed to him 'a genuine expression of the calm which comes of religious conflict resolved'.

> It must be added [Rees ended his review] that if Mr Betjeman is one of the most original of modern poets, he is also, in his mock-innocent way, one of the most perverted.
>
> > Kind o'er the *kinderbank* leans my Myfanwy
> > White o'er the play pen the sheen of her dress,
> > Fresh from the bathroom and soft in the nursery
> > Soap-scented fingers I long to caress.
>
> Is it an accident, given their common architectural tastes, that in his amatory exercises Mr Betjeman sometimes strangely reminds one of Ruskin?[51]

Andrew Wordsworth, who reviewed *Old Lights* for *Time and Tide*, had been at Marlborough with John – a son of the Bishop of Salisbury and a younger brother of Matthew Wordsworth with whom John ran *The Heretick* magazine. (He had gone on to teach at Westminster School with John Edward Bowle.) He made use of his inside knowledge in the review.

> When I was fourteen I thought school slang silly. Then I went to tea with John Betjeman and heard him use as much as possible but in inverted commas. It was the revealing light. Keats left Leigh Hunt 'Brimfull of the happiness Which in a little cottage he had found'. I left Betjeman's *bin* converted. The world of school could never again be dismissed as something you tried to avoid because its values were not of the aesthete and the intellectual. You were in it. *Barnes, tolly, oiler, bolly* – these were no longer the

words of Marlburians with false values; they were your own words, words by which the extraordinary business of being at a public school could be made fun of, yes, but also understood and controlled.

Betjeman has always chosen to live in the background in which he was brought up. Not for him the Waste Land, the Proletariat or the Tower, but the actual geographical world of his own life, the actual world sweating only in sports and in bed, of that slice of the middle-class he has lived through. He loves it and hates it all and knows all its slang, using it to control it, and, because he is a genius, to preserve it for ever in poetry of obsessional power.[52]

In March 1940 the *Times Literary Supplement* added its carefully measured encomium to the other tributes.

Because he has a definite aim and definite interests, and has limited himself to these, his verse, if minor, is not so through failing to be major. It is perfected achievement in its kind.[53]

13

IRELAND

It says much for the British Civil Service that, in an hour of grave peril for the nation, it has actually been able to find something for John Betjeman to do.

(Sir) Norman Costar, conversation with Dr Nicholas Mansergh, 1941

I think I was a spy.

John Betjeman, in conversation with Frank Delaney, 1982

On 24 January 1941 John's mother wrote to Philip Asprey: 'John and family go to Dublin next week, he has been transferred from the MoI to the Embassy there, a very lucrative post. I do hope the Huns don't invade Ireland.'[1] The British did not in fact have an embassy in Dublin; because of the ambiguous relationship between southern Ireland and Great Britain, the senior British diplomat in Dublin, Sir John Maffey, had the title 'United Kingdom Representative in Eire'.[2] John was to be his press attaché. Writing to Gerard Irvine on 27 January to give him his office address in Dublin, John added: 'I am very sad to be going.' He signed the letter 'Seán O'Betjemán'.[3]

Penelope was no better pleased. Having witnessed her mother's wearisome routine of entertaining at Aldershot and in India, she had sworn she would not marry anybody in the services. In marrying John she 'little thought that he would become a sort of bogus diplomat'.[4] Uprooting themselves from Uffington and finding a suitable home in Dublin was an ordeal. Penelope recalled:

We were given the names and address of two old maids, the Misses Hamilton, who had a house on the outskirts of Dublin – *just* country[5] – and took PGs [paying guests]: we could PG there until we owned a house. One of the sisters, Eva Hamilton, was rather a good watercolour painter. Oddly enough, my mother had had me painted by her in a Japanese dressing-gown when I was six. I'd forgotten her existence. The other sister was a market gardener. There would be great excitement because you'd find a heap of strawberries in the kitchen and think they were for supper: not at all, they were all taken to the market and sold.[6]

John went over on his own first. It was a cold, damp Irish winter, and the Misses Hamilton had only a small peat fire. 'John was so cold on one occasion', Penelope said, 'that he sat on the fire and I was furious because he had a new pair of trousers on and I had to do some invisible darns.'[7] She was not impressed by the ménage when she arrived. 'We had absolutely filthy food and never quite enough of it. Once, when some people came to dinner at the last minute, the cook Mary "stretched" the soup – held the tureen under a hot water tap and put a bit more pepper in.'[8] The Betjemans and Betty Evans, the nanny, stayed with the Hamiltons for three months. All that time, Penelope was looking for a house in Dun Laoghaire, Blackrock and Killiney – seaside suburbs of Dublin – but found nothing she liked. Then at a party she and John met Billy Kirkwood and his wife Peta, who was of the Jameson Whiskey family. 'They knew I was mad on horses,' Penelope recalled, 'so they said, "Why don't you have Collinstown? We're going to live in our other house outside Dublin, and we want to have Collinstown aired. You can have it on a caretakers' arrangement at £10 a month." There was no polo in the war so all the eleven polo ponies were turned out there and I was allowed to ride any I wanted. The house was beautiful, but in terrible condition and very damp.'[9] Collinstown was at Clondalkin, near Dublin, and next to an aerodrome – one of the first places the Germans would have overrun if they had invaded.

A further hazard of life at Collinstown was the Kirkwoods' maid, whom John called 'Mad Peg'.

She was completely dotty [Penelope recalled]. She had her hair down to her waist and, although she was fifty-one, she always referred to herself as a girl. We had an awful old Aga which didn't work very well. We were having a diplomatic lunch party one day and I came down and found her in prayer in front of the Aga because it had gone out.

Another day she went to church – John and I used to take it in turn to drive her to Mass, John would go one week, I'd go the next; one of us had to stay with Paul. John always liked his breakfast ready on the table when he came back, so when he took Mad Peg to church I would cook the breakfast. Well, on this particular occasion, Mad Peg had left the larder (the 'press', as they call a cupboard in Ireland) locked and I couldn't find the key anywhere to get at the bacon and eggs. So John came back and there was no breakfast ready. I was very cross with Mad Peg, but she said, 'You can't blame me: didn't the key get twisted in me glove?'[10]

The post of British press attaché in neutral Ireland was one of great sensitivity. Henry Maxwell, John's Ministry of Information colleague, heard that he was sent out on the suggestion of Brendan Bracken, whom Churchill had made Minister of Information. 'It was felt', Maxwell said, 'that the German Minister in Dublin, Eduard Hempel, was making much too good an impression on Eamon de Valera, the Irish leader; and that it would be a good idea to send out somebody of charm and wit to keep de Valera sweet, and the Irish press and public opinion sweet. And it worked: once John was out there, reports came in of improved Anglo-Irish relations.'[11]

Bracken may have had a hand in John's appointment; but the person most directly concerned with it was the head of the MoI's Empire Division, Harry Hodson, a fellow of All Souls[12] and a future editor of the *Sunday Times*.[13] Hodson thought John was 'the sort of chap who could get on with the Irish'.[14] It was not only his charm that qualified him; there were also his varied experience of Ireland over more than ten years, and the good contacts he had made while staying with Billy Clonmore, Pierce Synnott and the Longfords.[15] He had even had a taste of Northern Ireland while at Clandeboye.[16] And he was a poet, coming to a land where poets were more honoured than in his own.

Hodson thought highly of the report John had written after being sent on a preliminary visit to Ireland in 1940. It revealed that he had 'a keen sense of the situation there for propaganda'.[17] His report noted that the Irish Republican Army was immune to propaganda; that the Irish people would warm to Britain only if Partition were settled; that Britain should support de Valera because he was widely backed among the Irish and that the British press should choose its propaganda subjects carefully – no discussion of a possible German invasion of Eire, for example, and, above all, no criticism of Irish personalities.[18]

In early December 1940, Penelope Aitken, Sir John Maffey's daughter, wrote to her father after a visit to the MoI: 'I met John Betjeman, who is arriving over as your Press Attaché. I think he should be very good . . . The couple have a big reputation here, both rather eccentric and intellectual . . . He should be the sort of whimsical person the Irish will like and he likes them.'[19] Years later, John told Penelope Aitken that when she had come into the room that day he had thought her so beautiful that he went weak at the knees.[20]

John was made welcome at the Representative's office in Upper Mount Street, Dublin. He painted his third-floor room 'boudoir pink'[21] and hung it with Piper paintings of bombed London churches[22] – a political, as well as aesthetic, statement. The building stood in a Belgravia-like area where polished brass plates marked the offices of the Hospitals Commission, the Carnegie Foundation and the Fianna Fáil Party's headquarters. Outside No. 50, the office of the United Kingdom Representative, a policeman stood guard and CD-plated cars usually crowded the kerb.[23] Inside, Sir John Maffey sat behind a large desk, his Labrador beside him.[24] Maffey had been brought out of retirement to take up the Dublin post. He had been a most effective Governor-General of the Sudan; before that, as Chief Commissioner in Peshawar, he had won renown by freeing an English lady, Miss Mollie Ellis, from captivity by a gang of Afridis. At six foot four he was even taller than de Valera, the 'Long Fellow', and he towered above John.[25] The Dutch journalist Kees van Hoek described him in a book of 1943, *Diplomats in Dublin*:

> In his middle sixties, he is a miracle of youthful virility. Dressed in an impeccable dark, chalk-striped suit with a butterfly tie round his high collar, he is the archetype of the high Whitehall official . . . His full crop of grey hair, sprucely combed, would do credit to Toscanini . . . Clean-shaven, with a long, strong nose, a tight-lipped mouth, sparkling eyes underneath the straight line of his full eyebrows, he looks . . . like a friendly family lawyer, or could be, in the appropriate garb, a most dignified but likable Prince of the Church . . . Seldom has a more determined character hidden under so much charm of speech and manner.[26]

A colleague remembered Maffey's 'going out rather splendidly to bat on College Green. He did a half-day's work as a rule; on the other hand, he seemed to me to do what he did very well.' Maffey also had the quality essential in anybody for whom John worked: a developed sense of humour. He was himself a wit. When Hitler committed suicide in 1945, and de Valera, pedantically true to the letter of his policy, called on the German Minister to offer condolences, Maffey described the gesture as 'an act of conspicuous neutrality in the field'.

Maffey briefed John on the other diplomats in Dublin; and gradually he got to know them. The German Minister Plenipotentiary, Eduard Hempel, was a conservative career diplomat. He had been a cavalry officer in the Saxon Guards and was wounded in the First World War.[27] It interested John that Hempel's family had bought the house of John Addington Symonds's widow in Davos.[28] Hempel was married to an exceptionally beautiful woman[29] and they had three children who in 1941 ranged in age between six and ten. Kees van Hoek noted that a portrait of Hindenburg, not Hitler, hung behind Hempel's desk in Dublin, adding:

> Squarely built, Herr Hempel has a strongly hewn face, greying hair around the massive dome of his head, dark eyebrows round his stern eyes.

His urbanity is not of the effervescent type. Correct diplomat to the manner born, he can unbend with a winning quiet charm.[30]

He could also get very tetchy. In 1937, when a dockers' strike had delayed the delivery of his furniture, he had seriously suggested to the Minister of External Affairs, Joseph Walshe, that he should 'bring in the army to see to it'.[31] Hempel was not a Party man, but his First Secretary, Henning Thomsen, was regarded as a 'strutting Nazi'.[32] John was amused that his own opposite number, the German Press Attaché Karl Petersen, had the same name (though differently spelt) as the arch-villain of the Bulldog Drummond stories by 'Sapper'. Petersen was causing difficulties for Hempel by his drunken indiscretions.[33] There was some fraternizing between the British and Germans – 'The German diplomats used to come to Maffey's parties and vice-versa,' said Ruth-Ellen Moller, a granddaughter of the novelist Erskine Childers.[34] But John was asked not to fraternize with Petersen, 'because then Sir John wouldn't be able to cut him dead in the street'.[35]

The American Minister, David Gray, was in his seventies. He had a reputation as 'a testy old gentleman'. His father had edited the *Buffalo Courier* and he himself had been a journalist on the *New York Sunday World*.[36] His wife was Eleanor Roosevelt's aunt.[37] As a young man, the Nuncio Apostolic, Paschal Robinson, had been a friend of Mark Twain, while working on the *North American Review*;[38] and he had reported the Parnell case, in London.[39] Poland still had a consul-general in Dublin, W.M. Dobrzynski, whose surname John was to borrow in a satirical poem of the later 1940s.[40] The Japanese Consul, Setsuya Beppu, had served as an attaché in London in the 1920s.[41] In a letter of August 1941 to William Plomer, John described Beppu as 'a frightening little man, a kind of Eastern Strict Baptist, with a taste for sport'.[42] Beppu's Press Attaché, Mr Ishihashi (John called him 'Mr Itchy-Scratchy'),[43] went riding with Penelope until the attack on Pearl Harbor in December 1941, after which she was asked not to see him again.[44]

It was not the Germans and Japanese who gave Maffey and John most trouble. A delicate aspect of the two men's position was the poisoned relations between de Valera and Churchill. The two statesmen had disliked each other as young men; age had not mellowed them. Churchill remembered de Valera as a terrorist. De Valera was also the man who had done his best to scupper the 1922 treaty which Churchill, as Colonial Secretary, had signed with Michael Collins – the treaty which gave Ireland, not the home rule that de Valera wanted, but the status of a dominion. In Churchill's view, de Valera had 'broken the word of Ireland'.

What above all rankled with Churchill was that the three Irish ports which, under the 1922 treaty, were to be kept available for Britain's use in time of crisis, had been meekly ceded to de Valera by Neville Chamberlain's Government in 1938. Churchill regarded these ports – Queenstown (now Cobh), Berehaven and Lough Swilly – as 'sentinel towers'.[45] He protested in 1938 and warned that the ports might become 'nesting places for our enemies'. Throughout John's three years with Maffey, Churchill kept up a constant growl about the cession of the ports, with occasional threats that it might be necessary to seize them by force. These were the times when Maffey's calm diplomacy and John's wooing of the Irish press were most needed.

One day, while Maffey was talking to the Taoiseach, John doodled caricatures of de Valera on the back of an official document. It was a face of closed religion, with a clamped-shut, bigoted expression, a rigidity about the mouth. Too often it was a face 'unlighted by any smile'. John's friend Sean O'Faolain, who had fought alongside de Valera in the civil war, said he had 'a voice like a cracked or muffled bell, and an ordered restraint to his looks, as if all lusciousness had been pared away by bitter experience'.[46]

When Britain declared war on Germany in 1939, de Valera insisted that Ireland would be neutral. Many British people – Churchill among them – thought that Ireland's neutrality was craven. And as Maffey put it to de Valera in May 1940: 'Here is a maniacal force let loose in the world. It is not a time to talk of Anglo-Irish disputes . . .'[47] How long did de Valera imagine Ireland would remain free if Hitler conquered Britain? There were several other reasons for the Taoiseach's policy. Anti-British feeling was widespread in Eire. De Valera himself had been condemned to death by the British, and the Black and Tans' atrocities were not forgotten.[48] The propagandist commentary of a British Pathé film might suggest, with sublime euphemism, that 'Britain and Eire may not always have seen eye to eye in the past' and that 'today all that is forgotten in the common danger', but in fact old hatreds were not so easily obliterated. The novelist Elizabeth Bowen, in a secret report for the British Government in 1940, relayed a 'typical' Dublin comment: 'What right have the British to keep denouncing the Nazis? Haven't they been Nazis to us for centuries?'[49] Hempel reported back to Berlin a nationalist commonplace, 'England's difficulty is Ireland's opportunity.'[50]

In early 1941 when John took up his post, the Germans were winning. In 1940 Malcolm MacDonald, the British Dominions Secretary, had told London that de Valera 'was extremely gloomy about our prospects of winning the war . . . He was evidently very chary of throwing in his lot with us in these dark days . . .'[51] And

Kingsley Martin, editor of the *New Statesman*, who visited Dublin in
1941, later recalled:

> I was invited to spend the weekend with the British Representative
> [Maffey], now Lord Rugby, and also got to know John Betjeman, then
> Public Relations Officer in Dublin. Rugby took me out to dinner with a
> leading Irish politician. It was an embarrassing occasion, because I sat
> between two leading Dublin socialites, who took delight in scoring off a
> British radical. As a guest of the British Representative, I could not answer
> back. It was some time before I realized . . . that they were quite deliber-
> ately attempting to put themselves in the right with the Germans in case
> of a Nazi invasion. They wanted to be reported as being on the German
> side.[52]

De Valera warned Maffey that the country would be 'split from top
to bottom' if Eire were to enter the war. Herbert Shaw, a Protestant
and former southern Irish Unionist MP, thought that if de Valera
ceded the ports 'he might well be shot'. On 14 December 1941 de
Valera starkly stated the position: 'We can only be a friendly neutral . . . Our circumstances, our history, the incompleteness of our
national freedom through the partition of our country, make any
other policy impracticable.' Elizabeth Bowen, with her novelist's sensitivity, divined something more:

> This assertion of her neutrality [she wrote] is Eire's first *free* self-assertion:
> as such alone it would mean a great deal to her. Eire (and I think rightly)
> sees her neutrality as positive, not merely negative. She has invested her
> self-respect in it. It is typical of her intense and narrow view of herself that
> she cannot see that her attitude must appear to England an affair of blind-
> ness, egotism, escapism or sheer funk.[53]

Perhaps the most astute observation on the subject was made in
January 1940 by Frank Aiken, the Irish Minister for the Co-ordination
of Defensive Measures. 'In the modern total warfare [neutrality] is not
a condition of peace with both belligerents, but rather a condition of
limited warfare with both . . . In these dark days one of the most
important weapons of war is propaganda.'[54] Diplomatic niceties
could not dispel fear – German and Irish fears that Britain would seize
the treaty ports; British and Irish fears that Germany would invade
Eire. There was a characteristic grim wit in de Valera's comment on
these possibilities: 'First come, first served.'[55]

De Valera's position could not really be presented as heroic; but he
stuck to his lack of guns. He also knew that the majority of his

people wanted Britain to win; and Ireland's trade links with Britain
were important. He allowed Irish men and women to serve in the
British forces. If German airmen crash-landed in Ireland, they were
imprisoned. If British airmen came down – in Maffey's poetic phrase,
landing 'like exhausted birds on Irish shores'[56] – they were, when
possible, refuelled and allowed to leave. The Irish became more
co-operative after America entered the war and still more so after the
German capitulation at Stalingrad in February 1943. The German
Minister in Dublin was required to surrender the Legation's radio set
before D-Day.[57]

John's duties in Dublin were not confined to 'keeping sweet' de
Valera and the Irish press. He had also to send regular reports to
London. The reports went to the Dominions Office and to the
Ministry of Information. Dr Nicholas Mansergh, a young historian
who was later to be Master of St John's College, Cambridge, was
appointed by the MoI to be John's opposite number in London. He
was an Ascendancy Irishman. As a boy in Tipperary in 1919 he had
heard the shots ring out as two policemen were killed on the road to
the stone quarry at Soloheadbeg, just up the road from his home. This
was the act that opened the guerrilla fighting retrospectively known as
the Anglo-Irish War or the War of Independence.[58] He was educated
at St Columba's College, Dublin, the 'Eton of Ireland' ('just in time to
escape arms drill, because all the rifles had been seized by the IRA'),[59]
and read history at Oxford. He was taken into the MoI as 'a sort of
one-man Irish Office'.[60]

Before Mansergh could be appointed, his credentials had to be
cleared with the Ministry of External Affairs in Dublin. His writings
on Ireland were carefully examined, and he was invited to lunch three
times by Joseph Walshe, the Minister. ('I found that his main interest
at that time was to reconstitute the triple empire devised by
Charlemagne for his three sons in the year 800.')[61] Finally Walshe's
Ministry gave its approval, and John had 'what he had to have to be of
any use, a London link. He could then make representations from
Dublin, and the MoI and the Dominions Office could take action in
London, where the resources were.'[62]

The circle in which John moved in Dublin consisted mainly of Irish
Government ministers and civil servants, diplomats, Irish and visiting
British journalists and literary people. Sometimes he accompanied
Maffey to see de Valera; occasionally he was sent on his own as a 'mes-
senger boy'. John was virtually apolitical, the Irish leader steeped in
politics; yet perhaps the two men had more in common than either
would have acknowledged. Both had foreign names and forebears. (De
Valera, born in New York of a Spanish father, was once called 'the

Spanish onion in the Irish stew'.)[63] Each immersed himself in the culture of the land in which he grew up, and became a voice and a personification of that land's character.

If John paid attention during Maffey's encounters with de Valera, he may have picked up negotiating skills that would later be useful on Royal Commissions or committees. Lloyd George had said that negotiating with de Valera was 'like trying to pick up a blob of mercury with a fork'. De Valera had told his friend and chief press officer Frank Gallagher[64] the secret of negotiation: 'The greatest danger of all is reasonableness . . . Those who are anxious to be accommodating are lost.' It was said that if he could not get his own way he would do whatever he could to prevent anyone else getting theirs. Over the years he had refined the histrionics of hard bargaining – 'the shows of temper, the calculated hissing breathing through the nostrils . . . deliberate silences, the piercing accusatory glance . . .'

Maffey told John which of the Irish Government ministers he thought more or less friendly. He considered Seán MacEntee, Minister for Industry and Commerce and later Minister for Local Government and Health, 'a strong Anglophobe';[65] in spite of that, John sat with MacEntee in the front row of a concert and went on to drinks with the MacEntees at their home. Diplomacy is not the art of courting one's friends. In fact, John and Penelope became very friendly with the whole family. MacEntee's daughter Máire (now Mrs Conor Cruise O'Brien) recalls:

> Mr de Valera was his own foreign minister, but was not over-fond of entertaining diplomats and making small-talk, so he often delegated that task to my father. Both my parents absolutely loved the Betjemans. And – I was only a teenager – I think the Betjemans loved them, too. John wrote a very nice poem about my father's holiday house in Brittas Bay . . .[66]
>
> My father had been condemned to death by the British for his part in the Easter Rising of 1916 (he was released under the amnesty of 1917) – but I think he felt he had settled scores with them. He was emphatically *not* anti-British. He loved Shakespeare and Browning and wrote poetry in English himself.[67]

The MacEntees found both the Betjemans, 'in their different ways, marvellous company'.

> In those days being good company was far more important than it is now. People didn't have electronic entertainment – well, perhaps the odd radio set made out of cigar boxes. We got together to entertain each other. We sang after dinner and wrote extempore poems. As well as the Brittas Bay

verses, John wrote a poem about the Currans, an upmarket literary family, rather grand and rather precious –

Along the Dingle peninsula, the Dublin people go,
Some of them speaking the Gaelic and speaking it terrible slow;
Some of them wearing the Filleadh beag,* and some of them wearing
    the shawl;
But Con Curran's daughter Elizabeth is the most Gaelic of them all.

Con Curran – Constantine Peter Curran – was a friend of James Joyce, had been at University College, Dublin, with him in 1902. [Joyce died in the first month John was Press Attaché in Dublin, January 1941.] And Elizabeth Curran, Con's daughter, wrote articles on Irish art for Sean O'Faolain's magazine, *The Bell.*[68]

John's wit also helped to make him good company. 'What I like about the Church of Ireland', he told the MacEntees, 'is the Real Absence.'[69] On being introduced to Roger Chauviré, Professor of French at University College, Dublin, on a bathing expedition commemorated in a photograph, he insisted on talking appalling franglais, including the phrase 'Je pense ne.'[70] Máire MacEntee thought that he understood the Irish. 'His Irish poems are so full of instinctive sympathy for the gentle complexities of rural Irish society; and in most of them he is not, you notice, being satirical.'[71]

Máire accompanied her parents to a lunch the Betjemans held at Collinstown for Professor Joad, whom she thought a bore. Also of the party on that day was Mrs MacEntee's brother, Monsignor Patrick Browne, an extraordinary polymath. His Paris doctorate was in mathematics. He was interested in physics. But he had also translated Homer, Dante and Racine. 'He had a glorious singing voice,' Máire recalls. 'And he loved reciting poetry. You could start anywhere in Homer and he'd continue.'[72] He eventually became President of University College, Galway. Máire loved him: she and her brother Séamus had been partly brought up by him in his house at Dunquin, 'the most westerly house in Ireland', when their father was in jail or on the run. The Betjemans sometimes stayed there. 'John and my Uncle Paddy struck sparks off each other on religion,' Máire says. 'My uncle thought Anglicanism was the illiberal wing of the Church. He claimed that "What the French Church thinks today, the Church Universal thinks tomorrow." That annoyed John, and John would annoy my uncle back – but they were very fond of each other.'[73] Máire feels sure that conversations with Monsignor Browne were among the influences which led Penelope to Rome after the war. John and

* kilt

Penelope left Browne a bizarre souvenir. They decorated the dark walls of his study with large plasticine reliefs of scorpions and centipedes. 'They were all over the room,' Máire recalls. 'The house is now a ruin, but the reliefs are still there. My uncle wouldn't let them be removed. He said he liked the memory.'[74] Penelope, who struck Máire as 'a character out of an Angela Brazil schoolgirl novel', took her on a riding tour of the Wicklow Mountains. They stayed two nights at the house of Seán T. O'Kelly, the future President of Ireland, and his wife. Máire later wondered whether this was a planned 'cementing exercise', giving John access to people he wanted to cultivate, but decided it was just a gesture of friendship.[75]

Ruth-Ellen Moller has less happy memories of Penelope and horses. When John was in Dublin, her father, Erskine Childers (a son of the novelist of the same name shot by Michael Collins's faction in 1922), was secretary of the Federation of Irish Manufacturers, though he was soon to be one of de Valera's ministers and was another future President of Ireland. He and his American wife Ruth became friends of the Betjemans. One day, Penelope telephoned Childers and asked, 'Do your children ride?' Childers said they did. 'Well, send them over. I'd love to have an afternoon with them and they can do some riding with me.'

> I was twelve and my brother Erskine was ten [Ruth-Ellen Moller remembers]. We were at boarding school and we'd ride at school but we never hunted. We arrived at Collinstown – a Government car had picked us up – and John opened the door. He said, 'Wait a minute.' Then he called up the stairs, 'Penelope, your slaves for the ponies have arrived.' No answer; so he said, 'Propeller! Your slaves for the ponies are here.' Still no answer. He said, 'Dammit, I can't *stand* it,' and shouted, '*Filth!* The children are here to exercise your beastly ponies.' So Erskine and I just stood there in wonderment – wondering what was going to come down the stairs. Anyway, down she came and she took us by the hand and brought us out to the stables and put us on two ponies. John came out too and looked on rather bleakly, as if to say to Penelope, 'I hope you're going with them.' But she didn't come with us, we were on our own.
>
> We were not well up in various kinds of horses, so we had no idea we were on polo ponies – very dangerous to ride. She gave their rumps a good slap and off we went into the middle of yonder. And Erskine must either have put his knee into the pony's side or pulled on the rein – anyway, complete circle; he came down heavily, his head protected by his arm which broke in two places, the bones sticking out. I didn't know what to do. I thought he was going to die, he was absolutely unconscious and I thought, 'If I run to the house he'll be dead; I've got to stay here.' Eventually, some farm worker came across and carried Erskine back to the house. Penelope

paid little attention. She said, 'What a silly boy! I suppose the two of them will have to go to hospital.' But John was incredibly upset. And furious. Livid with Penelope for not going with us; furious with himself for not realizing what she was capable of. He drove us to the hospital – the nearest was near the main station – and stayed with us until my parents arrived. Erskine had a double compound fracture. He was never able to straighten his arm after that.[76]

Ruth-Ellen's parents often held parties at their house in Highfield Road, Dublin. She remembers one party at which John's diplomatic *savoir-faire* was urgently called upon.

The party was in honour of Udo Udoma,[77] the son of a Nigerian chief. He was very talented and had become president of the Philosophical Society of Trinity College, Dublin. I was allowed to stay up that night. After a while there was a hammering at the front door. My father said to John, 'I've got a horrible feeling this is going to be bad news' – because somebody had told him that Francis Macnamara, Dylan Thomas's father-in-law,[78] was going to gatecrash the party.

So John and my father – I was watching from the stairs – went to the door. My father was very tall and John wasn't; they couldn't stop Macnamara, he just burst in. My father said, 'Francis, you just have to behave yourself.' Macnamara was a *wild* man, much given to drink. So they went on back to the party. I crept back into the drawing-room. I had a feeling that something exciting was going to happen. When I went in, there wasn't a sign of Macnamara – I couldn't think where he had got to.

Udo Udoma was on the sofa beside my mother. Suddenly a huge hand came up from behind the sofa and grabbed his shoulder. Then a big head popped up and said, 'Hiya, nigger!' Deathly, horrified silence. My father tried to get hold of Macnamara but he couldn't. He dodged behind an armchair and said it again, even louder – 'HIYA, NIGGER!' Then he went back behind the sofa. John told my mother he would try to get him to leave but he came back and said he thought Macnamara had reached the 'incapable' stage. So my father, John and a well-known American war journalist, Raymond Gram Swing,[79] a very strong man, got hold of Macnamara, threw him out into the garden and locked the door. We were relieved and a little surprised that there was no further sound. The party progressed.

Because John's house was quite distant, he stayed the night with us. In the morning I heard him calling out to my father, 'Erskine! Erskine! You must get down here at once!' So my father rushed down in his dressing-gown – I was close behind, to see what the excitement was. I heard my father give an awful groan; and John was in hysterics. I went out on to the lawn. Cut into the turf was a huge swastika. In neutral Ireland! It was a terrible embarrassment. And Macnamara had just thrown the turf he removed over the fence into the next-door garden. So John and my father set to – scrambled over into the neighbours' garden to retrieve the turf and put it all back before breakfast.[80]

Various austerities, including petrol rationing, were forced on the Irish by British economic sanctions, intended to bring home to de Valera the consequences of neutrality. It was not officially admitted that the measures were punitive: the British Government, tongue in cheek, said they would be 'failing in their duty . . . if, while existing conditions continue, they did not give absolute priority to the urgent need of those engaged in the present war against aggression'. Petrol pumps ran dry and there were shortages of bread, coal, animal feeding stuffs, fertilizers, agricultural and other machinery, chemical and electrical goods, paper and cardboard. Maffey did not approve of the economic pressure; he was afraid that de Valera would tell his people that Britain was trying to coerce them into the war, or that sanctions were a preliminary towards more serious measures. Churchill, by contrast, wanted de Valera to be made fully aware that the sanctions were deliberate. When Lord Cranborne was planning to visit Dublin in February 1941 (in the event, the visit was postponed), Churchill ordered him not to leave 'a trail of courtesies, comforts and reassurances which ill consorts with the hard policy which it is our duty to pursue'. Churchill wanted there to be 'no humbug' about sanctions, but Maffey, ever the diplomat, thought they should be kept going 'on the right note'.

Censorship was another subject that could cause friction between the Irish Government and the British Representative's office. When John submitted to the censor an article by the English journalist and historian Joan Haslip[81] – it was intended for publication in the *World Review* – Jack Purcell, assistant controller of censorship, was directed by the Anglophobe Frank Aiken to inform John that the article, 'De Valera's Other Island', had been stopped. Purcell added that 'if there is much more of this sad-sympathy-with-the-mists-that-do-be-on-the-Irish-bogtrotters type of propaganda in the British press regarding Irish neutrality, it will be necessary to let the Irish people know about it and allow Irish publicists [to] reply'.[82] But another time the censor, in response to a direct appeal from John, helped him out by preventing the Roman Catholic paper *The Standard* from printing remarks which John's friend, C.E.M. Joad, had made on his visit to Dublin. Joad had argued for the legalization of abortion, increased access to contraception and divorce, the abolition of censorship and the repeal of anti-homosexual legislation. *The Standard* was eager to quote him 'as a representative of British degeneracy'; the censor closed down the story on the basis of preserving 'good relations' with Britain.[83]

Normally, the censor was less concerned to prevent information coming into Eire from outside than to suppress any propagandist material from within Eire that might compromise neutrality. British newspapers and magazines were on sale in Dublin throughout the war. Neither BBC nor German broadcasts were jammed. However, the Dublin cinemas were not allowed to show Charlie Chaplin's satire on Hitler, *The Great Dictator*. Where the Irish censor departed from strict neutrality, it was usually to avoid giving offence to the Germans rather than the British. The vast, Chestertonian editor of the *Irish Times*, R.M. Smyllie, was strongly Anglophile. As he never tired of reminding his readers, he had been in a German prisoner-of-war camp in the First World War. He was adept at sliding pro-British stories past the censor, and protested fiercely if he thought the censor was failing to be impartial. His biographer, Tony Gray, writes:

> A typical example of his artfulness occurred when I was editing the Book Page and we ran a short review of a schoolgirl's romance entitled *Worrals of the WAAFS*. When the proofs reached Dublin Castle, the review was immediately banned. Smyllie then re-wrote it carefully, giving the girls names like Gretchen, Eva and Lilli, and retitling the book *Lotte of the Luftwaffe*. The resultant review was passed by the censor without comment, and of course Smyllie then raised all hell on the grounds that this incident proved that the Irish censorship was biased in favour of the Germans. It didn't, of course; all it proved was that at this particular stage of the war the Irish Government ministers were far more afraid of the Germans than they were of the British.[84]

A spirited joker like this was likely to get on with John; and obviously it was in the interests of the British Press Attaché to cultivate the editor of the leading Irish newspaper. The two met often in the inner-sanctum 'snug' of the Palace Bar in Fleet Street, Dublin. At the back of the main bar, a door led through a screen, 'rather like the iconostasis in a Byzantine church',[85] into an area where journalists and other writers were served drinks by barmen in long white aprons. Cyril Connolly, who was brought to Dublin by John in 1941, thought it 'as warm and friendly as an alligator tank; its inhabitants, from a long process of mutual mastication, have a leathery look, and are as witty, hospitable and kindly a group as can be found anywhere'.[86]

> The Palace Bar [he added] is perhaps the last place of its kind in Europe, a *café littéraire* where one can walk in to have an intelligent discussion

with a stranger, listen to Seumas O'Sullivan on the early days of Joyce or discuss the national problem with the giant, Hemingway-like editor of *The Irish Times*. Here one may also gather varieties of anti-British opinion, and see the war as a bored spectator, as a pro-Pétain intellectual Catholic, as a pro-German, anti-Semitic Kerryman, as an Anglo-Irish Protestant disillusioned with England.[87]

Smyllie's special chair was always reserved for him. One of his columnists wrote: 'Looking at the editor, one frequently sees the left hand flying out as if in demonstration of some wide, generous idea; actually, however, it is merely a claw in search of a cigarette, a modest tax that is gladly paid by listening neophytes.' In 1940 the *Irish Times* had published a cartoon of the Palace Bar sanctum by the New Zealand caricaturist Alan Reeve, who depicted most of the regulars:[88] among them, the poet Patrick Kavanagh, the novelist and *Irish Times* columnist Brian Nolan (alias Flann O'Brien and Myles na gCopaleen), the poet Austin Clarke, who lived mainly on what he earned from Radio Éireann for a weekly poetry programme; the literary editor M.J. MacManus; the journalist and former trade unionist Cathal O'Shannon; the one-legged wit and raconteur G.J.C. Tynan 'Pussy' O'Mahony (father of the comedian Dave Allen);[89] and the poet mentioned by Connolly, Seumas O'Sullivan. John came to know all these men. He enjoyed the company of the Rabelaisian Kavanagh, who was profiled by *The Bell* magazine as 'a consommé of a boy'.

> He wears a tartan shirt with a Paisley tie, a Josephan sports jacket which would throw any self-respecting chameleon into convulsions, and a check cap in the cycling mode of *circa* 1895. He is constructed on the heroic scale. Rodin would have admired him as a model. At tea, a great root-like hand shoots across the table to the toast dish, casting a thunder-cloud shadow on the cloth. Patrick Kavanagh, without warning, suddenly crosses his legs, jerks the table a good two feet into the air, cups and dishes a-jingle-jangling, and continues the conversation as if no earthquake had occurred. Or he as suddenly hunches the enormous, mountainous shoulders, and chairs, table, walls even, seem to shiver with him.[90]

Kavanagh was usually in debt. John introduced him to John Lehmann, who published poems by him in *New Writing*, and to Cyril Connolly, who found space for him in *Horizon*.[91] 'He used [my father] mercilessly to help him promote his work,' writes Candida Lycett Green.[92] John helped many other writers and artists to 'place' their work, too. He obtained the painter Jack Yeats an exhibition at the National Gallery, London.[93]

Brian Nolan moonlighted from a civil service job to write his novels and articles. While John was in Dublin, Seán MacEntee made Nolan the secretary of an enquiry into a tragic fire in Cavan town. (A convent industrial school was burned down. Thirty-two children were killed. No nuns were injured. It was said that they had kept the doors locked because they did not want the firemen to see the young girls in their night clothes.) Nolan was congratulated on the 'care and consideration' of his report.[94]

Nolan's novel *At Swim-Two-Birds* (1939) was 'experimental' in the Joycean manner. That might not have recommended him to John; but, as Myles na gCopaleen, he was also the *Irish Times*'s star humorous columnist, and John found his 'Cruiskeen Lawn' column hilarious. Nolan liked monstrous puns. In August 1941 he suggested that the Russian Marshal Timoshenko was really an Irishman, Tim O'Shenko, who had played full-back for Garrytown in 1924–25.[95] He could also turn his hand to deft light verse –

> Let not the cups I won for golf
> Exclude a love of Hugo Wolf;
> Picasso can be reconciled
> With hunting lions in the wild;
> I do not fear my war with Leo
> Unfits me for the Archduke Trio.[96]

Nolan and John often met for a drink or lunch, and Nolan made a friendly reference to John in the 'Cruiskeen Lawn' column.

Chatting to writers in bars was all part of John's semi-cultural mission; but there were many more drudge-like aspects to his job, as he satirically indicated both in a letter to John Piper[97] and in a long, only half-spoof outline of a typical day's activities which he wrote for his own amusement or to relieve his frustration. What made a lot of work for John in Dublin, and for Nicholas Mansergh in London, was people trying to get round the rigorous rules of travel, including shipping space. 'The standard reply was a stone-walling reply,' Mansergh recalled. 'If a special exception was made, it was made for art, literature and general knowledge about the war.'[98] The two men decided to encourage European exiles with harrowing tales of Nazi persecution to visit Ireland. King Peter of Yugoslavia was brought over and given a guard of honour. 'But in general we encouraged youngish, not too high-ranking, officers from the exiled governments,' Mansergh said. 'They would go over to Ireland for two or three weeks and would say what Nazism had meant to other small countries.' One of the Polish exiles was 'a marvellously beautiful girl with nineteenth-century heroic features – the "bare breasts and banners" look.' Mansergh thought she would make a change from the usual men. John looked after her on her visit to Dublin and wrote back to Mansergh: 'Dear Doctor, if you can, please send urgently, more like our latest visitor. If you do so all the young men will be leaving this country to fight for them.'[99]

Although he received regular, and very entertaining, letters from John, Mansergh sometimes felt he was being kept in the dark about the Press Attaché's activities. On 1 August 1941 he wrote John a slightly pained letter.

MOST SECRET

My dear Betjeman,

The Censorship sent me the other day an extract from a letter written by Lady Rathdonnell to a friend in this country. The relevant sentence read: 'I am launched into the Fifth Column with this propaganda person to do with Sir John Maffey's outfit and saw them yesterday (also the head of the Communists, they're our Allies now you know!!) and not unfunny the whole thing.' I do not know whether the undignified appellation of 'propaganda person' refers to you. But the letter did raise one question in my mind. If since your visit to this country you have felt it possible to expand your propaganda work in certain directions, it would be a great help to me if you could let me know the lines along which you are working. There is no need to give details, but just a general indication of your plans.[100]

John underlined the last two sentences and irritably wrote across the bottom of the letter: 'Now what have I done to deserve this?!! I don't do propaganda work at all. It is a waste of time. No one believes propaganda.'[101] Robert Cole records that 'Betjeman compiled a report for the Empire Division [of the MoI] describing what *he* would do if *he* were a German propagandist in Eire, and, being Betjeman, he ended it with "*Heil Hitler!*"'[102]

Occasionally John came to London to report in person to Mansergh and to Professor Hugh Pugh in the Dominions Office in Downing Street. Mansergh was in the London University building where John had previously worked. 'Betjeman regarded my office as "dim",' he said. 'He asked the porter at the entrance where I was to be found, and he didn't know. Betjeman was rather shaken by this.'[103] Mansergh noted that John was usually able to get access to people in high positions. At the MoI John would call on Brendan Bracken himself, or one of the directors-general, Sir Walter Monckton or Sir Cyril Radcliffe. (He had first met Radcliffe and his antique-dealer brother at Camilla Russell's house in the 1930s.)[104] John was known at the MoI and his eccentricities were tolerated, even enjoyed. He was less cordially received at the Dominions Office, where the permanent under secretary was Sir Eric Machtig and the deputy under secretary was (Sir) John Stephenson. 'Machtig passed him on to Stephenson,' Mansergh remembered, 'but something had gone wrong and Stephenson thought Machtig should see Betjeman. Machtig was quite up to that sort of thing and declined to see him. So Betjeman retorted by inventing a fantasy that "Sir Eric Machtig doesn't exist". He did see Stephenson. He had to get a pass from the porter to see him. The porter asked, "What is it in connection with?" "Supply of lavatory paper." '[105]

Mansergh thought that John 'either consciously or subconsciously knew how to exploit the advantages of the curious triangular situation between the MoI, the Dominions Office and himself'.[106] Mansergh was mildly irritated at attempts to play him off against Pugh, though he was amused when John referred to one of the Dominions Office civil servants as 'some dreary pen-pusher at your end', and even more amused when (Sir) Norman Costar, Machtig's private secretary, remarked, after John had crossed him in some matter, 'It says much for the British Civil Service that, in an hour of grave peril for the nation, it has actually been able to find something for John Betjeman to do.'[107] John was in still less favour with the Dominions Office after the episode of the sticky diplomatic bag. One summer morning, Lord Cranborne, who had succeeded Anthony Eden as Dominions Secretary, found that the pile of letters on his desk was sticky. Enquiries were made, and it was found that the diplomatic bag in which the letters had arrived had been used by John to send a pound of butter over to a friend in London.[108]

John's visits to the MoI were never less than exhilarating for Mansergh.

Once, when Betjeman was in London on a week's visit, the Germans showed signs of attacking Bermuda. There were headlines in the papers. Betjeman came to a meeting of the Dominions Section and I remember well his coming into the Senate House room for the meeting, a little late, in marvellous Irish tweeds and looking sunburned and happy.

'Doctor, dear doctor, how nice of you to ask me round,' he said. 'Bermuda! I could *die* for Bermuda. Where is it?' This disrupted the morning's meeting. Then I had another meeting with him, and in the course of some great discussion about something, he heard that Joan Hunter Dunn was in the building. He had lost track of her. He was wildly excited – only stayed with me a minute or so longer – raced off to see her. Actually, I knew quite a lot about Joan Hunter Dunn, because my wife had been at school with her. They had played lacrosse together.[109]

Less often, Mansergh would go to see John in Dublin. Here, too, John impressed him by having 'influential contacts all over the place'. Mansergh admired his astuteness in keeping a balance between the people whose company he enjoyed and those with whom work had to be done. 'For all the pleasure that I knew Irish peers gave him, he didn't rely on their judgment.'[110] Mansergh heard the stories that were circulating in Dublin about John's more outrageous encounters with important people.

Seán Lemass was the deputy Prime Minister. Betjeman met him in Kildare Street. Betjeman was munching a Mars Bar. Lemass looked at this with some surprise and Betjeman's counter was to hand him the Mars Bar – 'Take a bite. It's very good.' Another time, Betjeman had lunch with George O'Brien, the economist, in the Kildare Street Club. O'Brien was rather a shy person, so he was horrified when, as they came into the dining-room, which was crowded with people having lunch, Betjeman said, 'I want to get a good view here,' and lay down flat on his back to admire the ceiling.[111]

When he visited John in Dublin, Mansergh noticed that 'he was very protective about the position of the Embassy [the British Representative's office], and so of course were the staff. If there had been any kind of rising the Embassy would have been the first target.' He thought that John was 'dedicated to being as co-operative as possible to the Irish while preserving the priorities of Britain's wartime interests', and felt that he was the ideal person to put across the idea that 'what the Embassy [sic] was really interested in was fostering cultural links – literature, the arts, and so on.'[112] Certainly John made himself popular on the Irish literary scene. He became a lasting friend of the writer Sean O'Faolain – novelist, short-story author, travel writer and editor of *The Bell* – and of Frank O'Connor, another master of the short story. 'I see Frank O'Connor quite a lot,' John wrote to his friend Oliver Stonor.[113] 'He is the best writer here. Very frustrated and unhappy and pro-us.'[114] The poetry editor of *The Bell*, Geoffrey Taylor, became John's most valued friend in Dublin. His widow, Mary, told John's daughter:

Penelope and John used to come over sometimes in the cart [to Airton House, Tallaght, a few miles from Collinstown] and John and Geoffrey

would closet themselves up and read poetry to each other for hours at a
stretch, while we sat in another room playing the piano and singing
'Brother James's Air' with a descant. I remember going in with some sandwiches once or twice and the atmosphere was absolutely electric . . .[115]

John spent time with O'Faolain's sometime lover Elizabeth Bowen
at her flat on St Stephen's Green. John Lehmann has described her at
that time as 'in high spirits, radiating charm and vitality, the slight
impediment in her speech giving an attractive touch of diffidence to
the eager flow of her wide-ranging conversation'.[116] A more evocative
profile of her – by Larry Morrow writing as 'The Bellman' – was
printed in *The Bell* in September 1942.

If you know your Holbein even tolerably well, you will have seen Elizabeth
Bowen many times – in a dozen or so of family portraits . . . the long,
heavily knuckled fingers, the high, almost boyish cheek-bones, the upper
lip, rose-petal coloured, slightly curled, showing the velvet side; the ring,
the bracelet, the ear-rings of whorled dull gold, which in some curious way
seem to be not so much ornaments as part of the wearer's body. Even
about her clothes – the floppy hat of dark brown felt, the folds of the
biscuit-coloured linen dress – there is the same timelessness.[117]

Bowen was both a British Intelligence agent and a contributor to the
New Statesman. She and John saw each other both professionally and
socially; though O'Faolain, in the tell-all revision of his autobiography, *Vive Moi!*, which was published in 1993 after Bowen and others
of his lovers had died, writes that she 'scornfully dismissed' John,
after having lunch with him in 1946, as 'that silly ass'.[118]

Through his continuing friendships with the Longfords and
Micheál MacLiammóir and Hilton Edwards, John was also involved
with the theatre in Dublin. In 1941 he attended the première of
MacLiammóir's play *Where Stars Walk*, a romantic comedy in which
MacLiammóir played a country bumpkin. Osbert Lancaster happened to be in Dublin and accompanied John.[119] Maffey was present
too; so were several Irish literary figures lately returned from exile.
For John, toiling to learn the Irish language, there were some memorable sights. MacLiammóir's biographer writes:

A dark blue Rolls Royce brought Ireland's first president, Dr Douglas
Hyde, founder of the Gaelic League, a genial scholarly man, whose translations of almost-forgotten Gaelic poetry were the chief influence on the
Irish literary revival at the turn of the century. Here he was, fifty years
later, smiling from his box in the theatre where his early plays had been

produced in the Irish language, eagerly absorbing a play which, in spite of its modern setting, clearly derived from that movement.[120]

In November 1941 the Gaiety's seventy-fifth anniversary was celebrated with a production of Shaw's *Caesar and Cleopatra*. John wrote a stirring prologue in rhyming couplets, spoken by MacLiammóir's cousin Anew McMaster –

> Only those floreated golden walls
> Can recollect the hundred curtain calls
> Of Hilda Moody's O Mimosa San
> In '97 when the Geisha ran.

It ended:

> The great tradition she has known before
> Goes on – with Edwards and MacLiammóir![121]

The different circles in which John moved – the novelists, the theatre group, artists, the 'Palace Bar crowd' – interlinked like Chinese rings. Brinsley MacNamara, shown in the 1940 cartoon of the Palace Bar, was not only a playwright and drama critic of the *Irish Times*, but a curator at the National Gallery of Ireland. Brendan Behan, whose first draft of *Borstal Boy* was published in *The Bell* in June 1942, was a friend of Kavanagh, another contributor to *The Bell*. Kavanagh was taken up by the formidable Archbishop of Dublin, John Charles McQuaid, who found him a job as film critic of *The Standard* and paid him a regular allowance.[122]

Archbishop McQuaid was one of the powerful Dublin figures whom John was most eager to court. John knew that he was close to de Valera and that he had been as responsible as anyone for drafting the Irish Constitution of 1937;[123] also, that through the priesthood he exercised an immense influence over the thinking of Irish people. John's great interest in religion was one of his many assets in a country where religion was all-pervasive. Dónal Ó Drisceoil has written:

> The assertion that Britain's war defended Christian civilisation against the anti-God Nazis formed one of the broad themes of British propaganda. The line was that while Catholics, Protestants and Orthodox might differ doctrinally they were as one as Christians under threat from the common neo-pagan foe.[124]

This 'line' was not necessarily accepted by the Irish. The Roman Catholic Church in Ireland had supported General Franco against 'godless Communism' in the Spanish Civil War. There was an Irish fascist movement, the Blueshirts: W.B. Yeats had indulged in 'a rather silly flirtation' with it,[125] and John knew the Blueshirt officer Dermott MacManus.[126] Like Franco, Hitler could be portrayed as anti-Communist. He was also anti-Semitic; and a strong case has been made that so were the Roman Catholic Church in Ireland, Archbishop McQuaid himself and even Pius XII, who has been called 'Hitler's Pope'.[127] There were, however, portents of German irreligion. In 1934, one of Eduard Hempel's predecessors as German Minister in Dublin, Dr Georg von Dehn, had followed the usual practice of kissing Paschal Robinson's ring as he left the Nunciature in Phoenix Park. A photograph of the incident had reached Hitler, who had insisted on von Dehn's instant dismissal.[128] Pope Pius XI had opened his encyclical of March 1937, 'mit brennender Sorge' ('with burning sorrow') at the condition of the Roman Catholic Church in Germany.[129] In that year the Nazis arrested Dr Otto Niemöller, pastor of the Protestant church in Dahlen. The *Irish Press* commented: 'No folly seems to be too extreme for the leaders of the Nazi Party.'[130]

John distributed copies of the Roman Catholic journals *The Universe* and *The Tablet* (the latter edited, since 1936, by his friend Douglas Woodruff);[131] organized broadcasts on St Patrick's Day;[132] publicized the exploits of Irish Catholics fighting in British forces; urged London to get *Picture Post* and *The Universe* to publish straightforward illustrated accounts of Nazi persecution of Polish Catholics;[133] and made friends with Peter O'Curry, editor of the influential Catholic *Standard*, setting out 'to persuade him of Nazi anti-Christianity and to steer him away from the anti-British slant taken in his paper'.[134] And to some extent he gained the interest of Archbishop McQuaid. In a letter of 1942, he gave the prelate his views on ecclesiastical architecture and, in effect, told him what he wanted to hear – that if English parish churches 'become simply & traditionally Catholic (the Communion Service, the Central Service & the Catholic teaching of the meaning of that service), so, I believe, we will enlarge the nucleus which is to bring England back to Catholicism'. Unfortunately, there were several ways in which, directly or indirectly, John managed to annoy McQuaid. In January 1941, when he brought over Count Jan Balinski from the Polish Research Centre in London, a branch of the exiled Polish Government, Balinski antagonized McQuaid by complaining about the Irish censor. In June 1941 McQuaid wrote to Archbishop William Godfrey, the Apostolic Delegate to Britain, to tell him how angry he was at 'the Balinski incident' and of 'the caution that I feel obliged to show in the future'.[135]

In December 1941 McQuaid again wrote to Godfrey, this time to complain of 'a scandalously offensive calumny' which had appeared in an article in the *Catholic Herald* written by a priest, Father John Heenan (the future Cardinal Archbishop of Westminster).[136] The article was the fourth in a series which Heenan had written after a visit sponsored by the British Government as part of a campaign run by John to counteract the isolationism imposed by neutrality and the censorship laws.[137] Heenan had been appalled by Dublin beggars and by teenage drinking and late-night dancing. 'It is disturbing', he wrote, 'that in Catholic Ireland degrading poverty should be tolerated.' McQuaid told Godfrey that the article had 'deeply angered both clergy and people in this country'.

There was more trouble in September 1942, over the Mercier Society[138] which, ten months earlier, McQuaid had allowed his friend Frank Duff[139] to set up under the auspices of the Legion of Mary. The society's objective was to bring about a better understanding between Protestants and Catholics. A joint committee of ten Catholics and eight Protestants was formed to select speakers for its meetings at the National University Buildings, St Stephen's Green; John was among the Protestants. The Archbishop had hoped that the society might be a means of converting Protestants to Roman Catholicism; instead, he was disturbed to find that it was a platform for questioning Catholic orthodoxy. He was outraged when the Church of Ireland Rector at Harold's Cross, the Rev. W.G. Proctor, attacked the primacy of Rome and papal infallibility. By September 1942 he was already wondering whether to close the society down.[140] He suggested that only Roman Catholic speakers should be invited, but this advice was disregarded.

The society's minutes, preserved at Archbishop's House in Drumcondra, Co. Dublin, record some lively interventions by John in the post-lecture discussions. After 'Communism and the Answer':

Mr Christie (a Catholic) treated on the widespread emigration of our labourers to England ... and of the likelihood that they would return with a materialistic outlook on life. There was great social work being done in Ireland today . . . We should, in accordance with Christian principles, promote a wider distribution of property. We should see the Redeemer in every human soul. Social services run by the State or Municipality were coldly run and could sap the independence and pride of those who depended on them.

Mr Bietjemiens [sic] said he had to rise to defend his country from aspersions. Irish immigrants were well taken care of in religious matters: the Ministry of Labour saw to it that Chaplains were provided and facilities given for attendance at Mass. You cannot, he added, generalize about England, and especially you can't generalize about its materialism. England was a country of moral individualists. Religious apathy is terrifying in England, but English individualism saves it from being directed into wrong channels. It seemed to him that one explanation of the reason why Spain went Communist was that, if you loved a thing very much, you could also hate it very much. That was always a big danger in any Catholic country.[141]

After a talk on 'The Liturgy' by an Anglican priest, John said, 'I have attended the Roman Mass and have watched the people at prayer. It is the tense silence at the moment of Consecration that I always think remarkable. I note the devotions of the people at Mass. Some say their beads; others use the little manuals. I would like to know what is the attitude of the Roman Church to the use of the Missal.'[142] A Lieutenant Dowling[143] 'ventured to answer Mr Betchman's [*sic*] question'.

> Among those who attended Mass there were many who were ignorant and even illiterate. They could not use the Missal. The Mass, as a spectacle, supplied the needs of these people. But the Church encouraged all those who could read and follow the Missal to do so. The Roman Missal was printed in Latin and English in parallel columns.[144]

In July 1943 John caused direct irritation to McQuaid. The Archbishop's secretary left McQuaid a note to say that 'the British Press Attaché (Mr Bietjiemens)' had telephoned asking for an interview on behalf of a Mr Van der Heijden who was examining into the conditions of Irish labourers in England.[145] The misspelling hardly suggests that John's was a name to conjure with at Drumcondra. Later, McQuaid wrote an irritable note at the bottom of the memo, in the finicky little hand which Brian Nolan used to enjoy imitating when he was McQuaid's pupil at Blackrock College. 'Mr W[alshe] phoned to say this man was a Catholic, a sugar magnate, over here to find Irish workers. It was most incorrect for him to call on me.'[146] A different side of McQuaid's nature was seen in his much friendlier notes to his protégé Patrick Kavanagh. One of these, accidentally dropped by Kavanagh in a pub, was picked up by Brendan Behan and mockingly read out.[147] To tease Kavanagh, Behan and a friend, Seán Daly, would play ritual scenes of kissing McQuaid's ring. 'Oh, the Archbishop is not such an ould bastard,' Kavanagh said.[148]

In September 1942 Kavanagh wrote a poem to celebrate the birth of the Betjemans' second child, Candida Rose.[149] She was born in the Rotunda Hospital, Dublin: Elizabeth Pakenham (later Lady

Longford) told Penelope that it was 'like being born in the Parthenon'.[150] On 22 September, John's mother, who was recovering from illness at her sister's house in Wimbledon, London, wrote to Penelope to congratulate her and to ask what 'woollies' the baby needed – 'I will at once start knitting.'[151] Paul, sturdy and flaxen-haired, was five that year. He took lessons a few miles away at Johnstown with a family named Warham who had a governess. John wrote a nonsense rhyme about him:

> There is a Paulie with no head,
> he runs about at the bottom of the bed
> There is a Paulie with no feet,
> he runs about at the bottom of the street
> There is a Paulie with no arms,
> he runs about and plays with the Warhams.[152]

Ruth-Ellen Childers (now Mrs Moller) and her brother Séamus thought the rhyme was 'a bit off. Perhaps it was innocuous, but we thought it odd that a father would write that about his son. We certainly wouldn't have liked to have a rhyme like that written about *us*.'[153]

Family life took second place to John's diplomatic duties. Even he, a natural socialite, found the pace gruelling.

> I am in hell [he wrote to John Piper]. A hell of my own choosing. I begin to hate Ireland and feel it is all playing at being a country . . . This eternal lunching out is getting me down and dining out and drinking and high tea . . . It feels like St John's Wood in Leicester.
>
> Thank goodness Propeller and the Egg and 'Bet' [Betty Evans] are happy enough. They like the country and Moti has arrived to cheer Propeller.[154]

Penelope was not in fact particularly happy, though she dutifully played her part as a diplomat's wife. In another letter to the Pipers, John wrote: 'Propeller presided at a luncheon I gave to sixteen fifth columnists the other day. It was funny but sad. We all went in taxis to look at a church afterwards – double bluff.'[155] Penelope wrote to Myfanwy Piper:

> As John has probably told you, we are both madly homesick and loathe all the social life here. We have to go to large cocktail parties, dinners and lunch parties and, worst of all, a special brand of Dublin party when you arrive after dinner: about nine pm and are expected to stay till at least two am . . .[156]

An important part of John's work was to look after visiting celebrities. The popular journalist Beverley Nichols was invited to stay at Collinstown, but found mushrooms growing on his bedroom walls in the damp mansion,[157] and moved into the Shelbourne Hotel.[158] In 1941 Kenneth Clark came over with his wife Jane. Churchill had asked him to discuss the treaty ports with de Valera. Like others, Clark noted that John 'had adopted the local colour so thoroughly that he signed his letters Seán O'Betjemán'.

In his company [Clark recalled in 1977] we visited Jane's birthplace in Merrion Square, the house in the suburbs in which she was brought up, and the beautiful Rococo Rotunda of which her mother, the first woman in Ireland to be a member of the College of Surgeons, had been the Master.[159]

Clark's meeting with the Taoiseach went well.

Incredible as it sounds, I found him sympathetic. He was above all a dialectician, who loved to argue the opposite point of view. I discovered that if I put the case *against* Ireland granting us the use of the treaty ports, he would argue, with great skill, the case in favour. Naturally he did not intend to follow this pro-English policy, but he was fully aware of its advantages, and even its moral justification, and all this I could report to Mr Churchill.[160]

John, just as certain as Clark that the art historian's mission was bound to fail, saw to it that he enjoyed the rest of his stay.

With my early admiration of Yeats, Synge and Lady Gregory [Clark wrote] I asked Seán O'Betjemán to take me out to Coole, but there were no wild swans; the whole place was derelict and was shortly afterwards pulled down . . . We also broke into the Abbey Theatre, which was a sordid building not much bigger than a village hall. The rooms seemed to be empty and, as we trod the half-lighted stage where *The Playboy of the Western World* had been hissed and booed, we felt suddenly inspired to perform an Abbey Theatre play of our own. We kept it up for quite a long time. Then the lights were suddenly put on, and we saw, sitting at the back of the auditorium, three rows of spectators. We left hurriedly by the stage door.[161]

Harold Nicolson caused embarrassment on a visit in March 1942. He flew to Dublin on an aeroplane which 'smelled of sick and all the windows were covered with butter-muslin so that one could not look out'.[162] On 16 March he attended the inaugural session of the Law

Society. Replying to a speech by the Auditor, T.D.E. Williams, which he considered 'a covert attack on England . . . designed to show that she has fallen from her high estate and reaped the penalty for many sins', Nicolson departed from his prepared text and said:

> Imperialism is dead, and, I devoutly hope, buried. If you were to picture the British lion as a rampant beast, red in tooth and claw, seeking whom it might devour, then you would get a completely false and distorted picture of our war aims. It would be much wiser to think of the British lion as an elderly, replete, self-satisfied, moth-eaten animal, whose tail in the last twenty years has been so frequently twisted that few hairs remain, but an animal which at this moment is alert and angry. We have suffered severe defeats and will have further disasters to meet in the future, but while these defeats and disasters have certainly diminished our conceit and destroyed our self-complacency, they have increased our pride.[163]

The next day, Nicolson wrote in his diary: 'St Patrick's Day. John Betjeman rings up to say that my speech went very well. I am, however, worried by the *Irish Times* and the *Independent*.'[164] One headline read, 'Britain, a moth-eaten lion'. This was not pleasing to Maffey and John; and Nicolson was anxious about the reception his remarks would get if reported in London. He had reason: the Conservative MP Walter Liddell tabled a Commons motion that Nicolson should be dismissed as a governor of the BBC for having made a 'defeatist' speech in Ireland.[165] The film star Leslie Howard came over and was entertained at Collinstown. Nicholas Mansergh thought him a particularly desirable visitor because he was Jewish. 'And after his visit he wrote a very sensitive report on Irish feelings. We might well have asked Howard to go back, but he was shot down nine or ten months later – the Germans thought they were shooting down Churchill.'[166]

In May 1943 Laurence Olivier came to Ireland to film the Battle of Agincourt for *Henry V*. Ireland was chosen because the skies above England were scored with the vapour trails of marauding Luftwaffe aircraft and defending Spitfires and because the able-bodied men of England were fighting a real war, while in Ireland extras could be easily and cheaply recruited. Olivier first came over on a reconnaissance trip accompanied by Dallas Bower, who seemed to appear at intervals in John's life like a recurring figure in an Anthony Powell novel.

Olivier and Bower arrived at Dun Laoghaire in the mail-boat and were met by John who took them to their Dublin hotel in a taxi. During the taxi-ride, John said, 'You do like Palestrina, don't you? I'm sure old Larry does, because he was a chorister; but I'm not certain whether you do, Dallas.'

Bower said, 'Well, yes, John, I do like Palestrina, of course I do, yes.'

'Ah, good,' John said. 'I'm afraid you'll both have to come with me to High Mass at Maynooth tomorrow morning.' (The next day was a Sunday.)

Olivier looked very dubious at this and said to Bower, when John had left them, 'What do you think of this?'

'My dear chap,' Bower said, 'we are absolutely in John Betjeman's hands and we must do whatever he says.' Later, he recalled, 'we realized that John knew exactly what he was doing – because on the Monday morning, all the Dublin newspapers had banner headlines, "LAURENCE OLIVIER ATTENDS HIGH MASS AT MAY-NOOTH", or words to that effect. And after that we had no trouble at all with the Irish Government.'[167]

John gave Olivier and Bower lunch with Edward Longford, who said, 'The man for you is Mervyn Powerscourt.' Longford pointed out that Lord Powerscourt's demesne at Enniskerry, Co. Wicklow – one of the scenic marvels of Ireland – had the advantage of a permanent Boy Scout camp in the grounds, in which Olivier's armies could be billeted. John drove Olivier and Bower to see him. 'Without John Betjeman, we could not have made that sequence there,' Bower believed. 'And, as it was wartime, we might not only have been unable to make the Agincourt sequence – we might not have been able to make the film at all.'[168]

Henry V's army had numbered 30,000, the French 60,000, and it was estimated that, to suggest such forces, at least 650 men and 150 horses would be needed. Men were recruited from all over Eire at £3 10s a week, with a bonus of £2 a week for any man who brought his own horse. Olivier's biographer John Cottrell records that 'Volunteers included such assorted types as a Dublin taxi-driver and an overweight jockey, but for the most part they were farm workers, with a stiffening of more disciplined men from the Irish Local Defence Force . . .'[169]

Various Irish notabilities came to the Powerscourt demesne to watch the filming. It was John's task to entertain them and, in Bower's words, 'keep them out of the actors' hair'. Seán T. O'Kelly, with whom Máire MacEntee and Penelope had stayed on their riding tour, was one of the sightseers.

Again John Betjeman knew exactly what to do [Dallas Bower said]. This little man very much wanted to see us at work. He brought his wife, and she took a liking to a lamp we had on one of the sets – took a shine to it, you might say. So John nudged me and said, could we let her have it? Of course we did. She was thrilled, and Seán T. O'Kelly was so pleased with us that he later held a party for all the actors and crew. Something very curious happened at it. Everyone else was enjoying themselves and drinking. Larry and John and I were invited into O'Kelly's study. When we sat down he went over and turned the key in the door. His intention was to tell us something of his experiences in British prisons. He was determined to get this over. And we sat there and listened and didn't make any comment. And in due course he said, 'Perhaps you'd like to join the others now,' and unlocked the door.[170]

O'Kelly's favourable report on the filming persuaded de Valera, who was convalescing from illness, to drive out to Powerscourt.

Mervyn Powerscourt was astounded that 'Dev' was coming [Bower recalled]. He said: 'Extraordinary thing. I suppose I'll have to fly the damn' flag. I put the damn' feller in jail in '16.'[171] We were briefed by John beforehand in the biggest possible way. He called all the actors and the film crew together and told them that during the whole time de Valera was with us, there must not be so much as a breath of talk about politics. Anyway, 'Dev' arrived and we gave him tea. And the first thing he said after sitting down and balancing a teacup and saucer on his knee, was: 'Now, about neutrality.' So I plunged in and said, 'Well, the start of *Henry V* is a bit political, but we're only here to make the *French* sequence.' He seemed to be satisfied with that, and very much enjoyed the filming he saw.[172]

Journalists also wanted to know how the film was progressing. Lord Castlerosse, a friend of John's from his *Evening Standard* days, told him he would like to meet Dallas Bower.

So John took us both to the Kildare Street Club for lunch on a Saturday [Bower recalled] – I thought that was the best day to choose, knowing something of Castlerosse's expansive habits. After a very long lunch, the three of us strolled into the neighbourhood of Merrion Square. John suddenly said, 'Oh, look, that's an interesting place; and it's just about time for the change of shift.'
    'What are you talking about?' said Castlerosse.
    'Nuns of the Perpetual Adoration,' said John. 'They are most important people. We can go in, I think the turnstiles are working.'
    It was a little chapel. 'Don't let the neon lighting upset you,' said John.
    'Nothing upsets me,' said Castlerosse – and considering what he had drunk at lunch I don't imagine anything would have.
    'Yes, well, there they are,' John said. 'They're very strange old girls and they never stop praying. You have to go through the turnstiles and put something in the box.'
    We got Castlerosse through the turnstile with some difficulty; he was

very stout. And John was quite right, it was rather like the Changing of the Guard. One shift of praying nuns was just going off duty and the next coming on.[173]

Bad weather washed out two weeks' shooting time on *Henry V*. Apart from that, horses caused the main anxiety. Penelope Betjeman recalled:

A most terrible thing happened. One of the horses got strangles, which is an extremely serious disease of the throat – they get a huge abscess and all the pus comes out and it goes through the ranks like wildfire. Every single horse caught it: it is terribly infectious and they can die of it. I don't think any of them did. But anyway Lord Powerscourt was in a fever lest his horses should get it and they had to be moved and all the wretched horses had to stand out in cavalry lines. So the Battle of Agincourt was deferred for six weeks, and we therefore saw a lot of Olivier. At one moment he was going to use my white charger Moti, but I said it wasn't correct as Arabs hadn't been imported to England by that date.[174]

Instead, Olivier was found an Irish grey gelding which he called Blanche King, from which he directed much of the filming.

If Penelope was in her element advising on the horses, John was in his, showing Dublin to Olivier and Olivier to Dublin. But here, too, not everything went smoothly. Christine Longford recalled:

John gave a party for Olivier, who came to our little repertory theatre and saw the show. It happened, just that night, that Sybil Thorndike was there, because she was the mother of one of our actors, Christopher Casson. I remember these well-known people kissing each other. And then John had a supper for Olivier, Edward and me and I'm not quite sure who else at the Gresham Hotel, after the show. And actors like to eat well after the show, and there were steaks; but this is a sad story. John had promised Olivier the best steak he could find. He enquired beforehand from the waiter and told him to be pretty careful. The best possible steak that could be found arrived. I mustn't libel the Gresham – it has changed its management since – but the steak was *tough*!

Up to then, Olivier had been so sweet and kind, and not patronizing to rep actors. He had told us who was good and who was less good, with little tips such as 'That boy would be good if he could manage to keep still.' (That was true, and that actor *did* manage to keep still afterwards.) But when the steak turned out to be not good, he showed all the temperament that an artist can show when disappointed of anything – he was very, very cross. John, of course, responded well and got him a nice pudding.[175]

The Gresham was one of the main meeting-places for the British and pro-British community in Dublin. Others included the Wicklow Hotel and Jammet's Restaurant, both of which were regarded by the Irish as Ascendancy haunts and had their windows broken, together with those of Maffey's office and the American Legation, at the end of the war. But the centre of pro-British society was the Shelbourne Hotel. Elizabeth Bowen wrote:

> The sequestration of Ireland created, for the Shelbourne, conditions very unlike those of the First World War. Hungry British journalists, as happy to be in Dublin as their forebears had been displeased, headed upon arrival for the hotel; first to eat, then to type gargantuan stories of Irish eating for the papers they happened to represent. Mystery men with sealed lips and locked brief-cases shot through the hall and up and down in the lift.[176]

She added: 'It was the rooted belief of all the Shelbourne chambermaids that those arriving from London were to be treated as casualties from bomb-shock: voices and footsteps were accordingly muted, soft ministrations were many, and in no night-nursery could one have been more fondly, soothingly tucked up in bed . . .'[177] In this luxurious, cushioned environment, the world of the pre-war Ascendancy, a Molly Keane world of affectations, brittleness and Bright Young People, seemed to survive. As a superannuated Bright Young Thing himself, John knew how to make himself interesting in this society. It was at a literary party in the Shelbourne in 1941 that he met the young British writer Sylvia Stevenson. She introduced him to her friend Eleanor Butler, whom he, in turn, was to introduce to her future husband, Billy Clonmore (later Earl of Wicklow).[178]

Eleanor Butler and John soon discovered a common interest in architecture. Her father, Professor R.M. Butler, had been Professor of Architecture at Trinity College and was 'one of the few people in Dublin at that time who knew anything about Georgian buildings'.[179] Eleanor brought John to see her father, who was recovering from a heart attack. John had learned to do some research into people before he met them. One thing he had found out about Butler was that his mother, by birth a German from Schleswig-Holstein, had become interested in the Irvingites, whose small sect, the Catholic Apostolic Church, had flourished in Germany. They had one little church in Dublin, one in Belfast and a number in England which had been designed in the late nineteenth century by some of the Gothic architects whom John most admired. So, instead of talking about Georgian Dublin, John plunged into the history of the Catholic Apostolic Church. By this date the Church was in decline, and Professor Butler, as the only descendant of anybody connected with it, had been appointed a trustee to wind up its affairs. When John began to say how fascinated he was by the Irvingites, Butler was not really interested. John was full of the correct terminology – the Catholic Apostolic Church called their pastors 'angels', and above them was a number of 'archangels'. Lady Wicklow recalled:

> John went on with his usual thing: 'Oooh, how marvellous! Are you visited by the *angels*? How often do you meet an *archangel*?' Well, up to a point my father went along with this and joked about it; but then John said, 'Really what I would like, Professor Butler, if you could arrange it, is to join the Catholic Apostolic Church in Ireland.' . . . About a week afterwards a friend, Senator Douglas, who was a leading Quaker, came to see my father and said, 'Have you met this fellow Betjeman?' My father said yes. And Douglas said, 'Well, it's an extraordinary thing, he's come to me and says he wants to become a Quaker.' So from that point on, my father always said of John, 'That *mountebank*!'[180]

John caused Butler more serious annoyance in 1942, by claiming to have 'discovered' a cache of drawings by the Irish Georgian architect Francis Johnston.[181] The story was splashed in the press; but Butler not only knew about the drawings, he had told John where they were.[182] To mollify the Butlers, John proposed that he and Eleanor should write a book on Johnston. 'But it was put on the long finger, and put on the long finger,' Lady Wicklow said in 1979. 'We never did the book; but John published a very good article on Johnston in 1946, in *Pavilion*, an art magazine edited by Myfanwy Piper.'[183]

To friends in England, John gave a lugubrious account of his life in Dublin. In April 1941 he wrote to Gerard Irvine: 'I am overworked, tired, unappreciated, persecuted and hopeless half the time. Yet if I can make some friends for England, I suppose I can do something. I have made a few, but I don't know what HMG's policy towards Ireland is, & if I did would either leave or stay on. We are all of us on the rack in this office. I long for polychromatic construction and bombs and friends again.'[184] But Eleanor Wicklow's recollection of John in these years is that 'He was always full of fun.'

> One never knew how much he was being funny and how much he was being naïve. I never could make up my mind. For instance, when he decided he was going to learn Irish, and he started attending Irish lessons. He and his wife and family were at Collinstown and petrol was very short and he didn't want to drive. So he used to go to the lessons on the Clondalkin bus. Whether it was the petrol, or whether it was a way of

making contacts, I don't know. For every half dozen people who were
devoted to him, half a dozen thought he was a subtle special agent: with
his poetry and architecture he could get in anywhere . . . John had this idea
that all the plots were hatched in the Gaelic League, and that if he wore a
whitish tweed cap and a tweed tie and Irish tweeds and looked as untidy
as he could and went on the Clondalkin bus with his Irish grammar
propped up in front of him, people would confide in him. The story goes –
I can't vouch for it, as I was never on the Clondalkin bus – that night after
night he used to be heard murmuring to himself, in Irish, 'The cow went
into the field. The cow went out of the field' – with the most junior Irish
textbooks. And Irish speakers would come to his aid when he made mis-
takes; and he got to know these people.[185]

Though John was fond of Eleanor Butler, she did not inspire one of
his extravagant crushes. 'I think the person he really fell for in Ireland',
she said in 1976, 'was Lady Hemphill, now Emily Villiers-Stuart. He
wrote one of his best poems about her, "Ireland with Emily".' Partly
from duty and partly from choice, John and Penelope devoted as much
time as possible to travelling round Ireland and staying in country
houses. They spent a weekend with Lord Dunsany ('Lord Insany') at
his half-medieval, half-Gothick castle.[186] They stayed with the
Longfords at Pakenham Hall[187] and the Chetwood-Aikens of
Woodbrook, near Portarlington in Queen's County (Laois), who were
related to Penelope.[188] The Betjemans met Emily, Lady Hemphill, at
the house of Terence Gray in Co. Cavan. 'Terence Gray was a colourful character,' Emily Villiers-Stuart recalled. 'He had a little goatee
beard, at a time when beards were uncommon. And he was very effete,
loved cooking and fancied himself as a master of the arts. (He wrote
on ballet for *The Bell*.)'[189] Emily Hemphill was a New England
American, daughter of a rich shoe manufacturer – the kind of heiress
who marries English lords in P.G. Wodehouse novels. She had married
Lord Hemphill, a Dublin lawyer, but by now the marriage was under
severe strain because of his chronic alcoholism.[190] She remembered
her first meeting with John at Gray's house.

I had heard of him, but hadn't yet met him. Somebody gave me something
of his to read, and I was reading it when he came in, so that was a good start.
This was during the war, when John was what I call Chief Spy. Well, he *was*
. . . Press Attaché it was called, but of course he spent most of his time spying
on the Germans. He was always on the lookout for hidden wireless sets.[191]

Emily Hemphill got on well with Penelope too at that first meeting.
They had horses and ponies in common. Emily spent most of her time

hunting. She would ride off (as there were no cars, she had to ride to meets) with a knapsack containing two evening dresses, beautifully folded by a maid, and boots and a mackintosh. After a long day of hunting, one of the long dresses would be worn.

The Hemphills lived at Tulira in Co. Galway, an accretion of 1880s Victorian Gothic around a much earlier building. The castle had been the home of Edward Martyn, a pioneer of the Gaelic Revival who had been a friend of Yeats; it was famous as Martyn's house in George Moore's *Hail and Farewell*.[192] The architect had incorporated the three marbles of Ireland in floors and the columns of the hall. Soon after meeting the Betjemans in Co. Cavan, Emily Hemphill invited them to stay at Tulira. She recalled:

John had a motor-car – *no* one had a motor-car then, the only people allowed to run one were priests, doctors, vets and race officials. But he was on the fringe of the diplomatic world, so he had one. Well, Penelope went off in the car straight away to look for a Connemara pony. So John and I had nothing but bicycles, and we went on the ride John describes in 'Ireland with Emily'. I said the nicest place we could go was where the St George family lived. John was thrilled with them, because they were rather aristo-cratic and very profligate, gamblers. The lovely Georgian house had been burned down. 'Let's go there,' I said, 'and let's go to the sea and swim.' So off we went, and picked up beer at a pub. Then he saw the ruins – very attractive ruins, a shell with lovely festoons of plasterwork hanging down like stalactites. And across the road was the mausoleum which he describes in the poem.[193] The door of that was hanging open, the sarcophagi had been robbed, the lead had been taken, naturally, and sheep used it as a refuge. After that, we did swim, halfway up Galway Harbour, about twenty miles from the Clare border. Then we bicycled back down the 'bohreens' (that means lanes) described in the poem.[194]

Penelope was miserable on that first visit to Tulira.

John absolutely fell for Emily, and I'll never forget the agony of jealousy, the only time I've ever felt jealousy, I think, when he stayed up talking to her till about 1.00 a.m. and I went up to bed and he never came in. In point of fact I needn't have worried a bit; she was already secretly engaged to someone called Ion Villiers-Stuart who lived in a very beau-tiful and famous house called Dromana which has now been pulled down. I mean, she wasn't in the least in love with John, but he was mad about her. She subsequently married Ion Villiers-Stuart, then he died beside her in bed after two years. She had to get a Reno divorce from Lord Hemphill, because you couldn't get a divorce in Ireland. Ion

Villiers-Stuart's wife, too, was an alcoholic, oddly enough; she died, and he married Emily.[195]

As at Pakenham Hall, John's favourite room at Tulira was the library. It contained a shelf of 1880s 'yellowbacks'. The one he liked best was called *Was It a Marriage?*, in three volumes. The book contained an illustration of a beautiful girl riding side-saddle, with the caption: 'Firefly's fetlocks seemed to be made of steel'. In hot pursuit was a wicked baron. Her parents were trying to make her marry this villain, but the man she loved – though neither realized they were in love – was the curate. John sat down and wrote a final chapter to the book. In it, the curate was Terence Gray. John also wrote a poem about Emily's school, again involving 'Father Terry'.

The idea voiced by both Eleanor Wicklow and Emily Villiers-Stuart, that John may have been a spy – for Britain, of course – has been treated with some derision;[196] but it deserves open-minded consideration. On the face of it, the notion of John Betjeman as a spy seems absurd: surely he would have been to espionage what Inspector Clouseau was to detection? Leaving aside the glib rejoinder, 'Who better to be a spy than the last person anyone would suspect?', it is perhaps more fitting to use the expression 'Intelligence agent' than the more emotive and sinister 'spy', with its undertones of betrayal.

The sceptics ask: 'But isn't it part of any diplomat's job – especially in wartime, in a neutral country – to keep his eyes skinned, be on the *qui vive* for nefarious activities by the representatives of enemy powers and other hostile groups?' No doubt it is; but there *is* a difference between a properly alert diplomat and a spy masquerading as a diplomat.[197] On the German side, the 'very correct' Hempel was still 'a veritable sleuth-hound, snooping after firms like McGee and Beck and Scott to uncover breaches of neutrality'.[198] He was not quite the 'innocent abroad' that he purported to be.[199] Rather absurdly, he was instructed to put red flowerpots in a particular window of the Legation to warn Nazi agents in Dublin if England was about to be invaded.[200] Hempel was in the dark about some of the agents and was embarrassed by the ones he did know about.[201] He thought their activities could compromise his attempts to convince de Valera that Germany intended to honour Ireland's neutrality. He was especially disturbed by the exploits of a German spy named Hermann Goertz.[202] Maud Gonne MacBride (the great love of Yeats's life), who was implicated in German espionage in Ireland, joked that Hempel was 'frightened out of his wits' by the very mention of Goertz's name.[203]

The degree to which it has simply been taken for granted, in Ireland, that John was a spy in 1940s Dublin is remarkable. John Feeney, writing in the Dublin *Sunday Independent* in 1978 about the demise of the Roman Catholic newspaper *The Standard*, wrote: 'John Betjeman, the poet laureate now, was the British spy during the war who was detailed to court the [*Standard*] staff away from their Nazi sympathies.'[204] Five years later, Robert Fisk wrote: 'Rumours still persist in Ireland that John Betjeman . . . was a British spy . . .' Fisk dismissed the idea. 'In fact, Betjeman – far from being anything so preposterous as a spy – was a cultural attaché in whom even Colonel [Dan] Bryan [responsible, as head of the Irish secret service G2, for monitoring foreigners in Ireland] could find nothing more suspicious than an interest in Gaelic poetry and a predisposition "to go around calling himself 'Seán' Betjemán".'[205] Fisk added a footnote: 'According to the Soviet spy Kim Philby, the British double agent Guy Burgess, who made a habit of brawling with his professional colleagues, "had been in trouble in Dublin" in the 1940s or early 1950s. But Philby did not make it clear if Burgess had at any time been in contact with Maffey. He certainly did not know Betjeman.'[206] There, as we have seen, Fisk was mistaken: John knew Burgess, and was in correspondence with him, in 1937.* Why did Fisk jump to the wrong conclusion on John's friendship with Burgess? Presumably because it seemed so unlikely. May he not, for exactly the same reason, have jumped to the wrong conclusion on the nature of John's rôle in Dublin?

John P. Duggan, in his book *Neutral Ireland and the Third Reich*, had no doubts about John's rôle, though he was light-hearted about it.

> The way John Betjeman of Maffey's staff related to Eire's *salon* society was symptomatic. He represented the acceptable face of espionage: he was a marvellous verbalizer, a lush and a bit of an eccentric, qualities which immediately endeared him to the natives. He was condescending about what he termed 'Irish gush', although he kept that to himself until he was back in Britain. Betjeman was Ireland's favourite spy, and his activities in this field could be laughed off. No one took them seriously.[207]

Duggan, again – like Fisk, normally a meticulous historian – is mistaken in suggesting that no one took seriously the idea of 'Betjeman, British spy'. In 1941 the IRA took it seriously enough to plan to assassinate John. In 1967 he received a letter from Diarmuid Brennan, of Stevenage, Hertfordshire, who wrote:

* See Chapter 10, 'Taking to the Air'.

Bertie

I was in Dublin in 1940–41. I was responsible for all matters relating to civilian Intelligence for the Army Council of the Irish Republican Army. My particular department was a sort of MI5 – internal, and counter intelligence. I was also in charge of IRA publicity. I had set up a dummy office in Westmoreland Street, next door to the *Irish Times*, and I used to mix socially with reporters, sub-editors and civil servants in the restaurants and pubs around that area, especially in the Palace Bar which was then regarded as Bob Smyllie's sub-office. I had been told about you at the British Embassy [*sic*]. You were, I remember, Press Attaché . . . and appeared to be the counterbalance to Petersen in the other place, though he, of course, did more scurrying around. Reports that came to me established Smyllie as a person of considerable standing with British Intelligence in Ireland; but we already had two people among the *Irish Times* sub-editors so we did not worry much over the Editor. Oddly, though, you became a source of much anxiety to the Army Council of the IRA. I got communications describing you as 'dangerous' and a *person of menace* to all of us. In short, you were depicted in the blackest of colours. It was decided to maintain daily contact with you so that we would know where you were precisely at any given moment. I used my office for this. I had registered as a publisher. I was, therefore, in a position to establish myself as a correspondent with the various embassies. The contact with your office was made through a woman whose name, I believe, was Lynam.[208] As soon as credentials were established it became a simple matter to make telephone calls and initiate references to you that more or less kept us informed of your whereabouts. You yourself telephoned a few times with news items; but I only remember one such item now. You came through with the news that the great film actor Leslie Howard was currently on holiday in County Kerry. I could not figure this as an item of dramatic interest but I went along with it. We discussed it at an IRA meeting that evening and, having eliminated all other reasons, decided that Leslie Howard was working for British Intelligence. Work [*sic*, for 'Word'?] was sent, accordingly, to an IRA commandant in Kerry named Dan O'Toole with the suggestion that the movements of Leslie Howard might be worth following![209]

Brennan's narrative jumped on a few months. He told John that after the arrest and abduction of the IRA chief of staff Stephen Hayes in mid-1941,[210] chaos invaded IRA council meetings. Some groups in Dublin wanted to save face by embarking on terrorist activities, which would '*stir* things with the British' and 'take the spotlight off the IRA internal difficulties'.[211] Among these groups was the Second Battalion of the Dublin Brigade. Brennan had a call from the Second Battalion staff, who were known as the 'Edward-Gees', after the cinema tough

guy Edward G. Robinson. They told Brennan they had picked a man
they had heard about, 'a fellow named Betjeman', and they wanted a
photograph of him right away. The Edward-Gees knew that the IRA
council had pictures of diplomats, journalists and civil servants, taken
by a street photographer. Brennan told them that in Betjeman's case
he had no street snapshot, but that he had a good studio picture.
However, by this stage he had come to the conclusion that the terrorist activity was 'going crazy'. He had also looked up John's poetry and
decided that he 'couldn't be much of a secret agent'. (In his letter of
1967 to John, he admitted, 'I may well be wrong.') So instead of giving
the Edward-Gees a photograph of John, he gave them one of his own
cousin, a Special Branch officer in the south of Ireland.

> They went off with it, enormously pleased. A few days later, I sent word
> to these two fellows and told them that one of our contacts in Dublin
> Castle – a Special Branch man – had passed on word that they had been
> spotted around the area of the British Embassy. I emphasized that as they
> were now under police surveillance they hadn't a chance of 'taking care'
> of you. This, I should stress, was pure invention; but they called off the
> job.[212]

The letter has to be read with the caution that any IRA document
merits. There is perhaps a touch of blarney about the story of the
photographs: possibly Brennan hoped to ingratiate himself with John
by this piece of uncharacteristic sentimentality. But there was no 'percentage' for Brennan in writing to tell John he had been on an IRA hit-
list. He could have made money by writing the story for a newspaper;
instead he just approached John privately. (In fact, he wrote, he had
tried to do so at Christmas 1950 at the offices of *Time and Tide*, but
John had introduced him to others he was entertaining as Gerald
Brenan, the writer of books on Spain. 'You then started discussing one
of the books which, fortunately, I had read. But I was only too glad to
make my departure as soon as a lull in the conversation allowed.')[213]
The main burden of Brennan's story, taken with the circumstantial
trimmings – such as the correct surname of John's assistant Joan
Lynam, newly appointed in 1941 – is convincing. John was luckier
than Cinna the poet, in *Julius Caesar*, who is first confused with a con-
spirator, then murdered for his bad verses.

John himself joked that he was a spy. In 1941 he wrote to Frank
O'Connor, 'Look at me, a bloody British spy (open) Press Attaché
here.'[214] Over forty years later, questioned about the Dublin years by
Frank Delaney, who was writing *Betjeman Country* (1983), he smiled
and murmured, 'I think I was a spy.'[215] These remarks could have been

a double-bluff. (Martial: 'Pauper videri Cinna vult, et est pauper' – 'Cinna wishes to appear poor – and he *is* poor.')

Is there any concrete evidence that John went beyond the alertness expected of a diplomat and ventured into the 'grey area' between diplomacy and espionage?[216] There are at least four pieces of evidence – one comparatively inconclusive, one stronger, and two that are hard to explain away. In 1941 Harry Hodson ordered John to 'find out about' Kees van Hoek – the Dutch journalist whose pen-portraits of Dublin diplomats were published in 1943.[217] Questions about the Dutchman had been raised by Dirk de Man of the Netherlands Government Press Service in London via C.H. de Saumarez of the MoI.[218] Hector Legge was a colleague of van Hoek on the *Sunday Independent*, and regarded him as 'certainly pro-German, and possibly a German agent'.

> Once I was visiting some people between Blackrock and Stillorgan [Legge recalled]. Their house overlooked Woodlands Park, Blackrock, the house of Karl Petersen, the German Press Attaché. And as we were standing in the garden, who should come out of that house but Petersen with van Hoek, who went as red as anything.[219]

John's links with Elizabeth Bowen are more significant. In his book about Anglo-Irish relations, *Paddy and Mr Punch* (1993), Professor R.F. Foster writes:

> Bowen's novel *The Heat of the Day* (1949) . . . was inspired by an aspect of her visits to Ireland which was not known at the time: the reports which she was furnishing to the Ministry of Information, who passed them to the Dominions Office and, eventually, the Foreign Secretary. They were also studied by John Betjeman, currently press attaché to the United Kingdom Representative in Dublin.[220]

In the novel, Bowen wrote of the central character, clearly based on herself:

> She was now . . . employed, in an organization better called Y.X.D., in secret, exacting, not unimportant work, to which the European position since 1940 gave ever-increasing point. The habit of guardedness was growing on her, as on many other people, reinforcing what was in her an existing bent . . .[221]

Bowen recycled some of her reports for an article in the *New Statesman*; but, Professor Foster notes, 'the original reports are more outspoken and personal; they also confront, much more clearly, the lack of understanding between Ireland and Britain . . .'[222] There is a large gap in the reports: Foster thinks the Foreign Office may have destroyed some of them. He adds:

> Writers, according to Bowen's friend Graham Greene, are in a sense fifth columnists, and in her position among her Irish acquaintances during wartime, this has a double application. Always fascinated by espionage, she was now a kind of spy. Her reports are headed 'Secret'; and she had proposed herself for the commission. Nobody in Ireland, apparently, knew of this commission. [The Fine Gael politician James] Dillon, discovering many years later that she had recorded and reported their conversations to the British government, was furious at what he saw as a betrayal of trust. It is unlikely that even O'Faolain knew what she was up to.[223]

So Bowen was 'a kind of spy' and John was privy to her reports. He was in the loop. She was an Irishwoman giving Irish secrets to the British; John was British, so the accusation of 'betrayal' made against her cannot justly be levelled at him. All the same, many of her friends (O'Faolain, for example) were his friends too.

The third fragment of evidence is presented by Robert Cole. He writes of the IRA plot to assassinate John:

> It came to nothing, and . . . responsible IRA leaders apparently never thought that Betjeman was other than what he appeared. But then, in January 1942, an Irish acquaintance on the West Coast begged Betjeman to come down because 'something very important has turned up about the fishing. It is urgent that you should come here and see me *now* . . .' Betjeman contacted Brigadier Woodhouse immediately, saying: 'This may be important.' Did 'fish' refer to German submarines? Was Betjeman acting as liaison with naval intelligence?[224]

The message John received was almost a parody of a 'spy' message. As he was no keen fisherman,[225] he would not have regarded any aspect of fishing as 'important'. And Cole's tentative hypothesis about naval Intelligence reminds us that, in the year after John left Dublin, he had a 'hush-hush' post with the Admiralty in England.*

The fourth piece of evidence looks even more like 'red meat'. In 1998 David O'Donoghue published his scholarly book *Hitler's Irish Voices: The Story of German Radio's Irish Service*. Part of the book is about Mrs Susan Hilton, who, although born in India of British parents,[226]

---

* See Chapter 15, 'Admiralty'.

had Irish connections. Using her maiden name, she began broadcasting to Ireland from Berlin in January 1942, and 'warned listeners against allowing Ireland to be turned into a battlefield following America's entry into the war'.[227] She had arrived in occupied Europe as a prisoner-of-war. 'The ship on which she had been travelling from Britain to Burma in 1940 was captured by a German warship in the Indian Ocean – and, having first refused to undertake a spying mission to Ireland, she escaped further incarceration by agreeing to write articles and later to broadcast for German Radio.'[228]

> On 26 March 1942 she used official German Radio notepaper to write a letter to her brother Edward, then living at the Moat House in Oldcastle, County Meath. The letter read:
>> My Dear Edward, by now you will have heard that I am here working at the above address [77 Kaiserdamm, Berlin]. Maybe you sometimes hear me. I speak mostly at 8.15 [p.m.] over the station Rennes and some other shortwave, but I never can remember . . . I am well and fortunate to be alive after the fun and games I have had all over the world. Cheerio, your many times devoted sister, Susan
>
> As well as being read by the Gestapo, the letter was intercepted by British Intelligence who tipped off their Irish counterparts in G2. It threw an unwelcome spotlight on Edward Sweney who never received his sister's letter but did become the subject of an official investigation. G2's contacts with MI5 were well developed at that stage of the war and so it was a British official, not an Irish one, who was despatched to check up on Edward Sweney at his poultry farm . . . Almost fifty years after the event, the latter recalled it in detail. The official sent to the Moat House was John Betjeman, then attached to the British diplomatic representation in Dublin, officially as a 'press and cultural attaché', but actually involved in intelligence work. Sweney remembers that Betjeman 'called at my place in the 1940s in a car when no one had cars, and asked whether the local church had pews in it or not. I told him I didn't know but suggested he could get a chair to stand on and look through the church windows to see for himself.'[229] Betjeman's question was a pretext to engage Sweney in conversation but the wily farmer did not take the bait. At around the same time Sweney also received a phone call from the German Minister in Dublin, Eduard Hempel, but he can no longer recall what Hempel said.[230]

The message about the 'fish' and the Edward Sweney affair suggest that, on at least two occasions, John trespassed into the 'grey area'. But, if he was a 'spy', he was an ineffectual one. James Bond would have left his car at a discreet distance from Sweney's poultry farm[231] if he intended to pose as an antiquarian fascinated by pews. If indeed

John had some kind of Intelligence rôle – and the evidence suggests he had – it is likely to have been only a minor and fitful aspect of his work, not – as implied by David O'Donoghue – a major task for which his formal title of press attaché was only a cover.

One piece of evidence which weights the balance against major Intelligence duties for John is the mock timetable he wrote of his typical day's work, 'A Representative Day in the Press Attaché's Office'. It was presumably written to amuse his secretary, Miss Whitehorn, and others of the staff at Upper Mount Street; perhaps it was also a sidelong way of making Maffey aware of some of his grievances. There is a clear element of spoofery in the document. No doubt John squeezed several days' events into the supposed account of one day in his life, rather as Pugin marshalled the domes and spires of several cities in the *capriccio* frontispiece to his *Contrasts*. But the exercise would have been less entertaining to Miss Whitehorn and Maffey if it had not resembled reality. If John had to cope with even a quarter of these pettifogging duties in his average day, then by Archimedes' Principle little time can have been left for Intelligence work. The only direct reference to espionage in the whole schedule is this:

3.35 [p.m.] Mr Shaw of Trinity has urgent business that he can't discuss over the telephone. (This turns out to be a spy scare).[232]

However, an earlier entry reads:

2.30 [p.m.] While Miss Whitehorn is typing my letters Dr Constantia Maxwell, Professor of Economic History at Trinity College, Dublin,[233] is announced. She asks if she may put a letter into the diplomatic bag which is addressed to a dentist in London and contains her own drawing of a tooth with an exposed nerve which is giving her great pain and which she alleges her dentist in D[ublin] is not competent to treat. Miss Whitehorn assures her that if speed in transit is essential the letter had better go by express post through the ordinary channel, and gives her the name of a dentist in Dublin who is eminently capable and who does Sir John's teeth and her own. Dr Maxwell leaves quite contented and pauses on the threshold to expound her theory that the final Axis *coup* will take the form of an invasion of Ireland.[234]

Professor Foster records in *Paddy and Mr Punch* that Elizabeth Bowen spent 'an afternoon *tête-à-tête* with Archbishop McQuaid of Dublin – an unlikely conjunction, set up by Constantia Maxwell of Trinity College on the pretext that her friend was interested in social work'.[235]

In the sustained *jeu d'esprit* of the Pooterish timetable, John may well have belittled his importance to add to the comedy: he depicts himself as put-upon dogsbody. But some observers thought him just such an insignificant figure. Hector Legge said in 1976: 'John Betjeman was small boys' stuff – Maffey's little boy. Nobody took him very seriously, and there wasn't much for him to do. The papers were all down to a minimum – the *Sunday Independent*, which I edited, was only four pages. So there wasn't much point in Betjeman's churning out press releases.'[236] Professor Foster has formed a similar impression of John's wartime rôle from the surviving documents in the Public Record Office, London. He writes that in Dublin John 'indulged in a camp Hibernian High Church fantasy'.[237]

John Lehmann, editor of *New Writing*, gave in his memoirs a more sympathetic and probably fairer assessment.

> John Betjeman had taken on a cultural liaison job in neutral Dublin in the UK Representative's office, and fulfilled his duties with immense aplomb and zest, charming the most suspicious among the local intelligentsia into at least keen interest if not wholehearted engagement with what writers and artists were thinking and doing in war-shattered Britain, and keeping an easy lead over his Axis opposite numbers all through the course; thus proving, not for the first or last time, that in such a job a dram of personality is worth a hogshead of bureaucracy. He acted, in fact, as a two-way channel between the countries, providing at the same time Irish intellectuals with a much-needed outlet into the wider Anglo-Saxon world of letters, the normal passages of which censorship, shipping dangers and every other kind of war-time restriction had all but dammed up. He managed to arrange a mutual exchange of *New Writing* and *The Bell*, and elicited stories or poems from some of the more interesting Irish writers which he sent over to me, with accompanying letters that would suddenly break mysteriously into Gaelic . . . I tried in vain to get him to send new poems of his own: 'only Tennysonian blank verse pours out of me,' he wrote in the Spring of 1942; but a few months later: 'I feel as though I shall never be able to write again.'[238]

Why did John and Penelope leave Ireland, late in 1943? Given their growing disenchantment with the pattern of their life there, John may well have been pulling strings. Some of his disaffection is seen in a letter he wrote Oliver Stonor in March 1943.

> We live in a large, wet, partly furnished house . . . Just now the daffodils are out on the 'lawn' and the avenue beeches are budding. It is what one would dream of as the ideal existence – if it weren't for Irish politics – and

what I have often longed for. But what is my reaction? Acute nostalgia for
Wolverhampton, as you divined. I have never worked so hard in my life
and with so little tangible results.[239]

On 14 June, 'Mr John Betjeman Leaving' was front-page news in the
Irish Times.[240] He received over seventy letters of regret.[241] Replying
to Frank Gallagher's, he gave palatable reasons for the move.

It all sounds rather like a bereavement and it is one. I am very depressed
at going. So many friends made, so much kindness. But I'm not leaving
until the middle of August, so far as I know, so we will meet again. And
Propeller will not leave until September.

The reasons for my going are not hard to explain to you, though they
might be to some people. When I was over in London last I was urgently
asked for by Minnie [the MoI]. I suppose I could have said 'no' and been
backed up from here. But then it occurred to Propeller and me that we
would either have to remain here permanently (and the job is unlikely to
go on after the war) or go back when we were wanted. We both have
responsibilities in England. First our village life where the Vicar (Anglo-
Catholic) [the Rev. George Bridle] is old and ill and wants us to help with
the church life of the village as we used to do; and second, the need to be
in England during all the post-war reconstruction schemes and to put in a
word, everywhere possible, for Christian bases. Living in Ireland has been
a wonderful experience, because it is a wholly Christian country. I am sure
it is my duty to go back and to help to remake England one so far as I can.
It would be not so easy to carry any weight either in the village or in public
work and writing, if people were to have justifications for saying, 'You
lived on eggs and bacon in comfort in Eire for the war and now you come
and tell us what we ought to do.' We obviously must share some of the
unpleasantness with them of wartime life. So that was why we decided I
had better accept the job offered me. Rough luck on Paul and Candida.[242]

The MacEntees gave an informal leaving party for John and
Penelope. 'Towards the end of it,' Ruth-Ellen Moller recalls, 'my
mother said to John, "Why don't you sing?" So he sang, in fluent Irish,
"Dark Rosaleen" – sixteen verses – with the tears pouring down his
face. My mother accompanied him on the piano. The tears were terrible, because others started to cry, too. The tears were genuine; but
the letters which have been published show he was glad to leave.'[243]
Frank Gallagher organized the formal leaving party in Dublin Castle.
Terence de Vere White,[244] another friend the Betjemans had made in
Dublin, remembered: 'The *gardaí* controlled the traffic as it piled up in
the Lower Castle Yard, and there must have been a sinking in the hearts

of many who had seen themselves as choice spirits.'[245] Gallagher made
the farewell speech. 'One thing', he said, 'they will carry with them as
proof of Irish hospitality. Came three. Went four . . .'[246]

On 25 August 1943 John and Penelope went together to say goodbye
to de Valera, who signed and dated a photograph of himself. Some
four months later, John, over lunch at Brooks's with James Lees-
Milne:

> Said he loved Ireland but not the Irish middle class. Only liked the country
> eccentrics like Penelope's distant relations, the Chetwode [sic]-Aikens.
> When they claimed to be cousins Penelope retorted, 'No, you can't be.
> Your branch was extinct fifty years ago.' When the Betjemans left Ireland,
> de Valera sent for them. Penelope said to him, 'My husband knows
> nothing of politics; or of journalism. He knows nothing at all.' She offered
> to plan an equestrian tour for de Valera, and her last words to him were,
> 'I hope you won't let the Irish roads deteriorate. I mean I hope you won't
> have them metalled and tarmacked.'[247]

DAILY HERALD

The *Daily Herald* was started as a serious political paper. It failed. When it copied the frivolities of successful rivals it equalled their success.

Frank Preston, Technical Books Adviser to Odhams Press, *Tribune*, 21 April 1944

My mornings are spent reviewing rubbish for the *Daily Herald* – once a week my articles appear and I thank God none of my friends see the paper.

John Betjeman, letter to Mabel Fitzgerald, 20 August 1944[1]

It was the fate of a rackety journalist called Tom Darlow that led to John's becoming freelance book critic of the *Daily Herald*. Early in 1940, Darlow, then the paper's deputy editor, asked to be released from desk duties to go to France as a war correspondent. The editor, Francis Williams, tried to persuade him to stay. He and Darlow had been colleagues and drinking companions on the *Sunday Express* in the 1920s. When they went to Soho or docklands in search of excitement, Darlow's build – he was six foot three inches tall and bulky in proportion – deterred rougher elements.[2] He was in revolt against his strict upbringing as the son of a Congregational minister. On the *Herald* he often caused trouble, Williams recalled, 'by disappearing for days at a time with a young woman to whom he was attached and then ringing up from a rather grand hotel somewhere to announce that he could not pay the bill and as he was most anxious not to give the paper a bad name, would I have the money to meet it dispatched forthwith';[3] but he was a good journalist and Williams enjoyed his company. Still, Darlow was insistent that he be sent to France. Reluctantly, Williams let him go. 'There after a few brilliant dispatches he died ...', Williams wrote. 'Fleet Street seemed empty without him.'[4]

Darlow was replaced as deputy editor by Percy Cudlipp, John's old boss on the *Evening Standard*, who 'had grown weary of Beaverbrook'.[5] Late in 1940, Williams resigned as editor of the *Herald*. He had been manoeuvred into doing so by the proprietor, Lord

Southwood, of whom he later wrote, 'I came to hate him more than any man I have ever known.'[6] Southwood made Percy Cudlipp editor. In 1943 Cudlipp needed a new book reviewer – a single writer who would select and pronounce on the books of the week. He chose John. Evidently he did not hold against him his naughtinesses as *Standard* film critic – the blazing row with the movie mogul, the 'scoop' fiasco, the muddled facts that upset Bruce Lockhart, the failure to track down the American star in her liner cabin. As film critic John had proved his ability to write entertainingly and had been a draw to advertisers. Cudlipp, himself a doggerel versifier, also admired John's poetry. And he felt about him rather as Francis Williams did about Darlow: he might be 'a bit of a handful', but he enjoyed having him around.

John began reviewing for the *Herald* in November 1943. His then agent, Edmund Cork, negotiated a fee of fourteen guineas a week, which was to increase to eighteen in July 1945. John used his first 'About Books' column to set out his stall.

> If you see a book at a booksellers which you like the look of, buy it while it is still there. Books are not rationed, but good books are scarce.[7]

Only two of the thirty words of this 'intro' are of more than one syllable: like George Orwell, in his journalism of this same period, John understood the power of plain writing – in this trait, both men were perhaps influenced by the Authorized Version of the Bible. In the rest of the article, John hammered the 'mad situation of English literature' in the war, by which publishers had become arbiters of public taste, because the public appetite for books was such that they would buy anything publishers chose to print.

John's second article in the *Herald* was headed 'Nothing Over One-and-Six' (that is, 1s 6d). Graham Greene's *Brighton Rock* was among the paperbacks he recommended.[8] By 24 November he was into his stride with a slyly satirical notice of A.G. Street's *Hitler's Whistle*:

> The leisurely, conversational writing of Farmer Street[9] is always to me like standing on market day in a country town and hearing someone hold forth on the price of hay.
>
> If you are in the mood, you think this is a breath of old England. If you are not, you think what an old bore the man is.[10]

But he conceded that the book contained a 'good evacuee story'.

> It concerns a maiden lady who lived in a small house in the country with one maid.

One morning the bell rang.

The maid admitted the visitor and then rushed upstairs. 'Please, mum,' she blurted out breathlessly, 'you've got to have two babies, and the man's downstairs.'[11]

John had only one serious disqualification as a writer for the *Herald*: his political views, or rather his lack of them. It was a Labour paper. Started as a strike journal in 1912, for several years it was edited by the Labour politician George Lansbury. It was the *Daily Express* of the left.

A casuist could make a debating case that John was a left-wing radical. He reverenced William Morris and had bought relics of the great Socialist poet–artist at the Kelmscott Manor sale in 1939.[12] He ran errands for the National Union of Railwaymen during the General Strike of 1926. He was a friend of Conrad Noel, the 'Red Vicar' of Thaxted. He hobnobbed with G.D.H. Cole (a frequent *Herald* contributor), with John Dugdale and Tom Driberg. At Sezincote he had met Clement Attlee, the future leader of the Labour Party. His relationship with Hugh Gaitskell, another future Labour leader, was much more intimate. Yet a third future Labour leader, Michael Foot, contributed a political column to the *Herald* when John was book critic. Foot wrote in 1970, reviewing for the *Evening Standard* 'the latest, enlarged, umpteenth' edition of the *Collected Poems*: 'How many of the anti-pollutionists or community-preservers of the 1970s may look for their inspiration to early Betjeman? . . . He anticipated and, maybe, excited the modern outcry against the desecration of England in general and London in particular . . .'[13] By that time John's 'We spray the fields and scatter/The poison on the ground' could be hailed as a hymn for ecologists. In 'The City' and 'Slough', John had blasted capitalists. 'But spare the bald young clerks who add/The profits of the stinking cad . . .' was almost Socialist orthodoxy.

It is not entirely preposterous to claim such left-wing credentials for John. He was a humane man, sickened by cruelty or devastation. But in truth he was virtually apolitical – and an apolitical man is clearly not much concerned with changing the status quo; so, by definition, he is at least a conservative with a small 'c'. The tug of all John's emotions was to the past and to a hierarchical society in which one might have the fun of climbing towards a summit. Though he was a friend of Auden and Spender he had no truck with their Socialism in the 1930s. For that reason, he received no mention in D.E.S. Maxwell's *Poets of the Thirties* (1969) or in Samuel Hyne's *The Auden Generation* (1976), though the poet Robin Skelton did include three of John's poems in *The Penguin Poets: Poets of the*

Thirties; and no portrait of him was shown in the National Portrait Gallery's 1980 exhibition 'Writers of the Thirties'. He took little interest in the Spanish Civil War. Through Harold Nicolson, he flirted with Oswald Mosley's fascist magazine *Action*. In 1945 he had a rubber stamp made, 'Telephone not allowed by Slave State'.[14] In 'Huxley Hall' he was to write, 'Comrades plot a Comrade's downfall "in the interests of the State"'. In 1992 Margaret Thatcher quoted, as an epitome of the Socialist nightmare, these lines from 'The Planster's Vision':

> I have a Vision of the Future, chum,
>> The workers' flats in fields of soya beans
>> Tower up like silver pencils, score on score:
> And Surging Millions hear the Challenge come
>> From microphones in communal canteens
>> 'No Right! No Wrong! All's perfect, evermore.'

When, after the Second World War, 'new estates' were built in the country to house Londoners who had been bombed out in the Blitz, John deplored the violence done to the landscape by 'these wretched little houses' and did not set against it the welfare of thousands of families. Politically he was closer to Evelyn Waugh than to Auden.

Luckily for John, neither the proprietor nor the editor of the *Herald* was zealous in adherence to Socialist dogma. 'Lord Southwood was really an absurd figure to be in charge of a Labour paper,' Michael Foot said. 'He was a small-minded man interested only in profits.'[15] Foot had a much higher regard for Percy Cudlipp, 'although maybe he was not a tremendously enthusiastic Socialist'.[16]

> He was an extremely efficient editor in every way [Foot said in 1990]. He could do anything on a newspaper. He could take anybody's copy and make it better; he could make up the paper; he could write the political leader; but he could also write poetry of his own peculiar debased kind – it didn't claim to be anything of any great moment . . .
> Percy was the brightest and best of all the Cudlipp family – Hugh[17] will contest it! – and certainly the most interested in light verse. His relationship with John Betjeman was a very close one; I often heard Percy talk about Betjeman.[18]

John was not required to toe the party line undeviatingly. In 1946 he wrote to the publisher William Collins that if he gave up his job at the British Council he would be 'at the mercy of the *Daily Herald* which may sack me at any moment for being a bloody reactionary and not the sort of reviewer they want. I don't trust them an inch.'[19] But, though he was sometimes reproved by Cudlipp, he was never fired.

One committed Socialist on the staff was Marjorie Proops, later the queen of agony aunts on the *Daily Mirror*. She was on the *Herald* throughout the war, first as a fashion artist, then as fashion editor, later as women's editor. Her overriding memory of the *Herald*'s offices in Long Acre (the building was demolished in 1984) was 'a persistent smell of rotting cabbages'. Covent Garden market was still below. 'I used to walk through the market every morning and knew all the porters. They gave me apples to have with my lunch. They used a lot of naughty words: of course, I didn't know what they were talking about.'[20]

The *Herald*'s star columnist was Hannen Swaffer, whom Southwood had enticed away from Beaverbrook. 'He always struck me as ten feet tall,' Marjorie Proops said. 'He was a man of importance – of self-importance, too. Simply disregarded lesser creatures like myself.'[21] Michael Foot has warmer memories of Swaffer.

> In the Twenties he was a theatre columnist on the *Daily Express*. He had his face slapped by actresses and there were other sensations. In those days he was considered a drunkard but by the time he got to the *Herald* he was a full-scale teetotaller because of all the disastrous things that had happened to him when he was drunk. He was a great gaunt fellow with cigarette ash spilling all over him.
>
> He was the most inaccurate journalist, I think, who ever lived. He could hardly tell a story without two printed corrections being required. But he was extremely kind to young journalists . . .
>
> He became a strong spiritualist. He would go to Percy Cudlipp's office and say he'd been talking to Northcliffe on the Other Side and this was Northcliffe's advice as to what the *Herald* should do . . .[22]

When Swaffer's *Stranger than Truth* was published in 1947, John gave it a friendly, but not unreservedly favourable, review. 'I do not review this book of short stories because its author is on the staff of the "Daily Herald". I review it as an example of the use of journalism in story-telling. You may not regard these tales – the best are those which deal with the stage and with Londoners – as masterpieces of concise prose. Their manner is often flowery. But they are stories. That is to say, from the first sentence you wonder what is going to happen.'[23] Marjorie Proops received a more flattering review, for her illustrations to Lillian Day's *Domestic Symphony* (1946), 'a high-speed comedy about a cute American girl of 16'. ('The drawings by Proops are really humorous – they are funny in themselves without the need for an explanation underneath and reflect the gaiety of the book.') Marje Proops said that she did not meet John often, because he had no desk at the *Herald*, but hand-delivered his copy to the cabbage-smelling office every Tuesday.[24] This chore was often combined with an architectural exploration. On 15 December 1946 he wrote:

> To each his private pleasure. Mine is looking at buildings old, new and middle-aged. So soon as I have delivered these reviews to the 'Daily Herald' I go off for the afternoon on a tram.
>
> Away in the suburbs I watch the sun redden behind high Victorian churches, children scamper over municipal asphalte [*sic*], cats dash into speckled laurel bushes, and I think myself back into my childhood.
>
> I am perfectly happy. Mr **J.M. Richards** clearly has the same pleasure. His book, THE CASTLES ON THE GROUND (*Architectural Press*, 8s. 6d.) is the first study of the modern suburb which looks at it from my own point of view that I have read . . .
>
> In effect, Mr Richards says it's no good being superior about 'Jerrybethan' and 'suburbia' and making pleas for simplicity and restraint and 'good taste'. The truth is that 90 people out of 100 *like* modern half-timbered villas and suburban life. What we must do is to see why they like them and to become fond of the suburbs ourselves.

This passage shows how winningly John could write when his interest was engaged. Often it was not. His mother 'gutted' many of the books for him and he frequently used her brief reports verbatim. Colonel Kolkhorst, by contrast, sent John long and minutely detailed reports, which had to be drastically boiled down in the *Herald*.[25] John's critiques were marred by a disinclination to write anything but good of the writers under review. One reason for this was that he was so acutely sensitive to adverse criticism himself that he shrank from visiting it on others. On 7 March 1945 he wrote: 'When a man lays bare his soul he should be treated kindly, whether he does it in prose or verse. Reviewers killed Keats . . . I feel qualms of conscience towards an author's feelings and would prefer not to review a book at all rather than review it unkindly.' A.L. Rowse had a more cynical explanation of John's benevolence: 'He didn't want to make enemies in the literary world.'[26]

On 6 September 1944 John wrote: 'I believe it is true to say that any book which is printed now sells out.' The reviewer might therefore be seen as redundant, but in public, at least, John bridled at the idea that book-reviewing was a frivolous, escapist activity which did not contribute to the war effort. On 13 September 1944 he wrote: '"You can no more win a war of ideas without books than you can win a naval battle without ships," said President Roosevelt. And this is a war of ideas, if ever there was one.' Earlier in the same year he had written, with unusual asperity:

> What harm there is in catchwords! Two of the latest are 'escapist' and 'sentimental'. As I propose to be both these things for a minute or two, I intend to defend myself (and you) first.
>
> An escapist is someone who seeks relief from one form of mental or physical activity in another.
>
> But escapism has grown into a catchword used by people with uneasy consciences to describe those who take an interest in things they are not interested in themselves, but would like to be if they could only summon the energy.
>
> It generally takes the form of giving somebody a dirty look for not going all out 100 per cent. for the WAR EFFORT all the time and never letting up – a physical impossibility for us all, because body and brain demand diversion as a rest.
>
> 'Sentimental' is a word used by people who are shy of admitting the existence of love, who dry up their tears in the cinema before the lights go up and then assert that they never cried after all . . .
>
> THE EAGLE AND THE DOVE, by **V. Sackville-West** (*Michael Joseph*, 10s. 6d. net) is both 'escapist' and 'sentimental', and all honour to the words, if we must use them . . .[27]

John was further discouraged by what seemed to him a shortage of English authors. Every week about a quarter of the books he received for review were by Americans.

> Another quarter are by journalists who have been out on some war front, and who seem to race one another to see who can get out a book on the very latest phase of the war first. This does not make for good reading.
>
> Another quarter consists of essays and pamphlets. The remaining quarter are the more usual English books.
>
> The explanation is quite simple. Every English writer of note who is not over age or physically disabled is doing some sort of war work and has no time to write at length.
>
> So I advise you, unless you see a new book warmly recommended, to content yourself with an old book or a reprint of an old one.[28]

An additional reason for recommending old books was that most of the new ones, because of shortages and war conditions, were so poorly produced. It was not only that John delighted in the 'physique' of well-printed, well-bound books. Having to read several books a week muzzily printed on greyish paper was affecting his eyes. In the *Herald* of 20 January 1944 he asked the printer to put a small drawing of a pair of spectacles against books printed in 'type so small that it may strain your eyes'.

Among the prose writers of the past whom John recommended were Walter Scott, Dickens, Thackeray (John thought *Vanity Fair* superior to any of Dickens's novels, though Dickens wrote 'magnificent passages'), Meade Falkner and Conrad. 'I remember "Bartimeus",[29] another fine sea-story writer, telling me that Conrad always retained a slight foreign accent, but that he had a most wonderful choice of words in his conversation.'[30] Edith Wharton was also praised: 'She was satirical, witty, profound – I remember her *House of Mirth*, about New York society, as a landmark in my reading.'[31] Reviewing Hilton Brown's 'appreciation'-cum-biography of Kipling in 1945, John wondered whether it was suitable for *Herald* readers – 'The subject is generally considered unutterably Tory.' But he recommended the work: 'It is the sort of book, were one a famous man, one would wish written about himself.' Hilton Brown's book was not a 'whitewash'. John learned from it that 'Kipling always idolized his superiors. He remained a schoolboy at heart and obeyed the prefects.' The book also suggested to John that 'All his life [Kipling] was to look for friends and find only fame.'[32]

The miserable hours of parsing with Mr Gidney at Marlborough paid off when John reviewed E.V. Rieu's translation of Homer's *Odyssey*.

> It does not, because it cannot, preserve the poetry. Indeed it is worth learning Greek simply to read Homer: just take one of Homer's great and best-known phrases, 'polyewfloizboyolasseez' (I write it phonetically). That means, literally translated, 'of the loud-sounding sea'.
>
> It doesn't seem great shakes in English. But roll the Greek over on your tongue again slowly and hear if it does not describe a breaker tumbling about in foam and finally hissing up the shingle.[33]

In the same review, John was for once severe, on a translation of Pushkin's poems by Walter Morison, and used his own poetic talents to damn it.

> 'They hear the thunder's roaring glee' – that line would be rejected for a school magazine. It may be literal but I blame the translator for using it.
>
> Only a great poet can translate a great lyric poet in poetry and great poets generally only know their own language. Let me show you what I mean: here is a famous verse from Coleridge['s] *Ancient Mariner*:

> The fair breeze blew, the white foam flew,
> The furrow follow'd free:
> We were the first that ever burst
> Into that silent sea.

Now imagine yourself a Russian with no English, reading a translation of it, the translator having said in his preface (as most translators do): 'I have so far as possible kept to the meaning, metre and rhyming scheme of the original.' Here is the same verse:

> The wind was fair, there was foam in air,
> The wake came on unbound
> No one before did ever explore
> That ocean free from sound.

The sense, metre and rhymes are there – but the poetry is gone![34]

Reviewing Edmund Blunden's *Shelley* (1946), John was torn between being gracious to Blunden, whom he admired, and giving the rough edge of his tongue to Shelley, whom he disliked for his atheism and inflated language. (Thomas Hardy's doubts about the existence of God he was prepared to overlook, as they were less 'arrogantly' expressed.) In the review, John compromised: 'Being a poet himself, Mr Blunden can quote from Shelley's poems in the course of this stormy life in such a way as to cause me to turn to my dusty copy and enjoy some of them for the first time. Though I agree with Tennyson that "Shelley was not worth Keats's little finger", he is, of course, a poet.'[35]

John made no mention of André Maurois' *Ariel*, the life of Shelley which had become the first Penguin book in 1935; but in reviewing William Blake's *Selected Poems* (Westhouse, 1947), chosen by Denis Saurat, he showed himself fully *au fait* with the politics of the Blake worship which was at the centre of the new romantic movement in poetry and art in the 1940s.

> Denis Saurat says in his introduction that 'the test is literary: there is none other.' If only he had read that excellent book of Ruthven Todd's, *Tracks in the Snow*, which appeared last year, he would have known more of Blake. For this great poet's religious beliefs mixed up with Swedenborg, Richard Brothers, Joanna Southcott and the beginnings of the Anglo-Israelites are an essential part of him, and Ruthven Todd is the first to have investigated them at all deeply.
>
> I do not believe there is such a thing as 'pure literature'. I think every man's writings are a part of his beliefs and his relation to the age in which

he lived. For this reason I think this handsome selection of Blake fails. The criterion of 'pure literature' by which it has been selected seems to me a false one.[36]

When Holbrook Jackson's edition of *The Complete Nonsense of Edward Lear* was published by Faber's in 1947, John drew a significant contrast. 'Lewis Carroll, by comparison, is a pedantic don in his nonsense poetry, but Lear was a true Victorian poet and a true artist. Most of us can bear poetry only if it has a story or sounds marvellous when it is read out and makes us want to shout and dance. Lear knew this. First he wrote his famous illustrated Limericks. Then he wrote whole poems which sounded like those of his friend Tennyson, and which were, in their mad way, as poetical.'[37]

In June 1945 John complained: 'Now we have a system of paper control which rigorously keeps down the printing of good literature, the slow-selling classic, in favour of what will sell off rapidly in a month.'[38] But, during the time he was reviewing for the *Herald*, several books were published which are now regarded as classics – among them Evelyn Waugh's *Brideshead Revisited*, Albert Camus' *The Outsider*, John Steinbeck's *Cannery Row*, L.P. Hartley's *Eustace and Hilda*, Joyce Cary's *The Horse's Mouth*, Malcolm Lowry's *Under the Volcano*, Elizabeth Bowen's *The Demon Lover* and Mervyn Peake's *Titus Groan*.

John's almost unerring recognition of exceptional quality is the most impressive aspect of his reviewing. Of course a critic who praises virtually everything he reviews is not going to miss many winners, but the purr of John's approval rose to a noticeably higher frequency – like a Geiger counter in the presence of uranium – when he encountered a masterpiece.

He found Camus' *The Outsider* 'so well written and profoundly disturbing that it is in a class by itself'.

What makes so short a book so moving, so true to its Paganism, is that although, by our own standards, this highly intelligent and physically attractive young man has no morals, no conscience, no motive in life, we still sympathize with him.

Throughout the trial we see that the French are imposing the alien moral and Christian code of Europe on a sun-soaked Pagan.

Seldom have I read a work which says so much in so short a space.[39]

In August 1944 John wrote of Cary's *The Horse's Mouth*:

Mr Cary is an important and exciting writer, there's no doubt about that. To use Tennyson's phrase, he is a Lord of Language.

He talks about the night getting 'as dark as the inside of a Cabinet Minister'. And here are rich people.

'Just then the Beeders came in. Sir William and Lady. Big man with a bald head and monkey fur on the back of his hands. Voice like a Liverpool dray on a rumbling bridge. Charming manners.'[40]

In May 1945 John wrote to Evelyn Waugh:

You are very much in my thoughts, for I am reading for a second time *Brideshead Revisited* since it has come in to me for review in the bloody old *Daily Herald*. It will get a spanking good notice. To me it is a great treat to read a book with a standard of values behind it. Christian values what is more. I shall have somehow to hint this fact to readers without letting it be apparent to the Editors, since recently I had a letter from them to say that I was using the paper for *Roman Catholic propaganda* and that 'The *Daily Herald* finds itself in conflict with the Catholic Church on several points.' I was also accused of 'Jesuitry'. This made me rather proud. Of course, I have not altered my tactics.[41]

John reviewed the book in June. 'Evelyn Waugh is about the only living writer whose novels I can read a second time with pleasure. This is because he hates writing and does not suffer from verbal diarrhoea, as do many lengthier novelists . . . His new novel is, I think, his best yet, and that is saying a lot.'[42]

T.F. Powys's *Bottle's Path* (1946) was his first collection of stories for ten years. John compared him favourably with Thomas Hardy, who 'understood the slowness, the sense of external laws which rule us, the graspingness, the weather, the nearness of birth and death in country life'. (John uses the word 'us' as a country-dweller in Uffington.) But Powys's writing is 'consciously simple' whereas Hardy's was 'unconsciously cumbrous'. John writes of Powys: 'Most of his stories are tremendous. And they have about them a sense of the Old Testament, of cruel deeds done down lonely lanes and of a miracle impending.'[43]

Reviewing Lowry's *Under the Volcano* (1947), John agreed with the publisher's blurb: the book was 'as ambitious as it is impressive'. He added: 'Another title might have been "A Day in the Life of a Dipsomaniac" . . . The effect of the writing is to make the reader feel drunk himself – a most convincing performance by the author.'[44]

L.P. Hartley's *Eustace and Hilda* (1947) completed the trilogy of novels begun with *The Shrimp and the Anemone* and *The Sixth Heaven*. John thought that the combined effect of the three books was one of 'mounting excellence'. He specially relished these novels because, like much of his own best work, they evoked what it was like to be a child.

[Eustace], the central figure, is an immortal portrayal of the delights and agonies of childhood and adolescence.

I cannot but envy the author of these books. He must feel immensely satisfied to have written a social novel which is in the class of George Meredith . . .[45]

If Hartley took John back to childhood, Seán O'Casey took him back to a past more recently left behind, in Ireland. Reviewing O'Casey's autobiography *Drums under the Windows* (1945) John wrote:

Seán O' Casey soars like a bird on his own eloquence. He hardly minds what he says for the joy he has in saying it. And as he writes I feel I am listening to the magniloquent talk of a Dublin pub.

I see the velvet-brown porter and through the windows of the snug inn* watch those green trams swish past the fine, seedy Georgian façades of Guinness-coloured Dublin brick.

O'Casey brings with him a smell of peat smoke and that world of internal strife which only those who know Ireland know . . .[46]

Another Irish writer who was high in John's regard was Elizabeth Bowen. David Daiches has suggested that it was only with the publication of *The Heat of the Day* in 1949 that she 'moved out of the ranks of interesting minor writers to become a major modern novelist'; but she received three admiring mentions from John in 1944–45. Reviewing *The Hotel*, her novel about the guests in a hotel in the south of France (23 March 1944), he called her 'one of the subtlest and most sensitive of modern . . . writers'. On 17 October 1945 he described her as 'one of the greatest exponents' of the short story and quoted extracts from her contribution to *New Writing* and *Daylight*. Two weeks later he wrote (revealing, not for the first or last time, the chip on his shoulder about being a book writer forced to take work as a journalist):[47] 'Nor should we assume that if you write for the newspapers you are spoiled for writing books. Elizabeth Bowen reviews novels in weekly periodicals. Yet I think I give her the palm for short-story writing in her latest book, THE DEMON LOVER (*Cape*, 7s. 6d.).'[48]

In the same issue, he devoted a paragraph to Steinbeck's *Cannery Row*, in which the American novelist had returned 'to the nomadic slum life he described in *The Grapes of Wrath* and *Tortilla Flat*'. John

---

* I suspect that what John wrote was 'through the windows of the snug I watch those green trams swish', using the word 'snug' as a noun; but that an officious sub-editor, thinking 'snug' was an adjective in need of a noun, inserted the word 'inn'.

disparaged 'the plot – if you can call it one', but added: 'Plot does not matter, since Steinbeck holds your attention and, what is more, teaches you, with his knowledge of human nature.'[49]

John was one of the most insular of English poets; yet he was not insular in his literary taste. In 1946 he gave high praise to Vladimir Nabokov's *The Real Life of Sebastian Knight*, acclaiming him as 'a novelist in the forefront'. He admired Nabokov's use of adjectives.

> See how he describes a European express train at night: 'The long sad sigh of brakes at dimly surmised stations, the upward slide of an embossed leather blind disclosing a platform . . . the clank of an invisible hammer testing wheels; the gliding move into darkness; the passing glimpse of a lone woman touching silver-bright things in her travelling case on the blue plush of a lighted compartment.'[50]

On the same day John reviewed Mervyn Peake's book *Titus Groan*, about the Earl of Groan and his mad sisters, Cora and Clarice. 'If you can tuck yourself into the dream world Mr Peake creates – and I was able to do so – this book is a cobwebby, candle-lit escape from life.'[51] (Only later editions of the book were enhanced by Peake's illustrations of Gothic 'gloomth'.)

In January 1947 John reviewed Saul Bellow's *Dangling Man*, published by John Lehmann. 'What happened to a man in America could not have happened to him in England. He expected to be called up, resigned his civilian job, had a year to wait before entering the United States Army. This is a diary of the year of waiting. It is in the best vein of sophisticated American prose.'[52]

Generations of critics had lauded some of the pre-twentieth-century classics John praised but there was no 'critical heritage' to tell him to admire *Dangling Man*, Bellow's first novel. The acuteness of John's talent-spotting was revealed also in his reception of two English writers in their twenties, Francis King and P.H. Newby. Of King's first novel *To the Dark Tower* (1946) John wrote, under the crosshead 'IT'S NOT NICE':

> I do not think 'nice' people will recommend TO THE DARK TOWER by **Francis King** (*Home and Van Thal*, 9s. 6d.). It is unhealthy, saturated with sex and physical violence; it is remorseless; it is a tale of despair . . .
>
> Though no 'nice' people will recommend *To the Dark Tower*, I will.
>
> Nothing escapes the author's eyes, not even the meals in the inefficient arty tea shoppe in Chelsea:
>
> 'After the apple course the plates were always lined with what looked

like toe-nails. Miss Plumpton was too haphazard to core an apple with any success.'

I find, on adding up, that I have to read over three hundred novels a year. Half a dozen of them would I wish to read again. This is one.[53]

Francis King was grateful to John. 'It's grotesque,' he wrote in 1992, 'but at that period my book shocked a number of critics. Pamela Hansford Johnson reviewed it in *John o' London's Weekly* and called it "disgusting". Henry Reed, who you'd have thought would be more liberal, began his review in *The Listener*, "'Let copulation thrive' seems to be Francis King's motto." So John Betjeman's review meant a great deal to me at that stage. He gave a good review to my second novel, too.'[54]

In the same year John also reviewed P.H. Newby's first novel, *A Journey to the Interior*. Newby was twenty-eight. John thought the book showed him to be 'a writer who is more than merely promising: a real writer who creates character and atmosphere with certainty and economy . . . There broods over it a power of mounting horror that captures you and drags you into the loneliness of the searcher's mind, made doubly lonely by his weird journey.'[55]

John had some blind spots. He found Thomas Mann unreadable – possibly because he saw in him the 'Teutonic thoroughness' that he deplored in Nikolaus Pevsner.[56] He found Mann's *Joseph the Provider* 'a porridge which went into lumps in my mouth'.[57] He similarly heard the chorus of admiration for Ivy Compton-Burnett, but would not join it. In January 1944, reviewing her *Elders and Betters*, he wrote:

An admirer tells me that had Æschylus and George Eliot married, their daughter might have been Miss Compton-Burnett.

I console myself by thinking that perhaps only one in a hundred readers reads this column. I protect myself by saying that only one in a hundred of these will enjoy Ivy Compton-Burnett.

I am not among them myself.

But I know she is a remarkable writer.[58]

'SHE'S ORIGINAL' said the crosshead above his review of the same author's *Manservant and Maidservant* three years later, however. 'Her style consists almost entirely of dialogue,' he wrote. 'In narrative in the usual sense she is not interested.' But he was relenting towards her slightly. He ended the notice: 'If you can enjoy Miss Compton-Burnett, every novel of hers is a major event in your reading life. I am just beginning to acquire a taste for her style.'[59]

He responded with the same respectful incomprehension to James Joyce's more revolutionary works. In 1947 'two rather heavy-handed

Americans', J. Campbell and H.M. Robinson, produced *A Skeleton Key to Finnegans Wake*. 'They show', John wrote, 'that this vast, unreadable work has a slowly evolving story.' John was prepared to give the key a fair trial. He thought it did make some faint sense of passages which seemed to be in 'language caught by an inattentive ear with only a drift of meaning in it'.

> If you know of an Irish person, get him to read this piece of *Finnegans Wake*, realizing, with the aid of the Key, that it describes nightfall on the banks of the Liffey and two washerwomen calling to one another across the broiling stream. You will then hear the gathering evening and the soft voices above the water:
> 'Dark hawks hear us. Night! Night! My ho head halls. I feel as heavy as yonder stone. Tell me of John or Shaun? Who were Shem and Shaun the living sons or daughters of? Tell me a tale of stem or stone. Beside the rivering water of, hither-and-thithering waters of. Night.'[60]

John was equally unenthusiastic about the modern movement in poetry. Two of the movement's leaders, Eliot and Auden, were friends of his, and he wrote carefully about them; but he could not conceal his distaste, which was more for their influence than for their own works. 'Please don't try to imitate Mr Eliot' was the headline above John's column on 18 October 1944.

> There is little doubt that the greatest established poet writing in Britain to-day is T.S. Eliot.
> There may be other potential great poets lurking among the pages of that excellent periodical 'Poetry', edited by Tambimuttu, in 'Horizon', and other periodicals like a new one called 'Prospect' (*Claremont Press*, Little Chalfont, Bucks, 9d.).
> But Eliot is established, and anyone who is interested in literature has heard of him.
> But not everyone likes him. They say he is obscure, that he doesn't scan or rhyme properly.
> Certainly his influence has been disastrous, for his mannerisms are easy to imitate. Eliot writes lines which are each their own rhythm and poem, and yet together they form a poem which is a sort of outer-covering to the numerous little poems which are each line.
> Imitators have hit on this manner of writing as an excuse for composing 'poems' which are really just prose sentences chopped up to look like Eliot on the printed page. Read the description of the sea . . . from Eliot's poem 'The Dry Salvages' in his new collection FOUR QUARTETS (*Faber*, 6s.) which are his four newest poems in one volume.

If you were to string these lines together like prose, they would be very odd prose and you would soon want to separate them again into Eliot's arrangement.[61]

In 1945 John wrote of his friend:

Wystan Auden, the poet, has reverted to religion. His new book, FOR THE TIME BEING (*Faber*, 8s. 6d.) contains one long poem on the birth of Our Lord and it is clear that its author has been influenced by the thinking of three other British writers from these islands who are in the United States – Aldous Huxley, Gerald Heard and Christopher Isherwood.

Though I cannot get the general drift of the whole poem, being too near to it in time, I find it flowering with mature and beautiful lyrics.[62]

By contrast with these restrained plaudits, there was heartfelt praise for Dylan Thomas in 1946: 'The Welsh poet, Dylan Thomas, is not only the best living Welsh poet, but is a great poet. His DEATHS AND ENTRANCES (*Dent*, 2s. 6d.) proves this. He is sometimes difficult, but always rewarding, rich and arresting . . .' Quoting 'A springful of larks on a rolling Cloud', John wrote: 'I wish there was space to quote more; for Dylan Thomas deserves a whole page of this paper and it is unfair to him to quote part of a stanza as I have done – it is too like cutting a bit out of a painting and asking you to judge the whole picture from it.'[63]

This was the highest praise John gave to any contemporary poet. That said much for his objectivity, because Thomas's floodtide lyricism is far removed from John's own poetic style.[64] When John discovered a poet of his own metal, such as William Plomer, D.B. Wyndham Lewis or 'Sagittarius', he praised freely but less ardently. He knew how the trick was done. In Plomer (who became a friend) he at once recognized a kindred creator. Plomer's *The Dorking Thigh* (1945) contained 'splendid poems for reciting to a not too squeamish audience'.[65]

Many of the writers John reviewed were people he knew, often friends. He seldom revealed that he knew them. It was not primarily a case of his giving friends special treatment; it was simply that he had come to know many of the leading and minor figures on the British and Irish literary scenes – at his schools and at Oxford, and in his later jobs. Then there was the happy chance of having Mary Renault as his nurse in the Acland Nursing Home, Oxford, in 1945 before she moved to South Africa. Reviewing her novel *Return Tonight* in 1947, he wrote, 'The authoress is so good and knowledgeable about doctors and hospitals and has a touch, terrible and tender, when she describes suffering.'[66]

From Dragon School days, there was 'Per' Mallalieu, the 'perfect boy' who challenged John to the aborted fight.[67] In 1944, while serving in the Royal Navy, he published a novel, *Very Ordinary Seaman*. John was not over-enthusiastic. 'The method of telling the tale is straight reporting: just journalism; there are no fine flights of description, no attempts at writing like Conrad, Melville or Hemingway. There isn't any attempt to disguise the boredom of much of life at sea . . .'[68] From Marlborough, there was John Edward Bowle;[69] from Oxford, there were A.L. Rowse, Margaret Lane, Christopher Sykes, Henry Yorke (Henry Green), Harold Acton, Peter Quennell, Osbert Lancaster and Wyndham Ketton-Cremer. Of Rowse's *West Country Stories* (1944), John wrote, somewhat stretching the truth, 'I had the inestimable privilege of spending most of my childhood in Cornwall, and I do not recollect reading better descriptions of the county than those of Mr Rowse.'[70]

When fate delivered C.S. Lewis's *The Great Divorce* into John's hands in 1946, the temptation for him to savage it must have been almost overwhelming. But he allowed himself just one barb: 'Mr C.S. Lewis may not be a master of style, but he is a provocative writer.'[71] Another old adversary, Geoffrey Grigson ('Griggers'), edited a collection of other writers' essays, poems and stories in 1946, *The Mint*. John magnanimously gave it a wholly favourable review.

He had copious compliments for 'society' friends of the pre-war years, such as Nancy Mitford and Cecil Beaton.[72] In December 1945 he wrote to Nancy Mitford:

My dear Nancy,

Cold from the G[reat] W[estern] R[ailway], in which I have just been finishing *The Pursuit of Love*, I write to tell you on this lovely *writing* paper how v. greatly I enjoyed it.

You have produced something that really is a monument to our friends. It is exactly how we used to talk at Biddesden.[73] In the beginning of the book I wondered how you were going to keep it up to the high standard you had set. By developing Linda as a character you subtly and gradually changed the key of the thing. It starts as a sort of *Diary of a Nobody* about the upper classes instead of the lower middles, as does that immortal work, and it develops into a very moving love story. You look down like a goddess on the world. It cannot be that the wonderful, unforgettable Uncle Matthew is really like Lord Redesdale, can it? He is my favourite character in the book. Gerald [Berners] and particularly Eddy [Sackville-West] are superb.[74] Oh you clever old girl. How I am going to break this lovely book to the drearies of the *Daily Herald*, I don't know. I shall enjoy trying. Clever, clever Nancy. I am proud to know you.[75]

John's Berkshire neighbours of the 1930s, Stuart Piggott and Lord Berners, were both well reviewed; and there was a pleasant mention, tinged with irony, of Gertrude Stein, whom he had met through Berners.[76] From his time on the *Evening Standard*, there was Howard Spring, the novelist. The lukewarmness of John's review of his work suggests some antipathy; when he called another writer 'a sort of Howard Spring', he clearly did not intend to flatter. From the Ministry of Information there were C. Day-Lewis and Arthur Calder-Marshall. Friends from Ireland included Lord Dunsany, Lord Longford and Patrick Kavanagh. John could hear Dunsany speaking in *The Donnellan Lectures* (1943, reviewed 1945) and thought he summed up superbly the difference between poetry and prose, thus:

'She and I were born about the same time, and used to live at Brighton.' You may anticipate a story when you hear those words, but you cannot be thrilled by the anticipation. Now take something similar, but said by a magician, Edgar Allan Poe:

> *I was a child and she was a child*
> *In a kingdom by the sea.*[77]

John liked to write about survivors from the nineteenth century, authors who had been young in the period he felt it galling to have missed, the 1890s. He was fascinated by Graham Robertson's autobiography *Time Was* (1945).

It tells you of the eighties and nineties, of William Morris 'looking like a burly sea captain with deep voice and brusque manner', of his long-chinned wife, the idol of Pre-Raphaelites; of the great libel case, Ruskin v. Whistler; of Bernhardt, Ellen Terry, Irving.

It ranks, in my opinion, with William Allingham's *Diaries* (why aren't they reprinted?) as *the* picture of literary life at the end of the last century.

Its author wrote an excellent play called *Pinkie and the Fairies* which some of us prefer to *Peter Pan*; collected first-rate Pre-Raphaelite pictures and the best Blakes and knew many of the great actors and writers of the day.

His account of Oscar Wilde's conversation is the most vivid I know . . .[78]

In 1946 (the year John reached forty), George Bernard Shaw celebrated his ninetieth birthday. It was characteristic of John, that in reviewing a birthday tribute (*G.B.S. 90*, edited by S. Winston) he should wonder what Shaw was thinking, and be conscious of the pathos of time's survivor.

He is one of the last giants of English literature alive and I cannot but think he feels lonely. He who started a lone revolutionary lives now a lonely victor.

For in this volume even Dean Inge must seem to him to be a new boy, James Bridie and Priestley right down in the infants' class, and even Lord Passfield, whose memory fails, is a younger contemporary by three years.[79]

That sensitivity to other people's loneliness is a recurring trait in John's poetry. 'Lonely Lilian' waits in vain for her friend Alice in 'The Flight from Bootle'. In 'Business Girls', the women having baths in Camden Town are urged, 'Rest you there, poor unbelov'd ones,/Lap your loneliness in heat/. . .' The heroine of 'Eunice' leaves 'her lonely cottage by the lonely oak'. The Platonist Bank Clerk's male friends marry and leave him to his collection of pipes. And Prince Charles is reminded, in 'A Ballad of the Investiture, 1969', 'And thus your lone-lier life began' – a last line which seems to carry a distant echo of Hopkins's gnomic 'leaves me a lonely began' in the last line of one of his 'terrible sonnets'.[80]

Some of the Victorian survivors did not outlast John's stint as book reviewer of the *Herald*. 'One of the saddest things to think', he wrote in March 1947, 'is that Forrest Reid will never write again. He died a few weeks ago.'[81] Three years earlier he had described a visit he made to Reid in Northern Ireland.

> I remember his bewilderment when I paid a pious pilgrimage to Mr Reid a year or two ago. I fancy he was surprised that anyone should pay such a pilgrimage.
>
> And some job I had to find where he lived, too. He is not in the Belfast telephone book and Belfast is not exactly a literary city, nor a small one.
>
> I got his address from a bookseller: for, like me, Forrest Reid collects old books and the walls of his little house, his study, the upstairs room and even the hall are lined with them.
>
> So now that a new book of his is out I want to recommend to you, not only this but any book by Forrest Reid which you can find in the library.[82]

The new book John was reviewing in 1944 was *Young Tom*. 'Terrifyingly,' he wrote, 'Mr Reid brings back one's own memories of some childhood misdeed, which leaves a scar on one's mind for life, but which the grown ups who were involved probably forgot a week afterwards.'[83] There are likely to have been two main reasons why John made his 'pilgrimage' to Forrest Reid. First, like John, he collected 1860s books with magnificent stamped and gilt bindings and illustrations by Millais, Arthur Hughes and other Pre-Raphaelites.

(Reid wrote the first book on the subject.)[84] But, also, John knew that Reid had written homosexual novels under a pseudonym; so he sought him out as he had sought out the Rev. E.E. Bradford and the Rev. S.E. Cottam and later corresponded with Siegfried Sassoon and Cecil Beaton about Sidney ('Jenny') Mavor, an old man who had been implicated, as a youth, in the Wilde scandal.[85] Himself susceptible to men as well as women, he was always interested in how others, especially writers, had dealt with their 'percentage'.[86]

John's account of his visit to Forrest Reid is one of many autobiographical fragments embedded in the *Herald* reviews. Some refer to the past; others are clues to his daily life and state of mind in the 1940s. In December 1945, reviewing new editions of *Treasure Island* and *Children of the New Forest*, he wrote, 'I know that as a boy I preferred a good book for a present even if it was second-hand, to a new book that was indifferent reading.'[87] Of William Maxwell's *The Folded Leaf* (1946), 'a profound and singularly beautiful story of the friendship of two American schoolboys . . .', he wrote, 'You will find this book reawakes in you the hell – the deep, scarring, thrilling hell – of adolescence.'[88] Nevil Shute's *Pastoral* (1944) revived memories of falling in love.

> You know that wonderful revelation of the beauty of the beloved – how first you just notice her face, how then you see the way her hair falls and then you suddenly realize that the shape of cheek or nose or lip is just the shape that was made for you, and then you realize that she doesn't think you are so awful as you know that you are really.
>
> Then she speaks to you and you read all sorts of things into the simplest remark. And then you both break down the barrier of that first delicious shyness and you are engaged.[89]

On 30 January 1944 John's column began: 'Deep out of the dark, as I write, they are ringing a muffled peal for someone in the village. First loud, as the unpadded side of the clapper strikes the bell. Then the same notes again, but this time muffled, as though men were ringing up in the stars. Infinitely distant and remote, though so familiar, those muffled bell-notes sounded. They reminded me of the book before me, BBC WAR REPORT . . . for so much of it was familiar, both near and far at once.'[90] His later poem 'Uffington' begins:

> Tonight we feel the muffled peal
> Hang on the village like a pall . . .[91]

John's interests and prejudices enlivened his reviews. Some of the
prejudices were the same as had coloured his film reviews – his wariness of children, for example. In March 1946 he wrote a piece to mark
the centenary of the births of the children's-book illustrators Kate
Greenaway and Randolph Caldecott. The review began deceptively:

> There are, I think, few sights so sad in the world as the sleeping innocence
> of children. The round heads on the pillow, the long-lashed shut eyes, the
> arm thrust out in unconscious abandon.
>   You wish, if you are a parent, that they could go on living in the clouds
> of glory which still hang about them.[92]

Having painted such innocence and charm, John disrupts them with
a reminder of original sin. 'And as you look at your sleeping children,
wishing the world of these artists could really be theirs – bang! crash!
the shuddering shock of one child's cruelty to another is upon
them . . .'[93]

In spite of his antipathy to 'kiddiz', John did not neglect to review
children's books. 'The toyshops may have let the children down, but
the bookshops have not,' he wrote just before Christmas 1944.[94] His
own children gave him insight into young children's tastes. 'I have been
trying to get *Grimm's Fairy Tales* for my son,' John wrote in 1944. 'He
has reached the age when he enjoys miraculous stories, especially
those involving the mystic numbers of three or seven – seven wishes
and three giants or three visitors and seven adventures for each.'[95] But
Grimm and Hans Andersen were 'unobtainable'. In 1947 he recommended, for children of eight and younger, Enid Blyton's twenty-one
new stories in *The Little White Duck.*[96]

John's interest was kindled by books on railways, religion and architecture. 'Red of the Midland Coaches!' he exclaimed in 1947. ' "Purple
brown and spilt milk" of the London and North-Western! Glorious
royal blue of the engines of the Caledonian! Ah! those many-coloured
days before British railways lost their personalities in the four great
groups in which we now know them! Perhaps their individualities will
revive when they are nationalized.' He was reviewing *Paddington to
Seagood* by Gilbert Thomas. It was, John wrote, 'the work of a
railway maniac. I am one, too, and a book so frank, so infectious, so
enthusiastic as this makes me forget that not all my readers are fond
of railways, though I suspect most of them are. A love of railways is a
gift, like a love of music.'[97]

The possibilities of atomic warfare turned his thoughts to religion
anew. Reviewing Bishop Hensley Henson's autobiography in 1946, he
wrote: 'The spring flowers that are now so full in the hedges may dis-

solve to nothing tomorrow as man tampers with the very substance of which the earth and all that is on it are made . . . More and more I turn to the books of those who have a belief in man's destiny . . .' He thought Henson, a former Bishop of Durham, 'a real mountain of a writer . . . In his writings . . . he does not come out as exactly lovable, but here is a man who will make mincemeat even of Bernard Shaw. He is what an Anglican bishop is meant to be and why people still listen to bishops; of recent times only bishops such as Temple, Gore, King, Frere and Headlam have been in the same class.'[98] John wrote with exceptional authority on the Church of England, and was correspondingly severe on writers who, in his view, misrepresented it. He called S.H. Lambert's *Portrait of Gideon Power* (1944) 'ridiculous as a portrait'. John had no quarrel with the 'mixed nature' of the clergyman depicted ('It is a common failing among us to imagine that clergymen ought to be perfect') but thought his 'very vague theology' was misplaced. 'No bishop in his senses would have ordained him.'[99]

Architecture was the other subject on which John was not prepared to be lenient towards standards below his own. There was high praise for John Summerson's *Georgian London* (1946) and G. Scott-Moncrieff's *Edinburgh* (1947). But the gloves came off for William Kent's *The Lost Treasures of London* ('The text is inadequate. Its information is culled from stock reference books . . .')[100] and for John Gloag's *The Englishman's Castle* ('The illustrations are almost without exception ignorant, wrong in colour, insensitive and misleading').

John's review of 30 December 1947, headed 'Handy Guide to Modern Novels', began:

> Mind you, I don't say it always works. But, as a general rule, you can tell what a novel is going to be like from its first sentence. Supposing you read this one:
>
>> His demob suit pinched him behind the shoulders, and the wet, rain-soaked streets of a typical London November day seemed singularly uninviting.
>
> Well, I can tell the book is unlikely to be any good. There are several obvious errors. His demob suit would have pinched him under the arms or drawn his shoulder-blades together, but it would not have pinched him *behind* the shoulders. If the streets were rain-soaked they were presumably wet. A 'typical London November day' means nothing definite. Foggy or dry or fair, or windy or cold?
>
> 'Singularly uninviting'. If it were a 'typical' day, it would not be *singularly* uninviting; it would be as uninviting as usual. In fact, this author is a bore who does not think before he writes, but just jabbers away, putting in needless dead words which add nothing to the picture.

John's columns would have been of value to a reader who wanted to be a writer. His most effective critical technique was comparison, either with another book in the week's batch, or with inventions of his own. His column of 31 July 1946 was headed 'How NOT to write'.

> If you want an example of bad writing, take this: 'Frank, aware that he looked guilty, made *frantic efforts* to *banish the maiden blush* which was *suffusing his face.*'
>
> I have italicized the outworn clichés which this writer brings into the sentence. What he means is 'Frank, aware that he looked guilty, tried not to blush.'
>
> Because he is writing a 'funny book' he thinks funniness consists in spinning out a sentence.
>
> I will not bother you with the name or author of this book. The publishers should not have wasted paper on it. They are to blame. Every page has dozens of such dead sentences.
>
> 'It was not, therefore, until the next morning that the *full tragedy of the previous night* was *laid bare to his horrified gaze*. The four rabbits were still *reposing* on the lawn and *with some distaste* he collected them up, *depositing* them in the tool shed.'
>
> This is a 'funny' way of saying 'He found the dead rabbits on the lawn next morning and put them in the tool shed.' Funny my foot! And no funnier tricked out in fourth-form frills.
>
> If you want an example of better writing, take this, which describes a wife saying good-bye to her husband at a station:
>
> > 'John has gone. The last brass carriage handle has disappeared, and the empty track yawns greasily in front of me.'
>
> That is felt and observed and simply described. Of course she could have said:
>
> > 'John has departed. The iron monster has steamed forth on its appointed journey, leaving to my distracted gaze a dreary expanse of shining rails.'
>
> But because she is an artist, she does not. I do not know her real name, this **Elizabeth Evelyn**, who writes NO PROMISE IN SUMMER (*Cape*, 8s. 6d.) . . .

Another telling comparison was made two months later, in a review headed 'Fewer Isms and Asms, please'.

> Which of these passages do you prefer? They both describe William IV, Sailor King, surely the most lovable monarch who ever sat on the English throne.

'The monarchy itself was becoming a reflection of the new demo-
cratic spirit, and though at times the royal language lacked restraint,
it was, nevertheless, symptomatic of a trend.'

Compare it with this description of William IV at a naval and military
dinner in 1835:

'. . . at which he made a very peculiar and inappropriate oration.
After holding forth at length about the equal opportunity afforded
to all classes in the Services, he illustrated his remarks with the observation, "Here, on my right, is my noble friend, descended from a line
of ancestry as ancient as my own; and here, on my left, a rear-
admiral, sprung from the very dregs of the people."'

They both say the same thing. But the first, how dull and colourless! The
second, how vivid, amusing and memorable! Let me beg of you to take
warning. Avoid reading too much about trends, spirits, -isms and -asms.[101]

Reviewing *A Book of Quotations* by Viscount Samuel, in August
1947, John wrote: 'A remark Lord Samuel made to me months ago
haunts me still and should be in this book.

'"You smoke too much," he said.

'"Do people die of oversmoking?" I asked him.

'"No," he said. "They do not die. They merely fade into inefficiency."'[102]

By 1947, John was fading into inefficiency as a book reviewer. His
notices were becoming ever shorter and more perfunctory. He made
no attempt to disguise the fact that reviewing had become a grinding
chore. Sometimes he frankly washed his hands of a book. In June 1947
he wrote: 'If you ask me what TREADMILL, by **Michael Harrison**, is
about, I don't know. All the same, I enjoyed it.'[103] In October he wrote
lamely of Betty Askwith's *The Admiral's Daughters*, 'I do not quite
know how to explain that this is a very good book, beyond simply
saying it is and adding that it is mature, sensitive and shocking at
once.'[104] It was clear that he was suffering from reviewer's fatigue. He
hated the work[105] and despised his readers. In October 1950, writing
a letter to congratulate Evelyn Waugh on his novel *Helena*, he referred
to 'my jaunty, vulgar review in the *Herald* – written to attract the cloth
caps as they hurry through to read "Templegate" on the back page'.[106]

The Waugh review was perhaps the last *Herald* notice over which
John took any trouble. It betrays the interplay of various tensions. Not
long before, John and Waugh had had a serious epistolary row over
religion, after Penelope's conversion.*[107] It must have been obvious to
John that *Helena* was far from the novelist's best work; and, on top of

* See Chapter 16, 'Farnborough'.

that, John was perfectly well aware that the novel's central character
was based on his wife, and with her active collaboration; and he may
have heard the rumours of Penelope's sleeping with Waugh.[108] He
began with a soaring compliment. 'Whatever Evelyn Waugh writes is
good. He will be remembered when you and I are forgotten.'[109] But
soon the review became personal, and it ended with a decided thumbs-
down.

> To turn this vague story into a novel, Evelyn Waugh has had to invent his
> saint's character. He makes St Helena a tough English hunting girl of the
> kind who features in most of his novels.
>
> She is clever and matter of fact. She puts up with the inconveniences of
> being divorced by her husband, neglected by her son and exiled from her
> native land.
>
> She has one perfectly clear aim after her conversion – to find the
> True Cross. Scheming daughters-in-law, vicious Romans and pseudo-
> philosophers from the East move her not. She has her way.
>
> The book, for all the genius in it, lacks for me a clear central character.
> St Helena is made an honest, downright sensible woman, but she doesn't
> seem to be a saint.[110]

In 1951, by mutual consent with Percy Cudlipp, and with no hard
feelings, John ceased to be the *Herald*'s book critic. Reviewing had not
been just a penance. Who writes must read: every writer needs to
refuel with new ideas and vocabulary. But for the *Herald* job, John
would not have read so intensively. He was forced to formulate opinions on things which did not naturally interest him. And some of the
books he read may have influenced his poetry. For example, he quoted
from 'Per' Mallalieu's *Very Ordinary Seaman* the words ' "What a
thing Eternity must be! Ever and ever without end . . ." For a split
second his mind held this unimaginable everlastingness, then recoiled
from it in terror more penetrating than anything he had felt during the
action.'[111] Of course John was familiar with 'World without end' as a
liturgical mantra; but Mallalieu's book probably crystallized the feelings instilled by John's Calvinist nursemaid long before, and provoked
the lines in his poem 'N.W.5. and N.6.':

> 'World without end.' It was not what she'ld do
> That frightened me so much as did her fear
> And guilt at endlessness. I caught them too,
> Hating to think of sphere succeeding sphere
> Into eternity and God's dread will
> I caught her terror then. I have it still.[112]

ADMIRALTY

In 1940 John received a letter from a young policeman in Southampton, John Arlott, who was a fan of his poetry and had read everything he had written. He asked if John would like to collaborate on an anthology. John politely declined. Arlott collaborated with George Rostrevor Hamilton instead. *Landmarks*, published in 1943, included Arlott's own poem 'Cricket at Worcester', in Betjeman style. John introduced Arlott to Geoffrey Grigson, who was then a BBC radio producer at Bristol. John told Grigson he had met 'a policeman who is mad about poetry, who might make an amusing broadcast'.[2] Arlott, whose lulling accent had the lawnmower burr of Hampshire, went on to become a famous cricket commentator; he was known as 'the voice of summer'.

At the end of 1943 John wrote from Garrards Farm to congratulate Arlott on *Landmarks*, which he promised to review in 'the bloody old *Daily Herald*'.[3] He was pleased that some of his own poems had been chosen: 'I've never appeared beside Wordsworth before and feel very honoured.'[4] He added: 'I am back home but being KILLED by the Min of Inf in London. A sadist in charge of the Films Division is trying to do me in.'[5]

By March John had managed to get himself moved to a section of 'P' Branch of the Admiralty, which was stationed in Bath. Though some of his former colleagues thought him disorganized and flippant, he had won the approval of senior figures – such as Sir John Maffey and Sir Kenneth Clark – whose opinions counted when appointments were being made. Their glowing commendations helped to gain him his new, responsible and 'hush-hush' post. He arrived in Bath in March 1944.[6] In April he had a letter from Honor Tracy, the future novelist and humorous journalist. He had known her at the Ministry of Information, where she served in the Japanese department. Clearly she felt for him something more than friendship; and it is possible that their affectionate relationship was later the inspiration for a Betjeman poem.* In the 1944 letter Tracy wrote:

> Please send me your Bath address because I am writing a farewell poem for you. At present I am drunk, I was picked out of the canal last night by PC Smith at two am. Case coming up on Tuesday . . . How I love you. I am very drunk. There is no need to read this letter to everyone who comes into your office. Don't tell Arthur [Calder-Marshall] about the canal.[7]

John's immediate superior in Bath was the novelist Richard Hughes, author of *A High Wind in Jamaica* (1929), an adventure story about a family of children captured by pirates. Hughes and John had at least known *of* each other since John was a schoolboy at Marlborough, when Hughes was one of three literary judges who chose a poem of his for the anthology *Public School Verse*.[8] Six years older than John, 'Diccon' Hughes had just overlapped with Robert Graves at Charterhouse and became a friend and protégé of the Graves family. At Oriel, Oxford, he achieved the rare distinction of a double Fourth; but while still an undergraduate he had a play produced in the West End, with Sybil Thorndike in the leading rôle; contributed articles to *The Spectator*; and had verse published in *Georgian Poetry*.[9] Also, between his Fourth in Classical 'Mods' and his Fourth in English, he had travelled steerage on an emigrant ship to New York. After Oxford he had voyaged down the Danube, written the first play ever broadcast on radio, lived in Morocco, moved to Wales, become a friend of Dylan Thomas and won fame with *A High Wind in Jamaica* and another sea novel, *In Hazard*.[10] When war broke out in 1939 he was considered too old for active duty in the Royal Navy. But through his friend Jack James, who was a godfather of his daughter Llecky and one of the 4,000 Admiralty staff whose departments had been evacuated to Bath soon after war was declared, he was offered a post as a temporary assistant in the Administrative Service.[11] He arrived in Bath in June 1940.[12]

* See Chapter 17, '*New Bats in Old Belfries*'.

Hughes had expected to be 'licking envelopes'; but in fact he was made personal assistant to the head of one of the departments. That head in turn answered to Jack James, who, with the rank of assistant secretary, was in charge of the Bath section of 'P' Branch. (The 'P' stood for Priority.) This was an independent secretariat within the Admiralty. Its task had originally been 'the rigid administration of production priorities';[13] but it had gradually become 'the administrative pivot of a very much wider field of work, wherever the Admiralty supply machinery came into contact with the ever more complex central machinery of Government and with the other supply departments'.[14] It was 'concerned', as Hughes wrote at the time,

> with all the broad problems of organizing ship-building, armament and supply: and I am now a sort of chief-of-staff and intelligence officer to the head of [my] branch. One of my special pigeons is extracting the meaning from a large complexity of facts, and trying to express it simply enough to be comprehensible to My Lords. It is rather like that time when I tried to write on Wave-mechanics for twelve-year-olds: only stuff for admirals, of course, has to be put far simpler than that.[15]

Returning to Bath in September 1940 after a short leave with his family, Hughes found that 'P' Branch had officially become the '*Production and* Priority Branch' and that he had been promoted to be 'Head of the General Section of the "P" Branch' and moved into a more luxurious room.[16] To begin with, Hughes, as a slightly Bohemian literary man, had felt out of his element in the Admiralty. 'I never thought to find myself a civil servant,' he wrote to an old family friend in July 1940.[17] But he soon grew into his rôle. His (and John's) friend Lance Sieveking, who, like Geoffrey Grigson, was then working for the BBC in Bristol, wrote that 'From having been quite one of the most unconventional characters one could hope to meet, he had become, almost overnight, a Higher Civil Servant of the most correct kind.' Even Hughes's beard, Sieveking noticed, had been formalized,

> so that it should be more in keeping with his new dignity. Up to then it had been a distinctly untidy and straggly affair. But by curling the two sides upwards with merciless severity he eventually forced the whole of the lower part of his face to confirm and support the impression created by his black trilby (or Eden) hat, his neat collar and tie, his official brief-case and his tightly-rolled umbrella.[18]

Sieveking was told that Hughes became 'such a stickler for the Correct Way of Doing Things that he struck terror into many of his colleagues who had spent all their lives in the Service'.[19] In December 1942 there was another significant promotion for Hughes. From now on, the Principal Priority Officer (head of 'P' Branch) was to be stationed in London; Hughes was left in charge at Bath as his 'vicar'.[20] In February 1943 he wrote to his wife that most of his energy was absorbed in:

> trying to make this extraordinary team pull together. They range in age from sixty-one to thirteen, in sex from male to female, in interests from beer and hunting to mathematics and the Social Revolution, in beauty from hideous to mildly pleasing: they work like niggers and they fight like cats and there are now 114 of them, & probably I shall wake up one morning and find that we have been abolished.[21]

Hughes later explained why so many Admiralty departments were moved to Bath within a few days of the outbreak of war: as early as 1936 the Government had been warned that, with the increased striking-power of aircraft, it might now be possible for an enemy 'to destroy the seat of government and with it the machinery of government in the first few days of a war, without having first won any general victory'.[22] Relocation of offices in the country was the obvious answer; but when should that happen? To embark on it in peace might precipitate the international catastrophe and alarm the citizenry. To do so in the first few weeks of war would interfere with the mobilization and deployment of the armed forces.

> One is reminded [Hughes wrote] of the dilemma of the Hibernian authority that had resolved to build a new gaol, resolved to build it from the materials of the old gaol, and resolved not to pull down the old gaol till the new gaol was built.[23]

That is typical of the pawky humour which constantly brightens Hughes's record of a dark time. Humour was always the most effective catalyst in any professional relationship with John. Hughes's taste for enlivening the most sober of subjects with a dash of wit is seen also in his account of the billeting difficulties in Bath.

> The war had already begun, and by this time Bath was rapidly filling up with private citizens from the metropolis and elsewhere, themselves fleeing from the aerial wrath to come of their own proper motion and at their own proper (fairly lavish) costs. Bath was a city accustomed to live off

visitors. If the Admiralty moved in, these private ones would have to go: and by contrast a bare guinea-a-week per head was all the Government proffered for board and lodging. Moreover the Government insisted on specified comforts: this horde of official lodgers might not be treated entirely as steerage passengers, even if they were only paying steerage fares (for example, Admiralty officers should *not*, it was laid down, be compelled to sleep two or more to a bed).[24]

After the Ministry of Health's local billeting officer had made almost no progress, Hughes adds, the Admiralty took over billeting themselves.

In many cases comforts in excess of the official minima were hospitably provided: as for the Government's guinea-a-week, usually private arrangements were concluded which at least reduced the financial burden on the hosts. Thus tension was gradually eased. Moreover it is related that the Admiralty's chief billeting officer developed his own rule-of-thumb for handling complaints. Guests who complained of their hosts were moved to the homes of hosts who had complained of their guests, to the better discipline of both . . .[25]

On whom one got billeted was a hit-or-miss affair. Hughes had struck particularly lucky. He was billeted on the elderly writer Horace Annesley Vachell, at Widcombe Manor, a fine house with an Italian fountain in its forecourt and a Greek temple in its grounds.[26] He found it a little tedious that Vachell insisted on dressing for dinner each night; but there were compensations. Vachell said: 'We will do our best to drink everything in my cellar before the damned Hun can get it . . .'[27] Hughes told Lance Sieveking: 'The port, particularly . . . was something that had to be tasted to be believed.'[28] John did not enjoy quite such luxury, but was happy with the lodgings the Admiralty found for him. He was billeted on Mrs Helen Holmes of 16 Macaulay Buildings, Widcombe Hill, Bath. He got on very well with Mrs Holmes, who remained a friend and correspondent for many years after he left Bath. In a letter of 1965 she recalled a practical joke he had played on her when he first knocked on her door. 'Do you remember the ragged rain coat you wore when you came to see me? & tried to fox me into thinking you a poor old beggar man?'[29]

Mrs Holmes was a widow of sixty-five, with an unmarried daughter, Joan. She made pin-money by the sort of Arts-and-Crafts work that John satirized as 'beating opals into copper'.[30] She crafted copper cigarette boxes lined with cedarwood, blue enamelled boxes with domed lids, moonstone necklaces, onyx and silver cufflinks, and silver dishes which could be used as 'either a sweet dish or ashtray'.[31] John, who had been elected an Honorary Brother of the Art Workers' Guild in 1937, eventually got her made a member too.[32] A warm, kindly woman with a lively mind, she enjoyed having intellectual arguments in the evenings with John and her other lodgers. In 1949 she wrote to him: 'I have often thought of you and longed for some of the old exhilarating conversations that made you tear your hair at my rash statements . . .'[33] And again, in 1954:

> Do you know that looking back on those war years, for me, brings back happy memories of pleasant evenings, sometimes very argumentative ones, because I just liked to contradict you and the other guests, to listen to the storm of talk aroused by my 'silly' ideas.[34]

One of her special bugbears was Modern Art. In 1945, when John gave her, for Christmas, a book entitled *Giovanni to Picasso*, she wrote in her thank-you letter:

> I infinitely prefer the first [that is, Giovanni]. I am afraid I have no use for Freaks in art any more than I should view the Freak show at the Village Fair.[35]

Some of the arguments were political. On 29 March 1945 one of Mrs Holmes's lodgers, named Alford, sent John a postal order for 2s 6d 'because the war was not over by 25 March 1945'.[36] In an accompanying letter he told John, 'I have increased my bet with Mrs Holmes from 6d to 1s. You will remember that Mrs Holmes [thought] that the British and Americans would be in Berlin first, whereas I thought that the Russians would be there first. We must be content to wait and see.'[37]

On 1 May 1944 John reported for duty. The Admiralty offices were in the Empire Hotel, a grotesque, cavernous building overlooking the Avon and its shop-lined Adam bridge. Built in the last three years of Victoria's reign, the hotel had been designed by the City architect C.E. Davis; that is probably why it was allowed to tower above the nearby Abbey. Pevsner described it as 'an unbelievable piece of *pompier* architecture';[38] and Charles Robertson, having described the hideous main bulk of the building in his *Architectural Guide* to Bath (1975), adds:

> Perched above is an astonishing row of dolls' houses with little or no relationship either to each other or to the block below. They are, in order, a mock cottage, with two bargeboard-and-plaster gables; a curly gable which Sir Nikolaus [Pevsner] identifies as 'Loire-style'; and a tower on the

angle . . . Someone has suggested that these are intended to symbolize the three estates of the realm . . .[39]

The Admiralty official Cyril Wallworth, who entered the service by examination in 1939 and by 1944 was assistant private secretary to the First Lord, recalls that, by and large, the career officials responded well to the influx of temporary administrative assistants, such as John.

As is well-known, people 'pulled together' in the war. Unless we won the bloody war, I was going to be shot or put in a concentration camp. One didn't have this spectre before one all the time – but, as Dr Johnson said, it concentrates a man's mind wonderfully! So we were all quite determined to win the war, and that welded us together.[40]

Some of John's colleagues in 'P' Branch, however, felt slightly resentfully that he was literally a 'Johnny-come-lately', who had missed the really hard work and the pressures that they had endured. 'The reason why he landed in our midst was never disclosed,' one of them later wrote.[41] The Battle of Britain had been won in 1940, but when Hughes had arrived at 'P' Branch, German U-boats were sinking 300,000 tons of shipping in the Atlantic each month. By 1942 the figure had risen to 500,000. In March 1943 the U-boat fleet sank 625,000 tons.[42] But that was the zenith of the German success. The main preoccupation of 'P' Branch then was to make the most effective use of shipyards. Hughes developed a system for obtaining up-to-date statistics, so that the yards where warships were being built would not become overloaded: man-hours were logged, also the numbers of men employed on ships at different stages of their construction.[43] Sometimes Hughes was asked to report to Churchill direct.[44]

After May 1943, in which month Admiral Dönitz lost forty-three U-boats, he withdrew the rest of his fleet from the north Atlantic until the autumn.[45] In the remainder of the war, there were only three months when the U-boats sank more than 100,000 tons.[46] But the pressure on 'P' Branch was still intense. The invasion of Sicily in the summer of 1943 was embarrassingly held up by a shortage of transport ships and landing-craft.[47] Far more would be needed for the invasion of France which the allies were planning for May 1944 – 'Operation Overlord'. This was to involve the largest invasion fleet in history, with 1,200 fighting ships, 10,000 aeroplanes, more than 10,000 landing-craft and more than 800 transport ships.[48] These preparations had all been made by the time John joined the Admiralty a month before D-Day.

He had also missed the heavy bomb raids on Bath. In April 1942, in retaliation for 'Bomber' Harris's raids on Lübeck, Rostock and Cologne, Hitler had ordered the so-called 'Baedeker raids' on un-defended English cities of special historic interest. Exeter was hit first. Hughes witnessed the raids on Bath. The first, on 25 April, he saw from the roof the Empire Hotel, where he was on fire-watching duty. 'I can't help it,' he wrote to his wife; 'it is a most beautiful sight . . . huge fires full of majesty and compounded of strange colours . . .'[49] He had sheltered behind a chimney-stack. When the bombers returned the next day, he was with Vachell. This time,

> Seeing Bath burn from the *outside* was horrible, not beautiful at all. An enormous smoke turned a bloody brown with flames stretching from the station right up through that lovely city to the top of the hill above the Circus. A filthy thing to see . . .[50]

Four hundred and seventeen people were killed. Many Bath residents took to the surrounding fields and woods, convinced the city would be flattened in the next raid.[51] But there were no more concerted attacks.

Hughes made John welcome; but the younger man was too untrained to be given much responsibility. There was so much for the 'new boy' to learn. Cyril Wallworth recalls:

> The temporary staff were totally unaware of how to work in a massive organization like the Admiralty. You had to decide the relative importance and urgency of papers that landed on your desk. A huge machine like the Admiralty has a huge inertia factor. If something had to be settled very quickly, the Admiralty could move quickly; but it took a disproportionate amount of effort to make it move. You had labels – 'Important', 'Most Important', 'Secret', 'Most Secret' and, after the Americans came in, 'Top Secret'. But none of those necessarily affected speed of action. 'Urgent' did. And if something was 'Very Urgent', you had to drop everything and run it round personally to various people and discuss it with them, taking notes which were added to the folder. All this had to be learnt by a new administrative assistant like John Betjeman.[52]

John found these bureaucratic procedures, as he wrote to Nancy Mitford after less than a fortnight in 'P' Branch, 'wonderfully boring'.[53] After a while Hughes found some limited use for his literary talents. He was put in charge of two publications which were circu-lated to Admiralty branches around the country: the 'Green 'un', as it was called, supplied up-to-date bulletins on the best places to find sup-plies of labour, steel, wood and so on; and the more 'hush-hush' 'Pink 'un' (originally the title of a famous Victorian sporting paper) gave reports on recent damage, for example, 'Don't try to find labour in Acton because it has been bombed.'[54] John had three people working for him in his office. One of them was Arnold Weinstock (later Lord Weinstock), who remembered him as 'frightfully scruffy' and chain-smoking, with a cigarette always hanging from his top lip.[55] Weinstock noticed that John swore a lot – a habit, it seemed to him, oddly at variance with his professed Christianity.[56] He also remembered John's using the staff as 'slave labour' for his book-reviewing.

> He was working for the *Daily Herald* at the time and he used to get all these trashy books sent to him. He'd give them to us to read and we said which ones we liked and he then reviewed our selection which he got to keep. He had this friend called Bryan Little who was in another section of the Admiralty and they'd bicycle off on architectural excursions all the time.[57]

The excursions resulted in a book by Bryan Little, *The Building of Bath*, published in 1947. John and Little often met for tea in the café part of Fortt's restaurant in Bath, which was not unlike a Lyons Corner House.[58] John was also elected to the Pepys Club for naval officers and senior civil servants, where 'one could get a drink in comfort'.[59]

Dawn Macleod, a young woman who was made John's personal assistant, has left two vivid accounts of 'P' Branch in 1944 and the impression he made there. In 1958 she asked John's permission to write about her wartime encounter with him in *Oasis of the North*, an autobiographical book mainly about her post-war life with the Highland landowner Mairi Sawyer of Inverewe, Wester Ross. He replied: 'Say what you like.'[60] But in fact, only too well aware of the thinness of John's skin, she wrote about him with a polite wariness. After describing her earlier friendship with the 'unworldly and elegant' Georgian poet Robert Nichols – who 'seemed . . . to have lived in a golden haze of unreality' – she continued:

> Twelve years after the completion of Robert Nichols's attempts to educate me, I met John Betjeman. (Though he doesn't, I think, refer to himself as a poet – and may dislike the description.) . . . Betjeman, with his tubby figure clad in mass-produced garments (clothes were rationed), writing verses about Edwardian villa-life and Victorian Gothic churches, seemed earthy – or perhaps bricks-and-mortary; and he was streets and lamp-posts away from the ideal of a poet imagined by any maiden born around 1912.
>
> *Dear* Mr Betjeman, don't think me rude! Anyone who could make a

Civil Service office amusing and lively, as you did, has genius enough to
stoke the warmest fires of gratitude and praise. Our essential part in the
war effort had been virtually completed before D-Day, and until you came
we found the ensuing boredom much harder to bear than bombing.[61]

In 1984, however, just six months after John's death, Dawn Macleod
felt free to write, in a *Spectator* article headed 'Betjeman at War', a
much more candid account. She began with a pen-portrait of Richard
Hughes, whose assistant she had been until John's arrival.

The bearded author of *A High Wind in Jamaica*, imposing as a rock-cut
temple Buddha, sat alone in the Principal's office, censing himself with
snuff. After chattering groups of clerks and typists had left adjacent rooms
and gone home for the night, he used to send for me. Then began prolonged consideration of reports which I had drafted . . . 'Dickon' [*sic*]
Hughes, a master of written English, knew how to shape my technically
informed but lumbering prose to suit his own finely-tuned ear.

What endless pains he took! . . . I felt like a novice monk under instruction by the Dalai Lama. The sonority of his voice took me back to the
awesome noise heard in childhood when a family friend, Sir Francis
Younghusband,[62] sounded a huge Tibetan trumpet in his garden at
Westerham.[63]

Dawn Macleod contrasted John with Hughes.

Betjeman proved to be a completely different fish: plain John Dory to a
lordly salmon. He sought no technical details and did not even feign interest in my talk of welded hulls, Oerlikon guns and the latest radar equipment. What, then, could a well-meaning personal assistant do for him?
His chief need, a shoulder to moan upon, had never been listed in Fleet
Orders. But this was autumn 1944, with the war all but won, the air-raids
on Bristol and Bath at an end, and a surfeit of tinned spam to fill our
shrunken stomachs. It seemed opportune to relax my official attitude a
little. While most of us felt cautiously cheerful, poor JB so hated being
confined to an office that he drooped and wilted day by day, appearing to
be on the brink of suicide or at best an early Victorian decline.

His curious complexion reminded me of some chameleons with whom
I once cohabited in the East. It kept changing its hue, not to match the
background but apparently influenced by some inner alchemy of thought
and emotion. At times he was a flat Egyptian yellow, which would turn by
stages to a lurid gypsy bronze with gold trimmings. In his most miserable
moods he displayed a countenance of ghastly peasoup green, truly alarming until you got used to it. After all, he never quite passed out: yet none

of us would have risked a sixpenny bet on his chances of living to be seventy-eight.[64]

Dawn Macleod thought that Hughes, although he made no comment, guessed that John's need for constant sympathy was a drain on her. Hughes's remedy was to take her and John on lunch-hour strolls around Bath's crescents and squares. She noticed how the architectural merits of any building were 'instantly reflected by the poet's countenance'.

His sagging cheeks puffed out, pink and soft. His wet-spaniel eyes developed glamorous sparkle. Without delay he launched us on a sea of inspired documentary, so that we lost our bearings and all track of time. On one occasion the punctilious Hughes disgraced himself by forgetting an appointment with a VIP.

We must have made an odd assortment of characters even for an ancient city accustomed to freaks, from Bladud to Beau Nash and Beckford. Richard Hughes, in harmony with his erect posture and stately, unmodern pace, was invariably well barbered and tailored, while roly-poly John Betjeman looked as if he slept in his clothes – and someone else's garments grabbed after a shipwreck at that . . .[65]

John's love of Bath comes across in a review of *Bath* by R.A.L. Smith which he wrote for the *Observer* in October 1944;[66] but so do the accidie and frustration he felt in that year. It did not help that the book was published by Batsford, with which firm he had had a series of rows when they published the Shell Guides in 1937–38.[67] The review begins with an attack on the 'plansters', analogous to John's poem 'The Planster's Vision', also written in 1944.

So many keen young careerists are manoeuvring for good executive positions in post-war planning: terrifying blocks of gleaming hygiene in glass and steel are visualized for the great new insect state of their dreams: civic centres, airports, community kitchens, community this and that, community crèches for the few eccentrics who would sooner have a child than a private aeroplane: so much of this kind of thing is in the air that the heart turns gratefully to any book, even this, on the largest stone memorial of England's eighteenth century, the City of Bath, a city far less blitzed than its exquisite and even more interesting, though not so obvious neighbour, Bristol.[68]

John conceded that the late Mr Smith had written a good *social* history of Bath; but the architectural side of the book, he complained,

was 'mere scissors and paste journalism'. He went on to indicate his
own preferences in the city – the sort of places he showed Hughes and
Dawn Macleod.

> There are far too many pictures of the Abbey, while many of the loveliest
> things still to be seen in Bath are neglected. There are no views of the subtle
> sweep of The Paragon, the seductive S-shape of Lansdowne [sic] Crescent
> where it curves to Somerset Place, the pillared gloom of Bath Street, the
> noble vista down Pulteney Street, intimate blocks in Alfred Street, North
> Parade, Cavendish Place, the fine extent of Kensington. There are no pic-
> tures of the acres of excellent, if modern late Georgian and early Victorian
> building which make Bath so beautiful and which deserve recognition by
> the camera – Sydney Place, Daniel Street, Norfolk and Widcombe
> Crescents, houses on Bathwick Hill and the numbers of delicate terraces
> and squares and bridges which will all too probably be swept away by rapa-
> cious plansters. A book such as this might have helped to save them.[69]

John lived to see his bleak prophecy fulfilled.* The 1944 review
shows that John's response to Bath's buildings was not just aesthetic,
but scholarly.

> The 'Concert Room' is really the Assembly Room; the terrace at Prior
> Park is not by either Wood but by H.E. Goodridge, an architect of Bath
> who, along with Attwood, Killigrew, Lightholder, Harcourt Masters and
> even such original Gothic Revivalists as G.P. Manners and James Wilson,
> should have been mentioned in a book which the publishers claim is 'one
> of the most complete and attractive "portraits" of a city that has yet been
> offered to the public'.[70]

One event in Dawn Macleod's life as John's assistant stood out in
her memory. She mentioned it briefly in *Oasis of the North*, but
twenty-six years later, in the *Spectator* article, pulled out all the stops
to describe it in its full absurdity.

> We had compiled a long and boring paper about some plant extension at
> a shipyard. In it, reference to 'a bed of retorts' was seized upon by my
> superior with infantile glee. Opening the docket out flat, he used the inside
> of its smooth cover to draw a picture of the great bed of Ware, at the
> Victoria & Albert Museum in London.[71] The illustration, perfect in every
> detail, showed the entire Retort family tucked up beneath a quilt, heads of

---

* In 1973 Adam Fergusson, a nephew of his old Oxford friend Michael Dugdale,
wrote *The Sack of Bath*, with some introductory verses by John.

all sizes in a row on the bolster. Having put his signature to the report and dropped it into the messenger's bag for Whitehall, the artist leaned back with a happy smile.

This euphoria did not last. He was utterly downcast next day, when the docket came back with a curt note attached: 'Please instruct your staff to refrain from scribbling on dockets.' It was that cruel word 'scribbling' which caused such pain. *Scribbling*. He read the insult aloud in a hoarse voice. His face, already green, turned eerily blue, the sort of leached colour seen during an eclipse of the sun.

For the first and only time in my life I tried a homeopathic remedy, using like to cure like. Outside in my car, some fine purple plums, picked from our orchard, waited for delivery to an aged aunt. She had to go without, for Betjeman's need was paramount. I fed him the luscious fruit, the blue bloom on the fat plum cheeks matching exactly his facial hue. Quickly he recovered, flushing crimson with pleasure. I still have the book of poems which he pressed upon me in gratitude. It is inscribed:

> from J. Betjeman
> Hell,
> Bath,
> 1944[72]

John had a few other solaces in Bath, besides Georgian architecture and homeopathic plums. Hughes took him to dinner with Vachell.[73] (The old man died in 1955, aged ninety-three.) And John's and Penelope's friend and mentor P. Morton Shand lived in Bath with his family. John and Shand were always 'on the same wavelength'. When Shand died in 1960, John wrote to his widow, Sybil:

> I am v sad to lose P. Morton Shand as I am sure you are. I can't say how I'll miss his wise selective eye at architecture, his unfailing loyalty & his gorgeous jokes about 'Yerb' [the architectural writer F.R. Yerbury], [John] Gloag, 'Mixwell Fry' [the architect Maxwell Fry] & all the other hoaxes he ridiculed. He really was the guardian of high principles in all criticism.[74]

The Shands lived in Darlington Place on Bathwick Hill, with a view right over the city. Morton Shand was becoming as knowledgeable on horticulture as on architecture. His front and back gardens were planted with apple trees, on which he was a leading expert. He also had the use of a neighbour's kitchen garden on the top of Bathwick Hill and bought some land opposite his house to prevent its being built on. 'He grew every possible vegetable,' his daughter Mary recalled. 'Some people suffered privations in the war, but I have to say I have

never eaten better. We had blue beans, white strawberries, yellow rasp-
berries and black radishes – before black radishes were at all known.'[75]

John visited the Shands often and was captivated by Morton
Shand's schoolgirl daughters, Elspeth and Mary, who were to marry,
respectively, the politician Geoffrey Howe (now Lord Howe) and the
architect James (later Sir James) Stirling.

John Betjeman was 'someone from London' [Lady Stirling remembers].
We grew up in the provinces; we didn't see many people from London.
There were wonderful conversations at dinner. He was so funny. Once I
was re-writing an essay we had been set at Bath High School, on 'Practical
Jokes'. My father had helped me with it, but it had still been returned for
me to do again. So John wrote me an essay on Practical Jokes. My English
teacher was just *flattened*. She couldn't do anything. One evening he was
fire-watching in Bath Abbey and I went up the tower with him. He pressed
the wrong button and the clock chimed one more stroke than it should
have.[76]

John had a special crush – romantic and platonic – on Mary, whom
he saw as some idealized figure from a medieval legend illustrated by
William Morris or Edward Burne-Jones.[77] He jotted down some rough
notes for a poem about her –

> Pale Pre-Raphaelite Mary Shand
> Swung her satchel and waved her hand;
> Her every step on the wet Bath pavement
> Bound me more in a ~~deep~~ sweet enslavement,
> Held me fast ~~with~~ by a braid and band
> Stitched with Knights
> Galahad, Guinevere riding by
> In a dark green forest of faerie-land
> Guinevere, stitched in gold and red
> Stitched with Iseult and fair Elaine
> And Arthur's champions riding through
> And brave King Arthur riding ahead
> To the blue-green forests of Faery-land
>
> What are they ——, these young girls doing,
> Too old for teaching, too young for wooing?[78]

To the best of Lady Stirling's knowledge, this inchoate poem was never
completed; but 'fair Elaine' was to reappear in John's poem
'Middlesex' (1954) as:

> Fair Elaine the bobby-soxer,
> Fresh-complexioned with Innoxa . . .[79]

and John later recycled the rhyme of 'pavement' and 'enslavement' in his much criticized Laureate poem about Princess Anne's first wedding.

Mary Shand was also, probably, the 'Mary' of a poem he wrote before he came to the Admiralty, 'An Archaeological Picnic' –

> Drink, Mary, drink your fizzy lemonade
>   And leave the king-cups, take your grey felt hat . . .[80]

Again there is a Pre-Raphaelite association, as the party enter a church –

> Green in a light which that sublime Burne-Jones
>   White-hot and wondering from the glass-kiln drew,
>   Gleams and re-gleams this Trans arcade anew.[81]

In the final stanza, which ends in bubbles of bathos, John makes it clear that Mary is still a child, and not for him.

> So stand you waiting, freckled innocence!
>   For me the squinch and squint and Trans arcade;
> For you, where meadow grass is evidence,
>   With flattened pattern, of our picnic made,
>   One bottle more of fizzy lemonade.[82]

'I would funnily meet John all over Bath, bump into him,' Lady Stirling recalls of his Admiralty days. 'He was the first person outside the family who got me interested in buildings and furniture.'[83] In 1946, when she had moved on to another school, Wycombe Abbey, he and Colonel Kolkhorst took out her and her friend Rosemary Craig, a sister of John's then secretary Diana Craig. 'Colonel Kolkhorst had a very fast open sports car – an MG perhaps,' Mary Stirling remembers. 'At one point I looked at the speedometer and it showed 100 m.p.h. They took us to the Pipers at Henley and got us drunk on Pimm's No. 1.'[84] Under her maiden name, Mary Shand became a well-known furniture designer. In 1962 she designed chairs (with R.D. Russell) for the rebuilt Coventry Cathedral; later, furniture for the Staff House at Liverpool University and for the Clore Gallery at the Tate, a building designed by her husband.[85] John kept in touch with the Stirlings, visiting them at their house in north London. The last time Mary saw him was at a 10 Downing Street reception in the early 1980s. 'He was in a wheelchair.'[86]

The poem 'An Archaeological Picnic', first published in *Horizon* in 1940, appeared in John's collection *New Bats in Old Belfries* (1945), as did his moving sestet 'In a Bath Teashop', about the transcendent power of love.

> 'Let us not speak, for the love we bear one another
>   Let us hold hands and look.'
> She, such a very ordinary little woman;
>   He, such a thumping crook;
> But both, for a moment, little lower than the angels
>   In the tea-shop's ingle-nook.[87]

John's poem 'Bristol' was also published in *New Bats in Old Belfries*. For him, the proximity of Bristol was one of the great compensations for being at 'P' Branch. As his review of R.A.L. Smith's book shows, he found Bristol 'even more interesting' than Bath. As he also observed, Bristol had been far worse hit in the Blitz. A historian of Bristol later wrote: 'For the first time a city which had always played safe with history, secretly disliking the political wars that interrupted trade with France, Spain and the American colonies, found violent history on its doorstep.'[88] To John, who had known Bristol before the war and lavished praise on it in a radio broadcast of 1937,[89] the damage inflicted by the Luftwaffe was agonizing. The greatest loss was St Peter's Hospital (1612), formerly the Bristol Mint. The ancient Temple Church, once at the centre of the city's weaving trade, was gutted. The seventeenth-century 'Dutch House', with its mock-medieval battlements, was destroyed; so was the Merchants' Hall, with parts of the Merchants' Almshouses. There was tragic wreckage among the Queen Anne houses of St James's Square. Mercifully, the Cathedral was largely unscathed, as were the Lord Mayor's Chapel and St Mary Redcliffe Church, in the muniment room of which Thomas Chatterton, Wordsworth's 'marvellous boy', had claimed to have found his forgeries of William Canynge.

John had three friends in Bristol. One was John Garrett, the flamboyant headmaster of Bristol Grammar School, who, with W.H. Auden, had compiled the anthology *The Poet's Tongue*. Another was the same school's art master, the painter Edward Wolfe – also, as it happened, a friend of Richard Hughes, who had met him in Morocco in 1927.[90] John knew Wolfe through Frederick Etchells. Like Etchells, Wolfe had been a member of the Bloomsbury Group's Omega Workshops; in 1918 Roger Fry had ranked him second only to Duncan Grant among the Omega artists.

John's third friend in Bristol was Mervyn Stockwood, the future

Bishop of Southwark, who since 1941 had been Vicar of St Matthew, Moorfields, Bristol, of which the roof had been severely charred in a German air raid on Good Friday 1941. John had first met Stockwood in 1939 at the table of Father Cyril Tomkinson, the ebullient and high-living Vicar of All Saints, Clifton.[91] (When that church was blitzed, Tomkinson became Vicar of one of John's favourite Victorian Gothic churches, All Saints, Margaret Street, London.) Stockwood, whose childhood was spent in Clifton, was an intense young cleric who had been converted to Socialism in 1937 by a Bristol speech of Sir Stafford Cripps, the future Labour Chancellor.[92] Stockwood had a deep, resonant voice that seemed designed to echo round cathedrals. He was a man in whom piety and sensuality seemed constantly at war: he was described as having 'the eyes of an angel, the mouth of a devil'.[93] Like Tomkinson, he was a *bon vivant* and a spirited talker. Some of John's friends could not understand his liking for Stockwood, whom they found vain, overbearing and bombastic. But the two men just 'clicked'; and they remained lifelong friends.

Penelope Betjeman once said, 'John likes all his friends to be homosexual.'[94] His three Bristol friends certainly answered the prescription. The broadcaster Robert Robinson, who encountered Garrett at Raynes Park Grammar School, where he was headmaster before coming to Bristol, regarded him as a great teacher, but wrote: 'At all times he was rumoured to be on the point of marriage with a strange actress called Martita Hunt, but was in fact as queer as a coot (not that these two last conditions need have been mutually exclusive).'[95]

Teddy Wolfe, a charming sprite of a man, eventually became a Royal Academician. Each year the canvases he submitted to be hung in the Summer Exhibition tended to be of burnous-clad Moroccan boys with wide brown eyes. He was one of the figures of the Swinging Sixties, when he held court in Narrow Street, Limehouse, with his lover, the playwright Jim O'Connor, and hand-painted ties for his friends with Omega-esque designs.[96] And Mervyn Stockwood's biographer, Michael De-la-Noy, writes of Stockwood: 'His heart he only ever gave to men . . .'[97]

The last line of John's poem 'Bristol and Clifton' was an in-joke intended specially to amuse Stockwood –

'I know the Inskips very well indeed.'[98]

The poem is largely a monologue by a pompous and insensitive churchwarden. In 1990 Bishop Stockwood said that although another Clifton church had claimed in its printed guide that it was the one in which the poem was set, the actual church John had in mind was

Emmanuel parish church, Clifton, a 'streaky-bacon' building of the 1860s.[99] Stockwood even knew who the pompous churchwarden was. And the Inskips? There were three brothers, the sons of a leading Bristol solicitor, all born in the 1870s and educated at Clifton College. James Inskip was Bishop of Barking from 1919 to 1948. Sir John Hampden Inskip became Lord Mayor of Bristol in 1931. And Thomas Inskip, first Viscount Caldecote, was made Minister for the Co-ordination of Defence in 1936. A.J.P. Taylor, in an introduction to Len Deighton's *Fighter: The True Story of the Battle of Britain* (1977), claimed that although Thomas Inskip was 'an unimpressive figure whose appointment had been dismissed as the most surprising since Caligula made his horse a consul', it was his insistence on building fighter planes, rather than bombers, that 'made British victory in the Battle of Britain possible'.[100] This conclusion must have come as a surprise to Deighton, who makes not a mention of Inskip in his book.

It was the Bristol alderman, Sir John Hampden Inskip, with whom the young Stockwood had a very public row. A right-wing Conservative, Inskip was balefully aware of Stockwood's growing links with the Labour Party. He accused him of using his pulpit to preach 'blatant socialist propaganda'.[101] Inskip was furious to hear that, in a sermon preached in Cambridge at the invitation of the Student Christian Movement, Stockwood's passionate indignation at the sale of British zinc to Japan had led him to incite the workers to strike. Inskip demanded Stockwood's dismissal.[102] It was rumoured that the police were taking an interest in the young man's seditious opinions. But Stockwood had already acquired the art of making friends in high places, which was to bring him much preferment in later life. William Temple, Archbishop of York and soon to be Archbishop of Canterbury, was particularly impressed and charmed by him, and 'saved his skin', while cautioning him to be more temperate in his public speaking.[103]

John's 1944 poem about Bristol was written in a mood of exalted melancholy and with none of the satire of 'Bristol and Clifton'. It begins:

> Green upon the flooded Avon shone the after-storm-wet sky
> Quick the struggling withy branches let the leaves of autumn fly
> And a star shone over Bristol, wonderfully far and high[104]

and ends with 'the mathematic pattern of a plain course on the bells'. Showing off the knowledge of campanology gained in Uffington, John added, in a footnote, the actual sequence of changes –

```
1   2   2   4   4   5   5   3   3   1   1
2   1   4   2   5   4   3   5   1   3   2
3   4   1   5   2   3   4   1   5   2   3
4   3   5   1   3   2   1   4   2   5   4
5   5   3   3   1   1   2   2   4   4   5
```

Most of the temporary administrative assistants in the Admiralty saw out the war in that service, then resumed careers that had been interrupted.[105] A very few of the temporary staff stayed on in the Admiralty after the war. Dawn Macleod was offered permanent tenure but baffled and annoyed her superiors by declining it because she wanted to live in Scotland.[106] John had absolutely no wish to stay at the Admiralty; he could not get out of it quickly enough. Even the more equable Hughes had written to his wife in 1942, 'O Lord how I hate this life, thinking about things all the time which have merely a practical value. Shall I ever get my mind clean again? Scrub it in sea-water & bleach it in stars and hang it up to dry in front of very warm love . . .'[107] Three months after describing his work to Nancy Mitford as 'wonderfully boring', John was calling it 'hellish'.[108] He left at the end of October 1944. On 31 October his colleague Pamela Barlow wrote to thank him for some flowers, adding, 'I do hope you will be happy in your new work.'[109] Morton Shand wrote on 4 December: 'The family are bitterly disappointed you've turned your back on Bath. Mary is already renouncing Anglicanism in consequence.'[110] In January 1945 Helen Holmes wrote to him on receiving a copy of the 'Bristol' poem.

> Many thanks for your long letter and typescript. I feel very honoured that you should take the trouble to send both. We are still hoping to see you and waiting the poem on the sister city Bath. We hear the Bells of Bristol *sometimes* at Bath. They are peculiarly sweet and touching. I don't think we hear them at Macaulay but in the Combe Down area.[111]

In December 1954, in another letter of their long correspondence, she wrote:

> I was looking through some old letters just now to find a lost document and came across a letter of yours dated 14.i.XLV and a poem, 'Bristol', which you composed on Widcombe Hill and sent to me. I have read and re-read it this afternoon instead of going on with my hunt for lost papers. It is just lovely, and again from our windows we see the flooded Avon and the after-storm-wet sky . . .[112]

FARNBOROUGH

This morning I met an old and revered friend, C——, who congratulated me on my forthcoming marriage and gave me some advice, based on his own experience; he has been married for more than thirty years and his marriage, he says, has been 'ideally happy'.

. . . He says that two things are tremendously important – first a mutual respect 'amounting almost to awe', so that there are certain spiritual privacies which are never invaded; secondly, a joint dislike of rows so that you change the subject the moment 'that "row" edge' comes into the voice . . .

Later in the evening I happened to meet John Betjeman, who is also happily married, told him what C—— had said, and asked him if he agreed with it.

'Yes,' he said. 'It's very good advice . . . but it's the advice of a man who has never been in love with his wife.'

Tom Driberg, diary for 26 April 1951, in *The Best of Both Worlds*,
London 1953

Early in 1945, Farmer Wheeler told the Betjemans that he needed Garrards Farm: his son Peter was going to live there. It was a bad blow for John, who never welcomed sudden changes in the pattern of his life. It intensified his dislike of Wheeler, which was to surface in his poem 'The Dear Old Village'. John and Penelope began house-hunting. They looked at a farmhouse at Stanford in the Vale, and another house at Avebury. Then Sir Ralph Glyn, the local MP, told them that the Old Rectory, Farnborough, was on the market,[1] a squarson's house of 1749 in grey vitrified brick with red-brick dressings, a panelled parapet and a columned porch. Penelope recalled in 1976:

My solicitor had been asked to come down from Market Drayton – they had been my family's solicitors for generations. He was going to come down and do all the bidding for me. But it so happened that the day the auction was to take place in the Town Hall, Wantage, coincided with VE Day[2] when all the trains were 'Sunday trains' and everything virtually came to a full stop. So the solicitor rang to say he was sorry, it was absolutely impossible for him to get down. So I then drove in in my four-wheel pony cart; and John was in an absolute state because he wanted the house much more than I did. It was a large Georgian house with no water and no light and a very large garden, twelve acres, and a gardener whose wages you had to pay, and I didn't think we were in that income group, quite honestly. And it wanted an awful lot doing to it. All the paint was horrible brown. It wasn't very attractive inside, it was just a very beautiful façade. But John was absolutely potty about it and was determined to get it whatever happened. He said it was like buying a Cézanne, a beautiful picture. So I drove my pony cart the seven miles from Uffington to Wantage, tied it up in the yard of the Bear Hotel and went across the square to bid for the house. Lord Chetwynd's agent was there. He had been told to go to £5,000. But I've got an awfully good technique, having done a lot of buying at furniture and other sales: I never come in until people have almost stopped, then I suddenly come in and bid up so quick that they're absolutely taken off their feet and think I'm going on to a million, so drop out. And I did that. I came in at about £4,500 and just bid up and up and up. We got it for £5,100.[3]

Because John and Penelope had married clandestinely, her parents, Lord and Lady Chetwode, had never given them a wedding present. Now, reconciled to John, Chetwode paid for the Farnborough house and gave it to the couple.[4] For the first time John, who had spent his life in little houses in north and south London, in London flats and then the Uffington farmhouse, was moving to a 'gentleman's house', rather as Evelyn Waugh, another north Londoner, had done when he bought Piers Court, Gloucestershire, in 1937. For the first time, too, John would have a library for his hundreds of antiquarian books. It was a topic of amused comment in the neighbourhood, that the Betjemans, on coming to the Old Rectory, *removed a bathroom*.[5] John was not renowned for cleanliness; in 1943 he contributed an article to the racy magazine *Lilliput* in praise of dirt.[6]

In June 1945 Penelope wrote to John, who was staying with Colonel Kolkhorst at Yarnton, 'We may have bitten off more than we can chew with Farnboro' but I regard it as a last stand against the slave state. If by taxation and filling in forms they make it impossible for us to live there, then we shall have to emigrate to St Helena as you once suggested.'[7] She had hopes of running a smallholding at Farnborough, the profits from which would enable John to give up his book-reviewing for the *Daily Herald* and devote himself to the work he enjoyed, writing poems and books on architecture and topography.[8]

The Betjemans found themselves having to explain to many of their friends that they were moving not to Farnborough in Hampshire, where in 1887 the Empress Eugénie had built a mausoleum for her husband (and where Joan Hunter Dunn had grown up), but to the

Berkshire Farnborough, near Wantage. With a population of just over a hundred, it was the highest village in Berkshire, situated idyllically amid ancient tracks, notably The Ridgeway. In 1952, Ian Yarrow wrote in his book on Berkshire: 'The road to Farnborough through West Ilsley is one of the most lovely downland drives imaginable, sweeping up and down, the verges glorious with knapweed and scabious, the rolling cornfields sometimes yellow with charlock and often blood-shot with poppies.'[9] History had hardly impinged on Farnborough since 1688, when William of Orange's Dutch troops marched through the village on their way from Newbury to London. Some of them ran-sacked the Roman Catholic chapel of the Eystons at East Hendred, drinking themselves drunk from the chalice and making a guy of the priest's vestments which they carried to Oxford and burned on a bonfire.[10] Lady Agnes Eyston still lived at East Hendred and became a friend of the Betjemans.[11] After Penelope was converted to Roman Catholicism in 1948, she sometimes took her children to Lady Agnes's chapel; but John, though he thought the Rector of Farnborough, the Rev. John Durno Steele, 'lazy and good natured, woolly-minded and useless', took his squirely duties seriously and continued to worship at the little village church, with its tower built of stones from Poughley Monastery, suppressed by Henry VIII. (Today a window by John Piper commemorates John's years as a parishioner.)

On 27 May 1945 John wrote to Evelyn Waugh:

Propeller's father has just bought Farnborough Rectory, Nr. Wantage for us:

1730-ish. Red brick seven hundred feet up on the downs. No water, no light, no heat. Beech trees all round. We shall be at Uffers till September at least.[12]

In the meantime, there was a medical problem that needed attention. 'I am feeling so ill and tired . . .' John wrote to Geoffrey Taylor on 8 June.[13] Later that month he went into the Acland Nursing Home,

Oxford, to have a sebaceous cyst removed from his stomach. He was nursed there by the historical novelist Mary Renault, who was nearing the end of her nursing career and was soon to emigrate to South Africa.[14] She remembered that John's window overlooked a girls' school and that he told her, 'The girls are just like St Trinian's' – the incorrigible school-girls of Ronald Searle's cartoons.[15] He was invited to convalesce at Friar's Oak, Beaulieu, Hampshire, the home of Jack and Vera MacKenzie, the father and stepmother of his Uffington friend Arthur MacKenzie. Their house was beside Beaulieu River. There he met Brigadier Buckland and his daughter Clemency, whom he introduced into one of his most poign-ant poems, 'Youth and Age on Beaulieu River, Hants'.*[16]

On 22 July John wrote to Penelope from Friar's Oak, heading the letter with a caricature of Candida, captioned 'WABA STAND ON WABA'S POWNIE TINKY BULL [Tinkerbell]' –

He was planning to remain with the MacKenzies until the Wednesday, when he would stay with Penelope, moving on to the Colonel's at Yarnton on the Thursday, with a morning visit to his doctor 'as he alone can determine my convalescence' – a euphemism for 'decide how many weeks he will sign me off work'.[17] John spent much of the summer of 1945 at Yarnton. It was handier for Oxford than either Uffington or Farnborough; in a time of petrol shortages, he could bicycle to work. Yarnton also took John out of the milieu of scream-ing children, horsiness, animals and rows with Penelope, into the relaxed bachelor ménage in the Tudor manor house. Osbert Lancaster joked that 'John liked large girls and the Colonel liked small boys';[18] but John was able to enter amusedly into the campery of Kolkhorst's circle, which included the dons John Bryson and Toby Strutt, the aes-thetes Hedley Hope-Nicholson and Stuart Hill, two servants, Fred and Souch, and Soda the dog. Bryson lived not far off, at Court Place,

* See Chapter 17, 'New Bats in Old Belfries'.

Iffley. John had known him since his undergraduate days, respecting him as a scholar 'who read Anglo Saxon, Finnish and probably Swedish and Faroese as easily as I read the gossip column of the *Cherwell*'.[19] In 1939 he had written him a poem, beginning:

> Ow Mister Broyson
> Yew are a noice one
> Oi 'aven't done with yew yet
> Ow you entoice one . . .[20]

Stuart Hill spent an hour and a half each morning putting on his make-up.[21] Hope-Nicholson, though married and the father of Marie-Jaqueline Lancaster who was to edit a book on John's friend Brian Howard, also applied a bit of 'slap'. In a libellous rhyme, John alluded to this habit and to his owning More Place in Chelsea, the former home of Sir Thomas More –

> H is for Hedley,
> Who lives in a Place;
> What he makes on his bottom
> He spends on his face.[22]

Another frequent visitor to Yarnton was Gerard Irvine, who used to bicycle over at weekends from St Stephen's House in Oxford, where he was training to be a clergyman. John had met Irvine through his former pupil at Heddon Court, Paul Miller. Miller had gone on to Haileybury, where Irvine was one of his best friends. He had introduced Irvine to John, who in turn – tempting Providence – had taken the two schoolboys to lunch with Tom Driberg in Fleet Street.[23] Irvine became a great family friend of the Betjemans and John's long correspondence with him – because the two men wrote to each other with utter candour on all subjects and with no posing or posturing – is one of the most reliable sources as to what John was thinking or feeling at any given time between the late 1930s and the early 1980s. Irvine's home was in Cheltenham and his father was a general – facts to which John made reference in his poem 'Cheltenham', published in *Old Lights for New Chancels* (1940) –

> Shall I forget the warm marquee
>   And the general's wife so soon,
> When my son's colleger* acted as tray
>   For an ice and a macaroon . . . ?

* Colleger = mortarboard.

Irvine had met Kolkhorst just before he became an Oxford undergraduate. In *Summoned by Bells* (1960) John recorded one dramatic encounter between the two. Addressing Kolkhorst in the poem, he wrote:

> No one believed you really were a don
> Till Gerard Irvine (now a parish priest)
> Went to your lecture on *Le Cid* and clapped.
> You swept towards him, gowned, and turned him out.[24]

John and Irvine enjoyed, as a sort of running pantomime, the feuds and crushes and goings-on at Yarnton. They browsed among the 'Uranian' (homosexual) books on what the Colonel archly called 'the Youth Club shelf'. They were amused by Kolkhorst's pretensions as a china collector: in 1945, when an expert on Chinese porcelain valued the collection, he concluded, or so John told Alan Pryce-Jones, that 'the Colonel had only paid a hundred and seventy-five per cent too much, not two hundred per cent, as I had feared'.[25] John and Irvine also chaffed the Colonel about his bachelor slovenliness, which his surly domestics did little to relieve. John evoked life at Yarnton in a premature poem on 'The Death of the UNIVERSITY READER IN SPANISH (the late Col. George Alfred Magee Kolkhorst RSVP)', of which he sent copies to Irvine and other friends:

> SODA is lying on the 'couch'
> And so is FRED and so is SOUCH.
> There is an air in every room
> At least of Thought, if not of Gloom.
> The Carpets shiver to themselves
> The Plates are silent on the shelves
> (And some of them are very old
> And some of them are not, I'm told).
> The toothbrushes in order ranged
> Are all remarkably unchanged
> (And these are older far in date
> Than any rug or any plate),
> The bits of sponge of various shades,
> The fifty years of razor blades,
> All these no evidence betray
> That 'tis *the Colonel*'s dying day . . .
>
> What glimpse of the Eternal flashes
> Across those long mascara-ed lashes?
> What meetings with the blessèd dead

Await that dear old cube-shaped head?
See like a spark from ETNA's Crater
The everlasting soul of PATER.
It flits about the room and rests
Beside *the Colonel*'s woollen vests.
And what is that thing over there
With neither face nor form nor hair?
Just disembodied Intellect?
It's dear old PLATO, I expect.
It has departed by itself
To browse about the Youth Club shelf . . .[26]

Kolkhorst retaliated with a poem cattily entitled 'JOHN BETJEMAN
or SELF-IMPORTANCE', which began:

Here I sit, up to the hilt
Dyed in sin and steeped in guilt.
Everybody else is white,
Only I am black as night.
Pleasures come and go in vain;
Pleasure hurts me more than pain.
Fame, success and schoolboy pashes
Are to me as dust and ashes.
Though I get more than my share
Of these things, they are but – air.
Others envy me my lot;
Little what that is they wot . . .[27]

Still continuing in John's voice, the poem describes how, when he
appears before the Angel with the Book, he will be seized by devils and
the Angel will denounce him –

'Fearful, unbelieving you,
Abominable liar, too;
Sorcerer, murderer, all in one,
Perched up there before the Throne:
Idolater, fornicator,
Of my chosen saints foul hater;
Brimstone is too good and fire
For the likes of such a liar . . .'[28]

One was as likely to find village boys as Oxford dons enjoying the
Colonel's hospitality. John brought his son Paul to Yarnton several

times. Kolkhorst at least affected to be in love with the 'golden lad'. (In 1937 he had declined to be his godfather, on the grounds that it would mean renouncing 'the Devil and all his works'. Tom Driberg was chosen instead.)

One other visitor to Yarnton was the future MP and notorious heterosexual Alan Clark. In 1949 John wrote to his father, Kenneth Clark: 'I remember how marvellous Alan was in the Boys' Club at Yarnton which he visited for about two minutes, joining in *boxing* – the greatest asset for a "social worker" – with terrific success.'[29] In 1999 Alan Clark recalled the occasion.

> One evening Betj. did take me out to Yarnton. In those days I was extremely innocent and didn't realise that the 'Colonel' hosted the Boys' Club and laid on an *ex tempore* gymnasium for them from motives that were voyeuristic if not actually predatory. I had been runner-up middle-weight champion at Eton the year before and so it was no problem for me when invited to 'spar' with one of the boys. Actually I have had guilt about it ever since because he was a pleasant self-effacing youth and I was much too rough with him.
>
> Later on the 'Colonel' tried to humiliate me (probably in retribution) by getting me to guess the prices of some of his carpets. By pure chance I got them all right. 'This boy hears voices,' said Kolkhorst.[30]

John was still at Yarnton on 23 September 1945, when he wrote to John Piper: 'You have been a true friend to me in my war years and lying back in bed in the Colonel's luxury I fully realise it. I have sciatica and shall be in bed for about a week more I gather.'[31] In October Piper and John travelled through Shropshire, doing further research for the Shell Guide to the county – a project which had been interrupted by the war. John was back at Yarnton on 3 November, when he sent Eileen Molony, a BBC Talks producer in Bristol, a letter beginning, 'Ah my darling dark yellow-stockinged Amazon'.[32] ('The whole organization is humming with interest and speculation as a result,' she reported.)[33] But by 2 December he was writing to Jock Murray from the Old Rectory, Farnborough. The family had moved into the house in time for Christmas. On 28 December, thanking Cyril Connolly for a Christmas present, a book illustrated by Dicky Doyle, John wrote:

> You and Lys[34] really must come here. It is bloody cold and rather like Collinstown and the house quite featureless inside. But if I can only get some drink and it is clear crisp weather, you will be enchanted with the place . . . Unluckily we have to fell fifteen beeches around the house. They have AMERICAN disease, which is INCURABLE.[35]

Early in 1946 he described his new home in a letter to Tom Driberg: 'Corking scenery. No light, water, no telephone allowed by Slave State – but what exquisite scenery; come and see your godson. He is charming and fair.'[36]

In January, John began a long campaign to obtain a public honour for Ninian Comper, which eventually led to the architect's knighthood. John thought he should be appointed to the Order of Merit, but wrote to Kenneth Clark on 28 January: 'Tom Boase does not think Comper "enough guns" for an OM. I doubt if he knows Comper's work.'[37] Boase, a historian of both medieval and Victorian art and architecture, became President of Magdalen College, Oxford, in 1947; the letter shows John's low opinion of the man with whom, seven years later, he was to have an ill-tempered battle over Magdalen's plan to create a rose garden opposite the college, in the High. In March, John asked Comper if he would design the lettering for a Memorial to his beloved friend Basil Dufferin, killed in the last days of the war.[38] John and Maureen Dufferin had decided on these words for the memorial at Clandeboye:

IN MEMORY OF
BASIL SHERIDAN,
4TH MARQUESS OF DUFFERIN AND AVA
CAPTAIN, ROYAL HORSE GUARDS

A MAN OF BRILLIANCE
AND OF MANY FRIENDS

HE WAS KILLED IN ACTION AT LETZE ON MARCH
25TH 1945 AT THE AGE OF THIRTY-FIVE,
RECAPTURING BURMA THE COUNTRY WHICH
HIS GRANDFATHER ANNEXED TO THE BRITISH
CROWN

On 18 April John attended Dufferin's memorial service at which, Evelyn Waugh wrote, 'White's turned up in good numbers.' Waugh made his first visit to Farnborough in October. He told Nancy Mitford that the house 'smelled like a village shop – oil, cheese, bacon, washing . . .' and that 'The Betjemans both put on Jaeger combinations on the 1st of September & keep them on for all purposes until the 2nd week of May. A horse sleeps in the kitchen.'[39] In his diary he wrote:

Wantage, Thursday 31 October 1946

In the late afternoon to stay with the Betjemans in a lightless, stuffy, cold, poky rectory among beech woods overlooking Wantage. Harness everywhere. A fine collection of nineteenth-century illustrated books. Delicious food cooked by Penelope. I brought sherry, burgundy, port. A daughter of grossly proletarian appearance and manner.[40]

John's comment on this, when the Waugh diaries were published in 1976, was: 'How very Evelyn, to write so readably and so inaccurately.'[41] Candida Lycett Green agrees the Rectory was cold, but denies that it was lightless or poky and that one could see Wantage from it.[42] As for her seeming 'proletarian', Waugh may have got that impression because, at that time, Candida's playmates in Farnborough spoke broad Berkshire and she picked up the accent – that pleasant yokel murmur in which, characteristically, a cactus is described as having 'noice little spoikes'. Candida recalls:

Most of the village children of our age, who numbered around a dozen, almost lived at the Rectory – except for Johnny Willoughby, who was kept indoors, and the Marshall girls, who lived two miles away in a remote farm cottage. Juney White became my best friend and Terry Carter my brother's . . . All the village children came on the trolley cart pulled by the Connemara mare, Tulira, who had come with us from Ireland, to lunch picnics on remote tracks and lost valleys around the Ridgeway, the ancient grass track that runs along the Downs.[43]

All drinking water had to be fetched daily in a bucket from a communal tap in the village street. In a small cottage by the tap lived Florrie and Pearl Wilkinson, sisters of Bob, Sis, Peter, Stella, Christine and Bill. Florrie, blonde and eighteen and Pearl, red-haired and sixteen, worked on one of the two main Farnborough farms. Candida remembers them as 'sunburnt and always singing the latest hits from the radio'.[44] John was greatly taken by Pearl and immortalized her in his poem 'Agricultural Caress' –

> Keep me from Florrie's sister Pearl!
> She puts my senses in a whirl,
> Weakens my knees and keeps me waiting
> Until my heart stops palpitating
> . . .
>
> God shrive me from this morning lust
> For supple farm girls: if you must,

> Send the cold daughter of an earl –
> But spare me Florrie's sister Pearl![45]

Because of its 'personal' character, John withheld publication of this poem for twenty years; and when it did finally appear, in *High and Low* (1966), he changed Florrie's name to Thelma, to avoid embarrassing the two women, and to throw scandalmongers off the scent. Florrie remembered John with affection, in particular his rowing her and Pearl up the Thames from Lechlade to look at a church.[46]

An exception to Berkshire accents in the village was Mr and Mrs Dowkes who ran the village shop. They came from the Midlands and John taught Paul and Candida to recite a rhyme about them –

> Hickory Dickory Dowkes,
> I'll tell you some Birmingham jokes.[47]

The children never realized that the nursery rhymes they learned were different from those chanted by other children. John's favourite was:

> Ba Ba centipede,
> Have you any jelly?
> No sir, no sir, it's all gone smelly.[48]

On days when he was reviewing books for the *Daily Herald*, the children were discouraged from going into his library. But on other days John invited them into the room, with its cornflower-blue walls and leaded window (an Edwardian addition) to be shown his book collection. ' "I *say*, look at this," he'd say, drawing in his breath with a whistling sound, on opening some book of aquatints, or showing us the illuminated pages of a Kelmscott Press volume,' Candida recalled, adding:

Going into JB's library was a treat. For me the most exciting thing was to open the right-hand drawer of his desk where he kept an enormous dead centipede in a glass case and also a cardboard cut-out souvenir which concertina'd into an optical illusion of the Crystal Palace in miniature. JB loved reading aloud and read us every book by Mrs Molesworth, every poem in Coventry Patmore's *A Child's Garland* and all M.R. James's ghost stories. We asked for these last again and again and once enacted one of them, *Lost Hearts*, in the hall and at the bottom of the stairs while an amazed village audience looked on.[49]

John often satirized interior decorators, with their 'scumbling', violent colour combinations and frequent campness;[50] but the former editor of *Decoration* was an uninhibited practitioner of what he had once preached. For Farnborough, wallpapers were ordered from the London firm of Green and Abbott: an ivy trellis for the main bedroom, a blue *art nouveau* design for John's dressing-room, a reddish Gilbert Scott design for the dining-room.[51] In effect, a Georgian interior was transformed into a Victorian one. As Osbert Lancaster recalled, 'It was like opening a plain wood tea-caddy and finding a William Burges casket inside.'[52] Intensifying the Victorian atmosphere, Pre-Raphaelite paintings were hung on the walls, Rossettis and two Holman Hunts, one of an amaryllis, the other of a girl holding an urn.[53] The Hunts were a loan from John's friend James Knapp-Fisher, who had bought the publishing firm of Sidgwick and Jackson. (John, who was asked to edit a children's series for the firm, usually referred to Sidgwick and Jackson as 'the hygienics' because of the medical books they published.)[54] By an odd coincidence, it was in the Rectory, in 1940, that William Gaunt had written his masterpiece about the artistic Brotherhood, *The Pre-Raphaelite Tragedy*.[55] John was thrilled to discover that an artist who had illustrated Kelmscott Press books for William Morris, Charles M. Gere, was still alive, aged eighty-three. He commissioned him to paint a portrait of Candida, who recalls: 'Four times JB drove me in the Vauxhall to Mr Gere's house in Painswick in Gloucestershire and I sat, bored and irritable, while JB talked to Mr Gere about all his Arts and Crafts friends.'[56]

Candida was only three, and Paul seven, when the family moved to Farnborough. Both of them attended the small village school until Paul left for the Dragon School.[57] This prep school was chosen not just because John had been there, but because, on Cornish holidays, the Betjemans saw a lot of the Lynam family, including Joc Lynam (son of 'Hum'), who had taken over as headmaster.[58] The winter of 1947 was the most severe in living memory. Farnborough was cut off for a month by huge snowdrifts. Miss Whitaker, the new schoolmistress, arrived the day before the snow fell, but the Pickford's van bringing her furniture got trapped on its way from Newbury.[59] The Betjemans took her into the Rectory. During the snow blockade, Penelope 'became the local heroine, riding Tulira down to Wantage to collect the mail and provisions, pulling a large sleigh behind, on which Florrie and Pearl rode to act as brakes'.[60] Paul and his school-friend Paul Knapp-Fisher, a nephew of James, were delighted that the snow prevented their returning to school. But there was a crisis when Paul Knapp-Fisher, whom John always called 'the quietest boy at the Dragon', went missing for several hours. He was found by John asleep in a snowdrift, suffering from hypothermia.[61] Apart from that it was a happy time of balaclava helmets and mittens, of sledging, snowball fights and snowmen. No one who was a child in 1947 ever forgot that winter.

Candida was just old enough to enjoy the fun. A pretty, fair-haired child, she was her father's pet. She was allowed great freedom and was seldom reprimanded. John often kissed the top of her head. He first called her 'Waba' or 'Wuba', then 'Wabz' or 'Wubz', then 'Wibbly' or 'Woebley', and finally 'Wibz'. That was the nickname that stuck; so she called him 'Dadz'.[62] Candida early showed literary gifts. The 'first remembered paeans of praise' came from him when she presented a poem she had written, clearly influenced by the M.R. James ghost stories John read the children. It began:

> Two young people sat at an old table
> Playing cards as fast as they were able.
> Suddenly the door came open with a creak
> And a woman walked in with a scar on her cheek.
> She beckoned to the two young horror-struck people
> And far away the old church steeple
> Struck twelve . . .[63]

As she grew older, Candida found she could make John laugh. He threw back his head and rocked with laughter when she read him this limerick:

> Wibberly Wobberly Wib
> She blew up her dad with a squib
> And when he was dead
> She cut off his head
> And scratched on his face with a nib.[64]

John made Candida laugh, too. She remembers:

He bought a stuffed crocodile in Tiverton and because my mother would not have it in the house, he kept it in the apple store and brought it out on fine days when he would put it in the long grass beside the path out towards Mr Laurence's farm. When people visited, he would walk them along the path and then suddenly clutch hold of their arm, feigning terror . . . He was also a good mimic; he could take off anyone and used to read stories to me in wildly differing regional accents – some days he would talk with an American accent in nothing but what he called Longfellow language, and by the evening we were all doing it:

If you talk like Hiawatha
You can talk for twenty minutes
Pass me please the bread and butter
Is it time to go to school now?

This activity put me off *Hiawatha* for life.[65]

In later life Candida realized that John had avoided household
chores and the discipline side of bringing up children; these were left
to Penelope. Paul and Candida connected John with treats and presents; Penelope with disagreeable work and crossness. The only physical work John undertook was preparing the paraffin lamps, trimming
the wicks and lighting the fires – all quite good fun for the children to
join in. To Penelope fell all the cooking, the vegetable gardening,
milking the cows, Buttercup and Daisy, morning and evening, feeding
the horses, goats, rabbits and chickens, and making the bright yellow
butter which Paul and Candida hated. (They much preferred the
whitish substance from the local shop, which Candida thought was
called 'shock butter'.) John was seldom found at the kitchen sink,
where Candida spent a lot of time complaining to her mother about
having to wash up. Penelope did all the ticking off over table manners
and all the bossing about. '*Will* you tidy your clothes? *Will* you brush
your teeth? *Will* you feed your rabbit?' Paul and Candida found these
'dreadfully dreary occupations', and soon learned that being near
their mother usually meant being given a job and being near their
father usually didn't.[66] Forced by their mother to do the things they
did not want to do, the children were often encouraged by John to
break the rules.[67] John's reluctance – perhaps incapacity – to be a
handyman or disciplinarian caused friction with Penelope, but that
was nothing new.

John's caricature of Candida in 1949

John only twice became really angry with Candida: once, when she tore plates out of a valuable book and stuck them up round the house and garden;[68] and again when she and her friend Terry Carter were in the attic and Terry stepped between the rafters and fell through the ceiling of John's dressing-room. 'Unfortunately he was in it at the time.'[69] In later years, as she became the dedicated custodian of her father's memory, Candida tended to dwell on the undoubted love she and her father had felt for each other. But there was another side to being John's child. He could be selfish and unconsciously cruel. In 1968 Candida told the *Daily Mail* journalist Catherine Stott:

He doesn't like babies at all. I doubt if he cared much about us before my brother or I reached the age of two. I mean, if he gets into a railway carriage with a baby in it he has a fit and jumps out.

My life before I was ten is mostly a blur but I remember being dragged round churches which I loathed and so did my brother. I mean, from the age of about four. And also my mother was mad on horses and she used to put me to rest on a horse when I was a baby, upright. Well, I got on with the horses in the end but I never got on with the churches until I was about twelve.

Oh they were so boring, they really were. I mean, every time we went for a drive we had to stop at a church like some people stop at pubs.

My brother and I used to sit outside and play among the graves. No, he didn't want to show us the churches, he just wanted to see them for himself![70]

Talking to Candida Crewe for a *Times* profile in 1991, she described another upsetting aspect of her childhood.

What frightened me a lot as a child was the family joke that I was betrothed to John Sparrow, the Warden of All Souls College. I genuinely thought it was true, that I was going to have to marry him. He was sort of bristly and wore thick tweed suits. When he came to lunch he would play along with the joke. I was terrified and would run away.[71]

It is extremely unlikely that John and Sparrow knew they were causing Candida distress; but the sustained joke suggests a curious insensitivity. Basil Dufferin's sister Veronica, who met John when she was a child, in the 1920s, also found it disconcerting that 'one never knew whether he was being serious, or not'.[72] John's treatment of Paul was equally misconceived. Candida writes: 'Alan Pryce-Jones's son David remembers JB coming down to Eton often and taking them both [David and Paul] out to tea. "I always felt mortified for Paul. John used to treat him in a childish way in front of me and I remember Paul curling up with embarrassment." . . . JB often behaved in exactly the same way to me as he did to Paul – but I took it to be the joke it was. I just told him to shut up. I don't think it was possible for my brother to do so.'[73]

Penelope kept in touch with her friends from Uffington days and sometimes invited them to Farnborough – among them, Paul's former nursemaid Betty Packford, who was very fond of Penelope but noted her eccentricities and her occasional thoughtlessness.

One day she said she was coming to fetch me for lunch and I spent most of the previous evening making a little blouse for my son, in yellow check, and a dress for my daughter, because I'd got a yellow check blouse myself. And we were all waiting outside in these rather nice new rig-outs, looking all alike, and we waited and waited and she didn't turn up. So eventually I had to bring them in, because I thought, 'Well, it's gone lunch hour now.' She rang up and said, 'Oh, by the way, was I going to fetch you today? I'm awfully sorry, I forgot. I'll come tomorrow.' Of course, all the clothes were dirty by then, that I'd taken so much trouble to make look nice.

We did go to lunch the next day. I gave my children strict instructions to make sure they used their knives and forks and didn't use their fingers. And when we got into lunch we had fish fingers with crisps. Well, there was my poor son trying to pick up crisps with a knife and fork, and there was Mrs Betjeman using her hands and gobbling up everything in sight. And when we had tea with her, it wasn't tea as the children knew it. It was crisps and sugar almonds and biscuits and milk – though I was allowed tea.[74]

The Betjemans had also remained friendly with Ken Freeman, who, as a boy, had been the first person they met when they arrived in Uffington. He was now a handsome young man, farming in a small way. The Betjemans caused considerable offence among the *haut ton* of the neighbourhood when they encouraged him in his romance with Judy Allen-Stevens.[75] Her father, Tom Allen-Stevens, was a rich land-owner at Wicklesham, with one of the finest dairy shorthorn herds in the country; he was exporting bulls for £500 at a time when the normal market price for a bull was £30 to £40.[76] The young couple were married in April 1949. 'You have no idea', said Jean Rome, 'of the huge divide there was, then, between a yeoman farmer like Ken Freeman and, say, a family like the Loyds [landowners at Lockinge, Wantage]. That John and Penelope abetted this love affair caused a lot of ill-feeling.'[77] John was unrepentant. He liked both Ken and Judy; he had read *Tom Jones*; and it was not so long, after all, since he himself had been regarded as a most 'unsuitable suitor'. Ken and Judy's marriage was a very happy one.

The Betjemans' own marriage could not exactly be described as unhappy; but it was turbulent. The friends from Uffington days observed that John and Penelope had not given up their habit of having rows in public. The rows had become a sort of ritual: point, counterpoint. The great crisis of the marriage came in 1947. A religious schism opened between the two. John had resigned from the Society of Friends in 1937,[78] and now, ten years on, was a fully committed Anglican. The first strong hint of a religious rift with Penelope appeared in a letter from John to Gerard Irvine on 20 March.

> Your prayers are asked for a quandary I am in. Propeller is toying, nay more than toying, with Rome (keep to yourself) and I do not feel any urge to go over. Indeed I think it would be *wrong* for me to go over, mainly betraying the Church of God. But it will not be at all wise to live in a divided family, as I shall, I suppose, have to do. For P will want the children over too. The Motto is, my dear Gerard, celibacy pays.[79]

Irvine replied:

> My advice is (for what it's worth) stay put. That is I know sound: it is a principle of moral theology to stay where you are when in doubt. You can't go over to Rome just because your wife has gone; or because it breaks up your family. Nor even because the Church of England has proved itself a false church (if you were to think that it had). You can only go over to Rome because you believe that what Rome says is true about the extent of the church, and the Pope and Anglican orders and all the rest. If you do believe that (and I suppose that you *don't*) you ought to go over whatever Penelope does.[80]

It has been claimed that Evelyn Waugh and Frank Pakenham (later Lord Longford) converted Penelope to Roman Catholicism; but in fact she made the decision quite independently, after experiencing 'a vision of the heavenly host' while on holiday in Assisi.[81] Nevertheless, Waugh was a close friend of hers; and as she moved Romewards he tried to bully John into joining her, in a series of hectoring letters. The bullying began in 1946. Although the two men were on friendly terms, the respect John felt for Waugh was tinged with terror. Of John's near-contemporaries, Waugh was the one who had really made it as a writer – and at a time when John was still a struggling prep-school master, with no books to his name. And John knew what venom Waugh could spurt at anyone he took against. As early as 1933, in a profile of Waugh for *Oxford and Cambridge* magazine, he had written:

This is the most terrifying task I have ever undertaken. Supposing you, reader, were asked to write about somebody who saw through you and could do you down, if he were so minded; supposing, too, that you also liked the person you were going to write about, what the hell would you do? . . . Whatever I say, whatever I write, I can see Evelyn, with his fierce eyes, reading it, criticizing it, objecting to it or ignoring it. I am terrified.[82]

In 1946 he let himself in for a similar ordeal when he rashly agreed to give a radio talk about Waugh. More dangerously still, he undertook to write 500 words to accompany a caricature of Waugh which Osbert Lancaster had drawn for the *Strand Magazine*. Waugh hated the drawing: it showed him bowler-hatted, pop-eyed and choleric on the steps of White's. In this year, too, Waugh was busy satirizing John in his novella *Scott-King's Modern Europe*. When it was published in 1947 he wrote to Penelope: 'I hope John did not resent the parody of his erotic rhapsodies in *Scott-King*.'[83] In the book John is unmistakably travestied as Mr Whitemaid, who, with the schoolmaster Scott-King, is attending a conference about the poet Bellorius in the republic of Neutralia (a thinly disguised Yugoslavia). Also apparently at the conference – though in fact she is with another group of physical training experts – is Miss Sveningen, a 'giant carnivore'.[84] Whitemaid thinks she looks superb in shorts,[85] but is disillusioned when she appears at a reception in a chocolate-coloured gown with a patent-leather belt.[86]

'The belt,' said Whitemaid, 'was more than flesh and blood could bear. Something snapped, here,' he said, touching his forehead. 'You must remember how she looked in shorts? A Valkyrie. Something from the heroic age. Like some god-like, some unimaginably strict school prefect, *a dormitory monitor*,' he said in a kind of ecstasy. 'Think of her striding between the beds, a pigtail, bare feet, in her hand a threatening hairbrush. Oh, Scott-King, do you think she rides a bicycle?'
    'I'm sure of it.'
    'In shorts?'
    'Certainly in shorts.'
    'I can imagine a whole life lived riding tandem behind her, through endless forests of conifers, and at midday sitting down among the pine needles to eat hard-boiled eggs. Think of those strong fingers peeling an egg, Scott-King, the brown of it, the white of it, the shine. Think of her *biting* it.'[87]

Waugh did not think much of John's radio talk about him, to which he listened on a borrowed 'apparatus'. 'Too much of it was quotation,' he complained in his diary; though he conceded that in reading a long passage from *Vile Bodies* John had 'succeeded in breathing life in those dry old bones'.[88] Waugh had appropriated John's love of Victorian architecture in *A Handful of Dust* (1934), in which he had teasingly given John a walk-on part as 'a very civil young man' from 'an architectural review';[89] and in *Brideshead Revisited* (1945) he had brazenly pirated John's teddy-bear, and his treatment of it, for Lord Sebastian Flyte. Beyond these minor sources of tension was Waugh's manifest affection for Penelope: there were persistent rumours of an affair.[90] John already knew in 1945 that Waugh was making Penelope the heroine of his novel *Helena* – which, when it appeared in 1950, was dedicated to her.

On 22 December 1946, a week after John's broadcast on him, Waugh wrote him his first long letter about religion. He had been reading John's contribution to *Five Sermons by Laymen*, and was 'painfully shocked' by it.

> Last time I met you you told me you did not believe in the Resurrection. Now I find you expounding Protestant devotional practices from the pulpit. This WILL NOT DO. You should be thinking of St Thomas More not of Henry Moore.[91]

Waugh had heard that Penelope intended to purchase John 'a year's respite from uncongenial work', perhaps with the produce of her smallholding. 'You must spend some of that time thinking,' Waugh urged. 'It is no good saying: "I don't happen to be logical."' He considered that John's ecclesiastical position was 'entirely without reason', adding:

> You must not suppose that there is anything more than the most superficial resemblance between Catholics & Anglo-Catholics. They may look alike to you. An Australian, however well-informed, simply cannot distinguish between a piece of Trust House timbering and a genuine Tudor building; an Englishman however uncultured knows at once.[92]

In a lost reply, John seems to have written – what he was to repeat in later letters – that he could not desert his local church.[93] Waugh, wrongly assuming that he meant Wantage Church (rather than Farnborough) snapped back on 9 January 1947:

> God forbid that I should pronounce damnation on the people of Wantage . . . I have no patience whatever with the plea of duty to a sinking ship. If your group at Wantage are the Catholic Church they are not

sinking. They are one with the angels & saints triumphant. If they are sinking it is because they should never have put to sea . . .

You cannot rely on a death bed conversion. Every hour you spend outside the Church is an hour lost. I well know the vast handicap of having started my Catholic life 27 years too late. Think what it must have been like for poor Charles II who only had a few minutes Catholic life![94]

Waugh's belief, expressed in the same letter, that John was 'being allowed to see a glimpse of the truth broad enough to damn you if you reject it now' was well calculated to revive the fear of hellfire instilled in him by his Calvinist nurse in early childhood, as he described in his poem 'N.W.5 & N.6'.[95]

John wrote back politely: 'I deeply appreciate your zeal on my soul's behalf. Indeed I have never been more exercised by a correspondence in my life.' But he put up a spirited defence of his position.

What I cannot believe – and this is a far more permanent carbuncle (you would call it) than my occasional doubts about the Resurrection – is that the C of E is *not* part of the Catholic Church. The Roman Communion could not have me unless I were convinced that the C of E was a heretical church. I do not doubt for an instant that the RC church is part of Christ's Body but I also do not doubt that the C of E is. For every heretical clergy-man in the C of E (if by heretical we both mean Protestant or what is far worse 'modernist') you quote to me, I can quote back, I am sure, two Catholic ones.[96]

Waugh returned to the charge on 14 January, ridiculing the claims of a church which came into being because Henry VIII could not obtain an annulment of his marriage to Catherine of Aragon. He further taunted John:

What you are saying is: 'When I am convinced of error I will receive instruction.' Are you expecting a divine revelation like Paul's? It's very pre-sumptuous. How can you be convinced of error *without* instruction? And how can you expect a Cowley Father to instruct you in the truth which he lacks himself? . . . All this 'waiting for God's good time' is intolerably wet. Time is a human conception & limitation. We make God's time for him.[97]

He apologized for having referred to John's Church of England advis-ers as 'a small group of homosexual curates' – 'No doubt there are thousands of them at the moment but they are still a pretty small group when assembled with all their colleagues since the Act of Supremacy. And where are their Saints & Miracles?'[98]

John sent back a short letter, maintaining that 'All I can do now is to read, pray and study the life of Our Lord. That I am doing.'[99] On 3 February he wrote again, to say that he found it hard to believe in 'the *certainty* of the Incarnation and Promise' and also that 'all the Wantage sisters, priests, missioners and parishioners of the many hundreds of Anglican Churches which are Catholic that I have known' were going to hell.[100]

It was a month or so later that John told Gerard Irvine of his fear that Penelope was about to defect to Rome. At the beginning of April Waugh thanked John for his words about him in the *Strand* but griped, 'why do you persist in cutting down my Catholic life? I was received in 1930.' He added: 'Awful about your obduracy in schism and heresy. Hell hell hell. Eternal damnation.'[101] By now, Waugh's letters had become a torment to John. Penelope, who unlike Waugh had to live with John, intervened to ask the novelist to lay off.

> Dearest Evelyn [she wrote in April],
>   I am very grateful to you for writing those letters to John tho' it is very disloyal of me to write to you and say that still I hope you will pray very hard indeed during the next few weeks for him because he is in a dreadful state he thinks you are the devil and wakes up in the middle of the night and raves and says he will leave me at once if I go over . . . However put yourself in his position: suppose Laura [Waugh's wife] were to wake up and say to you tomorrow morning 'I have had a revelation of the TRUTH it is only to be found in A. Huxley's Yogibogi sect, I shall join it.' You would not unnaturally be a little put out. You might even threaten to leave the old girl should she persist. Well John feels just like that. He thinks ROMAN Catholicism is a foreign religion which has no right to set up in this country, let alone try to make converts from what he regards as the true catholic church of the country. Your letters have brought it out in a remarkable way . . .[102]

Waugh did not take the hint. He shot another salvo at John in May:

> Can you not see how preposterous it is to go for advice to the very people whose position is in question? I say 'They are impostors & I can prove it.' You say: 'Well I must ask them first whether it is all right to examine the proofs.'
>   One deep root of error is that you regard religion as the source of pleasurable emotions & sensations and ask the question 'Am I not getting just as much out of the Church of England as I should from Catholicism?' The question should be 'What am I giving to God?' Nothing less than complete abandonment is any good. His will is plain as a pikestaff that there

shall be one fold & one shepherd and you spend all your time perpetuating a sixteenth century rift & influencing others to perpetuate it. I wouldn't give a thrush's egg for your chances of salvation at the moment.[103]

This drew a heated reply from John.

Religion first. Believe me I find it no pleasure. Indeed to worship here at Farnborough requires a great act of Faith. You say I have seen the light. I agree. But what I regard as the light which I have seen is the Catholic Church of which the C of E is a part. I do not feel any doubt about that ... It would be far *easier* (but against my conscience) to become RC. For in this village which has no Nonconformist chapel, the only bulwark against complete paganism is the church and its chief supporters are Propeller and me. If we were to desert it, there would be no one to whip up people to attend the services, to run the church organizations, to keep the dilatory and woolly-minded incumbent (who lives in another village) to the celebration of Communion services any Sunday. It is just because it is so disheartening and so difficult and so easy to betray, that we must keep this Christian witness going. In villages people still follow a lead and we are the only people here who will give a lead. I know that to desert this wounded and neglected church would be to betray Our Lord.[104]

John was particularly upset by Waugh's suggestion that he stayed in the Church of England for purely aesthetic reasons. 'Really you are wrong in thinking that I regard religion as "the source of pleasurable emotions and sensations". I used to, as an undergraduate, but it has been a stern struggle for the last fourteen years.'[105] Waugh riposted: 'Blind worm, who are you to lead? You should humbly follow.'[106] Penelope was by now so concerned at John's state of mind that she postponed her instruction. In a letter to her on 4 June 1947 Waugh at last promised to lay off John. 'I am by nature a bully and a scold and John's pertinacity in error brings out all that is worst in me. I am sorry ... But really when he says that the truth of the Petrine claims is dependent on his place of residence, the mind boggles. I think there is very clearly a devil at work in him ...'[107] Waugh also said that he could not conceive what John meant by ' "smart" Catholics'. Did he, he wondered, mean Mrs Sweeny (later the scandalous Margaret, Duchess of Argyll)? Penelope replied:

As far as I can make out John thinks the smart catholic set consists of you, Laura's relatives and Asquiths, the Pakenhams, D. Woodruff, C. Hollis[108] and in fact any English R.C. he knows. He thinks if I go C. and he doesn't you will all persecute him and there will be plots and counterplots and the

only thing for him to do is to get right away from it all and go and settle
on his own in Swindon for which city he has always had a great liking as
you know and where there is an old established Anglo colony. However he
saw Crackywilliamclonmorewicklow[109] last night who made him laugh a
lot about the whole thing and who told him your patience was at an end
which he thought very funny and altogether he seems less antagonistic
than he was . . .[110]

Indeed, the tension seemed to have eased. In July, while apologizing
for not attending a Pre-Raphaelite exhibition with Waugh ('I went
with Propeller a week or two ago'), John wrote to him affably, with no
mention of religion, telling him he wanted his opinion of a stained-
glass window which he was sure was by the Pre-Raphaelite Ford
Madox Brown.[111] In August Waugh, rarely a bearer of olive branches,
made a special effort to heal relations with John. He wrote in his
diary:

> To Farnborough to make my peace with the Betjemans. Successful in this.
> A drive with John looking at 1860 churches. Penelope seems resolved to
> enter the Church in the autumn.[112]

After his one night at Farnborough, he wrote to Nancy Mitford:
'Penelope [was] just off for a camping holiday in a nearby field'; and,
to Penelope herself: 'My heart bleeds for you in your wigwam.'[113] On
Boxing Day 1947, Waugh wrote to Nancy Mitford again.

> Betjeman delivered a Christmas Message on the wireless. First he said that
> as a little boy he had been a coward & a liar. Then he said he was sure all
> his listeners had been the same. Then he said that he had been convinced
> of the truth of the Incarnation the other day by hearing a choir boy sing
> 'Once in Royal David's City' in King's College Chapel.[114]

He could not resist teasing John about the broadcast.

> One listener at least deeply resented the insinuation in your Christmas
> Message that your listeners had all been cowards & liars in childhood.
> Properly brought up little boys are fantastically chivalrous. Later they
> deteriorate. How would you have felt if instead of a choir boy at
> Cambridge you had heard a muezzin in Isfahan?[115]

The more or less friendly badinage continued. In 1948, after John
had mispronounced the word 'lichen' in reading his poem 'Ireland
with Emily' on the wireless, Waugh sent him a postcard –

I lie itchin'
Because of the imperfections of my kitchen
While you are bikin'
Round Berks studying the lichen.[116]

But somehow the friendship was never the same again after the epistolary battering and Penelope's conversion. Waugh had proposed John for membership of the Beefsteak Club and he was elected in December 1947; but on 9 January 1948 Waugh wrote in his diary: 'To the Beefsteak to induct Betjeman, but he had taken ill or frighted and would not come.'[117] A year later, Waugh annoyed John by referring, in the Roman Catholic periodical *The Month*, to his 'jaunty sub-aestheticism of the Third Programme' ('whatever that may be!' John wrote in a testy letter).[118] In reply, Waugh conceded it was 'a villainous phrase,'[119] but the damage was done. Another year on, and Waugh was writing to Penelope: 'It is nice of you to ask me to visit you but (a) I don't think John likes me (b) I don't think I like your children (c) I know I detest all talk about the varying fads of heretics.'[120]

Penelope was received into the Roman Catholic Church on 9 March 1948 at St Aloysius, Oxford. It was, Waugh told her, St Catherine of Bologna's Day – 'She is the only Saint I have ever shaken hands with. She has been dead 500 years but sits bolt upright in a little chair in her nun's habit . . .'[121] It was an agonizing time for John. As so often through history, religion, intended as a beneficent force, had brought discord and misery. He could not follow Penelope. As she had told Waugh, he regarded Roman Catholicism as 'foreign'; and he 'hated "abroad"'. He had no taste for ecstasiated Bernini virgins, *baldacchini* and Salomonic columns. He preferred the more temperate beauties of English parish churches. If he 'went over to Rome', in defiance of all the indoctrination of his youth, he would be giving up not only those churches but most of the hymns he loved, and relinquishing the Authorized Version for intoned or gabbled Latin – a language which, from his days under Mr Gidney at Marlborough, had never been his forte. Rome would also mean submission to authority, which did not come easily to him. Rome stood for absolutism and infallibility, as against the easy latitudinarian ways of the Church of England.

Three days before Penelope's 'reception', John wrote to his friend Geoffrey Taylor that he was making himself scarce, in Cornwall, for the event, 'and for the recovery I am going to Denmark (paid for by the Danes) for a week the week after'.[122] He enclosed a poignant sonnet he had written on Penelope's apostasy.

> In the perspective of Eternity
>   The pain is nothing, now you go away
>   Above the steaming thatch how silver-grey
> Our chiming church tower, calling 'Come to me
> My Sunday-sleeping villagers!' And she,
>   Still half my life, kneels now with those who say
>   'Take courage, daughter. Never cease to pray
> God's grace will break him of his heresy.'
>
> I, present with our Church of England few
>   At the dear words of Consecration see
>   The chalice lifted, hear the sanctus chime
> And glance across to that familiar pew.
>   In the perspective of Eternity
>   The pain is nothing – but, ah God, in Time!

This poem, which became known as 'The Empty Pew', had been through several earlier versions. When it reached the page proofs of *A Few Late Chrysanthemums*, the third line from last read, 'And glance across to that deserted pew'.[123] Jock Murray thought the poem might cause Penelope distress and it was pulled out at the last moment. For the same reason I did not include it in the *Uncollected Poems* published in 1982, when both John and Penelope were still alive. It was first published in Volume One of John's *Letters*, edited by Candida Lycett Green in 1994.[124]

John told Susan Barnes in 1972: 'I had thought that however much Penelope and I quarrelled, at any rate the Church stayed the same – rather like old Archie, something you can always turn to. And Penelope was really very Anglican by temperament – the sort of person who always quarrels with the vicar.'[125] Now Penelope quarrelled with Father Wixted, priest of the 'hideous Roman Catholic church' in Wantage which she attended each Sunday, picking up on the way Irish farm labourers' children and the Italian servants of the local gentry.[126] Paul and Candida noticed little difference in life, except that a 'Hail Mary' was added to 'Our Father' at their nightly prayers. Candida remembers John's making fun of the 'Hail Marys' and reciting them in a broad Irish accent, 'which I assumed, not unnaturally, was how we were meant to say them – "Hooley Merry, methyr of Guard . . ."'[127]

In May 1949 John went into the Acland nursing home in Oxford for the removal of another cyst. This enforced distance from Farnborough and his marriage gave both him and Penelope a chance to reflect on their changed situation. Penelope wrote to him:

You must be really honest and admit we were never religiously at one in the Anglican Church. I wanted to become RC when Fr Burdett tried to convert us both and you said, 'You ought to try your own Church first.' Then I was completely converted to Catholicism by Fr Folky [Harton]'s book . . . When we went to Eire I became more and more convinced of the truth of the Roman claims and hoped that you were feeling the same way . . . Life simply is NOT long enough to go on like this and personally I think it would be idiotic to separate, we would neither of us be any happier and the children would be very *un*happy. Let us forgive and forget and both admit that we have colossal faults and different temperaments and different approaches to religion and have been very bad husbands and wives though I think we are BOTH good parents, and let us each lead our own lives as far as friends are concerned and not try to conceal things any more but let us LOVE AND BE HAPPY. Yours very truly, Morwenna Plym Woad. [Morwenna was the Cornish saint's name which Penelope had added to her own Christian names on being received into the Roman Catholic Church.][128]

John replied from the nursing home on 2 June. He had been suffering intense physical pain which, he thought, had 'an excellent purifying and clarifying property'. It had enabled him to realize that he must for a long time have been going through 'some sort of breakdown', marked by excessive bad temper. 'The peace of this place now I am out of pain makes me see how tiresome I have been and cruel and bullying. *Oi am very sorry.*' In response to a renewed suggestion by Penelope that she should pay for him to give up his uncongenial work for the *Daily Herald* and let her minister to him, he replied:

I don't really mind doing degrading work like book-reviewing (I doubt if I am now fit for anything better) provided I have your love. And having your love doesn't mean being told I have got it 'underneath all our quarrelling'. It doesn't ever entail on your part mending my clothes. It means seeing you and being with you *alone* much more than I am.

Whatever the circumstances of our marriage in its beginnings, I had grown to love you so much by the time Powlie was born, that you were more important to me than anything else. And you still are. I have always prayed in my heart that I will die before you because I feel that I could not live without you.[129]

Analyzing the course of their marriage, John thought that his main trouble had been jealousy. It had not been too acute at Uffington, where they saw a lot of each other and could always get together and make up after a row. But 'Ireland was just hell.' John's war work had taken him away from Penelope just when she needed him most. 'Farnborough gets me down because the farm and the children between them have taken you away from me so much that I only see you alone late in the evening when you and I are both tired and touchy. Or rather I am touchy and you are tired.' And now something had happened to take her further away still: her defection to Rome. 'That is really why I have an "obsession" about Rome, because I love you so much.' He asked for more time alone with her – ideally one full afternoon a week, including lunch and tea. So far, John's letter was all love and conciliation. But before ending it he had to address a topic of further contention. In her letter, Penelope had asked that Candida – now seven – should be brought up as a Roman Catholic. John made clear his resistance to this plan.

> The business of Wubz's being brought up RC is not easy unless I explain to you my fundamental religious longing, which is very difficult. I long for Jesus as a Man, I long to see Him, to be lifted up to Him, to love Him, not to injure Him as much as I do all the time. I *try* to long for Him when I don't long for Him, Jesus is the centre of my faith and the Sacraments are one of the ways by which I try to know Him. I have never doubted our Sacraments in the C of E and I see in Farnborough that the only witness to Jesus is our church there. I see Jesus on the Cross there, very much more crucified and suffering than say, at Wantage (C of E or RC). Each person who leaves Jesus here in Farnborough drives another nail in His Cross. That was how I felt (and I hope you won't mind my saying it) first when you left Farnborough for Rome. But now I know that it is God's will for you to go there, and so I must say I'm sorry I felt like that. But you do see, don't you, that if I let Wubz go I personally think I would be further wounding Our Lord in our feeble church in Farnborough, which one day may be a great one and a full one. It's just when things seem quite hopeless, as they do now, that they brighten. To let Wubz leave the C of E at present would, I think, be your will not God's will.[130]

A compromise was reached. Candida stayed within the Church of England but Penelope sometimes took her to Mass at East Hendred or in Wantage. Paul was at Church of England boarding schools.[131]

Gerard Irvine thinks that Penelope's conversion was 'the beginning of the end of John and Penelope's marriage'.[132] And Candida, although her childhood was not disrupted by the event, realized in retrospect that 'It was a watershed, for it saw the beginning of JB's being able to love other women whilst continuing to love my mother.'[133] He was smitten by a lady glider he met at a John Murray party, but nothing came of the encounter.[134] In June 1949 he fell in

love with Margaret Wintringham, the blonde, buxom wife of
Edmund Penning-Rowsell, the wine expert. The couple lived in
Hinton Parva, a village at the foot of the Berkshire Downs. They
were both Communists: John called them 'the Party Members'.[135]
He first met Margaret at a Swindon Poetry Society meeting. He was
lecturing on Lincolnshire poets – chiefly Tennyson and Jean Ingelow –
and asked if anybody in the audience was from Lincolnshire. She put
her hand up and they talked afterwards. Later he called in at the
Hinton Parva cottage, then took to visiting about once a week on his
way back from seeing his mother in Bath. In early autumn he went
to supper with Margaret and her husband and left behind his handkerchief, which seemed almost to take on the significance of the
handkerchief in *Othello* when Margaret returned it, washed and
ironed, with a note saying how much she had enjoyed doing it. He
tried unsuccessfully to get her work at the BBC but gave her children's books to review for *Time and Tide*. They met for coffee – this
was the decade of *Brief Encounter* – when John was on his way to
Bristol or London. He encouraged her in her poetry-writing. She
tried to convert him to Communism: he called her 'my
Stakhanovite'. Eve Disher,[136] the girlfriend of John's Marlborough
friend Sir Arthur Elton, wrote in October 1949: 'I hope she is plump-
ish and does rather *gaily* try to convert you. I suspect this is the worst
attack you've had – isn't it? Worse than the flier?'[137] Margaret often
brought her family to Sunday lunch at Farnborough. Penelope, who
referred to her as 'John's Poitry Girl', would take the children off in
the pony cart, Candida recalls, 'so that Margaret and JB could be
left alone to talk about poetry'.[138]

Was there more to it than that? John's main confidante in these
years was Anne Barnes, the wife of George Barnes, his friend and
patron at the BBC.* In July 1949 he wrote to her from Farnborough:

Like a fool I went there. With priggishness and self-righteousness, with
fear and love, I insisted on doing nothing. She – oh God I can't put it down
in ink or pencil or charcoal or anything – she put up with my priggishness.
And now what have I? Remorse, internal writhings, detestation of everything here, inability to concentrate, fear of her revenge on me and the
prospect of several more deliciously wonderful visits each with its sad
ending. Sad for her, self-righteous for me, misery for us both. Yet if one
'went the whole hog' as we used to say at Marlborough, the guilt would
be worse still and I wouldn't see her again.[139]

---

* See chapter 29, 'On the Air in the Fifties'.

It is the very voice of *Brief Encounter*. Three days later he wrote to
Anne Barnes again.

> I received a beautiful slap-in-the-eye from my Stakhanovite yesterday in
> the form of this quatrain:
>
>> For J.B.
>> Remember when in your philosophy
>> Human relationships take second place
>> Your chastity is founded on my charity
>> And through my grief you reach your State of Grace.
>
> Of course, she's quite right. If I'm not prepared to risk mortal sin, then I
> shouldn't go on with it. Anyhow she leaves today for three weeks in France
> and I shall begin to breathe again. She is very funny. But oh that Party line,
> that runs through her! It is shiveringly attractive and horrifying at once.
> There is always that delicious sense . . . that one has gone just a little too
> far.[140]

Margaret's trip to France was followed by the Betjemans' annual
holiday in Trebetherick, during which, he told Anne Barnes, 'I was
able to keep up a daily correspondence with Margaret Wintringham.
It loosened the emotional strain and crystallized our relationship, if I
may coin a few metaphors.'[141] Three months later John wrote to Cyril
Connolly: 'I would like to see you again very much indeed to tell you
about *Margaret Wintringham* and love.'[142] He was still writing to
Anne Barnes about Margaret in February 1950 ('There is no one like
you to discuss Love with . . .').

> It was Margaret Wintringham I want to talk to you about. This
> Communism is a bit boring. I don't think she is really keen on it. It is
> loyalty to her hubbie which keeps her in the party and unless she is loyal
> to her hubbie, her relationship with me will collapse. It is what is known
> as a vicious circle up in 'the Street', as we Newspaper boys call it. She looks
> if anything *more* attractive than she used to and has now completely
> resigned herself to the idea that her charm is Lincolnshire windblown land
> girl and not smart literary.[143]

In November he reported: 'Margaret Wintringham is terrific at the
moment. She broadcasts on the West. Her cheeks glow purple and her
hair flies wiry in the wind and she wears a grey woollen jersey and a
blue serge skirt and I have kept sex under foot as much as we can.'[144]
  In 1999 Edmund Penning-Rowsell wrote of his wife and John: 'She
was not in love with him';[145] but he disclosed this hitherto unpublished

letter which John wrote her in January 1951 from Hull, where he had been lecturing:

Darling Margaret,

If I were to strain my eyes from the top window here I *might* be able to see WINTERINGHAM which, I am sorry to tell you, is they say now no more than a suburb of Scunthorpe. Boot ah can ardly tell you darlin ow mooch it pleases me to be ere in Yorksheer where we are so near to Lincolnsheer & where everything reminds me of you, the red tarls on the ouses, pantarls that is, the old brick walls & all the loovly voices talkin north coontry. Ah've ad a loovly tarm looking at Ooll ah looked at Trinity House & the Dock Offices & t'owld bewk shops & then ah went ter loonch terday to Beverley Minster and that's grand, absolutely grand. The Gothic is very tall & thin Frenchifade boot all the people in the shops talk Yorksheer (Holderness kind) & it is very oonexpected . . . Boot in ma lecture at Ooll ah said that ah had lost my heart in Lincolnshire over theer across t'Oomber . . . Ah wish you were with me ere. Ah would feel ah was at home . . .

Ah'm thankful ter say that ah'll ave a secy next week (D.V.) & will ave the tarm to coom & see you mah darlin Margaret ah'm stook ere in your coontry & you aren't ere ah wish you were this wind would make you look woonderful ah to ave you with me on the Wowlds is the wish of

Your looving choom

JB[146]

Margaret disappeared from John's letters to Anne Barnes after 1950 and was gradually relegated to the status of old flame. But John and Margaret never lost track of each other. In fact, John remained on good terms with both the Penning-Rowsells. In the late 1950s Edmund, then working for Hulton's, edited a selection of his poems in their 'Pocket Poets' series. A decade later Margaret, watching the BBC films *Betjeman at Random*, wrote: 'WHAT a pleasure to hear you speaking poetry, I shouldn't think there is anyone alive who does it better.'[147] On 12 March 1972 Edmund wrote to John: 'Thirty-nine years ago today I first met Margaret Wintringham in Hyde Park.'[148] John replied: 'And to think of Margaret Wintringham's windswept cheeks and stormy grey-blue eyes and petulant suffering lips . . . Oh, to have been in Hyde Park thirty-nine years ago on 12th March and just have been a few yards ahead.'[149]

In 1950 another love-interest came into John's life: his new secretary Jill Menzies, whom he called 'Freckly Jill'. She was twenty-two, an Oxford graduate who had taken a course at St Godric's Secretarial College.[150] John interviewed her in the offices of *Time and Tide* and

appointed her even though she admitted she was not good at doing up
parcels – a skill useful when sending back review books. John had
already had two secretaries. The first, Ruth Webb, had arrived in
Farnborough in October 1948 and had left in December 1950 to
become a nurse and missionary. She was briefly succeeded by another
woman, described by John as 'nice but so barmy she had to go into a
loony bin'.[151] Providing John with a secretary was part of Penelope's
plan to relieve him of some of the chores that made him fractious; this
new luxury could be afforded because the Betjemans no longer had to
pay rent to Farmer Wheeler. Miss Webb, who came to John from the
Agricultural Research Centre in nearby Compton, had been warned
that 'he would be liverish in the mornings and in a very bad temper',
but that did not happen all the time. His main phobia, she recalled,
'was the possibility of getting marmalade between his wrists and his
cuffs at breakfast, which seemed to be easily done and would make
him shout "Oh God, Oh God!" '[152] In general, she and John got on
well and he was happy with her work; but she made on him nothing
like the impression of Jill Menzies, who arrived in Farnborough in
May 1951 and lived as one of the family. For her, Candida writes, 'he
developed a grand, long-lasting, platonic passion'. On 3 June John
wrote to George Barnes: 'On Tuesday I will be accompanied by my
new Scottish-Canadian C of E Secretary with freckles, grey eyes, tip-
tilted nose and grey flannel skirts and cream shirts and furry skin.'[153]
In later letters to others he rhapsodized about her 'sultry lips and
darkish hair', her 'tall hiking figure and high Scottish cheekbones',
and drew sketches of her –

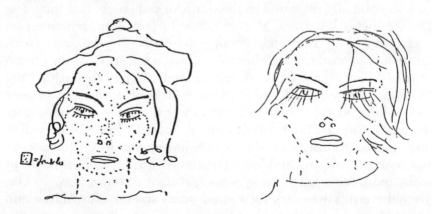

    The secretaries helped to bring some order into the haphazardness
of John's work – his book-reviewing for the *Daily Herald* and the
Daily Telegraph; radio scripts; poems for the *New Statesman* and
The Listener – and wrote kind letters of encouragement to the often

hopeless would-be poets who wrote to him enclosing their verses. From 1949 he put in an afternoon a week at the London offices of *Time and Tide,* as the magazine's literary adviser.* Having a secretary and becoming more 'organized' also allowed him some free time to drive off to Oxford and give talks to undergraduates. He enjoyed these jaunts, in which he could exercise his histrionic side. He learned what the young were thinking and became well known to those who were to become political and cultural leaders in Britain. Denis Healey, a future Chancellor of the Exchequer, invited him to talk about Victorian architecture. In 1946 the future drama critic Kenneth Tynan – like John, a Magdalen man, but unlike him a favoured pupil of C.S. Lewis – wrote to his friend Julian Holland:

> John Betjeman spoke on Thursday about Tennyson. He completely succeeded in rehabilitating him as a man: he was apparently a great wit and a humorist of boundless, spasmodic energy. In fact, Betjeman suggests that the last lines of 'Enoch Arden' 'The villagers had never seen a costlier funeral' may be intentionally amusing. Most Tennysonian anecdotes are of the Victorian lavatory kind. Here is one of [Tennyson's] favourites. Macready, playing Othello to a packed house, was horrified to notice that throughout the bedroom scene, there were incessant titters in the audience. Storming with rage, he went off; and as he did so, caught sight of a small white chamberpot under the bed. He rampaged across to the prop. man and in a voice strained with fury said: 'What is the meaning of that white chamberpot?' With a look of abject apology the man replied: 'I'm terribly sorry, sir, but we couldn't get a flowered one.'
>
> Another story of Tennyson: a female admirer requested a simile for sheep on a hillside. He snarled: 'Lice on an old blanket.'[154]

Sir Ludovic Kennedy, who, though older than Tynan, had had his university career deferred by wartime service in the RNVR, also remembers one of John's visits to Oxford. Kennedy was a founder member of the Oxford University Writers' Club, whose object was to gather together 'a score of hopeful scribblers like myself' and four times a term to invite some literary figure to address them. Fellow members included Michael Croft, subsequently director of the National Youth Theatre, Francis King, the novelist and critic, and Sir Alan Herbert's son John, later a director of Christie's. Among the eminent guests were Charles Morgan, Evelyn Waugh, Cyril Connolly, V.S. Pritchett, Elizabeth Bowen, John Lehmann – and John. Not all of

* See Chapter 24, 'Tame and Tade'.

them went down well with the undergraduate audience. Kennedy recalls Connolly's 'very soft, flabby, girlish way of speaking'.

> Perhaps we didn't always treat our guests with the reverence they expected or deserved [he adds], but at our time of life we were less concerned with which act [of a play] you wrote first than with the practicalities of living, in particular with how to exist while trying to complete a book or play. 'Be a roadsweeper,' said Evelyn Waugh helpfully, puffing at a Havana cigar. 'Become keeper of a railway crossing,' said John Betjeman with his Boy Scout smile, 'where there's only one train a day.'[155]

Penelope did not worry too much about John's undisguised 'pashes' for Margaret Wintringham and 'Freckly Jill'. They became her friends too, and that seemed to neutralize them as threats to her marriage. Apart from the couple's religious schism, life at Farnborough continued much as before. Penelope still ran the local Women's Institute and organized fêtes and gymkhanas. John usually kept as far away from horses as he could; but in 1950 he was inveigled into attending an event which inspired one of his funniest poems. Candida recalls:

> ... I was so proud of my achievements on a dock-tailed mare called Dinah at Mr and Mrs Glover's riding school, that I persuaded [my father] to make his first and only venture to a hunter trials. Mrs Glover ran the event in fields next to her riding school at Chieveley, which now lie under the Services at Exit 13 of the M4 motorway. There was a young woman called Diana Russell who arrived in a horsebox from East Woodhay with several ponies and usually won everything. She was brusque, jolly and competitive. JB's 'Hunter Trials' followed, beginning with the lines:

> > It's awf'lly bad luck on Diana,
> >   Her ponies have swallowed their bits;
> > She fished down their throats with a spanner
> >   And frightened them all into fits . . .[156]

The Betjemans kept up with all their old friends: the Pipers, the Lancasters, John Sparrow and Maurice Bowra. One friendship was maintained in the face of some controversy: that with Sir Oswald Mosley and his wife Diana, both of whom had been imprisoned in the war because of their pro-Nazi views. There is small doubt that, if Hitler had succeeded in invading Britain, Mosley would have been offered some kind of *Gauleiter* post; and after the war many members of 'society' ostracized the couple. John and Penelope had never got mixed up in Mosley's politics, although in the 1930s (as we have seen) Harold Nicolson, for a time a supporter of Mosley's New Party, had tried to persuade John to contribute to its fascist magazine, *Action!* The Betjemans had known Diana Mosley when she was 'one of the Mitford sisters' and during her marriage to John's friend Bryan Guinness (Lord Moyne). If John's serious proposal to Pamela Mitford or his light-hearted one to Nancy Mitford had been accepted, he would have been Diana's brother-in-law. Was he now to break off the long friendship because of a political scandal – because some people considered the Mosleys traitors? It was the classic dilemma crystallized by E.M. Forster: my country or my friend? Just as Forster prescribed, John chose his friend. The Mosleys had a house at Crux Easton, near Newmarket, and a working farm at Crowood in Wiltshire. Like Roy and Billa Harrod, who also refused to 'drop' the Mosleys, John and Penelope dined in both the houses. Nicholas Mosley, the politician's son by his first wife, Lady Cynthia, remembers:

> There would be the meals at which my father would hold forth as he loved to hold forth on his favourite themes – the world as a training-ground for spirits: the difficulties attendant on the vision that good can come out of evil. There was something so bright and assured about him that he held people entranced: the shooting-colonels and Swedish painters were entranced: my friends, who had expected – what? – stayed on and on to listen. He was like a dynamo switching lights on in people. Occasionally there was a brief fuse: a neighbour would ask a question about Hitler or Streicher perhaps: then what, in such circumstances, could be done? This was a time when the worst stories of German atrocities had not yet come out: there was not much news about the extermination camps, which were in territory overrun by Russia: the news was of Belsen and Dachau, the horrors of which could just conceivably be explained by the disease and starvation resulting from the chaos and bombing of the last stages of war. There would be just a flash from my father's eyes; a guillotine look from Diana's bright blue ones. The people who came to dine at Crux Easton and Crowood during these months were mostly friends of Diana's and my father's from very old days – John Betjeman, Gerald Berners, Daisy Fellowes. With them the talk would go off into fireworks of laughter. Sometimes these friends would bring friends of theirs who did not know quite what to expect: there would then be some wariness again; people sat on the edges of chairs as if my father might swoop like Dracula.[157]

Most of the people Paul and Candida met at Farnborough were of their parents' generation, or older. An exciting exception was Patrick Cullinan, who came to stay in April 1950. Today a well-known South African poet, he was then a seventeen-year-old schoolboy at Charterhouse – Osbert Lancaster's old school. He was the grandson of the 'Randlord' Sir Thomas Cullinan after whom the huge Cullinan Diamond was named.[158] He and John had met in January 1950 when John came to address the school's Poetry Society in the drawing-room of Cullinan's housemaster, Vincent 'Sniffy' Russell. John invited anyone who wrote poetry to send him their work. Cullinan sent him a poem entitled 'England 1950' and a short story. John wrote back enthusiastically. 'If you knew what a treat it is to have something worth considering sent to one after the heaps of mediocre verse [sent to *Time and Tide*], you would know how grateful I am to you.'[159] He was encouraging about 'England 1950', though it was not his sort of poem. And he thought Cullinan's story 'a most accomplished piece'.

> I shared with you in memory that feeling for inanimate objects as a child. They did make a world of their own for themselves. I had forgotten they did until your story reminded me of it. Or perhaps it put the idea into my head. Anyhow I like it a lot – or rather am greatly upset by the story which is what you desire. I hope your nurse did not fall on top of you into a pit in that terrifyingly sensual way.[160]

The story clearly inspired a passage in a radio talk John gave six months later, in which he revealed that, as a child, he believed that inanimate objects could feel and think.[161] His letter to Cullinan ended: 'Of course you will be a writer. Nothing will stop you whatever, not riches or poverty,[162] nor being made to do something else, not anything but illness. I am sure of that.'[163] Cullinan sent more poems. John wrote back, on Valentine's Day:[164]

> Your Joyce–Auden–Eliot MS hot from the soul . . . pleased me a lot.
>
> What I like in it is not the thought (if there is any) nor the emotions (turbulent) nor the transitions (inexplicable), but that same delight in words and ability to use them that I mentioned before.
>
> You may not agree with me, but I think
> 1) Poetry should not be private but easy for all to understand.
> 2) It should have tones of meaning beyond the surface one.
> 3) It should read out loud well.
> 4) It should be memorable.
> 5) It should very clearly not be prose.
>
> I would like to see what you did using rhyme (which often provides more inspiration than the human fancy can devise without it) & an accepted metre & writing quite clearly & obviously but out of anger, love or sadness, exaltation or self-pity whichever inspires you most.
>
> Your poems bring back to me my own delight when literature first opened to me & I wish I had your vigour & hope now.[165]

This correspondence was the beginning of what amounted to a series of seminars in prosody, in which John made clear his own very decided views while always insisting that Cullinan must 'be himself', the final arbiter in whatever he wrote.[166] 'Don't take the middle way. Take your own way. You will be able to make it comprehensible if you understand – or at any rate feel – it yourself.'

John came to Charterhouse again on 1 March. Cullinan wrote in his diary that day: 'Betjeman down. Read his own poems. Superb. V. encouraging.'[167] At the meeting, John suggested that the boy should come to stay at Farnborough. On 8 March he wrote to him:

> I have been in Leicester (not hunting foxes but churches) & lecturing rather coarsely to refined audiences . . .
>
> I look forward to your coming here. But will you enjoy it? You who have always lived in luxury may be horrified by the squalor, the lateness of meals (eaten in the kitchen), the noise of children, the smells of cooking, the dullness of the surrounding scenery, & my early morning nervous irritability. Will you be able to stand it? I am anxious. I hope you will for a day or two. Try the inside of a week & stay on if you can stand it. Do you ride? We can provide plenty of that . . . I dare not ride. It frightens me & makes me stiff. I am a coward to the very core in everything.[168]

Cullinan first went to stay at Farnborough on 6 April 1950.[169] His memory of the Rectory is of 'a dark but friendly kitchen where we had our meals and I remember John opening and decanting the most delicious bottles of claret'.[170] Cullinan's mother had died of a brain tumour the year before and his grief had made him introspective.[171] John helped him get over the tragedy. The youth had a blond lock of hair which constantly fell over his blue eyes. Candida, now eight, 'became completely transfixed by him and watched with fascination as he cleaned his teeth each morning with an almost supernatural vigour'.[172] His extravagant good looks, charm and vitality were not lost on John, either. In a letter to Candida in 1993, Cullinan tackled head-on the (not directly asked) question whether there was anything more to it than that.

> I don't think for a moment that JB worshipped me. I just think he needed to have some sort of acolyte at that period in his life – fortunately for me. We had so much fun together . . . Obviously, you would want to know if there was anything beyond our friendship, ie a physical relationship. There was nothing. Never at any stage was there any move from him or from me to get involved sexually. I was crazy about girls and, quite frankly, so was he.[173]

John drove him around England in his battered Vauxhall. In the car, the two recited poetry and told jokes. There were more jokes when they visited Lord Berners, who was ill in bed at Faringdon, 'a startling figure in a nightshirt and stocking cap'.

> He was depressed [Cullinan recalls] but soon chirped up when John began to read *Eric, or Little by Little*. John hammed it up outrageously, inserting all sorts of smutty asides and monstrous double entendres; Lord Berners and I were weak with laughter.[174]

On Cullinan's second visit to Farnborough, in April 1950, Penelope's father was staying. He told the young South African stories of his experiences in the Boer War – in particular, how he had allowed Kruger's train to escape capture by his troop because his horses were tired and needed a rest.

> Cullinan: 'But, Good Lord, sir, if you had captured Kruger then it would have shortened the war by at least a year!'
> Chetwode: 'Yes, I know.'
> Cullinan: 'But didn't anyone find out?'
> Chetwode: 'No. I never told anyone!' (Looking very pleased with himself.)[175]

Lord Chetwode died three months later. 'Very sad it will be for Penelope,' John wrote to Cullinan on 15 July. 'Losing one parent is bad enough. When you lose both, you suddenly know you have stepped out in loneliness, there's no one to back you up or even to quarrel with except other lonely people like yourself.'[176]

By now the poetry seminars had become a two-way traffic; Cullinan was venturing to comment on John's verses. He had presumably sent him a letter about 'Before the Anaesthetic, *or* A Real Fright' shortly before 8 August, when John replied:

> Indeed I had your flattering &, as usual, perceptive & stimulating letter. I'm glad you feel tantalized by the Anaesthetic lines, I'm glad you feel shut out from my private pre-occupation with death – it's no joke to be mixed up in it & it is not essential to our relationship – but I'm pleased & flattered & comforted to think you know it is there, my pre-occupation.[177]

In September 1950 another house guest arrived at Farnborough, a French girl called Françoise Allard, who wanted to learn English. 'One afternoon,' Candida remembers, 'she came downstairs after a rest and said proudly, "I have just had forty wanks." I didn't understand why

JB and Maurice Bowra exploded into laughter.'[178] Françoise's education was left very much to Penelope, while John continued to introduce Cullinan to his friends. The boy was taken to meet John Piper, who drew him a sketch of Myfanwy which he still possesses.[179] He was also brought into the circle of Colonel Kolkhorst, whom John caricatured in a letter to Cullinan on 6 October 1950 –

You are, of course, welcome to come out for the day on Sunday – if so, Betts [Pentofu] will know the goods in to fetch the Powlis in that van. Who is this? It's ye olde Squire of Yarntbune. love John

In that month, Cullinan went up to John's old college, Magdalen, Oxford. John visited him there, writing on 19 October: 'That was a v haunting afternoon in your rooms yesterday ... Looking out at those still misty elms from your window, I realised how exiled you must feel.'[180] Cullinan returned to Olifantsfontein in the Transvaal for the vacation. On 13 December John wrote to thank him for a present. 'I v much enjoy the Van der Hum this cold weather. Evelyn Waugh who has been staying with us told me he drank too much of it at the Wembley Exhibition in 1925 & was sick over the side of the Giant Racer.'[181] On the 29th John received two letters from Cullinan, and wrote back:

The two best things that could have happened to you have happened.
   (1) You are not sad or disillusioned or lonely on your return home but love it more than ever.
   (2) You are in the sweet agony of love (which brings one out in spots so

eat plenty of *tin*) than which there is O better for clearing the mind, fixing the muse & making everything more coloured so that one knows one is an artist in the full Pauline sense of knowing. I'm delighted.[182]

In the same letter he wrote, 'Osbert Lancaster has given me a water colour he did of the Colonel reading the lessons at Yarnton which is so *devastatingly* like, I dare not shew it to the Colonel.' Paul and Candida wrote to thank Cullinan for gifts of toffees. They told him about the 'flu epidemic. Penelope and Candida had both gone down with the illness and Paul had been sent home from school as sixty boys were in the sickroom. Candida wrote about her new pekinese, Marco Polo. At the top of Paul's letter, John caricatured both children.

Farnborough.
Wantage,
Berkshire.
Tel. Chaddleworth 202.

Cullinan stayed with the Betjemans again in 1951 and held a lunch party attended by John, his secretary Jill Menzies, Kolkhorst, the eccentric modern-languages don Enid Starkie and undergraduate friends of Cullinan's. 'That luncheon of yours was one of the best I can recollect,' John wrote on 24 May 1951. '. . . The Colonel sweated a lot which is his sign of pleasure, & there's no doubt that Enid Starkie was ravished (not physically). I liked all your friends a lot. Oh will such gaiety ever happen again?'[183] Five days later he wrote again to say how pleased he was that Kolkhorst had conducted 'your USA chums round his lovely old house with all its lovely old things lying on top of one another in hopeless *déshabillé*'. The last part of the letter was about Jill Menzies, whom Cullinan also found attractive. 'I am writing this opposite to her & dare not show her your letter. One gets a sudden cold jab if one goes too far. We looked at the Festival on S. Bank last night. In her excited ecstasy at the illuminations she laughed and smiled at me & touched my hand.'[184]

Cullinan's visits were cheering; but John had become depressed by life at Farnborough. That it was the scene of the first great rift in his

marriage had soured the place for him. In any case, essentially metro-
politan in temperament, he was ill suited to village life. Living in a
comparatively grand house brought unpalatable financial demands –
for roof repairs and fencing, for example. An estimate for putting
electricity down the drive showed it was beyond the Betjemans'
means.[185] As a possible escape-route, John, much against Penelope's
wishes, rented William Morris's old home, Kelmscott Manor, near
Lechlade – the idyllic 'Nowhere' of Morris's *News from Nowhere*.[186]
At first the idea of moving there seemed tempting. John wrote to
Cullinan from Farnborough:

> There is one of those damned dogs barking here & I cannot think. This
> village is a hell. Thank God there is a chance of taking Kelmscott Manor
> House . . . Then you, my dear Rimbaud, will be able to join Ned Jones[187]
> & me & Dante Gabriel[188] & you will write epics under the willows & I
> will wear tapestry & Dante Gabriel will paint pictures all to illustrate your
> long, Anglo-Saxon epics.[189]

But then John realized that family life at Kelmscott was likely to be
interrupted by bearded Fabian pilgrims in hairy suits, knocking at the
door; so the Betjemans never moved in.

John was upset when Fritz the cat, who had been with them since
Uffington days, died behind the boiler in the kitchen on the day after
Boxing Day 1950.[190] And he 'minded intensely' when the elm trees by
Farnborough Church were felled and the ancient barn next to their
garden was demolished by Mr Laurence, one of the local farmers.[191]
In 1951 John and Penelope decided to sell the Rectory and move to the
less isolated town of Wantage.

In the last months at Farnborough, John took time off to attend an
unmissable social event, the marriage of Tom Driberg in London on
30 June. Driberg's engagement to Ena Binfield, a Labour Party worker,
had been announced in *The Times* in February.[192] That this most confirmed of bachelors should choose to marry was a surprise to everyone, and a joke to many. (A House of Commons policeman muttered,
'Poor lady, she won't know which way to turn.')[193] Osbert Lancaster
and John went together to the service in St Mary's Church, at the
corner of Graham Terrace and Bourne Street, near Sloane Square.
Driberg wrote in his diary on the day of the wedding: 'As we went out
at the end, I remember seeing my old cronies John Betjeman and
Osbert Lancaster standing together regarding me quizzically.'[194] The
two men also attended the reception on the river terrace of the House
of Commons, where 'the most gawped-at visitors'[195] were Seretse
Khama, unofficial chief of the Bamangwato tribe in Bechuanaland,

and his English wife Ruth.[196] Later, Lancaster wrote an 'Ode on the Wedding of Thomas Driberg, Esq., MP'.

Hark! The joyous nuptial tune
Cleaves the jocund skies of June,
Triumphant anthems rend the air
All the way to Eaton Square.
In Pimlico the strains are heard
Of Palestrina and of Byrd,
And marshalled crowds in patience wait
The due arrival of the Great.

Within the Church a tight-packed throng
Hope the service won't be long,
A hope that I at once surmised
Unlikely to be realised;
For all experience has taught
The Very High are seldom short.
Flanked by chattering MPs,
BETJEMAN's down upon his knees.

Come to kindle Hymen's torch,
Yet still lingering in the porch,
Aneurin BEVAN and his wife,
Pose, with easy grace, for *Life*.
Ushers with extremist views
Show the Leftists to their pews,
But I, reactionary and grand,
Although on time, am left to stand.

Te laudamus Domine,
Chiefly in the key of A,
From CUDLIPP comes an angry belch,
For he can only sing in Welsh.
But look, they turn on every side
To see the coming of the bride,
Radiant, demure and neat,
She almost trips on BETJEMAN's feet.

But hark, the Bishop's on his toes
To ask if anybody knows
'Just impediment or cause . . .'
There follows then an awkward pause.
In every heart an anxious fear
Of what we half expect to hear.

Strike the organ! Beat the bell!
The Past is silent! All is well! . . .

Friends of yours and friends of mine,
Friends who toe the party line,
Labour friends who're gratified
At being allowed to kiss the bride.
Artistic friends, a few of whom
Are rather keen to kiss the groom.
Friends from Oxford, friends from pubs
And even friends from Wormwood Scrubs.

Friends we always thought were dead
Friends we know are off their head,
Girl-friends, boy-friends, friends ambiguous
Coloured friends from the Antiguas,
Friends ordained and friends unfrocked,
Friends who leave us slightly shocked,
All determined not to miss
So rare a spectacle as this![197]

In the same month, the Old Rectory, Farnborough, was auctioned at the Bear Hotel, Wantage. 'We have put a reserve of eight and a half thousand on it,' John wrote to Patrick Cullinan, 'and I don't think it'll reach the reserve. But the woodlice still walk on the landing here unperturbed. And what am I more than a woodlouse?'[198] The house was bought by the racing expert Patrick Lawrence and his wife Molly for £11,000.[199]

Candida, for whom Farnborough was 'my favourite place on earth', hated moving.

It was [for the Betjemans] the end of nearly twenty years of village life [she wrote]. That September we moved the five miles down the long hills to alien territory in red-brick Wantage. On the last trip down with the last of the furniture, Paul and I travelled on the trolley cart with my mother driving. Terry and Maureen Carter, Billy Wilkinson and my best friend, Juney White, came with us. I cried all the way and once the village children caught the Reliance bus from Wantage market-place back up the slow, steep crawl to Farnborough, I knew that things could never be as happy again.[200]

NEW BATS IN OLD BELFRIES

If all the English poetry of the last two decades was destroyed and scholars of a later century had only a volume of Betjeman, what would scholars write about the literary moods and standards of our time? Whatever they inferred they would be largely wrong, because Betjeman represents only himself and reflects no fashion . . .

The Listener, 14 February 1946

By December 1941, Jock Murray was already encouraging John to marshal enough poems for a further Betjeman collection. On 12 December John sent him, from Dublin, the manuscript 'of what little I have done of my Epic' – the long autobiographical poem of which the greater part was published in *Summoned by Bells* (1960).[1] In April 1943 Murray again pressed him to let him know what poems he had amassed. John replied: 'I have written one sonnet which I enclose and a satirical poem, also enclosed, signed Sylvia Paddington, in the *New Stateswoman*. You have the rest in Murray's. If these, with an extract from the Epic, are enough to make a book, let me know and go ahead, old boy.'[2] There were three afterthoughts.

> ps However did you hear of these compositions?
> pps Couldn't we bring it out very cheap in paper binding on Bromo [lavatory paper]? I like that style.
> ppps I am engaged on one more about Invasions at Poultry Farm, probably too indecent.[3]

In fact, 'Invasion Exercise on the Poultry Farm', with its daring themes of lesbian love and bondage, did appear in the next volume. One extract from the 'Epic' was chosen: 'Sunday Afternoon Service in St Enodoc Church, Cornwall'.

Plans for the book hung fire from mid-1943 to mid-1945. Not only was John busy with secret war work for the Admiralty at Bath:* Jock Murray was serving as a lance-bombardier, first experimenting with Molotov cocktails on Brighton beach; then involved with gliders for the landings at Arnhem; and latterly in Belfast.[4] (During his absence, the office was run by Noël Carrington,[5] brother of Lytton Strachey's ill-starred adorer,[6] with help from Jock's uncle, Sir John Murray.) But on 11 July 1945 John sent Jock 'what, with two other poems which I must ask you to get, should be enough to make a book'.[7] The two missing poems were 'A Lincolnshire Tale',† which was to be retrieved from the *Cornhill Magazine*, where it had appeared in April; and 'May-Day Song for North Oxford', which was with Cyril Connolly at *Horizon*. 'There might be a new poem if you wanted one,' John wrote. 'If we are cutting down, I think we could sacrifice the Bank Clerk Monody and Cheshire Lines which are very early work; and do you think the Poultry Farm ballad too indecent?'[8] 'Monody on the Death of a Platonist Bank Clerk', about a repressed homosexual, did not see the light of day until *High and Low* (1966), while 'Cheshire Lines' remained unpublished until 1982, two years before the poet's death.[9] Murray wrote on 19 July: 'It was very good to get the poems . . . If we get them all into proof we can then best decide if any should be taken out.'[10]

This proof survives: Murray later had it bound in leather. A blank had been left for the title, which John filled in, with his usual maladroitness in the matter of titles, 'ROPES & RINGERS'. The poems 'Cheshire Lines' and 'Monody' were printed but crossed out, as was 'To Uffington Ringers'. A poem printed with the heading 'Fragment of a Poem for Emily Hemphill' was changed to 'A Fragment for Emily', then to its final title, 'Ireland with Emily'. Some comic misprints were put right – as in 'Invasion Exercise', in which the printers had rendered 'I've trussed your missing paratroop' as 'I trust your missing paratroop'. Other lines were altered to improve them. The ambiguous 'But still you leave the world alone', in 'Before the Anaesthetic', became 'But still you go from here alone'. In 'Invasion Exercise', the line 'Stand Judy and a paratroop in confident embrace' was altered to 'Lie Judy and a paratroop in horrible embrace' – the new line intended to convey the revulsion of the lesbian Marty at her friend's sexual apostasy.

Basil Dufferin, of whose death in the Burma campaign John had heard on VE Day (8 May), was described in the original threnody as 'Curious, reckless, loyal –/The last of civilized Oxford'; in the revised version as 'Humorous, reckless, loyal –/My kind, heavy-lidded

* See Chapter 15, 'Admiralty'.
† See Chapter 19, 'A Lincolnshire Tale'.

companion'. The same poem was given a far more poignant and effective ending. In the original:

> Stop, oh many bells, stop
> on this hollow, unhallowed VE Day
> pouring on sunwarm stone,
>   luxuriant roses and creeper
> Your unremembering peal
> He has died in battle, in Burma.

In the revision:

> Stop, oh many bells, stop
> pouring on roses and creeper
> Your unremembering peal
> this hollow, unhallowed VE day –
> I am deaf to your notes and dead
> by a soldier's body in Burma.[11]

Thirty-five years later, John told James Lees-Milne that he had been
'more in love with Ava[12] than with any human being he had ever met
in the world. His Oxford career was ruined by this unrequited love for
"Little Bloody". He loved his gutter-snipe looks, his big, brown,
sensual eyes, sensual lips, dirtiness generally. Never received so much
as a touch of a hand on the shoulder.'[13] That day, Lees-Milne had just
met, for the first time, Basil Dufferin's daughter, the novelist Lady
Caroline Blackwood. When he mentioned this to John, 'He told me he
once saw her twenty years ago and was so moved by her resemblance
to Ava, and so attracted to her, that he decided he could never meet
her again.'[14]

On 20 July 1945 John, recovering in Beaulieu from his operation,
sent these suggestions to Jock Murray: ' "Grandsire" "Triples" "Bob
Major" "Bats in the Belfry" "Triple Bob" "A Ring of Twenty" "Call
Changes" "A Touch of Twenty" "Belfry Jottings" "Louvred Steeples"
"Spires & Towers" "Ropes & Ringers" "Mr Murray's Surprise
Method" "Homage to Newbolt". I don't know JB.'[15] Eventually *New
Bats in Old Belfries* was agreed on, as a neat counterpoise to *Old Lights
for New Chancels*. The volume included what was to be perhaps John's
most famous, most quoted poem, 'A Subaltern's Love-song'. It also
contained the cryptic poem whose title mystified Philip Larkin, 'The
Irish Unionist's Farewell to Greta Hellstrom in 1922', apparently a
poème à clef. In reviewing Patrick Taylor-Martin's *John Betjeman: His
Life and Work* (1983) in *The Observer*, Larkin wrote that for years he

had been waiting for someone to explain the poem, which Taylor-Martin had described as 'baffling'.[16] It is about a man saying a regretful farewell to a woman – allegedly 'my Swedish beauty' – in the small town of Dungarvan, Co. Waterford, Ireland; and it involves a car driving away from Dungarvan. The final stanza runs:

> Had I kissed and drawn you to me,
>   Had you yielded warm for cold,
> What a power had pounded through me
>   As I stroked your streaming gold!
> You were right to keep us parted:
>   Bound and parted we remain,
> Aching, if unbroken hearted –
>   Oh! Dungarvan in the rain.[17]

No celebrated Greta Hellstrom (or Hellström, as she would need to be) is known to Swedish history;[18] so it is natural to wonder whether the poem is a coded account of a meeting between John and a woman. If so, one could not rule out the possibility that he disguised the place of the meeting as well as the names of the couple; but the mention in the poem of the Comeragh Mountains (near Dungarvan) supports the Dungarvan location; and a paragraph printed in the *Dungarvan Leader* newspaper in 1984, after John's death, confirms it.

When we published 'Dungarvan in The Rain'[19] ten years ago in 1974 and another poem by the late Sir John, 'Moira McCavendish',[20] Mrs Stella Noonan (Kiely), a true-blue Dungarvanite residing in London, a regular reader of the 'Leader' with a great interest in the Old Boro', took the matter up with Sir John himself and he very kindly replied to her queries as to how these poems came to be written in the following terms:
   'I did meet a lady on a wet day in Dungarvan when she was staying in Helvick and I was in Dublin. I was driving on to a house (on the Blackwater River) which has now, I believe, been destroyed. The name Moira McCavendish was as fortuitous as Greta Hellstrom. They are there for their euphony and for their faces and figures in the memory of [John Betjeman].'[21]

Clearly, there is some dissimulation in that letter: as the *Leader* columnist slyly observes, 'With hindsight one could be excused for wondering now whether the name McCavendish was one which the poet thought of merely because of its pleasant sound!' The letter provokes the question: what else was he concealing? But at least he was admitting that the Dungarvan poem was about himself and that that place was the scene of the 'farewell'. Given that location, which was the country house referred to in the penultimate stanza of the poem?

> There is no one now to wonder
>   What eccentric sits in state
> While the beech trees rock and thunder
>   Round his gate-lodge and his gate.
> Gone – the ornamental plaster,
>   Gone – the overgrown demesne
> And the car goes fast, and faster,
>   From Dungarvan in the rain.[22]

The greatest country house within range of Dungarvan was Lismore Castle, a home of the Dukes of Devonshire. Since 1941 John's old friend Deborah Mitford had been Duchess of Devonshire (and years later he stayed at Lismore with his friend Lady Elizabeth Cavendish);[23] but neither the description of the house nor that of its owner, in the poem, fits. There is another house near Dungarvan which could be considered. In *Castles of Ireland* (1977), Brian de Breffny writes of Ballysaggartmore, Co. Waterford:

> Arthur Keily, a Waterford gentleman whose ambition was greater than his fortune, was seized with the desire to be in fashion and build a castle of historic appearance on his estate near Lismore. His wife was anxious to outshine her sister-in-law, Mrs John Keily, the châtelaine of Strancally Castle . . .[24] Mr and Mrs Arthur Keily's dream castle began with the approach – a splendid gateway with a lodge in the turrets. Then his funds were exhausted and the castle was never built. Fabulous gates led to an insignificant house where the Keilys continued to live.[25]

Such a folly *de grandeur* would certainly have interested John. The eccentric, the gate-lodge and gate match the poem's description; so does the buildings' desolation, to judge from the photograph in de Breffny's book. And what remains of the house overlooks the Blackwater River.[26]

There is, however, a stronger candidate. In the Betjeman archive at the University of Victoria, British Columbia, is a letter written to John on 21 September 1946 by Emily Villiers-Stuart (formerly Lady Hemphill), in which she thanks him for having been kind to her son Peter Patrick (now Lord Hemphill) on his visit to Oxford. The stationery on which the letter is written has the printed letterhead 'DROMANA, CAPPOQUIN, Co. WATERFORD', but Emily Villiers-Stuart has crossed this out and superscribed it 'Helvick Lodge, Tring,

Dungarvan'. Dromana was the home of Ion Villiers-Stuart. Mark Bence-Jones describes it as 'a house rising sheer from a ledge of rock high above one of the loveliest stretches of the Blackwater estuary, incorporating parts of the old castle of the Fitzgeralds, Lords of the Decies . . . The drawing-room or ballroom was a magnificent room extending into the great curved bow above the river . . .'[27] He records how in the 1840s Henry Villiers-Stuart, first and last Lord Stuart de Decies, 'gave the principal reception rooms cornices of early-Victorian plasterwork';[28] and notes that a part of the exotic complex of buildings has been demolished – in both cases, aspects of the house in the poem.

John told the *Leader*'s correspondent that the woman he met in Dungarvan was 'staying in Helvick'. Does that mean that the friend to whom he was saying farewell was Emily Hemphill (as she still was)? We know from Penelope that he found her very attractive. She was certainly the central figure of one poem in *New Bats*, 'Ireland with Emily'; was she the heroine of this one, too?

Once again, there is a rival candidate. The 'Dungarvan' poem appeared in the *Cornhill Magazine* in December 1945: for Murray's, who owned the periodical, this served the dual purpose of securing a plum contribution for the magazine and promoting the new book. On a postcard from Eire postmarked 4 (or possibly 24) December 1945, Honor Tracy wrote to John:

> Sean [O'Faolain] asked me who the girl in your *Cornhill* poem was: and I said with a little break in my voice that I didn't know. Then Reggie [Ross Williamson] rang up and asked who she was and again I had to say, but now weeping bitterly, that I could not say. How sad is life . . .[29]

Three explanations for this message might be postulated: first, that Honor Tracy did not know who the girl in the poem was, and was upset that John would not tell her; second, that she knew who the girl was, and was distressed that it was not herself; and third, that she *was* the girl in the poem, and was sad that John had not kissed and drawn her to him, or alternatively was regretful that she had not been responsive to him. It might seem tempting to plump for the third of these possibilities. We have already seen that Honor Tracy wrote to John as early as April 1944, 'How I love you.'* They had been friends at the Ministry of Information, where Tracy worked in the Japanese section and for a time as secretary to the Sinologist Arthur Waley, also in John's circle. In a handwritten postscript to a typewritten letter of 11

---

* See Chapter 15, 'Admiralty'.

September 1946 from the offices of Sean O'Faolain's magazine *The Bell* in Dublin she wrote, 'Dear, dear John'.[30] And a letter from her to John dated simply 'April 23' begins 'Dearest Johnny' and ends, 'It would be lovely to see you again, you forcibly illustrate my favourite maxim, namely, the ones we don't sleep with are the dearest and the best.'[31] That would fit with what he wrote in the poem.

Honor Tracy was a linguist, a humorist, novelist and journalist.[32] John gave her an introduction to Sean O'Faolain, who employed her after the war.[33] She was generally regarded as an uncomely woman. Máire Cruise O'Brien recalls her as 'the plainest woman', Ruth-Ellen Moller as 'very unattractive' and Frances Daly, companion of the veteran journalist Benedict Kiely, as 'the ugliest woman I ever saw; I was amazed when someone told me she was Sean O'Faolain's mistress'.[34] O'Faolain's biographer describes her as having 'a pug nose and a curiously quilted face in which the eyes were barely visible';[35] Peter Conradi refers to her 'rubicund and endearingly porcine features';[36] and the journalist Cathal O' Shannon said she had 'masses of flaming red hair and a huge arse; she became rather a nuisance in the Pearl Bar [in Fleet Street, Dublin], so thrusting and brash'.[37] Nevertheless, she began a long affair with O'Faolain in 1945. Her bared figure, he declared, 'would have delighted a Rubens, a Brueghel, a . . . Maillol, a fat-loving Titian'. To him she was 'charming, unbeautiful, fatal'.[38]

In Dublin Tracy was regarded, in spite of the affair with O'Faolain, as primarily a lesbian.[39] 'Honor . . . appeared to be one mainly for the ladies,' Professor John Bayley writes, adding:

> She was quite a character. Lesbian certainly – much attracted to Iris [Murdoch] and up to a point it was mutual. It didn't bother me at all & I once made a pass at her myself which amused her – she was quite game for a kiss & a cuddle, & being what my old tutor David Cecil used to call 'an old-fashioned Lesbian of the sound type' she never 'came out' & never admitted anything. She wanted to be thought hetero in fact. She was massive, carroty, but distinctly attractive, at least to me in early days. [John Bayley and Iris Murdoch first met Tracy in 1957.] There's a sort of sketch of her in Barbara Pym's first novel, *Some Tame Gazelle*. Pym knew her at Oxford (Pym a student, HT working at Blackwell's). I should think John Betjeman would have adored her ('Pam, I adore you, Pam') physical type, but not much more than that?[40]

Tracy's red hair conflicts with the 'streaming gold' of Greta Hellstrom's in the poem; but that could have been an exercise of poetic licence, as 'gold' rhymes with 'cold' and 'red' does not; also, 'streaming red' would suggest blood. If indeed Tracy was the woman in the poem, why did John not make a more robust pass at her? Her letters to him suggest that she would have welcomed one, though in the poem he seems – perhaps gallantly? – to depict *her* as applying the damper ('You were right to keep us parted'). First, he was married – though that had not deterred him in the past and was not to deter him in the future from having affairs with other women. Second, he may have found her, as so many others did, physically unalluring. Third, he was no doubt aware of her relationship with his friend Sean O'Faolain, and might have felt that advances to Tracy would be a betrayal of him. Honor? Emily? Cathleen Delaney (O'Dea), the 'Colleen'? Or a woman unknown? Larkin's question about the poem with the baffling title is only half answered. Like the 'Mr W.H.' conundrum, the matter is likely to remain a tantalizing mystery – unless, some day, a cache of hitherto unknown letters should come to light, with indisputable revelations. For the time being, because of the mention of Helvick in John's letter to the *Leader*'s correspondent and in Emily's letter, the most plausible hypothesis is that Emily was the object of a tactfully deflected pass by John, whose later letters to her suggest that he was still greatly smitten by her.

By September 1945 last-minute corrections were being made to *New Bats in Old Belfries*. At the eleventh hour, John sent a further poem for inclusion, 'Youth and Age on Beaulieu River, Hants'. At the twelfth hour, he realized that he had not asked permission of three women mentioned in three different poems: Emily Hemphill, of 'Ireland with Emily', Joan Hunter Dunn of 'A Subaltern's Love-song', and Clemency Buckland of the Beaulieu River poem. Emily cabled from Reno, Nevada, where she was getting a divorce from the drunken Lord Hemphill, 'OF COURSE DON'T OBJECT'.[41] The reference to Joan Hunter Dunn had the most terrifying legal implications, since at the end of the poem John claimed 'And now I'm engaged to Miss Joan Hunter Dunn', whereas in fact she had married H. Wycliffe Jackson on 20 January.[42] Fortunately she made no objection either.[43]

As with Joan Hunter Dunn, John had used Clemency Buckland's name *en clair*.[44] In reply to his request to print the poem, she wrote:

Dear Mr Betjeman,
   Thank you for your letter and the poem. It is alright, neither my father nor I mind your publishing it. It certainly came as a surprise though, we little thought this would come of just asking the time!
   I am glad you did write it, as it will commemorate for me some very happy evenings spent on the river. You see the MacKenzies got it wrong, it was a friend of mine with me, and not my brother. We had just borrowed his sharpie [the flat-bottomed, two-masted vessel mentioned in the poem].[45]

Unfortunately our time was all too short, and he has now got sent to America for some months. So I remember very well the times we met you. Would you mind keeping it private, though, please, as you doubtless know what gossip in small villages is like, and I do happen to like him very much.

I'm sorry if I have bored you with all that, but I thought I should explain things to you, after writing such a nice poem. I like it. And as you do ask my opinion, I think 'limbs' goes better than 'form', giving a clearer picture.

My father thought it might interest you to know that my grandmother had a poem written to her, by Robert Louis Stevenson, who was her first cousin. It was called 'To Minnie with a Looking Glass' . . .

Yours sincerely,
Clemency Buckland[46]

On 30 November Jock Murray sent John £50 advance on royalties. 'With luck,' he wrote, 'the NEW BATS will make their appearance about the 12th December. It has been something of a rush, but we may yet succeed.' There was, he added, 'a considerable scramble' for the autographed limited edition; he hoped John would be able to come to London on 10 or 11 December to sign these copies.[47] On 2 December John replied:

Thank you & Mr Murray [here John imitated the script on the brass plate on the front door of No. 50 Albemarle Street] for the unexpected but BY NO MEANS UNWELCOME cheque for £50. I will now be able to buy Christmas presents with the half the Slave State does not take to pay such people as those who mismanage the Petrol coupons in Reading.

I will come up on Monday or Tuesday next week to sign the special editions. I hope to heaven you have not printed more than 2000 copies. You will never sell them. By the way, do ask your advertising people not to refer to me as a SATIRIST in future. I spent a long time in the last book's preface explaining I wasn't a satirist then; I am even less of one now. What I write may not be poetry to TAMBIMUTTU, whoever he may be,[48] but it is certainly not SATIRE . . .[49]

Confounding John's gloomy prediction, bookshops were eagerly subscribing to *New Bats* before publication. By now, he even had a following in America. Terence and Elsa Holliday of the Holliday Bookshop, New York, who had seen an advertisement for the book in the *New Statesman*, asked Murray for forty copies 'in order that we might not disappoint our more fanatical enthusiasts'. Terence Holliday added: 'The books will be at least one assurance of a merry Christmas to us, even in these dreadful times. I am really sorry to add to your complications during this season; I can only plead that Betjeman is such a great favourite of ours, and of others whom we have inoculated with the virus.'[50] Murray replied that 'the edition has been considerably over-subscribed' and that he could only let them have fifteen copies from a cache of copies held back 'in case of urgent demands'.[51]

Murray did not quite manage to meet his self-imposed deadline of 12 December. *New Bats* was published on 19 December in two editions, one at 6s, the other (on better paper and signed) at 10s 6d. On 23 December Tom Driberg reviewed the book in *Reynolds News* ('Betjeman specializes in nostalgic, exact, topographical, metrically archaic, only half satirical descriptions of middle-class life . . . The thing about Betjeman that probably annoys some fools is that they don't know if they are meant to laugh or not'). But, because of the delayed publication, the main reviews did not appear until January and February 1946. Like *Old Lights*, the book was very well received by the *New Statesman*, *The Listener*, *The Spectator* and *Time and Tide*. The *New Statesman* critique was by the Australian-born journalist G.W. Stonier, who had recently resigned as the magazine's literary editor.

A new volume of poems by Mr Betjeman catches the eye at once [Stonier wrote]. Smaller, chaster than any other, it attracts us by its ornamental scroll or plaque to walk nearer; at a yard or so its tiny lettering can be read, title and author in the same size as the publisher; and the date at the foot – 1845, surely? No, there weren't dust-jackets then. Peel off the jacket; and the shiny granular red suggests – good heavens! – shorthand manuals, a thesis from Calcutta. One's alarm is given a new direction by the stick-on panel, hinting at winners of the Newdigate. Inside . . . once inside, we forget the book as an *objet* and begin reading. Henley-on-Thames: from a house-boat the poet surveys the sunny reaches, the ripples that slowly flap against the boat's side and 'flop away in gems' . . .

How fastidiously our dreaminess has been caught, shivered and mended again! Would Mr Betjeman prefer his river reaches without adolescent boat-loads? I doubt it. Compare *Henley-on-Thames*, say, with Thomson's Cockney lyrics and one is immediately made aware that Mr Betjeman commands a liveliness and a depth rare in light verse. What he writes is poetry.

> . . . And low the mists of evening lie
> And lightly skims the midge.[52]

Stonier quoted three stanzas of 'A Subaltern's Love-song', about Joan Hunter Dunn, and commented:

There is the flavour of keepsake and cartoon, mocking, sentimental, wittily abandoned, giving to the life on our doorstep (or verandah) the charm of a mezzotint. The tennis girl has, of course, other admirers outside the fold: notably Mr Osbert Lancaster and Miss Joyce Grenfell. One can imagine the first adding daisies to dropshots, the second retailing to us every monosyllable let fall during these rallies. But of all admirers Mr Betjeman is both the most passionate and the most equivocal. Does he, or doesn't he, care? A very difficult question to answer. Anyway, he must have her in his album, that album in which love-sets and sunsets, chancels and ghosts and Cricklewood laundries, the morning bathe and the evening bell, nestle so surprisingly.[53]

The anonymous *Listener* reviewer's fantasy of an archaeologist's looking back on the twentieth century was so similar to that of the *New Statesman*'s reviewer of *Old Lights* that one wonders whether 'Senex' had migrated from one magazine to the other in the intervening five years.

If all the English poetry of the last two decades was destroyed and the scholars of a later century had only a volume of Betjeman, what would these scholars write about the literary moods and standards of our time? Whatever they inferred they would be largely wrong, because Betjeman represents only himself and reflects no fashion either in subject or technique. An analytical scholar might say – 'Here we have a poet who represents a period of conscious and elaborate decadence; it is the kind of poetry, and there has been great poetry of this kind, which expresses nostalgia for an unreal Golden Age; the thirties and forties of the twentieth century were clearly decades of pastiche and sophistication, the poets looking back to the heroic age which stretched from Tennyson to Hardy'; and they might add – 'It was clearly a period in which poets and their public were particularly sensitive to sound and to metre, a fastidious, not a revolutionary, age'. How wrong such a scholar would be, in both his judgments; poetry today is in no sense decadent nor is its public fastidious; we are bullied to accept strange and original imagery buried in heavy and unmemorable metres. Poets after Eliot are not often quoted, nor does their poetry run in people's heads, as poetry used to do; 'interesting' or 'original' or 'I think there is something in it' is what the reader now says when he wants to praise. The scholar with his Betjeman fragments would know nothing of the self-conscious collective achievement which is Modern Poetry, the common idiom and the quickly submerged personalities. Betjeman is not Modern Poetry, and he is not submerged.[54]

The *Listener* reviewer found it exciting 'to read poems which are so sentimental, and also self-conscious, self-mocking, and often very funny'. It was, he thought, 'like listening to an exile making fun of his homesickness'.

> Betjeman is exiled in time not in space. He looks for the spirit of the English past which is his home, and he finds it lingering in odd places pathetically; he conveys not only the pathos but also the absurdity of the odd places, and of the people who live in them. It is not comic verse (the horrible hearty tradition) or sentimental verse, but comic-sentimental, usually something more than the mock-Victorian valentine, because of the extraordinary sensitiveness to the mood and life of places. Within a single idiom and attitude there is great variety in this book, certainly great differences of depth and interest. There are the easy running magazine poems which are always funny and have jingling metres. But there are also the lyrical and more metrically elaborate poems, which are sad and sentimental, with beautifully contrived mournful echoes and a depressing nostalgia for dying ways of life; the best and most original poems are the meeting-places of the two styles.[55]

If one had to choose any passage of criticism to sum up the strengths of John's poetry, this might be it; and John must have basked in the praise. He was probably less enchanted by the critic's concluding paragraph, printed opposite an advertisement for Pelmanism.[56]

> Perhaps the professor of a later century will say – 'Here is the little verse of the defeated bourgeois, who commemorates the last illusions and escapes which survived into the electric-atomic age, protecting himself with little jokes and pathetic apology. A minor poet, certainly; but must be read for historical interest. But don't be deceived by the jokes and the sophistication; very reactionary and above all religious; safer to read Thomas Hardy, as Betjeman probably did'.[57]

The Spectator again asked Goronwy Rees to review his friend's book. 'He has most strongly the Aristotelian virtue of seeing the natural metaphors of life, the similarity of dissimilars (I am sure Mr Betjeman will appreciate so donnish a compliment) . . . One can only say of him that his poems are both clever and good, and perhaps that as they become less clever they become even better.'[58] In *Time and Tide*, Paul Bloomfield called *New Bats* an 'enchanting little book' and wondered whether John's foreign surname had helped to make him extra-aware of English traits.

> No other good poet for a long time has been as entertaining as Mr Betjeman. His verse is in several respects unlike that of his best

contemporaries, and this gives him into the bargain a kind of rarity value. I should guess that most of his regular readers are particularly grateful for his unregenerate mundanity. He is not frightened by the 'conscious' – by the synthesis made by mind. He positively seems to delight in the ebullience of the body . . .

What Mr Betjeman writes is extravagantly amusing, and sometimes moving and beautiful. He vindicates the five senses and the five or more sensualities and sensibilities. He is very clever and resourceful; his works suggest a sociable, nosy, knowledgeable, eighteenth-century Whig whom the accident of birth (that is, of being born an Edwardian) has obliged to be a twentieth-century Tory – an eighteenth-century sceptic, moreover, whom the spread of republican precept, practice and uncouthness has forced to identify himself with twentieth-century Catholicism (Roman or Anglo I don't know). There is something else too. The name Betjeman may be as thoroughly naturalised in England as the name Bentinck; but I don't believe that any Englishman whose ancestors settled here as long ago as 1066 can ever see other Englishmen's characteristic foibles with the objectivity of one who happens to be called Disraeli, Rossetti, Wilde, Henry James, Beerbohm – or Betjeman . . .[59]

John feared the anonymous reviewers of the *Times Literary Supplement* even more than the left-wing ones of the *New Statesman*; but in fact the *TLS* review was one of the best that *New Bats* received. It was headed simply 'Mr Betjeman's Work'.

He sees life as something too great and too delicate to be reconstructed over a packet of cigarettes, and he therefore writes 'The Planster's Vision' . . . He's the John Clare of suburbia and of upriver places, and not least in North Oxford, where we find him as tuneable as his own bells . . .

Older readers, following him on the summer Thames, may be reminded of such accomplished holiday versemen as Ashby-Sterry[60] and Cholmondeley-Pennell;[61] but he has the advantage in imaginative concentration, and very seldom writes an 'easy' piece for all the outward semblance of ease in his compositions . . .[62]

In July 1946 *The Architectural Review* published a rather late notice of the book, by Hugh Casson. John and Casson knew each other well from working together on the *Review* and *Decoration*, and were outwardly friendly; but they had never really clicked. Casson was aware that John only paid lip-service – if that – to the Modern Movement, to which he himself was committed. Already plans were in train for a 1951 Festival of Britain, of which Casson was to be the architectural director.[63] As an architect of the brave new Britain, he could take only so much of what he clearly regarded as an increasingly tiresome pose; though, by the same standards, he was generous about John's more serious poems.

> . . . Mr Betjeman's belfry is no ivory tower. Sturdily built – to the design perhaps of Butterfield? – it stands firmly on English soil, buttressed with affection, ivy'd with nostalgia . . . And the bats, are they really new? Well, we've met some of them before – the toothbrush airing on the N. Oxford window-sill, Miss Hunter Dunn, 'Furnished and burnished by Aldershot sun', the poultry farm girls, the barking athlete, the village organist – but how nice to see again their familiar furry little faces and hear the effortless beating of their wings. And those of you who still think Mr Betjeman is just a funny man read the last verse of 'Parliament Hill Fields', or 'Before the Anaesthetic' or 'Sunday Afternoon Service in St Enodoc Church, Cornwall'. Send not to enquire, then, *Review* readers, for whom Mr Betjeman's bell tolls – it tolls for all of you – and each note is a summons.

Did the conflation of 'bell' and 'summons', in that last sentence, plant in John's mind the phrase which became the title of his verse autobiography, fourteen years later?

BRITISH COUNCIL

... Ormrod to Betjeman, 11 April 1945. The recipient of the last-named letter was the future Poet Laureate, whose brief career with the Council put him in charge of the Oxford outpost for a time. As a Council officer he evoked mixed feelings: some remember him for his charm and wit; but by most accounts he was a hopeless administrator who contributed little if anything to the Council's books and library work.

Douglas Coombs, *Spreading the Word: The Library Work of the British Council*, London 1988

If John had lived in the eighteenth century, he would probably have found himself a rich patron. At the *Daily Herald*, it was one of his *cris de coeur* that the only reason he took employment – the war effort apart – was to buy time to write poetry. By September 1944 he was as discontented at the Admiralty as he had become with all his previous jobs. He was flirting with the BBC, which was holding out the possibility of a staff post based in the Devon and Cornwall area. More attractive to him was the prospect of a senior appointment with the British Council, which he was discussing with Brian Kennedy-Cooke, director of the Council's production division. Kennedy-Cooke was one of a number of Council officials who had served in the Sudan – they were known as 'the Camel Corps' – and it is possible that Sir John Maffey, who had been Governor-General of the Sudan, recommended John to him. Kennedy-Cooke obtained John an interview with the Council's well-loved Secretary-General, A.J.S. White, who had served with the Indian Civil Service before the war. White was ten years – to the day – older than John. In 1984 he recalled the interview.

We had been to the same school and as he sat down I said, 'You were at Marlborough, weren't you?' To which he replied – 'That stinking place. Yes I was.' Hardly an ingratiating remark from a candidate for a job, as I and my four sons were very enthusiastic Old Marlburians and I was ten years his senior! But of course he was the last person one could expect (or want) an ingratiating remark from. I was glad I brought him into the Council though I think I may have had to invent that job for him!¹

John was to be assistant director, under Kennedy-Cooke, in charge of the books division. The British Council had been created as a voluntary body in 1934, and was essentially a trade propaganda organization, though its aims were expressed in high-flown language – 'To make the life and thought of the British peoples more widely known abroad; and to promote a mutual interchange of knowledge and ideas with other peoples'.² A prime aim of the campaign was to encourage the study and use of English.

A single department with a staff of two dealt with Books and Periodicals in 1939. By the end of 1943 work and staff had grown so much that there were three departments – Books, Periodicals, Publications – each under its own director. In Kennedy-Cooke's view, these directors had become warring 'primadonnas'. He thought that putting John in charge of them would make for harmony.³

On 26 September 1944 Kennedy-Cooke wrote to offer John the job.⁴ John replied from Uffington: 'Dear Brian, Your letter has proved a bombshell of delight . . . To begin with I prefer books to films and know something about their production. Another thing, I prefer Oxford to any town on earth. And it is near here.'⁵ But he explained that, to his chagrin, he could not immediately accept the offer.

> The Admiralty is gentlemanly but all for regulations. It will not willingly release me. The work I do with it is such as any cute businessman could do ten times better than I do it. The people I work with are almost all charmers. However, as my immediate superior, though nothing like as awful as Beddington, has proved himself incompetent at dealing with humans and has upset all my subordinates and even me slightly, I have had to make representations to try to get out. The BBC in Bristol, which was trying to get me at the same time as you when I originally left Minnie [the Ministry of Information], offered me a job as regional programme director for Devon and Cornwall, attractive enough until your definite offer came along. The Admiralty which is good and understanding on top may be willing to release me to do this and would I think be equally amenable to your suggestion . . .⁶

John added that he was writing to the BBC to say that he did not want to leave Berkshire and could not work in Devon or Cornwall. He asked for a week's grace until he should hear from the BBC.

> I hope I do not appear to be behaving like a prima donna or playing one group off against another . . . The prospect of working under you at a job

I know something about already is preferable of course to starting in a new medium and with the prospect of being separated for months at a time from my family.[7]

John then wrote a somewhat disingenuous letter to the BBC – a letter whose clear object was to make it impossible for the Corporation to offer him a job.

Dear Beadle,

So far as I can gather from spies on the uppermost boughs of the Admiralty tree I am going to be given my release by the end of this month and I do not think any gentlemanly etiquette will be endangered by my receiving a letter from the BBC offering me the job about which we have all talked.

I feel however before I take the step and you are committed to my services that I must in fairness to you raise two questions. In order to keep myself and family alive it will be necessary for me to continue my reviewing on the *Daily Herald* and pursuing my avocation as a poet.* I hope the BBC will extend this favour to me as did the Admiralty, and the Ministry of Information before that.

The other question is one of permanent home. I could not but be sensible of the wisdom of JS's suggestion that I should live for this Devon & Cornwall job in Cornwall in old Trebetherick which I know and love. But I am not the only person to be considered and I have discussed this aspect of the job with my wife. She feels, and I cannot blame her for I share the feeling myself, that we would be silly to leave this village [Uffington] except under compulsion. Our roots – eleven years of married life spent in the place – are here; our children have been brought up here and are part of the community; our friends are all here. Though I would not mind the uprooting if I were a bachelor I feel I owe a first duty to my family. I love Devon and Cornwall and I like the idea of a job and I should naturally spend a lot of my time down there. But I am not prepared to sacrifice this house and neighbourhood at the moment. Of course in the new Slave State the whole district may be ruined and our friends and neighbours may be turned out or killed. All sorts of things may happen but for the moment I do not want to commit myself to permanent residence with my family in Cornwall.

I feel this may be a serious obstacle to your offering me the job and I would not like to take it under false pretences.

If it is not, please do not hesitate to send off the fatal letter . . .[8]

---

* See Chapter 14, '*Daily Herald*'.

The ploy worked. The BBC backed off; the Admiralty gave John his release; and by January 1945 John was an officer of the British Council. He first worked at St James's House, South Leigh, Oxfordshire, where the books departments had temporary quarters. It had been a school for 'backward boys'; above the entrance was a carving of the hare and the tortoise, with the legend 'FESTINA LENTE'.[9] John found that he knew three of the staff already. Renée Tickell he had known at Oxford, where, like himself, she contributed to *Oxford Outlook*. She had taken a First and had written a novel about Oxford called *Neapolitan Ice* 'because it's about people who live in layers'.[10] In 1929 she had married Jerrard Tickell, who wrote the best-selling novel *Appointment with Venus*, about the kidnap of a cow from the Germans in the Channel Islands.[11] Molly Fernald he had also known at Oxford, as Molly Kidd. They used to drive out to the Spread Eagle inn in Thame together. She had married John's Marlborough and Oxford friend John Fernald, but by now they were divorced. 'There were those who called her Mrs *In*fernald,' Renée Tickell recalled. 'They had reason.'[12] Michael Hooker, who was Molly Fernald's personal assistant, said: 'She was very decisive – over-decisive, most people would think. If anybody said anything to her, she would seize the 'phone and immediately start a conversation before she had got all her facts. She was great fun and very loyal, a great fighter for her department, and very intolerant of red tape, which was a most necessary quality for anybody to have there.'[13]

A third Oxford friend was Jack Yates (who as an undergraduate had called himself Theodore). Between Oxford and the Council appointment he had been a prep-school master. Always an aesthete, he had developed into a richly camp figure. 'Jack had great affectations,' Hooker said, '– I think one would say "screaming queen" – but people once they got past this always liked him, he was so charming, so kind. And he entertained John Betjeman. He was a very memorable character: beaky nose, stepped very gingerly, delicately, like Agag.'[14]

Lady de Bunsen (then Joan Harmston and in charge of books for the Colonies) remembered:

There was a terrible housekeeper at South Leigh who gave out the biscuits. One day she made us all line up and take them. Major Longden, who was director of fine arts, was very irate and said, 'Tomorrow, I suppose, I'll have to sit up and beg for them.' Jack Yates just tossed his head and walked by, and afterwards he said to me, 'Did you see my *tantrum*?'[15]

John did not have to endure the South Leigh housekeeper for long. Shortly after he joined the Council, the books departments moved into

Oriel College, Oxford – exchanging the carved tortoise of St James's
House for a live college tortoise which had the Oriel coat of arms
painted on its shell. The catering still had its shortcomings. It was at
that time servants' wisdom that a pinch of salt improved a pot of
coffee. One day, when John complained about the taste of the coffee,
one of the maids, whom he called 'the Troglodytes', answered: '[*Sniff.*]
Well, I salt it and leave it in hot water all night – what more can I do?'[16]

In theory John was answerable to Brian Kennedy-Cooke for the ef-
ficiency of the book departments. In fact, however, almost all his dealings, by memorandum and by telephone, were with Kennedy-Cooke's
assistant, Joanna Collihole. 'John Betjeman was not remotely suitable
for the job,' she considered.

> I suppose he was what one would now call an administrator, but that was
> not his forte.
>
> Mrs Ormrod (now Lady Ormrod) was in charge of the books depart-
> ment. Its business was, during the war, to supply libraries in those coun-
> tries where you could send books. Joan Barton was in charge of the
> periodicals department. John Hampden was publications department.
> That department was very very busy during the war because it was pro-
> ducing English classics in the wide range of languages of our allies in the
> United Kingdom – for instance, enormous numbers of books were pub-
> lished in Polish for Polish pilots and seamen. Mrs Fernald was in charge of
> the book exports scheme. Renée Tickell was in charge of reviews.
>
> So there was this group of primadonnas, largely isolated down at Oriel
> College, getting awfully sick of being down in the country when they
> would much prefer to be up in London – and *he kept them sweet*. That, in
> my opinion, was John's greatest contribution.
>
> He was an appalling administrator. This is my view – rather pompous,
> I suppose. I was a good administrator. My business was to see that John
> provided Mr Kennedy-Cooke with what he needed in the way of confiden-
> tial reports and returns and all the things that didn't matter to John one
> iota. So he was always late; and he must have hated my guts . . .
>
> Where John was lucky was in having good directors under him. They
> could carry him, as good musicians can play on when the conductor is
> deficient. John was a good 'musician' but a bad conductor.[17]

Knowing what Miss Collihole thought of him, John went out of
his way to make his messages to her sound as maddeningly scatty as
possible. One of his memos to her that has survived (because he eventually crossed it through and used the rest of the sheet to write to one
of his assistants about poetry) begins: 'Miss Collihole from Mr
Betjeman III II XLV: I have bicycle oil on my hands which has got on

to the minutes. Miss Craig [John's secretary] is on leave – hence long-hand . . .'[18]

In view of her own difficulties with John, Joanna Collihole found it slightly galling that he got on so well with her boss, Brian Kennedy-Cooke. 'They liked each other very much,' she said. 'Mr Kennedy-Cooke found John enormously amusing – as *everybody* did! Of course he didn't have the irritations: my job was to keep the irritations away from him. John used to come up to London now and then and they'd go out and lunch together. *Long* lunches. John Hampden's venue was the Café Royal, because he had been a publisher and that was very much a publisher's place. You could get a lunch for 5s there; it was controlled prices. But Mr Kennedy-Cooke preferred a funny little restaurant in Hanover Square, where the Council was then.'[19]

Dr Michael Hooker, who worked in book exports and was later co-founder of Hooker Craigmyle, fund-raisers for charities, formed an impression of John similar to Miss Collihole's.

[He] was extraordinarily nice of course and everybody – well, they adored him, as they always do. I should think he was just about as big a disaster in the job as it was possible to be . . . he drifted through, keeping everybody very happy, but I should have thought he was totally miscast.[20]

John did not in fact manage to keep everybody happy; even in his limited mission of keeping the 'primadonnas' sweet he was not invariably successful. Mrs Ormrod, who had done more than anyone to create an effective books department, was not best pleased to have him put above her.

He suddenly turned up when we were fully established [Lady Ormrod[21] recalled]. I think I had about thirty staff by that time. I was told, 'He's going to be the head of this.' And he didn't know a damned thing about it, of course, poor chap.

I don't think he really liked me, because he knew I didn't really like him. He was a very warm-hearted, immediate sort of person who behaved instinctively, rather like a child does. He wanted to be liked. I don't think he was often disliked. I thought he was damned good company. But he didn't know a thing about anything, and he'd disappear – I don't know what idiot had appointed him – he'd disappear and wouldn't be in for days and he insisted that nothing should be sent out unless he was there. And if you really kept to that, which I couldn't, you could never answer urgent things. It was very tiresome, though he was great fun.

He had been appointed to pour oil on troubled waters. But he wasn't an oil-pourer! He was too honest, in a funny sort of dotty way. He'd take violent sides. I remember one meeting: he was in one of his furies about something. He'd been away for a week, and I think somebody had protested. And we all met. I said something and he didn't like it, and he was frightfully rude to me. He was intolerable.

. . . We were at Oriel, and the Council had been offered the possibility of a very fine house on the river. None of my people wanted to go, and it wouldn't have been suitable for me at all . . . And he accused me of influencing my staff not to go and I denied this, which was absolutely true . . . And he said, 'That's an absolute lie.' And I said, 'That is no way to speak to me; and it's not so.' . . . And he said, 'But you don't want to go.' And I said, 'No, I don't.' He said, 'Well, there you are, you've influenced your staff.' And he went on bullying me. So I got up and walked out and the meeting broke up.

At lunchtime, I was just going out when somebody tapped me on the shoulder, and it was Betjeman, smiling and saying, 'I was a swine to you this morning.' And I said, '*Why* were you a swine to me?' He said, 'I felt like it.' So I said, 'Well, that was very unkind, because you upset my whole morning, making me feel beastly.' . . . Then he said, 'Oh, let's stop this and go and have a look at Oxford.' So he put his arm in mine and out we went; and, you know, to be with him . . . I knew Oxford pretty well, but he'd say, 'Stand in this doorway and look at that corner . . .' and see this or that. He was wonderful to be with. We had a very happy lunchtime together. Really happy. It was typical, wasn't it?[22]

Of all the 'primadonnas', the one John found most congenial was Renée Tickell. He always called her Renée Haynes, her maiden name by which he had known her at Oxford, though in reference to her married name he made the Biblical pun, 'Renée, Renée Tickell, Upharsin'.[23] Michael Hooker said of Renée:

She was very kind, gentle, amused – not a wild sort of character, by any means, like John himself and Jack Yates, who would do outrageous things and take the initiative. John pulled her leg – he pulled all our legs. He had a habit, if he heard anybody's telephone ringing and not being answered, he would go into the office and answer it on behalf of the person, and see what happened. I think some pretty inconsequential conversations resulted. One day I was ringing up Renée, and I had my diary open which had all sorts of useless information printed in it at the front. The telephone rang for a bit, then I suddenly got this brisk voice: 'Renée 'aynes 'ere. 'Oo's that?' And I said, 'How many puncheons in a hogshead?' And John said 'No idea' and slammed the receiver down. He was rather annoyed: *he* made the jokes around there! The diary just happened to be in front of me, and I knew perfectly well who it was. He did behave in a very un-Civil Servant manner, some-times.[24]

Lady de Bunsen remembers John's scrawling 'I cannot read this it is too dull' on some lengthy minute 'over which several departments had chewed their pencils and thought of something to add before passing it up to him'. She noted that he took snuff, 'an antique habit that few of us had witnessed before' and that he proudly wore Henry James's old clothes.[25] Robert Milner, a young librarian, came to work in Mrs Ormrod's department on 15 January 1945.[26] He, too, recalls that John's 'mild eccentricities' were much discussed round the office, for example his habit of answering the telephone 'It is John Betjeman who speaks.' John was said to dictate letters lying on his back on the floor, though Milner did not witness this himself. Milner thought the eccen-tricity was partly natural to John, partly a 'persona' deliberately put on. 'He seemed, and perhaps felt, rather out of place in this milieu, and was clearly impatient with some of the wrangling and official-dom; but he took it usually with great good humour . . . No doubt there was personal friction; but I had the impression that he made a real effort to master a somewhat uncongenial job.'

A series of letters which Milner wrote to his wife Joan in the early months of 1945 gives a kind of cinematic view of John in action at the British Council.

South Leigh, Jan. 21

This is my day. A ting-a-ling-a-ling wakes me up at seven; & in a ¼ of an hour I get up & hurry round to a bathroom to shave, dress & make my bed. Then breakfast in the school-hall at a long table; & hurry down the lane in the half-light. The bus comes & turns round; so a chilly journey into Oxford, & we get out by St Mary's [the University Church, opposite Oriel College].

Now 5 days out of 6 I work in Books, under Mrs. Ormrod; if work is the word. I am really hanging about reading files & begging bits of work to do. I usually have a short session with Mrs. O. in wh she talks all the time, & then get shunted off for the rest of the day . . . I still know nothing definite [about a future posting], but surely I must soon. Mrs. O. has gone so far as to say 'When you go to France', & it seems generally assumed that I may go there.

T'other day I was introduced to John Betjeman. 'One of the librarians'. Where is he going? France or Italy probably says Mrs. O. Where does he want to go? France, I put in. Does he speak French? (I quaked at that.) My dear, he'll talk to you in Anglo-Saxon or anything you like. Can you really speak A.S.? says B. I can read a little: my wife taught it me.

He paces about catlike, his quizzical eye slyly following you: an odd creature, who deliberately plays the fool but is probably acute.

Jan. 23

Yesterday was my Periodicals day & I worked for Rosemary, at a subject index for periodicals. In comes Betjeman, & we simply gossip about this & that for about an hour, or more. 'But, dear thing' . . . he wd say, and 'I say, isn't this nice!' We talked about religion a good deal. He is quite nice I think.

Feb. 5

This morning I classified till eleven; looked up Mrs. O., & hung about her room till lunch; had lunch with her; back to the library to classify. Straight in comes Betjeman to look something up, & he stays talking until tea time. I was quite interested: he is an intelligent man. Among other things I had to give him a brief summary of Dewey.

[The American Melvil Dewey introduced the decimal classification of library books. Lady de Bunsen wrote of John: 'He found the whole idea of librarianship hilarious, and could hardly believe his ears when told that Rosemary Pearce had been called to London for an urgent and important meeting on catalogue cards . . . But he did concede, and on paper, that there was more to the job than "Deweyfying a shelf of *Britain in Pictures* in an African kraal." ']27

March 20

Betjeman produced a wonderful imitation of a broken egg, to be put on expensive carpets etc. – quite horrifying.

John enjoyed Milner's company, and took him up. He showed him round Oxford. 'I seem to remember', Milner wrote, 'tip-toeing across a lawn, at Pembroke [College] I presume, & peering through a window at Dr Johnson's teapot.' John sent Milner letters in the *art nouveau* 'art lettering' that he used only when writing to people who interested him.* The tone was markedly different from that of his memoranda to Miss Collihole.

In one of the *art nouveau* letters, John mentioned 'Miss Mole' who was Milner's library colleague and friend Rosemary Pearce. John had nicknames for most of the staff. 'How right he was unwittingly,' wrote Lady de Bunsen, 'about the wistful doe-eyed girl he called "the wronged village maiden".28 Rather less appropriate, and deliberately so, was his pet name for the first male librarian to be appointed [Robert Mann]. Him he called "Old Quick-Ref".'29 Joan Harmston

* See pp. 350-51.

and her colleagues were 'the Jolly Girls'. Michael Hooker recalled in 1981: 'I was the youngest, so I was called "Master Michael", and there was some sort of a story about my having been in a Victorian household as a small boy, and what nurse would say . . . He still calls me "Master Michael" – I'm nearly sixty – and occasionally writes letters to me as "Master Michael Hooker, PhD".'[30] John himself received a nickname from Jack Yates – 'the Bard'. Robert Milner remembered his living up to it.

> One morning at a staff meeting in his room he came in with a pleased look in the eye, & announced that he had written a new poem, which he proceeded to recite to us. So I was one of the first to hear the admirable little piece beginning –

> Belbroughton Road is bonny, where [sic] pinkly bursts the spray
> Of prunus and forsythia . . .[31]

John was not the only poet. He soon discovered that Joan Barton also wrote poetry. He gave her great encouragement. On the sheet of paper on which he had scratched out the beginning of the memo to Miss Collihole, he wrote:

Miss Barton
  From Mr Betjeman
You are a lovely poet. Make no doubt of it. Reading your poems all through again this morning I am soaked in the Bristol rain and moved beyond words by some passages in Nether Stowey which I have marked in pencil. I have also marked in pencil in an index with an X those I have liked particularly. Perhaps the one that gets me most is the one about the hospital – all except the last part about the landscape of morning which seems to me to be too abrupt a contrast and too full of sensitive observation for the type of observer who is watching through the previous stanzas . . .
  Only one criticism in a v good poem *Newgate Sands* you use two words which for me, at any rate, have no significance on account of over use 'unimaginable' and 'incredible'. I would have preferred more concrete and abrupt phraseology . . .
  John Betjeman
  IV. II. XLV[32]

In later years, when Joan Barton ran a bookshop in Marlborough with her former British Council junior and close friend Barbara Watson, John kept in touch and 'sold' her poetry to his influential friends. Philip Larkin included one of her poems in *The Oxford Book*

TELEPHONE: MAYFAIR 8484
TELEGRAMS: BRITCOUN LONDON

THE·BRITISH COUNCIL
3 HANOVER STREET
LONDON W1

YOUR REFERENCE

COUNCIL REFERENCE

ORIEL

I· VIII · MCMXLV

MY DEAR FELLER ⚬⚬ I THANK YOV

FOR YOVR FORMAL LETTER WITH

ITS FASCINATING ENCLOSVRE OF

IX·VII ⚬⚬ I NEVER RECEIVED ANY

LETTER OF XXI·V WHICH IT MENT-

IONS ⚬⚬ I ONLY RETVRNED AFTER

A LONG & MERCIFVLNESS ILLNESS

YESTERDAY ⚬⚬ I VNDERSTAND FROM

MISS MOLE THAT YOV RETVRN FOR A

BREATER ON XXXVIII XX ⚬⚬ PLEASE

MAKE K-C OR ME YOVR FIRST OR LAST

PORT OF CALL ⚬⚬ I MAY BE

AWAY. INT HAVE TOLD. K-C OF
YOUR /PROTECTED
      λ NEW MOVEMENTS α α I EXPECT
TO HAVE SOME LEAVE FOR TWO
WEEKS STARTING AUGUST XIVTH α α
WILL YOU BE ABLE TO SEE ME EITER
BEFORE MY LEAVE OR AFTER * ? α α
MISS CRACE HAS BAD PNEUMONIA
SO I HAVE DONE THIS ON MY OWN
TYPE WRITER α α MORE ANGLICAN
NEWS FROM PARIS PLEASE & ANY
NEW & VIEWS ON 'NXTH CENT. (LATE)
FRENCH GOTHIC WHEN WE MEET
YOURS JOHN BETJEMAN α α α
* PREFERABLY AFTER

of Twentieth-Century Verse. One of the letters C. Day-Lewis dictated to his wife in his last illness, when he was too weak to write, was to Joan Barton, telling her how much pleasure some of her poems had given him.[33]

While at South Leigh, John found that Alfred Grosch, the head of the packing department, was another poet. A genial, elderly man, he had formerly been a police constable and a probation officer. 'He and John used to have man-to-man chats about disturbed boys,' Lady de Bunsen recalled.[34] 'We all liked him,' Renée Tickell said,

> – but alas I can only remember two lines of a poem he wrote about our neighbourhood in South Leigh, which praised:

> An old-world residence of great charm
> Formerly known as Ivy Farm.

> You see how innocently Betjemanly he could be.[35]

When John arrived at the Council, Renée Tickell was suspicious of him. She had heard he was to be a 'general watchdog'. But he walked round talking to the staff and made himself very agreeable.[36] He wanted to know all about them. He learned that Anne Ormrod had run away from her home in Ealing when she was fifteen because she hated her father, the art expert Charles Lush.[37] Michael Hooker had been at Marlborough and told John the latest Gidney stories. Joan Harmston had worked on *John o' London's Weekly*, the middlebrow literary magazine. Joan Barton had been in the Hampshire land army; before that, in the accounts department of the Somerset County Council, where she learned that the first thing the men and women in the workhouse had to do, even in 1940, was to knit their own grave stockings.[38] John burst in on Margaret Barber, who worked for Molly Fernald, and, observing a printed pottery ashtray on her desk, said, 'I see you smoke Balkan Sobranies.'[39]

John wanted to know all about the staff's families, schools and ancestry as well. Renée Tickell was a cousin of Aldous Huxley and a friend of Hilaire Belloc and H.G. Wells. Joan Barton's father ran an art-materials shop in Whiteladies Road, Bristol – a street John often visited to broadcast for the BBC. She had never told her parents she wrote poetry. Her friend Barbara Watson was a granddaughter of A.G. Watson who was a Fellow of All Souls and a housemaster at Harrow; and a kinswoman of the celebrated Lady Ellenborough who had countless lovers and married a sheikh.[40] Michael Hooker was a descendant of Bishop Hooker whose statue stands outside Exeter Cathedral.

John was especially interested in everybody's religion. Jack Yates and Alfred Grosch were Roman Catholics; Robert Milner on the brink of becoming one. Renée Tickell was a spiritualist[41] who wrote books on extra-sensory perception. John Hampden was sarcastically described by John as 'a lapsed Methodist'. Rosemary Pearce had two aunts who were nuns in a convent at Wantage. 'Of course that thrilled him immensely,' she said; 'also, my grandmother on my mother's side was living at Clewer, a cluster of nunneries, and that interested him too.'[42] Lady de Bunsen remembered:

> He called himself a religious maniac, and he certainly caused consterna-
> tion and hagiographical research by dating appointments by Saints' days.
> St Simon and St Jude 2.30, St Vedast, 11 a.m. and so on . . . He loved to
> spend his time in the British Restaurant in Woodstock speculating on the
> denomination of everyone there: High Church, C of E (Middle Stump),
> Methodist and so on, and he was usually about right, if a generation or
> so back. To a lorry driver enjoying his sausage and mash he once asked
> politely, 'Excuse me, but you are a Baptist, aren't you?' The startled man
> collected his wits, and then replied good-naturedly, 'Well I suppose I am.
> That is, my mother was.'[43]

Late in 1945, the books division was moved from Oriel College to Blenheim Palace – the Duke of Marlborough's house, where Winston Churchill had been born. Most of the staff were to be housed in offices which were converted railway carriages in the Palace grounds; but a few rooms in the Palace, just vacated by MI5, the security service, were available, and for these there was ill-tempered competition. The practical Anne Ormrod quickly decided that she would much prefer to be in the trains. 'Everybody was fighting for rooms in the Palace, and bargaining. They were great, draughty rooms, and the tapestries were all covered with white dust-sheets, which had to be removed by men on ladders whenever the Duke wanted to show the tapestries to visitors. I wanted the trains, they were perfect for me. I had the end carriage and it had a telephone to the Continent. It had been the headquarters of the British staff until the Germans got to know where it was and threatened to bomb it – which was pretty nice for us, but we were expendable.'[44] Molly Fernald bagged a room in the Palace. 'Mrs Fernald had her own way with her,' said Margaret Barber. 'She said, "We're not going out in the *huts*." '[45] John Hampden was also in the Palace; and John, as head of the division, took the best room. Ralph Glasser, who worked for Molly Fernald, has written a brilliantly observed portrait of him *in situ*.

> Talking to John Betjeman in his room at Blenheim Palace, I happened to
> mention that I had come up to Oxford from the Gorbals. Part of the
> palace was in use by departments of the British Council, still in wartime

evacuation quarters. He was standing before one of the huge panels of biscuit-coloured plywood covering the walls of the little salon which, like most of the rooms put to office use, still carried this protection for delicate surfaces beneath. He had been chalking on it a complicated notation of change-ringing . . . His present duties could not have been burdensome; to judge from the vast arrangement of chalk marks he had drawn on the board, he had spent most of the morning at it. He turned, the loose lower lip, drawn to the left as always, sagging further, and searched my face, plainly wondering what to say, which was unusual for him. Then, resuming the habitual mandarin drawl, half-eager, half-blasé, said, 'You *must* tell me how the place struck you – I suppose "struck" is the word! Dear boy, did the architecture transform you?'[46]

John made himself an expert on the architecture of Blenheim. He produced a typewritten guidebook and set a competition for the office juniors to draw or paint anything they chose in the Palace and grounds. Diana Slessor, daughter of the then Air Marshal Sir John Slessor, won it with a neat drawing of some carvings on the staircase.[47] John was on hand to show visitors around. He enjoyed pointing out the three limpid eyes painted on the wainscot in the entrance hall. The story was that the ninth Duke, who married the scandalous American Consuelo Vanderbilt, had been obsessed with her beautiful eyes, and had asked a decorator to paint them in the hall; but the decorator, finding he had more space to fill than he had expected, gave extra value for money by painting in *three* eyes. Lady de Bunsen remembers the day an eastern European delegation came to the Palace. One of its members asked John whether he had any books on economics.

'Nothing at all!' he replied. 'But this is our [John Singer] Sargent. Rather good, don't you think?'[48]

A.J.P. Taylor recalled that on VE Day in May 1945, his son Giles had a holiday from the Dragon School. 'He and I bicycled out to Blenheim where we picnicked in the park. We also called on John Betjeman who conducted us over Housemaids' Heights, the extremely uncomfortable servants' quarters, not usually shown.'[49] The Duke of Marlborough was incensed when he learned that John was making so free with his house. He was particularly annoyed to hear that John had taken some visitors out on to the roof – 'treadin' on me leads', as the Duke put it.[50] John was forbidden to go roof-climbing again.

The Duke was not popular with the Council staff, nor they with him.

He was an old beast [Lady Ormrod said]. He would stamp about in a Norfolk jacket. If he could find a complaint he made it. He used to come and say to me, 'Would you please stop your staff doing something-or-other?' – whatever he could think of. And I used to say, 'In what way is it inconveniencing you?' And he didn't like that. One day he said, 'It is nothing to do with you what I think about it. This is *mine* and you are here by courtesy of *me*.' And I longed to say – but I hadn't the courage – 'And you're getting damned well paid for it.' He was paid enough to put in central heating in his part of the Palace.

One of the troubles was, you had to go to the loo in the Palace. You had really almost to be introduced to the loo – it was in a room twice the size of this [a fair-sized drawing-room], and on the door was somebody-or-other's name. When you opened it, in the far distance you could see a loo, then you swept up the steps.

The Duke complained to John Betjeman that people were jumping out of my train and walking to the Palace to relieve themselves and were wearing the grass out. And Betjeman replied, 'But, surely, Your Grace, you are aware that it is not permitted to use the train lavatory when the carriages are stationary.'[51]

John's secretary was Diana Craig. One of his first acts at South Leigh had been to prowl around looking at the secretaries. 'He stole Diana from me,' Rosemary Pearce complained. Barbara Watson thought Diana Craig 'a luscious-looking girl, rather plump, lovely fair hair'.[52] John used often to disappear with Diana Craig for the afternoon. 'He took her off to lunch, and sometimes took her to Magdalen Chapel. I shouldn't think Diana Craig had been in a church since she was baptized – *if* she was baptized.'[53]

Diana Craig figures with another Council secretary, Daphne Dunlop, in the one Betjeman poem directly inspired by his spell at the British Council. Entitled 'A Romance', it was not published until *Uncollected Poems* (1982), but it was a comic fantasy about the twenty-first birthday ball of a girl called Carol on the Council staff. It ends:

> 'Two thousand pounds it cost me,'
>   Said the Captain to his mate,
> 'And there's our daughter Carol
>   And she hasn't made a date.
> I fear we made the guest-list
>   Far too wide and vague
> When we asked that cold Miss Dunlop
>   And that fast Diana Craig.'[54]

Most of the Council staff at Blenheim took their lunches in the British Restaurant in a converted garage in Woodstock village. The

British Restaurants (but for Churchill's flair for public relations they would have been known as 'communal feeding centres') were set up all over the country, in cinemas, museums, clubs and garages, and sometimes in new buildings. Subsidized by the Government, they served cheap meals, mainly to ensure that the wives and children of men who were abroad did not go hungry. John sometimes ate at the British Restaurant: it was there that Joan Harmston saw him quizzing the lorry driver about his religion. But the homely standard fare was not to his taste. Happily for him, the Marlborough Arms in Woodstock had been taken over by Max Ehrsam, the Swiss restaurateur who in John's undergraduate days had presided over the George in Oxford.[55] 'John and Jack [Yates] welcomed Max with open arms,' Michael Hooker said. 'He was always known as "Max". There was a Mrs Max, but Mrs Max tended to change from year to year. He cooked marvellously, particularly when he was drunk – and the drunker he was, the better he cooked. His black-market contacts must have been superb, because he kept a very good table there.'[56] Hooker added:

> Some of the lunches tended to go on . . . and I remember John coming back to Blenheim Palace and lying on his back on the floor of a corridor and waggling his arms and legs in the air like the man turned into a beetle in Kafka's *Metamorphosis*. We tried our best to get him to behave. He wasn't at all drunk, he was playing a part. As the registry clerks went by carrying files from one department to another, he would call out, 'Miss Smith, I'm as tight as an owl!' And she would say, 'Yes, Mr Betjeman,' and walk on . . .
>
> I remember coming back from the Marlborough Arms on one occasion – *more* than one occasion, we always tried to egg him on to repeat this, because once John got into his stride, nothing would stop him. Good company rather than good food or drink, I think, probably had this stimulating effect. He would give a one-man performance of the OUDS [Oxford University Dramatic Society]. He would stand behind some curtains in one of the state rooms of Blenheim Palace where we had our offices, and would produce pseudo-Shakespeare by the yard. Somebody had 'engendered ten thousand horse' or something, and he would play the part of the prompter getting it wrong and he would come on to the stage and somehow, with another hand, drag himself back off. There were mutterings behind the curtain, between two or three imaginary people. I've never laughed so much before or since. I remember lying on the floor there, thinking my ribs were going to crack.[57]

Like Jack Yates, but far less often, John sometimes went abroad on Council work. The film-maker Michael Powell, who had had dealings with him at the MoI, encountered him in Dublin in the early spring of 1946; Powell was there for the christening of his son Kevin, whose god-mother lived in Dublin.

I had promised to be back [in London] in a week [Powell wrote], but mean-while I had met John Betjeman, who was representing the British Council in Dublin's fair city, and using it, the Council, to further his own ends as a poet and *bon viveur*. He had put into my hands a book entitled *My Story, by Paddy the Cope, as told to Peadar O'Donnell*,[58] and nothing would satisfy me but I must go to Donegal where Paddy was King of Dungloe . . . I decided to ride there on horseback.[59]

John knew Peadar O'Donnell, who succeeded Sean O'Faolain as editor of *The Bell* that year. And the story of Paddy the Cope had special interest for him as John had worked for Sir Horace Plunkett, the apostle of Irish land reform and co-operative creameries, in 1929.[60] ('The Cope' stood for 'the co-operative'.) In the early 1900s, Paddy, born and bred in Dungloe, was a 'little peasant', in the grip of the 'gombeen men', middlemen who supplied seed, fertilizers and tools to smallholders. At that time, Paddy met 'Jesus Christ . . . in the form of a young man with a wispy beard, a knickerbocker suit and a bicycle'.[61] This was George Russell ('A.E.'), the friend of Plunkett and Yeats. He was touring Ireland and telling the peasants of their rights and how they should organize. Under his spell, Paddy had formed a co-operative and begun to buy from big farms, by-passing the rapacious gombeen men. Michael Powell saw the resulting conflict as a subject for 'another of those films which only I would want to make and which I certainly should have made'.[62] He did ride to Dungloe.[63] There he offered Paddy the Cope £500 for a ten-year option on his story 'and he danced with delight'.[64] He was paid; but Powell was already at work on one of his masterpieces, *Black Narcissus*; in 1947 he began shooting another, *The Red Shoes*, and Paddy's gritty story was forgotten.

Back at Blenheim, the Duke of Marlborough was agitating for the British Council to be cleared out of his palace and grounds, bag and baggage. He had taken to going round with a spiked stick, ostenta-tiously stabbing at litter.[65] Later that year his wish was granted and the books division moved back to London. But by that time John had found himself another job, as secretary of the Oxford Preservation Trust.* He left little mark on the Council;[66] but, as usual, he had made more friends than enemies. He kept in touch with some of the friends, including Joan Harmston, whose surname, he told her, was one of his

* See Chapter 20, 'Oxford Preservation Trust'.

favourite Lincolnshire stations. On 27 January 1950 he wrote to her
from his home in Farnborough:

> I would very much like to come and see the Jolly Girls in Grosvenor Square
> on one of my journeys to Paddington and it will have to be in the month
> of May when, as you know, we all get so skittish and our thoughts turn to
> Austin Reed. You sound happy . . . I look back on those old Council days
> with great pleasure.
>   Yours sincerely, affectionately, nostalgically and everlastingly,
>   John Betjeman, Art Letterer[67]

A LINCOLNSHIRE TALE

Lincolnshire is . . . singularly beautiful and . . . a separate country. I would like to see it with its own flag and needing passports to get in.

John Betjeman, speech at the inaugural meeting of the
Lincolnshire Association, 1963

For Jack Yates, working for the British Council at Oriel was a kind of homecoming. Born in 1905, the year before John, he had been an undergraduate at the college, where he was a friend of A.J.P. Taylor, the historian – 'my most treasured friend until his death', Taylor wrote in his memoirs.[1] In those days Yates affectedly used his second Christian name of Theodore, 'though there was always a tough Yorkshire Jack underneath', Taylor wrote, adding:

Theodore, whom Innes Stewart[2] used to refer to, I think a little enviously, as 'your silly friend', had elegance and culture without intellect. Indeed he was lucky to get a fourth class in his final examination. Theodore had cast himself as a distinguished elderly man. He walked with a silverheaded ebony cane and he did not walk much. He stayed in bed until midday, dined every evening at the George and sat up half the night drinking whisky. I suppose I first took up with him because his room was a refuge from my own. But we had many tastes in common. He loved driving a fast car and I shared mine with him when my father gave me one. He had a good taste in both wine and cigars which I also shared.[3]

John had also been a friend of Yates at Oxford. Both 'aesthetes', the two moved in the same circles, the OUDS, Pusey House and the 'Georgeoisie'.[4] Osbert Lancaster caricatured Yates as a yaffling figure in his *Cherwell* series 'Seen in the George'.

In his unpublished autobiography, Jack Yates remembered how he had met John in their undergraduate days: 'Eric Walter White[5] . . . asked me to lunch in his Victorian lodgings in John Street to meet a bright-eyed, pink-faced boy just up from Marlborough called John Betjeman.

SEEN IN THE GEORGE.

Mr. Th--d-r-y-t-s.

Caricature by Osbert Lancaster, Isis, *24 May 1928*

That one was obviously going to enjoy his time at Oxford – Benediction at Pusey House, Skindles' Hotel, Maidenhead,[6] and all.'[7] John was amused by the way Yates used one or other of the three surviving hansom cabs in Oxford to travel round the city. He egged him on to describe his schooldays at Radley[8] and to tell the latest stories about the eccentric Provost of Oriel, the Rev. Lancelot Ridley Phelps, who, like the hansom cabs, was a Victorian survival.[9] John's friends Miles Sargent and Freddie Hood, librarians at Pusey House, got Yates in as a lodger in his fourth year. Taylor remembered him at that time.

My friends were somewhat broken up. Theodore was living at Pusey House, an Anglo-Catholic establishment. He would have liked to go into the church and could not decide which one. There were family problems in the background. Theodore's grandfather, a wealthy wool-manufacturer, had been a devout Methodist. Theodore's father however had become an Anglican priest, whereupon most of the Yates fortune passed to Mansfield College, a Methodist seminary.[10] Theodore was minded to go over to Rome but not at the risk of losing what remained of the Yates heritage. He drifted for some ten years. When war came, Theodore decided that it had been caused partly by his sin in not becoming a Roman Catholic. He was duly, if belatedly, converted. His repentance may have been aided by the fact that his father had died a little while before.[11]

Writing in his autobiography of his British Council years, when he lodged with A.J.P. Taylor, by then Vice-President of Magdalen, at Holywell Mill, Yates is chiefly interested in describing the huge exhibition he organized in Barcelona in 1944, representing every kind of publishing from novels to works on penicillin. That was, Yates thought, 'the climacteric, the peak of the graph of my life'.[14] Alan Taylor comments, with his usual wry cynicism: 'His religious conversion brought its reward. Spain was a principal target for the British Council and the Fascist government would only accept British emissaries who were Roman Catholics. Who more suitable than Theodore, who in addition looked very Spanish though he spoke none?'[15] Yates's niece, the artist Gill Foot, agreed. 'Jack used to enjoy a cup of tea on the train. One time the waiter asked, "Would you like some cream in it, sir?" Jack said, "Just a bit." "It's a *drop*, sir, with liquids," the waiter said, tactfully correcting the foreigner he took Jack to be.'[16]

After the war Yates found the British Council uncongenial. John Betjeman had left and the Books Division had been turfed out of Blenheim. Yates deplored the way 'all the militarized boys were being demobbed and bringing their impersonal ways into civilian life'.[17] His enthusiasm was frowned on. In his view, the British Council 'grew more and more like that organization which C.S. Lewis invented. It was all ADMIN. I said to myself, like the woman in *Peter Grimes* who has to go to the pub for her drugs, "This is no place for me." '[18] He did not like his new offices in Grosvenor Square, where a 'Roosevelt memorial layout' had been opened. One day in 1948 Yates sat with his deputy Peter Goodwin 'in this antiseptic garden wondering how we could get out of this antiseptic Council'.[19] Goodwin said he and a friend were thinking of breeding bees in Tobago.[20] Yates had something more literary in mind.

Despite his Yorkshire forbears, Yates himself was a native of Lincolnshire: his father was Vicar of St Michael's, Louth. At fifteen he had witnessed the great Louth flood of 1920, when the River Lud burst its banks and roared through the town – the wall round the vicarage garden fell 'like a pack of cards' and a hen house with chickens stranded in it was washed past.[21] In 1948 Yates's mother, Emily, was still living in a large William and Mary house in Louth with one 'faithful' not much younger than herself. Yates was deeply devoted to her – 'I sometimes wonder whether the umbilical cord was ever severed,' he wrote[22] – and he looked for some means of returning to Louth to live with her. In the middle of the town was a musty eighteenth-century bookshop with a tall mahogany bow window. It was unheated and lit by flickering gas. Miss Goulding, who had inherited it from her father, had not been near it for four years before she died. It seemed to have a thriving newspaper and magazine business, but there was less custom for the books in the dank and dim rooms. 'Was this the answer? Should I? Could I shake the dust of London off my feet, look after my mother and revive Goulding's as a bookshop with enough profit to keep me going?'[23] He decided to take the risk.

Established 1788.   2C, *Mercer-Row, South,* _____194

Lincs.

Dr. to J. W. GOULDING & SON,
(J. T. YATES)
Printers, Booksellers, Stationers and Bookbinders,
DEALERS IN PAPER HANGINGS.

HARROD'S CIRCULATING LIBRARY   SCHOOLS SUPPLIED WITH ALL REQUISITES

Goulding's Bookshop did not have much competition. Yates liked to recount how he had gone into the town's only other bookshop and asked if they had Pepys's Diary. 'No, only Lett's,' was the reply.[24] There had been a bookshop on the site of Yates's shop for over 200 years – long before the Gouldings took it over. At the top of the building was a large printing press which caused the floor to buckle. Yates installed good heating and lighting. He used the shop, Gill Foot thought, mainly 'to meet good friends and read good books';[25] but he had some lucrative contacts with schools, especially Roman Catholic ones such as Ampleforth. (He was a friend of the future Cardinal Hume, then a master there.)[26] He made money on school prizes.

John had already been to stay with Yates and his mother in The Mansion in their British Council days.[27] It was a handsome but cold house, and all visitors were given 'jimmies' – 'shawls which seemed to have been knitted with punt-poles', recalls Yates's Louth neighbour and friend Dr David Crook.[28] The jimmies were named after a friend of Yates, Dr Jimmy Thierens, who lived in Ramsgate. 'Everybody wore a jimmy in the evening,' Gill Foot said, '– but Dr Thierens wore one all the time, and wrapped himself up completely, like a mummy.'[29]

When Yates moved back to Louth, John became a regular guest. 'He stayed about twice a year,' Gill Foot remembered.[30]

John was predisposed towards Lincolnshire. His mother's family, the Dawsons, were Lincolnshire folk. 'My grandfather', he told the Lincolnshire Association in 1963, 'was a Spalding builder who went bankrupt.'[31] John admired the Lincolnshire poet Jean Ingelow, to whom Tennyson exclaimed, 'Miss Ingelow, I do declare you do the trick better than I do.'[32] And Lincolnshire was the county where Tennyson himself had lived.

In the late 1920s John stayed in Kirkby-on-Bain with Canon Felix Blakiston, the father of his friend Noel Blakiston, and was 'first excited by the county'. With comic variation, the place-name was absorbed into his poem of 1945, 'A Lincolnshire Tale' –

> Kirkby with Muckby-cum-Sparrowby-cum-Spinx
> Is down a long lane in the county of Lincs.[33]

John liked the place-names of Lincolnshire – Clixby, Claxby, Claxby Pluckacre, Ashby Puerorum, Bag Enderby. Gill Foot remembered his glee on encountering a signpost on the Spilsby–Boston road which read 'TO MAVIS ENDERBY AND OLD BOLINGBROKE'. Somebody had scrawled underneath '– the gift of a son'.[34]

He loved Lincolnshire because, he said later, in 1963, 'it is so beautiful, so unobtrusively beautiful, and from the landsman's point of view it is saved from much hideous destruction by the Humber stopping things going straight through'.[35] Little had changed in almost twenty years.

I shall not forget yesterday morning, Sunday morning. I stayed with my friend Jack Yates in Westgate, Louth. It was a lovely clear morning, pale sharp early winter, late autumn sun. My panelled bedroom with thick, 1680-ish panes of glass, panelled rooms throughout, little garden opposite, walled garden behind. My room looked down the curve of Westgate, and I could see in that sharp winter morning sunlight the different browns and reds and pale biscuit of the brick which is such a feature of Lincs; dark red for the seventeenth century and rather brighter reds for later periods until you get the yellow brick of the Regency. And I saw the curve of these houses, each with its garden and a little bit of lawn and a shadowy cedar, arching round past the winter trees and that spire of Louth which was sharp in the winter sunlight, superbly proportioned. You will notice always in Lincolnshire, in village and town, where there is an old church tower and a road leading to it, the road curves round so that you see two sides of the tower.[36]

John did not care to join Yates for his early-morning run, in pyjamas, along the sea-front at Humberstone.[37] After breakfast, the two men would set out for a day of exploration, often accompanied by Emily Yates. Sometimes they went by car, sometimes by bus. The old bus services had an Emett atmosphere about them[38] and carried, besides the passengers, chickens, ducklings, piglets and sacks of produce. The places associated with Tennyson were visited, from Parker's in Mercer Row, Louth, where his *Poems of Two Brothers* was first printed, to Somersby Rectory where he grew up, and Harringdon Hall, whose garden was the one into which 'Maud' was invited to come.[39] Another favourite trip was to Woodhall Spa, described by John as 'that unexpected Bournemouth-like settlement in the middle of Lincolnshire'.[40] The place is also mentioned in his poem 'House of Rest'.[41]

Whether or not she was to be of the party, Emily Yates prepared a picnic hamper for each expedition, with bottles of wine as well as food. Jack Yates usually found a brook in which to cool the white wines, tying strings round the bottle necks. A Yates picnic was not a casual affair. A linen tablecloth was spread out, with napkins in ivory rings. The wine was drunk from stemmed glasses, not plastic beakers or paper cups. At home in the evenings, swaddled in their jimmies, the two men and Emily would play a card game called Mikiuno in front of the fire with its surround of blue-and-white Dutch tiles. Or sometimes Yates would take John along to the Louth Naturalists', Antiquarian and Literary Society of which he was for a time president, ('the Gnats and Ants', as he called it).[42]

There was plenty to interest John in Louth itself. As early as 1935 he had written an article in praise of its Methodist chapel. Writing on 'The Buildings of Louth' in *Lincolnshire Life* (Autumn 1962) Jack Yates directed attention to the Mansion House (formerly the Assembly Rooms) in Upgate, especially 'the fine ceiling in the further chamber into which have been screwed a number of particularly vicious pig-trough lights'. He added:

> Finally, there is the Betjemanesque frolic which can be made in the town. James Fowler . . . provides the polychromatic church of St Michael and All Angels, mysteriously dark, with delicate arcading like a Fra Angelico Annunciation, screening the Lady Chapel . . .
>
> 'Now take me,' said the poet, 'to something that looks like Beaconsfield.' So I took him to St Mary's Lane and it did. As you go outwards from any good market town it tends to look the same as anywhere else in the United Kingdom, it is only in its heart that you will find its individuality . . .

The architect James Fowler of Louth was in fact a pet abomination of both Yates and John. He had over-restored many old churches in north Lincolnshire, with undistinguished windows, encaustic tiles and alabaster reredoses. John mentioned Fowler in his poem 'Norfolk':

> The church is just the same, though now I know
> Fowler of Louth restored it.[43]

Happily, there were many Lincolnshire churches that had not been 'Fowlerized'. On 18 June 1946 John wrote to his friend George Barnes: 'Doing a church crawl in the marsh here and in the wolds. This county is an unspoilt Sussex only with better churches. Keep it dark.'[44] Two of the churches John visited with Jack Yates inspired poems, 'A Lincolnshire Tale' (1945) and 'A Lincolnshire Church' (1948). In the collection of John's *Church Poems* which John Murray issued in 1981 with illustrations by John Piper, these two poems were respectively illustrated with drawings of Goltho Church and Horsington Church. As John Betjeman was still living when that book appeared, it might wrongly be assumed that these juxtapositions of poem and drawing had his blessing, and that the churches described in the poems are to be identified with those in Piper's fine sketches.[45]

In fact 'A Lincolnshire Tale' is clearly a Gothick fantasia inspired by various of John's memories and observations. It cannot be related to one church only. In the opening lines John has in mind Canon Blakiston's Kirkby-on-Bain. ('Sparrowby' was a tease for John Sparrow.) Yet there is another Lincolnshire church which, more than any other, tallies with that in the poem: Langton-by-Spilsby (also known as Langton-by-Partney), a small Georgian building about three miles north-nor'west of Tennyson's Somersby.[46] It serves the village where Dr Johnson's scholarly friend and butt Bennet Langton lived. Johnson visited him there and worshipped in the church.[47]

Whereas 'A Lincolnshire Tale' blends different churches, the slightly later poem 'A Lincolnshire Church' is about one only, and that readily identifiable. The church John had in mind was St Margaret's, Huttoft, about four miles south of Sutton-on-Sea. The lines which enable us to identify the church with certainty are these:

> There in the lighted East
> He stood in that lowering sunlight,
> An Indian Christian priest.
> And why he was here in Lincolnshire

> I neither asked nor knew,
> Nor whether his flock was many
> Nor whether his flock was few
> I thought of the heaving waters
> That bore him from sun glare harsh
> Of some Indian Anglican Mission
> To this green enormous marsh . . .[48]

The Vicar of Huttoft from 1943 to 1959 was the Rev. Theophilus Caleb, an Indian.[49] He died in a tractor accident in November 1959 and was buried in Huttoft graveyard.[50]

Three times in the poem John writes of the marsh,[51] and that certainly is the dominant and seemingly endless feature of the landscape in which Huttoft lies. In his phrase 'the green enormous marsh', he may have been echoing, consciously or unconsciously, 'the waste enormous marsh' in these lines from Tennyson's 'Ode to Memory' –

> A sand-built ridge
> Of heaped hills that mound the sea
> O'er blown with murmurs harsh
> Or even a lowly cottage whence we see
> stretched wide and wild the waste
> enormous marsh.

Henry Thorold, the squire of Marston, Lincolnshire,[52] who later went on many church crawls with Jack Yates and John, said that John's Huttoft poem was sent to Emily Yates as a bread-and-butter letter, thanking her for her hospitality.[53] Thorold was as well known a Lincolnshire character as Jack Yates, and the two had much in common – both bachelors devoted to their mothers, both deeply religious (though Thorold was in Anglican orders), both lovers of good architecture and of good food and drink. The Thorolds had been at Marston since 1372. Marston Hall, a sixteenth-century building of Ancaster stone, was 'first base' for many of the Betjeman–Yates–Thorold expeditions.

John and Yates remained friends well beyond the 1940s. When, in 1960, Jack Yates had the first of three heart attacks and gave up his bookshop, John, who always moved swiftly to help friends in distress, said to Henry Thorold, 'Dear boy, our friend Jack is a bit bored, I'm afraid, now that he hasn't got the bookshop. I was thinking, we really do need a Shell Guide to dear old Lincolnshire and I was wondering if you'd like to do it together.' He added: 'Of course, Jack'll do all the work, and . . . you can have some jollies round together.' John then went to Yates and said, 'I say, old man, I've just been talking to Henry and I think that you and he ought to do a Shell Guide to Lincolnshire together, because after all we do need one. He'll do all the work, of course, because you don't want to be overdoing things now with your heart. But you could have some expeditions together, and I thought you might enjoy it.'

As John's career took off, Yates's foundered, with an almost exact counterpoise, as if they were at either end of a seesaw. Yates became a local politician and was elected to the Lincolnshire County Council as a very right-wing Independent. (From 1969 to 1974 the Conservative MP for Louth was the young Jeffrey Archer, the future novelist, peer and convict.) Yates was harried and hounded by the Labour Party, which eventually brought him down with accusations of corruption.[54] He was hard hit by the death of his adored mother at the age of ninety-seven. He gave up the bookshop, but was knocked back again when Ted Knight, a handsome young man to whom he had entrusted it, disappeared – 'did a bunk', as Thorold put it.[55] John, who stayed with Yates soon after Knight absconded, sympathized, aware that his friend's infatuation with Knight had caused what business sense he ever had to fly out of the bow window of Goulding's; but, strapped for cash himself, there was little he could do to help. Yates died in 1971, the year John became Poet Laureate. John attended the thronged funeral service in Louth. Gill Foot commissioned the letterer Philip Pape to engrave these words on the gravestone:

> He was a devoted son,
> a scholarly defender of
> beauty, an understanding
> ally of youth, a staunch
> friend, a bon viveur, and a
> believer in the love of God.[56]

Years later, John wrote to Thorold: 'My dear Henry, last week I took up your Lincolnshire Guide, thinking of you and our late friend Jack and read it as though it were a thriller. Such it proved to be. It is funnier and succincter than any Shell guide. Norton Disney is the funniest entry I know.'[57]

OXFORD PRESERVATION TRUST

Christ Church and Magdalen and, in a lesser degree, most of the other colleges of Oxford, were large land-owners, according to Kelly's Directory for 1887, in just the districts which have been 'developed' in the most merciless way round Oxford since then.

Now these colleges are paying for the past stupidity by subscribing to the Oxford Preservation Trust. This Trust was founded in 1926 to compete with the jerry-builder. Anyone can see that it was founded sixty years too late.

John Betjeman, *An Oxford University Chest*, London 1938[1]

Between 1946 and 1948 John was secretary of the Oxford Preservation Trust; but on this episode in his history there is a puzzling lacuna in the printed records of his life. He omitted any mention of it from his *Who's Who* entry. No allusion to it appeared in any of the obituaries, even that in the *Oxford Times*. He seems not to have spoken of it to either of his early biographers, Derek Stanford or Patrick Taylor-Martin. A natural place for him to have recalled it would have been in his contribution, 'A Preservationist's Progress', to *The Future of the Past*, edited by Jane Fawcett in 1976: but still there is not even a glancing reference. It was as if John had taken to heart the advice of Walter Pater to Oscar Wilde. When Wilde was an Oxford undergraduate, he complained, 'There seems to be a conspiracy of silence about my work.' Pater murmured: 'Perhaps you should join it, Mr Wilde.'

John was happy enough to be offered the job in 1946. The pay seemed good: £300 a year for a minimum of one day's work a week; he was allowed to continue reviewing for the *Daily Herald*. His office was in one of the most historic rooms in the city, the Painted Room in the Cornmarket, part of the old Crown Tavern where Shakespeare was alleged to have slept. John was allowed to recruit Diana Craig, his British Council secretary, as assistant secretary of the Trust. He liked writing letters on the Trust's impressive stationery, printed with a

representation of the OPT's official seal, not unlike that of a medieval abbot. It was a job for which he was well cast. He had known Oxford since his prep-school days in the Great War, and was nothing if not a preservationist.

The Oxford Preservation Trust had been founded in 1926 by Sir Michael Sadler,[2] Master of University College, and others who wanted to preserve the old Oxford and to ensure that any new building was in keeping with the old. In particular, they were alarmed at industrial encroachment on the outskirts of Oxford by the Cowley motor works of Lord Nuffield – 'William Morris the Second', as John ironically called him in *An Oxford University Chest*.[3] Industrialization was leading to a rapid increase in the population which had to be housed. Sadler summarized the Trust's aims in a poetical and tactful manifesto:

> Oxford is growing. Its growth may be guided but should not be grudged ... The beauty of Oxford is one of the treasures of the world. Within her borders some things must be kept at any cost untouched ... Colleges may justly be called upon to count the conservation of the city's beauty as in itself a profit to the education for which they are trustees.[4]

Sadler had died in 1943, and others of the original Trustees, including the sub-Stracheyesque historian Philip Guedalla, had resigned. Among the most influential of the Trustees in 1946 were Lionel Curtis, the Rev. J.M. Thompson and H.S. Goodhart-Rendel. John was on good terms with all three. Curtis, who had fought in the Boer War, had become acting town clerk of Johannesburg and was now a fellow of All Souls.[5] John knew him through his Magdalen friend Lionel Perry.[6] Perry's father and Curtis had both been members of Lord Milner's 'Kindergarten';[7] Lionel Perry had been named after Curtis, who was his godfather. A further link between Curtis and John was John

Sparrow of All Souls. It was he who suggested to Curtis that John would make a good secretary for the OPT.[8]

Lionel Perry took John to meet Curtis at the old man's thatched house in the Oxfordshire village of Kidlington, where Curtis, as A.L. Rowse recalled, 'paddled his canoe, reared his ducks, planted his willow plantation, cut up his timber, reconstructed the boy-scouting out-of-door life he had known in his South African years – in the intervals of vaticinating about the British Commonwealth, writing such works as *Civitas Dei* and regurgitating blueprints for the universe.'[9] John made a good impression. 'He and my godfather were utterly different people,' Perry said, 'but my godfather was charmable, and John knew how to charm.'[10] John was already a friend of J.M. Thompson, his favourite don at Magdalen.[11] Thompson was a key figure in the Trust, with the title 'Convener'. The architect Goodhart-Rendel John had known and praised in his days on *The Architectural Review*.[12]

In the early 1940s the English Speaking Union occupied the Painted Room offices, and the Union's secretary, Helen FitzRandolph, also acted as secretary of the OPT.[13] But in December 1945 the Union's lease of the premises was due to end and Miss FitzRandolph would cease to work for the Trust. A new, permanent, secretary was needed who would do as much as possible of the work previously done by the convener and the Oxford secretary, and in due course also that of the treasurer and the land agent of the Trust. This work included the usual routines of administration: arranging meetings, keeping minutes, circulating acta and agenda, keeping archives and carrying on correspondence. It also involved cultivating good relations with the City Council, County Council, the Council for the Preservation of Rural England and other local and national bodies. On top of that, the Trustees felt it should be the secretary's duty to increase the Trust's income and to keep them informed of opportunities for extending their work in Oxford and its neighbourhood. All this they thought might be done part-time in the first instance, but the secretary should 'endeavour so to extend the membership and activities of the Trust as to make his post a whole-time one'.

John was duly interviewed and at a meeting of the Trustees in Lionel Curtis's All Souls rooms on 28 April 1946 it was agreed unanimously that he be appointed, the Trust to bear as well the cost of an assistant secretary, who would also act as caretaker of the Painted Room. It was open to the public most days. Combined admission receipts and postcard sales for the previous year amounted to £400. The position would be reviewed at the end of the first year, when it was hoped that an increase in the Trust's revenue would enable it to raise John's salary: payment by results.[14]

The next day, Thompson wrote to him:

Dear Betjeman,
At yesterday's meeting all went as merrily as a marriage bell. I read your letter. It was at once said by people like Sir Arthur Salter [Independent MP for Oxford] and [A.B.] Emden that we ought not to tie you down by strict rules; & in short you were approved Secretary on your own terms . . . I needn't say how pleased I am it has ended so.[15]

There was just time for Thompson to squeeze a crowing mention of John's appointment into the Trust's printed annual report.

The Trust counts itself fortunate to have been able to secure . . . a man already distinguished as a writer about architecture and English city life, in close touch with other societies most akin to the Trust, and above all a devoted student and admirer of Oxford. Mr John Betjeman, an old Magdalen man, comes to the work of the Trust not only with these qualifications, but with considerable experience of Government work during the war . . . We look forward with confidence to the lively and intelligent direction he is sure to give to the work of the Trust.[16]

Diana Craig and John moved into the Painted Room and the adjoining office in September and were given £100 to spend on essential office furniture.[17] Even at Blenheim, John had not had an office so splendidly appointed. The Painted Room was on the second floor of No.3 Cornmarket Street, above a J. Lyons restaurant. The ground floor had formerly been occupied by Hookham's, a gentleman's outfitters.[18] The building behind the shop front had been part of the Crown Tavern kept between 1564 and 1581 by John Davenant, the father of the dramatist and Poet Laureate Sir William Davenant to whom Shakespeare 'stood godfather' in Oxford.[19] In 1934 E.W. Attwood, who owned Hookham's, stripped away seventeenth-century panelling in the upper rooms and revealed remarkable Tudor wall-paintings. Against a rich orange-scarlet background, probably of red ochre mined on Shotover Hill, were painted stylized flowers and fruit – white Canterbury bells, windflowers, roses, passion flowers and grapes. The materials used for colouring were lime, charcoal and ochre; the fixative, beer. Over the fireplace was painted the Christian monogram IHS and around the room ran a set of pious verse exhortations known as 'the Girdle of Holiness'.[20]

John Aubrey tells how Shakespeare 'was wont to go into Oxfordshire once a year and did in his journey lye at this house in Oxon, where he was exceedingly respected'.[21] It became settled belief

that the Painted Room was the poet's bedroom. By the time of John's
appointment, a panelled screen mounted on rollers had been set in
front of the floral wall. He would draw it back with a flourish to surprise visitors. Osbert Lancaster liked the paintings but said he thought
the rooms were rather dark. 'What was good enough for Shakespeare
is good enough for me,' John said.[22]

John attended his first meeting of the Trustees informally on 26
May 1946 in Curtis's rooms at All Souls, though his appointment was
from 16 September and he did not begin taking the minutes (in un-
usually legible handwriting) until October.[23] E.W. Attwood, the man
who had discovered the murals in the Painted Room and never let
anyone forget it, was one of the Trustees present. John was also introduced to Lord Macclesfield, Lord Esher (shortly to be replaced as a
Trustee by his son, Lionel Brett), H.V. Ferguson whose company
owned the *Oxford Mail* and the *Oxford Times*, Sir Arthur Salter, Sir
Arthur Curgenven who had been a judge in Madras, and Alderman
Sam Smith, a dwarfish man who had worked his way up from a mill
job in Bradford to teaching at Ruskin College for working men and
serving on Oxford's City Council.[24]

The minutes of the previous meeting, which were read out and
signed, gave John an immediate insight into the nature of the Trust's
work and its manner of working:

> 27 *St Giles*. St John's [College] wished to pull down this building and the
> Town Planning Committee had consented, without consulting the Trust.
> The committee recommended that, as this house is amongst those build-
> ings scheduled by the Trust as worthy of preservation, and this fact was
> known to the Planning Committee, the attention of the Town Clerk be
> called to this break-down in a valuable custom of cooperation.[25]

That, John realized, was the Trust's courtly way of saying: 'How dare
you!' It was resolved that letters were to be sent both to the Town Clerk
and to the President of St John's.[26] The courtly approach sometimes
worked: in subsequent minutes, John was able to record that, while the
interior of 27 St Giles was 'beyond repair', St John's had agreed to
retain the façade and roof.[27]

The Trust was, however, an impotent body. It had no statutory
powers. Too often it was reduced to asking plaintively, 'Can something
be done . . . ?' Much depended, as those who appointed John understood, on diplomatic relations between the secretary and the Town
Clerk and other officials. As Lionel Perry and almost everybody else
observed, John knew how to charm; but there was another aspect to
his character which sometimes militated against his power to do so. If

he was involved, as often happened with the OPT, in a business dispute over land or buildings, he was inclined to interpret the opposing point of view – even when it was expressed with no animosity – as hostile criticism directed at himself. Then he bridled and spat back. This trait was aggravated as John's work-load became heavier.

In the first months there was little sign of bile, though there was a touch of it in the minute he wrote on 'Cherwell Dredging' on 29 October 1946: 'The Secretary was instructed to write to Sir Ralph Glyn [an acquaintance of John's from Uffington days][28] asking him, as a Thames conservator . . . whether dredging operations necessitated the felling of trees on river banks, as had been done on the New Cut above Gosford, and whether it was beyond the wit of man to devise a dredging plant which did not cause the destruction of trees.'[29] The minute immediately after the 'Cherwell Dredging' item reads:

> BINSEY POPLARS. The Secretary to arrange with the Town Clerk for Mr Emden, Mr Sanzen-Baker and himself to visit these sites with the Parks Superintendent.[30]

Though John was never an enthusiastic Hopkinsian, he knew Hopkins's poem 'Binsey Poplars'; and the Town Clerk's name was Harry Plowman – phonetically, at least, the title of another Hopkins poem.

In every job he held, John needed a *bête noire*, somebody on whom he could vent the frustration he felt at not being free to write poetry. Harry Plowman was the official with whom he had most dealings while with the OPT. The Town Clerk was, by all accounts, a likeable and intelligent man, but John seems to have taken against him and his tough, no-nonsense memos. Perhaps as John's duties increased, Plowman made it too obvious that he thought he was getting out of his depth, and teased him a little about his inefficiency. There can be small doubt that John had Plowman in his sights when he wrote his poem 'The Town Clerk's Views', published in *Selected Poems* in 1948, a few months after he left the Trust. The poem begins:

> 'Yes, the Town Clerk will see you.' In I went.
> He was, like all Town Clerks, from north of Trent;
> A man with bye-laws busy in his head
> Whose Mayor and Council followed where he led.
> His most capacious brain will make us cower,
> His only weakness is a lust for power –
> And that is not a weakness, people think,
> When unaccompanied by bribes or drink.

> So let us hear this cool careerist tell
> His plans to turn our country into hell.[31]

Later in the poem are the pointed lines

> Oxford is growing up to date at last,
> Cambridge, I fear, is living in the past.[32]

John Edwards, who was Plowman's deputy at the town hall, remembers the Town Clerk as 'a consummate advocate and diplomat, coupling this with great charm, imperturbability, and a sense of humour'.[33] Loyal to Plowman's memory, Edwards does not think he would have been capable of formulating the philistine opinions with which he is credited throughout the poem. 'Moreover, on no occasion would there be any question of HP sending for the Secretary of the OPT to hold forth about general national planning.'[34] But Edwards admits that when John arrived at the Town Clerk's department, he might well have been invited in with some such formula as the first line. 'In view of line 2, it should be mentioned that HP was a Londoner, but as he had been Town Clerk of Burnley, Lancs, before coming to Oxford, JB might be pardoned for thinking he was a northerner. As to line 4, I can quite imagine that anyone not familiar with Council procedure might be given this impression at a meeting of the City Council, whereas all HP would be trying to do from time to time would be to see that the Council did not stray too far from its own standing orders.'[35] John is unlikely to have had regular dealings with any other town clerks. It is probably safe to conclude that Plowman is being 'got at' in what was largely a work of John's imagination, a generalized onslaught on the town planners.

John's job was no sinecure; he put effort into it and he got results. Many of his tasks were on a small scale, such as finding out who had responsibility for a particular towpath, or answering such letters as that which arrived from P.C. Henderson of Magdalen on 9 October 1947: 'Dear Sir, Will you use your Influence, Good Offices etc etc to get removed from the front of the Angel Café a monstrous black and white chef who advertises "cheap 'students'' meals" in pasteboard?'[36] More significant campaigns in which John took part were over the gasworks; the future of Oxford Prison; the fate of the Clarendon Hotel in the Cornmarket; the Army's requisitioning of land at Shotover; and the ownership of South Park, Headington. Both the OPT and the Council opposed the then Gas Company's proposal to double the size of its works by an additional 'retort house' only half a mile from Carfax, near Folly Bridge. It may have been through

John's influence – or even from his hand – that an editorial on the subject appeared in *The Architect and Building News* in June 1947:

> As bizarre a relic of the Age of Nonplanning as exists anywhere is the gasworks at Oxford. The manner in which it smites the eye of the eager visitor, craning from the train window for his first view of the city of his dreams, is something altogether unique. So many romantic voyagers have experienced its devastating *frisson* . . . that it has long ranked as the most celebrated eyesore in the country. Naturally therefore, a proposal for an immediate and large extension of the works on the present site is causing considerable local uproar.

John Edwards recalls: 'There were endless inquiries both local and before committees of Parliament. The opposition to the gasworks extension was eventually successful, and must have saved a good many red faces when natural gas was discovered shortly afterwards.'[37]

With Oxford Prison there were two difficulties: to get the Home Office to make up its mind whether it intended to vacate it by 1950; and, if so, to what use the building should be put. John favoured the idea of an Oxford City Museum, which was indeed eventually established in the former prison.[38] Over the Clarendon Hotel, the OPT was less successful. One of John's angriest minutes (meeting of 19 January 1947) reads: '*Clarendon Hotel*. The Vice-Chancellor read an illiterate & evasive letter he had received from the Board of Trade. The Mayor and Alderman Smith agreed to report the City's views as to the future use of this building at the next meeting.'[39] The local inquiry as to whether the hotel might be demolished to build a new Woolworth's store was not held until after John had resigned; Harold Macmillan, who in 1961 was to be the hammer of the Euston Arch, upheld Woolworth's case and the hotel was pulled down, together with a fine Victorian Gothic shop in the Cornmarket with a Dickensian name, Grimbly Hughes.

What little power the Trust had sprang from its owning valuable stretches of land in Oxfordshire which had been acquired by gift, bequest or purchase. In all, it owned about 500 acres in Oxfordshire. It was proud of having saved, in the 1930s, the fields on Boar's Hill which still command one of the best views of the city. To the west, near the Trout Inn at Godstow, it had thirteen acres. Above the Trout Inn are Wytham Hill and the Wytham Woods mentioned in Arnold's *The Scholar Gypsy*. The Trust had joined with the University in acquiring the Wytham estate on generous terms from the owner, Colonel R.W. ffennell (the former Rand magnate Schumacher, whom Lionel Curtis had known since his South African days).[40] The Trust held 181 acres in Shotover, an amphitheatre of hills and downs, and kept a supervising eye on a further 254 acres owned by the City and University. During the war Shotover was requisitioned for military training. 'The hillside was sadly hacked about by tanks and guns,' wrote Sam Smith.[41] Lord Simon was particularly exercised about the state of Shotover. He told a meeting of the Trust in 1948:

> This stretch of unspoilt country which lies at our very doors – which . . . is as essential to Oxford as Hampstead Heath is to London, and which, moreover, was acquired in perpetuity for the protection of Oxford by the exertions of the Oxford Preservation Trust – is threatened with the continuance after the war of military use which . . . is calculated to turn this beautiful piece of natural scenery into a local Aldershot.[42]

To polite laughter, Simon joked that the ancient name of Shotover, 'found with a different spelling in Domesday Book', did not imply that the land was meant to be shot over. He added:

> Where is the horror at the destruction of beauty which even our fighting departments should feel? In the days of the Blitz, Hitler never let a bomb fall on Oxford: I do not say that this was a reaction due to his aesthetic sensibility. But it may well have been due to the fact that even he realised that to destroy the beauties of Oxford would bring upon him in double measure the execration of the world.[43]

John was in a position to do something about Shotover. In 1946 his old friend Frank Pakenham (by now Lord Pakenham) had become Parliamentary Under Secretary at the War Office. John arranged for him to meet the Trustees. It was agreed that damaging military manoeuvres at Shotover would cease, and that the land would become a public camping site. Though this decision was not implemented until John had left the Trust, he and the Old Boy Network deserve the credit for it.[44]

The affair of South Park was an example of the arm-wrestling which sometimes took place between the OPT and the Council. The Trust's fifty-four acres of South Park lay east of the city centre, not far from Magdalen Bridge. In 1932 the estate had been bought by the Trust from Emily Alicia Morrell, one of the Oxford brewing family and a kinswoman of Lady Ottoline Morrell's husband Philip. During the war the Trust managed to fend off the requisitioning of part of the land for Food Ministry offices. In 1944 the Trust offered to sell it to Oxford Council for the price it had paid for it, but Harry Plowman wrote to J.M. Thompson to explain that, much as the offer was appreciated, the Council could not accept it because of the wartime prohibition imposed by the Treasury on capital expenditure by local authorities. Plowman said he hoped the Trust would keep the matter open until the Council's normal powers were restored.[45]

In 1947 the Trustees instructed John to raise the matter again with the Town Clerk. On 2 May he wrote Plowman a very businesslike letter, offering to sell the Park to the City 'at the same figure that the Trustees paid for it, plus a rate of interest from the date of its purchase by them'.[46] The Trustees had paid £23,155 for the Park in 1932 and had spent £353 on improvements. In an internal memo of 13 May, the Council noted sharply that the Trust's offer had changed.[47] It is doubtful that it was any financial acumen of John's that had prompted these new terms; but the Town Clerk may have thought that it was – after all, the main change in the Council since 1944 had been John's arrival as secretary.

And there was another potential source of friction. John, as usual on chummy terms with the local press, had jumped the gun by feeding them with stories about the proposed sale. Plowman irritably commented: 'Although there has been a good deal of Press publicity . . . the matter has indeed not even reached the stage where one can say with any certainty that the Council will buy the property at all.'[48] Writing to John on 15 May 1947, he asked whether he fully realized 'that if 5% simple interest from 1932 were charged the total payment in respect of interest alone would amount to over £17,000?' It was not, he pointed out, as if the Trust had purchased the property at the request of the Council.[49]

On 29 May John wrote to tell Plowman that he was unable to find in the records 'any copy of the Rev. J.M. Thompson's letter to you about South Park, dated 23rd December 1944'. He said he would be most grateful if Plowman would be kind enough to send him a copy to show the Trustees.[50] Plowman drily replied the next day: 'I think that in the circumstances it would be as well if I were to let you have copies not only of [that letter of the Rev. Mr. Thompson] but also of his letter of 11th December of that year, my reply of the 6th February, 1945 and Mr Thompson's final letter of 24th February, 1945, which had the effect of closing the matter for the time being.'[51] Perhaps Plowman was just being helpful, but somebody as sensitive to nuances as John might have felt that he was being teased about the muddle of his filing system. Was Plowman implying that he was, in the language of the day, 'running a Fred Karno's Circus'?

Perhaps feeling that he could smooth things over better in person than in niggling memos, John suggested that he and a Trust deputation should wait on Plowman and the Parks and Cemeteries Committee of the Council.[52] Plowman riposted that since the next meeting of the Committee was rather far off, it might be better for John to put the Trust's views in writing.[53] John disagreed.[54] The matter dragged on. Eventually the Trust climbed down and offered the property for £20,000.[55]

The Council, however, was still unhappy with the price. In November 1949, after John had left, the Trust began to feel that it was losing public sympathy by holding on to the Park. Sam Smith, who succeeded John as secretary, suggested that the Trust should make a gift of the Park to the City: what it lost in revenues it would gain in prestige. He wrote: 'Regrettable as it may be, few Oxford citizens give due credit to the Trust for having preserved the Park as an open space. A favourite topic of Alderman Smewin when Mayor (and since) has been the disservice of retention of the Park from public use . . .'[56] (John Edwards recalls Smewin as 'a signalman on the Great Western Railway and a Socialist of the old school whose favourite slogan was, "The University is driving the workers out of the City." ')[57]

In 1951 Sam Smith's advice was finally followed and the deeds of South Park were handed over to the Mayor by the University's Chancellor, Lord Halifax, on behalf of the Trust at a ceremony in the Mayor's Parlour. The Morrell Trustees imposed a few restrictions, including the picturesque condition that the lower end of the Park should be 'kept free of all structures and buildings so as to preserve what was known as the "Turner View" of Oxford, being an aspect of a picture by J.M.W. Turner from the south side of Headington Hill looking across the City'.[58] One distant result of the Council's purchase of the Headington estates was their lease of Headington Hill House, in the 1970s, to the infamous publisher Robert Maxwell at a pepper-corn rent.

John's two years at the OPT were a critical period in the history of British town planning. The Council was required to prepare a devel-opment plan under the Town and Planning Act 1947, and to that end commissioned Dr Thomas Sharp to advise it. Five years older than John, Sharp had been educated at Council schools and had worked for twenty years in local government before becoming a town and country planning lecturer at Durham University. While preparing his report for the Oxford Council, he rented from them the floor below the Painted Room. Against all the prognostics, the pugnacious Sharp got on well with John, often joining him and Diana Craig for tea. John was to describe him as 'our most sensitive and controversial town planner'.[59] Most of those who had dealings with Sharp found him considerably more controversial than sensitive. John Edwards recalled: 'Through his inability to compromise, and his bluntness in argument and inability to suffer fools gladly, he was unable to fit in with the process of planning by committee. Perhaps it was TS's misfortune to have been born too late; the age which produced Brunel and Telford might have found him better employment than our own was able to.'[60]

Sharp's report on the city, *Oxford Replanned*, was published as a book in 1948, before John left the Trust. The lavish avant-garde production showed that post-war paper shortages and austerities were coming to an end. It was part of John's job to canvass opinions about the report from the Trustees, college heads and others who had, or thought they had, a right to be consulted. On 21 January 1948 he wrote to J.M. Richards at the Architectural Press:

Dear Boy

For goodness sake help me, and I repeat, for goodness sake help me.

Here am I Secretary of the Oxford Preservation Trust & asked to obtain 27 copies of Thomas Sharp's Plan for Oxford on the day of publication, for distribution to each of my Trustees. Oh for God's sake get them for me. I will send you a cheque so soon as you tell me you can get them. Ask old AED, ask the Regans, ask Tatters, ask Mr Pierson, ask Obscurity himself, but get them for me.

Thomas Sharp has moved into this old-world building with me, and very happy we are together . . .[61]

Sharp's main recommendations were that the Morris and Pressed Steel factories be moved from Oxford as soon as possible to 'a more favourable location'; that the High should be by-passed by a 'Merton Mall' (as opposed to a road through Christ Church Meadows); and that the city should expand the shopping area near Carfax, rather than develop embryonic areas in North Oxford, Cowley and Headington.[62] The proposals quickly attracted strong criticism. L. Bellinger, vice-president of the Oxford Trades and Labour Council, gave the *Oxford Mail* his view that Sharp was 'trying to put the clock back' and that he was 'an idealist living in the 16th century'. Bellinger added: 'The future prosperity of this country depends on industry, and it is no good trying to re-establish Oxford University with a monastic atmosphere. It seems to me that the report, which shows so much concern for the University, might have been issued by the Oxford Preservation Trust.'[63] Perhaps John's teatime conversations with Sharp had had some effect. Bellinger had a helpful suggestion for the planners: rather than move the Morris works from Cowley, why not move the University buildings out to Wytham?[64]

As early as November 1946, less than two months after he had taken up the post, John made it acidly clear that he was finding it uncongenial. His outburst was the result of a sarcastic postcard which R.C.K. Ensor, the distinguished historian and also a Trustee, sent J.M. Thompson on 12 November: 'When we appointed a secretary, prospect was held out of a special campaign which he would conduct to recruit our membership and multiply our funds on a quite outstanding scale. Is *anything* being done about it?'[65] Thompson made the mistake of sending this to John, commenting, 'You will notice from the last paragraph which way the wind may be blowing amongst some of the Curators: not Yours ever JMT.'[66] John wrote straight off to Ensor in his most acerbic manner:

> The Convener has sent to me your post-card of Tuesday, November 12. As it refers personally to me, I hope you will not mind a personal reply to it, & I am, of course, perfectly prepared for you to make its contents known to Trustees who may feel the same way as you do about my work. When I was interviewed by a Committee of the Trustees for this post, I made it clear in my preliminary letter if the Trust wanted someone who would organize appeals for funds, I was not the person. The art of appealing to the public for money is highly specialized, and should be done by the sort of person who is used to appealing for money for hospitals. There are plenty of such people, and they are salaried posts. It may well be that the most urgent matter for the Trust at the moment is getting more funds; if this is so – & I think you might bring it up at a Trustees' Meeting – I am perfectly prepared to resign in order that an Appeals Secretary may be appointed. I doubt whether the funds of the Trust would stand the payment of two of us . . .
>
> I should add that I would really suffer no loss of face or sense of personal slight, if an Appeals Secretary is considered necessary in my place. Indeed in some ways my resignation would come as rather a relief to me. I joined the Trust on the understanding that I should work for a minimum of two days a week. Rarely have I been able to get through the work in under four, & this does not include having to come into Trustees' Meetings on Sunday mornings and to other Sunday meetings. If you will look at this matter from my point of view, you may even be doing me a kindness by pressing for my resignation. At the moment I receive £350 a year from the Trust, I do not think it could afford more, & I would not like to take more; while for reviewing in the 'Daily Herald' once a week I receive £900 a year, which enables me to continue the work of the Trust at the salary it offers. I could make as much as this again by writing, & I really have the choice before me of Preserving Oxford, or writing books, in my spare time.
>
> Up to now the Preservation of Oxford has won.[67]

Ensor knew how to deal with this tantrum. On 21 November he replied from his home in High Wycombe, Bucks:

> When I wrote to the Convenor, I had no idea of 'pressing for your resignation'; if I had, I should not have put it on a post-card.
>
> But when you were appointed – at what most of us felt was too low a stipend – we were encouraged to hope that the new dispensation would include a new effort to increase the Trust's income, which would enable us, *inter alia*, to pay you better.
>
> How far this effort would be your personal concern, and how far we might have recourse to a special 'appeal' agency, was hardly, I think, discussed. But it is unusual that the Secretary of a Trust or society of this kind should entirely disinterest himself in the problems of membership and income, with some aspects of which nobody, ordinarily speaking, can deal as well as he.[68]

John seems to have made his peace with Ensor, though he is unlikely to have forgiven him. And one result of John's *cri de coeur* was that Sir Malcolm Stewart, president of the Associated Portland Cement Manufacturers and a Trustee, increased his salary by £300 a year from his own pocket.[69] But as time went on there were further signs that John was chafing against the restrictions the job put on his freedom. As so often before, novelty degenerated into routine, routine into drudgery. One Trustee, John Johnson, printer to the University,[70] complained that he had missed a meeting because he had not been notified of it. John said a letter had been sent: 'I think it *must* have got lost in the post.'[71] He tried to make life more amusing for himself. His irrepressible facetiousness showed up in the minutes:

> RICHARD I (Lionheart). Mr Curtis proposed that a plaque should be put up in Beaumont Street where he was born, if he was born in Beaumont Street.[72]

Sometimes, like most of his previous employers, the Trustees became impatient with his antics. One chastened minute shows John being reproved for exceeding his competence:

> YOUTH HOSTELS ASSOCIATION. Secretary had been over hasty in assuming a member of this Association should be on Plans Committee. Letter to be written asking him to submit matters to Trust and promising to invite him when specific matters concerned him.[73]

There was illness, too. On 5 February 1948 John wrote to a Mr R.E. Enthoven of Wootton: 'Dear Mr Enthoven, I write this from bed, ill . . .'[74] On 9 February Diana Craig wrote to tell Miss M. Whibley of Dorset County Museum that John had been away sick for two weeks.[75] It is unlikely he was malingering. His *Angst* over Penelope's defection to Rome may have caused stress which exacerbated the ill health he had suffered since his operation for the removal of a cyst in 1945.

In June 1948 John resigned from the Trust; Diana Craig resigned at the same time. Recording the annual general meeting in Brasenose College on Saturday 26 June, John wrote in the minutes:

> *Resignation of Secretariat* ~~was accepted with regret~~, Mr Betjeman as Secretary and Miss Craig as Assistant Secretary was accepted with much regret. The appointment of Alderman Sam Smith as Secretary, with effect from the date of transfer of change, is approved . . .[76]

'It was thought', the Trust's annual report for 1949 recorded, 'that on his appointment as Secretary to the Trust in 1946 Mr John Betjeman would be able to undertake whole-time work, but this has unfortunately proved impossible. Pressure of other commitments compelled him to resign in October [in fact he resigned in June but left in October] and the Trust lost the asset of his lively and accomplished mind.'[77] Evidently John remained on good terms with the Trust, as the annual report for 1950 shows that he gave the first lecture to the Trust's newly formed Junior Common Rooms branch. The subject was 'Nineteenth-century Buildings in Oxford', and it was illustrated by lantern slides. 'The large attendance augured well for the future.'[78]

The Trust forgave John for deserting it; but did he forgive himself? The absence of any later mention of his secretaryship suggests a deliberate or subconscious attempt to wipe the episode from his record. Did he perhaps feel that his credibility as a passionate preservationist would be impaired if people learned how he had not made more of the biggest chance he ever had to preserve? In Oxford his authority as a preservationist was never taken quite seriously again. In 1962, when he expostulated to President Boase of Magdalen that his college's new Waynflete Building, on the other side of Magdalen Bridge, was 'a hideous monstrosity that will ruin Oxford for ever', Boase felt able to treat the criticism dismissively, patting it away with a droll Irish bull – 'Oh, I don't know, John; it's not as ugly as it looks, you know.'[79]

ON THE AIR IN THE FORTIES

I find that he sounded sincere, convinced and vigorous ... We get a bigger correspondence after his talks down here [Bristol] than we get after talks by any other speaker ...

Geoffrey Grigson, memorandum to Winifred Salmon of the BBC,
September 1943

In the six years before his abrupt exit from the Oxford Preservation Trust, John had steadily built up his reputation as a 'natural' on the radio. Earlier, his wartime service in the Ministry of Information and in Ireland had caused a big gap in his broadcasting career, though on one visit to London, in 1943, he had taken part in *The Brains Trust*, the weekly discussion of current affairs and other topics, with Professors C.E.M. Joad and Julian Huxley. In February of that year he had also given a heartfelt talk on 'Coming Home – or England Revisited'.

It is something really terrible, this longing for England we get when we are away. The other month I found my eyes getting wet (fortunately there was no one about) at the sight of moonlight on a willow stump covered with ivy. It reminded me of a willowy brook in the Berkshire village where we used to live before the war ...

I do not believe we are fighting for the privilege of living in a highly developed community of ants. That is what the Nazis want. For me, at any rate, England stands for the Church of England, eccentric incumbents, oil-lit churches, Women's Institutes, modest village inns, arguments about cow-parsley on the altar, the noise of mowing machines on Sunday afternoons, local newspapers, local auctions, the poetry of Tennyson, Crabbe, Hardy and Matthew Arnold, local talent, local concerts, a visit to the cinema, branch line trains, light railways, leaning on gates and looking across fields.[1]

On 18 September 1943, John wrote to Ronald Boswell from the Films Division, Ministry of Information, 'Here I am back, grinding at the mill.'[2] Shortly afterwards, Geoffrey Grigson, who worked at the BBC's Bristol studios, told Winifred Salmon, the assistant director of talks, London, that John wanted to talk on 'war weariness'. Grigson commented:

> That would be too bald a title, and would, perhaps, put you off, but he means the state of mind after several years of war, the necessity for thought and silence and some point of meditation in one's life. Things that he would mention are the feeling one had of being *cared for* during the blitzes, not cared for by the ARP but cared for by one's fellow human beings. The way people lose that feeling and are rather nastier to each other now things are going better. His own experience of fire-watching in St Paul's and caring for a building that intensely matters.
>
> I believe he would do a talk of this kind really well. Last Thursday was the first time I'd produced him myself and he seemed to me to have control over his speaking, and a marvellous ability to be on the listeners' side.[3]

Winifred Salmon sent a lukewarm reply.

> By all means encourage Betjeman to talk about war-weariness, but I see certain snags in this.
> (a) that having lived in Dublin for so large a part of the war he has less excuse than most people to be war-weary;
> (b) that his particular voice and manner (no offence intended) might make a good many people think that he was weary before the war began. He must contrive to sound entirely sincere . . .[4]

Grigson replied:

> You rather suggest that Betjeman might not sound sincere or that, as a broadcaster, he sounds tired. That isn't my impression of him on the air. Whatever one may know about him oneself, I find that he sounds sincere, convinced and vigorous. The fact remains that we get a bigger correspondence after his talks down here than we get after talks by any other speaker, and that correspondence is always 99% appreciative.[5]

John might have been surprised if he could have seen this inter-office correspondence. He had been ill-disposed towards 'Griggers' ever since, in their Oxford days, Grigson had rejected his poem 'The Arrest of Oscar Wilde at the Cadogan Hotel' for an undergraduate magazine. In John's view, Grigson was a sucker for avant-gardism in verse; and Grigson made no secret that he thought John's poetry indefensibly anachronistic. It was magnanimous of Grigson to praise John to Winifred Salmon in 1943; only four years earlier, John had had to write him a grovelling apology for using something very close to his name for a character in a published short story about commercial travellers. ('There is your name in cold print and if I found my own name in such a position I would be furious.')[6] The story began:

> 'Now 'oo was the old boy as used to be with Consolidated Dried Fruits before Lemon come on? Grogson, was it?'
>   'No, not Grogson – let me think . . .'[7]

Grigson continued to recommend John. In 1944 he suggested to Godfrey James, in the London Talks Department, that he should ask him to review books. 'As you know,' Grigson wrote, 'he's a kindly and engaging broadcaster, doesn't set himself a low standard, or one too far from the centre of common taste . . .'[8] James replied: 'Yes – I'd love to have Betjeman on fiction.'[9] John had given his first talk on books in 1939, confessing, 'What the roulette table is to the gambler, the second-hand bookshop is to me.'[10] He mentioned a copy of one of the two 1599 editions of Shakespeare's *Venus and Adonis* which had been found at Lamport Hall, Northamptonshire (the home of his Oxford friend the film actor Sir Gyles Isham) and sold for £15,000 in 1919. John said that if he found the rare pamphlet for which Shelley was sent down from Oxford, *The Necessity of Atheism*, 'I should sell it at once, buy a car and a vacuum cleaner for my wife to clean the books in our house at present . . .'[11]

In November 1943 he had given a talk on 'Secondhand Books' which opened with an extraordinary passage, reminiscent of Metaphysical poetry.

> I notice everywhere that the habit of reading is growing. Enforced confinement in some ARP post, transport difficulties, black-out, bad weather, higher education; – they all drive us to books. And a very good thing, too. How I hate a room without books. It is, to me, a room without a soul. 'Yap; yap; yap;' explosive people sitting in luxury suites, hard electric light, ash trays, thick carpets, a whacking great wireless set pouring out, perhaps these very words, and 'yap-yap-yap' the talk goes on, just to while away the time. I wouldn't mind at all if the people in this interior I visualize were reading books or even had some books to read. But when people just talk for the sake of talking and because they have lost the ability to read, I feel they are fooling with eternity. I suddenly see them as so many skeletons and the jaws of their skulls going up and down in all this luxury,

up and down, up and down, and their souls getting smaller and smaller. But perhaps I am unsympathetic. For I am someone who would much sooner read than talk. Indeed, I would prefer a Quaker silence to talk, any day. In fact, perhaps you'd rather I shut up. But I won't . . .[12]

In 1946 John asked Ronald Boswell for a higher than usual fee for giving a talk on Evelyn Waugh – 'I have had to re-read all the works of Evelyn Waugh, which takes me at least four full days.'[13] A few days after the Waugh talk was broadcast, John's friend Terence de Vere White wrote to him: 'I had the pleasure of listening to you on the Third Programme. You have a very charming voice. Everyone says that and they have never noticed the tiny substratum of petulance until I point it out.'[14] As we have seen, Waugh himself was not impressed by the talk.[15]

In the same year, the idea that Malcolm Brereton had mooted over ten years before, of John's writing 'a short story especially adapted to the microphone', was at last realized. Asked by Ronald Lewin of the Talks Department to write a story for Christmas, John wrote a ghost story, initially entitled 'The Church Crawler'. Later he suggested it should instead be called 'Seeking Whom He May Devour': on 2 December Lewin wrote, 'I am adopting immediately your awe-inspiring second title.' He added: 'If your final script is based, as you suggested it might be, on an actual experience which you and John Piper shared, I wonder if you could let me have a short paragraph about that experience as I feel that it would be most welcome to the *Radio Times*.'[16]

John wrote back: 'John Piper and Oliver Stonor have given permission for their names to be used. John Piper has heard the story, it's more or less what happened at a place called Wolfhamcote, in Warwickshire. I have disguised it in appearance. I mean it happened except for the ghost. The cinema manager is apocryphal.'[17] On 18 December, with Christmas only a week off, Lewin wrote: 'I am a little unhappy about the ending. You build the story up to what looks as if it is going to be a big climax, and it all ends "not with a bang but a whimper".'[18] John sent a 'simpler' version on 21 December, apologizing for being 'down to the wire'. He added: 'I now have learned that you cannot try in the space of 1800–2000 words to describe two or three places in a short story. The setting must be one place. A useful lesson to me, but rough luck on you.'[19] Lewin replied that the new version had 'much greater unity'.[20] John received twenty guineas for giving two readings of it on Christmas Day.[21] (Repeats were not recorded in those days.)

Ingredients of future poems are found in two of John's radio talks. In 1937, in a talk on Exeter, he said: 'Another part of Exeter that still survives almost intact, is the Georgian district . . . Walk in the miniature dell of beech and ilex-shaded lawns called Rougemont Gardens . . .'[22] Later in the talk he again referred to the Exeter trees – 'copper beech, beech, oak, and best of all the ilex whose olive leaves look grand against the yellow, red or cheerful plaster'. The ilex re-appeared in his poem 'Exeter', published in *Continual Dew* that year –

> The doctor's intellectual wife
>   Sat under the ilex tree
> The Cathedral bells pealed over the wall
>   But never a bell heard she
> And the sun played shadowgraphs on her book
>   Which was writ by A. Huxléy.

A much more developed blueprint for a poem formed part of his talk 'Christmas Nostalgia', transmitted on 25 December 1947.

> Last week I was in the most beautiful building in Britain – King's College, Cambridge. You know it. It is a forest glade of old coloured glass, and between the great windows columns of shafted stone shoot up and up to fountain out into a shower of exquisite fan-vaulting. It is the swan-song of Perpendicular architecture, so immense, so vast, so superbly propor-tioned, so mysterious, that no one can enter it without gasping. All the school children of Cambridge had filed into a Carol service and there they were in the candle light of the dark oak stalls. We stood waiting for the choir to come in and as we stood there the first verse of the opening carol was sung beyond us, behind the screen, away in the mighty splendour of the nave. A treble solo floated up to the distant vaulting
>
> *Once in Royal David's City* . . .
>
> It was clear, pure, distinct. And as I heard it, I knew once more – knew despite myself – that this story was the Truth.[23]

There – even down to certain phrases – is the inspiration for John's poem 'Sunday Morning, King's Cambridge', published in *A Few Late Chrysanthemums* (1954). But in a 1949 recital of his poems on the radio, with his own commentary, his listeners were not only given an early version of the poem, but were made party to the very workings of the poet's mind.

> Well, there's one other [poem] I might as well give you on a more serious topographical note, before we come to the suburbs, which is 'King's at Cambridge'.

Do you know King's at Cambridge? I always think Cambridge really beats Oxford . . . Its architecture. And I'm trying to do a poem on King's Chapel. Haven't finished it yet. Keep writing the last verse and it doesn't work. Sounds too grand. Sounds like a sort of state poem in *The Sunday Times* when I get the – when I put the last verse on, so I'm just going to read you the first two. I've crossed out the last one. I don't know whether they are much good, but King's Chapel really is such a blaze of glory and beauty, especially inside, that I've always wanted to get it into verse. If you can compose the last verse in this metre I should be very grateful and would give anybody who writes it full acknowledgement . . .

> File you out from yellow candle light
> Fair choristers of King's,
> And leave to shadowy silence
> These canopied Renaissance stalls.
> In blazing glass above the dark
> Go skies and thrones and wings,
> Blue, ruby, gold and green
> Between the whiteness of the walls.
> And with what rich precision
> The stonework soars and springs
> To fountain out, to spreading vault
> A shower that never falls.*

Then, I've tried to give the impression of how all the colours that you see in Cambridge, and Cambridge is full of them in its stonework and in its meadows, and in all its scenery, its flint, and everything outside and in its sky. They're all – they become transmuted through this stained glass, just into pearl on the stone shafts that go sprouting up the walls and bursting into the fountains I've described of fan-vaulting.

> The white of windy Cambridge courts,
> The cobbles brown and dry,
> The gold of plaster Gothic

* In the published version the first stanza reads:

> File into yellow candle light, fair choristers of King's
>   Lost in the shadowy silence of canopied Renaissance stalls
> In blazing glass above the dark glow skies and thrones and wings
>   Blue, ruby, gold and green between the whiteness of the walls
> And with what rich precision the stonework soars and springs
>   To fountain out a spreading vault – a shower that never falls.

With ivy overgrown.
The apple red, the silver fronts
The deep green flats and high
The yellowing elm trees circled out
On islands of their own.
Oh! Here beyond all colours change
That catch the flying sky,
To waves of pearly light that heave
Along the shafted stone.*

And now I don't know how to complete it, you see. One wants to get the impression, really, that brings King's Chapel finally to life when one's inside it, which is when the organ is going, and that choir is singing, so brilliantly conducted by – run by, Boris Ord, you know. Then you get such a sort of fourth dimension in the place. It's absolutely the one experience, I think, that England has got above any country in the world, in the way of architecture and music welded together. That last verse, I don't think I shall ever be able to write it. But I hope somebody will one day write a poem about King's Chapel. Wordsworth's sonnet, to me, though very wonderful, doesn't quite bring it off as I should like to see it done, to hear it done, by some great man. It can never be done.†24

In 1943 John became one of the new 'question-masters' of the *Brains Trust*.25 He was scheduled to appear with Joad and Robert Boothby in April 1948, but on 17 March the talks producer Anna Kallin received a message from her secretary: 'Mrs Betjeman telephoned and said Mr Betjeman is in Denmark (Palace Hotel, Copenhagen) and will not be back until Good Friday. Mrs Betjeman said that he was so angry last time he was on the Brains Trust that he would not be on it again!!!'26

Later that year, John plotted with Basil Taylor of the BBC (an art historian responsible for establishing Stubbs as one of the great British

---

* In the published version the second stanza is almost the same; except that the twelve lines are regrouped into six lines; 'the deep green flats' become 'the wide green flats'; and 'beyond' (presumably a typist's error in the BBC script) is corrected to 'behold'.
† As published, the third stanza John wrote was as follows:

In far East Anglian churches, the clasped hands lying long
    Recumbent on sepulchral slabs or effigied in brass
Buttress with prayer this vaulted roof so white and light and strong
    And countless congregations as the generations pass
Join choir and great crowned organ case, in centuries of song
    To praise Eternity contained in Time and coloured glass.

artists)[27] to make a programme about Ninian Comper. He wrote to Taylor on 10 October: 'Comper is diffident, indeed far too terrified to speak on the wireless. But I think I shall have to do this by means of conversation with him, pointing out to him that it is not at all alarming as he does not have to go to the BBC but all those nice chaps in grey flannel trousers and pipes come and stick wires about in his house instead. Love and kisses . . .'[28]

On 19 February 1949 the BBC recorded a debate in the village hall of Letcombe Bassett at the foot of the Berkshire Downs. The subject was the recent decision by Wantage Rural District Council that nothing should be done to preserve the 'dilapidated' village of Letcombe.*[29] In the debate John opposed his old friend Thomas Sharp under the chairmanship of Sir Ralph Glyn, MP for North Berkshire. The hall was packed with Letcombe villagers, who protested loudly when Sharp said of the village, 'It is a slum, a rural slum.' John pounced on that in his reply.

> Well, good people of Letcombe Bassett sitting in this hall – and a good many more standing – I want to tell you at once that I'm not on the same side as my friend Thomas Sharp. No, I'm not on his side, I'm on yours. I wonder how you like being described to the country at large as 'slum-dwellers' – it's a grave injustice to you, and first of all, I want to put that injustice right by congratulating you on the tremendous stand you've made against the tyranny of small local officials. (HEAR, HEARS) That is what you've done as no other village in England *has* done in this century: you've made history by asserting your right to be treated fairly by these officials, who should be your servants, not your masters . . . My dear slum-dwellers (SUBDUED LAUGHTER) . . . I would be proud to be called a 'slum-dweller', if I could also say I lived in Letcombe Bassett – it's an honourable title.[30]

Letcome Bassett was saved, though there was to be one later spoliation. In the 1970s a planning application for a modern house at the head of the cress beds on an ancient spring was rejected; but on appeal to Michael Heseltine at the Department of the Environment it was granted.[31]

The 1949 radio debate was considered of such quality that it was transcribed in 1953 in *The Oxford Book of English Talk*,[32] in company with Dame Margery Kempe, Sir Thomas More, Charles I and his accusers, and Dr Johnson and John Wilkes. In 2000, Dot Wordsworth wrote in a *Spectator* column on pronunciation:

* See also Chapter 23, 'A Preservationist in The Making'.

I think I have detected an illuminating error in a transcription of a wireless debate from 1949 in which John Betjeman took part. The transcription . . . has Betjeman saying this: 'Even you, Sharp, admit that the draining could be done for £8,500 – which today is not a prohibitive course.' I suspect that Betjeman said not *course* but *cost*, rhyming with *horsed*. It was even then a dated pronunciation of the vowel in words such as *cross*, *lost* and *frost*. A truly historical curiosity.[33]

'THE BETJE-BUS'

Mr John Betjeman is, for me, the most interesting figure in English poetry today . . . He is developing on seven-league boots . . .

Frank O'Connor, reviewing *Selected Poems* in the *Evening News*, 6 October 1948

In June 1946 Jock Murray and John began discussing a new book which would bring together poems from the three earlier Murray volumes. Though it was early decided that a selection would be made, both men referred to the book as *Collected Poems* until just before publication. 'I would prefer to leave the selection to you or to who you like to get,' John wrote to Murray on 22 June.[1] Murray asked whether there were any poems John would like to omit. 'As far as possible,' Murray thought, 'they should all be included.'[2] On 10 July the publisher wrote again to ask for any new poems that had appeared in magazines since *New Bats in Old Belfries*.[3] He had asked John Sparrow and Peter Quennell to read through the earlier volumes and give their views. In sending the three books to Sparrow, Murray added: 'Apparently the Cornish Saga has got a new lease of life and we may be publishing that separately.'[4]

Quennell marked with an 'X' 'the poems I like least. Naturally this doesn't mean that I don't like them.' He blacklisted five poems from *Continual Dew* (including 'Slough'), three from *Old Lights* and two from *New Bats*. Sparrow's advice was to select only the best – 'the best *poetry*, light or serious – not the most typical . . .' He wanted to include twelve poems of the thirty-three in *Continual Dew*, eleven of the twenty-one in *Old Lights* and fourteen of the twenty-four in *New Bats*.[5] So Quennell's and Sparrow's estimates of the three books, in terms of quality, were strikingly similar: both men thought Betjeman the poet had improved over the years. Murray agreed with Sparrow that 'The ideal is certainly only to include the very best.'[6]

Sparrow wanted to discuss with John not only the selection, but also the arrangement of the poems under thematic headings. And indeed it was soon accepted – though exactly when, how or why is unclear from the Murray archives – that he would be a sort of ringmaster for the selection. It was also agreed that he would write a preface to it. Sparrow had been one of John's closest friends since they were undergraduates together.[7] To have him, with his double First and All Souls fellowship, introduce the poems might not confer gravitas on them; but it would set on them a seal of Establishment recognition which John, for all his pot-shots at society's grandees, craved. Sparrow's attitude to him was unengagingly *de haut en bas*. For his friend, he would deign to dip a fastidious toe into the popular market; but in return he expected absolute control over the contents of the book. His strictures on the poems he wanted excluded were severe. There was perhaps an element of jealousy in this. Though he held the blue riband of academe, he published little more than a few collections of essays. His poems never caught on. His name was unknown to the man in the street – except, possibly, in 1962 when he suggested that D.H. Lawrence had introduced buggery into *Lady Chatterley's Lover*.[8] It was satisfying to subject John to his authority.

A chance for Sparrow to slap John down came in mid-August 1946, when Murray suggested a new possibility to the poet. Murray were founder members of the Guild Books, a cheap reprint series selling at one shilling. Would John like his book to be published in this series? An edition of about 40,000 was envisaged. The author would get two guineas per thousand. One drawback was that illustrations would be needed if the poems appeared as a Guild Book.[9] John replied that he was all in favour of the idea 'because I like to think my verse is comprehensible enough to the ordinary person for publication in such a series, though it would be a dead loss to the publishers – 5000 would be the sale at the most'.[10] He thought that the book should be illustrated with line drawings by John Piper. But Sparrow would not hear of the idea. An elitist if ever there was one, he did not want his selection and preface to be issued in a cheap edition. He wanted something for bibliophiles to gloat over. The Guild Books idea was dropped.

On 28 August Sparrow reported to Murray that he and John had spent 'a most satisfactory weekend' together. Dashing Murray's hopes for a rather inclusive selection, he wrote: 'We both agreed vehemently that what would be best . . . is a comparatively small selection of his really good poetry. We also agreed on which were his best poems.' He urged: 'Do not try and persuade John to agree to a more inclusive selection, on the plea of "What the Public wants", "Must have old favourites" etc. I think that a rigidly limited selection would show up John for the poet that he is.'[11]

Jock Murray had asked his friend the publisher Martin Secker for his advice on a title for the book. Secker wrote: 'It is time to get away from bats and belfreys [*sic*] and churches, and I would therefore respectfully suggest *Collected Verses*.'[12] On 5 September Murray wrote to Sparrow that he envisaged a book of about ninety pages. He hoped that the poems 'Hymn' and 'The Arrest of Oscar Wilde at the Cadogan Hotel', which Sparrow wanted to leave out, would be reprieved. Sparrow grudgingly made the concession of including them at the end of the book under the 'disparrowging' heading 'Juvenilia'. By mid-January 1947 the poems had been sent off for galley proof. Murray wrote to John: 'We have added the new one about the church in N London "St Saviour's, Aberdeen Park, Highbury, London N" and you also sent us the new one about the illness of a son "A Child Ill", but surely there are others which are candidates for inclusion . . .'[13] John had sent J.C. Trewin part of the Cornish 'Epic' for his *West Country Magazine*.[14] Sparrow received a copy of the poem. '*Excellent*,' he wrote to Murray, adding that he had insisted that John make improvements to 'Ireland with Emily'.[15] *Murray's Buckinghamshire Guide*, edited by John Piper and John, was also going through the press.[16] The proofs of the first section of photographs were ready.

W.H. Auden, who was living in Long Island, New York, selected and wrote the introduction to an American collection of John's poems – a book quite distinct from Sparrow's selection. It was issued in 1947 as *Slick but not Streamlined*. John's daughter, Candida Lycett Green, recalls that her father detested this title.[17] Auden wrote to John on 9 August: 'I was furious about the title they gave your book but the sales department insisted . . .'[18] He said he had wanted to call the book *Betjeman's Bust*. This was probably disingenuous. In his 'Verse-letter to C. Day-Lewis' (1929), Auden had described the poetaster Humbert Wolfe,[19] whom he despised, in these contemptuous lines:

> While Wolfe, the typists' poet, made us sick
> Whose thoughts are dapper and whose lines are slick.

It seems rather too much of a coincidence that the epithet 'slick' should occur in the American title too; and was it really likely that an American publisher's sales department would have thought of such an untempting title and insisted on it in defiance of the anthologist's wishes? It is more probable that Auden, like Sparrow, slightly resented his old Oxford friend's growing fame, and intended to put him in his place. He was also, perhaps, not amused by the suggestion in *The Listener* by 'Beachcomber', reviewing *Continual Dew*, that he, Auden, had 'begun to imitate' John. With the honesty that belongs to great poets, Auden

candidly admitted his jealousy of John in the first sentence of his introduction; and while the tone of this piece was friendly, its effect was to
depreciate John by treating him as a very English joke.

It is difficult to write seriously about a man one has sung hymns with or
judiciously about a poet whose work makes one violently jealous.
Normally when I read good poetry, for example Mr Eliot's line

> The place of solitude where three dreams cross

my reaction is one of delighted admiration; a standard of excellence has
been set in one way which I must try to live up to in mine: but when I read
such lines of Mr Betjeman as

> And that mauve hat three cherries decorate
> Next week shall topple from its trembling perch
> While wet fields reek like some long empty church

I am, frankly, rather annoyed because they are not by me. My feeling is
similar to that one has when, on arriving at some long-favorite picnic spot
in the woods, one finds that another trespasser has discovered it too.
   Indeed, like a character in a tale by Hoffman, I can never make up my
mind whether Mr Betjeman was born after the flesh or whether he was
magically begotten by myself in a punt on the Cherwell one summer
evening in 1926. I have no memory of company on the outward journey
on that occasion; I only know that *two* of us returned . . . Even if there was
a real Betjeman once, I am afraid that he has been evicted and his place
taken by the obstinate spirit of my favorite aunt Daisy. She was said to be
what is called 'mentally retarded' . . . She had one obsession; being totally
deaf in one ear, she would implore us to promise that, when she died, we
would not bury her too deep, for then she might never hear the last
trumpet. Sure enough, at her funeral, when the coffin was being lowered
into the grave, it stuck halfway down and refused to budge. It is my secret
conviction that she fooled us all about being buried and that it is her dear
chilblained mittened hand which now prompts Mr Betjeman's pen.[20]

Having thus equated John with a mentally retarded old aunt, Auden
commends his 'topophilic' verse, pausing to add snidely: 'It is one of
my constant regrets that I am too short-sighted, too much of a
Thinking Type, to attempt this sort of poetry . . .'[21] Thus the idea of
John as a non-intellectual, mindlessly registering his quaint impressions of the visible world, is reinforced. When John had worked on
The Architectural Review, his bosses had drummed it into him that he

was not to mistake the 'Modernistic' or *moderne* (or Art Deco) style for the Modern: the former was a bastardized version of the latter, and could not be regarded as part of the Modern Movement or the International Style.[22] The title *Slick but not Streamlined* seemed to be making the same point about John's poetry.

Somewhat in contradiction of his preface, Auden mainly chose John's more serious poems and omitted such popular favourites as 'A Subaltern's Love-song' and 'Slough'. In February 1947 John sent Jock Murray Auden's preface to forward to Sparrow. Murray commented on it: 'It is certainly odd, but then the public for whom he is writing is also odd and requires a rather unusual form of stimulant.'[23] Returning the Auden preface to Murray on 25 February, Sparrow wrote, 'I read it nearly to the end before turning to see who it was by. I had no idea it was Auden – and had already nearly been made sick by it before I saw his name. It really is frightful – not just bad Auden, but bad with a badness of its own, and cheaper than I could have thought possible. I suppose that JB cannot prohibit its appearance, and I am afraid he may not much want to.'[24]

On 1 August Murray sent Sparrow the first instalment of the printers' marked galley proof of John's poems.[25] Murray was still pressing John for more poems to add to the selection. He replied on 27 August: 'It is not the fees but lack of inspiration, tiredness, dispiritedness and complete cessation that compel me to say I have nothing. The firm of Murray is instead benefiting from our work on Bucks which has taken up two days a week for months now – and very enjoyable too.'[26] Murray wrote to him the next day: 'The Bucks glossary is a stupendous work! I am full of admiration for your energy and learning!'[27]

Both John and Murray were becoming concerned about Sparrow's preface. Constantly promised, it had not arrived. Sparrow was a notorious procrastinator. It did not help that he had resumed his practice at the Bar. In his letter of 27 August John wrote: 'I suggest that in lieu of Spansbury [Sparrow] who seems so dilatory you use W. Plomer's BBC talk on my verse as a preface.'[28] (In the wireless talk Plomer had set out to explain how John differed from his contemporaries, such as Auden and Spender.) On 19 September Murray wrote again to Sparrow to ask for the preface – 'or is it really becoming too much of a burden? You must tell me truthfully.' Sparrow replied: 'My preface – I *am writing* it!' and asked what length he could be allowed.[29] About three thousand words, Murray answered; though it could run to six thousand or ten thousand if Sparrow felt inspired.[30] Meanwhile John did send in some new poems. Sparrow included 'Indoor Games near Newbury' but rejected 'The Dear Old Village'. He wrote to Murray from All Souls on 7 October: 'You will believe it when you see it but I

SLICK

BUT NOT

Streamlined

POEMS & SHORT PIECES BY

John Betjeman

SELECTED, & WITH AN
INTRODUCTION BY

W. H. AUDEN

GARDEN CITY, N. Y. 1947
DOUBLEDAY & COMPANY, INC.

can positively say that I have this day handed IT to the Porter at the Lodge here, to be dispatched by registered post as soon as the Post Office opens tomorrow.'[31] In reply, Murray sent a telegram: 'CAN ALMOST HEAR THE PREFACE APPROACHING. BEATERS ALL LINED UP UNDER COVER. MURRAY.'[32] In November Sparrow wrote: 'After so much suspense it can hardly be anything but disappointing.'[33]

In fact, Murray was delighted with the preface, an urbane, thoughtful and entertaining piece. Sparrow had two main themes. He wanted to show that John was pre-eminently a poet of place (Harold Acton was to call him 'the genius of the *genius loci*').[34] And he tried to distance him from his early 'amusing' phase, and to illustrate his new maturity. The essay began:

> In the Preface to his second collection of verses – *Old Lights for New Chancels* – John Betjeman described the kind of poetry he most enjoys; and it is the kind to which the best of his own poetry belongs. Most of the pieces in that book, and in his later volume – *New Bats in Old Belfries* – are inspired by what he calls his 'topographical predilection': they describe a scene, or convey the atmosphere of a place. If there are figures in the foreground, they are subordinate to their setting and somehow expressive of it; and even when the poem tells a story the incidents seem to be designed to make the landscape articulate, to give a voice, as it were, to the atmosphere of the Lincolnshire fens or the lakes of Westmeath or the London suburbs.[35]

Sparrow could not altogether refrain from patronizing John.

> In his earliest verses, collected in *Mount Zion* and *Continual Dew*, Mr Betjeman was in danger of yielding to the seduction of the 'original' and the 'amusing'; he seemed content to lose himself in his new-found wonder-land of Victorian and post-Victorian architecture . . .
>
> His sense of period, and of certain periods in particular; his eye for detail; his relish for architectural and ecclesiastical eccentricities; his evident delight in this newly discovered field of poetry and his evident facility in exploiting it – all these threatened to inhibit any effort to extend his range of subject or of feeling. And here his admirers were his enemies: for his early verses gained him an audience of devotees who seemed to ask only that he should continue to amuse them by further variations on the theme of his own invention:

> Oh worship the Lord in the beauty of ugliness!

It looked, indeed, as if Mr Betjeman was fated to end his days as the Laureate of the suburbs and the Gothic Revival . . .[36]

Sparrow was especially scornful of the 'juvenilia', such as 'The Arrest of Oscar Wilde at the Cadogan Hotel' – 'an attempt to create an atmosphere of "period" by wheeling the old stage properties – the astrakhan coat, the hock and seltzer, *The Yellow Book* – all too conscientiously into place'.[37] But in his peroration he paid tribute to 'an increase in his power of pleasing', and added:

> It would be unnatural not to attempt some forecast of his future development. Its next stage I think is indicated clearly enough by the extracts from an unfinished poem which will be found at the end of this Selection ['Fragments of a Cornish Poem: Sunday Afternoon Service in St Enodoc; North Coast Recollections']. In the Idyll or Verse Tale he has discovered . . . he has it in him to produce a poem which will prove, in its own strange way, a masterpiece.[38]

Sparrow was having second thoughts about some of the poems he had turned down. 'I have been haunted for days', he wrote to Murray on 25 November, 'by the feeling that we ought to have included *Invasion Exercise on the Poultry Farm* in the Selection . . .'[39] There was still time, and it was reprieved. However, Sparrow was adamant in refusing to admit 'Myfanwy at Oxford'. He also had reservations about a new poem, 'Sunday Morning, King's Cambridge'. After Jock Murray had passed these and other criticisms on to John, the poet replied, on Christmas Day 1947:

> I am delighted with Spansbury's comments, on which I find myself in complete agreement with the dear old thing. With others I am not.
> But before I deal with these I will tell you one thing I must write to him about (and I have not yet had time to do so) and that is the Preface. I said I would like to be as dead about it, but there is an inaccuracy in the beginning which, since I am alive, I MUST correct. I am not a pure poet of place. I bear no resemblance to Bloomfield or Clare and very little to Crabbe and only a little to Cowper but much more to him than the other three. This means to say that I write (and I know this) primarily with *people* in mind and relate the people to the background. When I am describing Nature, it is *always* with a view to the social background or the sense of Man's impotence before the vastness of the Creator. That is what makes my satirical poetry and the earlier stuff different (and I think feebler) than the later. You will also find this in my prose work. For instance, the only merit of Ghastly Good Taste was that it treated architecture sociologically.

So when we come to his quotations of me as a poet of place he does not really mean purely place. The Henley poem which he quotes is wartime Henley superseding fashionable river Henley. It is full of people. The Trebetherick quotation is an evocation of childhood and the child's sense of wonder at the force of the sea and rain. The Lincolnshire poem he quotes is not on the same plane. It is primarily a narrative poem intended to give a Monty James thrill and hence the East Anglian setting. The Irish poem is much more a descriptive one, but its primary impulse was to present-day Irish Catholicism and the dead Protestantism of the dear old drinking hunting Somerville & Ross landlords in a setting of all Ireland from E to W so that when he goes on, quite rightly, to decry my earlier verse, he really means that there I was in danger of becoming purely a poet of place and architecture and pastiche and he does not mean that I have emerged from all this into a poet of place. Had I done so, I would be no different from John Drinkwater. This only refers to the first four pages. One matter he does omit and that is that I write of what I describe, whether it is a town or a tennis girl, with *love*.

I will therefore write explaining this to Spansbury.[40]

John was upset that Sparrow wanted to omit 'Sunday Morning, King's Cambridge'. After dealing with Sparrow's textual criticisms of the poem ('I always pronounce Renaissance Rēnaïssănce'), he burst out: 'But this poem is a corker! and Spansbury is mad not to include it, though I admit it gives the lie to his theory about my being a poet of place; back your own judgment, Jock; you know it is the best poem I've ever written; so do I.'[41] In sending Sparrow's comments to John, Murray had written, 'If you think his suggestions are improvements and decide to adopt them, I personally very much hope that he will, in the end, include it.'[42] But in the upshot the King's, Cambridge poem was left out of *Selected Poems*; it appeared in *A Few Late Chrysanthemums* (1954).

Also on Christmas Day, John wrote a long letter to Sparrow. (How much time was left for festivities with the children?) All the points he had made to Murray were reiterated more crisply and emphatically. John added: 'When you describe my "amatory" poems really it would be better to call them "sexy". All my better poems are Amatory in that they are written from a love of the people and place they describe. They are written with love and, I like to think, reverential understanding . . . Also my view of the world is that man is born to fulfil the purposes of his Creator i.e. to Praise his Creator, to stand in awe of Him and to dread Him. In this way I differ from most modern poets, who are agnostics and have an idea that Man is the centre of the Universe or is a helpless bubble blown about by uncontrolled forces. I dare say

I don't show that much in my verse except in the choice of subject (in the non-sexy poems). But on the social plane, old boy, I know that is my motive for writing.'[43] Sparrow, who tended to think he knew better than others, disregarded all John's comments. In the published preface John was still described as a poet of place.

Sparrow, too, was busy at his writing-desk on Christmas Day 1947. He had thought of a fiendish practical joke to play on John, and was writing to Murray to ask him to connive at it. Knowing how cross John was at the title of Auden's American selection, he proposed to write him this letter: 'Auden has bagged the obvious title for the selection, which I myself suggested and had in mind to use – so I have had to fall back on my second string, *Queer but not Quaint*. Jock Murray approves. I hope you do too.'[44] Sparrow wrote to Murray, 'I hope this takes him in. It will certainly make him sit up. If so, keep up the deception as long as you think fit.'[45] To give added plausibility to the imposture, Sparrow even suggested that Murray should have a fake proof printed of the title. It is unlikely that Murray agreed to carry the joke that far. He knew how thin-skinned John was.

For the same reason, Murray asked Myfanwy Piper whether she thought John's complaints about Sparrow's preface were fair. She replied:

> a) . . . it wasn't a question of creating a *taste* for Gothick or anything else that JB makes fashionable because he, JB, is really, not just fashionably, in love with the subjects and that love is greater than taste . . .
>
> b) . . . JB doesn't satirize things because he doesn't hate them: what he does satirize is the absence of love which he does savagely.[46]

Murray paraphrased these remarks and passed them on to Sparrow as his own observations, without mentioning Myfanwy. Murray also wrote to John that he would do his best to persuade Sparrow to include the King's, Cambridge poem, 'but I think it is a bad thing to persuade JS against his opinion, as the selection is to be his'.[47] Sparrow remained implacably opposed to the poem. On 22 January 1948 he told Murray he thought it should be 'kept for a later book'.[48]

On 4 March Murray wrote to the printer, William Clowes, 'We shall be sending you shortly a printing order for 4000 copies of Betjeman's *Collected Poems*.'[49] There was also to be a limited edition of 100 copies on handmade paper, with marbled endpapers from Douglas Cockerell of Letchworth, Herts. John returned to Murray what he called 'the Spansburied proofs' on 3 March, making a last vain plea that 'Myfanwy at Oxford' should be used instead of 'Invasion Exercise' ('but it is not a vital matter').[50] On 3 May Murray wrote to him that 'The Collected, Selected Opus will be the advance guard of the autumn season – that is to say a September book.'[51] The title *Selected Poems* was finally decided on. In letters to Sparrow about last-minute corrections, Murray referred to the book as 'the Betje-bus'.

Murray sent John the first completed copy on 16 September and asked him to lunch on 4 October (Sparrow was invited too) to 'drink a health'. John replied two days later: 'I am DELIGHTED with the book of Selected Poems and with the preface by Spansbury. I cannot bring myself to read the verses.'[52] The book was published on 5 October 1948. The next day, it was reviewed in the *Evening News* by the short-story writer Frank O'Connor – John's friend from Dublin days – under the heading 'A POET FOR ALL'.

Mr John Betjeman is, for me, the most interesting figure in English poetry today. He approaches you with the most disarming air of being really a disappointed contributor to *Punch* who has been barred from its pages owing to his eccentric passion for Victorian bric-à-brac. This is he on Oscar Wilde's arrest, an early effort:–

'One astrakhan coat is at Willis's –
    Another one's at the Savoy:
Do fetch my morocco portmanteau,
    And bring them on later, dear boy.'

Mr John Sparrow, who introduces Mr Betjeman's *Selected Poems* (Murray 8s 6d), apologises for this, but the attitude – half passion, half pose – is familiar enough. It is a young poet's way of deliberately marking the distance between himself and reality, of nailing his poetic colours to the mast. With Yeats it was fairies; with Betjeman, Victoriana.

Poets usually live to regret it, and I expect to see Mr Betjeman wince at the word [*sic*] 'box pews', like Yeats in later life at the word 'fairies'. In their mature work it lingers on as mere affectation, as when Mr Betjeman entitles one beautiful poem 'Before the Anaesthetic *or* A Terrible Fright', for which he deserves to have his ears boxed.

Some of the poems reviewed in this column three years ago he has revised, and his revisions show growing awareness of his strength and weakness.

The newest poems in the selection (unfortunately dispersed in the tiresome arrangement) represent an advance which astonishes even me who never took Mr Betjeman seriously in his pose as the funny little man. Watch how the Victorian affectation has been transmuted in the exquisite poem on Highbury church!

Only the church remains, where carriages used to throng
  And my mother stepped out in flounces and my father stepped
                                              out in spats
  To shadowy stained-glass matins or gas-lit evensong
  And back in a country quiet with doffing of chimney hats.

The jingle has weakened the second line, but nobody can mistake that for minor verse.

Mr Sparrow seems to be writing something perilously like nonsense when he says that 'the gift of poetry was not bestowed on Mr Betjeman to enable him to unlock his heart.' Betjeman is, I think, a religious poet in the line of Donne and Hopkins, with the same crude, unqualified tension between his love of God and his natural sensuality, though in him the sensuality is mostly expressed in adolescent terms. He is developing on seven-league boots . . .[53]

In *Time and Tide*, under the heading 'Mr A and Mr B', Seán Rafferty reviewed John's *Selected Poems* with Auden's *The Age of Anxiety* – a poem which Auden had dedicated to John, perhaps to mollify him after his protests about *Slick but not Streamlined*.

Nothing but a new poem by Mr Auden [Rafferty wrote] would permit the mention of Mr Betjeman's name at the end of a review: that most of his poems, chosen and excellently prefaced by Mr John Sparrow, are already familiar is a faint excuse. It might be possible to overpraise Mr Betjeman from sheer relief: how unusual, reading one's contemporaries, to understand first and puzzle afterwards instead of puzzling dismally all the time. Captain Webb,

  Dripping and still he rose over the sill and faded away in the wall

is as immortal as an Ingoldsby Legend and if I were forced to bet on any modern poet's survival, I should put my money on Mr Betjeman in a Gothic niche . . .[54]

The Spectator also bracketed Auden and Betjeman, in a review by H.A.L. Craig. Craig thought John deserved the dedication of *The Age of Anxiety*. 'Indeed, John Betjeman deserves much, for he is that rarity, a poet who chooses his own limitations and is completely successful within them. Auden sets himself a big test, and fails; Betjeman a lesser test, and passes it, taking again the prize of the senior freshman year. This is not to belittle Betjeman, but to place him . . . John Betjeman is a minor poet, but an original one. The exactness of his expression, the lightness with which he lays down serious moods, the

disarming way he codifies the unwritten and terrifying laws of middle-
class behaviour, are the works of a master.'[55] The anonymous reviewer
in *The Listener* also praised John. 'This descendant of Crabbe,
Calverley and Praed, this poet of the local gazette, of parish, school
or regimental magazine, writes with assurance, wit and style.'[56] The
reviewer thought that the tender last lines of 'Parliament Hill Fields'
were 'almost Blake-like' –

> And my childish wave of pity, seeing children carrying down
> Sheaves of drooping dandelions to the courts of Kentish Town.

John's old school friend Andrew Wordsworth, who had reviewed
Old Lights for *Time and Tide*, now wrote on *Selected Poems* for the
New Statesman. Once again he recalled visiting John in his 'bin', or
study, at the age of fourteen, and the revelation of John's use of
schoolboy slang 'in inverted commas'. He continued:

In his poetry Mr Betjeman has always been able to capture 'the language
really used by men', and especially by men when they are most vividly representative of their class or type. Just as it has always been found funny
that people should be of different sexes (it is strictly incongruous) it is
funny too, that people should be of different classes; and the funniest
moment of this joke is when they are pinpointed by an eccentric but
exactly centred blasphemy upon the holiness of the English language.
Pleasure in being in a different drawer from other people is called snobbery and it is generally allied with contempt. Mr Betjeman has not always
been free from it. His *Varsity Students Rag* begins:

> I'm afraid the fellows in Putney rather wish they had
> The social ease and manners of a 'varsity undergrad,
> For tho' they're awf'lly decent and up to a lark as a rule,
> You want to have the 'varsity touch after a public school.

This is very funny because the observation in 1929 of the 'fast' undergraduate from a minor public school is wonderfully correct. But the poem
is distasteful because it is contemptuous and lacking in sympathy. No
other poem by Mr Betjeman is in this category. The most important point
about him is that he likes people very much indeed, even, or perhaps especially, when he is appalled by them.[57]

Of John Sparrow's preface, Wordsworth commented that it was 'in
the manner of homage for a seventieth birthday' (precisely what
Sparrow was asked to do, twenty-eight years later, in a television

broadcast to mark John's reaching seventy). Wordsworth added: 'There is, I expect, a secret joke in writing pompously about these poems – incongruity about incongruity. So it is perhaps funny of Mr Sparrow not to say that they are funny.'[58]

John was receiving attention in the literary pages for another reason in 1948 and early 1949. In 1948 he contributed an introduction to *The Eighteen Nineties*, an anthology by Martin Secker. Many remembered the 'Naughty Nineties' with affection in the post-war austerity, but John reminded his readers that it was a world 'which ended in prison and disgrace for Wilde, suicide for Crackanthorpe and John Davidson, premature death for Beardsley, Dowson, Lionel Johnson, religion for some, drink and drugs for others . . .'[59] Evelyn Waugh gave the book a waspish review in the Roman Catholic periodical *The Month*. It began with the complaint that, though Phil May was a much better draughtsman than Max Beerbohm, he had no place in the anthology.[60] John could not be blamed for that; but he took exception to comments aimed at himself – not least a reference to the 'jaunty sub-aestheticism of the Third Programme' – at a time when relations between the two men were particularly sensitive because of their acerbic exchange of letters about Penelope's conversion.*[61] Waugh only half apologized.[62]

On 27 November 1948 John wrote to Jock Murray: 'IF my poems are doing well, can you let me have an idea of how much money I shall be getting by, let us say, December 31st? I ask because I am, I see, over-drawn on all sides and must probably consider selling a few colour plate books which, thank God, I have, as visible capital. I don't expect much will be coming in from *Bucks*.'[63] His royalties on *Selected Poems* were £176 2s 5d by the end of the year.[64]

* See Chapter 16, 'Farnborough'.

A PRESERVATIONIST IN THE MAKING

The most important name of all [in writings on Victorian architecture] will not appear in my footnotes because his influence has not been exerted through learned articles, but through poetry and conversation. It is that of Mr John Betjeman, one of the few original minds of our generation. His first interest in Gothic Revival architecture may have been part of his overflowing love of the neglected; but his sensitive response to architecture, as to everything which expresses human needs and affections, allowed him to see through the distorting fog of fashion, and to recognize the living force of the Gothic Revival in Voysey and in Mr J.N. Comper. The changed point of view which underlies all recent articles on nineteenth-century architecture . . . is due directly to the stimulus of his talk; which proves once again that history is not to be found solely in files and learned publications, but in human contacts and in the radiation of a single personality.

Kenneth Clark, letter to Michael Sadleir (dated July 1949), prefacing
The Gothic Revival, London 1950 edition

John had the same belief about architectural appreciation as Freud had about the human psyche: that experiences in early childhood are crucially formative. 'What makes you like architecture', he wrote in 1971, 'are the things you have seen and reacted to as a child.'[1] The first buildings he could remember were on Highgate West Hill. 'I did not realize that some of them were charming Georgian.'[2] He thought that tall buildings near his parents' house, in a Pimlico style, were very ugly. 'One of them was lived in by some people called Garnett. I think they were the British Museum lot,[3] and I used to call out "Ugly Garnetts!" '[4] So as early as that – before the First World War – he was exercising his own taste, deciding for himself what he liked and disliked. The spiky skyline of Holly Village, Highgate, built by Alfred Darbyshire in 1864 to house Baroness Burdett-Coutts's servants, gave him a frisson of horror.[5] Also, he thought that anything in grey or stock brick was ugly and that red brick was beautiful. 'I remember my father telling me that this was not so.'[6]

In his early years, before 'the Devil [came]'[7] to sour relations between father and son, John paid much attention to Ernest Betjemann's decided views on architecture. When Glenhurst Avenue was built near John's birthplace, Parliament Hill Mansions, the boy thought its bow-windowed red-brick houses, of 'Metroland' style, were beautiful. 'My father told me they were awful. I now see [1971] that he was right.'[8]

What made John realize that there was 'more than surface' in architecture was *The Ghost Stories of an Antiquary* by M.R. James, which 'Skipper' Lynam used to read the boys at the Dragon School. 'Those stories', John said, 'bring out the Norfolk landscape, Perpendicular churches, Georgian squires' houses in red brick, Strawberry Hill Gothick, mezzotints and the eighteenth century as well as the Middle Ages – and with that touch of horror which is essential to keep one's attention.'[9] M.R. James's eclecticism was a good antidote to the indoctrination that John was receiving from the Dragon School master 'Tortoise' Haynes, who believed that the dog-tooth Norman arch at the entrance to Iffley Church was the *summa* of English architecture.[10] John picked up architectural terms from a book in the 'Shown to the Children' series by T.E. and C. Jack. 'It ran through the whole lot – Norm, Dec, E.E., Perp and then a quick bit about St Paul's, and then it said, "What is your favourite style? Does it begin with a G?" By then mine didn't, but it does now,'[11] he wrote in 1971.

On sketching expeditions at Marlborough, in the 1920s, he became infatuated with Ramsbury Manor, a classical building of the late seventeenth century.[12] During the school holidays, he explored the City of London churches, which he had already discovered in holidays from the Dragon School.[13] He took John Bowle on a memorable tour of them, on an open-topped bus.[14] 'There were a lot more of them then than there are now,' John said in 1971. 'I have always preferred unimportant things to ones which are well known, and so I found churches which have since been pulled down, with box-pews in them and clear glass windows, and very lazy rectors, and very uncooperative churchwardens, such as St Katharine Coleman . . .'[15] He also began buying second-hand books, among them Thomas H. Shepherd's *Metropolitan Improvements* – 'steel-engravings of London in the 1820s, the sort of things that are now tinted in by watercolour and put on to dinner mats.'[16]

And then my eyes were opened by looking at a book called *Monumental Classic Architecture in Great Britain and Ireland* by A.E. Richardson.[17] That was folio with whacking great sepia photographs by Bedford Lemere. Those pictures opened up a world to me that I did not know existed – that you could go beyond Sir Christopher Wren and even admire Somerset House, and still more the Greek Revival, and notice things like Waterloo Bridge, and the British Museum, and branches of the Bank of England, in the Romano-Greek style, in Bristol and Birmingham.[18]

At Marlborough, too, John waged his first conservation campaign. In the new introduction, 'An Aesthete's Apologia', which he wrote for Anthony Blond's reissue of *Ghastly Good Taste* in 1971, he recalled how offended he had been at school that the grotto Lady Hertford had caused to be built in the eighteenth century was used as a potato shed and kept locked.[19] As so often in the future, he had used the press to express his anger and to try to remedy the situation – in this case, in the school magazine.[20]

Letters sent in his Oxford days show John's continuing interest in eighteenth-century architecture. Writing to Pierce Synnott in 1927, he praised 'a beautiful baroque church at Edgware built by an eighteenth-century Duke of Chandos'[21] and a church of 1760 at West Wycombe, where the politician Bubb Dodington, Lord Melcombe, was buried.[22] A taste for the Georgian, let alone the Victorian, was revolutionary enough at that time. Looking back, as president of the Georgian Group, in 1969, John's friend Lord Rosse said, 'It must be remembered that the period between the wars was that of Jacobean cocktail bars and spurious Knole sofas, when Georgian buildings were dismissed as dull square boxes.'[23] Rennie's Waterloo Bridge was destroyed in 1934; and the destruction of Adelphi Terrace, London, an Adam building, in 1937, provoked the formation of the Georgian Group, in which John took part with Douglas Goldring, the older poet viewed by some as a proto-Betjeman.[24]

Through Alan Pryce-Jones, John was brought, in the late 1920s, into the circle of Sir John Squire, editor of the *London Mercury*.[25] John much admired a poem Squire had written attacking the Bishop of London in 1919, when the prelate planned to demolish nineteen City churches.[26] John, too, used verse as a weapon against those who threatened or destroyed Georgian architecture. In 1932, when Sir Reginald Blomfield, architect of the new Lambeth Bridge, the new Regent Street and the new part of Carlton House Terrace, was incautious enough to say that 'The Regency did not produce "gems", either in architecture or anything else,'[27] John wrote '1930 Commercial Style' with furious irony –

> How nice to watch the buildings go
> From Regent Street to Savile Row.
> How nice to know, despite it all,

> We need not grumble when they fall;
> For ain't the big new Quadrant lined
> With facings 'Architect-designed'?[28]

More than anybody else, John is credited – and rightly – with having established the taste for the Victorian; but he was not the first in the field, and his own appreciation of Victorian work was slow to develop. Harold Acton, Robert Byron and Henry Green (Henry Yorke) had all collected Victoriana before they came to Oxford;[29] and Osbert Sitwell had indulged a similar taste before them, not only in his collections, but also, like John, in poems.[30] John, in his changing attitude to the Victorians, passed through all the stages that James Laver has ascribed to style revivals: hostility, amused tolerance, romantic appreciation and scholarly investigation. In 1923 his lifelong friend Philip Harding recorded in the minutes of the Marlborough literary society how John had read a paper on early-Victorian art and literature 'which he very aptly illustrated by passing round examples to prove to what artistic depths the Victorians had debased themselves'.[31] Six months later, the school magazine reported John's first speech at the debating society, 'eloquently recalling the exhibition of 1851 with scorn'.[32]

It was also while he was at Marlborough that he wrote, at sixteen, an 'Ode on a Mid-Victorian Centre Ornament'. Hitherto unpublished, it runs:

> Oh thou maid of buxom beauty!
>   Lifting up to hold the cake,
> An impossible creation,
>   Which is surely a mistake,
> I have often wept in thinking
>   How terribly your arms must ache.
>
> Oh thou fish in beauty trailing
>   At each corner, are you dead?
> If you are not I will warn you
>   'Lie the other way instead:
> Staying long in that position
>   Makes the blood run to your head.'
>
> Oh you thousand strange devices,
>   Can you tell me what you mean
> By trailing creepy curly tendrils
>   Over every varied scene,
> Infringing on the neat inscription
>   'A presentation to the Dean . . .'?[33]

John claimed that at Oxford he had 'reacted against the Greek Revival and certainly against genuine Gothic, which merely seemed funny and rather pathetic . . . I started to like the Gothick Revival with a "k" as hinted at in M.R. James's stories, when it was Perpendicular revival of the 1820s and 30s. I could now see the merits of the Houses of Parliament. And this was in the 1920s, when of course the prevailing taste was all in favour of the classical, and being as like Wren as possible.'[34] His taste for the Gothick was stimulated by his stay in 1927 at Shelton Abbey in Ireland, Lord Clonmore's Gothick home.[35]

However, in his undergraduate days John was far from being an enthusiast for Victorian Gothic. In 1927 he illustrated in *The Cherwell* the Gothick Revival porch of 5 Norham Gardens, North Oxford, and wrote: 'I have found that for which I have long been searching – the worst and most senseless building in Oxford.'[36] But while an undergraduate he did show a sort of liking for at least one Victorian building, in a letter to his Magdalen friend Lionel Perry:

> I am in the Grill Room not of Oddenino's, nor of the Café Royal nor even of the Troc[adero] but of the Crystal Palace. Here I am encased in Paxton's Great Masterpiece looking over the suburbs of South London . . . I shall boat on the lake this afternoon and read Hemans,[37] looking up at the Crystal Palace like a great waterfall among the trees . . .
>
> Dear [Prince] Albert has left his mark here by appearing in every little niche round the concert room where the names of great people are written round the walls in blue and yellow and gold and red – HERCULES – MENDELSSOHN – MME PAGANINI – APOLLO – everybody.
>
> Even as I write, a man has entered the 'Grill Room' with real Dandiacal whiskers.[38]

There seems to be genuine admiration in this, though the use of capital initials for 'Great Masterpiece' suggests that John wanted to leave open the option of being taken to be facetious. The mention of the bewhiskered dandy illustrates his characteristic relating of architecture to the sort of people for whom it was created. When he joined *The Architectural Review* in 1930, the Crystal Palace was one of the few Victorian buildings he was permitted to admire. In its metal-and-glass construction it was seen as a precursor of the Modern Movement.

John's earliest two letters to *The Times*, written in 1926[39] and 1927, give the impression that he was still, in general, vehemently anti-Victorian. To a church-lover, the main thing the Victorians represented was the over-zealous 'restoration' of old churches, which William Morris had abominated as 'scrape'. In his second letter to *The Times*, published in November 1927, John went so far as to suggest that, wherever possible, the 'restorations' should be undone.

> There is a great need for an Æsthetic Commission to enforce the destruction of church ornamentation of the latter half of the last century. I do not think I shall be considered eccentric for wishing my own memorial to take the form of the removal of the pitch-pine pews, marble pulpit, or 1880 East window from my own parish church.[40]

He 'recycled' some of the ingredients of the letter, more tellingly, in his poem 'Hymn', which was first published in the *Isis*, the undergraduate magazine, as 'To the Blessed St Aubin'[41] in October 1928. Also in 1928 John wrote to the publishers Ward, Lock about their guidebook to Leamington: 'Unless your author is writing in a spirit of satire, I do not think he could call the iron and glass pavilion in the Jephson Gardens "handsome" . . . Please do not think that I want to be unpleasant or that I am too modern, but I do believe that nowadays the greater enormities of the Gothic Revival and of Victorian smugness are at a discount.'[42]

Sneering at Victorian buildings was *de rigueur* for staff on *The Architectural Review*. Again, in June 1931 John wrote a letter to the newspaper in defence of modernism. He used his office address; and his views would have been entirely in keeping with those of his boss, Hubert de Cronin Hastings.

> No wonder modern architecture is generally imitative and sterile if such an opinion as was expressed by one of your correspondents on 3 June is common – 'it seems even more important to set up something beautiful than something new.' Medieval architects, whom your correspondent so much admires, were not conscious that they were building in a 'style'. Although the eighteenth century may have imitated, in its detail, Classic decoration, it was a 'new' spirit which overruled all questions of style that gave Oxford her crowning architectural glory, the Radcliffe Camera, contrasting so boldly and well with the Gothic that surrounds it. The goodness of architecture does not depend upon its style; when it was built the Parthenon was not classified as 'Doric'.[43]

In 1932 John mounted the first of his campaigns to try to save a historic piece of architecture – John Rennie's Waterloo Bridge (1810–17). He was in favour of reconditioning the bridge, and in *The Times* put forward precise, practical suggestions as to how that operation could be financed.[44] He failed: the bridge was destroyed and a new one was designed by Sir Giles Gilbert Scott. John's defence of a pre-Victorian bridge – 'industrial architecture' – would not have jarred on de Cronin Hastings. But four months later, in an address at Painters' Hall to the Incorporated Institute of British Decorators, John made some remarks about the International Style that were distinctly 'off message'. He was only twenty-five; but his speech was reported at length in the home news pages of *The Times*. Part of the talk was wholly in line with *Architectural Review* dogma.

In a paper entitled 'From Bad to Worse' Mr JOHN BETJEMAN said he was tired of those people who decorated the interior of fashionable houses in Mayfair–Ecclesiastical–Spanish or South-Kensington–Monumental–Queen Anne, and he yawned when an architect said to him, as one did the other day, 'Oh yes, I can run you up something in Tudor antique or in jazz modern [Art Deco] just as well.' 'Decorate' was the wrong word unless it meant the same as 'build', because architecture and decoration were insep-arable . . .

In a later passage of the speech, John suddenly veered away from *Architectural Review* orthodoxy and revealed what he really felt about the Modern Movement.

After referring to the architecture of today as 'chaos', Mr Betjeman spoke pessimistically of the future. Architecture, he said, would not consist of the varying indigenous styles of a county or a country, but of one style for a continent. The increase of transport, the spread of knowledge, the uni-versality of many materials would cause most of Europe to have the same style. We were being levelled down . . . The motor-car had become more important than the house, the petrol than a picture. In the house the sitting-room was less important than the kitchen, and artists would be required to dispense with mere ornament and create things severely of use.[45]

John's somewhat pontifical *Times* letters of the late 1920s suggest a man implacably hostile to all things Victorian; but even then in talk with his close friends he revealed a more catholic taste. Kenneth Clark, whose pioneering book *The Gothic Revival* was published in 1928, later acknowledged that John was one of the people who had opened his eyes to Victorian architecture.[46] In 1930, Evelyn Waugh, in his travel book *Labels*, called John 'the chief living authority' on the *art nouveau* architecture of Antoni Gaudí.[47] In 1933, reprinting the 'Church's restoration' poem in *Ghastly Good Taste*, John added: 'But it is tiresome to laugh at Victorian solecisms. It has been done too often. For those who wish to read a far from laughable study of the earlier part of the Gothic Revival, I can recommend Mr Kenneth Clark's book on that subject.'[48] Here was a distinct thawing. As we have seen, in 1934 John wrote to Bryan Guinness that he was going to stay in the (Victorian Gothic) Charing Cross Hotel, London, 'as I am very fond of it there . . .'[49] In that year, too, Evelyn Waugh, in *A Handful of Dust*, teasingly associated John with the appreciation of Victorian architecture.* An appreciation of Victorian art and architecture was among the many bonds between Waugh and John, before differences over religion caused their rift.[50] John gave the novelist a Victorian wash-hand stand by William Burges, which was known in the Waugh household as 'the Betjeman Benefaction'.[51] Waugh's interest in the Victorians may have been engaged by his kinship with the Pre-Raphaelite painter William Holman Hunt.[52] (His first book was on another Pre-Raphaelite, Dante Gabriel Rossetti.) But probably the same things drew both men to the Victorian age: a voyeurist fascination with the period just before their births and with the security and imperial splendours of a supposed golden age disrupted by the Great War; the appeal of a time when religion was a dominant force, at the centre of life; an architecture not stripped of beguiling ornament by the Modern Movement; and an aesthetic not undermined by cubism, vorticism and other twentieth-century fads. ('Modern art is all bosh, isn't it?' Cordelia asks Charles Ryder in *Brideshead Revisited*. 'Great bosh.')[53]

On 8 February 1936, at twenty-nine, John was for the second time the subject of a news report in *The Times*: 'OXFORD ARCHITECTURE CRITICIZED'. In a lecture on 'Modern Oxford Architecture' he had said that the factors which had made such a muddle of the city were antiquarianism and a desire to preserve. There was, he said, no point in preserving 'an early English arch or a squalid little block of medieval buildings' if undergraduates were to be forced to live miles down the Iffley, Banbury and Botley roads. Better build 'new and higher blocks of college buildings as they did in the eighteenth century'. The buildings need not be of steel and glass, but they could be convenient and up to date. 'Modesty and the desire to leave everything to the specialists, without knowing who the good specialists were, had resulted in the present architectural disasters of Oxford.'

De Cronin Hastings may well have rapped John across the knuckles for his outburst against the Modern Movement in the paper to the British Decorators in 1932. By 1936 John had left the staff of *The Architectural Review*; but he was still a contributor, and Hastings would have had nothing to complain of in the speech about Oxford

---

* See Chapter 16, 'Farnborough'.

architecture, in which John showed himself, so to speak, more Catholic than the Pope. He would have liked, he said, 'to see a planned university and a planned city, one collegiate and the other industrial'.

> Industry was giving us a new sort of landscape with a beauty of its own. The mistake that we made was to be ashamed of the strange creations of industry – huge buildings of glass and steel, pylons, wires, factories, chimneys and power stations. Oxford had been allowed to sprawl over the countryside, and the industrial city had been allowed to encroach to the feet of its famous buildings. 'It has become one of the lost causes, architecturally. The only decent approach to it is by way of a punt down the Cherwell.'

He spoke of 'the dull design of the new Bodleian, the waste of space and money at Rhodes House; the hideous example and messy appearance of St Peter's Hall'. He blamed the University authorities for much of the muddle.[54]

A year later, the Judicial Committee of the Privy Council in London held an inquiry into a scheme for the removal of All Hallows Church, Lombard Street, proposed by the Ecclesiastical Commissioners and opposed by the City Corporation, the Conference of Learned Societies and P.A. Moleno, a parishioner.[55] A report by the Society for the Protection of Ancient Buildings recalled the steps taken in 1919 to try to secure the demolition of nineteen City churches and the sale of their sites which the Society had helped to defeat. All Hallows had been one of the churches threatened then. Rebuilt by Wren after the Great Fire, it was known as 'the church invisible' because it was so constructed that it could hardly be seen from any street. It had woodwork and fittings of great beauty, an organ by Renatus Harris and a marble font probably by Grinling Gibbons. The lowest estimate of the site's value was £150,000; but as H.B. Vaisey said, opening the case for the Corporation of London, 'Many people are shocked, and very rightly shocked, at the idea of having that consecrated site used for a joint stock bank.'[56] Nevertheless on 7 February 1937 three law lords agreed that the church should be demolished, so that 'money from the centre of London should go to the suburbs'.[57] On 5 March a magisterial letter from John was published in *The Times*. 'It is daring indeed of any architect to think that he will do as well as Wren in arranging that beautiful woodwork in a building of his own,' he wrote.[58] He admitted that the once handsome interior of All Hallows had never recovered from a Victorian 'restoration'; but he argued that the fittings should on no account be redistributed among several churches.

The tragedy of St Katharine Coleman must not be repeated. This City church was removed, in pursuance of the Bishop of London's policy, shortly after the First World War. It had one of the few unspoiled Georgian interiors in the country ... Its magnificent pulpit and Communion rail now lost all significance in a huge, not unlovely, new church in Acton. What became of the old organ, its case, the gallery columns, the font and the acres of fine joinery in the box pews I have never discovered.[59]

On 7 March, the veteran Arts and Crafts designer C.R. Ashbee wrote to John to congratulate him on his 'good letter in the *Times*'.[60]

Though John was always at his most passionate in defending the City of London, especially its churches, he had homes in the country for much of his life, and often intervened in disputes on rural issues. In July 1937 he again wrote to *The Times* to support the Dowager Duchess of Norfolk, who had written to the paper about rural housing and who had asserted that 'There is a class in this country simply at the mercy of the local authority.'[61] John agreed: council houses were too big for old-age pensioners, even if they could afford them, and old people were not strong enough to start a new garden on virgin soil.[62] Beyond the tender concern for pensioners that the letter might suggest was probably the desire to score a point against the balefully regarded 'local authority' (the very word 'authority' was a red rag to John) and to release bile at the council houses springing up in Uffington.

By 1937, John's conversion to Victorian architecture was well advanced. In that year he warned John Summerson that the 'magnificent' Mary Ward Settlement in Tavistock Place, London, an early 1900s building by Dunbar Smith and Cecil Brewer, was to be demolished, and suggested it should be photographed.[63] A month later he wrote to Bryan Guinness, after the Crystal Palace had burned down: 'I haven't recovered yet.'[64] Osbert Lancaster had written to John on the night of the fire:

The only consolation which this disaster could possibly afford would be in the event of your muse drawing inspiration from so horrid a conflagration. I think we have the right to expect an epic fragment celebrating Paxton's masterpiece and its shocking fate in heroic couplets from your pen ... Quick, quick, before Auden or Spender seize it as a peg on which to hang some dreary Communist didacticism – a convenient symbol for ... spectacular social collapse ...[65]

In 1938 John's passion for Victorian Gothic is seen in full spate in a letter to Sir Giles Gilbert Scott. 'I am intensely interested in the work of George Gilbert Scott Junior who was, Mr Comper tells me, your father . . . I am prepared to travel as far as my purse will allow in search of his buildings.'[66] From then on, John's proselytizing on behalf of the Victorians was unflagging, in poetry and prose and on radio and television.

At the same time, he continued to have a bee in his bonnet about 'antiquarianism' – the word he had used disparagingly in his 1936 lecture on modern Oxford architecture. Quirkishly, he gave this word much the same sense as 'traditionalism'. In 1939 Virginia and Leonard Woolf published his booklet *Antiquarian Prejudice* at the Hogarth Press, a hard-hitting polemic which had much in common with Robert Byron's squib of 1937, 'How We Celebrate the Coronation: A Word to London's Visitors'.[67] 'The clergy are medievalists to a man,' John complained.[68]

> . . . Hey presto! before we know where we are there will be a box-pew cleared away to make a children's corner, a decent classic monument destroyed to reveal a conjectured wall-painting, fresh surface for the work of Professor Tristram,[69] a Royal Arms removed as 'not devotional' . . .[70]

He thought that antiquarianism (in his idiosyncratic sense) also ruined much contemporary architecture. 'What makes the new Regent Street such a grimy joke? Why is South Africa House so hideous?[71] First, there is the timidity miscalled "tradition", but really antiquarianism, which enslaves be-knighted architects . . .'[72] He had special scorn for St John's Wood in north London, 'where some of the most arrogant, staring, badly-planned travesties of Queen Anne architecture flare up in place of the decent Early Victorian stucco which once made that district a sun-reflecting half-village among laburnums and pollarded limes'.[73] He derided those 'experts' who had 'that wonderful gift of turning life to death, of interest to ashes',[74] and railed against those who responded to art and architecture, not with the instinct of an aesthete, but with the scholarly apparatus and attention to detail of a researcher. 'Research is the curse of our age.'[75]

> Perhaps long ago the expert really did like aquatints, but now he only likes knowing about first proofs, raw state, etc., etc. His word for 'beautiful' has become 'interesting'.[76]

John was not only firing early shots in what was to become a full-blooded vendetta against the immigrant German scholar Nikolaus Pevsner;* he was attacking the growing industry of professional art history.

---

* See the chapter ' "Vic. Soc." and "The Dok" ' in the third volume of the present work.

If the tremendous amount of money that has been lavished on founding the Courtauld Institute – an institute for breeding art critics and antique dealers of the more expensive sort – had instead been given as a fund for the encouragement and support of living artists, those among my readers who are creative workers would be able to have the more chance of earning a livelihood by what they like best. It is symptomatic of this age of anti-quarianism that a thing like the Courtauld Institute exists.[77]

The rant of the pamphlet was muddled. It contained an outburst against jazz modern or *moderne* (Art Deco), which was not primarily an 'antiquarian' style, but rather a bastardized, domesticated version of cubism.[78] However, the central message was clear: no amount of scholarly research could compensate for the lack of aesthetic sensitiv-ity, taste, a 'good eye'.

John wrote no letters to *The Times* during the war period; he was preoccupied, and as a civil servant could not express private views in the press without permission. When he did write again, in July 1946, it was in the spirit of the French comedian who was put in a concen-tration camp when the Germans occupied Paris and who, on return-ing to the stage after the Liberation, began his act: 'As I was saying, before I was so rudely interrupted . . .' Once again, John was indig-nant about new houses in the country, particularly as they were for staff of the atomic research station at Harwell. He deplored the plan that 'the two ancient and unspoiled towns of Abingdon and Wantage' should have their populations 'disproportionately increased'. The two towns were 'workable units' as they stood, 'and we know from experi-ence during the war how dangerous it is to monkey about with the population figures of old-established towns'.[79] To describe Wantage as 'unspoiled' was stretching the truth; here John was a protester of the kind later known as a 'nimby' – 'not in my back yard'.

He consistently opposed new housing for workers, at least on his doorstep. But on one subject his views changed. The pylons which, in his Oxford lecture of 1936, were among the creations of industry that were 'giving us a new sort of landscape with a beauty of its own', had by April 1947 become eyesores. In that month he attacked the Post Office's proposal to erect a television relay station on White Horse Hill.

The strange chalk dragon, the great bowl of the manger, the green rampart of Uffington Castle, comprise one of the fairest downland scenes in England. The beauty of this hill, with its wide views from the rippling sea of wind-blown grass, was in its remoteness from the present age, when one stood on it. And from the vast vale below, its beauty was in the bare-ness of the noble outline of down. Both remoteness and outline the Post

Office now intends to destroy in the interests of television, which it naturally considers more important . . . Of all hill sites to choose for the erec-
tion of masts and a hut, I can think of none more unfortunate.[80]

On 30 April, Henry Strauss MP asked a Parliamentary question
about the masts. The reply came from William Paling, who lives in
Commons lore as the victim of a classic Churchill joke. (Paling called
Churchill a dirty dog. Churchill replied: 'If the honourable member
would care to accompany me outside this House, I will show him what
a dirty dog does to a Paling.')[81] Paling said the White Horse Hill
station was 'one of three small relay stations required in connection
with research into the transmission of television signals by radio from
Bristol and Cardiff'.[82] The very next day, before John and his allies
could remuster, Post Office engineers took White Horse Hill. John
immediately wrote again to *The Times*.

> The Post Office has now [1 May] put up two clumps of poles about 300
> yards south of the Ridgeway from White Horse Hill, on an elevated
> ridge of grassdown. The Nissen huts and the full number of poles have
> not yet arrived . . . The age-old view of grass and fields and distant barns
> and ricks is interrupted by these gimcrack-looking clusters of Post
> Office engineering . . . If the experience we in this district have suffered
> from the behaviour of Government departments over Harwell is any cri-
> terion, we shall never be told of the damage to be done until after the
> event.[83]

In the light of his later fame as a 'television personality', it seems
ironic that John should have made a fuss about television relay masts.
If he had made such a complaint ten years later, the Post Office could
fairly have accused him of willing the end without willing the means.
    In 1948 John waged a quirkish and partially successful campaign to
preserve 'Colour on the Railway'. On 6 February he wrote:

> Now, when the British Transport Commission is considering the livery of
> our railways, comes the time to draw public attention to that beautiful and
> too long neglected subject.
>   The colours of engines and carriages in the pre-grouping days were not
> only, for the most part, attractive in themselves, but they emphasized the
> regional variety of our landscape, which is its especial merit. There were
> Great Eastern districts, even M[idland] and G[reat] N[orthern] districts,
> and for myself I still associate Scottish hills with those superb blue
> Caledonian engines. Countless people must have regretted the covering of
> the chocolate and cream carriages of the L[ondon] and N[orth] W[estern]

with that vulgar Midland red, which grew drabber and drabber with the L[ondon] M[idland] and S[cottish].[84]

Behind these liverish remarks on liveries might be discerned a broader theme, of reactionary disgruntlement over nationalization; but, in a Britain still crimped by post-war austerity and rationing, John's letter struck a nerve. By 14 February it had become a news story in *The Times*. 'Mr John Betjeman's letter to the Editor of *The Times*, published on February 6, on the livery of railway engines and coaches has attracted a large number of replies from readers almost unanimous in their desire for brighter colours.'[85] For locomotives blue, preferably the bright blue of the old Caledonian Railway, seemed the favourite.

The railway-colours letter not only provoked a news report; it also inspired a *Times* Fourth Leader characteristic of that facetious genre.

MR JOHN BETJEMAN's plea for beauty and variety of colour in our nationalized railway engines must evoke sympathy from all whose 'sense of heraldry', as he so well calls it, rebels against the dingy and the uniform. Everyone loves an engine and the sight of it storming through a station, dragging its little whirlwind of waste paper behind it, is one that never ceases to thrill. But many people, though they retain this youthful passion, do not retain MR BETJEMAN's youthfully accurate memory and power of observation.

> *Some like monarchs glow*
> *With richest purple some are blue*

and also green; but for them the engine passes in all too quick a flash and which hue denotes, or used to denote, which line is a question which finds them regrettably vague.

They are on surer ground . . . in dwelling on the insides of railway carriages which they can contemplate at greater leisure . . .[86]

The leader went on to contrast the interiors of first-, second- and third-class carriages, with equal pawkiness. But British Railways took John seriously, recognizing his trouble-making potential. Like the good tactician he was, General Sir William Slim, chairman of the BR executive, made a pre-emptive strike on 18 February, conceding just enough of John's plan, to keep him quiet: in May the executive would put into service about eight main-line trains, each painted in a different colour.[87] John described the concessions as 'Slim pickings'.[88]

Towards the end of 1948, he took a leading part in a much more significant controversy. On 30 October, F.T. Barrett, chairman of the parish
meeting of the Berkshire village of Letcombe Bassett, wrote to *The
Times* to say that a threat of such serious import hung over the village
'that it must concern all who dwell in small villages'.[89] Letcombe
Bassett, with its thatched cottages and barns, an old church, elms and
beeches above watercress beds in a gorge of the downs, was 'a singularly
beautiful place'. Swift had stayed there: it was from Letcombe that he
had written his famous letter of farewell to the Earl of Oxford: 'I have
said enough; and, like one at your levee, having made my bow, I shrink
back into the crowd.' The village appears as Cresscombe in Hardy's
Jude the Obscure. 'Indeed [Barrett wrote], Arabella's cottage of that
novel is likely to be one of the casualties in what may happen.'[90]

Rather than build twelve new cottages and recondition the existing
ones (involving main sewerage at a cost of £4,500), Wantage Rural
District Council seemed disposed to take the advice of a Reading planning officer and 'disrupt the whole village community'. Its plan was to
shift most of the population, against its will, to a larger neighbouring
village. Letcombe Bassett would then be left as 'a few farms and associated dwellings, and a sprinkling of cottages which may, or may not,
be taken by retired people, and with the church in decay'. Barrett
added: 'If, instead of being one of the loveliest villages in Berkshire,
Bassett were a nest of bungalows, the plan would still be sinister, for
it strikes at the root of an Englishman's love of his home surroundings . . . Are all our small villages to be allowed to decay, while their
luckless inhabitants are shifted to "larger units"?'[91]

In November, Dr C.S. Orwin of The Malt House, Blewbury,
Didcot, wrote to *The Times*, ridiculing the village's houses and assert-
ing that 'there are no buildings of historical or architectural importance in Letcombe Bassett . . .'[92] This was more than John could bear.
On 3 December he wrote to *The Times*:

> I must join issue with Dr Orwin on a number of matters which arise from
> his letter . . . First, no purpose is served by his listing, as he does, the few
> modern and unattractive buildings in Letcombe Bassett and omitting the
> many old and humbly beautiful ones which preponderate. On the same
> principle, I could produce a proportionately greater list of ugly buildings
> in the village of Blewbury from which he writes. His final paragraph
> comes as a shock. He implies that because there is now no school or resi-
> dent priest or 'social institution' (there *is* an excellent inn) or athletic club,
> therefore 150 people should be moved elsewhere. This is rather like saying
> that because a person who can be cured is ill, it is wiser, if it is cheaper, to
> kill him . . .[93]

John applauded the Minister Lewis Silkin's statement that he was opposed to the destruction of small villages, and his assurance that the people of Letcombe would be allowed to speak for themselves at a public enquiry. As we have seen, John also made a radio broadcast about Letcombe with Thomas Sharp.* On 15 December 1948 H.J.C. Neobard, Clerk of the Council at Shire Hall, Reading, wrote to *The Times*: 'In view of the publicity given to the development of this village, the planning committee of the Berkshire County Council wishes it to be known that no decision has been reached by the council as to the future planning of Letcombe Bassett.' The white flag was being shown, and Letcombe was saved.

Writing from Denchworth Manor, by Wantage, John's friend Compton Mackenzie, never one to pull his punches, started another conservation row with a letter to *The Times* on 17 September 1949.

Is it too late for sane, decent and civilized public opinion to shame Mr Silkin into withdrawing the permission he has accorded a private company to quarry along the whole length of Dulcote Hill and thereby ruin the natural frame of the lovely city of Wells? . . . 'Progress must come before sentiment,' the Minister . . . warned . . . But why stop at the frame? Why not sell the stones of Wells Cathedral and indeed the stones of every old edifice in England which has survived the Reformation and the German blitz?

On 24 September, in response to questions in the House, Silkin said he would take legal advice to see whether he had the power to reopen the inquiry. On 1 October, J. Foster Yeoman, a director of the quarrying company in question, wrote what he no doubt intended to be a reassuring letter. The inquiry had been held in 1947. The Government inspector had made his report. In April 1949 the Minister had given permission for some quarrying to go ahead: it would be undesirable, he said, to 'sterilize' – that is, leave untouched – the deposits of valuable limestone in the area; but he also laid down strict conditions to protect Wells and the western extremity of the hill. In his letter, Yeoman declared that he would obey the Minister; but he added a protest about the restrictions imposed, which, he wrote, would deprive his company of 'millions of tons of high quality stone . . . for the loss of which no redress is available to the shareholders'. This letter provoked one of John's most stinging attacks. He excoriated the company which intended 'to slice the top off Dulcote Hill'. Yeoman, he wrote, was 'hardly fair to those who object to such a drastic

* See Chapter 21, 'On the Air in the Forties'.

operation to a panorama so beautiful that it is of national and even dollar-earning interest'. No one had minded quarrying on Dulcote Hill for the last seventy years, because it had all been done on the side of the hill that did not face Wells. There was so much limestone in the area that 'the protection of Dulcote Hill from decapitation' was not going to 'sterilize the whole of the valuable deposits of limestone in this area'. The stone was certainly very fine, but there was more else-where, 'all the way from Frome to the sea'. It was not true to say the shareholders had no redress. Under the Town and Country Planning Act, if quarrying were stopped, they would be compensated.

> Finally, I do not see how there can be a 'reasonable' or any other kind of 'balance between the claims of amenity and the requirements of product-ive industry'. As well try to balance the claims of Wells Cathedral against those of dried eggs. There can be plenty of dried eggs so long as we have hens and chemicals and factories. But there is only one Wells. So there is plenty of limestone, but only one Dulcote Hill and one Wells of which it is a part.[94]

By 12 October 1949 the story had escalated into *The Times*'s main home news item. 'THE THREAT TO WELLS: CATHEDRAL SETTING ENDANGERED', though a *Times* reporter who visited Wells found to his surprise that 'of the 5,000 citizens of Wells, not more than a score or so really care'. The MP for Wells, Dennis Boles, who was on John's side, wrote to *The Times* on 20 December:

> We seem to have taken every reasonable step open to us to dissuade the Minister [Lewis Silkin] . . . from allowing the mutilation of our cherished countryside around Wells Cathedral. Neither to the north nor to the south has he met us. We in Somerset feel that we have failed as trustees in guard-ing our trust from the depredations of materialists . . . We must run no risk that ever again shall any of our Somerset shrines be at the mercy of a despoiler. It seems that in being able to mobilize public opinion early, to inform the public in time of any future threat, lies our best hope of pro-tection.

Boles announced that a Somerset (or Wells) Protection Society was to be formed. Here was another lesson for John: prevention was better than cure. Such thinking was behind the foundation of the Victorian Society eight years later, though its founders were to learn that public opinion had to be educated before it could be mobilized.

'TAME AND TADE'

I walked one day (it must, I think, have been in 1940) to the city to find the head of a famous firm of solicitors . . . The houses on either side of his had been bombed the night before and no longer existed. But his own office, standing up alone looking very tall and thin, had been only comparatively slightly blasted. He apologised for being in his extremely dirty shirtsleeves. 'I spent the morning scrubbing the floors,' he explained, 'there was no one else to do it.'

The spirit which was expressed in those words is one we have always tried to keep in *Time and Tide*. It applies to all of us. Those who cannot conform to it seldom stay with us very long.

Lady Rhondda, *Time and Tide Anthology*, edited by Anthony Lejeune,
London 1956

'I'm making some changes next week in the organization
    And though I admire
Your work for me, John, yet the need to increase circulation
    Means you must retire . . .'

John Betjeman, 'Caprice', *High and Low*, London 1966

After leaving the Oxford Preservation Trust in 1948, John made his living for a while as a freelance journalist, contributing promiscuously to *The Strand* (magazine), *The Listener* (spin-offs from his broadcasts), the *Church Observer*, the *Evening Standard*, *The Architectural Review*, *The Countrygoer*, the *Cornhill Magazine*, *The Harrovian* (the magazine of Harrow School), *Horizon*, *The Observer*, *Leader Magazine* and *The Author*. This kind of work continued for years but became more of a sideline than a lifeline in 1949, when John wrote to T.S. Eliot, 'I have become "Literary Advazer" to *Tame and Tade* which means going in on Mondays from two-thirty till five and distributing the books.'[1] He asked Eliot if he would review Ezra Pound's cantos, which he confessed he did not himself understand. 'The pay is *awful*,' he warned him.[2] Eliot declined the untempting offer and the commission went instead to Wolf Mankowitz, who wrote: 'Put simply, the situation of Pound seems to be that of an enthusiastic doctor beginning with an intense interest in the source and cure of a dangerous disease and finishing as a dreadful example of the disease itself.'[3]

John sometimes called himself 'literary adviser', sometimes 'literary editor' of the magazine. He succeeded the historian C.V. Wedgwood, who had been literary editor since 1943. How he got the job is not known. Under Veronica Wedgwood he was already a contributor of poems and reviews, and she may have recommended him to the magazine's formidable founder-proprietor-editor, Lady Rhondda; or he may have had more powerful backing. Anthony Lejeune, the son of John's old film-reviewing colleague C.A. Lejeune, joined the staff in 1956, three years after John left it. He was recommended by Sir Compton Mackenzie.[4] John, too, was a friend of 'Monty' Mackenzie.

Lady Rhondda founded *Time and Tide* in 1920 as an independent political and literary magazine. She was born Margaret Haig Thomas in 1883, daughter of David Alfred Thomas, a coal owner and politician. A militant suffragette, she jumped on to the running-board of Asquith's car and was roughly handled by the crowd; burned the contents of a pillar box with a chemical bomb; was sent to Usk Jail and went on hunger strike. She was returning from America with her father in the *Lusitania* in 1915 when the ship was torpedoed; both were saved, though she floated in a lifebelt three hours before being picked up unconscious. In 1918 David Thomas was created Viscount Rhondda with special remainder to his daughter 'in default of heirs male of his body'. A month later he died and Margaret inherited the title and a fortune. In a long legal dispute she claimed the right to sit in the House of Lords, an attempt which was finally defeated largely by the opposition of Lord Birkenhead.[5]

Though she married in 1908 (Sir) Humphrey Mackworth, later the seventh baronet, of Caerleon-on-Usk, the two were amicably divorced in 1923. Lady Rhondda was widely regarded as a lesbian. She surrounded herself with others of like tastes, such as the novelist Winifred Holtby (who died young in 1935) and Theodora Bosanquet, with whom she lived.[6] *Time and Tide*, it was said, wait for no *man*. Confusingly known as 'Bosie', Theodora Bosanquet had once been secretary to Henry James and had preceded Veronica Wedgwood as literary editor (1935–43). She was still coming into the office in John's time, arriving each morning on her motor-bike dressed from head to foot in black leather.[7] Veronica Wedgwood lived with the high-ranking civil servant Jacqueline Hope-Wallace, sister of Philip Hope-Wallace, the magazine's flamboyantly camp drama critic.

John found Lady Rhondda a difficult taskmistress, and he was not alone in that. Vera Brittain wrote glowingly of her in *Testament of*

Friendship, the book in which she recalled her own intense relationship with Winifred Holtby;[8] but when Brittain's diaries were published in 1986, almost thirty years after Lady Rhondda's death, a less flattering portrait appeared. Lady Rhondda would never allow her staff any initiative; she did not work hard enough herself, was just 'a rich leisured woman who runs the paper as a hobby'; and she had been Winifred Holtby's evil genius – 'used her time, health & energy, & gave little worth having in return for all that she took'. Holtby's letters revealed, Brittain thought, Lady Rhondda's 'selfishness and possessiveness' when, 'even in the appalling days of work & correspondence after [Holtby's] father's death she was apparently still expected to do Notes for T. & T.'[9] John may not have been the ideal employee, but Lady Rhondda was far from being the ideal boss.

In its early days, *Time and Tide* had been 'aggressively feminist', but by the time John joined the staff in 1949 that stance had been greatly relaxed. By 1958, when Lady Rhondda died, the magazine was considered right-wing and women's rights were seldom mentioned. Circulation had come to matter to the proprietress at least as much as influence. She had poured almost a quarter of a million pounds into subsidizing the magazine; now she wanted to see it profitable.

Reginald Langbridge, a cousin of the novelist Charles Morgan, joined *Time and Tide* as business manager in 1952, when John was literary editor. He had previously been publicity manager of Hutchinson's, the publishers, and deputy publicity manager of the *Daily Express*. He recalled:

> When I was buying advertising space for Hutchinson's I was told by the *Time and Tide* people that they hadn't got any net sales figures but they thought they were in the region of 30,000. They weren't. Its sales were around 10,000 a year, whereas *The Spectator* was around 40,000 and the *New Statesman* probably around 30,000. Those were *Time and Tide*'s main rivals, with *John o' London's Weekly* offering some competition on the literary side.
>
> The thing that lingers most in my mind, about *Time and Tide*, is the day I had to give the print order, which was rather an ordeal. Quite honestly, Lady Rhondda didn't mind if you increased the print order by several thousand every week regardless of whether there was any demand for it. She said, 'Ah! The sales are going up at last!' In fact, I was told by the outgoing man, 'All you've got to do to keep your job is to increase the print order every week.' Well, I refused to do that. I thought, I'll try to get it up by fair means but I'm not doing that, it would be so awkward to explain eventually. But the basement was always absolutely stuffed with returned copies. They had to get a van to come and collect them every so often,

because you couldn't get any more in. W.H. Smith used to return them by the sack-load.

What the newsagents were saying at that time was 'We want features' – especially the extracts from new books. That suddenly became the great thing in the Fifties. You couldn't open any newspaper or magazine that hadn't something that caught the eye and ran for three or four issues. So I said to Lady Rhondda, 'Well, could we have features of some sort? Book extracts, perhaps?' She said, 'Oh no, I don't think we can do that, that's common. We don't want to downgrade the style of the magazine.'[10]

In 1949, when John arrived at the offices of *Time and Tide* in Bloomsbury Street, where the ill-starred *Decoration* had also been based, Margaret Rhondda was sixty-six. Asked what she had looked like, John described her in Seven Dwarfs terms, 'stumpy, dumpy and grumpy'.[11] Reggie Langbridge answered the same question: 'Like a charwoman. She dressed either in black or in very dark colours, and appeared never to do her hair.'[12] Anthony Lejeune was more charitable: 'In looks she was sturdily built with curly hair and a very determined mouth and jaw, softened by a hint of ready laughter.'[13] Her control over the magazine was absolute. 'Not a comma went in without her approval,' Lejeune says.[14] In 1949 she seems to have allowed John little discretion, as his influence on the magazine is scarcely discernible. But from 1950 he made his presence felt in three ways: by importing his friends as reviewers, by contributing articles and poems himself, and by setting and judging imaginative literary competitions. Among the reviewers he inherited from Veronica Wedgwood was C.S. Lewis. One can only guess at the embarrassment he suffered in dealing with his hated former tutor. John did commission one review from Lewis in 1950.[15] After that his name disappeared from the roll of contributors, which now included Gerard Irvine, Roy and Billa Harrod, Stuart Piggott, Jack Yates, Renée Haynes (Tickell), Robert Bruce Lockhart, Randolph Churchill and other friends. John was happy enough to inherit Wolf Mankowitz, who had met Veronica Wedgwood when doing research for his book on her ancestor, the potter.[16] And John soon made friends with Rose Macaulay, whose Anglicanism was of the same dye as his own, and who also became a friend of Gerard Irvine at this time. The acute and incisive Rose Macaulay found John a somewhat woolly thinker ('one can never bring him down to exact facts', she wrote),[17] but the two remained affectionate friends long after he left *Time and Tide*.

John's literary acquaintance was so various that he could find apt reviewers for most books: horses for courses. There was Christopher

Blunt for Peter Seaby's *The Story of the English Coinage*; Christine Longford for Liam O'Flaherty's novel *Insurrection*; Father Harton for Thomas Merton's *The Ascent to Truth*; Sibyl Harton for *St Teresa of Avila and Other Essays and Addresses* by E. Allison Peers. Colonel Kolkhorst would write on almost anything, from Catalan poetry to *How to Identify Persian Rugs*. R.C.K. Ensor had been sufficiently forgiven for his tart letter at the Oxford Preservation Trust to be invited to review Beatrice Webb's *Diaries*. Evelyn Waugh wrote rare reviews for John. He praised *The Königsmark Drawings* of Rex Whistler, who had been killed in the war. ('His untimely death leaves us with no sense of frustration. All his promise was fulfilled.') Richard Amaral Howden, the eccentric psychiatrist of Maidstone Jail, who wrote John letters in different-coloured inks, gave a measured and (for its time) enlightened review of Gordon Westwood's *Society and the Homosexual*.

The 'Men and Books' feature enabled John to print longer articles by writers he admired. Denton Welch's 'A Morning with Lord Berners in "The Ancient Seat of Learning"' appeared posthumously on 5 July 1952. It was not a flattering portrait. Welch, who had met Berners at the Randolph Hotel, Oxford, was put out that Berners did not offer to buy a portrait he had painted of him. John felt it necessary to preface the article with a mitigating paragraph.

> This account of Lord Berners is so like how he seemed at a first meeting that it is worth printing. But those who knew him well know that it was a façade to hide his great shyness.
>
> In extenuation of the picture incident, it should be said that Lord Berners did not ask Denton Welch to paint his portrait as Robinson Crusoe, from a photograph. He received a fan letter asking him to allow it to be done. When he saw the portrait he did not like it. He asked Denton Welch to come to stay at Faringdon House, but Denton Welch died the very week he was supposed to be coming. Had they met more often, Mr Welch would have understood the shyness of Lord Berners. He was so shy that he could hardly bring himself to speak to someone when he first met them, and could never make a public speech.

Another contributor to 'Men and Books' was the novelist and autobiographer Jocelyn Brooke (who, coincidentally, wrote a preface to Denton Welch's *Journals* when they were first published). His article 'Silver Age' (7 July 1951) was a discursive, nostalgic piece. Brooke finds on a shelf a copy of *Oxford Poetry, 1928*. It reminds him of the undergraduate days he shared with John, who is twice mentioned in the article.

By 1928 the 'great' days of the twenties were over, and we (at Oxford) were living in a kind of Silver Age. The aesthetes had departed – leaving their silk handkerchiefs, cigarette ends and other testimony of summer nights; the friends, the loitering heirs of city directors, wore grey suède shoes and tittered over *Valmouth* in their digs in Beaumont Street, or ogled the hearties in the Café of the Super Cinema . . .

John borrowed Brooke's idea seven years later. When he was asked to write an article about his undergraduate days for the Oxford magazine *Parson's Pleasure*, he headed it 'The Silver Age of Aesthetes: A Picture of Oxford during the Twenties'.[18]

In one respect, at least, John was a hands-on editor: he wrote many of the reviews himself. In August 1950 he gave pride of place to his own long review of the *Recollections of Thomas Graham Jackson*, edited by Basil H. Jackson. He was very familiar with the work of the Oxford architect, and had used the expression 'Anglo-Jackson' in his poem 'Myfanwy at Oxford' (*Old Lights for New Chancels*, 1940). Jackson struck him as 'a likeable man'. His architecture, a development of the Jacobean style pioneered by Norman Shaw, compared favourably, John thought, with 'the ponderous, yet unconvinced monumentality of most of our later public and collegiate buildings'. John headed his review 'The Diary of a Somebody'.[19]

On 21 October he contributed an entertaining piece on book 'blurbs', a natural sequel to his earlier *Daily Herald* article on reviewers' terms. Blurbs were the publisher's way of helping the reviewer. 'Reviewing is a dreadful sweat and the refuge of the defeated . . . One book in 500 is really worth reading and sad is the lot of the dreary hack who has to be bright about the other 499.' But the publisher's hint was coded. John thought this glossary might be helpful.

'No ordinary War Book' –
   Yet one more book about the war.
'Fully illustrated' –
   More than one picture.
'Has long been known as an authority' –
   Has written one other book on this subject.
'The world-famous authority' –
   Has written two books on this subject.
'Grimly authentic background' –
   Squalid.
'Quietly sustained with much penetrating character-drawing' –
   Dully written and without any plot.

'This best-selling writer is well up to her usual form' –
This silly book is just like her last one.

For the Christmas issue of 1950, John devised with Osbert
Lancaster 'TIME & TIDE'S Game of SNAKES & LADDERS TO
LITERARY SUCCESS'* – an exercise similar to the 'Sociall Snakes &
Ladderes' they had published in *The Cherwell* as undergraduates.

The years John was at *Time and Tide* were those of the Festival of
Britain, the King's death and the accession and coronation of Queen
Elizabeth II. There were expectations of a new English renaissance, a
second Elizabethan age. The Festival of 1951 was ostensibly a commemoration of the anniversary of the Great Exhibition of 1851, but
symbolically it was more: a defiant statement of Britain's recovery
from war and austerity. John's feelings about the Festival were ambiva-
lent. The 'Crystal Palace' aspect attracted him, and he was all for
having some fun. On the other hand, the Festival had been a Labour
Government ('Slave State') initiative;[20] Evelyn Waugh attacked it in
prose, Noël Coward in a song. Significantly, John took only a negligible
part in the Festival,[21] though eleven years later, when asked to help with
a Festival of London, he wrote amusing lyrics and performed alongside
Sir John Gielgud and Tommy Steele.[22] At the same time, he did not
want to be too rude about the South Bank celebrations, as the director-
general of the Festival was Sir Gerald Barry, who had published poems
of his in 1933;[23] Hugh Casson, his colleague from the 'Archie Rev' and
Decoration, was the architectural director, and two of his best friends,
John Piper and Osbert Lancaster, were involved in designing fanciful
structures for the Battersea Pleasure Gardens. The conflict between
these feelings is clear in the article he wrote for *Time and Tide* (5 May
1951) after visiting the South Bank with Peter Fleetwood-Hesketh in
tow as artist. John thought 'the prettiest building in the exhibition' was
the 1851 Centenary Pavilion designed by Hugh Casson and made of
cast iron from moulds still in stock at Macfarlane's.

He liked some of the up-to-date buildings too. 'The Regatta
Restaurant by Messrs Black & Gibson . . . seems built of crystal
and planks. It surveys the lovely outline of the Royal Palace of
Westminster, Shaw's Scotland Yard and the domes and turrets
of Colonel Edis' Whitehall Court across the sliding water.' The hater
of pylons had an approving word for the Skylon, 'though it is best at
night. In the day I am for ever wanting to pull it by its end on elastic
and see if it shoots to the moon.'

* See pp. 430–31.

TIME & TIDE'S

Game

of

SNAKES & LADDERS

TO

Literary Success

devised by

Osbert Lancaster &
J. Betjeman

and

DRAWN BY

OSBERT LANCASTER

To play this game of Snakes and Ladders, remove the *CHILDREN'S CHRISTMAS NUMBER* by lifting the points of the two outer staples (pages xii and xiii) which bind it into the body of the paper, slip out the Supplement and press the staples back into position.

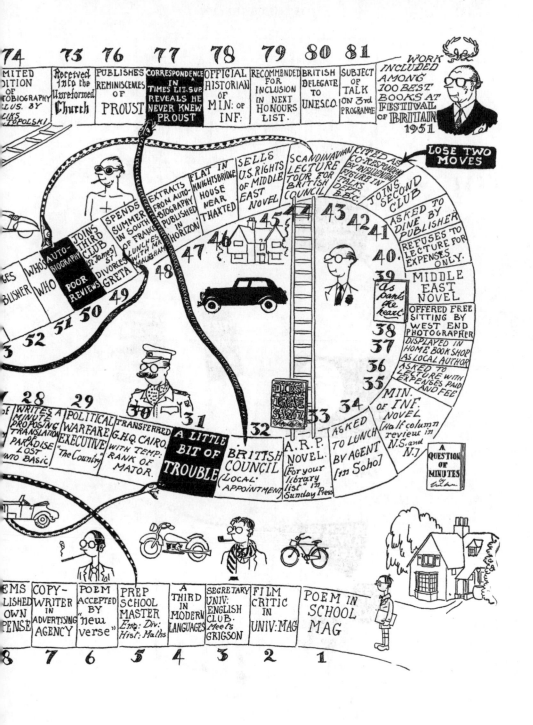

74 LIMITED EDITION OF AUTOBIOGRAPHY ILLUS. BY FELIKS TOPOLSKI

75 Received into the Unreformed Church

76 PUBLISHES REMINISCENCES OF PROUST

77 CORRESPONDENCE IN TIMES LIT: SUP: REVEALS HE NEVER KNEW PROUST

78 OFFICIAL HISTORIAN OF MIN: OF INF:

79 RECOMMENDED FOR INCLUSION IN NEXT HONOURS LIST.

80 BRITISH DELEGATE TO UNESCO.

81 SUBJECT OF TALK ON 3rd PROGRAMME

WORK INCLUDED AMONG 100 BEST BOOKS AT FESTIVAL OF BRITAIN 1951

LOSE TWO MOVES

JOINS THIRD CLUB
St James St

SPENDS SUMMER IN SOUTH OF FRANCE LUNCHES WITH MAUGHAM

DIVORCES GRETA

EXTRACTS FROM AUTO-BIOGRAPHY PUBLISHED IN HORIZON

FLAT IN KNIGHTSBRIDGE HOUSE NEAR THAXTED

SELLS U.S. RIGHTS OF MIDDLE EAST NOVEL

SCANDINAVIAN LECTURE TOUR FOR BRITISH COUNCIL

CITED AS CO-RESPONDENT BY INFLUENTIAL FIGURE IN TALKS DEPT: B.B.C.

JOINS SECOND CLUB

ASKED TO DINE BY PUBLISHER

REFUSES TO LECTURE FOR EXPENSES ONLY.

45 **44** **43** **42** **41**

40

46 **47** **48**

MIDDLE EAST NOVEL

39 "As pants the heart"

OFFERED FREE SITTING BY WEST END PHOTOGRAPHER

38

37 DISPLAYED IN HOME BOOK SHOP AS LOCAL AUTHOR

36

35 ASKED TO LECTURE WITH EXPENSES PAID AND FEE

WHO'S AUTO-BIOGRAPHY WHO
POOR REVIEWS

49 **50** **51** **52**

MIN. OF INF. NOVEL [Half column review in N.S. and N.Y.]

A QUESTION OF MINUTES

DIES IRAE SWOT

33 **34**

28 WRITES A MINUTE PROPOSING TRANSLATION OF PARADISE LOST INTO BASIC

29 POLITICAL WARFARE EXECUTIVE "The Country"

30 TRANSFERRED G.H.Q. CAIRO. WITH TEMP: RANK OF MAJOR.

31

32 BRITISH COUNCIL (LOCAL APPOINTMENT)

A LITTLE BIT OF TROUBLE

A.R.P. NOVEL [For your library list in Sunday Press]

ASKED TO LUNCH BY AGENT [in Soho]

POEMS PUBLISHED OWN EXPENSE

COPY-WRITER IN ADVERTISING AGENCY

POEM ACCEPTED BY "new verse"

PREP SCHOOL MASTER Eng: Div: Hist: Maths

A THIRD IN MODERN LANGUAGES

SECRETARY UNIV: ENGLISH CLUB: Meets GRIGSON

FILM CRITIC IN UNIV: MAG

POEM IN SCHOOL MAG

8 **7** **6** **5** **4** **3** **2** **1**

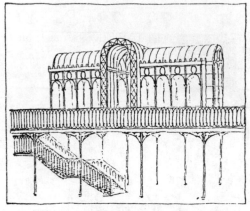

1851

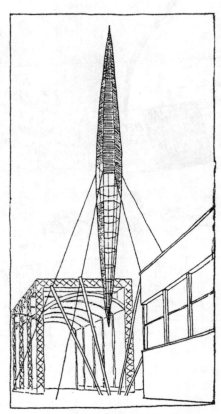

Perpendicular

The Royal Festival Hall was, he thought, 'forbidding outside',[24] but the Dome of Discovery was a disappointment inside, because the many exhibits and decorations put it out of scale.

He conceded that there were few really ugly buildings. 'The most notable are the kiosks illustrated here and the hideous walls on the Homes and Gardens Pavilion, which are snail-pointed like a scraped Victorian church.' He concluded: 'I went to the Festival Buildings expecting to find gambolling functionalists trying to be funny. I returned over that endless Bailey bridge exhausted but enchanted.'

On 16 June 1951, John contributed to *Time and Tide* an article unrelated to books, one of the most vitriolic things he ever wrote in prose or verse. Headed 'A Martyr to Income Tax', it was provoked by a paragraph he had read in the *News of the World*. James Morrison, a forty-nine-year-old boot-repairer, who had boasted in a public house that he was successfully 'diddling' the Inland Revenue by claiming allowances for two children he did not have and a 'dependent' mother-in-law who was dead, was reported to the authorities by one of his listeners and was jailed for four months for fraud. John wrote that this was 'a picture of such horror that I have been thinking about it ever since'.

Let us examine the queue of stinkers lined up before us . . .

Of course we do not quarrel with the law. There is obviously an Act of Parliament which enables one man to sentence another to four months' imprisonment for defrauding the State. No one questions that, just as no

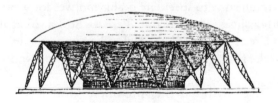

1951

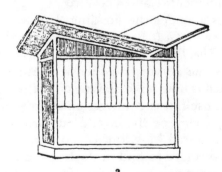

?

one questions the State's right to pay out our money for atomic research, community centres and the destruction of small village schools.

Similarly we dare not challenge the Minister of Transport's right to ruin old towns with concrete lamp-standards. If we did, his PRO would be hot on our tracks. But one of the surprising things about this case is that Mr James Morrison is a boot-repairer. I have seen many men glide by me in long new motor-cars with a wireless set in the dashboard. They were obviously not boot-repairers . . . And there are those restaurants where the waiter will buy your bill from you if you have paid in cash, and sell it to an executive who can show it in for expenses. I doubt if Mr James Morrison did that kind of thing. He was a boot-repairer. But it will not do if we have mere manual workers defrauding the State. We will have authors trying to do it next.

Though John is often accused of having been snobbish and apolitical, the emotions of this article were genuine. But his rant is not from the far left; rather it is the polemic of a Tory inveighing against the intrusive state and siding with the individual and his right to privacy, even in a public house. Still more, it is the rhetoric of a Christian denouncing the Pharisees: 'He that is without sin among you, let him first cast a stone . . .' (John 8: 7). The article continues:

Perhaps Mr Morrison . . . was under the influence. Who was the listener who took advantage of this? We do not know his name. Perhaps it is just as well, as some of us might want to do him an injury . . .

And it is interesting to speculate on his motives for writing. They could be either priggishness or vengeance. Perhaps he is a young man, fresh from a course in Civics . . . Perhaps he feels a loyalty to the Inland Revenue, as a soldier to the Flag. Perhaps he is willing to die for National Savings . . .

Whatever motives inspired the informer, John writes, 'he is a neo-Nazi, a traitor to the mutual trust of human society, a humourless prude, a pedant, a hypocrite and a coward'.

In February 1952, under the heading 'Faraway Fairways', John reviewed *A History of Golf in Britain* by Bernard Darwin (golfing correspondent of *The Times*) and others. 'Golf is a beautiful game,' he wrote. 'It tests the nerves and then it soothes them. It can be played alone (which is how I like playing it best) when the player can quietly cheat to himself. It encourages an eye for landscape. It turns a dreary stretch of clay or the coniferous aridity of some sandy waste into an enchanted kingdom of contours, hazards and distances.'[25] He was diverted to find in the book, alongside pictures of Miss Cecil Leitch swinging a driver in 1920 and Alf Padgham in the rough at Walton Heath, a mid-fourteenth-century stained-glass window from Gloucester Cathedral showing a man in a white shirt 'taking a golf swing at a yellow egg'. John was specially interested in the poems about golf and golfers quoted in the book. The one he liked best was Thomas Matheson's 'The Goff' (1743) about a maker of early golf balls, which were leather-skinned and stuffed with feathers —

> He crams and sweats, yet crams and urges more,
> Till scarce the turgid glove contains its store;
> The dreaded falcon's pride here blended lies
> With pigeon's glossy down of various dyes;
> The lark's small pinions join the common stock,
> And yellow glory of the martial cock.

The poems about golf in this book may have inspired John to have a go himself. His 'Seaside Golf' ('How straight it flew, how long it flew . . .') appeared in the Summer Number of *Punch* in July 1953.

On 5 July he contributed to the 'Men and Books' section a long article headed 'Mither Tongue', reviewing an anthology of *Scottish Verse 1851–1951* selected by Douglas Young. John had a mild antipathy to Scotland. It was not an irrational hatred, such as envenomed T.W.H. Crosland's *The Unspeakable Scot*; rather it was an affectionate tease, of the kind Dr Johnson practised on Boswell. After hearing his Dragon School master 'Bruno' Brown sing 'A lum hat wantin' a croon', John invented the hybrid language he called 'Skitch'.[26] In 1929 he wrote to Patrick Balfour of 'boulders behind which Burns took down his trousers and ruins where Sir Walter Scott took down his sheep dog'.[27] At Uffington he had amused Stuart Piggott with his parody of the pretentious Scottish Nationalist poet Hugh MacDiarmid.* John, then, might seem an unfair choice as reviewer of an anthology of Scottish verse. But he liked the book. It was, he wrote, what an anthology should be. 'It will be of little use to the exam-passer and the person who likes to find something he knows already without having to buy separate volumes of a poet.'

> Its compiler loves poetry and clearly has read hundreds of volumes. One can visualize the years of affectionate research that have gone into it. First he must have read those squalid-looking volumes bound in dark green or brown and printed locally in the 'sixties or 'seventies, the product of some poor weaver or eccentric laird. Amid pages of rot, one poem or perhaps

* See Chapter 1, 'Uffington'.

two emerge which are not facetious imitations of Burns or trite Scoticizing of Moore and Byron. He has also read poems in old local newspapers. By the 'nineties he comes to the Celtic Revival, heavy type on deckle-edged paper, devices of writhing Celtic knots and sad ponderosities purporting to be translations of Ossian, the Immortal Hour sort of poetry . . . Then come the late Lane books and the beginning of the Harold Monro Poetry Bookshop era. What multitudes of private press books he must have read, what angular lino-cuts must he have seen spoiling the effect of a good poem on the opposite page, what thin books of undergraduate muses, what expensive little items printed in exile at Ditchling or Chipping Campden, until he came to the stark political volumes of the 'thirties and the even starker paper-bound poetic pamphlets of today . . .

Douglas Young, John added, had presented him with thirty-four poets of whom he had not heard and of whom he wished to read more, and with four he had not considered as good as they obviously were, John Davidson, R.L. Stevenson, William Soutar and G.S. Fraser. However, he aired his distaste for dialect poems and renewed his charge on MacDiarmid.

In 1851 dialect was generally used for satire and comic verse only. Today, though I do not like to write anything anti-regional, I must say that I think it is rather over-done and can become contrived. Mr T.S. Law's 'Epitaph' begins:

> Yird him, yird snod the muckle nyaff o him.
> Swith noo, hap him wi stoor an stanes, swith, owre
> The sumph whause glinkin glisk o a sowl was dim
> As tynt luve taivert wi a tüme luve's glower.

Even with the aid of the glossary, this has a very specialized hand-woven appeal. There is also a certain humourlessness about welding Scottish and Party-Member sentiment, which is what Hugh MacDiarmid does in 'The Seamless Garment' when he talks to a mine worker cousin:

> Lenin and Rilke baith gied still mair skill,
>   Coopers o Stobo, to a greater concern
> Than you devote to claith in the mill.

In the issue of 2 May 1953 John allotted himself a full page to write on a subject on which he could claim to be a world authority: humorous works about the Church of England. The article, headed 'Trivia Anglicana', was formally a review of satirical poems by the Rev. S.J.

Forrest, Vicar of Leighton Buzzard. John must have been aware that Forrest's humorous verse was far inferior to his own, but he praised his 'splendid satire on interdenominationalism' which ends:

> There's room for brave agnostic
> For Hindu or Parsee
> Or devotee of Islam
> (So very C of E),
> And if uniting parties
> At Bishops take offence
> We'll consecrate the ladies
> And take our orders thence.

He did not live to see the Synod authorize women priests, forty years later.

John was much exercised at this time by unsympathetic additions to church architecture. On 5 December 1953 he and John Piper contributed to *Time and Tide* a feature headed 'Glories of English Craftsmanship – Electricity and the Old Churches'. The illustrations, specially drawn by Piper from 'authentic examples in Buckinghamshire', showed how electrical fittings were ruining church architecture. John supplied trenchant captions.

Reviewing *Teapots and Quails*, a new book of unpublished nonsense verse by Edward Lear (13 December 1953) John wrote that it would be 'a delight to the non-intellectual visual-minded person such as your reviewer, just as a new book for children by Lewis Carroll will delight the intellectual which your reviewer is not'. He thought it was wrong that Carroll and Lear should always be mentioned together, when they had nothing more in common 'than being Victorian, being eccentric, and being writers of nonsense verse and prose in their spare time'. He had a particular affection for Lear, because as a child, as he describes in *Summoned by Bells*,

> Once on a stall in Farringdon Road I found
> An atlas folio of great lithographs,
> *Views of Ionian Isles*, flyleaf inscribed
> By Edward Lear – and bought it for a bob.[29]

In the review he writes:

Besides having an awed sense of the wonder of creation whether in the wing of a bird or the shape of a mountain, he also could imply an extremely funny line in drawing them. He can make a bear lovable, funny

Nestling into the usual English skyline see this old Buckinghamshire church tower. If a thing expresses its purpose it must be beautiful, mustn't it? This old tower expresses a dead age, but the sensitive craftsmen who put up these poles and wires and masts have brought the blessings of science to millions. They are electrically-minded Trade Union men. Who are we to complain if we think their work looks shoddy, temporary and ridiculous? A civilization has the architecture it deserves. And we are highly civilized, aren't we?

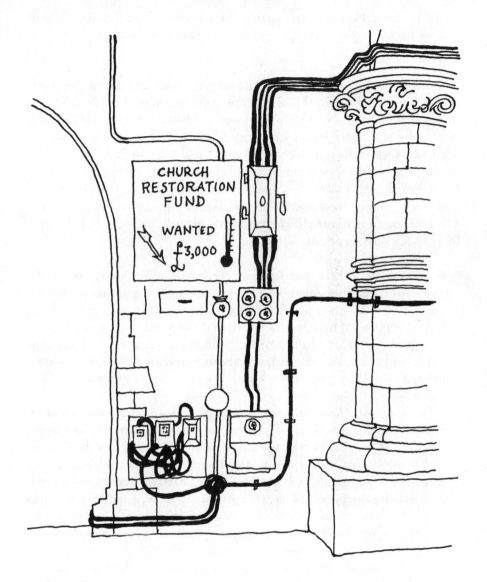

Perhaps the prettiest and most ingenious wall decoration of all is to be found here on the west and most prominent wall of the most beautiful medieval church in the Aylesbury district

and pathetic. He can make a pair of scissors into a personality without drawing a face on it or trying to twist it into semblance of the human form.

During the years John was literary editor, several of his own poems were printed in the magazine: among them 'Original Sin on the Sussex Coast' (8 December 1951), 'Hunter Trials' (5 January 1952), the elaborate spoof of Longfellow in 'A Literary Discovery', with all its footnotes (6 December 1952) and 'Devonshire Street, W1' (8 August 1953). Young poets were encouraged, including Edward Lucie-Smith and James Kirkup, an 'out' homosexual who later won notoriety when his poem about Christ provoked Mrs Mary Whitehouse to instigate the last trial for blasphemy held in Britain.[30] In 1988 Kirkup recalled:

It was while I held the Gregory Fellowship in Poetry at Leeds, 1950–1952, that Betjeman wrote to me asking if I had any poems for *Time and Tide*. I had just finished a long poem, about Leeds, which I believe was one of his favourite provincial cities (the Pugin church, etc.). The poem was 'City of the North',[31] and in a letter in reply to my contribution he was very enthusiastic about it and suggested it should be printed with illustrations . . . But in the end . . . he gradually backed down.[32]

He once invited me to lunch at Kettner's to sound me out about an ancestor, Seymour Stocker Kirkup, one of 'the Pisan Circle' and a noted medium. He was also not a bad artist (painted Trelawney as the Giaour) and some of his works are in the Bargello in Florence and in the Keats–Shelley Museum in Rome. He claimed to have been created a Papal Baron for his discovery of Giotto's portrait of Dante,[33] and Betjeman was amused by the title he arrogated to himself of 'Barone' . . . He was an intimate of Swinburne also, and I got the impression Betjeman wanted to write something about this odd character who obviously appealed to his sense of humour and his interest in rather weird literary and religious relics.[34]

The Leeds poem was never used, but John did print a number of Kirkup's louche verses. He failed, though, to get a poem by Tom Driberg into the magazine. Entitled 'Cycle with Masks', it was an almost parodic exercise in free verse,[35] not unlike his 'Spring Carol' of 1927 which had been guyed (probably by John) in the *Cherwell*.[36] In his diary of 1952, published in 1953, Driberg wrote of 'Cycle with Masks': 'I showed it to one or two friends: John Freeman was non-committal; Nye Bevan approved of it; Tony Crosland roared with laughter and said it was the greatest nonsense he had ever read.'[37] Driberg recorded those reactions in May. Five months later, he wrote in his diary:

> That unfortunate (and, no doubt, unworthy) poem, *Cycle with Masks*, having been rejected by three literary editors in quick succession, I was naturally delighted when John Betjeman said he liked it very much and asked me to let him have it for *Time and Tide* (whose literary side he helps to look after).
>
> They kept it for some time. Then it came back, with the following remarkable letter from the editor of *Time and Tide*, Lady Rhondda:

> Dear Mr Driberg,
>
> John Betjeman has given me your poem of which he thinks highly, as does Theodora Bosanquet, to whom I showed it.
>
> But I am, I am afraid, a little worried. Our views – yours and *Time and Tide*'s – are so extremely widely divergent that I cannot feel it to be suitable that you should appear in its columns. It would seem to me really almost as unsuitable as if the Archbishop of Canterbury were to be printed in the *New Statesman*!
>
> So I am very regretfully returning it.
>
> Yours sincerely,
> Margaret Rhondda

> To which I have replied:

> Dear Lady Rhondda,
>
> Thank you for taking the trouble to write to me personally about my poem, and for writing so candidly.
>
> I am surprised to learn your reason for rejecting the poem, for I had thought that political tests were applied to non-political writings only in Soviet Russia and possibly in some quarters in the USA. However, I suppose that such literary applications of the doctrine of infection by association are but a small part of the *Gleichschaltung* to which we are being subjected in the course of the Cold War; and, in any case, your editorial discretion is absolute.
>
> Yours sincerely
> Tom Driberg[38]

This episode may well have raised, in Lady Rhondda's mind, doubts about John's judgement.

While encouraging such young poets as Lucie-Smith and Kirkup, John did not neglect the older ones. On 6 December 1952 three poems by Siegfried Sassoon were reproduced in his own distinctive handwriting, with caricatures in the margin. Earlier in the year, Sassoon had sent John a copy of his privately printed *Emblems of Experience*. John wrote to him on 19 April:

Dear Sassoon,

I am thrilled, pleased & honoured to have three beautiful EMBLEMS OF EXPERIENCE signed by you & presented to me. It is so nice to find you, here in a later volume, an even finer poet than in those early volumes which I possess. I have now read through your poems twice out loud to myself, which is the best test. The words roll out full of sound & depth like they do in my beloved Tennyson. And the melancholy in every poem of yours, I welcome so very warmly. It is like the melancholy of Hood, that constant sense of Eternity . . . The poem I like best of all is *The Messenger*.

I understand it particularly because at the moment my mother is dying in a Nursing Home in Bath with her faculties gradually going & clinging as hard as she can to the threads of reason & memory left to her. I thank you very deeply for these poems . . . I do not think poetry is looking up (despite the efforts of know-all reviewers who write anonymous attacks on all they understand & only praise the obscure while missing the good in the clear) . . .

I hope I shall one day be allowed to come & see you at Heytesbury & we might make a tour to Upton Lovell & call on Sidney Mavor ('Jenny' Mavor, Wilde's & Alfred Taylor's friend), aged 83, if he is still alive.

I don't blame you a bit for publishing your poems privately & beautifully. That is just what you ought to do. I hope eventually all good poets will. But one needs the cash to do it.[39]

The long illness of his mother contributed to John's lowness of spirits in the *Time and Tide* years. She was the one person who had always had faith in him – 'The Only John', as she wrote on a baby-photograph of her son for Penelope.[40] Her love was unconditional. In the autumn of 1952 she lay dying in the Bath nursing-home. John's daughter recalls: 'JB and I used to visit her together. She sat swathed in shawls, forlorn and tiny on a window seat. After our last visit she wrote to JB, "I was so glad to see you and Candida yesterday. It was very kind of you to come. Give Candida my love and tell her the eau de cologne she gave me is sprinkled on my handkerchief and the scent of it wafts across the room. All love, Bess." '[41] In the final stages of his mother's illness, John visited her alone, staying in Bath with John Walsham, his childhood friend from Trebetherick who worked in the Admiralty, and his wife Sheila. He was with Bess when she died on the evening of 13 December and returned exhausted to the Walshams' house. 'He sat down with a glass of whisky,' Candida writes, 'and the telephone immediately rang. (Granny Bess had been an inveterate telephoner.) He said to Sheila, "Oh, my *God*, she's come alive again." '[42]

Colonel Kolkhorst wrote to John on 23 December: 'I think you saw a lot more of her latterly. That is a good thing. It will be a real consolation to you now that you pleased her and were dutiful. Duty, I found, came a lot into the picture on these occasions . . . As a son one is given the initiative; one has a special power to do right. Your Victorians – like the Romans – knew this; and it fortified them . . .'[43] But John knew he had not always been so dutiful. After Bess's death he wrote the moving poem 'Remorse', which ends:

> Protestant and Catholic, the wrong and the right of them,
>   Unimportant they seem in the face of death –
> But my neglect and unkindness – to lose the sight of them
>   I would listen even again to that labouring breath.[44]

It was well for him not to be too much on his own in this despondent state of mind. Aspects of his work were cheering. Veronica Wedgwood, in a preface to the Reviews section of the 1956 *Time and Tide* anthology, wrote:

The book room of a weekly paper has an atmosphere of its own, it is more social and apparently, although deceptively, more leisured than other departments. Reviewers – some of them anyway – drop in to exchange the time of day, an exchange which may easily turn into a discussion of contemporary trends in philosophy, the prospects of the novel, or even the ethics of reviewing. The weekly pressure of work rises regularly towards press day: Book Supplements and Book Numbers at intervals make tables and floor awash with corrected galleys, while the telephone rings incessantly. But between times there is, all the same – there must be – time for the leisurely expansion and discussion of ideas, time for simply pottering among the books. This alternation of tranquillity with activity gives its peculiarly genial, informal air to the book room.

Veronica Wedgwood was a historian, and was keenly interested in politics. In his depressed mood, John felt out of tune with the magazine's earnest political campaigning. In December 1950 he contributed a poem entitled 'The Weary Journalist', satirizing the stock of clichés on which the magazine drew so heavily. The poem may not have been intended as autobiographical in every detail but it is unlikely to have endeared him to Lady Rhondda.

Here, on this far North London height
I sit and write and write and write.
I pull the nothings from my head
And weigh[t] them round with lumps of lead
Then plonk them down upon the page
In finely simulated rage.
Whither Democracy? I ask
And what the Nature of her Task?
Whither Bulgaria and Peru?
What Crisis are they passing through?
Before my readers can reply
Essential Factors flutter by
Parlous, indeed, is their condition
Until they find a Key Position.
To keep their Tendencies in Check
I push them through a Bottleneck
From which they Challenge me and frown
And Fling their Tattered Gauntlets down.
And Vital Problems sit and trill
Outside upon my window sill
And Lies are wrapped around in Tissues
And oh! the crowds of Vital Issues.
I ache in all my mental joints
Nigh stabbed to death by Focal Points.
But all the time I know, I know
That ev'ry twinkling light below
Shines on a Worker in his Vest
(True symbol of the Great Oppress'd)
And he, like all unheeding fools,
Is filling in his football pools.[45]

One of the few parts of his job that John really enjoyed was setting
some of the weekly literary competitions. On 1 March 1952 he set:
'Competitors are asked to compose the most outrageously far-fetched
or pretentious advertisement they can think of.' On 26 April 1952: ' "A
Thing of Beauty is a Joy for Ever." Turn this into not more than 200
words of prose; the style may be pseudo-learned, sweet and sentimental, *Times* pontifical, German-pedantic-conceited, or any other form
of cliché-ridden boredom. The prize (£4) will be awarded to the
dullest and hollowest entry.'

Another competition he set (29 December 1951) brought him
lasting and not altogether welcome renown. Competitors were asked
to add a final verse to his poem 'How to Get On in Society'. The poem,

beginning 'Phone for the fish-knives, Norman' was a collection of the words and phrases that upper-class people were not supposed to use. It was already in existence in 1949, when Randolph Churchill, who had heard the first line from somebody, asked him for a copy.[46] In his report on the *Time and Tide* competition, on 19 January 1952, John wrote that he had been 'dazzled by yards of splendid verses from over a hundred entrants'. 'Mopev' had sent in not one final verse but an entire poem, which John said he thought better than his own. The first two stanzas were:

> Would you care for a smoke or a sherry?
>   The cocktail cabinet's there.
> No, the savoury spread and the vitamin bread's
>   In the cubby hole under the stair.
>
> Has Uncle gone out on his cycle?
>   He left making terrible sounds,
> Saying 'Just what the medico ordered'.
>   I'm afraid he'll get lost in the grounds.

John awarded the first prize to 'HMB'[47] for this verse:

> Your pochette's on the pouffe by the cake-stand
>   Beneath your fur-fabric coatee.
> Now, before we remove to the study
>   Let me pass you these chocs from Paris.

John liked the way this entrant used rhyme to get in one more *faux pas*. Honourable mention went to Rani Sinha's:

> The WC's locked from the inside;
>   Just beat on the door, there's a dear.
> Ask Father to slide out the papers
>   And tell him the bathroom is clear.

Rose Macaulay disapproved of John's poem. She wrote to her friend Father Hamilton Johnson, on 19 February 1952:

'Genteel' in English (not 'Gentile') has suffered some curious changes of meaning. It was, only a century ago, complimentary; 'A very genteel young man,' or woman, meant, as it did with Jane Austen, one with gentlemanly or gentlewomanly manners and breeding. But now . . . it is applied to the class between high and low; it is 'genteel' to say 'sufficient' instead of

'enough', 'serviette', 'preserve' for jam, 'wealthy' for rich . . . A rather snob
campaign of ridicule goes on against these, which tho' often amusing (I
have often taken part in it, adding words and phrases to the taboo list –
John Betjeman has lately composed a poem bringing in most of them), is
really perhaps a pity, and only exacerbates class war. It isn't, in fact, very
good manners or *gentle*.[48]

John's friend Nancy Mitford had started the hunt for 'social errors'
in her novel *The Pursuit of Love* (1945), in which 'Uncle Matthew' (the
character based on her father, Lord Redesdale) attacked the vulgariz-
ing effects of education on Fanny's vocabulary –

'Education! I was always led to suppose that no educated person ever
spoke of notepaper, and yet I hear poor Fanny asking Sadie for notepaper.
What is this education? Fanny talks about mirrors and mantelpieces,
handbags and perfume, she takes sugar in her coffee, has a tassel on her
umbrella, and I have no doubt that, if she is fortunate enough to catch a
husband, she will call his father and mother Father and Mother. Will the
wonderful education she is getting make up to the unhappy brute for all
these endless pinpricks? Fancy hearing one's wife talk about notepaper –
the irritation!'[49]

When John, who had once light-heartedly proposed marriage to
Nancy Mitford, wrote her a fan letter about the novel in December
1945, he showed that he had read the 'notepaper' passage by joking, 'I
write to tell you on this lovely *writing* paper how v. greatly I enjoyed
it,' and added that Uncle Matthew was his favourite character in the
book. It may well have been the 'social errors' passage in *The Pursuit
of Love* that inspired him to write 'How to Get On in Society'.[50]

In 1954 Nancy Mitford met Professor Alan Ross, a philologist from
Birmingham University, who told her he was writing an article on
sociological linguistics for a learned Finnish journal, to be entitled 'U
and Non-U', denoting upper-class and non-upper-class usage. In 1955
she wrote an article for *Encounter* entitled 'The English
Aristocracy',[51] based on his material. 'Of course it was all a tremendous joke,' writes Mitford's biographer Selina Hastings; 'but a joke
which Nancy herself more than half took seriously.'

The issue of *Encounter* sold out almost immediately. It provoked a
flood of letters, newspaper articles and cartoons, and a *New Yorker*
poem by Ogden Nash, 'MS Found Under a Serviette in a Lovely
Home'. In 1956 Hamish Hamilton reprinted the essay in book form
under the title *Noblesse Oblige*, together with Ross's original article,
John's poem, a piece by Peter Fleming ('Strix' of *The Spectator*) on

'Posh Lingo' and an open letter by Evelyn Waugh, 'To the Honble Mrs Peter Rodd [Nancy Mitford] On a Very Serious Subject'. The book was illustrated by Osbert Lancaster: John's poem faced a drawing of a 'cosy lounge' with Art Deco clock, brick 'mantelpiece', pouffe, neo-classical table-cigarette-lighter and the inevitable flying ducks on the wall. By the end of the year nearly 14,000 copies of *Noblesse Oblige* had been sold in Britain; in America 10,000 went in the first week. Nancy Mitford's sister, the Duchess of Devonshire, dismissively said: 'If it's me, it's "U"' – a quip quickly appropriated by Osbert Lancaster for a pocket cartoon of Maudie Littlehampton. The book made John's poem famous, rather to his embarrassment, as it seemed likely to link his name for ever with petty snobberies. 'JB never thought of his verses as anything but a journalistic joke,' his daughter writes.[52] As Gertrude Stein said to Stuart Piggott and John, 'not one of my *major* works'. In later years, to absolve himself of guilt for the poem, John invented – deliberately or unconsciously – a fable about its origin, which he retailed on a radio programme in 1974. 'The *New Statesman*, I think it was, set a competition to write a poem on this subject in my style. I didn't dare to enter, in case I lorst. But when the competition was over and the results had come out, I had a try myself and wrote this . . .' It made a more amusing story than the true one, and exonerated John by implying that he had merely 'had a flutter' on a slightly disreputable game rather than dealing the cards himself.

Towards the end of 1953, Lady Rhondda invited him to lunch (U: 'luncheon') at the Caprice restaurant in Arlington Street, St James's, where a table was permanently reserved for her. Over the coffee, she told him he was fired. In her forthright way, she probably thought she was doing the right thing in breaking the news to him herself, rather than delegating the task to some underling; but John felt ambushed and humiliated. Relations between them had been deteriorating for some time. John had enlivened the magazine, but circulation had not risen; indeed, because of Reggie Langbridge's honesty, it must have seemed to Lady Rhondda that it was suddenly falling. When Anthony Lejeune asked her why she had dismissed John, she said that the reviews he commissioned never came in on time or to length or about the right books.[53] A woman sub-editor who worked on the magazine with John and liked him thought that the last straw may have been an exchange which she overheard between the proprietress and the literary editor.

'Mr Betjeman!'
'Yes, Lady Rhondda?'
'I want to give the magazine a more European flavour.'

'Oh, so do I, Lady Rhondda, and you will be glad to hear that I have just ordered a review of a book on the architecture of fourteenth-century Spanish monasteries.'[54]

That was not what Lady Rhondda had in mind at all.

In 1956 John wrote a poem entitled 'Caprice' about being fired from *Time and Tide*. In 1957, as a visiting professor in Cincinnati, Ohio, he recited it to a party of academics under the seal of silence.[55] When the poem was first published, the last six lines were omitted as, in John's words, 'too strong meat'; they have since been restored to the version in the *Collected Poems*.

CAPRICE*

I sat only two tables off from the one I was sacked at
　　　　Just three years ago,
And here was another meringue like the one which I hacked at
　　　　When pride was brought low
And the coffee arrived – the place which she had to use tact at
　　　　For striking the blow.

'I'm making some changes next week in the organization
　　　　And though I admire
Your work for me, John, yet the need to increase circulation
　　　　Means you must retire;
An outlook more global than yours is the qualification
　　　　I really require.'

O sickness of sudden betrayal! O purblind Creator!
　　　　Oh friendship denied!
I stood on the pavement and wondered which loss was the greater,
　　　　The cash or the pride?
Explanations to make to subordinates, bills to pay later
　　　　Churned up my inside.

I fell on my feet. But what of those others, worse treated,
　　　　Your memory's ghosts,
In gloomy bed-sitters in Fulham, ill-fed and unheated,
　　　　Applying for posts?
Do they haunt their successors and you as you sit here repleted
　　　　With entrées and roasts?

Anthony Lejeune, to whom John gave a typescript of the poem dated 'April 1956', comments: 'To the best of my knowledge, none

---

* A restaurant in Arlington House [John Betjeman's footnote].

of the girls Lady Rhondda sacked did starve in gloomy bed-sitters. On the contrary, they married stockbrokers and lived in very upmarket Fulham.'[56] He says that John remained indignant about Lady Rhondda's treatment of him. 'Whether justly or not, we can't tell . . . one of Margaret Rhondda's great weaknesses (of which she was quite well aware) was that she was a bad judge of people; she trusted some dreadful crooks, who exploited her ruthlessly, but, conversely, she suddenly lost faith – often for quite trivial or misconceived reasons – in people who would have served her well and nothing could restore them to her good books. Whether she and John ever met subsequently I can't remember; but he did compose, with Osbert Lancaster, some delightful Christmas features for us when I was there; so he can't have borne too lasting a grudge.'[57]

After Lady Rhondda's death, *Time and Tide* limped along under different proprietors. In 1965 Anthony Lejeune said in a BBC talk on weekly magazines that it was 'weirdly changed'.[58] In February 1977 the once feminist publication was relaunched as 'The Business Man's Weekly Newspaper'. It survived only until July 1979.

25

WANTAGE

I hear with uncertain feelings that you are leaving the Downs and establishing yourself in a country town. Of course many respectable burgher families have started in that way. Do not be over-ambitious, but perhaps we shall see you or your descendants 'landed' again.

Lionel Perry, letter to John Betjeman, 12 July 1951[1]

Penelope remembered how she and John found The Mead, their new house in Wantage. 'A friend in the [Roman Catholic] congregation at Wantage called Mrs Baker, who'd married a Tate & Lyle sugar magnate who died, said, "Why on earth don't you buy our house?" It had never entered my head to live in Wantage, but in the end we did buy it. John went down to see it and said, "Yes, we must have this." It was lovely for him because there was a very High "spiky" church just across the fields.'[2]

The Betjemans' friend Douglas Woodruff, who lived not far off at Abingdon, believed that The Mead stood on the site of the palace of King Alfred the Great, whose axe-brandishing statue by Queen Victoria's nephew, Count Gleichen, dominates the town's market square.[3] But there was nothing ancient about the house. In moving to it, John was certainly practising what he preached. With its Gothic gables and bargeboarded porch, it was almost a caricature of the kind of Victorian building he was famous for admiring. He decorated the interior with Gothic wallpapers from Watts and Company, the church furnishers.[4] 'I was mortified,' Candida later wrote. 'All I craved were regency stripes'[5] – the Fifties fashion which John satirized in a poem.[6] The pictures were brass-rubbings in Arts and Crafts frames, Penelope's aquatints of India and 'voluptuous Pre-Raphaelites'.[7]

The house came with seven acres of land, later increased to nine before Penelope began selling off fields to pay for the upkeep of her ponies. There were nineteenth-century stables. During the Second World War, Colonel D.C. Robinson, a former Gloucestershire crick-eter who lived at The Mead then, had set up a milking parlour and a chicken house to ensure he always had dairy produce in the time of rationing. At the entrance to the drive was a Victorian lodge where Mr Gardner lived, the Betjemans' part-time chauffeur. Dick Squires, the son of their neighbour Dr Vaughan Squires, noticed that the usually genial John was sometimes 'horrid' to Gardner.

> There was a very naughty side to John. When he got annoyed, he could be very unkind to what you might call 'the humble folk' – and I was very much surprised at this. Once he and I were going to lunch somewhere in Smithfield Market, and an innocent little chap in the car park told him where to park his car. John suddenly went almost white with rage.
>
> It was partly to do with cars, I think – letting off his resentment of having to rely on motor cars and his intense dislike of anything mechanical. And Gardner, who was very loyal to the Betjemans, drove one of those old shooting-brakes . . . 'half-timbered cars', as John's friend Barry Humphries once said. Gardner was a lovely chap . . . but if things weren't going well and John got rattled, he used to be very unkind and . . . [call him] 'that fool Gardner!' and so on.[8]

Around the house were five paddocks. One contained the stables. One Penelope ploughed up, Dick Squires remembers, 'when she had a craze for a small and terrifying Caterpillar tractor she bought, which kept spilling her backwards up apple trees'.[9] In two of the paddocks, always grassed, she kept her ponies, with a large notice saying 'Please give the ponies CARROTS not SUGAR LUMPS' because sugar was bad for their teeth. The fifth paddock was the eponymous mead – in other words, it flooded in winter. Also on the estate was a cottage known as The Gogs, where Mr O'Brien, the Betjemans' gardener, lived with his family. He had come to work for Colonel Robinson in 1932 and had been inherited by each subsequent owner. The O'Briens' garden was damp, rat-infested and littered with old prams and packing-cases; but their children were healthy and had 'extraordinary natural charm'. Their daughter Margaret became a protégé of Penelope's. 'She made quite a name for herself in the horse world,' Squires said. 'She went very posh and could pass for a deb.'[10]

As well as looking after the grounds, O'Brien did odd jobs about the house. Unlike Gardner, he did not suffer in silence when John became autocratic.

> I used to clean his shoes [he recalled] . . . When [he] came home, if he was in a little bit of a hurry, he never undone the shoelaces . . . So I cleaned the shoes and sent them back with the shoelaces still done up. He said to me one day, 'O'Brien, you never undone me shoelaces.' I turned round and

said, 'Mr Betjeman, if you'm too bloody lazy to do it, *I'm* not going to do it.'[11]

O'Brien took no nonsense from Penelope, either.

Mrs Betjeman said to me, 'I can't afford to keep you on.' She said, 'Will you work out a six months' notice?' I said, 'Look here, madam, I'll have a week.' I said, 'I can't be on suspense for six months.' I finished up on the Thursday before Good Friday. So anyway I was paid up, and I was in bed in the cottage, when up the stairs comes Mr Betjeman. 'O'Brien!' he says. 'O'Brien, get up!' I said, 'What's wrong, then, sir?' He says, 'That bloody tree-killer's been at it again.' And that was Miss Candida's pony, called Dirk. I had already finished in their service, mind you. So I had to get up and put some barbed wire round a tree, on the Good Friday morning, and he gave me a five pound note. So I said to Mrs Betjeman, I said, 'He's given me £5, it's too much to take.' She said, 'You keep it, O'Brien.' She says, 'I'll put it on his account.' It later turned out that he had taken the money out of Miss Candida's money-box.[12]

In fact, O'Brien stayed on as gardener for a further year. He did not become any more deferential. One day, when John was going on holiday in the shooting-brake, he said, 'Don't forget my teddy-bear, O'Brien.' O'Brien asked, 'What's the good of having, like, teddy-bears in the back of the car, sir?' John replied: 'Well, if anyone looks in that car, O'Brien, he'll say, "That's only kids' things."'[13] When John came home from London, Penelope was usually with the ponies, or sawing wood; so John would chat with O'Brien about the day's adventures.

He got in the train at Paddington once [O'Brien recalled]. He got in the carriage and there was only one man in this carriage. Mr Betjeman was going as far as Reading. This particular day he was writing on some scrap paper he had kept from his days at the Ministry of Information. This chap on the opposite seat said, 'What! Writing on Government paper?' Mr Betjeman looked at him and was beat for an answer. When he got to Reading, he opened the carriage door and he had a brilliant brainwave. He put his hand in his pocket and took out twopence and he said, 'Here you are, you poor bloody old ratepayer.'[14]

The Betjemans took on a Spanish maid called Failla. Their friends were delighted: now one could get a meal on time and did not have to do the washing-up afterwards. But there was one contretemps with Failla.

Penelope was very proud of speaking fluent German, French, Italian and
Spanish [Dick Squires recalls]. But there was a disaster with this new
Spanish maid. Penelope tried to explain to her, in Spanish, what a Moral
Welfare Clinic was. She said she was having a tea for the Moral Welfare.
And she explained to the maid in very bad Spanish that it was all the ladies
who had babies and hadn't got any husbands and that the money from the
tea party was in aid of this. But she phrased it slightly wrong; so the
Spanish maid sat upstairs in one of the bedroom windows and looked at
all the ladies who were arriving – Lady This and Lady That, all the local
nobs – and said, 'Not her as *well?*'[15]

The Squires were already friends of the Betjemans. The Letcombe
Brook, mentioned by John in two of his poems about Wantage, separated The Mead's ground from the Squires' garden. Dr Vaughan Squires
was fifty-six in 1951, his wife Ottilie twelve years younger. He had
become the Betjemans' doctor when they lived at Farnborough. 'My
husband went up to Farnborough to see Candida once,' Ottilie remembered, 'when Candida was still riding quite a small pony, and he had to
examine her throat while she was sitting on the pony, because Penelope
said she didn't want to lift her off and on again.'[16] Dr Squires shared
Penelope's love of horses.[17] Their two children, Dick and Judy, were,
respectively, about the same age as Paul and Candida. Sometimes
Vaughan and Ottilie played tennis with the Betjemans. 'John wasn't
too bad at tennis,' said Ottilie, 'though he was slightly playing the fool;
he insisted on playing in a Turkish fez, a red one with a tassel.'[18]

It has been said of the second Earl of Ashburnham, an ancestor of
Swinburne, that 'he gravitated naturally to the rich'.[19] The same could
fairly be said of John and Penelope, though there were exceptions, rich
people whom they did not court. John could not stand the
Wroughtons, whose land was near The Mead. One friend of the
Betjemans thought that John had particularly taken against Michael
Wroughton when he sat opposite him in a first-class carriage in a train
from London and Wroughton said, 'My luggage is with my man, in
third-class.'[20] John's poem 'County' begins 'God save me from the
Porkers' and contains these lines:

> Loud talk of meets and marriages
>   And tax evasion's heard
> In many first-class carriages
>   While servants travel third . . .[21]

The Betjemans' greatest friends, among the local landowners, were
the Loyds of Lockinge and the Barings of Ardington. The Loyds'

fortune came from the Victorian S.J. Loyd, later Lord Overstone, a self-made banker from Northampton. His daughter developed an existing Georgian house into a vast mansion of geometric brickwork, and was, with over 20,000 acres, the largest landowner in Berkshire. The Betjemans became friends with Christopher ('Larch') Loyd of Betterton House – in 1944, the largely Victorian house had been demolished – and his sisters Hester ('Heck') and Catherine ('Ag').

Hester remembered her first encounter with Penelope. She 'brought Paul over when he was a baby; and she suddenly decided to breast-feed him. I had never seen that done, in a drawing-room. Then she proceeded to give my mother a tremendous lecture on that aspect of life, and I remember sitting there with my jaw gaping.'[22] John struck her as equally out of the ordinary when she met him at dinner-parties. 'If he was really amused by something, he'd pick up the table-napkin and throw it over his face, shrieking away underneath it.'[23] John discovered that Hester was interested in poetry.

> There was a train strike while John and Penelope were living at Wantage [she recalled]. John wanted to get to London and I was going to London anyway so he asked if I would drive him up. It was in the days when there was no motorway . . . It took about two hours . . . And he had a book with him, in the passenger seat – R.S. Thomas's *Song at the Year's Turning*. He said, 'This has just come out and it's marvellous.' And he read out one of the poems, 'Night and Morning' –

> > One night of tempest I arose and went
> > Along the Menai shore on greening bent;
> > The wind was strong and savage swung the tide
> > And the waves blustered on Caernarvon side.
> >
> > But on the morrow, when I passed that way,
> > On Menai shore the hush of heaven lay;
> > The wind was gentle and the sea a flower
> > And the sun slumbered on Caernarvon tower.

> Then and there, I learned that off by heart, by making John repeat it; and so often since then, if I've been on a sea shore – or just feeling fed up with things – I've remembered that poem and John sitting beside me with bundles of papers and his old bag, in my car.[24]

John also talked to Hester about his own poetry. 'The easy poems come very easily to him,' she suggested in 1976; 'but the soul-searching poems like "Norfolk" are real sweat and labour, and I think he shirks that task of really delving into what he most minds about.'[25]

Mollie and Desmond Baring, who were of much the same age as the Betjemans,[26] lived at Ardington House, an assured Baroque building of 1719–20 by Thomas Strong. Mollie Baring had been at RADA with Vivien Leigh and could do an imitation of Penelope almost as life-like as Joyce Grenfell's. Her father was the successful racehorse-owner Ben Warner, who also founded the Queen's Hotels Group (later taken over by Moat Houses). Desmond Baring, related to the banking Barings, ran the hotels group for his father-in-law.

The Betjemans were still at Farnborough when the Barings first encountered them. Mollie Baring recalled:

I had met Penelope at some local function. She realized that we had children of similar age. I was invited to bring my children to Farnborough. My second son Nigel couldn't go, but I set off with Peter, who was then, I suppose, nine or ten, and Anne, who was four or five. It was rather foggy. When we got there, Penelope said: 'I thought we'd do a scene from the Nativity,' and I said, 'Er, yes, how lovely.' She said, 'Peter, you can be one of the shepherds – you go round and put the candles on the tree.' Well, he thought that was marvellous: live candles, you know. 'You can be one of the shepherds, and Candida and Anne will be angels.' The Powlie [Paul] and Peter brought in a toy lamb. The little girls knelt there. Penelope suddenly thrust a torch at me and said, 'You flash that on the Virgin's face.' And I did. In the middle of that, John came home from London. He said, 'How very nice to meet you. Has she given you a drink yet?' And I said, 'No, we've had tea.' 'Oh Lord,' he said, 'how awful. Slip out whenever you can and join me in that little room on the left.' We had drinks and we found an awful lot to talk about together. And of course Penelope never had a drink at all, and I was considered a frightfully bad influence on John.[27]

During the move from Farnborough, Candida stayed at Ardington House and became great friends with the Barings' daughter Anne, whom John always called 'Arne', after Dr Arne who wrote 'Rule Britannia'. Paul was a friend of the Barings' sons, Peter and Nigel. As for their parents, Mollie felt it was 'a friendship that absolutely "went" – surprisingly, because we were not in John's world at all'.

We were at that time very much in the racing world; and even Penelope, though she loved horses, was not interested in racing. But we all got on so well . . . We saw each other almost every day . . . I don't think [John] ever got off the train at Didcot without calling in at Ardington. We spent about twenty Christmases together. The start of that was Penelope saying, 'We'll all come over to you Christmas-time.' I said, 'Well, I'm not sure that John will enjoy it [because there would be so much talk of racing] . . .

I was quite apprehensive, but John took to [it] all . . . like a fish to water. He was fascinated by the betting. Off the drawing-room was a little room where there were possibly some racing notes and a telephone. He always called it 'the betting room' – 'Is Dezzie sitting in the betting room?' Once, John found in there a Queen's Hotels letter with the directors' names at the top, and notice of a meeting. And under the typed part he wrote, in disguised handwriting: 'We've decided to sack Angus (who was the most upright and correct chairman). We might keep Ben Warner (my father) and we'll co-opt so-and-so.' Desmond found it on his desk and fell for it. 'What on earth is going on?' he said. I twigged it immediately. And John would ask absurd, off-target questions, like 'What won the four-thirty at Newton Abbot, Dezzie?' – when in fact it was Derby Day.[28]

When the Betjemans came to lunch or dinner, Mollie's gramophone records of Mantovani or Bing Crosby would be playing. Desmond would dispense sloe gin or White Lady cocktails and with a circular movement of his arm would intone, 'Here's to all who wish us well, And all the rest can go to hell.'[29] Mollie was the livelier one of the couple. Her juicy gossip usually began with the phrase, 'We are led to believe . . .'[30] But Desmond had his own quiet humour. If one of his children was successful at something, he would say, 'Winner trained by Baring.' On Anne's arriving home late from hunting, he asked, 'When are you going to get that horse fitted with headlights?'[31]
Anne (now Dalgety) remembers:

Penelope was always very busy and never sat down for a moment. Consequently, not much attention was paid to supplying John with the creature comforts he so enjoyed. When one went to the Mead, John would be tucked away in his library, the room on the right of the front door, keeping well out of the way, so as not to be involved, or expected to take part, in anything practical or outdoors. His library was rather dark, packed full of books, but warm and cosy. He'd love people to come in there and talk. Here he kept his drink, far enough away from Penelope [for her] not to be aware of how much or how often it was consumed. When we arrived in the house Moll would disappear into this room, while Dez would go and find Penelope, probably to discuss the price of hay, or the most efficient way of mucking out.[32]

By the mid-1950s, Anne adds, the two families had become 'so intertwined that no important decision could be made in either household, without consultation with the other'.

Many an evening would be spent chewing over the future of one or other of us. Despite her disregard for comforts, Penelope was a brilliant cook and often in the summer we would go over for dinner in the garden at the Mead, with the ponies so close that they were practically at the table. John would read to us and bring alive a verse of a poem that, until that moment, had gone unnoticed, or misunderstood.[33]

Through his catering contacts, Desmond was able to obtain exceptional wines. 'Oh, a Margaux! It never lets one down,' John wrote to him after a gift of a magnum.[34] He created a comic persona for Desmond. Mollie Baring recalled: 'John had the theory that the more drink he and Desmond had, the gayer he himself would become, but Dezzie would get quieter and quieter. And once John got hold of something like that, he never let go. He would look across the table at me and say, "It's going marvellously, darling – Dezzie hasn't said a word." It was a running joke . . .'[35] Penelope, who stuck to ginger beer, was very disapproving about the drinking. After one dinner she said John smelt of 'dead codskins', opened all his whisky bottles and poured the contents down the sink. 'I gave her a real ticking-off over that,' said Mollie Baring. 'I said, "There are plenty of old gentlemen in Wantage who would have enjoyed that." '[36] Mollie remembered a later dinner-party held by the interior decorator Oswin Bateman-Brown.

> We had dinner at his cottage on a New Year's Eve. It was a most gorgeous evening. Except for Penelope, we all had too much to drink and we went outside and listened to the church bells ringing. And she suddenly said, 'I am *disgusted* with you all,' and marched home. The next day, I asked her why. She said, 'Well, all you did, darling, was repeat yourself.' It upset Oswin, because we all liked drinking but Penelope liked eating chocolates, and he found she had demolished two of his Christmas boxes of chocolates.[37]

Near the Barings, at Mandhill, Ardington, lived Sir Ralph Glyn (later Lord Glyn), the local MP who may have 'found' the Old Rectory, Farnborough, for the Betjemans. As a politician he was best known for having inspected the Groundnut Scheme in East Africa.[38] 'Wonderful to think what our chaps are doing out there,' he commented on his return; in six months, the scheme collapsed.[39] 'He was a kind of Squire Western figure,' said Dick Squires.

> My father went to see his wife when she was ill (her first husband would have been Lord Long had he not been killed in the Great War). It was

Christmastime. 'I say, Squires,' Glyn said, 'would you care for a guinea fowl?' 'Thank you very much,' my Pa said. So Sir Ralph reached for his twelve-bore, stepped on to the back lawn and shot a bird down from a beech tree in his garden, in the twilight.[40]

Penelope and John called him 'The Ogre', but were fond of him and often visited Mandhill. Another friend was Lord Norrie, of The Ham, Wantage, a military man who had been Governor-General of New Zealand. 'He was a bit like Harold Macmillan, but with more of a twinkle in his eye,' Squires said. 'He wore racy braces – bright red felt with horses' heads and brass buckles.'[41] At Pusey House, near Faringdon, was Michael Hornby, who became chairman of W.H. Smith. His wife Nicolette was Penelope's schoolfriend. The Hornbys took part, with the Pipers, the Barings and the Knights, in evening singsongs at The Mead.[42]

Moving to Wantage brought John and Penelope geographically near to their old friend Frederick Etchells and his wife, the wood-engraver Hester Sainsbury, who interested John particularly as a niece of the painter H.S. Tuke, 'the Boucher of the Boy Scouts'. John, Etchells and Piper took a 'nature cure' at Edstone Hall, Stratford-on-Avon.[43] John wrote to his mother that he was apprehensive about the cure – 'no smoking, no drinking and raw cabbage and nuts'.[44] The three men were caught buying forbidden food and drink locally, and were asked to leave.[45]

Pat and Molly Lawrence, who had bought the Old Rectory at Farnborough, stayed with the Betjemans for six weeks as paying guests, while the architect Hugh Vaux, recommended by John, put bathrooms and a ballroom into their house. The Lawrences noticed how John teased Penelope with 'regulation jokes'. The favourite was: 'Penelope, why does your head come to a point?' Or he would say to the family's pekinese: 'Are you a *pig*, Marco Polo? Are you a *chicken*?'[46] The Lawrences named their son Mark because they had become so used to hearing Penelope call out to the dog – '*Marco! Marco! Marco!*'[47]

On 6 December 1951, John wrote to his BBC friend George Barnes: 'My new friend Elizabeth Cavendish is just our kind of girl. She is as bracing and witty and kind and keen on drink as Anne [Barnes's wife]. I long for you to meet her.'[48] Lady Elizabeth Cavendish, then twenty-five, was a daughter of the tenth Duke of Devonshire. She and John had first met on 29 May, at a London dinner party held by Lady Pamela Berry.[49] John had known Lady Pamela for over twenty years as she was the sister of his Oxford friend Freddy Birkenhead. She often invited him to dinner, *sans* Penelope, and usually asked him to sing for his supper by reciting some of his poems.[50] John thought it as well to keep in with her, as her husband Michael (later Lord Hartwell) had great power at the *Daily Telegraph*, for which John began reviewing books that year.[51] Neither John nor Elizabeth thought that the dinner-party in Lord North Street was going to be anything more than the usual agreeable mix of the Berrys' artistic, literary and political friends; but to historians of espionage that evening is counted as a critical moment in the dénouement of a great scandal. Among the other guests were Anthony Blunt, who by now was Director of the Courtauld Institute of Art; Sydney Butler, wife of the politician R.A. Butler; and Isaiah Berlin.[52] Also expected for dinner was another friend of John's, the diplomat Guy Burgess. These people were loosely linked in an Establishment mesh: R.A Butler, John and Blunt had all been at Marlborough; the Courtauld Institute was named after Sydney Butler's father, Sir Samuel Courtauld; Blunt and Burgess had been together at Trinity College, Cambridge, where R.A. Butler's father had earlier been Master; and Michael Berry and Burgess had been friends at Eton, where Berry had tried to get him elected to the exclusive Eton Society – 'Pop' – but had failed because 'The majority simply "preferred not to have him".'[53] Now, twenty years on, Burgess had asked Berry to give him a dinner-party and a job on the *Telegraph*.[54] In his book *The Climate of Treason* (1979), Andrew Boyle wrote in all innocence:

> The press lord had intended to tell Guy over dinner . . . that there would be no immediate opening for him on the staff of the *Daily Telegraph*.[55] When Blunt . . . had arrived, alone and rather downcast, having waited in vain for Burgess to join him at the Reform Club as arranged, Hartwell said lightly that their friend was not noted for his punctuality. They lingered, and there was an empty place at table when they sat down thoughtfully to dine. Blunt evidently did not enjoy the meal. He appeared sickly, pale and increasingly distraught. Suddenly he got up and said apologetically: 'I feel I must go now and look for him.'
>
> Only the day before, Blunt had dismissed with disdainful logic the theorizing of Goronwy Rees about the likely destination of Burgess.[56] Hartwell learnt later that the eminent art critic and connoisseur, prostrated by his unavailing efforts to solve the mystery of Guy's disappearance, had taken to his bed, sick with anxiety.[57]

On 25 May, four days before the dinner-party, Burgess had left England with Donald Maclean, another diplomat spying for the Russians, who was due to be interrogated by MI6 on the 28th. We now know that, by the day of the dinner, Blunt was not only fully aware of Burgess's defection, but had managed to scoop up two incriminating letters from his flat.[58] Blunt's distress at dinner – Hartwell recalled that he 'went noticeably white'[59] – may be ascribed to his fear that MI6 would now turn the heat on him. As Burgess's close friend, he was bound to fall under suspicion, perhaps be exposed as a spy.[60]

Somewhat off-target as it now seems, Boyle's account at least shows how things appeared to the Berrys and their guests on 29 May. Oblivious of any historical undercurrents, John and Elizabeth gazed at each other. 'They did not speak to each other that night,' writes Candida Lycett Green, 'not did they need to. It only took seconds . . . for JB and Elizabeth to know that they had fallen in love.'[61] Here, love was not blind, but dumb.

In that year, Lady Elizabeth had become a lady-in-waiting to Princess Margaret. She was just three days younger than the Queen; her mother had been a childhood friend of the Queen Mother, and Elizabeth had known the two princesses since children's parties at 145 Piccadilly. ('It can't have been easy for Princess Elizabeth,' she commented in a television programme about the Queen in 2001, 'always being curtseyed to, and with everybody falling silent when she entered the room.') Princess Margaret's biographer writes of Elizabeth Cavendish: 'Like Princess Margaret, she had also been brought up in palaces with chilly State rooms beneath painted Verrio ceilings . . . and, like Margaret, she set little store by such trappings.'[62]

We catch a flamelit glimpse of Elizabeth in adolescence, in a letter of 1943 from Kathleen 'Kick' Kennedy, sister of the future American President, to her father, Joseph P. Kennedy, describing a London party attended by Irving Berlin:

> The party ended at 1.00 . . . However we had an incident before it was all over. Lord Edward Fitzmaurice, a young Guardsman of 21, had rather too much to drink and set a match to Elizabeth Cavendish's new evening dress. She is Billy [Lord Hartington]'s younger sister and it was the first party she had ever been to so we were all afraid it might have scared her away from other parties. She stayed on and told her mother, 'before I was set on fire the boys didn't pay much attention to me, but afterwards I was very popular. An American boy put the flames out' . . . Angie Laycock said that she said to her brave husband Gen Laycock[63] 'why didn't you do something about putting those flames out?' He replied, 'I thought it was a firework display.'[64]

Kick Kennedy married Lord Hartington; Elizabeth tried to console her when he was shot and killed by a sniper in Belgium in 1944. She later recalled:

I never met anyone so desperately unhappy in my life. I had to sleep in her room night after night. Her mother had tried to convince her that she had committed a sin in this marriage, so that in addition to losing her husband, she worried about losing her soul.[65]

Elizabeth became a friend of John F. Kennedy too; in 1948 Kennedy met Kick at Lismore, the Duke of Devonshire's estate in Co. Waterford; shortly afterwards, Kennedy fell ill with Addison's Disease in London, and Elizabeth visited him. The three vignettes from Elizabeth's youth reveal something of her character: her sang-froid and ability to deal with an emergency; her sense of humour; her enjoyment of attention from young men; and her compassion. All were brought into play in her long relationship with John.

The day after the dinner-party in Lord North Street, Pamela Berry rang Elizabeth to tell her the sensational news of Burgess's disappearance. She also mentioned that she was trying to get John to take a trip to Copenhagen on the Camroses' yacht *Virginia*.[66] She added that he was unhappy, that 'his marriage was going wrong' and that he would come on the yacht only if she came too.[67] Elizabeth agreed to join the party. Alan Pryce-Jones, by now editor of the *Times Literary Supplement*, was also on board with his wife Poppy. 'It is often said that John hates "abroad",' Pryce-Jones said in 1976, 'but I can tell you he certainly didn't hate "abroad" on that voyage!'[68] After that, John's friends had to get used to the idea that, although he and Penelope were still together, he had 'found someone else'. How serious the affair was became clear in 1952 when he took Elizabeth, not Penelope, on holiday with the Barneses in France.[69]

In *Summoned by Bells* (1960), John wrote of his childhood love for a little girl in Highgate, adding:

> . . . all my loves since then
> Have had a look of Peggy Purey-Cust.[70]

Comparing photographs of Peggy as a child and Elizabeth as she was when John met her, one can see that both had the same kind of patrician good looks, with fair hair and a slight natural frown in the set of the eyes.[71] John nicknamed Elizabeth 'Feeble' (or 'Phoeble') because she wasn't – rather as short men get called 'Lofty'. He liked dominant women, but it amused him to keep up a teasing pretence that Elizabeth was shy, nervous and ineffectual. 'Come and meet the palest, wispiest, least-known lady-in-waiting in the world,' he wrote to a friend.[72] Because Elizabeth was tall and willowy, and Princess Margaret was not, John referred to the Princess as 'Little Friend'.[73] Elizabeth could be very winning and had a varied set of friends, including the Bohemian, slightly raffish group known as 'the Princess Margaret set'.[74] But a word sometimes used to describe her was 'reserved', and her reserve could be misconstrued as coolness or hauteur. The American critic Edmund Wilson, who admired John's poetry, was told by him at a London party in 1954 that he had invited 'a jolly girl' to join them. 'This turned out to be some titled lady,' Wilson wrote in his diary. 'She did not seem particularly jolly.'[75]

Not all John's friends welcomed his new romance. 'Is it not about time you gave your heart a rest, for a little while, anyway?' Colonel Kolkhorst asked in 1951. 'You have been at it non-stop now for I don't know how many donkeys' years. It is not good for you.'[76] Some friends, who loved and were loyal to Penelope, were frosty towards Elizabeth. At first, Penelope herself was not too concerned. 'John had had crushes before,' she said in 1976. 'But always, I met those girls, they became my friends too and somehow that sort of "defanged" the thing and John lost interest after a while. But with Elizabeth it was different. She just wouldn't agree to see me.'[77] Penelope's friends were not the only people who looked with disfavour on John's relationship with Elizabeth. Some of her own friends and relations saw her as 'throwing away her life' on a married man twenty years her senior. She had not been without admirers – among them Evelyn Waugh's brother-in-law Auberon Herbert.[78] Iris Murdoch and John Bayley recalled how, when they had stayed with Elizabeth's first cousin Lord David Cecil, at Cranborne, Dorset, in the early 1950s, he had expressed disapproval of the liaison.[79] It is likely that her nearer relations, too, were less than happy with the situation. But, as with John's relations with the Chetwodes in the 1930s, he was able to disarm criticism and to win over his detractors. Dick Squires remembered David Cecil rolling up to The Mead in a Bentley, about 1953. 'Penelope was weeding in the drive, pulling up dandelions in her jodhpurs, when he arrived. "My God, David! I'd completely forgotten you were coming to lunch. I must finish this weeding. Can you possibly scramble some eggs?" And there was poor Lord David, who had probably never cooked an egg in his life, having to go into the kitchen. Luckily, John was there and helped him.'[80] The Devonshires were soon placated, too. John had known the Duchess, the former Deborah Mitford, since the days when he had proposed marriage to two of her sisters. He also made a hit with the Dowager Duchess, Elizabeth's mother, whose house at Edensor, Derbyshire, 'was like another home' for John.[81] She enjoyed talking to him about the pomps of the 'old days'.[82] In October 1951 Evelyn Waugh wrote to Nancy Mitford: 'Betjeman has the flu and has retired to the house of the Dowager Duchess of Devonshire where he is waited on & washed by Lady Elizabeth while the high-church butler reads *The Unlucky Family* aloud to him. Meanwhile he has sold Penelope's house & purchased a villa in the centre of Wantage – "Oh the joy of being back in real suburbia old boy" – and has left Penelope quite unaided to make the move.'[83] In 1953 John wrote to Penelope from Derbyshire:

> Nooni nooni nooni noewke
> Er oobby went off for to stay with a duke
>
> Nibberly Nobberly nibberly nob
> Er ooby was clearly a bit of a snob
>
> Nibberly Nobberly Nibberly nidz
> But not sooch a snob as is two little kidz.[84]

In later years the Devonshires even placed a bust of John on the staircase at Chatsworth.

When John was with Elizabeth, she ministered to his comfort in a way that Penelope rarely did. Penelope could cook superbly, but most visitors to The Mead had to take pot luck. The episode of Lord David and the scrambled eggs was not unusual. Life at The Mead was often chaotic. In August 1953 Lady Silvia Combe, Penelope's old schoolfriend whom she called 'Cackle', visited her there. Shortly afterward she wrote an account. Although John was away at the time, this vignette is an unrivalled evocation of everyday life in the Betjeman ménage. As Lady Silvia arrived at the house, a man was turning into the drive with a yapping pekinese in his car. 'The Warden' (John Sparrow), who was staying and hated dogs, told her he wished she had run over Marco Polo and added: 'I was asked to lunch by Penelope before being given a jumping lesson, but she only appeared at *three*, there was no horse, and the entire afternoon has been spent transporting to and from the timber yard enormous planks of wood to make wings for her gymkhana jumps.'[85] Sparrow took Lady Silvia's case up to what he guessed would be her room, but warned, 'For goodness sake don't leave your hairbrush lying about on the dressing table. Last time I was here the daughter of the house cut all the bristles off mine, and with my own nail scissors, what's more!'[86]

The sound of a car stopping and a piercing shriek from the drive, 'Gina, fare mangiare alle anitre!', announced the return of Penelope, who, on seeing Lady Silvia, said, 'God, I quite forgot you were coming today, but it's nice to see you, Cackle.' (Gina was a new maid. The garbled Italian was intended to mean 'Go and feed the ducks!') They went into the dining-room.

The table was devoid of cups and the usual paraphernalia associated with afternoon tea. Instead a charming young lady was already seated there, with Bible and prayer books laid out before her. 'Oh God!' said Penelope. 'I quite forgot you were coming for your Catechism lesson. However, as you're here, you can help get the tea and also milk Clara. Gina won't give us any tea today, as she's always cross on wash day, and John's had his four Frog cousins to stay for the weekend so she'll be crosser than ever.'

A loaf of bread was suddenly hurled through the hatch, the catechist miraculously produced some cups and a tiny pot of tea. Half a Swiss roll and two partially nibbled biscuits were pulled by Penelope out of the pocket of her milking smock (which I felt would not exactly match the standards set by the Milk Marketing Board for their country-fresh dairy maids). 'I saved these from the W.I. [Women's Institute] tea,' she said. 'In these days one simply can't afford to waste anything.'[87]

They had hardly begun eating when Mr Levy arrived, a 'grey-faced, grey-suited' musician who had been examining the girls of St Mary's School, Wantage, on their piano-playing. 'Mr Levy sat down, and after eyeing the two half nibbled biscuits, the *passé* Swiss roll and the khaki-coloured tea, said that he'd already had tea, thank you.'

Not another remark did he make except when asked whether he didn't miss the Stones very much who'd left his neighbourhood. 'No, why should I?' he replied. 'I left Newbury two years ago. Why does *everyone* think I live there still?' he plaintively added. This temporarily silenced the conversation until Penelope looked at me and burst into uncontrollable giggles. 'Do have some cake, Cackle, it's delicious,' she said, and on seeing my hesitation, the Warden put in, 'You'd better, you won't get any dinner tonight, judging by my lunch.' Penelope shrieked, 'What do you mean? Cackle will have a delicious dinner, we've got a riding mistress coming who's so mean, she only eats when she's asked out, and I've ordered *Uove in Purgatorio*.' 'John's got a book about Purgatory by his bed,' said the Warden musingly.

Suddenly Penelope remembered that Clara had yet to be milked and the religious instruction still to be administered, so she said, 'Now you'd better all go home, the Warden must give Mr Levy a lift in that precious car of his, and Cackle must help with the cows, although she's too incompetent to milk them.' 'My car doesn't happen to be going in Mr Levy's direction,' said the Warden firmly and, as we all thought, quite finally. 'Then,' said Mr Levy with a sudden startling display of spirit, 'if your car does not intend to travel in my direction, *it must be coaxed to do so!*'[88]

Visiting the Betjemans for a day or so could be stimulating, but being their neighbour could be more testing. 'We were all very fond of Penelope,' said Ottilie Squires, 'but I don't think I've ever known anybody who could use other people so much.'

> She was so bright, she found just running the house was boring. So she gave lectures or went out in a pony-trap. Somehow she always needed your help more than you needed hers. She used to palm off Candida on us. Candida, who was older than my youngest, could be delightful; but she could also do everything she could to upset – like when nanny went to get the pudding course from the kitchen downstairs Candida would put stew on the chair, that sort of thing.[89]

Dick Squires also remembered Candida's naughtiness. 'One day my sister came in with wet knickers and my old man said, "Why have you wet your knickers?" "Well, Candida told me to." '[90] He also remembered Candida's bloodcurdling threat to Georgie Sale.

> The Sales were our other next-door neighbours – on the opposite side of us from the Betjemans [he explained]. Mr Sale was ex-Indian Army, a hydrologist and a grumpy lot of hot air. His wife was a large, forceful lady who looked her most frightening in guide uniform. Penelope called her 'Britannia'. Mrs Sale always called her husband 'Husband'. There were two elder boys and then Georgie, who drove us all mad, always knew the answer to everything. But he was terrorized by Candida. At a children's party we held, he came up looking very frightened and said, 'Ottilie (he always copied his parents in calling my parents by their Christian names), please help me, Candida and her friends say they are going to hang me.'[91]

Mollie Baring recalled: 'Ann had had a bad go of 'flu and Vaughan Squires came over to see her. I said to him, "I think Candida's coming over," and he said, "Well, if she can stand Candida she must be well, she can take anybody." Candida used to do *such* naughty things. Perhaps it was because she did not get enough attention from either of her parents.'[92]

'I'm sure it came as a shock to John, sometimes, to realize he'd *got* children,' said Ottilie Squires. 'That was the impression I got. The children rather did what they liked and then suddenly Penelope would realize that things were getting out of hand and she'd say, "Breakfast at eight o'clock; you've got to be down and you've got to make your beds and tidy your bedrooms." But it never lasted for more than about two weeks, and then they'd slip back into the old ways.'[93]

Now that the children were growing up, John became more interested in them. Though he was satirical about the horse world, he was proud when Candida won prizes on her pony Dirk – 'the tree-killer' – and amused when asked by a Post Office assistant whether he was related to the little girl who was carrying off all the trophies.[94] He took her sketching and was pleased when Miss Wimpress, the art teacher at St Mary's, Wantage, complimented her on her drawing.[95] He went to the cinema with the children; Candida remembers his explaining the plot of *The Third Man* (1949).[96] Every Christmas holiday he took them to see the Crazy Gang.[97] Every summer he drove them down to Trebetherick for two weeks. On the way down, he fumed behind long-distance lorries[98] and stopped at nearly every church. One year he tried surfing but realized on emerging from the sea that he had lost his trunks. He walked up the beach with the surfboard held in front of him and Candida walking behind him, both helpless with laughter.[99]

Paul was at Eton much of the time. He was embarrassed when his father turned up at the school in his usual harum-scarum clothes, sometimes to give poetry readings.[100] John was mortified when told about this and tried to look smarter. Paul's housemaster, Oliver Van Oss, had been at Magdalen with John and had acted with him in college plays. 'Paul's reports are good, he is an entertaining and independent boy with a clear mind, rather too clear at times,' Van Oss wrote to John in 1952. 'He likes things to be definite. He proved a hopeless library fag and was dethroned for casualness, etc. He has also become rather a good footballer. Very much of a character is Betjie and I value his presence a lot.'[101] In the school holidays Paul saw a lot of Dick Squires, who was about the same age.

> Paul was keen on jazz at that time, and so was I [Squires recalled]. He was always one stage ahead of me in liking a different form of jazz . . . It was the Brubeck Storyville concert that first got me hooked, but Paul was one stage more advanced in liking Coltrane, Miles Davis and so on . . . We used to play music for hours. We had a huge old-fashioned gramophone with a horn up in the hay-loft. One was able to put hawthorn spikes into it as needles.[102]

Dick Squires found John much more approachable than the fathers of his other friends. 'His great charm was his marvellous capacity for listening, very carefully, to what you had to say; he then added his own very amusing, witty reply, which was utterly in sequence with what you'd been saying – so you kidded yourself it was the most amusing thing you ever said in your life, especially when he gave one of his high-pitched, almost soundless laughs, like a dog-whistle.'[103] But Squires also observed some of his drawbacks as a paterfamilias.

He was very extravagant. We were in the kitchen of The Mead once, and the charlady's daughter was going to get married the following week. On hearing this, John immediately said, 'This calls for a celebration!' and rushed down the cellar and pulled out the cork of a very smart vintage champagne. Penelope was outraged at the very idea of drinking at eleven o'clock in the morning; and the charlady's daughter probably couldn't tell the difference between vintage champagne and ginger beer.[104]

If John's idea of entertaining annoyed Penelope, hers annoyed him still more. 'The trouble was, John liked comforts,' Mollie Baring said. 'He adored coming to Ardington and having tea and crumpets. At The Mead he wasn't allowed to have tea because Penelope was much too busy to bother to make him tea.'[105] Dick Squires remembered that 'he loved an evening with good wine, good friends, a bit of style. And he hated Penelope coming in, in jodhpurs, to put the spuds on at quarter-to-eight.'[106] Mollie Baring thought that 'It was because he was always semi-ashamed that the food wasn't going to be good, that he overdid the wine . . . We drank and drank to make up for the fact that we hadn't had roast beef, or something.'[107] John also objected to some of the people Penelope asked to dinner. She was teaching the Roman Catholic catechism to a number of Irish teenagers in Wantage and would invite a sixteen-year-old boy or girl to stay on for dinner. John could get on with anyone, but if the other guests were Cyril Connolly and Lord David Cecil, and conversation ranged from Oxford gossip to Proust to *risqué* jokes, he felt that neither the teenager nor the literary grandees would be at ease. Candida, too, resented her mother's foisting her catechumens on her – 'trying to force a friendship between myself and a certain Sean Connolly whom I loathed'.[108]

Other aspects of life at Wantage which John found disagreeable were litter (he waged a constant war on fish-and-chip wrappings) and the proximity of the Harwell Atomic Research Station, whose staff he called 'the Atomics'.[109] London, always a lure to him, was made yet more tempting by the chance to be with Elizabeth Cavendish; and in 1954 he rented a London flat.* But he did his best to fit into Wantage life. He became a churchwarden at the Church of St Peter and St Paul, 'the Cathedral of the Vale', and a governor of Candida's school. He opened church bazaars. In 1953 he took part in a Coronation Pageant organized by Penelope and filmed by Tommy Clyde, father of the actor Jeremy Clyde. And he appeared in local Brains Trusts held in St Mary's School and the Corn Exchange, both as a question-master and as a panellist. One question was, 'Would the panel prefer to look

---

* See Chapter 28, 'Cloth Fair and Rotherhithe'.

clever and be stupid, or look stupid and be clever?' John replied that
he would rather look stupid and be clever. A voice from the audience:
'Your wish is granted!'[110]

The Betjemans were usually short of money. John and Penelope
were both extravagant in their own ways: he in travelling first-class to
London and back, and paying for expensive lunches;[111] she in keeping
her ponies and buying carts. Penelope decided she must think of ways
to make extra money. First she set up The Mead Waterfowl Farm.
Reynolds Stone made a Bewick-like engraving as a letterhead for stationery and price lists. Aylesbury ducks were offered at two guineas
each; more exotic breeds and geese and ganders cost more.[112]

I had about five hundred ducks and geese [Penelope recalled]. I got my
initial Aylesburys from 'Ducky' Weston at Aylesbury, a wonderful old gentleman. Very sad: the family had been breeding ducks since the eighteenth
century, but his son was only interested in films and would not continue
the business – rather like John's not entering his father's firm. I always
thought Aylesbury ducks had orange beaks, but they don't. They have
pale, flesh-coloured beaks. The Peking have the orange beaks. And there
was someone called Colonel Appleyard who invented a duck called Silver
Appleyard – absolutely beautiful, very good table birds *and* very ornamental. And we had Roman geese – small geese, suitable for the small ovens of
small families. They were supposed to be descended from the geese that
gave warning on the Capitol.[113]

John did not help with the ducks. 'He wasn't interested; he couldn't
be expected to be, going up and down to London,' Penelope said.

An unfortunate thing happened [she added]. I had some ornamental
ducks just to look pretty called Black East Indian: they were beautiful,
black with a few green feathers, peacocky colour. They never made any
noise except when John came down. Then they would come outside our
bedroom window at five o'clock a.m. – they were loose, not kept in a

pen – and quack *without stopping*. He made such a fuss, I had to get rid of them.[114]

Because Penelope was a novice duck-farmer, there were some bad mishaps.

I bought an incubator, specially for water-fowl [she remembered]. Water-fowl were very difficult to incubate then. There have been great improvements since, but in those days it was frightfully difficult to get them to hatch out properly and on one terrible occasion about two hundred and fifty eggs were all scorched; the thing got up to too great a heat and all the poor little ducklings were roasted in their shells. So after that I put my duck eggs under broody hens from the Lockinge estate, only about two miles away. I'd put twelve duck eggs under a large hen, or six goose eggs.[115]

There was a further disaster when stinking pigswill for the geese over-turned in the back of the Betjemans' car.[116] And the duck farm never yielded adequate profits.

It was never really a paying concern [Penelope recalled] but you could set your tax against the losses and it meant you could keep one man, who got £5 a week and a very nice cottage. It more or less broke even, because the feeding stuffs cost about £250. It meant you could run your car and pay part of the telephone bill. And of course we often had delicious ducks for lunch or dinner.[117]

The Betjemans' next venture was John's idea.

John gets manias for people [Penelope said in 1978]. He got a mania for a very sad married couple in Wantage, Peter and Dorothy Martin. Mr Martin was a failed actor who dealt in a small way in antiques and she was rather literary and had a lending library, 6d a book. And she wasn't making much money because the county library had started and people were getting their books free, so naturally they weren't going to pay poor Dorothy her sixpences for the lending library. So John suggested that he and they should start a sort of cafeteria in conjunction with the books, which was what the Newman Bookshop in Oxford was doing very suc-cessfully. John rented an upstairs room from the chemist who lived on the opposite side of the road. It was in a funny little long building on a sort of island site. Dorothy had the ground floor and the chemist had most of the upstairs floor and John managed to rent just one end, where the cooking would be done. They called the café 'King Alfred's Kitchen', and John was a director of it.[118]

DIRECTORS:
JOHN BETJEMAN
P. B. MARTIN   TELEPHONE
D. MARTIN   WANTAGE 353

King Alfred's Kitchen
AND BOOKSHOP   (P. B. & D. MARTIN, LTD.)
THE CAFE WITH THE HOME-MADE SPECIALITIES : CAKES & PRESERVES
WANTAGE, BERKS.

Penelope, who was still running the duck farm, did not want to get involved with the café.

However, the trouble was that neither John nor the Martins knew the first thing about cooking – but, I mean, not the first *thing*. So I said I would try to find a cook and teach her. I did find them a cook, an awfully pretty young woman whose husband worked in the atomic research thing at Harwell. She knew a certain amount about cooking and I taught her a few things like soufflés; but she had such terrible equipment that they couldn't do very much. They only had a tiny electric stove meant for a family of two; it was just hopeless. One day I went in to have lunch and I said, 'Dorothy, what's for lunch today?' And she said, 'Oh, I couldn't care less; ask Mary' – the cook upstairs. In point of fact there was nothing but Spam salad with a lot of rather dirty lettuce. I was getting very worried about it. It was bad for our reputation in Wantage.[119]

After the restaurant had been open for almost a year, Penelope offered – 'Dorothy was looking very drawn and worried' – to run it for a fortnight while she took a holiday. It was agreed that Dorothy would go away on her own and that Peter Martin would stay in Wantage and help Penelope – 'emptying the dustbins, that sort of thing'.

But the day after she went on holiday he took a job at the atomic research station, so I was left to carry the whole baby. I found to my great surprise and horror that they were buying nut-and-date loaves on the opposite side of Wantage market square, a cake shop, and removing the trade labels and selling them in King Alfred's Kitchen as home-made. And I said to John, 'This is going to be a scandal – you are one of the leading Anglicans in England, and it will be the same sort of scandal as Joad and his railway ticket.'[120] And he got in an absolute panic. But anyway I managed to build up – just doing perfectly simple, straightforward, reasonably good cooking – from one 'regular' a day for lunch, to twenty, in a fortnight. I had the most awful difficulty because there was only that little stove; and one day I went down into the restaurant and I found two customers sitting opposite each other, each holding one half of a table – it had split in two. When Dorothy came home from holiday, John said he and the Martins must have a meeting and decide what to do; this state of affairs could not go on. I'd love to have been behind a curtain when the Board meeting, so to speak, occurred.[121]

At the meeting, the Martins resigned.

So then I really *was* left to carry the baby. I said to John, 'We'll have to build up our reputation after this disgrace – those awful cakes and things. I will run it for you for six months and then you can try and sell it as a going concern.' But then I realized the full horror of the situation: which was, that John had got a 'repairing lease' of twenty-one years, of which only seven years had elapsed while the Martins had their library. It was a most appalling prospect. We had to pay not only our own repairs but the repairs of the chemist's part, too. We were building up our custom, because of the reasonably good food – which was very important if we wanted to get any money at all. But I told John, 'I have to have proper equipment.' The first thing that happened was that I fell through the upstairs floor; so the kitchen had to be completely refloored – a much stronger floor as we were going to have much heavier equipment. We bought a commercial gas stove, a lovely big stove. We were able to do much more food. The next thing that happened, the roof badly needed repairing. The chemist said we would have to do that, and we had to close for a fortnight while the roof was done at a cost of £200, in those days a colossal amount. We bought new tables and chairs, and a local artist painted some murals. One was of goats; another was a still life of an oil lamp on a window-sill – you looked through the window at the White Horse.[122]

There was a grand reopening in 1956 by Father Trevor Huddleston, who had recently become the most famous Church of England priest (the sacerdotal equivalent of C.S. Lewis in the laity) with the publication of his book *Naught for your Comfort*, exposing the malevolence of apartheid in South Africa. Archbishop Huddleston recalled in 1990:

At that time the Community of St Mary the Virgin at Wantage and my own Community of the Resurrection at Mirfield were in close contact . . . In the summer we were able to take over the girls' school and have a summer school . . . for about a week. People gave lectures; and John Betjeman always used to come and read. I can remember he read

Tennyson. And I suppose it was in the course of that that King Alfred's Kitchen came up and he said to me, 'I want you to come and bless it.' His wife, though a Roman Catholic, was equally keen on this.

. . . I suppose Betjeman was quite poor in those days: he needed to turn a few pennies. I mean, his name wasn't nearly so well known in those days, certainly not as a national figure. It was quite difficult to get people into the Kitchen, but they did come in. It was a mixture of people – some of them from the summer school. I was moving about the country a lot talking about South Africa and that was a help, because it drew into the place people who were interested in that side of things.[123]

The restaurant became a meeting-place for Wantage folk and a popular rendezvous for undergraduates motoring out from Oxford. 'Everything was beautifully done,' recalled Kathleen Philip, a local historian who helped out in the café. 'You used to get a "King Alfred Special" – ice cream, nuts and burnt sugar, with chocolate sauce in little pots.'[124] There was the odd mistake; two scones were burned black. Penelope put them into the window with a label: 'Original cakes burnt by King Alfred the Great'.[125] More local girls and women were recruited as part-time waitresses. When one of them, Christine Carter, complained to Penelope that a regular customer had been pinching her bottom, Penelope said, 'I can't afford to lose such a good customer. I can't tell him off,' and put her behind the counter instead.[126] Another of Penelope's helpers, Di Cox, remembered her equally pragmatic solution of another problem.

She'd usually have three different menus for the day but there would always be one that went better than the others, and towards the end of the day she'd be running out of it but she'd never like to say it was 'off'. 'Mustn't say it's *orf*,' she said. So one day she'd done spaghetti bolognese and a chicken thing in sauce and some other concoction, and everybody had gone for spaghetti bolognese. So near the end, when somebody was asking for it, 'Oh,' she said, 'put the chicken in with the spaghetti bolognese – they'll never know. Just mix it in. They won't dare to ask what it is.' And she was right.[127]

Dick Squires recalled a day when Penelope had been cooking sausages for late breakfasts. 'And you know what a frying-pan looks like when you've done a lot of frying and haven't changed the fat. Well, a vicar ordered an omelette and he sent it back to the kitchen with a note on the plate that said: "Please will you do me another omelette. This one looks as if it has been cooked in a coal-scuttle." '[128] At its best, the cooking was exceptionally good; but Penelope periodically went on foreign tours,[129] leaving the catering to others. In any case, she wearied of the 'caff'. 'She was always too busy,' Mollie Baring said. 'The worst period for all her friends was the café. She got very tired, very irritable, and she and John lost a lot of money on it.'[130] Candida remembers that her father 'complained about the funds he had to keep pouring into the "caff" '.[131] For a long time the repairing lease deterred people from taking it off the Betjemans' hands. 'I felt it was going to be a millstone round our necks for ever,' Penelope said.[132]

Both John and Penelope still allowed themselves some extravagances. He bought a new Peugeot 203 estate car – 'the first and last smart car we ever owned', Candida writes.[133] Penelope acquired first a Vespa motor-scooter, then a 500cc Norton motor-bike. Even she came to realize that the motor-bike was too powerful for her; but Paul enjoyed riding it. Dick Squires recalled:

> Paul was riding the bike one day when he saw a car come out of a drive. It drove straight into the road in front of him. He went into the side of it, doing some body damage to the bike but not hurting himself. The car belonged to Father Wixted, the Irish Roman Catholic priest in Wantage with whom Penelope had quarrelled – she went to services in Hendred instead.
>
> At the court hearing the judge said, 'Did you not see Father Wixted in the entrance of his drive, and why did you not slow down?'
>
> Paul replied: 'I certainly saw a car, but did not know it was Father Wixted. Knowing what a reputation he has in a motor car, if I had known it was him I would not only have slowed down but I would have got off my motor-cycle and walked.'[134]

Paul was coming to the end of his time at Eton. Unlike his father, he excelled in gymnastics.[135] Van Oss wrote to John in the Lent term of 1955: 'Paul has an alert and critical mind . . . I mean that he gets the answers right, but seems desperately anxious to leave next half [that is, term]. He is vividly aware that his parents are unusual and gifted people, with strongly individual personalities. This makes him watchful and wary even in religious matters. He very much wants to be himself and not JB's son. It may be an argument against Oxford, I don't know . . .'[136] This was a wise and prophetic assessment; but in discussing Paul's future another factor had to be taken into account. In the mid-1950s, every fit young male had to do two years' National Service in the armed forces. On John's fiftieth birthday (28 August 1956) he wrote a long letter to Penelope, heading it 'The 50th birthday of a failure'. Penelope had written to him about Paul and about The Mead. John addressed them 'in order of importance', putting 'The

Powlie' first. He thought there was no harm in Paul's sitting an entrance examination to an Oxford college while waiting to be called up.

> Trinity might be able to take him now. But if you think, & I'm inclined to think with you if you do, that National Service in a good regiment w^d be the making of him, then even if the P[owlie] passes the exam to Trinity, he should do national service first. I don't think this is a decision we should leave to him. We should make it ourselves.[137]

It is curious to find John, never gung-ho or instinct with *esprit de corps*, suggesting that army service could be the 'making' of his son; odder still to find one who rebelled against an authoritarian father, intent on deciding for his nineteen-year-old son what was best for him. But the birthday letter shows that John had gone to some trouble on Paul's behalf. He had written to Michael Hornby, Michael Balcon and Sylvester Gates,[138] as 'three representative business men', to ask whether they thought an Oxford degree was a help in getting a job in business, 'as the Powlie, though not an academic type, will have to earn its own living'. In the event, Paul did his National Service, then went to Oxford.

On The Mead, John wrote: 'I feel like you do. I think we must do all we can to go on living here. I honestly don't think it's worth my giving up London as I would lose a profitable source of income which comes through my being in London. All my entertainment of people (reciprocal by the way), rent, cleaning & secretary are tax free because they count as business.'[139] The rest of the letter was, in effect, a politely phrased request for Penelope to reduce her housekeeping expenses at The Mead. He wanted them kept down to £60 a month. He added a postscript: 'If you think we can't do it, it's up to you to sell the Mead. I will abide by whatever decision you make about selling. The only thing I can't do is fork out more cash.'[140]

As so often, when practical action was needed, John was relying on Penelope to take it. 'Just look helpless' was one of his adages. But reaching fifty meant more to him than a suitable time to take stock and make plans. On 31 August he published a *cri de coeur* in the *Spectator* column he was by then writing:

> This week I had my fiftieth birthday. I had felt it coming on for some time. Standing nude in the bathroom two months ago, I suddenly realised I could not see my toes any more because my stomach was in the way. I started reviewing my past life first through a magnifying mist of self-pity – never quite made the grade, not taken seriously by the *Times*

Literary Supplement, Penguin Books, the Courtauld, the Warburg, the *Listener*, the University Appointments Board, the Museums Association, the Library Association, the Institute of Sanitary Engineers. I thought of the many people at school with me who were now knights and politicians. I wanted to cry. Then I thought of my many friends who are now dead, and terror of eternity made me want to scream.[141]

It is the mark of a poet that he can express what he feels more powerfully in a few lines of verse than in several of prose. In a poem about Archibald, John wrote:

> The bear who sits above my bed
>   More agèd now he is to see,
> His woollen eyes have thinner thread,
>   But still he seems to say to me,
> In double-doom notes, like a knell:
>   'You're half a century nearer Hell.'[142]

FIRST AND LAST LOVES

In another age or another country, Mr Betjeman would not be a 'failed literary gent' . . . but a national celebrity and arbiter of taste.

Cyril Connolly, *Sunday Times*, 14 September 1952

Evoking the Oxford of the 1920s in *Summoned by Bells*, John took his readers on a tour of 'Oxford's epitome' –

> The place they call the House
> That shelters A.L. Rowse . . .[1]

The rather obvious rhyme, which Auden was also to use in a later poem, was a dash of poetic licence: Rowse had indeed been an undergraduate at Christ Church ('the House'), but in November 1925, a month after John came up to Oxford, was elected a fellow of All Souls and vowed never again to set foot in Christ Church, which, he considered, had reneged on a promise to offer him a Studentship (fellowship).[2] That petulant vow was characteristic of Rowse, whose experiences had made him even more sensitive to slights than John. The son of a Cornish workman, he had won a scholarship to the most aristocratic of Oxford colleges and had been a 'swotapotamus', studying to the exclusion of all student treats.

He was of the 'Brideshead Generation' – born the same year as Evelyn Waugh – but despised the aesthetes who frittered away their time with parties and pranks, drunkenness and drag. He had taken the best history First of his year. Having passed through the gauntlet of exams, he allowed himself to relax a little. He attended Lady Ottoline Morrell's parties at Garsington;[3] dabbled in left-wing politics;[4] and made friends with a number of the new generation of undergraduates. He has described how W.H. Auden invited him to his rooms, darkened with drawn curtains.[5] Auden had not quite raised the nerve to try to seduce him. Not that Rowse would have been likely to succumb; though homosexual – in the 1930s he fell in love with the German intellectual Adam von Trott[6] – he was, in the 1920s, too repressed; and anyway, fellows of All Souls ought, he felt, to keep undergraduates at a respectful distance.

Though John was Auden's friend, he did not meet Rowse in his undergraduate days. But when John worked for the British Council at Oriel College in 1945, he came to know him well. In the meantime the don had published three books including *Tudor Cornwall* (1941), which some historians regard as his best work, though it inspired a famous pun by John Sparrow – 'I prefer Stuart Hampshire' (the Oxford philosopher).[7] In the Forties Rowse had also published two books of accomplished verse and the first of several autobiographies, *A Cornish Childhood*. Rowse shone when writing about himself – the subject which interested him more than any other. He was infinitely flatterable; and in that art John had few rivals. The two men's love of Cornwall was another bond. It was pleasant for John to be able to escape from his uncongenial duties and the inter-departmental squabbles at the British Council to take tea with Rowse in his beautiful rooms at All Souls. He found ways of jolting Rowse out of his normal routine, too: some the older man enjoyed; of others he at least affected to disapprove.

> John brought [Ninian] Comper to lunch with me in our Buttery [Rowse recalled]. 'Sir Niminy Piminy' said he had been asked to design vestments for the Archbishop of Paris, Cardinal Verdier. 'I absolutely *powdered* them with *fleurs-de-lys.*' He [John] took me in his dirty ramshackle old grey car across the Cotswolds to introduce me to Cheltenham. And to Stockcross, near Newbury, to see the chapel in the church which Comper had decorated, and in which he had designed the stained glass window, with a handsome young sailor in it.
>
> John and Jack Yates discovered that at that famous pub the Trout Inn, up the river at Wolvercote, there was a good-looking blue-eyed boy in the kitchen whom they called Chick, Chickabiddy etc. And they corralled me, took me up there to look in the kitchen window and chortle at Chick. Of course he knew what the score was. But what was the point of the exercise? It was very like John, up to his games, but I was not much amused. It was not like the domestic life of All Souls.[8]

It was Rowse, in 1945, who suggested to John the idea for what was to be his best prose book. John wrote to Jock Murray from Oxford on 6 February 1945:

> I have made the acquaintance of A.L. Rowse since I have been here and I find that he thinks a lot of my work. He says I ought to publish the

broadcasts, articles &c I have written on topography and architecture in a single illustrated volume. He says it would sell like hot cakes. What do you think? Of course some of the broadcasts may not be bad, in fact one of them is in a little horrible text book of 'Selected Modern Essays' by Macmillan. It looks very funny with schoolmaster's 'Notes' at the end. Osbert is in the same book equally dottily annotated.

If you think you would like to publish such a book, I could certainly produce – if the BBC, Listener, Evening Standard, Archie Rev, The Studio &c have them – a corking fat volume which we could then start to cut down.

Let me know what you think.[9]

Murray replied that he thought the plan was a good one.[10] He warned John that the wartime paper shortage might affect the date of publication but asked him to collect copies of his articles and send them to him. He was sure that the selection should represent 'a connected thread of interest, and topography and architecture certainly look like providing the thread'. Jock, who was almost as adept at flattery as John, remembered 'one very good article in the *Evening Standard* on railway stations which should be included'.[11]

Surprisingly, considering the eagerness of both these letters, nothing further was heard or done about the 'collected prose' project for three years; and even then it was only an initiative from another publisher that goaded the two men into action. In December 1948 John wrote to Murray, 'I have written to Odhams declining their kind offer to produce my essays in a single volume and have told them my first loyalty is to you.'[12] Another five months passed and it became clear to Murray that, for John, gathering together his broadcasts and articles was a chore with little appeal. It would not get done unless somebody else did it. So he volunteered the services of his secretary, who wrote off to the *Daily Express*, the *New Statesman*, *The Architectural Review* and other magazines to which John had contributed, asking for their help in listing his pieces. The *Express* sent a long list in May 1949, though John and Murray decided that John's home hints, including 'Worm Holes in your Furniture Are Made by Beetles' (26 March 1936), should probably be omitted from his collected prose.[13] In June, the poet's secretary Miss Webb was continuing to retrieve his articles and it was arranged that John and Murray would spend a weekend making the first selection.[14] What Murray would really have liked from John was not an anthology of his previously published essays and broadcast talks, but an entirely new book. 'In any sleepless moments,' he wrote, 'we will both try to think of the kind of subject with which you could deal in a continuous book of, say, 40–50,000 words to be published as a book which will have a really great success. If only we could think of the right subject, the success would naturally follow, you writing as you do.'[15] No such book was ever delivered: mettlesome as he was, John lacked stamina. A fragment of verse on the back of a cigarette packet was one thing; a sustained book of prose another.

Between them, Murray's secretary and John's managed to track down even the more recondite of his articles – 'A Matter of Metre' written for *Coal*, the magazine of the National Coal Board; 'Church Crawling' from *Leader* magazine (April 1949) and one of five sermons by laymen delivered at St Matthew's Church, Northampton (on 5 May 1946) – though none of these pieces made it to the final selection. On 12 August 1949 Miss Webb wrote to Jock Murray from Farnborough to apologize for a delay in sending off the prose articles.[16] When Miss Webb later left John's employ, his adored new secretary Jill Menzies took over the work of marshalling the prose pieces, but there seems still to have been no hurry on anyone's part.

In November 1951 Myfanwy Piper was brought in to make the final selection of articles and broadcasts, to save John from the anguish of 'murdering his own babies'. In the Acknowledgements John wrote: 'She read through many pages of dead papers, yellowing typescripts and periodicals, and with her sure critical perception weeded out much that was topical, sentimental, journalistic, pretentious and dull. Even so she has left you with plenty to complain about. But that is my fault, not hers.' Myfanwy also thought of a title for the book – *First and Last Loves*. John Piper made drawings of Nonconformist chapels and designed the dust-jacket. In April 1952 John wrote an introduction to the book. Headed 'Love is Dead', it reflected his depressed state of mind at the time. Jock Murray had written to John on 23 November 1951: 'Here is the galley proof of "Love is Dead" . . . If you see any way in which you can naturally give a paragraph with a ray of hope it would, I know, be a good thing. Myfanwy and I are meeting at Hampstead [at the Murrays' house] on Sunday over the other part of the proofs.'[17] John did not take the hint; 'Love is Dead' is among the bleakest of his writings.

Publication was finally achieved on 10 September 1952. Jock Murray sent 'birthday greetings' for that day.

> I know you are a little nervous and off-hand about your paternity of *First and Last Loves*, but at any rate I have enough pride for both of us. I am delighted that we should be publishing it and I know that it will make a lot of people happy.
>
> If you had your way, I suspect that no review copies would have gone

out. I have done everything in my power to prevent your being wounded,
but it would have been no act of friendship to withhold those review
copies that you would have wished us to withhold; indeed, for friendship's
sake I have gone further than any publisher should go and, therefore –
keep it to yourself – Osbert [Lancaster] will be dealing with the *Listener*
copy and the *Times Literary Supplement* is in reasonable hands. I did see
the *Times Literary Supplement* which you mention in your postcard and
see entirely what you mean but that is not something that one must sit
under.[18]

The reviews were generally excellent. John had the happy knack of
being reviewed by friends. They gathered, like a theatre claque, to
applaud his work. Osbert Lancaster, in a flagrant infringement of
reviewing etiquette, wrote notices of the book in both the *Daily
Telegraph* and *The Listener*. In the *Listener* review he remarked that
'No task is more difficult for a writer on art than to persuade people
to see merit in the unfashionable, and nothing is ever as unfashionable
as the immediate past.' Betjeman, as Sir Kenneth Clark had 'generously pointed out in his preface to his own work on the Gothic
Revival', had done more than anyone to rehabilitate the Victorians.
'The secret of his success is that for Mr Betjeman all works of art exist
in their human context.' Lancaster had a special word of praise for the
introduction which had given Jock Murray qualms. 'Some may think
that the preface "Love is Dead" bears little relevance to the essays
which follow; few lovers of good, minatory hell-fire prose will wish
that it had been omitted. Since Ruskin we have become unaccustomed
to passion in writing of this sort and our responses are the poorer.'[19]
In the *Telegraph* review he again compared John with Ruskin – both
masters of *saeva indignatio*. He suggested that it was John's being a
poet, 'and a poet deeply concerned with his fellow human beings', that
gave his writings their unique importance in 'an age of Art for the Art
Historian's sake' – 'For, almost alone among contemporary writers on
art, he is capable of whisking a building or a town out of the sterilized
oxygen-tent in which the professional antiquarians have placed it . . .
He is aware not only of the Saxon mouldings round the font but also
of the tin bowl from the chain stores which the churchworker has left
on top.'[20]

A particularly friendly review appeared in *John o' London's
Weekly*, the lower-middlebrow literary magazine. The notice was by
John Pudney, a poet whom John had known before the war and at the
Ministry of Information. He tried to explain how John differed from
other, more superficial, tastemakers.

If John Betjeman were an intellectual and nothing more, he would be a menace. He would be one of those fashion-forming literary *couturiers*, arbiters of a voguish taste, who declare that 'we shall all go a little more Edwardian', or who suddenly discover that gasometers, ruins, cricket pavilions or Oxford Circus are 'really rather fun'. What saves John Betjeman from becoming the Dior of letters is simply feeling.

Forgive me for using such a plain, old-fashioned word to describe an ornate character. It just happens to encompass entirely the really impressive qualities of the prose-writing Betjeman revealed in *First and Last Loves* . . . his first volume of essays to be published since *Ghastly Good Taste* – the stimulus of which, though it only seemed to hit us yesterday, came, I see, as far back as the mid-thirties.

It always seemed to me that Betjeman was born a legend in those far-off days. I am sure there are many who watched his growth and development. Indeed I have met some who claim to have seen him in his embryonic stages. For me, however, he was always a complete, original and legendary character to whom one might be fleetingly introduced in the too-bright, too-functional surroundings of the period when Advertising was holding hands with Art.[21]

The Spectator gave the book to Jocelyn Brooke, himself a virtuoso of nostalgia.

We live, says Mr Betjeman, in an age not of the Common Man but of the Average Man: 'There is a refinement about him which pervades everything he touches and sees. His books are chosen for him by the librarians . . . the walls of his room are in quiet pastel shades, he has cereals for breakfast, and he likes everything in moderation, be it beer, religion or tobacco.' It so happened that I read the first chapters of this book travelling down from London to Canterbury on what used to be the old South Eastern and Chatham Railway; and, as the train sped through those eerie and disquieting suburbs which, as Mr Betjeman says, 'once seemed to me so lovely with their freckled tennis-girls and their youths in club blazers', I too sighed for the yapping Sealyhams ('Mind the terrier when you call'), the calceolarias and the clean-limbed, Rossall-or-Repton heroes of my youth. For Ghastly Good Taste has triumphed all along the line (and not only the S.E. & C.R.); the tennis-girls are 'taking up' ballet-dancing, Van Gogh reproductions have replaced those jolly little sketches of Clovelly which the Mater dashed off on her honeymoon, the spiky and incense-haunted glories of St Aidan's have made way for the tumescent Romanesque of the Church of Christ Scientist. An age has passed – but its passing has at least been justly celebrated by one of the most original and gifted poets of our time . . .[22]

Brooke knew the tenor of anti-Betjeman gibes. 'It has been said of
Mr Betjeman that his tongue, at one period, became so firmly wedged
in his cheek that he has never been able to get it out again. It may well
be true; not everyone, certainly, will share his whole-hearted admiration for the Manchester Town Hall or for Norman Shaw's New
Zealand Chambers in Leadenhall Street. But does it matter? For Mr
Betjeman Victorian architecture has become an article of faith.'[23]

The review in the *New Statesman* was less fulsome. There, too, the
reviewer was a friend; but that friend was John Summerson, by nature
a supercilious carper – somebody said he kept his lip in curlers. He
began with a prolonged sneer at the very convention of anthologizing
a living author. There was no real sting for John in this ironic pre-
amble, and Summerson conceded that 'Mr John Betjeman is a writer
worth collecting.' But he immediately launched into another reserva-
tion. 'At first sight one would think he would collect easily and well;
but I am not at all sure that he does. There is a spikiness, a brittleness
about his pieces, so that they do not lie quite easily together.'
Summerson thought John's essays should be bound up with pretentious papers by other people – 'just so that they have companions to
embarrass'.

> That is part of Mr Betjeman's function and his art. What an embarrass-
> ing, what an out-of-step, singular author he is! There is nobody like him,
> nobody with that particular intuition for knowing when a thing has been
> forgotten but is not yet decently out of date, for recognizing the vanishing
> point of some word – 'electrolier', 'metro-land' – and bringing it back to
> use with a shock of pathos so striking that these resurrected words
> become Betjeman-words. He has created an attitude, a myth perhaps,
> almost a dialect.[24]

Even this acute analysis of John's gifts had a light frosting of
disdain; and there was more to come. 'Mr Betjeman is an architectural writer. For years he has embarrassed the profession by liking the
wrong architects, praising the wrong buildings and enjoying architecture very extensively for the wrong reasons, praising, liking and
enjoying wherever he finds what it is his mission to seek – sheer
neglect.'[25] John writes about buildings not as form, but as evocation.
'In this he is like Dickens, except that Dickens never bothered with the
machinery of styles, whereas Betjeman bothers tremendously and
loves to put in the names of all the architects, and the more hopelessly
forgotten the names the more delighted he is with them.' Just when
Summerson seems to be moving in for the *coup de grâce* – 'He has
transferred the snobbery of the collector of old china or Japanese

prints to a sphere where collecting is mercifully impossible . . .' – he suddenly reprieves him: 'and where its snobbery becomes on the one hand extremely funny, and on the other hand (and let this not be over-looked) utterly absorbing to anybody with a feeling for architecture and the oddity of mankind. Mr Betjeman is a serious student who can never keep an absolutely straight face; but he is a serious student.'[26] This barbed tribute paid, Summerson cannot quite bring himself to end on a complimentary note. Some of the essays are 'dullish broad-casts (where the author's reading style and diction carry off what cold print does not)'. A sympathetic essay on 'our ugliest buildings' – Nonconformist chapels – is accompanied by the 'mocking scribbles' of John Piper, 'who also contributes what no Betjeman book would be complete without – a folding plate'. The review ends: 'There is one thing I forgot to say about his book, which is that it is prefaced by one of the most savage Jeremiads on English life today that I have ever read. It is a little embarrassing.'[27] It was just this irresistible tendency to deprecate, even when he felt much admiration, that lured Summerson, nine years later, into writing the article on the Euston Arch which led Sir William Haley to write the dismissive *Times* leader which in turn encouraged Harold Macmillan and his Transport Minister Ernest Marples to ignore John and the other protesters who wanted to save the arch.[28]

Evelyn Waugh, writing in *The Month*, also laced praise with severities – warning John off his own territory of prose, satirizing his narrative methods and reprobating his, to Waugh, illogical allegiance to the Church of England. The piece began with high commenda-tion.

> In the small, shrinking, perhaps vanishing society which honours beauty and humour, Mr Betjeman is literally a household word. His name has passed into the vernacular as surely as Spooner and Banting.[29] 'A Betjeman character', 'a Betjeman house', have plain meanings. His poems are the best remembered, the most quoted, of any writer's save Mr Belloc. Are there circles where after-dinner revellers leap to their feet uninvited and declaim Mr Stephen Spender's verses for the sheer delight of hearing them again? . . . 'Betjemanism' is a mood of the moment like Existentialism. His following is among the gayest element of his contemporaries . . .[30]

However, the review soon lapses into a series of complaints. 'The col-lection', Waugh thinks, 'does not show Mr Betjeman at the top of his form. He is, first and last, a poet – one of high technical ability – and prose does not become him.' Not only that, too many of the pieces in the collection were broadcasts and still bore 'the awful stains of their birth – the jauntiness, the intrusive, false intimacy, the sentimentality – which seem inseparable from the medium'.

Waugh pokes fun at the set pattern of the typical Betjeman essay.

The normal process of Betjemanizing is first the undesired stop in a provincial English town, then the 'discovery' there of a rather peculiar police station, *circa* 1880; the enquiry and identification of its architect. Further research reveals that a Methodist Chapel in another town is by the same hand. Then the hunt is up. More buildings are identified. The obscure name is uttered with a reverence befitting Bernini. The senile master is found to be alive, in distressed circumstances in a northern suburb of London. He is a 'character'; he has vague, personal memories of other long dead, equally revered contemporaries. In his last years he is either rejuvenated or else driven mad to find himself the object of pilgrimage. It is all very beguiling and beside it there flourishes a genuine, sound love of the simpler sorts of craftsmanship.[31]

Waugh is scathing about John's religious interests. 'Theology is totally closed to him, but he has sung hymns in every kind of protestant conventicle and acquired an *expertise* in Anglican deviations. Show him the hassocks in a country church and he will know unerringly whether the incumbent was educated at Cambridge or Durham . . . *First and Last Loves* has an instructive chapter on Nonconformity. It is regrettable that he omits from this category that vigorous Nonconformist body, the Catholic Church.' Waugh adds: 'He rants against State control, but he is a member of the Church of England. In the face of that prodigious State usurpation laments about the colour of nationalized railway engines lose their poignancy.' Waugh sympathizes with the message of the 'Love is Dead' preface, which he interprets: 'There is nothing to look forward to . . . The game is up.' But he points out that John's own name 'would be on the list of guilty men' who had helped bring about the wretched mass-produced Britain that he execrates. 'In January 1938 there was an architectural exhibition in London of all that Mr Betjeman now deplores. The exhibitors called themselves the MARS group. Their catalogue had a preface by Bernard Shaw exulting over the destruction of Adelphi Terrace . . . And in the group beside Arup, Gropius, Chermayeff, Lubetkin and Zweigenthal stands the name of Mr Betjeman.'[32]

Other reviewers were less ambiguously critical. The bookman Daniel George, speaking on the BBC's General Overseas Service on 13 October 1952, found the book 'rather frivolous' – 'I often felt a little irritated by his lighthearted assumption of superiority and by his humorous touches of what intolerant readers might regard as intellectual snobbery. I think he's just a big tease.' When he read 'Love is Dead', George felt, 'O Lord, here it all is again, the old familiar diatribe.' He was suspicious of a writer 'whose Utopia is in the past'.[33] Under the heading 'Betjeman's Bogey', the young art philosopher John Berger mounted a more forceful attack on John's alleged snobbery in the socialist paper *Tribune*,[34] and concluded by asking 'why bother to consider the book at all? Because it shows, I think, how silly an imaginative and knowledgeable writer can become, if he loses touch with the real issues of the time.'

A number of reviewers agreed with John Summerson that the introductory essay was too extreme. Edmund Penning-Rowsell, writing in *World Review*, found in it 'a dispirited note, a tone of defeat, which is at variance with the zest for life and people which is Mr Betjeman's most engaging quality'.[35] Hugh Casson also took exception to 'Love is Dead'. Although he was ostensibly a friend of John's, he knew that John and Osbert Lancaster were hostile to modern architecture of the kind he practised. He wrote in the *RIBA Journal*:

Of course we have met his loved ones many times before and though perhaps we love some of them less for themselves than because we love Mr Betjeman, it is nice to see them, like favourite toys lifted once more out of the cupboard for an affectionate pat before, a little dog-eared and threadbare now perhaps, they are put away once more.

Nevertheless we must admit that like all great lovers Mr B is also a great hater – at least in his prose works. (In his matchless verses spleen is always defeated in the end by compassion.) . . . Any genuine lover of architecture must sometimes find it hard to love those of us who practise it but somehow, as is often liable to happen, Mr B's stings are so keenly directed that the reader begins to feel sympathy and not scorn for the victim. What, after all, Mr B, is so basically unsympathetic about a senior Civil Servant downing his breakfast Weetabix at Esher before catching the 8.45 to Waterloo? Surely he needs your sympathy no less than your lonely business girl crouched over her Kensington gas-ring? And the vicar's wife hanging the Margaret Tarrant up in the Children's Corner surely needs kindness, not coshing?[36]

By contrast, Cyril Connolly, reviewing the book in the *Sunday Times*, admired the preface more than anything else in the book. 'It is a cry of despair from the heart,' he wrote, 'and I would like to see it plop through every letter-box in the country for the despair is under control and the simple artless sentences state facts with but an undercurrent of contempt . . .' Where John writes, 'Almost any age seems civilized except that in which I live,' Connolly comments:

Is he right or is this a disease? I would answer that for any poet the 'paradise lost' is a necessary hallucination. Mr Betjeman is a scholar poet and in these essays we can enjoy the mixture at various strengths: scholarly, as in his analysis of Victorian architecture; half and half, as in the delightful catalogue of London railway termini . . . and purely poetical, as in his descriptions of coastal resorts and Cornish beaches. Only in some of the broadcasts does he lapse into poetical prose. Exclamation marks do not supply the warmth of the voice. One imagines a crazy fellow in a blazer rushing in with a straw boater: 'Ventnor! Here we are in Ventnor West!' or 'Sidmouth! Silvery pink and creamy Sidmouth, farewell!'[37]

Having had his fun at John's expense, Connolly gives him his vote. 'In another age or another country, Mr Betjeman would not be a "failed literary gent", by which I suppose him to mean a scholar and a poet who makes his living as a journalist, but a national celebrity and arbiter of taste. Lovers of good writing would hang on his words. Lovers of good building would submit him their plans. He would not be relegated to the limbo of the professional humorist or the clever fellow . . .'[38]

A FEW LATE
CHRYSANTHEMUMS

It is rather as though something friendly, familiar and furry and easily frightened had turned at bay and bitten one in the bathroom.

Geoffrey Taylor, *Time and Tide*, 17 July 1954

Betjeman's Chrysanthemums have set off again like a firework . . .

John G. Murray, letter to Mark Clowes, 7 January 1955

In mid-1952 Jock Murray and John were already making plans to publish a volume of *Collected Poems* to follow the 'selected prose' of *First and Last Loves*. John wrote to Murray on 6 June: 'I would like to see my Collected Verse published cheaply, in paper, with a cover by Walter Crane of daffodills [*sic*] and bluebells. I would call it *Jocund and Blythe*.'[1] On 18 July Murray wrote John a more businesslike letter, asking him to list the poems that had not been included in *Selected Poems* but which he would like to see in the *Collected* volume.[2] As with *First and Last Loves*, there was a hiatus between thought and deed. The *Collected Poems* were not published until 1958. In the meantime, another slim volume of new poems was issued by Murray in 1954, entitled – perfectly in character with John's new-found pose of premature Grand-Old-Mannishness – *A Few Late Chrysanthemums*.

In February 1953 Jock Murray's secretary was checking with newspaper and magazine offices to find out where John's newer poems, not yet in volume form, had first appeared – *Harper's Bazaar*, *Time and Tide*, *Punch*, *The Cornhill*, *Horizon*, *Church Times*, *Harlequin* and *The Harrovian* ('Harrow on the Hill').[3] John prophetically wrote to Murray on 17 May: 'I think that if we put in "Phone for the Fishknives" ["How to Get On in Society"] I will be dogged by the blasted thing as I am even now dogged by Westminster Abbey, so let's leave it out.'[4] However, Murray persuaded him to leave it in. On

28 May Murray sent John a complete set of the poems to be considered for the slim volume. He knew that John had doubts about publishing 'Easter 1948' ('The Empty Pew') and 'Dr Ramsden', an elegy for a don at John's favourite – because 'dimmest' – Oxford college, Pembroke.[5] The Easter poem was 'too personal' and might upset Penelope; the Dr Ramsden poem might give offence to the don's surviving colleagues at Pembroke College. 'I am sure that Dr Ramsden must go in, he is so good,' Murray wrote; but added, 'I would not mind leaving *Deux Poésies françaises* out.' Murray had also read through a separate batch that both men had agreed were 'doubtfuls'. Of 'The Dear Old Village' he wrote, 'You are rather fond of this and inclined to inclusion and so am I, but I am quite sure that it should either be cut or changed where you deal with the beastly farmer, because now some of that part reads as an excrescence on a beautiful poem. The farmer goes on too long.' John had let his hatred for Farmer Wheeler of Uffington run away with him. ' "Station Syren" I think could be included,' Murray wrote, 'though I am a little doubtful of the last two lines of the second verse.'[6]

'Easter 1948' was omitted. The French poems were also axed, but 'Dr Ramsden' went in, as 'I.M. Walter Ramsden, ob. March 26 1947, Pembroke College, Oxford', though John first asked the Master and Senior Tutor for their blessing. John had written to Murray on 20 July: 'I think if you left out the third stanza in the Dr Ramsden poem we might be able to print it. I dare not approach Salt & Drake & Homes Dudden.[7] That fool [R.B.] MacCallum[8] approached Drake some years ago who rather naturally did not want the poem published. Homes Dudden might give permission if we left out the third verse.'[9] The verse was struck out and John steeled himself to write to Homes Dudden and H.L. Drake. The letter to Dudden was sugared with praise of the don's biography of Henry Fielding. Homes Dudden replied from the Dudley Hotel in Hove that he thought the 'very striking poem on Dr Ramsden' should certainly be published, though he was glad John had deleted 'the purely fictional stanza'.[10] Drake wrote from St David's, Pembrokeshire, to say that he was 'entirely in accord with the Master's *imprimatur*', but thought that Ramsden's Christian name, Walter, should be added and that 'Winter 1947–48 is hardly a correct description of the date of his death which actually took place on March 26th 1947'.[11] John made the alterations suggested for the Ramsden poem. He also toned down – but not greatly – the 'farmer' passage in 'The Dear Old Village' and decided to include 'Station Syren' ('She sat with a Warwick Deeping . . .').

In August 1953 it was still intended that he should write an introduction to the volume. On the 7th, Murray urged him to write it 'as soon as you can' and to 'use it to get as much off your chest as you like'.[12] The process of selection continued. Murray wrote on 11 August: 'I have read "Sacerdos in Aeternum" again and while still in part moved by it, doubts creep in. Its slightly dated flavour gives for some strange reason a hint of "The Young Reciter" and I think that this would become more pronounced in the cold light of print.'[13] The poem was rejected. Also in August, John's secretary sent Murray two new poems, 'Essex' and 'Norfolk', both recalling happy childhood events associated with John's father. Murray thought 'Essex' was 'splendid, evocative and a fine addition to the volume'. On 24 August he wrote: ' "Norfolk" is very moving, and it goes to the printer immediately. Have you in mind that the introduction to the new volume might be an enjoyable Cornish holiday task?'[14]

Two days later, John replied from Trebetherick, where the family was taking its annual fortnight's holiday, 'If you will send me galley proofs I will write the preface. I cannot till then as I cannot remember them all.'[15] But by 17 October he had decided there was no need for a preface, 'except a sentence of thankfulness on my part for the unexpected popularity of my verse, which can appear above the list of acknowledgments. I might also add that I expect soon to be unfashionable and forgotten.'[16]

Meanwhile the two men had agreed that McKnight Kauffer, who had designed the wrapper for Continual Dew, would not be the ideal jacket-designer for this book. John thought he 'would not grasp it enough' and suggested instead a jacket 'like some of those home hobby books you publish'.[17] Murray agreed that the poems should be divided into three sections headed 'Light', 'Medium' and 'Gloomy', the last, in John's words, 'concerned with death and self-pity'.[18]

As usual, John had a lot of suggestions for titles. Myfanwy Piper had thought of A Few Late Chrysanthemums and he liked that; but 'The most honest title would be Gloom, Lust & Self Pity', and Murray might also like to consider Baker Street and Other Poems, Neither Jocund nor Blythe, Grandsire Doubles,[19] Cemetery Verses or Necropolis. 'This last', John added, 'has a good "twenties" ring about it.'[20] (Was he thinking of Fritz Lang's 1926 film Metropolis?) A postcard followed on 21 October: 'Elizabeth and I thought also of these titles: Skin in the Coffee, Jam on the Handle, Marmalade on the Wrists, The Struggle for Freedom, Whither Democracy?, Dying Dahlias, Painful Extractions.'[21] Jock Murray blandly thanked him for the suggestions and made no further comment on them. On 27 October he wrote to John: 'O[sbert] L[ancaster] suggested A Justification by Works but it looks to me as though up to the present A Few Late Chrysanthemums has it.'[22]

Murray was disappointed that there was to be no provocative

preface like those for *Old Lights* and *First and Last Loves*. He asked
John at least to supply a 'blurb' for the front jacket flap. Well aware
that a blurb is no vehicle for false modesty, John wrote:

> This new volume contains poems written since the appearance of *Selected
> Poems* in 1948. The poems, which are divided into groups – Medium,
> Light and Gloomy – have great variety of subject and mood but through
> all of them there is that magic which escapes definition but which can so
> unmistakably be identified with Mr Betjeman. Whatever the subject or the
> mood – a sports girl, a gas lamp or Perpendicular arch – Mr Betjeman,
> with a deceptive simplicity that covers extreme technical skill, engages the
> heart, both his and ours. Throughout the wit and music of his poetry it is
> evident that he is a passionate observer.[23]

On 21 December, returning the corrected galley proofs, John
enclosed a new poem on Middlesex, another on All Saints' Day called
'Spirit and Clay', which he had 'unearthed from a drawer', and 'two
poems which we unaccountably omitted' – 'Hunter Trials' from *Time
and Tide*, which qualified for the 'Light' section, and 'To a Child Aged
Eight' – 'which doesn't seem to me too bad, which appeared in a periodical *The Wind & the Rain*'.[24] He had thought up 'two good titles
for the book' – *Elevenses* or *Morning Coffee at Bobby's*. 'I think they
sum up just where I stand in literature – with Uncle Tom [Eliot] as
dinner, de la Mare, and Blunden, Spender, Auden and Day-Lewis as
lunch, the younger poets as breakfast and Andrew Young as tea.'[25]
John took some time off at Christmas. He wrote to Jock Murray on
27 December:

> How very kind of you to remember your old and failing author with that
> very nice bottle of bubbly which we imbibed with Batsford's man
> [Edmund] Penning-Rowsell today.
>   Old Patrick [Kinross] who is staying with us eat [*sic*] and drank too
> much and now has a temperature. Peter Venables who bullied him at
> Winchester [and] is now an RC priest came to call today and I took him
> with old Patrick, whose temperature passed to more than 100 when we
> took it during Peter V's visit which he had not been expecting.
>   The Italian maid was ill all through Christmas so we had a nice time at
> the sink . . .[26]

On 6 January 1954 Jock Murray received a new poem by John,
'Greenaway'.[27] That day, he wrote to John: 'We did scratch our heads
fairly hard over "A Child Ill" and decided against it. I cannot help
hoping you will hold to that decision. I have consulted two good

friends who are reasonably intelligent and who have also voted for its omission. Do you agree?'[28] John shot back an enquiry as to who the 'two friends' were. Murray answered: they were his wife and Mervyn Horder.[29] John overruled the three critics and 'A Child Ill' was included. Another small problem was sorted out: one of the poems had appeared in the *New Statesman* under the larky pseudonym 'Sylvia Paddington'; in the acknowledgements to the new book 'the author's sister, Sylvia Paddington' was warmly thanked.

Page proofs were ready by mid-February. One set was sent to John Sparrow, who wrote to Murray: 'Betjeman's new poems are $\alpha+++$, to use our old-fashioned academic ratings. I expected a scanty bunch of draggled old flowers – and instead I find that it is perhaps the best of the collections you have yet published for him. Some of the new ones, e.g. "Remorse", are as good as, if not better than, anything he has yet written. "Congratulations" to you both!'[30] Murray wrote back, on 16 February, that he might later ask permission to quote Sparrow's opinion. 'I am going through the proofs now and it will take a lot of chasing to get them out of JB . . .'[31] John returned his set on 24 February. 'I think it unlikely', he wrote, 'that the book will have any success and I should not print more than a few hundred copies.'[32]

One of the many things that Jock Murray and John had in common was their Church of England religion. Murray and his family worshipped at the 1745 parish church of Hampstead, in whose graveyard John Constable is buried. On 12 March 1954 the poet wrote to the publisher about the controversial philosopher C.E.M. Joad,[33] who had become a friend of John's through their appearances together on the radio programme *The Brains Trust*:

Would you be able to come at 10 a.m. on St Patrick's Day, that is to say Tuesday next, March 17th, to Joad's house, 4 East Heath Road, Hampstead, where Mervyn [Horder], Captain Bog [Alan Pryce-Jones], Rose Macaulay and I hope to be present when he receives Holy Communion. Father Whiteman, [of] the Grosvenor Chapel, is bringing the Blessed Sacrament and if you wish to make your own communion too then he will be very pleased for you to do so. I ought to tell you that though this sounds very peculiar it is at Joad's wish and Father Whiteman's recommendation for old Joad has missed the presence of other Christians when he receives his Communion.[34]

Murray was happy to attend the service for the lapsed atheist.

In April Jock Murray needed all his considerable powers of diplomacy to dissuade John from sending an irate letter to the editor of *The Times*. Earlier in the year, John had become involved in a campaign for what would later be called the Public Lending Right – the right of authors to be paid for library borrowings of their books. In April, incensed by a letter in *The Times* from the president of the Booksellers' Association, John sent Murray a copy of the letter he proposed to send to *The Times* in retaliation:

Sir, –

Your correspondent, the President of the Booksellers' Association, Mr Cadness Page, raises an irrelevant subject when he claims that the incomes of the signatories of the original letter on authors' rights are 'comparable with those of the heads of other professions and trades'. If he has seen my income tax returns over the last three years, which I presume he has done, in order to make this statement, he will have discovered that for the years 1951, 1952 and 1953 I have received a total of £546 from my publishers. He is good enough to say that I am an author who has 'arrived'. If I have done so this has not been through publishers but through not being rich enough to make a living from them. Indeed, I have accepted hackwork and written rubbish in newspapers and talked rubbish on the BBC. My relations with my publishers are admirable considering how little I earn from them.

I do not see how Mr Cadness Page can be as disinterested as he claims to be. As a bookseller he never gets less than 33⅓ per cent of the published price of a book and an author gets 12½ per cent. Would he, or the protesting publishers, care to swap incomes with me from published books? I am open to the first offer.

Yours faithfully,
John Betjeman[35]

Possibly John sent Murray a copy of this acrid letter partly as an oblique way of expressing dissatisfaction with what he felt to be slim pickings from his books. Certainly Murray was very anxious to dissuade him from sending the letter to *The Times*. Whether from a gentlemanly feeling that one did not bare one's personal finances in public or from a fear that what John had been paid might indeed seem unprincely, he wrote to John on 30 April 1954:

I do not think that you should enter the fray with a public airing of your personal accounts: first because your total literary and broadcasting earnings must be considered as a whole if your argument is to be relevant and these would probably compare not unfavourably with the earnings of heads of other professions. Secondly, because despite all the appeals and meagre temptations from publishers you are not a writer of *books*. All that your poor present publisher can do is to persuade you to collect your published works in a book form which can produce a little extra money.

Thirdly because the figures you give of book earnings over three years ought to be related to the fact that during that period only one book of collected essays was published.

My personal answer to your letter would be that I would gladly exceed your book earnings over three years in an advance of royalties if you would write a book! But this you know already and there have been several plans for possible books which are still on the shelf. (Confusing metaphor.) I have a sneaking belief that it is not really so much the money as the personal inclination and the character of your particular genius that keeps you from writing books . . .[36]

A *Few Late Chrysanthemums* was published on 2 July 1954: the main run was of 6,000 copies, and fifty special copies were printed on hand-made paper with full buckram binding. John was sent his first copy on 9 June. He thanked Murray and said, 'it looks very nice', but asked whether there was going to be any lettering on the spine – 'It looks a bit SPCK [Society for the Promotion of Christian Knowledge] without it.'[37] He was also irritated to find 'Huxley Hall' set in four-line stanzas, not in couplets like Tennyson's *Loxley Hall* of which it was a parody. Murray replied: 'We thought a lot about the lettering on the spine but decided against it. Had the title been composed of short words like "Bat" or "Belfries" we might have managed it, but as it is, the title would have had to appear longways down the spine, which is always tiresome and I rather like its present pristine simplicity which, strangely enough, seems to me to have nothing SPCK about it!'[38]

'I dread the reviews,' John wrote to Murray on 2 July.[39] Murray himself was privately worried about the reception the book might get. There had been a disquieting portent. John Gibbins, the firm's zealous publicity manager, had written to Webster Evans, the editor of *John o' London's Weekly*, asking whether he would consider commissioning a review by Lord David Cecil, who had wanted to review the book for *The Observer* but had found it already bespoke. Evans replied:

The copy of *A Few Late Chrysanthemums* reached me yesterday and I was able to read right through it last night. I cannot help feeling that it does not contain the best of Betjeman's work, in fact I found many of these poems curiously brittle in quality. On the whole I feel it would be a mistake for me to allow Lord David Cecil to do a separate article about the book but I am asking Richard Church to include it in a review of two or three other recent books of verse . . .[40]

Webster may have been piqued that his magazine was second choice to the *Observer*, and may also have meant to slap down an uppity publisher trying to teach him his business. All the same, it was a dispiriting first reaction from the press, and Evans's comments were not shown to John.

The most significant reviews, in terms of reaching large numbers of potential readers, were in *The Observer* and the *Sunday Times*. Both appeared on 11 July. The *Observer* review, by the paper's resident critic John Raymond (it was a sign of John's growing celebrity that it was headed simply 'Mr Betjeman'), was damning.

> In far too many of the poems contained in this new slim volume Mr Betjeman has traded his unique sense of place for the all too fashionable sense of Guilt. The exchange is entirely to his disadvantage. It often makes him quite unrecognizable. He has, temporarily at least, lost his magnificent knack of walking the sentimental-ironical tightrope. The Sussex tenderfoot, the strayed reveller in Kildare churchyards, Miss Joan Hunter Dunn's swooning tennis opponent, has thrown on a surplice and is making cruel faces at us from the Lady Chapel.
>
> There is a loss in awareness, precision, technique. The rhymes and cadences are no longer inevitable. They click all too neatly and mechanically together, like the combination of a well-oiled and expensive safe . . . The old magic has fled. There is nothing in this book comparable to 'Youth and Age on Beaulieu River, Hants.'

Raymond thought there were two reasons for the decline he saw in John's verse. 'The first is technical and peculiar to the poet, the second is the result of the contemporary *Zeitgeist*.'

> In Mr Betjeman's earlier poems place was all-important. The men and women were accidental figures; they completed or merged into the landscape. In this book, the morons tend to crowd out the conifers. Secondly, Mr Betjeman, like Mr Waugh and so many other Christian Right-wingers of our time, has deliberately opted for disgust and misanthropy. Because the world is not nearly as pleasant a place for him as it was in 1924 or '34, he seems determined to sulk.

Waugh himself reviewed the book in the *Sunday Times*: the notice was headed 'Mr Betjeman's Bouquet'. Now that John had moved off Waugh's turf and back into verse, the novelist was prepared to praise his friend once more, and his review must have given John some salve for Raymond's.

> Mr John Betjeman is a happy example of consistent fertility. He is not one of those poets who, like athletes who broke records in early youth, become

eminent spectators in middle age; nor does he, like so many of his juniors, complain that it is impossible to write poetry when burdened with the duty of earning his living. Despite multifarious other activities he continues to produce a book of new verses every five years or so. His 1954 volume is longer than either 'New Bats in Old Belfries' or 'Old Lights for New Chancels', and is fully their equal in quality . . . He has named it *A Few Late Chrysanthemums*. At first glance those mid-Victorian exotics, heavy and haunting in scent, rich in autumnal colours, might seem a happy epithet. But those ragged mops of petals? – no, in form Mr Betjeman's poems have the crisp precision of the iris.

For the most part, the other critics were polarized into the Raymond camp or the Waugh camp: those who thought the new book an unfortunate departure and those who thought the poetry as good as ever. (A third group maintained that the poetry had never been any good.) The critics who saw the book as a falling-away disliked two aspects in particular: its melancholy, and the acerbity of its satire, especially in 'The Dear Old Village' – the poem about which Jock Murray had had qualms. Geoffrey Taylor in *Time and Tide*: 'It is rather as though something friendly, familiar and furry and easily frightened had turned at bay and bitten one in the bathroom.'[41] Derwent May in *Truth*: 'The wit has almost entirely faded, the illness and horror taken full possession.'[42] J.M.D. Pringle in the *Sydney Morning Herald*: 'The poet who seemed so original when he stuck to tennis parties at the vicarage and the church's restoration in 1883, has some formidable competition when he turns to death and sin.'[43] The poet D.J. Enright in *The Month*: 'There are few signs of "passion" about the present collection. Signs of bad temper there are in plenty. "Mum, the Persil-user" – so what?'[44] The young poet Anthony Thwaite in the Oxford magazine *The Isis*: 'While painting and comedy can become great only through a slight twist of observation, or "reportage", even great verse must have something more – a dash of rich, animal vigour. This Mr Betjeman lacks, and in its place is a peevishness and querulousness, which sour all but his most jolly or most devout poems.'[45] There were the usual complaints about John's right-wingism and snobbery. *The Listener* on 'How to Get On in Society': 'Mr Betjeman lays himself open to charges of pharisaism and snobbery. There are plenty of well-bred people who would be astonished to know that the use of fish-knives is as inadmissible as to speak of "kiddies" and "serviettes". It is not always possible to be funny at nobody's expense, but it is a little uncomfortable to think that many readers will feel a self-righteous, class-conscious glow on being jocularly invited to share Mr Betjeman's knowledge of taboos prevalent among the superior.'[46]

The most punishing onslaught on the book, apart from Raymond's, came in *The Critics* programme on BBC radio on 1 August. The session was chaired by John's friend John Summerson, but he held the stance of a strictly impartial chairman and did nothing to restrain the participants from savaging him. Walter Allen[47] thought that the book contained nothing as good as his best work. E. Arnot Robertson,[48] in what might have been part of Peter Sellers's later take-off of *The Critics*, said: 'I think he did admirable work in his early days, when he was showing us that Victoriana was not wholly ridiculous – that it was possible to love a girl with hairy legs and hairy arms – but we've accepted that for a very long time, and I felt that these – these rather *tousled* chrysanthemums, as they are – had very little to show us.'[49]

In the same programme, Robert Furneaux-Jordan, who as a modern architect was no friend of John's, said:

> . . . I say with regret that I think something's happened to him, I think he's intelligent enough to realise it himself, with his sad title 'A Few Late Chrysanthemums'; and what I think has happened is that his nostalgia, and his perceptiveness and his satire, his Butterfield chancels and his tennis courts in suburban Surrey, and his Baker Street Station and all the rest of it, have merged and dissolved themselves into one thing, which is a misanthropy – a hate and dislike for the present.[50]

By grouping some of the poems under the heading 'Gloom', John no doubt invited the complaints that he was 'mournful', 'mopish', 'sentimental' and 'sour' – the *New Statesman* reviewer wrote of 'a prevailing slightly liverish note'.[51] But a few of the critics welcomed the new, less comedic Betjeman. In a radio broadcast, the Cornish poet Charles Causley said: 'I think his new book is his best. Some of the poems touch depths of feeling, and reach heights of imaginative invention, that I don't think Betjeman himself knew he possessed.'[52] Gerald Bullett wrote in the *Literary Guide* of 'Devonshire Street, W1', '[It] is one of the most simple and heartrending things I have ever read.'[53]

In the BBC's *Wednesday Book Programme*, Christopher Marsden defended John from the charge of being merely a maundering nostalgic.

> In a peculiar sort of way I suppose he's the best-known, here, of all the English poets. Say the names, in averagely educated circles, of Eliot, Auden, Dylan Thomas – some sort of picture is registered on the negative. But say Betjeman and at once the Surrey pinewoods, encaustic tiles in Victorian Gothic churches, tennis girls in shorts, fried fish shops – a curious mixture of love and hate for the rustic and for the urban scene in England – is firmly imprinted . . . In poetry he is a traditionalist who is, in

36. John in Ireland in 1941, with Paul

37. Candida with her Christmas presents, Dublin 1942

38. R.M. Smyllie, editor of the *Irish Times*, with Penelope in Dublin's Fleet Street. John is at right, in the flat cap

39. *Left to right*: Séamus MacEntee, Roger Chauviré, Professor of French at University College, Dublin, Paul Betjeman, Margaret MacEntee and John in 1942

40. Máire MacEntee, daughter of the Irish Government minister Seán MacEntee

41. Monsignor Patrick Browne, Máire's uncle, with Margaret MacEntee

42. P. Morton Shand, an old friend with whom John renewed contact while at the Admiralty in Bath

43. John had a crush on Shand's daughter Mary, and put her in his poem 'An Archaeological Picnic'

44. The Old Rectory, Farnborough, Berkshire, where the Betjemans lived from 1945 to 1951

45. Patrick Cullinan, the South African poet. John met him while lecturing at Charterhouse and invited him to stay at Farnborough. Candida, then eight, thought him dazzlingly handsome

46. Penelope, John, Candida and Paul in the garden at Farnborough

47. Mrs (later Lady) Ormrod was junior to John at the British Council, where she was one of the few who resisted his charm

48. Renée Tickell, another of John's British Council colleagues

49. The Rev. Gerard Irvine. The car, a 1929 Pontiac,
had formerly belonged to John Buchan. John met
Irvine in the 1930s, when the future priest was a
schoolboy. They were lifelong friends, and Irvine is
mentioned in John's autobiographical poem
Summoned by Bells (1960)

50. Margaret Wintringham, with whom John fell in
love in the 1940s. She was married to Edmund
Penning-Rowsell, the expert on wine

51. John at The Mead in Wantage

52. John in his library at
The Mead

53. and 54. Desmond and Mollie Baring. The Betjeman family were often at Ardington House, the Barings' home near Wantage

55. Anthony Barnes, son of John's BBC friend and patron Sir George Barnes. He confided in John his teenage problems

56. Paul Betjeman during his National Service

57. *Left to right*: Lady Elizabeth Cavendish,
Anne Barnes, George Barnes and John, on
holiday in France, *c.* 1952

58. Princess Margaret with Lady Elizabeth
Cavendish

59. The room in Rotherhithe which in 1958 Antony Armstrong-Jones (now Lord Snowdon) lent to John, whose house in Cloth Fair had been gutted by fire. At top left is the hammock into which Lady Elizabeth Cavendish gamely tried to jump

60. John with Sister (now Doctor) Winifred Hector, whom he often met when he visited patients at St Bart's Hospital

61. John and Penelope at The Mead in the 1950s

62. George Elliston, the
deplorable versifier who
established a chair of poetry
at the University of Cincinnati.
John was visiting professor
in 1957

63. The Vernon Manor Hotel in
Cincinnati, where the Betjemans
stayed. Penelope found the
central heating 'ghastly'

64. and 65. Van Meter Ames, the professor and poet who kept a diary of John's time in Cincinnati, and his wife Betty

66. Elizabeth Bettman in the 1950s. She realized John's marriage was breaking up at the same time as her own to Judge Gilbert Bettman of Cincinnati

67. John with Elizabeth Bettman when she visited Wantage later. Penelope wrote on the back of this photograph 'Garden study entitled " – LUST – " '

"If I hadn't married . . .   *I should still be . . .*   *a schoolmaster . . .*

extremely quaint . . .   *and cranky by now . . .*   *but very happy, I'm sure"*

68. These photographs accompanied an article on John in *Everywoman* in 1960. The captions quote a remark he made during the interview

69. Princess Margaret presents the Duff Cooper Prize to John in 1958 for *Collected Poems*

70. John signing copies of *First and Last Loves* (1952) at the *Sunday Times* Book Exhibition in 1955. To his right is his publisher and friend Jock Murray

71. John painted by his cousin, Doris Lurot Betjeman, in 1956. He would not sit long enough for more than a sketch to be made. Penelope, looking in on the sitting, said to Doris, 'Oh, I see *you're* the real genius of the family.' The artist caught the seriousness, determination and melancholy behind the poet's usual public image. That year he was fifty. He wrote in the *Spectator*: 'I thought of the many people at school with me who were now knights and politicians. I wanted to cry. Then I thought of my many friends who are now dead, and terror of eternity made me want to scream.'

an odd way, the most modern of all our poets. He is slap up-to-date. And, in exchange, he will endure the retribution of soon becoming incomprehensible. He is like an eighteenth-century satirist. He needs footnotes as soon as he is written.[54]

From Betjeman loyalists came a chorus of praise. In spite of the editor's reservations, Richard Church gave it a good notice in *John o' London's Weekly*.[55] G.B. Stern was enthusiastic in *The Sketch*.[56] John Arlott, who from his days as a young policeman had been a collector of Betjeman first editions, wrote a 'rave' in *The Spectator*.[57] Eric Gillett, the man who had suggested the title for *Ghastly Good Taste* in 1933, wrote in the *National and English Review*: 'His touch is as light as that of a burglar trying to pick a lock without waking a sleeping household.'[58] The *South Wales Argus* of Newport, Monmouthshire (now Gwent), noted with pleasure that 'the three church bells in "The Dear Old Village" ring "Lin-lan-lone" – the title of a drama which Lyn Harding brought to the Newport Lyceum when the world was young'.[59] The *Church Times* reviewer suggested that 'It is because he believes in the eternal that he can see both the charm and the irrelevance of the transitory.'[60]

On 14 July 1954 *The Times* sympathetically assessed John's current standing.

> In an age which positively enjoys wrestling with words, and far more readily spends its time upon the sibylline than the enjoyable, he has built up a steady following, both in England and America, by employing for the most part the easy grace which in the past has been associated with names like Tom Moore, Thomas Haines Bayly, and Jean Ingelow . . .
>
> He is often in love – but with the gym tunic quite as much as with its wearer . . . He suffers agonizing twinges of guilt, but bravely incurs the reproaches of a delicate conscience by going on exactly as before. And all this is set down in strains of deceptive innocence . . . while the reader, ever prepared to be amused, suddenly finds his heart touched as well by an entirely original skill.

An anonymous critic in *Reader's Review* gave general praise, explaining that 'the "failures" in this book are the price paid for a poet on the move, one who refuses to stand still, consolidating old ground and repeating old successes'.[61] That made a pleasant change from the stock criticism of any new Betjeman book – 'the mixture as before'. The critic added: 'His worst poems are also unique in the sense that they read like imitation Betjeman and remind you of the quality of the real article.'[62]

Murray had sold 1,000 copies before publication. On 12 August Jock Murray sent John a progress report. 'The Chrysanthemums are going well and are in great demand. They have certainly been given quite a lot of space in the press and are now approaching the 3,000 mark. Congratulations! A few critics show a rather appealing obtuseness but the majority have been intelligent and have hearts as well as intellects.'[63]

In October *The Spectator* gave John a page and a quarter to reply to his critics. He resisted the temptation to slang them back; modestly agreed with the poet G.S. Fraser that he was 'not at his best in Joyce Grenfell or *New Statesman* Competition mood'; accepted the provincial press's advice that he should keep off satire and anger. He allowed himself one jab: 'I was not addressing myself to the *vieux jeu avant garde* – if I may string four French words together – which still lingers on in the "Critics" programme of the BBC.'[64]

The article contained the most cogent description John ever gave of his method of writing poetry.

Verse-writers will know the lengthy and painful business of giving birth to a poem. First there is the thrilling or terrifying recollection of a place, a person or a mood which hammers inside the head saying, 'Go on! Go on! It is your duty to make a poem out of it.' Then a line or a phrase suggests itself. Next comes the selection of a metre. I am a traditionalist in metres and have made few experiments. The rhythms of Tennyson, Crabbe, Hawker, Dowson, Hardy, James Elroy Flecker, Moore and Hymns A & M are generally buzzing about in my brain and I choose one from these which seems to me to suit the theme. On the backs of cigarette packets and old letters, I write down my lines, crossing out and changing. When I reach home I transfer the whole to foolscap and cross out and change again. Then I start reciting the lines aloud, either driving a car or on solitary walks, until the sound of the words satisfies me. Then I try reading the poem out to a patient friend whose criticisms I gladly accept, provided they are of detail only. After that I may have the courage to send it all to a magazine.[65]

In the *Sunday Times* 'Books of the Year' selections, *A Few Late Chrysanthemums* was chosen by Evelyn Waugh, Lord David Cecil and Malcolm Muggeridge – enough votes to put it ahead of any other non-fiction work. Waugh bracketed it with Elizabeth David's *Italian Food* and *Private's Progress*, a novel by Alan Hackney. Cecil thought John's book 'especially memorable because in it the scene is strengthened by a darker and more tragic note'. Muggeridge wrote that the book was that which had given him 'most unalloyed delight this past year', and that John was 'easily my favourite contemporary poet', conveying 'as no one else can, the curious spiritual twilight in which we live, with its lengthening shadows and grotesque shapes . . .'[66] Jock Murray wrote to the printer Mark Clowes on 7 January 1955: 'Betjeman's Chrysanthemums have set off again like a firework thanks to the famous men's choices . . . Many thanks for getting the binding of the balance in on Friday afternoon. We have sold 700 of these already, so if we are to make chrysanthemums while the sun shines and before the frost the urgency is great . . .'[67]

At the suggestion of Eric Walter White[68] of the Arts Council, Jock Murray had delayed publication of *A Few Late Chrysanthemums* to allow it to be submitted to the Poetry Book Club for their summer selection of books. It was not selected; but, as consolation, in 1955 William Foyle, the bookseller, awarded John the £250 Foyle Poetry Prize. The cheque was presented to him at one of Miss Christina Foyle's literary lunches, at the Dorchester Hotel on 11 March – William Foyle's seventieth birthday, as it happened. Among those present were the Duchess of Devonshire, Rose Macaulay, John Neville from the Old Vic, Laurie Lee, John Edward Bowle, and John's aunt Mrs Simpson Harvey, who sat next to the diarist from the *Daily Telegraph* and proudly told him of her nephew's earliest verse. 'Written in 1914 at the age of seven, it was a patriotic piece entitled "A Call to Arms".' Bowle told the *Telegraph* man how he and John had jointly edited *The Heretick* at Marlborough.[69]

The diarist wrote his paragraph; but the sensational event of the luncheon became a big news story in most of the papers, including the *Telegraph*. John's cheque was presented by the eighty-four-year-old Lord Samuel, whom he had known at the Oxford Preservation Trust. Praising John as a rare contemporary poet who was comprehensible, Samuel made an intemperate attack on modern poetry. Having examined some anthologies of modern verse, he said he had been 'appalled to find the degree to which the vice of obscurity was afflicting English verse'.[70] It was, he thought, 'self-conscious posturing'.[71] To illustrate what he meant, Samuel quoted, in a 'stumbling' voice for comic effect, from Dylan Thomas's 'A Grief Ago' –

> A grief ago,
> She who was who I hold, the fate and flower,
> Or, water-lammed, from the scythe-sided thorn,
> Hell, wind, and sea . . .

The *Daily Sketch* recorded what happened next. 'Up sprang 46-year-old [Stephen] Spender. He bristled with indignation, glared at

Lord Samuel and stalked out of the door.'[72] 'Afterwards,' the *Daily Mail* reported, 'he said he was "furious" and "disgusted" and went on: "I was a great admirer of Dylan Thomas, and was the first person to write to him about his poetry. It seems that if you are going to give £250 to a modern poet you have to denounce modern poetry. It is the price you have to pay."'[73] The drama of Spender's exit turned into farce when he bumbled by mistake into the Dorchester's kitchens, from which he emerged sweating, blinking and 'poppy-faced'.[74] The whole incident made such an impression on the Bloomsbury novelist David Garnett, who was present, that he recalled it in a letter to Sylvia Townsend Warner seventeen years later, when the publisher of one of his own books was suggesting it might be promoted by a Foyle's luncheon:

> One of Miss Christina Foyle's literary luncheons! Have you been the object of one? I went to one given for Betjeman when Lord Samuel gave a long speech. He, Samuel, is what the Stracheys called a death packet, and I dozed off to find Stephen Spender, sitting next to me, on his feet and majestically walking out in the middle of his Lordship making an attack on the poetry of Dylan Thomas.[75]

Although Spender had been seated at the 'top table', he was some way from the speakers, and John did not see him leave.

> Mr Betjeman stopped staring intently at the ceiling [the *Manchester Guardian* reported] and rose hesitantly to his feet. He said that he hoped Mr Foyle's prize will encourage all poets because 'poets don't hate each other like some other people do who are in a less creative capacity, shall we say.' Turning to Lord Samuel, he said that some very great poetry seemed difficult when it first appeared – Mr Eliot's for example – but that after ten years it became a commonplace. Poets are prophets.[76]

The *Birmingham Post* quoted a fragment of John's speech. '[He] rejoiced that the cheque now safely stored in his wallet would do a good deal to put straighter his overdraft.'[77] *The Bookseller* printed another sally: 'He himself had struck lucky, he was fashionable, he said; "but, my goodness, I'm in for it in ten years' time!"'[78]

CLOTH FAIR AND ROTHERHITHE

This was the nicest place in London to live in, because everything could be reached on foot, down alleys and passages.

John Betjeman, 'The City', *Observer Magazine*, 24 July 1977

In the 1920s John's friend Patrick Balfour (later Lord Kinross) had given him shelter in 'The Yeo', his house in Yeoman's Row, South Kensington.[1] In the 1950s he again, for a time, offered him a London *pied-à-terre*. By now, Kinross lived in Warwick Avenue in London's Little Venice near the Grand Union Canal. He was a member of what John christened 'the Paddington set': in the same area lived Lady Diana Cooper, the composer Lennox Berkeley and his wife Freda, the painter Adrian Daintrey,[2] Princess Margaret's friend Judy Montagu and William Wilberforce Winkworth, the authority on oriental art. After a brief, predictably unsuccessful marriage, Kinross had reverted to the ways of a confirmed bachelor. He was making a name for himself as a travel writer, particularly on Turkey; and while he was away John was given the run of the Warwick Avenue house.

In May 1953, much to John's dismay, his secretary Jill Menzies resigned. 'I think I was getting too fond of him,' she said. 'I thought it would upset Penelope if I stayed.'[3] This may have been a polite way of saying, 'I think he was getting too fond of me.' Just before she left, John took her and Christopher Hollis to the Garrick Club. She had never been anywhere like it before and her excitement showed as she came down the stairs after leaving her coat in the ladies' cloakroom.[4] Later, John wrote the poem 'A Russell Flint' and sent it to her.[5]

> I could not speak for amazement at your beauty
> As you came down the Garrick stair,
> Grey-green eyes like the turbulent Atlantic
> And floppy schoolgirl hair.

I could see you in a Sussex teashop,
Dressed in peasant weave and brogues,
Turning over, as firelight shone on brassware,
Last year's tea-stained *Vogues* . . .

The poem was published in *High and Low* (1966).

To take Jill Menzies' place, John appointed a new part-time secretary, Anita Dent, the daughter of Major Leonard Dent, a friend of his and John Piper's who lived near Reading and collected Rowlandson paintings.[6] She agreed to accept the same salary as Freckly Jill, £3 10s a week, with her keep.[7] John warned her she might need to work for Kinross as well, as he was not sure he could afford her on his own; but in the event, even when Kinross was in England, he never had enough work to make this plan feasible.[8] Anita Dent worked for John three days a week. She remembered that his room in the Little Venice house was referred to as 'the Holy Church' and was crammed with books for review.[9]

John's cuckoo-nesting in Kinross's house was inexpensive, and he liked Little Venice; but he felt the need of a London flat of his own. He wrote to Kinross from Warwick Avenue on 29 June 1954:

> What with the wireless and *Punch* and the *Telegraph* I have so much to do in London that I think I will have to take a flat in London and furnish it with half my books from home – ie architectural books. The Holy Church would be too small a room. There would not be room here without altering the character of the house and moving a lot of my furniture and I think I will have to be on my own if I am to work in London and use Wantage for recreation.[10]

The reasons John gave for moving were plausible enough; but no doubt he also wanted Elizabeth Cavendish to be able to visit him without the threat of a sudden incursion by the gossipy Kinross, or in view of Kinross's neighbours who might tattle to him and others. John had found somewhere suitable to live. His letter to Kinross continued:

> I've heard of a very cheap flat in the City in Cloth Fair (Seely and Paget, my dear) which may serve the purpose. Three guineas a week in all but I would have to put in a bed, chairs, table and bookshelves. That means if I do get it, that I would move there in Aug[ust] or early Sept[ember]. So I'd better give in a reluctant notice to your house which has been very nice and increasingly funny.[11]

He added that 'A dear little kiddy from the slum house next door threw a brick through the window when it was playing at thieves with its sub-normal companion. But the gardener has mended the pane.' Another morsel of news concerned a new public lavatory in Warwick Avenue. 'The amenity is finished and a lovely gents blocks Lennox's view but not ours. No kiddiz unaccompanied are allowed into the amenity and it is full of refugees.'[12]

As one familiar with homosexual society in London, Kinross would have known exactly what John meant by the arch 'my dear' after the names of the architects Seely and Paget, who owned the Cloth Fair flat. Paul Paget and Jack Seely, who had succeeded his father as Lord Mottistone in 1947, were not just architectural partners; they were a couple.[13] They had met as undergraduates at Trinity College, Cambridge, in the early 1920s.[14] Seely, who had served in the First World War, was slightly the elder. Paget, whose father became Bishop of Chester, enjoyed acting and looking at old buildings; so did Seely. After university, Paget first went into a bank and was then assistant private secretary to his uncle, the Cabinet minister Sir Samuel Hoare (later Lord Templewood).[15] Hoare wanted Paget to go into politics; instead, Paget set up an architectural practice with Seely. Their influential parents bought them an office in Queen Anne's Gate and the two set up house together nearby. It was said that Seely drew the buildings and Paget made them stand up. They became well known for their adaptations of old buildings, creating the celebrated Art Deco interior for the Courtaulds in Edward IV's Eltham Palace,[16] and restoring Lambeth Palace, the Deanery and canons' houses at Westminster Abbey, Charterhouse, Eton and some City churches. The buildings they designed themselves were in general less admired, though Nikolaus Pevsner praised the Palladian shooting box they built for Hoare in Norfolk in 1939.

In an interview with Clive Aslet in 1985, Paget, who died later that year, described how he and Seely had moved house and office from Queen Anne's Gate to Cloth Fair.

When the practice was going reasonably well the partner said, 'You know, I think we ought to be in the City.' He gave the word, and every weekend was spent in hunting round for a possible property in the City. And . . . it was quite incredible luck because we chanced across this ancient little street with a pre-Fire of London house for sale for £3,000 freehold. It's unbelievable. We persuaded the parents to provide the necessary cash, and of course it did prove to be wildly rewarding – a wonderful shop window. We spent blissfully happy years there.

We went there in 1930. Then my father, who was on the point of retiring from being Bishop of Chester, was like most bishops and had got nowhere to go. He got rather miserable about the thought of retiring. We

were able to buy the next door property, so I had some very beautifully
engraved notepaper with the heading 39 Cloth Fair; and I wrote to him
and said: 'Here is your new address.'

My father was very, very reluctant, so I employed an artist [Roland Pym]
to do a decoration in the bathroom. I remember offering an illustration of
this to the then very popular weekly glossy called *The Tatler* and this was
published as 'Bathroom for a Bishop'. You can imagine that my father
found it of some embarrassment when facing his other bishops at the
Athenaeum Club.

In the end we bought the street. John Betjeman, with whom we had
come into contact over a battle about a television mast in the Isle of Wight,
came down to lunch and said, 'But of course I've got to live here.' So he
moved in next door.[17]

Mottistone's family home, Mottistone Magna, was on the Isle of
Wight: John's daughter Candida, who stayed there with him in 1955
when she was thirteen, remembers that 'the touches of discreet
modernity and close-fitting tartan carpets made an indelible impression on me'.[18] John knew the peer through their mutual friend George
Barnes, of the BBC. Congratulating Barnes on his knighthood in
October 1953, John wrote: 'You are now higher than Paget and well
on your way to being Seely.'[19] Mottistone was among the thirty or so
guests at a dinner-party which John helped organize to celebrate Sir
Ninian Comper's ninetieth birthday in June 1954.[20] John moved into
43 Cloth Fair in August.[21]

It was the brief Fifties lull between Hitler's bombs in the 1940s and
the 'new brutalist' architecture of the 1960s – the 'eggbox' buildings
which in John's view 'nearly killed' the City's character.[22] He was
returning to his roots – to the land of his fathers, the 'cavernous
streets' where his ancestors had lived and worked from the eighteenth
century to the twentieth. Aldersgate Street, where his immigrant
great-great-grandfather, George Betjemann, had lived, was just a step
away, and Pentonville Road, where his father had made dressing-tables
for maharajahs, was not far off. John had explored the City since
childhood, had known it intimately before much of it was lost in the
Blitz. He expressed his affection for it in several poems.

In 1977, five years after leaving Cloth Fair, he described in the
Observer Magazine what it had been like to live in the City.

This was the nicest place in London to live in, because everything could be
reached on foot, down alleys and passages. Like all county towns it had a
bit of every trade. I was lucky enough to live in Cloth Fair where there was
still a shop which sold cloth. On some weekly nights there was bell-ringing

from the tower of St Bartholomew the Great, just such bells as the walled city must have heard when there were 106 churches in its square mile. Behind me was Smithfield meat market with its cheerful, Chaucerian characters and medieval-looking handbarrows ... Just over the boundary were the rag trade and the print and down in Clerkenwell the clocks. Southward, the City became a river port with wharves and cobbled quays and a smell of fish from Billingsgate where alleys plunged steeply to the river.

There was still a sense of sewers where Fleet Ditch flows under Farringdon Street and Fleet Street climbs westward through the journalists to the Temple and the Law. East of the City at Aldgate Pump I could sense the Orient, and at Beaver Hall, on a Sunday, business was brisk in the fur trade while the rest of the City was silent. What makes the City so different from all London is its secrecy. It is really a village of about 400 people who know each other and whose words are their bond. If they break their word they are out. All this secret life is sealed by those medieval guilds, the City companies with their livery halls, bumbledom and beadles.[23]

In that atmospheric *mise en scène*, John curiously failed to mention St Bartholomew's Hospital (St Bart's), though he had close links with it when at Cloth Fair. Like the church of St Bartholomew the Great, which he attended most Sundays, it had been founded in 1123 by Henry I's court jester, Rahaere.[24] The twin foundations were among the four great medieval institutions of the area, with Smithfield meat market and the riotous Bartholomew Fair, already centuries old when Ben Jonson wrote his play about it. (Looking at a copy of the first edition of 1631, John noted from the title-page, and thought it amusingly apt, that the play had been 'ACTED IN THE YEARE, 1614 By the Lady ELIZABETHS SERVANTS'.)[25] The meat market and the hospital represented butchery and healing – or, as cynics maintained, butchery and butchery. When John took friends to breakfast in a Smithfield workers' café, it was a favourite joke to suggest that meat porters in bloodied aprons were surgeons fresh from the operating theatre.[26] John knew that the diamond-shaped arena of Smithfield had been a killing field – and not just for animals. There William Wallace, the Scottish patriot, was executed in 1305; Wat Tyler, the leader of the Peasants' Revolt, was stabbed to death by the Lord Mayor of London in 1381. There – as recalled by Shakespeare in *Henry VI* – the heads of Lord Say and Sele and Sir James Cromer were brought to the rebel clothier, Jack Cade, in 1450.[27]

The district was rich in cultural history, too. Dryden's first published poem had been issued in 1659 by a printer near Little St

Bartholomew's Hospital.[28] William Hogarth had been born in 1697 in Bartholomew Close, a courtyard wedged between St Bart's Hospital and the church.[29] His history paintings are on the staircase of the hospital, whose Augustan façade looms over the market. In 1725 Benjamin Franklin spent a year as a journeyman in the printing house of Samuel Palmer in what had been the Lady Chapel of St Bartholomew the Great.[30] But John was less interested in the early history of Smithfield than in the Victorian architecture of the market, a great brick shell with a glass roof. In 1949 he sent John Summerson a verse riddle about its architect, Sir Horace Jones (1819–87), who also designed Tower Bridge.[31]

As the name of John's street suggested, the cloth trade had been dominant in the district. In 1833 the Lady Chapel which had housed Samuel Palmer's press was taken over by a lace and fringe factory, jutting into the presbytery.[32] It proved impossible to dislodge it until 1885, after which the chapel was restored by Sir Aston Webb – the architect mentioned in John's poem 'Cheshire' – who named one of his sons Rahaere. When John moved into Cloth Fair there was still a textiles shop at No. 40 – Mitchell, Inman & Co., gone now, but *in situ* in 1977 when John gave this thumbnail sketch of it in the *Observer Magazine*: 'Mahogany counters and cupboards from 1800, stock of felts and cloths stacked in huge rolls looks unchanging, too. Wholesalers but happy to retail.'[33] The firm provided the tweed for the Woolsack in the House of Lords.

John bought from Mitchell, Inman several yards of altarcloth to be cut into curtains for his Cloth Fair flat. As he had done at Farnborough, he created a Victorian interior in a much earlier house. 'William Morris came too,' Candida remembers. 'His willow pattern wallpaper graced the narrow stairway, which led to the red "Bird and Anemone" in the sitting room where a sketch of Belfast by Sir Charles Nicholson hung above the fireplace.'[34] John's rooms overlooked No. 45 Cloth Fair, the Elizabethan house where 'the Partners', as Mottistone and Paget were always known, lived. Like St Bartholomew the Great, the Partners' house had escaped the Great Fire of London, which only licked the alleys south of Smithfield, blackening the northeast side of St Sepulchre's Church. The Partners' house, where John was always welcome, was sumptuously furnished in interior-decorator style. They had two baths, side by side, and no curtains over the bathroom window. John would take his visitors to a window of his flat overlooking No. 45, saying, 'If we stand here, we may be able to see my landlords in their baths.'[35] Eventually Mottistone and Paget grew tired of being a *tableau vivant* and tourist attraction. After John left Cloth Fair, they had the window that overlooked them blocked up and painted by Brian Thomas with a *trompe l'oeil* of 'The Sailor's Return'. Paget was amused to hear a tourist guide to the City telling his charges, 'Here is a very interesting case of a window that was blocked up at the time of the window tax.'[36]

Candida often visited and sometimes stayed at Cloth Fair. She would be treated to lunch at Coltman's restaurant in Aldersgate, where there were bentwood chairs on a sawdust floor and John would be served champagne in a pewter mug. She noticed that on Thursday mornings John disappeared. 'I never thought to ask why, but years later I discovered it was something he never talked about to anyone.'[37] Through the hospital chaplain, Mr Bush, whom he met at church on Sundays, he began visiting patients in St Bart's.[38] He made friends with two of the hospital's Sisters, Winifred Hector and Mary Bland. The two had arrived at St Bart's on the same day in 1935 and had had to deal with the City casualties of the Blitz.[39] Winifred Hector was the daughter of a Taunton railwayman ('*In loco parentis*' was her stock joke about that). To the younger nurses she was a daunting figure. 'When I entered the nurses' canteen, it went quiet,' she recalls. 'They called me "The Shadow of the Hawk".'[40] She was formidably capable. In 1957 she published *Modern Nursing: Theory and Practice*, which sold over 200,000 copies before it became outdated. Mary Bland was a gentler person who had been a teacher of folk-dancing and a performer on the penny whistle before going into nursing. John was amused that the Sisters took the names of the wards for which they were responsible, so Winifred Hector was Sister Fleet Street and Mary Bland was Sister Percivall Pott. (Pott was a famous eighteenth-century surgeon, whose portrait by Reynolds hangs at the hospital.) Mary Bland recalled that John 'named the sister who was in charge of all the cleaning ladies, "Sister Floors" and the sister in charge of the skin department in the outpatients, "Sister Skins". He would say, "Please can I go and see Sister Skins?" '[41]

He came to coffee in Mary Bland's room every Thursday morning and then visited the patients in her ward. 'He was able to make all the patients laugh,' she remembered, '– he was a wonderful mimic.'[42] She thought that it was his horror of death which 'helped him to see dying patients'.[43] Hugh Dunn was a cancer patient in Percivall Pott ward. His widow wrote to Candida in 1994: 'Your father certainly cheered up his days by his visits when they discussed London before and after the war. Mr Betjeman was at the time a very busy man but he still found time to visit us, and attend Hugh's funeral at Mortlake Crematorium.'[44] A much younger patient in Percivall Pott, whom John visited every Thursday, was David Johnson, who was being treated for bone cancer. John sent him letters, too. David was twelve when John wrote to him, on 17 April 1957:

Dear David,
   I hope to be able to come to see you tomorrow (Thursday) afternoon.

That knight has moved along to yet another bottle of sherry. You can see some
more on the right waiting for their corks to be drawn. Those on the left are
empty. A man with a pork pie hat on has been sketching the next house to me
here (it is the only pre-fire house left in the City) for two days. You or I could
have sketched it [in] less than two hours. I wonder why he takes so long.
   I will telephone your mother tomorrow, about the time of my arrival. I
hope Richard's measles are better. This repulsive Biro pen gives my hands
the measles. I must go and wash them.
   Love from John Betjeman[45]

A week later, John wrote to David, who was back at his parents'
home in the Vale, north London:

My dear David,
   As I cannot come to see you all at the Vale this week, I am writing a letter
to you instead and please will you thank Richard for his letter telling me
of the trick you played on him. I am very amused by it. I am writing this
coming down in the train from Doncaster. There are not enough seats on
it and I am very uncomfortable squashed between businessmen with pipes
who are travelling at their firm's expense.

This reads the same backwards and is the longest sentence of its kind to do so which I know of – LIVE DIRT UP A SIDETRACK CARTED IS A PUTRID EVIL. The Secretary of the Royal Fine Art Commission who is travelling with me and to whom I showed this sentence said did I know what Napoleon said when he was defeated? I expect you do. It was ABLE WAS I ERE I SAW ELBA. The skill of that one is that the words themselves fit. He also asked me what was the first remark made by a man to a woman. And when I said I didn't know, he told me it was MADAM I'M ADAM . . .[46]

David Johnson died in July 1957.

In December 1956 John's visits to terminal-cancer patients inspired a poem. Mary Bland was given the holograph manuscript, inscribed to her, and the poem was published in the *London Magazine*, at that time edited by John Lehmann.

> Now from his remoteness in a stillness unaccountable
> He drags himself to earth again to say goodbye to me
> His final generosity when almost insurmountable
> The barriers and mountains he has crossed again must be.[47]

Poetry inspired by hospital visits: the mind tracks back a century to Walt Whitman's visiting the wounded in the American Civil War and later writing:

> Thus in silence in dreams' projections
> Returning, resuming, I thread my way through the hospitals . . .
> I sit by the restless all the dark night, some are so young,
> Some suffer so much . . .[48]

Whitman's biographers have given much space to speculating on the motives for his hospital visits.[49] Why did John visit Bart's? Simple kindness was probably his principal reason for becoming a visitor, coupled with the fact that the hospital was virtually on his doorstep. But perhaps also, in talking with the dying, he was confronting his deepest fears. His poem 'Five o'Clock Shadow', again a result of his experiences at Bart's, ends:

> This is the time of day when the weight of bedclothes
> Is harder to bear than a sharp incision of steel.
> The endless anonymous croak of a cheap transistor
> Intensifies the lonely terror I feel.[50]

In his poem 'St Bartholomew's Hospital', John wrote that the ghost of Rahaere 'teaches us never to fear to die'.[51]

There was a lighter side to his long association with the hospital. Winifred Hector remembers him, surrounded by a gaggle of nurses on an upper floor, pointing out the spires and towers of the City churches. John and Elizabeth socialized with the Sisters. It was known that he was married, but the Sisters had seen too much of life to be censorious (as many people in the Fifties would have been) about the evidently close friendship. In October 1957 John wrote to the Duchess of Devonshire, Elizabeth's sister-in-law:

> Poor Feeble Elizabeth has had a bad throat. Before she got ill she went to a party of Bart's nurses in a functional flat. I saw her there. She looked quite different from everyone else sitting on a divan.[52]

When John was invited to make a television film about the City, he asked Winifred Hector if she would agree to be interviewed by him on the programme. She said she would and they arranged to meet in front of the hospital. The Sister dressed in her best 'civvy' clothes for the occasion but when John saw her, his face fell. 'I wanted you to be in your uniform!' he said. So Sister Fleet Street returned to her ward and re-emerged in her crisp apron, black belt with silver buckle and starched headdress. It was a fine day and the two were filmed sitting together on a bench in the open. John was one of the few people who were not frightened by Winifred Hector. He asked her provocative, even cheeky, questions, drawing from her her particular brand of grimly humorous repartee. Still photographs were also taken; when

Osbert Lancaster was shown one of them, in which John was scream-
ing with laughter while the nurse sat sternly beside him, he said it
looked like 'a loonie's outing from the asylum with his attendant'.[53]

In May 1958, when John's secretary Anita Dent announced that she
was leaving to get married, John took on in her place Tory Dennistoun
(now Lady Oaksey), the daughter of the racehorse trainer Ginger
Dennistoun who trained at Letcombe Regis and was a friend of the
Betjemans. She worked for John four days a week for seven pounds.

> John was a lovely employer and I was *hopeless* [she told Candida in 1994].
> Sometimes he would sigh and gaze wistfully at a photograph on the man-
> telpiece of a pretty girl, saying, 'Oh, for Freckly Jill!' – his perfect secre-
> tary . . . Archie, propped up on the top of a bookcase, looked over us all
> the time and probably saw me forget to turn off the Stenorette tape
> machine one night. I always suspected it was the cause of the fire which
> nearly destroyed the house, but John never blamed me.[54]

The fire damage was severe and John had to move out while the flat
was restored. He wrote to Candida on 26 November 1958:

> Through the kindness of Tony Armstrong-Jones, the photographer, who
> has just gone to the USA for a month, I have been lent a room in
> Rotherhithe while 43 is being repaired . . . It is so nice I never want to leave
> it and I long to take you to see it. I sleep there at nights and am writing this
> now in it with the sound of a spring tide lapping against the walls under
> my window.[55]

Antony Armstrong-Jones was the son of Lady Rosse, with whom
John had founded the Victorian Society in 1957. Rotherhithe Street
SE16 is the longest street in London. Pier-like, it stretched between
Cherry Garden Street and Cow Lane, with the Thames on one side
and the Surrey Commercial Docks on the other. It was from this
waterfront that the *Mayflower* sailed to Plymouth to take on board
the Pilgrim Fathers. Among the warehouses and blitzed sites opposite
the Victorian headquarters of the river police was a row of eighteenth-
century houses which ships' masters had built right on the river bank,
so they could keep an eye on their vessels at their moorings. No. 59
was the shabbiest of these. It looked across moored barges and tugs to
a tangled skyline of cranes and the portal of Tower Bridge, with the
dome of St Paul's beyond; at the back of the Georgian street façades
was a Dickensian jumble of wooden platforms and wharves. In 1954
William Glenton, a London shipping reporter, had bought the house
as a combined home and office. Paint on the panelled interiors was

flaking and some of the wooden floors sloped so badly that 'it was like being on the deck of a listing ship'.[56] An upstairs room overhung the Thames, with a view of a mile and a half of the river from London Bridge to Limehouse.

Glenton was a tough character who thought he had been lucky not to be hanged during the war when he and other ratings of the Royal Navy ship HMS *Lothian* had mutinied at Balboa against living conditions on the lower deck. They had refused to take the ship to sea on the way to the Pacific campaign and were court-martialled. Glenton was confined to ship for six months.[57] Now he divided his time between the waterfront and Fleet Street and used a bare ground-floor room of the Rotherhithe house to hold high-spirited parties with journalist friends. He also frequented the local pubs. At one of them he met some 'Chelsea-ites' in search of excitement in the East End. One of them asked if he would help him find a *pied-à-terre* along the river for a friend.[58] The friend turned out to be Armstrong-Jones, who said he could get no peace at his Pimlico studio now he had become a well-known 'society' photographer. Glenton and Armstrong-Jones cruised dockland in the latter's Morris 1000 saloon, with no success. Then Armstrong-Jones asked if he might lodge in Glenton's house, 'in the empty room overlooking the river on the ground floor'. Glenton agreed to this.[59]

At the time, Armstrong-Jones's girlfriend was Jacqui Chan, a Chinese model from Trinidad. Glenton remembered the couple 'like a pair of goblin tailors', stitching together squares of matting as part of a comprehensive decorative scheme. He was amazed at the bric-à-brac Armstrong-Jones brought into the house.[60] 'When he arrived in his car, now a Borgward station wagon, with the first of several loads of fittings, I thought he must have raided the Victoria & Albert Museum.'[61] Among other exotic *objets*, Glenton noted a golden cage containing three stuffed lovebirds, a stand carved in the shape of a Nubian page boy, a large ornate mirror, a miniature brass catafalque, dusty wax flowers and a blue glass rolling-pin. Later there arrived a rocking-chair with a basketwork back, a papier-mâché chair inset with mother-of-pearl, a life-size portrait of an eighteenth-century admiral on his flagship and a fishnet hammock.[62] Armstrong-Jones tried to hang the hammock between two hooks with knots which Glenton regarded as 'great-grannies'; Glenton secured it with seamanlike bends.[63] Armstrong-Jones stood out in dockland. He usually wore a fancy suede jacket, tight jeans and chukka boots.[64] He brought down fashion models to pose them against the river background, to the wolf whistles of appreciative dockers. He held parties, but they were not like Glenton's roistering press binges; instead, the old house echoed with 'the high-pitched chatter of debs, models and aesthetic young men . . .'.[65]

Armstrong-Jones was in the 'arty' circle of Elizabeth Cavendish and it was at a dinner-party given by her at her mother's house in Cheyne Walk, Chelsea, in February 1957, that he had first met Princess Margaret.[66] The Princess's biographer, Helen Cathcart, writes: 'Tony, who loved investing himself with an air of mystery, had occasionally spoken to Elizabeth Cavendish of a Room (which had seemed even then to be invested with capital letters) where he could escape at times from the bustle of his studio to work in peace and quiet.'[67] In March 1958, just back from inspecting, in Germany, two regiments of which she was Colonel-in-Chief,[68] Margaret crossed the Thames by the Deptford ferry, 'incognito, muffled up and unrecognizable', to have drinks with Armstrong-Jones in the Rotherhithe flat, after an official visit with Lady Elizabeth to the Dockland Settlement in the Isle of Dogs.[69] As the romance between Margaret and Armstrong-Jones intensified, the Princess often visited the Room.

In November 1958 William Glenton received a telephone call from Pimlico.

Speaking more excitedly than usual [he recalled], Tony asked if I could do him a great favour. Would I mind if a friend of his were to use The Room for several weeks? I imagined it would be someone of around Tony's age and of his usual circle. When he told me who it was I hardly knew what to think.

My house, with its broken-down, half-starved look, certainly did seem more appropriate for a poet than a fashionable photographer – but the beaming, well-fed, almost Pickwickian figure of John Betjeman, who appeared a few hours later on my doorstep, looked in no way like the conventional idea of the threadbare, starving poet. When Tony had told me who it was that wanted somewhere temporary to live, I knew of John Betjeman sufficiently well to be surprised, but I had never even seen a photograph of him. Now that I was getting my first look at him I was even more startled. But it was pleasant astonishment, for he radiated a warm friendliness that made me respond enthusiastically. He captured my attention so well that I hardly paid any notice to the tall, obviously well-bred woman in her thirties who had arrived with him by car. Indeed, she seemed to prefer to remain in the background while John explained how he had the night before been made homeless by a fire at his own ancient house in Cloth Fair ... He became as excited as a small boy when he saw The Room and then the view from it. 'Oh, how jolly! This is going to be fun! I shan't want to go back to my own place.'[70]

John insisted on seeing the rest of the house; but, an hour later, the woman with him reminded him that he was late for an appointment.

With his coat flapping and with wisps of grey hair poking out from beneath the wide-brimmed, well-dented trilby clutched to his balding head like the feathers escaping from a cushion, John rushed out of the house shouting promises not to be in late that evening. They had both gone before I realized that I had not been introduced to his female companion. Perhaps she was his secretary, I thought . . .[71]

As a friendly gesture, Glenton took a cup of coffee down to John the next morning. The guest came to the door in his striped pyjamas, sleepy but cheerful. 'I've never slept so well for years,' he said. 'I'm almost glad there was a fire.'[72] He explained about the lorries that rattled past Cloth Fair on their way to Smithfield meat market. The two men talked for a long time, as they were often to do in the weeks John spent in the house; but John found the view distracting.

> While still in his pyjamas he stood at the open windows, watching the river craft bustling by with all the deep satisfaction of a boy studying a demonstration of model trains. He seemed unable to tear himself away, and then, suddenly, he began throwing off his pyjamas and putting on his suit, in a frantic hurry to be on time for his first appointment of the day. He was still buttoning up his clothes as he rushed from the house.[73]

It seemed to Glenton that John always had 'some desperate business to perform, making it additionally difficult for me to realize that he was a poet and not some slightly eccentric businessman'.[74] Glenton could not understand 'the need for his constant rushing here and there' until, later, he learned that John had been involved in preparations for the imminent publication of his *Collected Poems*.* Glenton never saw him at work on a poem. John was constantly looking out of the windows.

> He wanted to know the reason for everything he could see, and to find out more about the people who worked on the river he went with me to several of the waterfront pubs. The watermen, bargehands and dockers he met knew little of, and cared even less about, poetry – but John's genuine and enthusiastic interest in them won them over, and they spent hours yarning about their work to him.[75]

When John and Glenton talked on their own, the subject of death often came up. 'Nothing frightens me more than the thought of dying,' John said.[76] Later, when the first big cigarette-cancer scare

* See Chapter 35, '"A Really Thrilling Moment of Triumph"'.

made news in Britain, 'John saw the smoke haze he constantly spread around himself as a pall of death and the ash clinging to his clothes as a bodily fungus. He made a great effort to give up cigarettes but would sometimes find himself absentmindedly lighting one.'[77] This was not the only instance of John's absentmindedness.

Once, soon after he came to stay, he returned to the house at midnight to find he had forgotten his key. When his banging on the door failed to wake me, asleep right at the top of the house, he thought, as he told me later, of finding his way to a hotel. But not knowing of any in the district he decided boldly to knock on the door of one of my neighbours in the row – for he remembered that most of the houses were connected at the back by a terrace of flat roofs. In the hope of persuading whoever answered his knocking to let him clamber across the roof to my house, he banged away at one of the doors. After several minutes he heard the shuffling of slippers and then a nervous: 'Who's there?'[78]

Luckily for John, the owner of the house, a woman doctor, was not only an admirer of his poetry but also knew his face well from photographs. 'John, who had expected a chilly reception, found himself being given a cheerful welcome.'

He had the greatest difficulty in persuading the doctor not to make him a cup of tea, even prepare him a meal – but when he followed her up the narrow stairs to the roof he found his luck had run out. While all the other flat roofs at the back of the houses were connected, there was a six-foot gap between hers and the next one.

   John's only alternative was somehow to scramble up on the sloping roof that linked the main parts of the houses and edge his way along the gutter. It was a precarious task that even I, several stone lighter than John, would never have attempted in broad daylight – let alone in the dark. The doctor tried her best to dissuade him. Yet, having got so far, to the point of getting the doctor out of bed, he felt he had to make the attempt. Clinging to a drainpipe and slowly heaving himself up, with a great deal of puffing and bruised arms and legs, he somehow got to the guttering. There were only those six feet to cross before he could lower himself down to the next flat roof and safety, but it could have been as long as a circus high wire as he edged along inch by inch, the old cast-iron gutter creaking and bending under his great weight. As the doctor told me later, she kept her eyes shut and said a prayer, at any moment expecting her favourite living poet to become her lately beloved deceased poet. But he made it. Waving her a silent goodbye as he crossed the remaining rooftops, he tiptoed into my house and gladly to bed.[79]

This daredevil exploit gives the lie to John's frequent description of himself as 'a physical coward'. There was a sequel. A few days later Glenton met a detective from the river police headquarters. The officer told Glenton he had been on duty and had seen John performing his 'minor Everest attempt'. At first he had thought he was a cat burglar, but thought better of it because 'judging by the hard work the old boy was making of it . . . it couldn't be any self-respecting villain'.[80]

When John left the Rotherhithe house – leaving an electric toaster as a thank-you present – Glenton was sorry to see him go. John was regretful too, and promised to visit him again as soon as he could. Knowing of John's busier public life ahead, Glenton did not expect to see him again; but two weeks later he reappeared at the house. 'As on the first visit he arrived with the tall, unknown woman, but this time Tony was with them. He, too, appeared to be a close friend of the woman's, and some of the mystery was cleared up when he introduced her to me. "Do meet Lady Elizabeth Cavendish," he said.'[81]

The visit of this oddly assorted trio [Glenton adds] signified a definite change in Tony's use of The Room. He never again used it to bring down any of his usual Chelsea friends or for any large parties. The people who did come down with him were older, and just two or three in number at the most. Lady Elizabeth was usually one of them, and proved to my surprise that she could be much jollier and less dignified than I thought. The three, including Betjeman, acted like happy playmates, as though they shared some secret joke.[82]

One evening Armstrong-Jones decided to test his friends' athletic prowess by seeing which of them could get into the fishnet hammock the easiest and quickest way.

He, of course, leaped in and out of it in a matter of seconds [Glenton recalled], while John, carrying a far greater weight disadvantage, had to be almost levered in. I wondered if Lady Elizabeth, who is somewhere around six feet tall and has very lanky legs, would even bother to try. But she was as keen as both the others, and with great glee threw herself up into the hammock. Instead of landing inside it, however, she went right over the top – and crashed to the hard floor on the other side. We rushed to pick her up, thinking she must have broken a few bones or cracked her head, but she brushed us off and once again tried to get in the hammock. This time she succeeded, and she lay sprawled along its full length like a highly bred saluki dog.[83]

Glenton remembered that evening not only for its fun but because it was the last time, for several months, that Armstrong-Jones invited

The river front of Rotherhithe Street, by Leonora Ison

him to join his guests. Glenton had the feeling that his tenant was becoming 'exceptionally secretive'.[84] One day, about teatime, Glenton entered the house and met Lady Elizabeth coming down the stairs. They discussed the weather with strained casualness, 'and then Lady Elizabeth, who must have felt that some explanation of her presence alone was necessary, told me that she had just dropped by to tidy Tony's Room. With no further explanation she excused herself and hurried out to her car . . .'[85] Later that evening, Glenton discovered that a roll of violet-tinted toilet paper had been hung in the lavatory. 'It did not need my reporting intuition to make me realize that there had to be some very special reason for a duke's daughter to act as a home help.'[86] A fortnight later, he was glancing through a glossy magazine at his barber's and came across a photograph of Lady Elizabeth with a caption identifying her as a lady-in-waiting to Princess Margaret. An 'almost unbelievable thought' entered his head.[87] Then, returning from a newspaper assignment, he was about to go up the stairs when the door of Armstrong-Jones's room opened and silhouetted against candle-light was 'the unmistakable figure' of the Princess.[88] Helen Cathcart writes, 'Here was a working journalist with the greatest romantic scoop story of the century within a floor's depth of his typewriter. Yet to his lasting honour Mr Glenton kept the secret through all its developments, until the demolition men razed 59 Rotherhithe Street . . .'[89]

Princess Margaret and Armstrong-Jones (by now Lord Snowdon)
continued to use the Room as a hideaway after their marriage in
1960.[90] But in September 1963 John wrote to Leonora Ison, who illustrated his articles about architecture in the *Daily Telegraph*:* 'There is
a serious threat from the LCC [London County Council] to the sole
surviving houses that hang over the Thames in London – namely No's
59 onwards Rotherhithe Street (west of Rotherhithe underground
station & near the Union public house).'[92] He asked her to get in touch
with Glenton and suggested she draw the houses '*from the river* – at
low tide on the shore, at high tide from a boat'.[93] But, in spite of John's
public pleading and some behind-the-scenes agitation by Margaret,[94]
Glenton received an eviction order, and soon the Room was rubble.
Only Ison's fine drawings survive to show John's temporary refuge of
1958.[94]

The street façade of Rotherhithe Street, by Leonora Ison

* See the chapter 'Men and Buildings' in the third volume of the present work.

ON THE AIR IN THE FIFTIES

Sky and sun and the sea! The greatness of things was in you
    And thus you refrained your soul.
Let others fuss over academical detail,
    You saw people whole.

John Betjeman, 'The Commander' (a poem about Sir George Barnes of
the BBC), *High and Low*, London 1966

At a time when the BBC was still standing on its dignity (radio announcers were required to wear evening dress at the microphone), John was lucky to gain the trust and admiration of a number of senior officials, who were not deterred by his irreverence and occasional facetiousness. Chief among these was George Barnes, the first head of the Third Programme.[1] His acquaintance with John began inauspiciously with the contretemps over Captain Newbolt* but developed into one of the great friendships of both their lives. In March 1944 Barnes invited John to lunch at the Oriental Club in London.[2] On 6 April, writing to tell Barnes that he was going to the Admiralty, John addressed him for the first time as 'Dear George'.[3] Barnes reciprocated with 'Dear John', but grumbled that he deplored 'this modern habit of using Christian names'.[4] Later that month he invited John down to his home, Prawls, near Tenterden, Kent, giving him the advice – 'hardly necessary in your case' – to wear his oldest clothes.[5] John met Barnes's wife Anne and the couple's thirteen-year-old son Anthony, whom he called 'Little Prawls'. Barnes himself was soon given a Betjeman nickname, too.

> John always called my father 'The Commander' [Anthony Barnes recalls].
> My father had been at Dartmouth Naval College; he desperately wanted to

---

* See Chapter 10, 'Taking to the Air'.

be in the Navy, but because of the cuts after the First World War and his poor health he had to give up that career. He always regretted it. When Independent Television started, there was a Commander Brownrigg at Associated Rediffusion, so John's nickname was particularly embarrassing to my father. John would go round saying, 'Do you know my friend Commander George Barnes, who has made a little niche for himself in television?'[6]

Prawls became almost a second home to John. Anthony Barnes looked forward to his visits.

He was hugely funny. Made my parents laugh a lot, which in a way made things easier – I mean, the whole family was enlivened by his being there. There were take-offs of planners who destroyed everything beautiful. John invented this wonderful character called Ken Arlington (the village just along the Royal Military Canal from us was Kenarlington) who was a garage mechanic and he'd either landed on D-Day or just after, and the thing that gave him the greatest pleasure was shooting the heads off the statues on French cathedrals.[7] One of the people John took off was some young 'forward planning'-type Oxford don. He did an impression of the voice and everything else. I think it may have been based on the young Harold Wilson.[8]

John also sent George Barnes importunate letters from an imaginary broadcaster-writer called Howard Output. ('I have just completed a play . . . The theme is topical, being the triumph of democracy over dictatorship, with a human appeal in an ex-Fighter Pilot who comes home to find his wife divorced . . .')[9]

Barnes shared John's sense of humour. 'My father was fun to be with,' Anthony Barnes recalls. 'Like John, he teased a lot.'[10] But there were unspoken limits. John wrote to Anne Barnes of 'that delicious sense (which the Commander . . . manages to carry) that one has gone a little too far'.[11] Barnes, too, was interested in architecture. On John's first visit to Prawls in 1944 they bicycled to the churches of Romney Marsh and had an argument as to whether lichen should be pronounced 'litchen' or 'liken'.[12] In 'The Commander', the poem he wrote after Barnes's death from cancer in 1960, John wrote:

> I remembered our shared delight in architecture and nature
> As bicycling we went
> By saffron-spotted palings to crumbling box-pewed churches
> Down hazel lanes in Kent.

I remembered on winter evenings, with wine and the family round you,
   Your reading Dickens aloud
And the laughs we used to have at your gift for administration
   For you were not proud . . .[13]

Sometimes John brought Paul with him to Kent. Paul enjoyed playing with Anthony's Bassett-Lowke model railway in the Barnes's attic.[14]

Anne Barnes, a don's daughter, was much more withdrawn than George. 'She was very shy, very private,' her son says. 'She hated the public part of my father's life.'[15] John was very fond of her. They confided in each other. He told her about his love for Margaret Wintringham and his pain over Penelope's conversion. She told him of her concern about her friend Lady Bates, wife of Sir Percy Bates[16] who ran the Cunard Line. The Bateses' son Eddie was killed late in the Second World War. 'Lady Bates for a number of years was convinced that she could get in touch with him,' Anthony Barnes remembers. 'This my mother found very distressing, and she talked about it with John. It was a case where the "confidant" thing went the other way.'[17]

Anne Barnes was bilingual; her second language was French. By slow degrees she managed to overcome John's antipathy to 'abroad' and he went with the family on holidays to France. In 1949 they travelled to Auxerre, Chartres and Vézelay – 'and then he went racing back to stay with Diana Cooper[18] in Paris and got 'flu on the way', Anthony Barnes recalls.[19] In 1950 they went to Albi and Armentières. 'But he was desperate to get back to Vincent's Garage in Reading, where his car was,' Barnes says. 'He was genuinely terribly homesick.'[20] After the 1951 holiday, John wrote to George Barnes: 'Oh, *wasn't* it fun! The best ever, ole man. And Bourges. I shall remember that all my life. Oh ta ever so. My breath is still bad from all that overeating.'[21] The 1952 holiday was cut short by Bess Betjeman's illness. Anthony Barnes took a photograph of John 'lying on the ground at Le Touquet in a sulk because the 'plane was delayed. I think my father delivered us to Prawls and then took John straight to his mother.'[22]

In 1953 George Barnes was conducting the Queen around the BBC's Lime Grove television studios when, to his astonishment, she told him to kneel and knighted him with a sword that had been smuggled in from Buckingham Palace.[23] John read the news in the morning paper. He wrote to Barnes on 19 October: 'Penelope and I laughed so much when we saw *The Times* this morning that I brought up my breakfast with the coughing fit induced by my delighted laughter . . .'[24] He sent him a comic drawing of the dubbing.[25]

The last holiday John spent with the Barnes family was in 1954. 'We went to Cognac and looked at a lot of the Romanesque churches in that part of France,' Anthony Barnes recalls. 'The emphasis that time was very much on humble parish churches. There was always tension between my father and John: my father was longing to see the big and famous buildings; but John, left to himself, would have pottered around small ones. They worked out a very good compromise. We certainly saw some big abbeys in western France. Elizabeth Cavendish was with us on that holiday and we stayed with an old friend of my father and mother called Anne Rockley, near Tours.'[26]

John took a kindly interest in Anthony. The boy came to stay at Farnborough in 1950. 'I remember Candida very wild about the house – she was about eight – and Jill Menzies with the freckles. And John showed me "the highest signed photograph of de Valera in Berkshire", which was near the top of the stairs.'[27] He went for a drive with John and Lord Berners.

> We were driving through Little Barrington in Oxfordshire, with houses across a strip of green and we were going very slowly looking for houses. John was driving. And there was someone behind who was getting more and more irritated at the slowness of our progress. And in the end when we came to a stop, he came along and put his face through the window and told us what he thought of us. And Berners turned to him and said, 'I'm so sorry, my friend is a little hard of hearing.' And then, of course, shrieks of laughter before the man was out of earshot.[28]

When Anthony was at Eton, he wrote to John about his problems. He was particularly unhappy on a Navy training-ship at Corsham in October 1949. 'I should have thought it was *boredom* which was the worst thing about your ordeal,' John wrote to him. 'The Homo petty officer sounds interesting. I'm never very worried – not so much as I should be – about sexual irregularity. I find I hate *power maniacs* more than sex-maniacs or anyone else and will forgive the wildest sensual excesses for a spark of kindness, generosity and humour in the profligate.'[29] Barnes recalls, of the petty officer: 'Luckily he didn't come anywhere near me and he got into trouble shortly afterwards. He was a fairly scary figure to us new recruits.'[30]

A week later, Anthony Barnes wrote to John about an affair he had started at Eton with another boy. John wrote to him: 'I had better not write too openly on the subject you mention for fear that letters are read by your comrades in arms. But of course the affair is a splendid

thing and probably will prove the deepest, purest and most remembered emotional incident of your life . . . Don't bother yourself about
the rights and wrongs of that sort of love in relation to the Faith. The
whole question, so long as it is love, is Academic. When it turns into
lust (and there often is a certain amount of lust can drive out love or
an affair can be wholly lust) then whether it is hetero or homo makes
little difference . . .'[31] When Candida Lycett Green published her
father's letters, she asked Anthony Barnes if he would prefer her to
exclude that letter. But Barnes, by then twice married, asked her to
leave it in 'because it showed a side of John which wasn't always
visible. It showed, too, in the letter he wrote me when my father was
dying – and in his hospital visiting of which there is no detailed
record.'[32] John also turned Anthony Barnes into a confirmed church-
crawler; in later life he became director of the Redundant Churches
Trust.

George Barnes, much as he enjoyed John's vivacity and humour,
respected his intellect and wanted to try him out on some doughtier
subject. 'My dear John,' he wrote to him in December 1944 –

I wish you would do some work in addition to expressing willingness. For
instance, the idea which I put to you some time ago that some kind of
broadcast series might be devised to illustrate the great clashes of thought
in this country in recent years . . . What about the Oxford Movement? . . .
Other subjects which I have in mind are: the controversy over Darwin's
theories on evolution, and the first impact of Wesleyanism. Of course you
will want to do the Gothic revival. That might come later, but is too visual
and too narrow to start with.[33]

He was still badgering John to tackle the Oxford Movement almost
a year later, but 'I expect', he conceded, 'your illness [the sebaceous
cyst which required the operation in Oxford] has prevented you from
doing anything more about it.'[34] John never delivered a talk on the
Oxford Movement, Wesleyanism or Darwin; but Barnes continued to
press him to give talks on the Third. In January 1947 he extended an
irresistible invitation: he would send John somewhere he had not been
before, the choice of place to be his.[35] John chose Aberdeen, 'the birthplace of James Gibbs and J.N. Comper, and, I believe, the Adam
Brothers'.[36] He stayed at the Douglas Hotel from 3 to 10 May.[37] His
talk, *Aberdeen Granite*, produced by Anna Kallin, went out on 28 July.
He ended it with a light-hearted poem he had written about the city,
which he attributed to 'a little known Victorian poet'.[38] In April 1948
John was annoyed to hear that the disc recording of *Aberdeen Granite*
had been destroyed. 'I am not a bit surprised,' he wrote to Kallin.

'Who wants to hear about <u>A</u>berdeen when we have <u>A</u>tomic Energy, <u>A</u>rchitectonics, <u>A</u>eroplanes, <u>A</u>nti-Vivisectionists, & so many more important things, not forgetting <u>A</u>ccounts.'[39]

Besides Barnes, John had two other great allies at the BBC: Harman Grisewood[40] and Douglas Cleverdon.[41] Both had known him at Oxford.[42] It had been Grisewood who had insisted on John's expulsion from the Oxford University Dramatic Society for publishing a spoof photograph of the OUDS rehearsing;[43] but the friendship had been soon patched up. Grisewood had joined the BBC as an announcer in 1933 and succeeded Barnes as Controller of the Third Programme in 1948.[44] Cleverdon had been an antiquarian bookseller in Bristol before joining the BBC in 1939. He was to be midwife to Dylan Thomas at the difficult birth of *Under Milk Wood*.[45] Cleverdon wrote to John in December 1945 commissioning a talk on 'How to Look at a Town'.[46] He was also in charge in 1947 when Osbert Lancaster and John read extracts from *The Adventures of Mr Verdant Green*, the first Oxford novel. (John and Lancaster got the giggles so badly that Cleverdon was almost sacked.)[47] In 1949 Grisewood, as head of the Third Programme, suggested a programme of poems by John, to be read by the author. John replied: 'I should adore reading my poetry for two lots of fifteen minutes.'[48] In an internal BBC memo of November 1950, Grisewood wrote that his ideal Christmas-week broadcaster would be 'John Betjeman – not on Victorian architecture'.[49] He would prefer him to Peter Fleming or Harold Nicolson, he said. 'I think John Betjeman could be made to turn in something very good if he was bullied a bit.'[50] Ronald Lewin of Features answered: 'Miss Molony[51] usually manages to bully John Betjeman to some purpose.'[52] That Christmas, Eileen Molony persuaded John to contribute one of his most spirited talks, on the Victorian musician Theo Marzials.[53] It was so successful that she asked for more talks on Victorian musicians. However, when John suggested Tosti,[54] Frederick Clay and Lord Henry Somerset, she said he would have to convince her that they had the same 'microphone magic' as Marzials.[55] In 1951 Lewin suggested to Molony that John should do a spoof 'How to Make Stained Glass' called 'The Tram with the Stained Glass Windows', adding, 'I remember him doing a brilliant improvisation on this theme when he was asked to give a level test for a recording.'[56] When Molony asked John, he replied: 'The writing of such a talk is bound to depend on mood. If you don't mind waiting for the talk, I don't mind waiting for the mood. Love and kisses . . .'[57]

John was never close to his other Oxford contemporary who made a career in the BBC, Louis MacNeice; but he socialized with Grisewood and Cleverdon. When Grisewood died in 1997, Cleverdon's widow Nest wrote in *The Independent*:

One other memory of Harman: a lunch at our Albany Street house in the Fifties; the guests were mostly members of OUDS thirty years before – John Betjeman, Osbert Lancaster, J.T. Yates, John Crow.[58] Conversation became more and more hilarious, and luncheon ended in an unforgettable cod-Shakespeare scene – Osbert as a pompous King, John Betjeman as an obsequious Archbishop, Harman's gnome-like figure skipping in and out as the Messenger with ever more and more unsuitable Tidings. Eventually they all left for Broadcasting House, in no fit state for the recording which had been planned, and I was left giggling into the washing up.[59]

Another friend at the BBC was Hallam Tennyson, the poet's grandson. In July 1950 John gave a talk on 'Tennyson as a Humorist', a theme he was later to develop in a television film.[60] In 1951, when asked to speak on the Festival of Britain, he entitled his talk 'Festival Oddities'.

Like you, I was not mad keen on the Festival at first. The word itself stood in my mind for the very reverse of feasting – discussion groups, processions, scaffolding, youth parliaments, some extra geraniums outside the Town Hall, and that sort of thing. Had the money been spent on giving us a dozen oysters each – and I would have yours if you didn't like shellfish – then that would at least have been the beginning of the feast a festival should be.

But now the Festival is here I like it very much . . . The greatest thing the Festival has done for London is to reintroduce the Thames into a life of pleasure . . .[61]

In 1952 he presented a series called 'Landscape with Houses', each centring on a famous building. After the first, on William Morris's house Kelmscott Manor, Sir Sydney Cockerell,[62] the private press printer, wrote: 'I have just been listening to your enchanting talk on Kelmscott Manor which brought tears to my eyes again and again, so dear has it been to me since I first stayed there with Morris sixty years ago.'[63] Next, John turned to William Burges's Cardiff Castle.[64] At that date it was still thought most eccentric to praise a Victorian building; but John did not pussyfoot. 'A great brain has made this place,' he declared. 'I don't see how anyone could fail to be impressed by its weird beauty . . . You see people coming out blinking their eyes, awed into silence, punch-drunk as it were, from the force of this Victorian dream of the Middle Ages.'[65]

John also became known as a broadcaster who did not need a script. He was effective impromptu, in conversations or panel games. A rare exception was a discussion with Rose Macaulay, in 1954, on 'Changes in Morals'. Elizabeth Rowley, Talks Organizer of the Home Service and the Light Programme, thought the result was 'rather thin in parts' and insisted on a second session.[66] John agreed to it, but wrote truculently: 'I don't think you can have an interesting conversation and then go over it again trying to be more interesting.'[67] The same year, he took part in a programme patronizingly entitled 'Foreigners', in which he interviewed a Turk, Dr Fahir Iz. This is how he introduced him:

> Good evening. When you were naughty and self-willed as a child, did your parents ever call you a regular Turk?
>
> When you hear the word 'Turk', do you think of that or do you think of Turkish cigarettes? Do you think of the 'terrible Turk' or of Turkish Delight? Do you think of 'the Sick Man of Europe' or do you think of 'baths', 'carpets' or 'cigarettes'?
>
> I have with me in the studio Dr Fahir Iz, a real live Turk.
>
> The questions I am going to ask Dr Iz are not intended to be insulting. They are being asked from the point of view of an insular fool, which I am.[68]

Often John was paired with Gilbert Harding,[69] the former schoolmaster known for his curmudgeonliness. (On *Housewives' Choice* Harding rasped: 'No, Mrs Smith, you may *not* have "Bless This House". Here is Mozart's Divertimento in D♭ Major.' To a man who

Caricature of Gilbert Harding by Nicolas Bentley

said he was a gentleman farmer: 'I suppose that means you're neither.') John's charm and Harding's crustiness made a nice antithesis; and the two men liked each other. In January 1955 the BBC producer Archie Gordon wrote to John: 'Last Thursday with Gilbert Harding was a huge success – he has had some delightful letters about both of you . . . Kenneth Adam[70] was so pleased with your reading of the two poems . . . Gilbert and I keep going on at each other to find a date for the Commander and you and us to go to the Crazy Gang.'[71]

Also in 1955, asked to take part in a programme called *Something to Say*, John sent the producer Pat Dixon four topics on which he would be happy to talk:

(1) The uglification of England by chain stores, electricity and motor cars;
(2) My idea of female beauty;
(3) The futility of the examination system;
(4) The preservation of canals and railways, particularly branch lines on railways.[72]

Freddy Grisewood, Harman's better-known cousin, records in his memoirs that John was one of the most popular panellists on the programme Grisewood presented, *Any Questions*.[73]

In 1956 there was a gap in John's broadcasting career. His then agents, Pearn, Pollinger, were pressing for an inclusive contract for both radio and television broadcasts: could something be worked out like the arrangement with Malcolm Muggeridge, who received £1,500 a year for a maximum of twenty-six television programmes? Consulted on this, the Head of Talks (Television) reported that John was 'not such tremendously good value as a Television performer as we first thought, largely because he will not take sufficient trouble'.[74] For their part, the radio producers felt that John's hesitations, which seemed engaging on television, just came out as awkward pauses on the radio. So on 30 April 1956 a polite refusal was sent to Pearn, Pollinger.[75] Mortified, John immediately brought down an iron curtain. On 2 May he wrote to Michael Wharton of the BBC: 'The subject you suggest is one that I mind about a great deal, but alas! I find I really cannot take on any more work at the moment. I wish I could say yes to you, but I mustn't.'[76] On 18 May he wrote an ill-tempered note to Miss Kirwan of the BBC: 'Forty-six letters today owing to the blasted wireless. Life insupportable.'[77] The idea of an 'all-in' contract for John, that would secure his services exclusively to the BBC, was revived from time to time, once through Barnes's initiative and again in negotiation with the bookings manager, Holland Bennett, who had been at Marlborough with John. Twice John was actually offered contracts; but either his agent of the time pressed for better terms or John became anxious about the work commitment involved, and the plans collapsed.

However, financial need soon forced John to end his strike and accept freelance work. In February 1958 Pat Dixon persuaded him to be a panellist in *These Foolish Things*. Different sounds would be played to the panel to provoke 'a series of interesting, amusing or dramatic stories'. The sounds would be: the Angelus, a sneeze, a poetry reading by Edith Evans, the music of a Russian dance, and bolts being drawn on a heavy door.[78] The same month, Archie Gordon booked him to talk with Mary Chubb, who had been a pupil with John at Byron House school before the First World War.[79] 'Now a word about Miss Chubb,' Gordon wrote. 'She realised a great ambition in being secretary to various archaeological expeditions to the Middle East in the thirties and has broadcast and written about these trips. During the war she slipped off her bicycle on a greasy road in front of a lorry and had to have a leg amputated. When I asked her if she would do a talk for "Woman's Hour" about the readjustment of her life consequent on this accident she agreed, but insisted that it should be called "One Foot in the Grave".'[80] John said he would meet Mary Chubb, but declined to talk on Kenneth Grahame to celebrate the approaching centenary of the novelist's birth, surprisingly disclosing to Robert Moore of the BBC that he had not read *The Wind in the Willows* 'and am too old to start it now'.[81] This may have been true; or perhaps he was still playing hard to get.

'CITY AND SUBURBAN'

At my public school the most unsympathetic schoolmaster it has ever been my misfortune to come across [A.R. Gidney] said to me when returning one of my essays, 'Betjeman, do you want to end up writing little paragraphs in the periodicals?' I said, 'No, sir.'

John Betjeman, 'A Spectator's Notebook', *The Spectator*, 27 August 1954

From 1954 to 1958 John wrote a weekly column for *The Spectator* under the heading 'City and Suburban'. In a decade that relished whimsy and nostalgia,[1] his rôle was that of the resident eccentric. He was encouraged to be as quirkishly Betjemanesque as he liked. His main topic was architectural conservation, with frequent 'casualty lists' of buildings demolished or threatened;* but he also wrote about the railways, class distinctions, schools, horror comics, etiquette and accents, and relayed some good jokes, well told if not always pristine. There were intermittent flashes of autobiography.

The Spectator was setting a new course after a year of editorial turmoil. In 1953 Wilson Harris, who had been editor for twenty years, was sacked.[2] Though Harris had raised the circulation to 40,000, the proprietors thought the magazine would do even better under a younger man. They left Harris's deputy, Walter Taplin, in charge while they looked for one, settling for the blind political commentator T.E. Utley, who joined the staff with the assurance that the succession would be his. But shortly afterwards the proprietors sold the magazine to a rich young barrister, Ian Gilmour (later Secretary of Defence and Lord Privy Seal in a Conservative Government, and now Lord Gilmour of Craigmillar). After a power struggle among the senior staff, Utley left in disgust and Gilmour decided he had picked up enough journalistic technique to edit the paper himself. He was editor for the whole of John's stint as columnist, leaving one year after him to become Conservative MP for Isleworth.

---

* See Chapter 32, 'Preservationist's Progress'.

The Spectator was known as a Conservative magazine, but Brian Inglis, Gilmour's assistant editor, thought he 'appeared more in sympathy with Labour'. Gilmour took on 'the Establishment' – a term first brought into popular usage by *The Spectator*'s political columnist, Henry Fairlie. Gilmour wrote exposés of the conduct of the police and the prosecution in the case which led to the conviction of Lord Montagu of Beaulieu for homosexual offences; he vigorously backed the campaign for the abolition of capital punishment, denouncing the Home Secretary in 1955 for his decision not to reprieve Ruth Ellis, the last woman to be hanged in England; and he opposed the Government over the Suez invasion of 1956. As Inglis later wrote, 'People in libraries and clubs who had regarded *The Spectator* as a soporific were woken up to the fact that it was now beginning to mount a challenge to the *New Statesman* as the journal to be picked up first.'[3]

Poets forced to make a living by journalism tend to regard themselves, or be regarded, as prostituting their talents. *The Spectator*'s offices at 99 Gower Street, London (the magazine had not yet moved to Dickens's Doughty Street) had been a Victorian brothel, run by an adventuress called Angel Anna, who claimed to be the daughter of the mad King Ludwig of Bavaria by the Spanish dancer Lola Montez.[4] Behind the house, in what was previously a garden, a two-storey pier had been built for Anna's clients. 'The cubicles were tiny, even for a brothel's requirements,' Inglis wrote.[5] Peter Fleming surmised that they might have been designed 'either as oubliettes for very minor poets or as ferret hutches for very large ferrets'.[6] Peter Fleming – Ian's brother – was a fellow columnist with John, under the pseudonym 'Strix' (Latin for screech-owl). Brian Inglis occupied a cubicle. An Irishman who had worked for Smyllie at the *Irish Times*,[7] he had missed John's spell as press attaché in Dublin, because he was serving with the RAF, but knew him through John's successor, Reggie Ross-Williamson – who showed him a book of Betjeman poems inscribed by the author with a reference to 'Joan Hunter Dunn, whom we both loved'.[8] Inglis had also been at the Dragon School, twenty years after John.[9]

Another Old Dragon contributor was the *Spectator*'s sports correspondent, J.P.W. Mallalieu – the 'Percy Mandeville' of *Summoned by Bells*.[10] John's Berkshire neighbour and friend Compton Mackenzie also had a weekly column, 'Sidelight'. His reservoir of nostalgia was even deeper than John's: in his column of 13 August 1954 he recalled an encounter with Maxim Gorky on Capri in 1914 and described being taken by his parents, in 1886, to meet Thomas Hughes, who inscribed for him a copy of *Tom Brown's Schooldays*. Bernard Levin came to *The Spectator* from the failing magazine *Truth*. Cyril Ray joined the staff as an expert on foreign affairs and wine. A constellation of book reviewers included Evelyn Waugh, Angus Wilson, Kingsley Amis, Patrick Campbell, John Wain, Robert Conquest and Hesketh Pearson. Salaries and fees were low. When Ray was employed at a 'pittance',[11] Levin marched in on Gilmour to protest. *The Spectator* could not afford more, he was told. 'You own it,' Levin said. 'Why not sell a couple of grouse moors?'[12] John received £8 a column.[13] But Gilmour did jazz up the *Spectator* parties from the staid affairs they had been under the old proprietorship.[14] It was at one of these parties that John first became a friend of Kingsley Amis.

John's first 'City and Suburban' column appeared in October 1954, but he made his début in the paper on 12 March. At the start, he seems to have been typecast as a specialist on religion. Only later does his column give us a view of the range of his preoccupations in his fifties. His first article was about the Greater London Crusade of the young American evangelist Billy Graham. John admitted that he himself was 'an Anglo-Catholic to whom the revivalistic approach is unattractive'; but he was fair to Graham. 'I think he must be cynical indeed who affects to despise the crusade,' he wrote. He was sure that Graham, a Baptist, would be prepared to understand a sacramental approach to Christ. 'He is not an emotional speaker, despite his wonderful eloquence. It is obviously within his power to make people weep and scream "Alleluyah". But he restrains himself. He has the great Evangelical love of Our Lord as Man.'[15]

In April, John wrote less indulgently on 'Selling our Churches' – an article provoked by the Bishop of London's selling the site of St Peter's, Windmill Street, London, for £150,000. 'Many will remember how, travelling on top of a bus down Charing Cross Road, one used to see a great crucifix on the dark red brick east wall of St Mary-the-Virgin's church, with the words under it: "Is it nothing to you, all you that pass by?" Apparently it *was* nothing . . .'[16]

On 27 August he was allowed to try his hand at 'A Spectator's Notebook' and used most of the space to protest about the Bishop of Ripon's 'determination to pull down the beautiful eighteenth-century church of Holy Trinity, Leeds, which stands in the heart of that city and is, as it were, the St Martin's-in-the-Fields of those crowded industrial streets'.[17]

The Archdeacon of Leeds, C.O. Ellison, replied in a letter more than a column long. As the Bishop of Ripon was in America, the Archdeacon took it on himself to say that 'Mr John Betjeman unfortunately misrepresented the facts.'[18] The Pastoral Committee, he wrote, was bound to question the existence of three or four churches near the centre of the city. 'Holy Trinity is one of these churches, and

it stands on an extremely valuable site in the midst of shops.' He
added, 'The wish to preserve Holy Trinity church for its undoubted
architectural interest and merit is a natural one, but to wish to keep it
for this reason alone is to shirk reality and to ignore the spiritual and
pastoral needs of the population as a whole.'[19] This was too much for
John. On 1 October a derisive poem by him appeared in the magazine,
entitled 'Not Necessarily Leeds'.

> I wish you could meet our delightful Archdeacon
> There is not a thing he's unable to speak on.
> And if what he says does not seem to you clear,
> You will have to admit he's extremely sincere.
>
> Yes, he is a man with his feet on the ground,
> His financial arrangements are clever and sound.
> I find as his Bishop I'm daily delighted
> To think of the livings his skill has united.
>
> Let me take for example St Peter the Least
> Which was staffed by a most irresponsible priest;
> There are fewer less prejudiced persons than I
> But the services there were impossibly High.
>
> Its strange congregation was culled from afar,
> And you know how eclectic such worshippers are.
> The stipend was small but the site was worth more
> Than any old church I have sold here before.[20]

John's views prevailed, and the church was saved.

In September 1954 John wrote another 'Spectator's Notebook'. He
deplored expense accounts, horror comics and 'The New Hubris'.
The attack on expense accounts presaged his future satire of 'executives'.

What an appalling fascination for me has that increasing class of people
which eats only on expense accounts. You find some cheap foreign restaurant where the food is good and where the customers are simple guzzlers
like yourself, who pay for their meals out of their earnings. Women and
men are in fairly equal proportion at the tables. Then one day you notice
a group of men in the corner who are receiving extra attention. Two of
them are sleek and neatly dressed and have put on flesh early, thanks to
well-organized expense accounts. With them is a bewildered technical
consultant, not used to this sort of place, pulling at his ears and straight-
ening his tie. The host is anxious to impress his guests with his influential

position in the firm, so he orders a vinegary drink masquerading as sherry, oysters, champagne, lobsters and various other expensive things which have never been the specialities of the house. You come again in a month's time and the restaurant is changed. You are no longer welcome, prices are doubled and the food has deteriorated. Men predominate at the tables and one or two hard-faced business women add a scarcely feminine note. You do not go there again, but the restaurant proprietor is making a fortune . . .[21]

'Horror comics' were seen by many (as, later in the Fifties, were rock 'n' roll and bubble-gum) as American imports undermining British culture. In February 1955 the novelist Joyce Cary contributed an article on the subject to *The Spectator* opposing censorship of what children read. ('I write as one who was a gang leader of criminal youth.')[22] In September 1954 John, as the father of a seventeen-year-old son, took a different view.

I have a friend who works in East London who found a paperbound book of strip cartoons, printed in America and republished here, on a seven-year-old child who was on remand. Every story in the book was in favour of criminals, and crime came out on top. One showed a little girl whose parents quarrelled and who wanted to go and live with her auntie. The mother's lover arrived and the child heard them plotting. The father returned and was shot. The last cartoons were as follows. 'First mummy was electrocuted. She went first, because she was a lady,' and there was a picture of the event underneath. 'Then mummy's boy friend was electrocuted. And wasn't I glad, because then I was able to go and live with auntie.' The final picture showed the little girl giving an enormous wink and saying, 'And nobody found out that it was I who shot daddy.'[23]

John defined his third topic, 'The New Hubris', as the insistence that there are two sides to every question, and that a strongly expressed opinion should never go unchallenged.

That entertaining talker, Christopher Sykes,[24] gave me a delightful hypothetical example of this sort of thing. An announcement appears in the paper that St Paul's must be pulled down as it is a waste of a valuable building site. You or I rise up in fury and write a letter to the paper saying this is an iniquitous idea. We express ourselves in unmoderated language. After a day or two a letter comes from some academic art historian saying that there is no need to get hot under the collar, let us look at this dispassionately, there are two sides to every case. St Paul's is indeed a beautiful building. On the other hand the site is very valuable in these times of economic distress. Let us pull down half St Paul's and use the other half as a building site . . .[25]

John made a good showing in these trial pieces. With his vivacity and pugnacity he caught the essence of the new *Spectator* – a pleasant-tasting cocktail with a kick to it. On 8 October 1954 he was given more than a page to review the reviewers of his latest book, *A Few Late Chrysanthemums* – another chance to mix wit and acerbity.* In the first of his 'City and Suburban' columns, 15 October, the main paragraph was about the superiority of Cambridge to Oxford, because of the industrialization of Oxford ('Much as I love Oxford, one of whose sent-down sons I can claim to be . . .'). Then a note on missionary pamphlets and a passage in favour of Australia House, London – anticipating by decades the architectural historians' interest in what John called 'the Edwardian baroque which goes with banks, town halls and civic state'.[26]

One thing that the columns reveal is how peripatetic John was in these years. He was constantly on the move across Britain. Why did he travel so much? Partly, perhaps, to check up on the buildings which his readers warned him were falling into decay or otherwise threatened. Partly because he enjoyed journeys by train in that last age of steam. Possibly, too, the column began to write him – a common fate of diarists who may begin to do interesting things just to have something worth putting in the diary. On a Sunday in late November 1954 he went to Bath. 'The Avon had overflowed its banks . . . That unworthy little building down in the wooded meadows, which is used for concerts, now that no one can bring themselves to reconstruct the Assembly Rooms, was well under water. A bill outside it announced Moiseiwitsch, and I imagined the grand piano floating about over the soaked parquet and bumping into the trivial decoration of this outsize army hut.'[27]

A week later he was on the Wiltshire Downs near 'the remote and desolate RAF camp at Yatesbury'.[28] The road was full of airmen thumbing lifts; John drove three of them into Chippenham. In February 1955, motoring near Hull, he spied the Italianate towers of Tranby Croft, a Victorian house which had been the scene of the baccarat scandal involving Edward VII when he was Prince of Wales.[29] 'It is now a girl's school, and the headmistress told a friend of mine that the girls know one of the rooms as the Baccarat Room. "And what is it used for now?" "Prayers." '[30] Eight years later, John's daughter married Rupert Lycett Green, a kinsman of one of the baccarat players of Tranby Croft.

---

* See Chapter 27, 'A Few Late Chrysanthemums'.

Ascension Day 1955 dawned fine in the City, so John cancelled all his engagements and gave himself a 'Church holiday'. He went to Liverpool Street Station and took the first train he saw. It carried him to Harwich; then he took the ferry across to Felixstowe.[31] (The visit may have inspired his poem 'Felixstowe, or The Last of Her Order'.) His friendship with Lady Elizabeth Cavendish brought him more than once to Derbyshire; in June 1955 he complained of the new power station 'mercilessly destroying the gentle skyline' at Willington.[32]

John was at Cowes in Cowes Week, 'and actually visited the Squadron lawn, wrongly dressed in a London suit and a yachting cap. What was worse, I visibly flinched when a gun went off at the end of a race.'[33] In November he was in 'the black, impressive borough of Huddersfield' and noted with horror plastic 'leaded lights' being stuck on windows of farms in the West Riding.[34] He was in Gloucester, with Penelope and Candida, in January 1956;[35] at Sutton Benger, near Chippenham, in February;[36] at Whitstable, with two friends, for an oyster orgy, in March.[37]

Early in December 1956, John stayed in Brighton to recover from influenza. ('How restful it was to go to sleep to the sound of crashing waves and rattling shingle.')[38] Just before Christmas he went to Maidstone, Kent, which had 'always seemed to me like Chelmsford, Reading and High Wycombe, an infuriating traffic block on the way to somewhere else'.[39] This time he discovered St Luke's Church (architect Seth Smith, 1896–97) 'in the most fantastic version of art nouveau Gothic I have ever seen'.[40] In January 1957 he attended a function in the vast Grosvenor Room of the Grand Hotel, Birmingham.

> What Conservative and Liberal cigar-smoke, I thought, must have curled up to those gods and goddesses in plaster above the pilastered walls, what strains from Strauss, Sullivan and *The Immortal Hour* must have poured from that Edwardian gallery . . . Italianate, exuberant and convinced, a place which makes you feel important howsoever dim you be. As I first remember it, this great hall was stained dark as port wine and richly gilded. What was my dismay to see that our timid age had redecorated this splendid plaster work in pale biscuit colour and the palest of pale nursing-home greens. It now looks like Queen Victoria dressed only in her underclothes.[41]

Trains, like buildings, were a staple ingredient of John's column. Like most of the largely Conservative readers of *The Spectator*, he thought the British railway system should not have been nationalized by the post-war Labour Government, and he was full of complaints. In December 1955 he wrote:

In order not to offend countries on the Continent, British Railways have decided to abolish third class and call it second. I wonder what is going to happen to the second-class carriages on the continental boat trains? I think this absurd slavery to formalism is just the same as that futile erasure of the old company lettering that went on when British Railways were started. It descended even to the tea-cups.[42]

He waged a running vendetta against Sir Brian Robertson,[43] the retired general who was chairman of British Railways. After visiting Cheshire in April 1956, John wrote:

Oh sad Sir Brian Robertson, England's most unpopular general, how heavily hung your spirit over my train journey from Congleton to Oxford! I remember Mr Chuter Ede[44] telling me that the idea behind the nationalization of the railways was that they should be a public service and not run from the profit motive. All the way along I saw sad little, weedgrown branch lines curving away to forgotten termini in midland towns. This devastation the general leaves in his trail is due to his determination to make the railways show a profit rather than perform a public service.[45]

John had another go at Robertson the next week, on returning from his visit to Ireland.

In Dublin I learned sad railway news. The Great Northern Railway of Ireland is being bludgeoned by the Transport Commission of Northern Ireland, which is obviously in close touch with Sir Brian Robertson, that unhappy General, into shutting many of its branch lines in its north-western section. An inquiry was being held and the south was resisting. If these branch lines are shut it will mean that Bundoran becomes more motor-coaches than houses, that the thousands of pilgrims who go to Lough Derg will have to find other means of transport – already we are being told that the closing here is an anti-Catholic move by Northern Ireland – but it also means the end of the last horse-drawn railway in these islands. I refer to the branch from Fintona Junction to Fintona.[46]

By contrast, he praised the façade of Blackfriars Station, built for the London, Chatham and Dover Railway in 1874: 'Here, engraved on the brick and surviving all wars, is a thrilling inducement to the citizens of London and the employees of *The Times* opposite to travel. Darmstadt, Herne Bay, Warsaw, Margate are some of the names I recall.'[47] One of the names engraved on the portals of Blackfriars was St Petersburg, which, in the 1950s, when the city was called Leningrad, seemed an exotic reminder of the Romanovs, Pushkin and the

Diaghilev Ballet. John once went to the ticket office and demanded 'A day return to St Petersburg, please.' Unfazed, the ticket clerk said, 'I'm afraid you'll have to go to Victoria for that, sir.'[48]

Religion, from High Church observances to Muggletonian survivals, continued to be a dominant interest. In June 1956 John was at Fulham Palace, which he had imagined was a dull house. ('I suppose this was because I had always heard about it from clergymen and they rarely like Georgian.')[49] He was pleased to find instead a Gothic lodge, a Tudor courtyard with diaper-patterned brickwork, and a house designed by Samuel Pepys Cockerell, the architect of Sezincote.[50] The reason he was at Fulham was to hear the Mirfield Fathers Hugh Bishop and Trevor Huddleston appeal for funds to send a community of contemplative nuns to Basutoland. 'The nuns to go out are from the Society of the Precious Blood, an Anglican Order at Burnham Abbey, Bucks. This place has in my own experience caused what seem like miracles to happen when I have asked for its prayers about particular personal problems.'[51]

On 30 August 1957, John began his column:

I would like to record something about Monsignor Ronald Knox[52] which may otherwise go unnoticed. At a time when there is a strain in the relations between the Church of England and Roman Catholics in some quarters, it ought to be mentioned. The chimes in the beautiful Parish Church of Mells were in need of repair, and Ronnie Knox wrote to me to ask me to come and open a fête in aid of them. This was held in the gardens of the Manor House where Mrs Asquith[53] lives and where Ronnie spent the last years of his life. Many prominent Roman Catholics had helped the vicar to organize the fête. Of course, it rained, like it always does at village fêtes, but Ronnie, though he was then very ill, came out into the rain to the little opening ceremony. I think he had much affection for the Church of his birth, and he certainly greatly appreciated its variety and added to its humour.[54]

John's rosy view of Knox on this occasion can be offset by Knox's less kindly memory of John, which Anthony Powell recorded in his journal over thirty years later:

V [Powell's wife, Lady Violet] recalled that when Betjeman was staying with the Clives[55] at Whitfield, the house was not yet 'on the grid' for electricity, so Betjeman could not use his electric razor. Someone therefore had to drive him to the nearest house in the neighbourhood (in fact on the outskirts of Hereford), which had electricity laid on. (Betjeman was then not Poet Laureate, tho' widely known from TV, other public appearances.)

V told this story to Ronnie Knox (Katherine Asquith's chaplain at Mells), who burst out: 'What a hypocrite that man is!' It turned out that an electric carillon had recently been installed at Mells Church and Betjeman had been invited down to speak in celebration of its arrival. His speech fiercely inveighed against modern, especially electrical, technology, regretting the old days of bell-ringing by hand. A slightly piquant trimming to this story is that the Mells chimes played hymns, which Ronnie had more than once mentioned greatly disturbed him, possibly hymns reminding him too vividly of his own apostasy from the Church of England.[56]

Knox's attitude toward John would have been coloured by his own friendship with Evelyn Waugh, his knowledge of Penelope's conversion and of Waugh's unsuccessful attempts to convert John. And John himself was not always in the sunny ecumenical mood of the paragraph about Mells. Speculating in 1954 as to who would be the new Head of Religion at the BBC, he wrote: 'Whoever it is, I hope we will not have too much of this oecumenical attitude' (by which, if one denomination was allowed a programme, another must be given a programme too).[57] When stuck for a subject, John could always fall back on the sport of archdeacon-baiting, which for him never palled. 'I am very flattered', he wrote in August 1955, 'by a remark made about these weekly notes of mine by Mrs Victor Rickard, the novelist. She told a friend that they were just as though they were written by an archdeacon on a bicycle. On second thoughts, perhaps I am not so flattered. When one thinks of the destruction of churches brought about by modern archdeacons, St George's, Tiverton, St Philip's, Buckingham Palace Road, St Agnes's, Kennington, to name a few recent cases, one begins to see the point of that medieval question, "Can an archdeacon be saved?"'[58]

The Spectator did not have an obituaries column; so when John read of the deaths of people he had known or admired, he paid tribute to them. The bushy-eyebrowed music-hall comedian George Robey died in November 1954. 'I saw him for the last time', John wrote, 'at the Hackney Empire more than a year ago . . . George Robey's jokes may sometimes have been coarse, but their coarseness was traditional and not shocking. Do you remember the one about two old cockney ladies at the bar? One says to the other, "Are you going to have another?" "No, it's the way me coat does up."'[59] In March 1955 he recorded the death of Professor A.L. Dixon, Senior Fellow of Magdalen, Oxford, 'one of the last people to have known Max Beerbohm as an undergraduate'.[60] (Dixon had been a young don at

Merton when Max was up.) Professor Dawkins, the authority on ancient Greek vases, died in May 1955.

He was returning to Exeter College [John wrote] from his favourite after-lunch walk in the beautiful gardens of Wadham when he fell down and died instantly in the road outside Wadham. He was eighty-three but seemed ageless. Hundreds of undergraduates from the early Twenties until today have known him. They have visited those cream-panelled rooms with Ethelbert White paintings and Greek ikons on the wall, books and papers littered everywhere. They have received those abominably typed postcards . . . with a '¼' and a '£' instead of capital letters . . . They will remember his squeaky voice and the witty things he said in it – that same voice which entertained Baron Corvo and Norman Douglas.[61]

A third Oxford don died in June 1955, Dr Homes Dudden, the Master of Pembroke, who only the year before had given John his blessing to publish the poem about Walter Ramsden in *A Few Late Chrysanthemums*.* 'His majestic eighteenth-century appearance fitted his scholarly mind and charm of conversation,' John wrote.[62] The long life of Max Beerbohm ended in May 1956. John recalled his visit to Faringdon,† adding: 'He detested power maniacs, particularly politicians . . . Just because he saw through people he was considered a satirist. He was nothing of the sort. He was a most affectionate and penetrating portrait artist.'[63]

In his obituary notes, John revealed details of his subjects which would never have appeared in *The Times* but which evoked them more vividly than any formal *in memoriam*. In October 1957 Lord Dunsany, who had been fond of both John and Penelope, died.

Unexpected things roused him to anger [John wrote]. One of them was manufactured salt in advertised brands (he mistrusted everything that was branded and advertised) – if he found this on a dinner table, no matter whose house it was, he would say, 'Send for some ordinary kitchen salt and bring two glasses of water.' He would then pour some of the branded salt into one glass and the kitchen salt into another. The kitchen salt dissolved, but the branded salt left a white deposit at the bottom of the other glass which he said was either chalk or ground-up bones.[64]

In the second of his columns, John wrote defensively: 'I suppose nearly everything I have written this week can be called "nostalgic". It

---

* See Chapter 27, '*A Few Late Chrysanthemums*'.
† See Chapter 1, 'Uffington'.

is a scientific word for "sentimental" and sounds like a form of catarrh. It is, of course, a term of contempt when used by people who believe in youth parliaments, the future, the kiddiz, civics and free thought, if one can be said to believe in free thought. I regard "nostalgic" as a term of praise, myself, for it implies reverence and a sense of the past . . .'[65] In many of his paragraphs he lamented what had gone or gloated over archaisms that had managed to survive. In November 1954 he wrote:

> Now that streets and rooms are dark by tea-time, I notice more than ever the horrors of modern electric light. I see my tea looking like green custard under the strip lighting of a café, and cakes look mouldy and toast looks like cardboard . . . I have been trying in vain to find those crinkly glass shades from which the old-fashioned bulb burst like a flower . . .[66]

In December 1954 he was saddened that *Doidge's Western Annual* had ceased publication.

> No longer will we have those Devon dialect stories in the manner of the veteran Eden Philpotts, no longer the poems and puzzles and lists of fairs and photographs of the Mayor and Aldermen of Plymouth; no longer will we unfold the colour plate, that sweet reminder of cottage art, showing Lustleigh Combe or a clapper bridge on Dartmoor. But I was thankful to buy, on Chesterfield station this week, *John Hartley's Original Clock Almanack* for 1955, originally published ninety years ago and still printed in a Victorian style in Bradford. Everything in it is in deepest dialect, except for the advertisements for things like Himalayan Brain Food, Nepha the Mystic, and Nerve Control remedies and other medicaments . . .[67]

In the hot summer of 1955, John took to wearing a boater and a bow tie in London.

> In Bond Street the glances of the women and men were so contemptuous at this ageing Teddy Boy[68] that I had to take off my hat and expose my bald head to the sun. But in the City old faces beamed with joy to see a straw boater again, and two strangers stopped me to ask where I had bought it. I can't tell you because that would be advertising, but the hat is cheap and cool.[69]

Most of John's columns were brightened by jokes, some supplied by friends.

> William Plomer has told me a story which can be used with effect when giving away prizes and talking to the parents about how they should bring

up their children. A woman was sitting on a bus with her child on her lap. The child was sucking a lollipop – one of those sticky things on a wooden stick. Presently another woman, wearing a fur coat, came and sat beside them. The child took the lollipop out of its mouth and started to wipe it on the fur coat of the lady in the next seat. 'Don't do that, Mavis!' said the mother. 'If you do, you'll get 'airs all over it.'[70]

A 'new train of deliciously futile thought' was set up by a story about surnames and place names. 'The late Lord Salisbury is said to have sent the following telegram to his son: CRANBORNE, CRAN-BORNE. ARRIVING SEVEN SEVEN SALISBURY – SALIS-BURY.'[71] John was tickled to hear from the County Surveyor of Northamptonshire that he had received a letter addressed to 'The Countess of Ayr'.[72] And a friend in the City of London told him he had 'lately seen a man working a pneumatic drill there and wearing a deaf-aid'.

In private, John enjoyed scatology; but in judging whether a risqué joke might be passed as fit for *Spectator* readers he was more circum-spect than the editor, twenty years his junior. A friend whose son was at Winchester College showed him a circular the school had sent to all parents, advising them that fees were to be increased by a certain amount *per annum*. The typist had missed out one of the 'n's in the Latin phrase; and John's friend had written to the school to say that, if it was all the same to them, he would prefer to continue paying through the nose. 'I urged him to put the story in his column,' Lord Gilmour recalls, 'but he never did.'[73]

Some of the jokes were good old chestnuts. When President Truman was given an honorary degree at Oxford in 1956, John raked up the story of the American in England and the don. 'An American, refer-ring to the little colleges in the Turl, said he could never distinguish between Lincoln and Jesus. The don replied, "Very few Americans can."'[74] So many readers wrote in to say they had heard this years before that John tended to introduce jokes, in future, with 'Probably you have all heard this, but . . .' or 'If this appeared in *Punch* many years ago, you will, of course, tell me . . .' There was no need for such disclaimers when he treated his readers to Chaplinesque mishaps from his own life.

Last Sunday [he wrote in October 1955] I succumbed, not for the first time, to that shocking form of self-indulgence, reading my verse aloud to an audience. It was in part of the Royal Festival Hall, a sort of ante-room with accommodation for small audiences for unpopular things like poetry. The audience was marvellous, and I strutted about like a peacock, eaten

up with my own compositions and thrilled by an unwonted sense of ora-
torical power. Shall I go on the halls, I thought? Or stand for Parliament?
Suddenly my balloon was pricked. There in the middle of the second row
was a man reading a book. Well, I thought, perhaps he's following the
verses in the book itself. He must be a very keen student of my work. I
went on reciting with more animation still, and looked again and saw that
he was not reading my book, but some sort of travel pamphlet with photographs. In the interval I hurried down to the bar and was waylaid by
a young lady asking for an autograph. She was accompanied by the
pamphlet-reader. I made some pleasant remark to him, only to find that
he was a Turk who did not understand a word of English.[75]

In some of the columns the germ of a Betjeman poem is found. On
29 October 1954 John laments that 'Aldersgate Street Station as our
fathers and grandfathers, and, for younger readers, great-grandfathers
knew it, is to be destroyed . . . No longer will we be able to ascend those
dizzy heights of branching iron staircases to where the bombed refresh-
ment room reminds us of how once there used to be written, in white
china letters, on its plate-glass windows "Afternoon Teas a
Speciality".'[76] In an extra article on 'The City Churches' he wrote of
the models of old London which used to be in the London Museum
and which enabled one to imagine oneself back in the medieval City.
'With this picture of a walled city, with red roofs and white stone and
many turrets and a wide, slow-flowing Thames, held up from the sea
by the sluice of waters under London Bridge, leave Kensington and go
to Aldersgate Street.'[77] This sentence anticipates the fourth stanza of
his poem 'Monody on the Death of Aldersgate Street Station' –

> Then would the years fall off and Thames run slowly;
>   Out into marshy meadow-land flowed the Fleet:
> And the walled-in City of London, smelly and holy,
>   Had a tinkling mass house in every cavernous street.[78]

On 12 November 1954 John wrote:

I was watching an opening meet of foxhounds last week and interested to
see that the majority of the field were men. Foxhunting friends tell me that
I would witness the same phenomenon all over England. Yet whenever I see
a riding school cantering over a field in the wake of a weather-beaten riding
mistress . . . girls predominate. I hope this paragraph will cheer the parents
of horse-mad daughters. The mania generally dies down before marriage.[79]

Shortly afterwards he wrote 'Winthrop Mackworth Redivivus', which
includes these lines:

> I'm afraid that that Riding School did it,
>   The one where we sent her to stay;
> Were she horse-mad before, then she hid it
>   Or her analyst kept it at bay . . .[80]

At that date, John's own daughter, aged twelve, was 'horse-mad'.

John's poem 'A Lincolnshire Church' was published in *Selected Poems* (1948); but a 'City and Suburban' paragraph of August 1956 suggests the source of a line in it which Philip Larkin admired. 'I believe', John wrote, 'that Mr O.G.S. Crawford, the distinguished archaeologist, used to keep a photographic record of vandalisms he noticed when travelling around and he called it "Bloody Old Britain." '[81] In 'A Lincolnshire Church' John wrote:

> Dear old, bloody old England
> Of telegraph poles and tin,
> Seemingly so indifferent
> And with so little soul to win . . .[82]

Another *Spectator* paragraph indicates the origin of the first line of a later Betjeman poem. In August 1957 John wrote, 'Warwickshire is the county which Henry James called "unmitigated England". I was there last week for some Shakespeare plays.'[83] John's 'Great Central Railway: Sheffield Victoria to Banbury' begins:

> 'Unmitigated England'
>   Came swinging down the line
> That day the February sun
>   Did crisp and crystal shine . . .[84]

Most of the autobiographical vignettes in *The Spectator* were pure clowning; but at times a Pagliacci pathos showed through. In his opening paragraph on 31 August 1956 about his fiftieth birthday three days before he wrote:

Fifty. Not much longer for this world, every day more precious. I must begin cleaning up this earthly house so as to leave things tidy for my wife and children. And there it was that real frustration set in. I don't know whether it is the same with you as it is with me, but every time, as a self-employed person, I have income-tax demands, I have to sell a little more of my dwindling capital.[85]

It was heartfelt, but there at the end was the authentic *Spectator* voice. It did not occur to John that his column might be read by people with no capital to sell, living from hand to mouth. When he noticed such people at all, his sympathy was at best ambiguous. In August 1957 he walked around some new London council estates.

'The awful equality of it all is frightening,' a friend said to me. And that is true. If you are lucky enough to have one of these new workers' flats, there is not much chance of showing individuality. You will take your washing to the launderette on the ground floor with everyone else. Your kitchen will have the same units as everyone else's; your rooms will be the same as your neighbour's; only in the curtains you hang across the sheets of glass will you be able to be different.[86]

From the Stanley Arms pub in Pimlico, London ('neo-Regency inside and New Statesmanish young architects with their girls in tight trousers and mares'-tails')[87] he looked out on new blocks built by Westminster City Council and the recently built Elgar House, a building he liked, though 'maybe it has no place for someone like me . . .'.[88] Equality is a disagreeable proposition only to those on the upper side of inequality. John took it for granted that his readers had been at public schools. In January 1956 he wrote:

I do not think anyone will dare to answer the questions in print asked below, except to say that I am a snob and a cad for bringing up so tricky a subject. It would be hypocritical of you to say it does not interest you.

1. Apart from Harrow and Eton, which are the best public schools?
2. What do you mean by the 'best'? Answer this truthfully.
3. Is Rugby above Winchester?
4. Put these schools in their order: Sherborne, Uppingham, Tonbridge, Charterhouse, Wellington, Rugby, Winchester, Clifton, Marlborough, Shrewsbury, Haileybury, Gresham's, Lancing, Malvern, Cheltenham, Radley, Repton.
5. Do you equate co-education with specialization? i.e. is Bedales as good as Oundle?
6. Are Gordonstoun and Dartington public schools?
7. Can a grammar school be a public school?
8. Is a grammar school above a high school?
9. Where do denominational schools stand?
10. Is a day school with boarders, like Westminster, better than one all day-boys?
11. Apart from preparatory schools, which privately-run boarding schools are not public schools? Why not?
12. Are Scottish schools above English ones – apart from Harrow and Eton?[89]

Of course this was what the Mitford sisters would have called a 'tease'. John returned to the subject of schools in September 1956.

I remember Canon Demant[90] saying to me that as soon as a nation started discussing education it was a sign of decadence. Let me discuss it here. Is it still true that there are two roundabouts which never touch each other? The one, State school and red-brick university or 'student' at Oxford or Cambridge and a career in the Civil Service or local government with a pension at the end, the other private school, public school and an undergraduate at Oxford or Cambridge and luck or influence afterwards?[91]

This time a reader wrote in to charge John with snobbery – Graham Hough, a future Professor of English at Cambridge, educated at Prescot Grammar School.

Sir, – The point of Mr Betjeman's suburban drooling frequently escapes me: I am particularly baffled by his antithesis between a 'student' at Oxford or Cambridge and an undergraduate at Oxford or Cambridge. This distinction is unknown at Cambridge [Hough was then a fellow of Christ's College], and I should be glad to know what Mr Betjeman supposes it to be.[92]

Later, in his valedictory column of 1958, John wrote, 'I am even grateful to those many correspondents I have infuriated . . . I was particularly glad at one time to have stirred so placid a writer as Mr Graham Hough into a positively interesting fury.'[93]

John would probably have pleaded guilty to the charge of 'mischievous silliness' levelled at him by Hough. He ended one column: 'Is this all a bit arch and E.V. Lucas-y and 4th-Leaderish? Yes, it is, and all the better for that. This column is the home of lost causes.'[94] In 1956, at the height of the Suez crisis, he complained of people who cornered him and made him discuss politics.

Because I write in this paper, people assume that I share its Editor's views about Suez, and I expect if I had read them I would have shared them for a time, for I am always persuaded by the last argument I have heard. But I don't know what the views of this paper about Suez are, because I never read the political stuff in front. I take the *Spectator* to see whether there are any misprints in this column and for the book reviews and for dear old Strix and the angry letters.[95]

This airy assertion brought a sharp rebuke from Ian K. McDougall of San Francisco.

Sir, – I have just read, in your Christmas number, 'City and Suburban' by
Betjeman.

I have lost all respect for this dodo as of this moment. I would remind
him that 'that political stuff in front' is more than people's opinions. It is
the very essence of our survival in these modern times . . . BAD LAWS ARE
ALWAYS MADE BY GOOD PEOPLE WHO DON'T VOTE. How can
Betjeman expect to get support from all those from whom he seeks it, to
preserve old buildings and streets, if they share his views in relation to, shall
we say, election of borough councilmen, and if they feel that such 'political stuff' is not for them? Such blindness is folly of a supreme nature . . . To
the block with this hermit.[96]

Francis Schwarzenberger of New York sprang to John's defence: 'I just
cannot let the insults to Mr Betjeman . . . pass without comment . . .
Actually, Mr Betjeman pointed out that the world's difficulties, "the
political stuff" included, in all their vital significance, must not excuse
disregard or lack of care for the precious heritage of the nation which
will survive, God willing, the great international and political crises . . .
Let us hope and pray that Mr Betjeman continues his panoramic
perusal of our times from his peculiar point of vantage . . .'[97]

In one of his columns, John quoted Herbert Morrison's description
of the Victorian politician Charles Bradlaugh: 'a devout atheist'. In a
comparable oxymoron, John might have been described as 'militantly
apolitical'. As he saw it, he had been hired by Gilmour to entertain,
not to analyse or pontificate. At least a third of every 'City and
Suburban' column consisted of things that had struck John as quaint,
curious or comic. In February 1955 he noted:

At just about the time that I am writing this, Monday afternoon,
Parliament is transferring the Cocos Keeling Islands from the Crown
Colony of Singapore to the Government of Australia. The Cocos Keeling
Islands are too small to be marked on my atlas, but they have 552 people
on them, and I like to think that somewhere in the Colonial Office there is
a door with a man's name on it and 'Cocos Keeling Islands' printed under
it in brackets, and that somewhere on the Islands there is an English
Residency with portraits of former Residents round the dining-room
walls. I do not like to think of this Whitehall official returning disconso-
late on the Southern Electric to Esher tonight, his job gone . . .[98]

John was always intrigued by outlandish or recherché jobs. Having
been told by Dr Cyril Joad that there was an Agricultural Officer for
the County of London, he set out to find whether that post still
existed. He was referred to various other officials and pestered them

with queries about sending ducks to Dulwich, sheep to Bermondsey and a cow to Canonbury.[99] He telephoned the City Remembrancer to ask exactly what it was he had to remember. John's old school friend Sir Arthur Elton introduced him to G.W. Noakes, the official magic-lantern projectionist to the Royal Albert Hall. With Elton and Robert Aickman, of the Inland Waterways Association, John visited Noakes at Southend in 1956 to see the Noakesoscope invented by his father, D.W. Noakes, 'whose Dioramic Lectures delighted town hall and philosophical society audiences in the Nineties'.[100] John thought the Noakesoscope was better than Cinerama. ('Most magical effects are obtained, such as night falling on Leighton Buzzard.')[101]

John was no doubt right in thinking that most of his readers found of absorbing interest nice points of etiquette, snobbery and accent. It was the decade of Nancy Mitford's *Noblesse Oblige*, the guide to 'U' and 'Non-U' usage to which he contributed. In November 1954 he wished someone would publish a little book on the correct etiquette for typed letters.

Rich and influential people who write to me by typewriter leave, I notice, a blank at the top and bottom and write in 'My dear Betjeman' or 'My dear John' at the top in long hand, and also sign 'Yours sincerely' or 'With much love' in long hand above their signatures. Those who are frightened by their secretaries correct the typewritten part in ink. Those who frighten their secretaries either have the mistake rubbed out or the letter done again. But there are further subtleties, and I notice that employees of the BBC delight to put 'Dictated by . . . and signed in his absence by . . .' To them I always reply with a letter signed 'Written by his secretary and signed in her absence by J. BETJEMAN'.[102]

Etiquette was not just a matter of academic interest to John. Bad manners could goad him into a choleric outburst, as in October 1957.

'Excuse me,' said a lady to me when I was crossing Hammersmith Broadway. She elbowed me off the traffic island and asserted her rights on the zebra crossing in front of a bus. When people say 'Excuse me' I always reply 'No', and they look round, as this lady did, risking her life in doing so, in pained amazement. 'Excuse me' is only one of the phrases current today which has lost its original meaning. Today it means 'Get out of the way.' 'Can I help you, sir?' means 'What the hell are you doing here?'[103] 'With due respect' . . . means 'I have no respect for your opinions at all.' For years now 'To be frank' has meant 'To be unpardonably rude'.[104]

In the same column, John complained that on a visit to Kingsdown, a leafy suburb of Bristol, he had listened in vain for 'the intrusive liquid' which had once been common speech in that part of Bristol. 'Ernest Bevin had it. He used to put "l's" on to words ending with an "a" or an "o" – "idea-l", "banana-l" . . .'[105] John was fascinated by pronunciation. He could with equal ease mimic station announcers ('Chipnem', 'Margit', 'Ramsgit', 'East Grinstid')[106] or an old-fashioned City gent ('I orften see a putty gel in an orf-white bloose playing goff with an orf-cer feller, where I stay from Saturday to Monday. Just now I saw her going into an otel. She must have lorst her bloose in the larndry as the one she was wearing was cawfee coloured.')[107] (He missed out 'laylock' for 'lilac' and 'balcōny'.) On some points of pronunciation he sought his readers' advice. Which of the following was 'correct'?

> Marlybun, Marrerbun, Mary Lee Bone
> Paul Maul, Pal Mal, Pell Mell
> The Mal, The Maul, The Mell
> Brumpton, Brompton
> Hoban, Holeborn, Hollbun
> Suthuk, South Walk, Southwahk
> Grenidge, Grinach, Green Witch.[108]

The next week, Austin Duncan-Jones sent in the correct pronunciation for all the names (including 'Marryb'n') and David Leggatt, chief librarian of Greenwich Public Libraries, reminded John that Edward Lear made 'Greenwich' rhyme with 'spinach'.[109]

Enthusiastic 'audience participation' was part of the fun. Most weeks, readers' letters about the column were published. R. Lush, manager of the De Vere Hotel, Kensington, wrote: 'I am interested in the paragraph "Railway Sandwich-de-luxe" by your columnist John Betjeman. By what reasoning does he consider 7s 6d expensive for two rounds of tongue sandwiches and a pot of coffee?'[110] Another correspondent wrote: 'I am sure I will not be the only Australian to register protest against Mr Betjeman's remark that an "untidy car park surrounded by wooden shacks" would be in any way in keeping with the town of Wagga Wagga. I can only assume that Mr Betjeman has never seen Wagga . . .'[111] Other letters from less aggrieved readers entered into the spirit of John's badinage. In January 1957 he suggested an 'enjoyable exercise of the imagination', inventing characters for the names of villages and railway stations.

Harold Wood (Essex), I always think, is a most exemplary man of about forty who goes to the City every day and is fully insured and has a wife and two 'kiddiz'. Patrick Brompton (Yorks) is not so exemplary and I think he is in rep. and belongs to a rather decadent set in Wolverhampton. Leonard Stanley (Glos) is not his real name. His neighbour, Stanley Pontlarge (Worcs), is a plumber with a large walrus moustache and belly. Broughton Poggs (Oxon) has written some verse dramas of country life. Langton Maltravers (Dorset) is a BBC producer on the Light [Programme] but thinks he ought to be employed by the Third.[112]

After that appeared, the novelist Jocelyn Brooke wrote in:

Sir, – Surely Mr Betjeman's game of place names can be played in reverse?
   I, for one, am well acquainted with the charming village of Compton Burnett (Dorset) and its neighbour, Hodgson Burnett, nor should the visitor overlook Malcolm Muggeridge, famous for its annual folk-dancing festival (not to be confused with Nether Muggeridge). Cowper Powys (Merioneth) and Morgan Forster (Mon) are both well worth a visit; so is Townsend Warner (Bucks), noted for its ancient ducking-stool. Mr Betjeman would, I am sure, appreciate the *art nouveau* bar at Sackville West (the East station has no buffet); and connoisseurs may derive a similar frisson from Graham Greene, that seedy and shabby-genteel suburb between Walthamstow and Brentwood.[113]

John enjoyed talking to readers who talked back. He complained to Brian Inglis (so Inglis recalled) that 'he got no feed-back (not a term, I suspect, he would ever have used) from the *Telegraph* column'.*[114] But, always morbidly sensitive to criticism of any kind, John did not appreciate the brickbats that arrived with the bouquets. Candida remembers that 'He had become tired of the constant complaints about his articles that they printed in the *Spectator* . . .'[115] In October 1957 John wrote to Michael Berry asking whether he would commission a regular feature on architecture for the *Daily Telegraph*, with an illustration, 'which unfortunately I cannot put in the *Spectator*'.[116] Berry agreed to this and John resigned from *The Spectator* in January 1958 – although the first of his 'Men and Buildings' columns did not appear in the *Telegraph* until April, and the column did not become a regular commitment until May 1959.†

---

* It is not clear whether Inglis was referring to John's book reviews in the *Telegraph*, or to his later 'Men and Buildings' column. See the chapters on each in the third volume.
† See the chapter on 'Men and Buildings' in the third volume.

'This is the last paragraph I shall be writing in "City and Suburban",' John wrote in *The Spectator* of 10 January 1958. 'I have not been sacked, but the effort, week after week, of compiling this column is proving too much for me . . .'[117] On the same day, 'A Spectator's Notebook' paid tribute to him in an affectionate farewell.

'I should like to see John Betjeman added to his own casualty list,' a truculent correspondent informed the *Spectator* recently, but I wonder whether – now that 'City and Suburban' is to be with us no more – he will not come to regret his words . . . For myself (if a colleague may be permitted to write the *valete*) I have not always seen eye to eye with him about many of his enthusiasms . . . But I entirely agree with another correspondent who, in answer to a recent *Spectator* questionnaire, called him 'always constructive in his destructive criticism of official vandalism' . . . I suppose there could be no higher praise than to say that . . . unlike in the case of most columnists . . . the appointment of a successor has never even been considered. 'City and Suburban' *is* John Betjeman; that is all.[118]

TELEVISION PERSONALITY

I was not there at the end of your television programme so I did not have an opportunity of finding out what you thought about it. Does the medium interest you any more now that you have practical experience of it? I enjoyed your programme, and as we discussed it afterwards we all agreed that you had a Television personality capable of development.

Mary Adams, letter to John Betjeman, 19 June 1951

In 1959 *Punch* ran a series of autobiographical articles under the heading 'Turning Point'. Eminent people were asked to describe 'moments of crisis and redirection' in their lives. On 18 November the contributor was Mary Adams. Even then, on the brink of the 1960s, she was an exceptional figure – a woman with high rank in BBC Television. But she had been given similar power more than twenty years before: she was the first woman producer at the BBC.

Born at Hermitage, Berkshire, in 1898, Mary Adams had become a research scientist at Cambridge.[1] In 1928 she gave six talks on heredity on BBC radio and was 'seized by the teaching possibilities of broadcasting'.[2] She applied to join the BBC and was accepted. She recalled her first day on the staff:

> . . . I arrived at Savoy Hill one sunny Monday morning. The doors opened before me. Everyone sprang to attention as I entered. Charwomen rose from their kneeling, little lads saluted, striped trousers knocked at the knees. When I got into the lift I saw the reason why. I had preceded the boss: John Reith himself, in a frock coat.
>
> It took me no time at all to realise that (a) the boss mattered, (b) that women didn't.[3]

The disadvantage of her gender, in the male-dominated BBC, did not hold her back. In January 1937 she was appointed a producer in the still fledgling enterprise of television. Her *Times* obituary in 1984 was to describe her as 'one of the formative minds in the development of talks on television'. It portrayed her as 'vivacious, tenacious, persuasive, continually bubbling with ideas'.[4] At the same time, the obituarist did not disguise that some of Mary Adams's colleagues found her exasperating. 'She was a typical pioneer. Ever eager to press on to new ground, she would not stay to tidy up that on which she was at any moment standing. She had little use for formal procedures . . . She was the despair of administrators.'[5]

Luckily it was this rule-breaker, humorous and open to new ideas, who first invited John to appear on television, and arranged his programmes. On 31 May 1937 she wrote to him:

> I don't know whether you have seen the television screen, or whether its problems interest you, but I should very much like you to come up to Alexandra Palace [then the headquarters of BBC Television] and discuss with us the possibilities of this new medium.
>
> We have in front of us a period of experimentation, and we should like to think that you were interested in how it can best be used.[6]

Unfortunately, John turned up at Alexandra Palace on a day she was away. 'I was greatly disappointed to have missed you,' she wrote on 13 July, 'but I hear you provided those who remained with a certain amount of fun . . . It occurred to me that it might be possible to give a television programme showing how Guide Books are made.'[7] On the same day she sent him a second note: 'If you don't like the Guide Book idea, what about having a shot at a *Museum*?'[8] In reply, John wrote, with a visionary prescience:

> I was interested by television. But I feel . . . that these initial stages are a little boring. The value of television seems to me to be its possibility of outside work. I mean, when television cameras can show to millions of people actual scenes of shooting and dying in Spain, then it will become the most valuable propaganda medium in the world. When it can actually drive down the Great Worst Road picking up the noises, and then catch the silence of a cathedral close, it will awaken people to the repulsiveness of their surroundings. Beside this, 'How to Make a Guide Book' seems an unimportant thing, but more important to me than Museums which I simply loathe – except the Soane, Saffron Walden, Dulwich Art Gallery and minor provincial collections.[9]

He added that he would like to try to make a programme on guidebooks, but he reminded Mary Adams that she and he had last met to discuss the possibility of a radio series on parish churches. 'I would have provided an excellent series of talks in my opinion. Parish churches are my pet hobby. As it was, you chose Mr Greening Lambourne [*sic*, for Lamborn],[10] a dull and inaccurate man and I was interviewed and turned down by your assistant – a Mr Wilson with a pink art-silk tie, unless I am mistaken.'[11]

An essential element of an English upbringing, in John's generation, was the undesirability of ever revealing to others that one was upset. There was as yet no tremor in the stiff upper lip. Showing emotion – 'getting in a flap' – was for 'volatile' foreigners. In this respect, John was un-English. When he was hurt, he showed it. He almost flaunted his vulnerability, though with an attitude of 'How dare they?' Mary Adams knew how to smooth the ruffled feathers. She agreed with John that the choice of Greening Lambourn had been a *big* mistake. She was still keen that John should be filmed in a museum; but, after sending her assistant, Andrew Miller Jones, 'nosing about the Soane Museum', she resignedly reported to John, 'Lovely stuff, but a Curator who doesn't like publicity.'[12] So it was decided to proceed with *How to Make a Guide-Book*.

On 14 September 1937 – just a week before the programme went out – John sent Mary Adams his ideas for it. The setting, he suggested, should resemble a village hall. There should be a blackboard. He also asked her to procure these objects:

a good-sized Cornish pastie
a waste paper basket
a hanging oil lamp.[13]

He enclosed a sketch, with self-portrait, to show what he meant.

John received eight guineas for this first television appearance. In her instructions to her crew, Mary Adams wrote: '[The programme] Opens on Betjeman sitting on bench with large basket on the ground in front of him. Various objects will be withdrawn from the basket and shown. On two occasions Mr Betjeman will rise and draw on blackboard near him. If this is on a separate camera, cue will be given by producer.'[14] Two years later, when asked to summarize John's performance of 1937, Andrew Miller Jones wrote:

John Betjeman drew us several types of tourists, and suggested the appropriate guide book for them. The bulk of the talk, however, dealt with a guide book for ordinary folk. He showed a milking stool, a piece of Cotswold stone, some wild flowers, a weather cock made from the hub of a cart wheel, and several other objects of interest which are not referred to

in the average guide book containing a preponderance of information on ecclesiastical architecture.[15]

Mary Adams sent John a 'still' of his performance, as a souvenir. He wrote back:

Thank you so much for the excruciatingly funny photograph. I shall certainly have it framed. It is the maddest thing I ever saw.

But it gives me an idea. Might not I become a sort of Harry Tate of Television and give talks on 'How to Make a Motor Car' in a nice intimate style, using objects even more ridiculous than those I used for 'How to Make a Guide Book'? I might do 'How to Make a Television Set', 'What to Do with Old Razor Blades', 'A New Use for Carriages', 'How to make an Omelette', 'Interior Decoration in the Falkland Islands', etc. It would be most enjoyable. Think of the objects one could select.[16]

In 1971 Mary Adams sent John a photograph of himself advertising that first television programme of his over thirty years before. He wrote back:

I so well remember coming to the Ally Pally [Alexandra Palace] and you giving me my first job in telly, and I suppose that man on the blackboard which was one of my drawings, was there to show you the boring sort of antiquary who looks at fonts and can't see the wood for the trees, and I think those extraordinary objects by which I am surrounded are there to show that guide books ought to be about significant objects like weather vanes, whatever their dates. It's the most happy memory for me, my darling Directress, for I remember, too, how one used to look out from your room on to that pathetic little garden, surrounded by hurdles which Mr Middleton had made; and was I with you that day when we walked into the depths of the Palace, and found ourselves in a huge theatre, and Gracie Fields[17] rehearsing to an empty house?[18]

John took part in a few more television programmes before the service closed down for the duration of the war. A photograph shows him blindfolded as a participant in a 'Tactile Bee' at Alexandra Palace, with Christopher Stone as master of ceremonies and Andrew Miller Jones as scorer.[19] (The object of the game was to identify things, such as a lady's elasticated swimming costume, from their feel.) But his television career did not really take off again until the early 1950s, when George Barnes was promoted to be Head of Television. On 3 June 1951 John wrote to Barnes, 'I am coming to Ally Pally on Tuesday morning for a lot of underpaid tripe I am doing with Griggers [Geoffrey Grigson]. I hope I shall see you.'[20] John and Grigson were to discuss guidebooks – John as joint editor of Murray's Guides,[21] Grigson as general editor of the 'About Britain' guides published for the Festival of Britain that year by Collins. The producer, David Bryson, wrote to warn John that he would be needed from 10.15 a.m. to 3.20 p.m., because of 'the Satanic time-consuming powers of Television'.[22] Bryson took the precaution of booking a table in the canteen, preceded by 'hospitality' in Dressing Room 12 – 'Whisky, gin, sherry, vermouth, lime, orange, soda and twenty cigarettes'.[23]

Mary Adams was still involved in television. On 19 June she wrote to John, 'I was not there at the end of your television programme so I did not have an opportunity of finding out what you thought about it. Does the medium interest you any more now that you have had practical experience of it? I enjoyed your programme and as we discussed it afterwards we all agreed that you had a Television personality capable of development.'[24] She suggested he might like to appear fortnightly over three months, adding: 'I thought that John Betjeman talking about something that had excited him during the week might make quite a dent on viewers. You could choose something you hated or something you liked.'[25]

John replied that he did not want to commit himself to a fortnightly series. 'Strain, lack of experience and finance are some of the considerations.'[26] What would interest him, he wrote, would be to make a film about a church – say Harefield or Tottenham, both in Middlesex. 'I was very interested when you said to me that you thought there was far too much talk and not enough silence in television. A church might enable one to use silence . . .'[27] On receiving this, Mary Adams, who did not give up easily, sent George Barnes a memo: 'You see what John Betjeman says in his letter. It looks pretty final, but could you have a word with him please?'[28] Barnes did so, but John repeated that he would prefer to film a church. On 14 August 1951 he wrote to Barnes from Alderney, where he and his family were staying with T.H. White:[29] 'I will be back in England on Sept. 1 from Denmark. I will then visit a church. I think Tottenham is a good choice. But I must see incumbent & see church before writing a detailed script.'[30] On 20 August, Pat Stapley in Barnes's office minuted that John would be starting on his script about 9 September.[31] After that, there is no further mention of the proposed Tottenham film in the BBC archives. John may have had second thoughts about it; and Mary Adams, in her memo of 25 June to Barnes, had deterrently pointed out that the kind of outside broadcast John was proposing would require 'expensive lighting'.

In September 1951 a new idea was put to John by Peter de Francia of Television Talks: would he like to interview the architect Basil Spence,[32] who had been commissioned to rebuild the bombed Coventry Cathedral?[33] John eagerly accepted; but on 12 October de Francia noted that Spence was 'reluctant to have any discussion concerning the proposed building'.[34] It may just have been that he feared a grilling by John – a notorious scourge of contemporary architects – as he later agreed to be interviewed by Rooney Pelletier, a BBC staff officer who later rose to be a Controller.[35]

George Barnes continued to canvass the idea of bringing John into television. In 1952 he goaded his Programmes Controller, Cecil McGivern, into taking action. McGivern was described by the veteran television critic Peter Black as 'the true architect of BBC Television . . . a short white-faced man with greying hair and thick-lensed glasses, a compulsive smoker, a prickly and difficult man to know unless one was close to him in the work in which he so passionately believed. To him television was the most important communicator ever put into man's hands . . .'[36] On 14 July 1952 McGivern wrote to his assistant,

Stephen McCormack: 'D Tel B [Barnes] is very anxious that John Betjeman be used in television somewhere . . . Can you please devise a means of using him on a film sequence in *London Town* or *About Britain*, a sequence involving a historic home, a castle, a cathedral etc?'[37] These were two topical 'soft news' programmes, both presented by Richard Dimbleby,[38] the best-known television journalist of the day.

McCormack wrote to John, who invited him to come to Wantage on 10 or 11 September and stay the night if he wished. 'Say what you look like – a beard? A moustache? A red tie? 6 feet high?'[39] The visit was made, but on 17 October John wrote to McCormack:

> How nice our interview was, how amiable, how inspiring, but since then not a word from your script writer, not a sound on the telephone, not a knock on the front door . . .
> Yours sincerely,
> John Barnsbury Ally Pally Betjeman, M. San. I.[40]

McCormack apologized and asked John to present a feature about lamp posts on *London Town*. That was one of John's pet subjects; but now his mother was dying in Bath and he had to turn the idea down. But in 1954 he made the earliest programme of his that is preserved in the BBC's recorded archives – *Conversation Piece*, a televised chat with Lord David Cecil and A.L. Rowse.[41] In the same year he agreed to take part in a programme called *Where on Earth*. Inviting him to join Peter Fleming and Merlin Minshall, David Attenborough, then a talks producer, told him that the idea was to show 'much-travelled people' pictures of places and buildings to identify.[42] John was ill-travelled, except in England, but knew he would be able to give value by jokes, aesthetic verdicts and ridiculous guesses. Sir David Attenborough recalls that one photograph was of burning-ghats in Benares, 'all temples, turrets, burning pyres and naked people washing themselves in the Ganges'. After the rest of the team had rather surprisingly failed to identify this scene, John, 'after a moment of bafflement, responded triumphantly, "Got it – the Thames just above Maidenhead!"'[43]

John liked this kind of panel programme which required him to do no gruelling research, but just live by his wits. In November 1955 Nancy Thomas, a production assistant on Television Talks, asked him to take part in an 'art' version of the popular quiz *Animal, Vegetable, Mineral?*[44] The show, which ran from 1952 to 1958, was a brainchild of Mary Adams, who had adapted it from an American programme called *What in the World?*[45] Museums and galleries submitted objects from their collections, challenging the panel of the night to identify them. Dr Glyn Daniel chaired the series, but its star was his fellow archaeologist Sir Mortimer Wheeler, craggily handsome, mustachioed and bombastic. Wheeler said: 'It is no good picking up something and saying "This is a Samoan cake mould" – viewers want to see how you arrived at your decision. They are interested in watching your process of thought.'[46] He had a large following, especially among women. Bernard Levin claimed that one lady, having heard that Sir Mortimer liked sherry, always stood a glass of it on her television set if he was present in the box below.[47] When John was on the panel with Wheeler, the two showmen egged each other on in a kind of contest of Edwardian courtliness. However, in 1955 Mrs Thomas wanted John to chair a session in which Sir Gerald Kelly, Sir James Mann and Sir Owen Morshead would try to identify paintings. John replied: 'I shall be delighted to act as chairman. Less embarrassing than not knowing the answers.'[48] The same month, Marie Bingham wrote to him:

> In the *Twice Twenty* programme for older women on 12th December, we are hoping to present an eight or nine minute spot on 'What Shall I Buy Him?' This of course refers to Christmas presents, and we wondered if you would find it amusing to air your views on the 'horrors' that you must have received in the past, and indeed may receive in the future.[49]

The sculptor Michael Ayrton[50] was to appear with John in the programme. In December John received five guineas for discussing a proposed Edinburgh car park with Malcolm Muggeridge.[51]

Though in demand for off-the-cuff contributions of this kind, he was still not being offered by the BBC the kind of television programmes he wanted to make. What sharply changed the BBC's mind was the growing threat from commercial television from the mid-1950s on. John's old friend Kenneth Clark was head of the Independent Television Authority; another old friend, Sidney Bernstein, founded Granada Television. And Jack Beddington of Shell was still around to help until his death in 1959.

The Shell films which John made with Peter Mills had the running title *Discovering Britain*. John wrote to John Piper in July 1955, 'I don't think I've enjoyed anything so much since our Shell and Murray Guide days. Of course the secret is keeping the camera on the move, whether looking at a flower, or a box pew or a painted ceiling.'[52] He described Peter Mills as 'a fast motor maniac', but thought him 'just the chap for these films and as funny as you and I are in the same way . . .'.[53] Paul and Candida went on location for some of the filming.[54]

George Barnes saw the Shell films. Annoyed that the competition had been allowed to steal a march on him, he gave orders that every reasonable inducement was to be offered John to persuade him to make television films. A programme on parish churches was commissioned.[55] For the first time, BBC viewers were to see John's arts as a cicerone: the way he took off his shapeless hat and gazed reverently upwards before entering a church; the conspiratorial gesture with which he beckoned them into the gloom to peer at a carved bench-end. On 22 February 1956, Barnes gave his initial opinion of the film in a memo to the producer, John Read.

> I enjoyed my first view of this film today. I felt that the commentary was a little bit didactic, but I can see the difficulty of finding a theme for a subject so diverse as this. I am sure you were right to concentrate on the churches of one part of the country . . .
>
> I should much enjoy to screen this film for Betjeman with you present. At the same time could we not borrow prints of his Shell films and see the whole lot through together?[56]

A new series was planned on 'The Englishman's Home' – meaning stately homes. 'The building', John told Barnes, 'should be more important than the commentator who should let the building speak for itself as much as possible and draw people's attention to what they might not notice, not emphasize the obvious . . .'[57] John was to receive 50 guineas a programme; but after filming at Syon House and Uppark, he wrote to Miss Knight of Programme Bookings to argue that this was not enough. He pointed out that for a 'light entertainment' programme he received a minimum of 25 guineas, usually with a lunch and drink thrown in and only half an hour's work, with perhaps a quarter of an hour's rehearsal. 'All is smooth and merry and well paid.'[58] But for an 'Englishman's Home' programme, he had to visit the house with the producer to work out which rooms should be filmed ('a day and very often a long journey by train'); then spend two hours at the studio dubbing the preliminary film ('a whole morning'); then on the day of the transmission he had to be at the house in question for most of the day, with two half-hour rehearsals.[59] As a result of this remonstrance, his fee was raised to £60 a programme. Three further houses were filmed: Berkeley Castle, Castle Ashby and Tower House, Kensington, with its eccentric Victorian décor by William Burges – the house that was to be bequeathed to him in 1962.

The casual television work that he found so untaxing and congenial continued to be offered. In 1956 the BBC asked John's old school friend Anthony Blunt, director of the Courtauld Institute, whether he would take part in an 'architectural' *Animal, Vegetable, Mineral?* at the Soane Museum with John and Sir John Summerson.[60] He replied:

'I hate *Animal, Vegetable, Mineral?* more than anything in the world and have always refused to do it, but the constitution of the panel is tempting, and so is the idea of doing architecture.'[61] He agreed to appear. In December 1956 Glyn Daniel retired as chairman of the programme, and Nancy Thomas asked John if he would take over, at thirty guineas a programme. He replied: 'My dear thing, I should love it. It is money for jam and it is a pleasure.'[62]

PRESERVATIONIST'S PROGRESS

John Betjeman was anxious about the effect of boisterous schoolchildren on certain pleached limes, a well-trained fig, a wistaria and a tulip tree. He allowed his anxiety to be published . . .

John-Paul Flintoff, *Comp: A Survivor's Tale*, London 1999 edn.

In August 1950 John launched what was to become one of his most tenacious crusades, in a *Times* letter headed 'UGLY LAMP POSTS'. He was sure he was not the only one to object to 'the present craze for erecting lamp posts like concrete gibbets with corpse lights dangling off them in old country towns'. He had seen a catalogue of some of these standards which advertised on its cover that the contents had been 'passed by the Royal Fine Art Commission'. Could it really be true that the Commission approved their being set up in old and beautiful towns?[1]

In 1951, almost twenty years after the fight to rescue Carlton House Terrace from Sir Reginald Blomfield's plans, he again took the lead in a campaign to save the building. The Ministry of Works had asked the architect Louis de Soissons to incorporate part of the Terrace in a new Foreign Office building. John wrote to *The Times* on 8 February: 'The new design looks top-heavy on Nash's Doric plinth. It overpowers Benjamin Wyatt's beautifully related Duke of York's column, sentinel between the terraces. It is ridiculous to say that "the essential character of Nash's work has been preserved".' On 12 February Correlli Barnett, then an undergraduate at Exeter College, Oxford, and later the author of books on government and war, wrote to *The Times* to support John, calling the proposed de Soissons additions 'lifeless neo-Georgian attics'. A letter from Sir Alfred Bossom appeared on 17 February. As an architect, he had built skyscrapers in New York. As an MP he had been, like William Paling, the object of one of Churchill's witticisms ('Bossom? Neither one thing nor the other').[2] Bossom wrote as one who had lived at Carlton House Terrace for the past twenty-five years. Lady Thatcher has described how in that year, 1951, she and Denis Thatcher held their wedding reception in Bossom's 'beautiful flat' there.[3] Bossom thought the alterations would be 'seriously detrimental to the building's dignity.'

On 23 February Lord Rea complained of the inadequate opportunity given to the public 'to digest and pronounce upon' Government plans of this kind. 'Such schemes seem to be produced *ex cathedra* on these aesthetic matters as if they were departmental trivia to be put into operation tomorrow morning or next week.' The pressure building up had its effect. On 20 April 1951 the Town Planning Committee told the Minister of Works that the appearance of the existing Carlton House Terrace building should be retained 'substantially intact'. Later, de Soissons was asked to modify his plans.

In September 1952 John and others, including Frederick Etchells and the Bishop of Oxford, recorded that on the next Sunday, the centenary of A.W.N. Pugin's death, the Rev. B.F.L. Clarke, author of *Nineteenth Century Church Builders*, would preach Pugin's memorial sermon in the church of Tubney, Berkshire (1848), one of the architect's few Anglican designs. They wanted to raise £1,000 to restore the church.[4] The sermon and the appeal symbolized the growing movement to rehabilitate the Victorians.

There was another side to the medallic image of John Betjeman, gallant preserver of Britain's heritage. Sometimes his mission was not so much to save the old as to prevent the new. In this rôle he could seem just a benighted reactionary. In February 1953 he and Osbert Lancaster appeared together in a *Times* news story, as objectors to the proposal of the LCC to acquire a site of eight and a quarter acres at Campden Hill, Kensington, London, for the construction of a secondary school for 2,200 children. At a public inquiry, Lancaster, supported by John, protested against the provision of 'huge permanent schools that would be but partially occupied after a few years'.[5] This was an argument they did not win. Holland Park Comprehensive was built and became the most famous school of its kind in the country. Forty-five years later, in his half-historical, half-autobiographical book *Comp*, John-Paul Flintoff gave a bilious account of the early opposition to the school, at which he was a pupil from 1979 to 1986. He quoted some of the letters from rich residents of Campden Hill to local papers. One described the school as 'a ghastly, gargantuan gasometer'; another as 'an educational abortion, a vast factory, mass-producing units for the prefabrication of the classless dictatorship of the proletariat'.[6] Flintoff singled out John for special ridicule.

In the best traditions of middle-class protest, the school's opponents founded a pressure group, the Campden Hill Preservation Society. Members included the South African High Commissioner, the widow of a former governor of the Bank of England and the future Poet Laureate, John Betjeman. All of them opposed the idea of grubby teenaged rowdies, and angular, 'modern' municipal buildings, popping up in their midst – but each of them had other arguments, too. The South African Commission, London apologists for a regime founded upon racial segregation, can't, presumably, have been chuffed at the thought of 'blecks' mixing with whites. Lady Norman opposed the plan because it involved a compulsory purchase order on her own home, Thorpe Lodge. Here, after a hard day in Threadneedle Street, Her Ladyship's late husband Baron (Montagu) Norman of St Clere had tried to take his mind off the complexity of the gold standard, and the sheer effort involved in keeping sterling a hard currency; he'd sit with Her Ladyship, beside the grand Medici fireplace, cheerily admiring the works of art they had collected, or the rare species of tree and flower they'd assembled in the garden.

And that's where the conservationist poet stepped in: John Betjeman was anxious about the effect of boisterous schoolchildren on certain pleached limes, a wall-trained fig, a wistaria and a tulip tree. He allowed his anxiety to be published, but after a public inquiry the purchase order was pushed through.[7]

In May 1954 W.M. Atkins, Librarian of St Paul's Cathedral, and A.J. Macdonald, who had the oddly self-contradictory title Rural Dean of the City of London, suggested in *The Times* that the City churches which had been bombed should not be rebuilt and that their sites should be sold to provide money for new churches elsewhere.[8] John wrote in protest against this idea – 'as one of thousands of Anglican laymen who work in London and as a member of the church council of one of the guild churches in the City . . .'.[9]

No one will deny the urgent need for churches on new building estates, but I am sure it is an unadventurous and too worldly policy for the Church to rob Peter to pay Paul . . .

To assume that because the nation is not at the moment given to church-going such will always be the state and we should therefore sell our churches is surely a denial of the Christian virtue of hope.[10]

When John pleaded for a church to be spared, he could do so, sincerely, on two grounds: it was fine architecture, and it was also the House of God. More sceptical preservationists might envy him the faith which gave an extra fervour to his pleas; but sometimes the demands of the Church conflicted with those of architecture, and it is noticeable that, whenever that happened, John always found reasons to take the side of architecture.[11] The divergence of interests was particularly acute in the case of Holy Trinity Church, Leeds. In October 1954 Lord Rosse and Sir Mortimer Wheeler wrote to *The Times* to denounce the diocesan pastoral committee of Ripon, which was seeking to demolish the church to pay for 'a scheme of pastoral reorganization'. The church was, the correspondents wrote, a noble building by William Halfpenny, built in 1726–27. On 27 October, Father Jonathan Graham of Leeds wrote to put the opposing case. He thought that the choice was between 'a living Church ministering to the needs of the living and a museum piece . . .'. As we have seen, John wrote a poem in *The Spectator* attacking the Archdeacon of Leeds over his plans.* He also wrote to *The Times*, acidly suggesting that 'great buildings of the past, like Holy Trinity, Leeds, are a more lasting monument to the Christian faith than bishops and archdeacons . . .'.[12] On 9 November 1954 a *Times* leader on the church commented that 'There will be widespread relief if second thoughts prevail' – as indeed they did.

In April 1955 the Inland Waterways Association appealed for £25,000 for a campaign against the closure of canals. The next day, C. Dexter Watts of Stroud, Gloucestershire, wrote to *The Times* to point out that nearly all the National Coal Board's output was rail-borne. A rail strike was threatened and, Watts wrote, canals would be the obvious alternative transport – 'except that many canals are rapidly falling into disrepair from sheer neglect'.[13] In May, Lionel Curtis, John's old champion at the Oxford Preservation Trust, wrote to *The Times* without consulting John first, 'Mr John Betjeman should receive support from everyone who enjoys the best form of holiday, i.e., camping out by waterway . . . We should all join in Mr Betjeman's movement to prevent Parliament from taking from us one of our best amenities.'[14] John, surprised to find himself suddenly hailed as the head of a movement, wrote on 18 May:

> I am glad to learn that Mr Lionel Curtis joins us in wanting to save the Oxford Canal. As a canal enthusiast he will also want to save the Kennet and Avon Canal, whose beam engine at the summit near Bedwyn, Wiltshire, still pumps the water as it did in the eighteenth century . . . But I am not the instigator of the public movement to save our canals. Mr Curtis should join the Inland Waterways Association, 35 Great James's [*sic*, for James] Street, London WC1, whose founder is Mr Robert Aickman and whose president is Sir Alan Herbert.

* See Chapter 30, ' "City and Suburban" '.

Lionel Curtis's elevating John into leader of the canals campaign is the first example of a trait that was to become endemic, and later chronic, in British preservation – the idea that no respectable campaign could afford to be without John's name. The enemies of conservation were thus able to depict him as a sort of 'Rentaprotest'; even his friends at *Private Eye* satirized him as bleating, 'It's those awful *developers*, old thing . . .' His main contribution to the canals campaign was made in 1974 when, in the presence of Queen Elizabeth the Queen Mother and Robert Aickman, he declaimed a specially composed poem at the opening of the Upper Avon at Stratford.[15]

In December 1955 he was appointed to the art commission of Westminster Cathedral, and Cambridge University announced that he was to be Rede Lecturer the next year. In January 1956 he wrote with Nevill Coghill, C. Day-Lewis, Gerald Finzi and Ralph Vaughan Williams to deplore the Arts Council's decision to close down all its regional offices. 'A central control, we fear, will have the same effect as an absentee landlord.'[16]

As his fiftieth birthday approached, John needed all his new-found kudos in the bruising campaign to save the Imperial Institute, London, a building of 1887–93 by Thomas Edward Collcutt. There was a Cold War drive to match the Soviet Union's technology; the Government had decided to demolish the Imperial Institute to make way for a more spacious block. John wrote to *The Times* on 13 February 1956: 'If this masterpiece is to be taken down by the Government it will surely be the first time a British Government has committed such a crime for many years.' Even Hugh Casson, who as a contemporary architect was not always on John's side in conservation debates, was moved to write to *The Times*: 'Sir, I protest. The Imperial Institute is not, as its would-be destroyers would suggest, just another quaint old crock beloved by a few perverse "Victoriamaniacs". It is unquestionably a masterpiece, one of the finest buildings of its period not only in England but in Europe.'[17] But R. Long of the Imperial Institute strongly supported the Government's decision to demolish 'this anachronism', and suggested that the 'Victorian sentimentalists' should be left 'to contemplate the splendours of the Albert Memorial'.[18] Nikolaus Pevsner wrote in February 1956 pleading for 'a new start on the site'.[19] But, although the tower was spared, the rest of Collcutt's building was torn down. In an outburst of contrition for having promoted the Modern Movement, P. Morton Shand, writing to John two years later, singled out the new Institute building, with its offensive 'cladding', as a prime example of the horrors to which the Movement had led. 'Thank heavens you were able to save the tower of the Imperial Institute, but just look at the accepted model of the sort of penitentiary cantonment which is going to surround it!'[20]

Albert Bridge, spanning the Thames between Cheyne Walk and the western boundary of Battersea Park, was threatened in May 1957. The LCC wanted to demolish it and build a larger bridge. 'The structure has its modest degree of loveliness,' an LCC spokesman said, 'but is regarded as having ceased to be a useful bridge for purposes of carrying modern traffic.'[21] Built in 1873, Albert Bridge was the second-oldest of the ten bridges maintained by the LCC between Hammersmith and Waterloo Bridge. Only Westminster Bridge, opened in 1862, was older. The LCC appointed the engineers Rendel, Palmer and Tritton to report on the matter.

John's friend Richard Church, the poet and novelist, wrote to *The Times* that he had known the bridge since his childhood. 'This fairy-tale structure is part of the aesthetic character of the approach to that unique marshland where William Blake and subsequent writers lived . . . Without the Albert Bridge, Battersea will lose much of its distinction. This graceful signature in suspended iron gives an authority to the Park, and an introduction to Chelsea. A concrete bridge can never work with such grace . . .'[22] On 7 June I.D. Hill of the Royal College of Science wrote: 'It seems to me that the retention of the Albert Bridge because your correspondent enjoyed swinging on it when he was young is carrying democracy too far.'[23] The letter contained less amusingly disobliging remarks. John swung in to Church's – and the bridge's – defence.

I question the statement of your correspondent of June 7, Mr Hill, that it is a sign of progress when a nation destroys the buildings of the days of greatness. I cannot believe he wants this country to be all airports, glass towers and sodium lights . . .

He ends his letter by bringing democracy into the argument. It will be a sign of a return to democracy when the aesthetic opinions of scientists are not always preferred to those of people who have been educated in the liberal arts.[24]

J.E. Rupp of Chelmsford commented on this: 'Why drag in the Imperial Institute, glass towers and sodium lights when a clear analogy is at hand? I thought the Battle of Albert Bridge was fought – and lost – at Waterloo.'[25] (He was referring to the demolition of the old Waterloo Bridge in 1934.)* But the Battle of Albert Bridge was not lost. Perhaps less through Church's and John's eloquence than through the disinclination of the influential residents of Cheyne Walk

* See Chapter 23, 'A Preservationist in the Making'.

to have increased traffic thundering over a big new concrete bridge near their front doors, the LCC scheme was abandoned. Today the bridge remains, festooned with fairy lights at night – a Whistlerian vision.

As the 1950s advanced, John found that more and more often he was resisting threats to such Victorian structures as the Imperial Institute and Albert Bridge. By now, the merits of good eighteenth-century architecture were generally acknowledged. Thanks largely to his proselytizing in verse and broadcasts, there had even been a slight shift in public opinion on the Victorians. We get some idea of what the general public thought about Victorian architecture in the Fifties from Agatha Christie's murder novel of 1952, *They Do It with Mirrors*.

> 'Have you been to Stonygates before?'
> 'No, never. I've heard a great deal about it, of course.'
> 'It's pretty ghastly, really,' said Gina cheerfully. 'A sort of Gothic monstrosity. What Steve calls Best Victorian Lavatory period. But it's fun, too, in a way.'[26]

In 1952, then, an intelligent lay person probably found Victorian architecture ugly. (In that year, John wrote: 'Everybody is busy running down the Victorians';[27] a *New Yorker* cartoon of four years earlier showed two girls visiting a man's apartment littered with Victoriana. 'Don't admire anything,' one of the girls whispers to the other. 'He might give it to you.')[28] But at the same time the character in Christie's novel allows the possibility that a Victorian building can be 'fun', can even be regarded with affection. ('"Hideous, isn't it?" said Gina affectionately.')[29] Even this small concession suggested that the public's mind was not absolutely closed to the appreciation of Victoriana. However, the enthusiasts for Victorian buildings were still a small group and the words 'Albert Memorial' were still good for a laugh. John and his pro-Victorian friends came to realize that architecture of the later nineteenth century needed its own pressure group to fight for it. In 1957 they founded the Victorian Society.

In October 1957 John was once again called on to defend John Nash stucco – not, this time, Carlton House Terrace, but the terraces of Regent's Park. On 19 October he ambushed the Crown Commissioners, in a *Times* letter signed by a formidable list of *eminenti* – William Holford, Ralph Vaughan Williams, Lord Mottistone, Arthur Bryant, Kenneth Clark, Richard Costain, Philip Hendy (director of the National Gallery), Basil Burton, Henry Moore, Basil Spence and Woodrow Wyatt. They understood that the Commissioners were on the brink of announcing a decision on the future of the terraces.

The letter continued in a tone of sweet reasonableness: 'Charged as they are with the responsibility of prudent estate management, it may well be that a part of [the Commissioners'] decision will be to pull down all or some of the terraces and use the sites for more profitable development, perhaps new blocks of flats or offices.'[30] But, if that was what the Commissioners thought, they must think again. The signatories felt that the Nash façades were designed to be seen as a whole, and 'would lose much of their attraction and merit if they [were] even partially mutilated'.[31] Not all art-lovers shared this view. On 22 October, R. Gainsborough, editor of *Art News and Review*, wrote, 'These gloomy terraces have overshadowed the park for long enough; built in imitation stone for an upper class . . . they have outlived their utility. Not only are the buildings worn out, but the aesthetic on which they are founded has outlived its day.' He wanted London to be rid of 'this pastiche of the Acropolis'.

In the top *Times* letter of 24 October, John replied with scathing irony.

How shocking it is, to carry the arguments of your correspondent of today, Mr Gainsborough, a stage further, that so many outmoded memorials of our decadence survive in London alone: St Paul's Cathedral, for instance, with its wasteful dome, and those of Wren's City churches built in imitation of Italian architects who in their turn imitated Greece.

If he finds the Nash Terraces gloomy, I dread to think of what he has to say about the Temple, Somerset House, Queen Anne's Gate, and other buildings of an age earlier than Nash which we have foolishly allowed to survive. As for Eaton and Belgrave Squares and towns like Cheltenham and Brighton, built in the stucco which your correspondent and the late Sir Reginald Blomfield and John Ruskin so deeply disapprove, such offensive memorials of class distinction should obviously be destroyed.

In his letter, Gainsborough had said that building is an act of faith in the future and that he had great faith in the power of modern architecture to create something worth crossing the oceans to visit. John commented:

Bucklersbury House, at present rising to dwarf the City of London, certainly shows great faith in future rents, and such glorious structures as the new building in St James's Park with the art school fish engraved on its spandrels show the care we can take over detail today.

I see your correspondent is the editor of a paper about art if not architecture. Certainly his views, if not original, are at any rate like the sillier ones of the Victorian Age with which I, Sir, am sometimes malevolently connected.

The modernist architect Maxwell Fry, John's old adversary (who later called him 'a bloody nuisance'),[32] wrote on the same day: 'In the past 25 years we have developed an architecture to fit our needs, and if it is not good enough for Regent's Park it never will be.' Stella Margetson of St John's Wood, London, disagreed: 'Alas, Britain cannot "build it". Atomic power stations, perhaps – but the "pastiche" of American, Swedish or Le Corbusier concrete and glass favoured by modern architects does not add up to an English style of domestic architecture.'[33] T. Bedford suggested that the buildings in Regent's Park should be gutted but the outer shells kept[34] – and this was precisely the compromise later reached.

John's campaign to save the Regent's Park Terraces showed that he had learned from his failure, four years earlier, to prevent Magdalen College creating a 'suburban' rose garden in the High Street, Oxford.* Now he mobilized all the media. The young presenter Woodrow Wyatt, himself a kinsman of Regency architects,[35] made a plea for the terraces on a television news programme and elsewhere. Almost thirty years later, in 1986, Wyatt – by now the Toad of Toad Hall of his generation,[36] a confidant of both Margaret Thatcher and Rupert Murdoch – was agreeably reminded of his efforts on behalf of the stucco façades at a dinner party held by Elizabeth Jane Howard, the novelist and former wife of Kingsley Amis. Self-pluming as ever, Wyatt wrote in his diary:

> Peter Parker[37] and his wife[38] were there. So were Anthony Hobson[39] and his wife[40] whom I have not seen for years. When we were in Wiltshire they were about an hour's drive away and we used to meet often. He was a senior partner in Sotheby's and writes learned books about such subjects as the Renaissance library . . . He recalls that I saved Regent's Park Terraces with John Betjeman. I am delighted that someone should remember what we did. John Summerson[41] was in on it too: I did a television programme on *Panorama*[42] and some other broadcasts.[43]

In 2002 Anthony Hobson recalled that Wyatt and John also took more direct action over the terraces.

> I lived in Chester Place, the smallest houses in Regent's Park, from 1952 to 1961. The Crown Commissioners wanted to pull down the [John] Nash/[Decimus] Burton terraces and erect modern blocks of flats. Woodrow Wyatt and Betj went to the Prime Minister, Macmillan, and got it stopped.[44]

* See B. Hillier, 'The Boase Garden', *The Betjemanian,* Vol. 9, 1997–1998, pp. 10–38.

CINCINNATI

Maybe Betjeman was eccentric by English standards, but by American standards he seemed like a good old Joe.

John Wulsin, interview, 1989

I can't remember what he said about his stay in Cincinnati – except that he loathed it.

Sir Stephen Spender, letter to the author, 3 September 1987

On 6 October 1946 Miss George Elliston died in Madisonville, Ohio, at the age of sixty-three.[1] From 1901 until 1942 she had been on the editorial staff of the *Cincinnati Times-Star*. As a young woman, she was a tough reporter: she had obtained an 'exclusive' from a murderer on his way to the electric chair and was proud of having climbed into a fifth-storey window to steal a photograph to accompany another scoop. Later she became the paper's social editor, a powerful arbiter of who was who in Cincinnati society. She also had a reputation as the dewiest of poetesses. Her 'Every Day Poems' in the *Times-Star* mixed sentimentality and moral uplift in the manner of Ella Wheeler Wilcox and Patience Strong.

For young Cincinnatians of the 1940s, such as Judge Gilbert Bettman (his mother Iphigene worked with Elliston on the newspaper), Elliston's poems became a kind of in-joke.[2] Her poem 'When Hands Are Cups' illustrates her talent for bathos. It begins:

> That was a strange sweet day you drank
> Your water from my hands,
> (We had forgotten paper cups)
> All that heart understands . . .

Risible as it was, Elliston's verse had its defenders. Cincinnati hostesses also soon realized that a sure way to get their parties mentioned in her social column was to commission an ode to be read to their guests – sometimes by the poet herself, dressed in gypsy costume or druidic robes.

During her lifetime, it was generally believed that, with all her fame as a Cincinnati 'character', George Elliston was poor as a church mouse. She wore cast-off clothes given to her by the society ladies whose parties she wrote up; even on her deathbed she borrowed $10 from a friend. Yet her will revealed that she had left $250,000 to found a chair of poetry at the University of Cincinnati. The will stipulated that the Elliston Chair was always to be held by a poet, not by an academic. The person responsible for choosing the first was William S. Clark II, chairman of the English department at UC. Clark hoped he could persuade T.S. Eliot to accept the post. As it happened, Eliot had been in the same class at Harvard as one of the leading citizens of Cincinnati, Lucien Wulsin II. The two men had 'roomed' together and had been editors of the *Harvard Advocate* in 1909–10.[3] Wulsin had no great regard for Eliot ('Tommy was a hare-brained writer who didn't have much substance to him,' he said).[4] But he wrote to Eliot, who agreed to give the first series of lectures in 1951. At the last moment, however, Eliot backed out, pleading pressure of work, and Clark was forced to make a hurried second choice. He chose the old-fashioned American poet Robert P. Tristram Coffin, a descendant of an early whaling family of Nantucket. He was not a success. The subject-matter of his works – which included *Ballads of Square-Toed Americans* – was the 'homefolk' and countryside of Maine. He had little to say likely to exhilarate teenage students, or even older people, who before long dominated the audience.[5] Coffin was at least 'safe'. Some of the Elliston Poets who followed him were more strikingly unsatisfactory. John Berryman, who held the chair in 1952, was an alcoholic. 'I used to think that he drank . . . to calm his intensity,' said Elizabeth Bettman, Judge Bettman's then wife.[6] George Ford, a lecturer in Clark's department, thought that Berryman's wife Eileen watched the poet 'like an engine-tender watching the gauge on a boiler'.[7] Berryman's immediate successor, Stephen Spender (1953), was at first refused a visa by the American Embassy in London, because he had been a self-confessed Communist for a few weeks in 1937.[8] There were awkward questions from the press when he arrived in Cincinnati; and on a subsequent visit to the city he was forbidden to speak on campus.[9]

The biggest disaster was the tenure of Robert Lowell in 1954. He went to the Gaiety strip club twice a day. Returning to his lodgings on one occasion, having run out of money, he jumped from a moving taxi to avoid paying.[10] There was further trouble when his estranged wife, the poet Elizabeth Hardwick, descended on Cincinnati, convinced that the Bettmans were encouraging Lowell in his plan to marry his Italian lover Giovanna Madonia.[11] His behaviour on the lecture platform was so bizarre and belligerent that William Clark asked some of his strongest and biggest lecturers to sit in the front row in case there should be any violence.[12] In his last lecture, Lowell declaimed what seemed to some a rambling panegyric of Hitler,[13] and was carried off to the Jewish Hospital in a van, yelling: 'I want my lawyer, Gilbert Bettman!'[14] With Elizabeth Hardwick's blessing he was certified and given 'warm bath treatment' and electric-shock therapy.[15]

After this débâcle, William Clark told Keith Stewart, a lecturer in his department, that in future he was going to be far more stringent in vetting candidates. 'I don't want any lushes [alcoholics], commies, homos, loonies, women, Catholics, Irish or Jews,' he said.[16] The Elliston Poets for 1955 and 1956 had already been signed up: respectively, Robert Frost, as American as the flag, and Peter Viereck, whom Van Wyck Brooks had hailed as 'the promised man who is going to lead modern poetry out of the waste-land'. Surely there would be no difficulties with *them*? Unfortunately, there were. Frost offended everyone by refusing to stay in Cincinnati for more than one weekend. And some left-wing and Jewish students protested about Viereck's appointment because they confused him with his father, who had been imprisoned during the war for pro-Nazi sympathies.[17]

Stephen Spender, who had charmed Clark, was asked whom he would recommend for 1957. He suggested John Betjeman. 'You won't have any trouble with him,' he said.[18] But this time Clark was taking no chances. In June 1955 he and his wife Gladys went to England to see for themselves whether John Betjeman would be suitable. Spender had already told John about the chair, in particular about the $3,000 he could expect for giving five lectures and some 'workshops'. At about three dollars to the pound, this was a tempting prospect for the hard-up Betjemans, and Penelope made sure that the Clarks' visit to Wantage would be both enjoyable and impressive. The VIP treatment was to include a tour of Faringdon House and Lockinge, and a picnic on the downs.[19]

As soon as the Clarks arrived back in Cincinnati, Clark wrote to offer John the post. Quite apart from the Betjemans' charm, erudition and fluency as conversationalists, Gladys (regarded as a bit of a snob by some of the academic establishment in Cincinnati)[20] had been impressed by their grand friends and by Penelope's 'Honourable'. John asked Penelope whether she would accompany him. She was dubious as to whether she would enjoy '*Chinchin-náti*' – as she insisted on pronouncing the city, in the Italian manner – but it was a good pretext to get John away from Elizabeth Cavendish. So she agreed; but she made it part of the bargain that, if she 'did her time' in Cincinnati, she should be allowed to take Candida on holiday to Italy afterwards.[21] John himself wrote to a friend in June 1956:

> I go there (Cinci[nnati]) for March next year and am absolutely dreading it as I saw a film called *Storm Centre* which obviously was just like suburban USA, very priggish and good and humourless and intense and psychological, and public libraries taken very seriously.[22]

A press release about John was based on information supplied by Penelope.

> A very important part of his life is his old Teddy Bear Archie, whom he was given when three years old so that Archie is now 47 and very patched. He takes him everywhere with him but will NOT bring him to the USA in case the customs officials might cut him open for suspected contraband. Archie is very Low Church and an archaeologist and very much disapproves of drink and levity of any kind. Recently when Betjeman's French cousin Doris Lurot Betjeman (a portrait painter of some note who exhibits annually in the salon) came all the way over from Paris on purpose to paint his [John's] portrait, she got so fed up in trying and failing to make him sit that she painted an excellent portrait of Archie instead which now hangs in Betjeman's London flat.[23]

By the time the *Cincinnati Enquirer* got round to announcing the appointment, in February, Archie had become the story, which was ungrammatically headed: 'Teddy Bears Are A Passion (Like Elvis) Of Famous British Poet'.[24] (This was intended to mean that Elvis also liked teddy bears, not that John had a mania for Presley's music.) 'The university suspects [Mr and Mrs Betjeman] will provide for Cincinnatians a refreshing interlude of new ideas, peppered with just the right amount of humor.'[25]

Penelope wrote to her old schoolfriend, Lady Silvia Combe, on 19 March:

> It was very stupid of me to go by sea, recollecting, as I did, how much I disliked the P & O voyages to India in the old days, but I thought these enormous liners never moved, however rough. Although they have stabilizers on them to prevent them rolling, they pitch and toss like a little paper boat in a rough bath! I was sick two days without stopping . . . We were dumped in Halifax, Nova Scotia, the most god-forsaken outpost of Empire on earth, and . . . after 2 deadly days we were transferred to a little Cunard liner, the *Saxonia* . . . We were delayed a further day by a snow

blizzard and then took a final two days to reach New York but again we had to wait a whole day . . . until the tide was right to dock without the help of tugs! Luckily it was perfect weather, and by the time we finally cruised up to our dock number 92, the sun was setting and the skyscrapers looked like a fantastic fairyland.[26] I forgot to say that I was again sick for most of the two days on the *Saxonia*![27]

John and Penelope spent one night at the Algonquin Hotel as guests of the *New Yorker*. The magazine wanted to publish a profile of John, and sent Brendan Gill to interview him. Gill wrote:

> He sat sipping a bourbon on the rocks and bubbling over with delight at the American scene: 'My first visit you know,' he said. 'I ordered a bourbon because I understand it's the authentic American drink. I mean to be thoroughly American during my stay at Cinci – I hope it isn't disrespectful of me to call Cinci Cinci so soon.[28]

(John had got it wrong. The accepted abbreviation of Cincinnati is not 'Cinci', but 'Cinti'.) John also told Gill that he thought the Woolworth Building – an early skyscraper – 'enchanting . . . all that Gothic work so high in the air, so close to eternity!'[29]

In Cincinnati, the University had booked them into the Vernon Manor Hotel, an ungainly mock-Tudor building on the edge of the leafy campus. Allegedly modelled on Hatfield House, it had been built at a cost of $1.5 million in 1924 as an 'apartment hotel', though there were also hotel rooms and restaurants open to the public. On panelling above the Tudor-style fireplace in the bar was the Vernon family's motto, '*NIL CONSCIRE SIBI*' ('To have nothing on one's conscience' – a phrase from the Epistles of Horace).

On 27 February, the *Cincinnati Times-Star* sent a reporter to the hotel to interview the Betjemans. John had evidently decided to be an English 'card'. He was photographed in a three-piece Prince of Wales check suit with revers on the waistcoat. He was smoking with a black cigarette-holder and from his neck dangled a spy-glass on a string. In the *Times-Star* photograph he grins toothily; behind sits Penelope with her usual down-at-mouth expression. John said all the right things. 'I want to see as many streets as I can,' he told the reporter. 'I want to be able to walk down them and date the houses and know the people who lived in them.' He crouched on a sofa to get a better look at a view from the window. 'Your Mount Adams looks awfully good,' he said. 'I want to go and see some of the less known and less modernized towns around here.'[30]

John's public-relations act was undermined by Penelope's forthrightness. The *Times-Star* reporter commented:

The Betjemans (Mrs Betjeman is along), used to England's open fireplaces and chilly rooms, very well may be forced out into the weather by central heating.

The stocky, tweedy lecturer was smoking a cigaret in a short holder and fiddling with the radiator in his room. He had already opened his window about a foot.

'It's ghastly,' Mrs Betjeman complained. 'I can't stand the heat.'[31]

On 4 March, the Clarks held a party for the Betjemans at their home in Hyde Park, Cincinnati. Two days later, John was to give the first of his Elliston lectures, on 'The Visual and Sensual Approach to Poetry'. Van Meter Ames, the University's professor of philosophy and himself a published poet, recorded both events in his journal:

7 March 1957. Monday evening was the Clark party for this year's Elliston poet, John Betjeman and his wife Penelope, who runs his farm near Oxford and is a famous cook . . . Much interested in Indian thought, and from it discovered western mysticism, Von Hügel and then St Theresa and was converted to Catholicism, after being 'damn glad I wasn't a Christian' . . . Didn't get much impression of her husband, and Betty [Ames, Van Meter's wife] and Liz Bettman were afraid he would not be interesting, and all he drank was grapefruit juice. But I caught a glimpse of the red lining in his coat and thought he might surprise us.

Sure enough he did, in his first lecture yesterday. Simply captivated the full house in 127 McMicken [Hall]. When the photographer thought he had finished snapping him, Betjeman opened his coat to cause a universal gasp over the flaming lining and equally red broad suspenders [braces]. Then he took the coat off and proceeded in his shirtsleeves which he rolled up.[32]

The UC News Record of 14 March contained a report on John's lecture, by Phyllis Cohen. He had begun his talk, characteristically, 'I've got some notes here, and let us hope they are in the right order.' Laughter had 'rippled through the audience' and humour had 'punctuated Mr Betjeman's clever and interesting discourse'. 'We are all poets,' John assured his audience, '– anyone who can dance . . . anyone with a sense of rhythm.' He added: 'I have been informed that Americans are considerably less inhibited than Englishmen.' Phyllis Cohen wrote: 'He spoke very informally and was completely at ease, removing and replacing his eye glasses at intervals as he leaned forward in addressing the audience. Mr Betjeman's affable personality literally charmed the group.'[33]

The same issue of the News Record carried an interview with John

by Hal Maier. 'My first lecture here was the most stimulating experience I have ever had on the speaker's platform,' John told Maier. 'I felt
as if I were being carried along on the crest of a wave. Such an immediate welcome is not usually apparent in England . . .' Asked his first
impression of the University of Cincinnati, John said: 'It is impossible
for me to understand how anyone could possibly get any work done
in a co-educational university. If I had been here as an undergraduate
I would have been in love all the time because your American co-eds
are so beautiful.'[34]

Very few undergraduates were admitted to John's lectures. 'As far as
the Clarks were concerned,' Keith Stewart said, 'the Elliston chair was a
social appointment, not a teaching one. The lectures were for select
members of the community, not for the students.'[35] But John did meet
some undergraduates and recent graduates in the poetry 'workshops'
which were among his duties as Elliston Poet. Completely at home on
the public platform, he was daunted by the idea of a workshop: the very
word, jarringly modern in an academic context, had, for him, unhappy
associations with his father's cabinet-making firm. The workshop consisted of eight to twelve people, about evenly divided between the sexes.
One member was Alvin Greenberg, later a novelist and poet and professor of English literature at Macallister University. In 1957 he was twenty-
five. He had graduated from UC in English in 1954, had been briefly in
the Army, had married and was working in Cincinnati in the family wine
business. Greenberg had attended Peter Viereck's workshop in 1956.

> So now I was delighted to be back . . . Workshops were always a real high
> point in the year for me. Betjeman was just a delightful person to be with –
> a wonderful spirit, and he always had that smile. I think it was also fairly
> evident, early on, that he didn't have the slightest idea what to do with us.
>
> That was the time when the teaching of creative writing was just begin-
> ning to make inroads into the American universities . . . I'm sure it wasn't
> being done at the British universities. Betjeman was in a totally unfamil-
> iar setting. It was not just that he was a traditionalist while we, being
> young, tended to be avant-garde. I think he didn't know what to expect of
> us, or exactly what it was one did, teaching in a workshop.
>
> We played games. We played a lot of games. We had a wonderful time.
> We wrote poems in class, based on ideas that he gave us (he was very con-
> cerned about correct scansion); and we did the Dadaist game called 'The
> Exquisite Corpse', a poetry-writing game – somebody starts with a line
> and passes it to the next person, who adds a line to it, then folds over the
> top line. It is called 'The Exquisite Corpse' because the Dadaists called
> things anything they wanted. In fact, there's an American literary journal
> now called *The Exquisite Corpse*.[36]

The game was exactly that which John had played with the Pipers and other friends in the 1930s and 1940s. For this, at least, he was well prepared.

When John arrived in the city, Alvin Greenberg, like most other Cincinnatians, did not know his poetry. He bought some, and was charmed by it, because of its subject-matter, rhythms and tones, but was also 'kind of baffled by anybody writing in the 1950s in the idiom of the turn of the century'.[37] It did not, though, occur to Greenberg or to anyone else in the workshop to tax John with his traditionalism or tease him about it. The era of 1960s 'student unrest' had not yet dawned.

Aside from the workshops, John's timetable was arranged by William and Gladys Clark, and the Betjemans saw a lot of them. Clark was a tall, handsome New Englander of fifty-six. He was considered autocratic. 'Some people thought him a benevolent despot,' said Alvin Greenberg. 'I wasn't sure about the "benevolent".'[38] Gladys Clark was also a New Englander, Vassar-educated. A faculty wife spoke of her 'frozen smile'. There was much humour, on campus, at the Clarks' expense. People complained of the interminable slide shows of their holidays, and laughed at the rugs that Gladys stitched from her husband's old tweed suits.

'I think John Betjeman enjoyed being lionized,' said Keith Stewart's wife Betty. 'The Clarks encouraged that. They had several parties at the beginning of the poet's visit – only people they thought would entertain the poet, because he was always "The Poet", "this year's Poet"; and if you wanted to have anything to do with The Poet, you had to talk to Gladys, who kept his calendar. She scheduled everything for him. I think the Clarks loved being part of all the Poet business . . . This was the annual excitement. And I felt dreadfully sorry for the Poet, because I don't like to go out three times a day – it was too much.'[39] Keith Stewart thinks that 'Betjeman was perhaps a quintessential Elliston Poet as the Clarks perceived the rôle.'[40] John Wulsin, Lucien's son and in 1957 a young surgeon, said: 'Maybe Betjeman was eccentric by English standards, but by American standards he seemed like a good old Joe.'[41] Elizabeth Bettman said: 'He put himself out enormously. He made a conscious effort, it seemed to me, every time I saw him, to entertain and to give pleasure.'[42]

Liz Bettman was the woman who overcame Clark's resistance to having women in the English department. 'I *broke* him,' she joked. 'After me, he let women in.' Clark had a crush on her 'but he was, for him, very shy about it'.[43] She was the young, attractive wife of Gilbert Bettman, who was forty in 1957 and had been elected a municipal judge in Cincinnati two years before. 'Liz is a bit wild,' was a general, if affectionate, view. She was a red-hot radical on almost every political and social issue. As a Vassar student just before the war she had done house-to-house campaigning for Franklin Roosevelt.[44] In the 1940s she had flouted southern rules by taking black children into the Coney Island fair on the bank of the Ohio River, and was often arrested for this. 'If Liz could have been black, she would have been,' a friend said.[45] An unlikely person, perhaps, for the conservative Clarks to entrust with any aspect of entertaining the Betjemans – but she was shiningly sincere, sympathetic and learned in English literature, and had become a friend of visiting poets as disparate as Spender, Berryman and Lowell. When the Betjemans arrived, the Clarks gave Liz Bettman two special assignments. First, she was to stand guard over the Poet so that would-be writers could not batten on to him. 'There would always be a line of ladies panting to read him their manuscripts; and I had to stand there and say, no.'[46] Also, Liz was to be John's chauffeuse in Cincinnati. He was captivated by her: she seemed an American Joan Hunter Dunn. At first, she 'found it hard to get past his bonhomie'; but later, when she was driving him to his appointments or on sightseeing jaunts, their relationship grew a little closer. He would give her sidelong looks from the passenger seat and would 'gently interrogate' her about her private life. 'I knew he was trying to get me to talk about my marriage, which he realized was already a little rocky. What I didn't realize was that his marriage was rocky too.'[47]

Gil and Liz Bettman were at the centre of a group of young Cincinnatians, part town and part gown, who were having the good time they had missed out on during the war. Gil himself had been with the field artillery at Okinawa. John Wulsin, as a Navy medical officer, had gone into Tokyo Bay on a landing ship tank, had been assigned to Marine headquarters on Guam, and had also served in Korea in the early 1950s. George Ford had been in the Canadian artillery. Alister ('Hamish') Cameron, a classics lecturer who was of the group,[48] had had a hush-hush job with the Office of Strategic Services, counterespionage. 'We all drank too much and stayed up too late,' Liz Bettman recalled. 'Berryman really got us started on the drinking. And we used to go swimming in the nude in my mother-in-law's pool at Elmhurst Place.' The gaiety of the group's parties in the 1950s is caught in a verse thank-you letter which Van Meter Ames sent the Bettmans. In it he described Hamish Cameron's party-piece of pretending a chair was a set of bagpipes – an act to which John and Penelope were also treated.

George Ford made the ladies ecstatic,
He whirled them and held them while Pat
All in white and Peg all in silk
Were held in the arms of Wyman and Van . . .

When Hamish, sobering more
Than was human,
Stiffened and stood, marched down the floor,
Turned short and returned with a chair
That he held to his lips in the air,
Gave his moustache a twist to the side
To fill the fat pipes with his pride,
Shrilling out
The wild notes of the Scot,
The answer of Hamish to gloom:

The ultimate toot,
The absolute squeak of the truth.[49]

John threw himself manfully into the party-going. After being sighted with the misleading grapefruit juice at the first Clark soirée, he took to strong martinis. Penelope, as ever, was much less keen on parties. In her letter to Lady Silvia Combe she wrote: 'The Americans are, as one has always heard, the most friendly and hospitable people in the world, and we are asked out to every meal and meet new people every day, so that we are nearly mad and shall need a long rest-cure on our return.'[50] Every member of the English department held a dinner-party for the Betjemans.

The evening went well as I recall [the lecturer Hugh Maclean wrote]. My sense now is that they recognized at once that we were rather shy people socially, and made nice efforts to fit in. Penelope rather endeared herself to me by inspecting the house, making cheerful remarks; then to the kitchen at last, and the frigidaire ('All you Americans have *enormous* ice-boxes!'), she threw the ice-box door open, spotted [his wife] Janet's large chocolate cake for the dessert, swiped her forefinger across the side, tasted with gusto, and smiled hugely at us – 'Delicious!' It was all done with great style, and broke the ice.[51]

George Ford and his wife Pat also held a dinner, but Ford was not as taken with John as others of the faculty. Though Ford figures as one of the revellers in Van Meter Ames's poem, he and his wife were slightly older and staider than the rest of the set. John and Ford did not really hit it off. Some members of the English department thought

that Ford's nose was put out of joint by Betjeman's popularity in
Cincinnati. 'Ford was a top-flight Dickensian,' said one of them, 'and
his attitude was that he didn't have anything to learn about Victorian
literature from John Betjeman. Also, George Ford liked to think of
himself as very British, or at least very Canadian – and now here was
John Betjeman, the genuine British article.'[52]

George Ford himself wrote:

I got to know Spender very well and also Berryman, but Betjeman was
more friendly with the townies than with the gownies. Because my special
interest as a scholar and critic has been Victorian literature, he seemed
to regard me as someone he did not need to convert to his opinions.
Whereas . . . he discovered that here were people not ordinarily attracted
to the Victorian scene . . . and he keenly enjoyed opening their eyes and
ears . . . He dazzled and delighted them with his hyperbolic talk . . .[53]

Another Cincinnatian who found John disconcerting was Walter
Langsam, the seventeen-year-old son of the University's President.
Unlike most of his contemporaries in Cincinnati, Langsam was
already an admirer of John's poetry when the Betjemans arrived. So
he badgered his father into holding a dinner-party for the poet. When
the meal was over, Langsam senior tactfully led the other guests into
the drawing-room, so that his son would have some time alone with
John. The tête-à-tête did not go at all as the young man hoped.

Betjeman had an *idée fixe* that Americans are terrified of the subject of
death and that they cannot bear to talk about it. (Jessica Mitford's *The
American Way of Death* later dealt with all that.) All I wanted to talk
about, of course, was poetry. All he wanted to talk about was death. I was
seventeen. I had not known anybody who had died and I was not in the
slightest interested in death. But he went on and on questioning me – and
the more I denied any knowledge of death, the more convinced he became
that, yes, Americans *were* terrified of talking about death. When my
father *finally* came back into the room . . . I was longing to be rescued.
Dying to be rescued![54]

Of all the UC academics (if one excepts Liz Bettman, who in 1957
was still only on the fringe of the English department) John liked Van
Meter Ames best. The Professor of Philosophy, whose own philosophy was close to Zen Buddhism, was a tall, earth-father sort of man,
with deep-gazing eyes. 'Van Meter Ames was a kind of saint on earth,'
Gil Bettman said. 'He was a warm, decent human being. He had the
luxury of having a wife, Betty, who had money . . . He had an infinitely

enquiring mind. Somehow you could feel Van taking the wonderful things out of a tree or the grass or the sunshine or the moisture in the air and translating them into human warmth. But he wasn't fey. He was ready to take courageous positions.'[55] A little on edge in the foreign setting, John found he could relax in the company of this calm, profound man, who reminded him of John Piper. He wrote to Ames after his return to England that he greatly admired his book-length poem *Out of Iowa* (1936) – 'especially the lawn-mower part'.[56]

In spite of these friendships with UC teachers, it was probably true, as George Ford suggests, that John saw more of the 'townies' than of the 'gownies'. Wherever he and Penelope went, he was interested in meeting the 'aristocracy', she in seeing and if possible riding the best horses – 'nobs and cobs'.[57] The Longworths had been the royal family of Cincinnati, but they were almost extinct. Their fortune was made from viticulture until disease destroyed the wine industry of south-western Ohio in the late 1850s.[58] John met Alice Roosevelt Longworth, whose husband had died in 1931. A daughter of President Theodore Roosevelt, she was the subject of the popular song 'Alice Blue Gown'. It was she who was supposed to have said, 'If you have nothing good to say about anyone, come and sit by me.' She and her husband had run the Rookwood Pottery in Cincinnati, whose decorative wares John admired on several Cincinnati buildings. (Alice Longworth died in 1987, aged one hundred.)

The most spectacular use of Rookwood tiles was in the interior of the Carew Tower on Vine Street, an Art Deco masterpiece and pre-cisely the sort of building John had been taught to despise as *moderne* in his years on *The Architectural Review*. The skyscraper had been put up in 1930, at a cost of $30 million, by John J. Emery, the heir to a fortune made in the lamp-oil and candle industry of Cincinnati from the 1840s. In 1957 John J. Emery – 'Jack' to everyone – and his wife Irene ('Babs') were the richest people in Cincinnati. They held a party for the Betjemans at Peterloon, their pseudo-Georgian house of 1930 in the grand suburb of Indian Hill, where no house was allowed to stand on fewer than five acres. (The Emerys had 1,200 acres.)[59] They also took John to see Mariemont, the quaint half-timbered village which Jack's aunt, Mary Emery, had built on the outskirts of Cincinnati in the late 1920s – stockbroker's Tudor *in excelsis*. In 1948 Jack Emery had raised one of the few modern buildings in Cincinnati which John unreservedly praised (that did not necessarily mean that he unreservedly admired it), the Terrace Plaza hotel designed by Skidmore, Owings and Merrill, with specially commissioned art-works by Joan Miró, Alexander Calder and Saul Steinberg. By 1957 the Terrace Plaza had become the Terrace Hilton: Emery had sold it to the Hilton chain the year before. The works of art went to the Cincinnati Art Museum.

John saw less of the Emerys than of their daughter Melissa, who with her husband Addison Lanier attended all his lectures. The Laniers had been married four years before and had two young children. 'When the Betjemans came to dinner at our farmhouse in Indian Hill, each of them was obliged to feed a child with a bottle,' Melissa Lanier recalled. 'John Betjeman was fascinated that my mother's father was Charles Dana Gibson, the artist, and that my grandmother had been one of the "Gibson Girls". She was born Irene Langhorne and her sister was Nancy Astor. I think it may have been Nancy Astor who gave the Betjemans an introduction to my parents.'[60] John was greatly taken by Melissa's looks. He inscribed three of his books for her and her husband. In *First and Last Loves* he wrote: 'To all the girls of Bryn Mawr but in particular to Melissa Lanier, the loveliest sophomore of her semester and her husband Cincinnati 1957.'[61] (Melissa had attended Bryn Mawr College, near Philadelphia.)

Like the Emerys and the Tafts,[62] the Wulsin family (of Baldwin Pianos) had been prominent in Cincinnati since the nineteenth century. By the 1950s, radio and television had largely replaced the piano as the centre of home entertainment; but the Wulsins had long since invested the profits from piano sales, in land. In the 1920s Lucien Wulsin had bought 500 acres in Indian Hill. When John and Penelope dined at the Wulsins' house, The Hermitage, they were waited on by liveried servants. Lucien Wulsin mounted Penelope on one of his horses for the local Camargo Hunt. She wrote far from flattering accounts of the Hunt in her letters to Mollie Baring and Lady Silvia Combe. Some of the American riders were equally critical of her. She had not come to Cincinnati prepared to ride – 'so I just wore rat-catcher', she wrote.[63] This shocked the huntsmen of Indian Hill, as Lucien Wulsin's daughter-in-law Rosamund recalled.

> My father-in-law mounted her on one of his horses, a great big clumsy Irish hunter. She didn't have her regalia with her. That didn't bother her one bit, because she was such an absolutely superb horsewoman. So she went out there, where everybody else was all dressed-up with the right hat and the right boots. She went out there in loafers, scruffy American loafers; no socks on her ankles and ill-fitting jodhpurs that belonged to somebody else. Now most Masters, even here [in Indian Hill], will not allow somebody to appear like that. But she, being Penelope, got away with it.[64]

Penelope gave Rosamund Wulsin another surprise. In 1957 Rosamund and John Wulsin were living in the Mount Auburn district, two blocks from the Vernon Manor hotel. One day Penelope arrived at the front door at 7.00 a.m. uninvited.

> The doorbell rang. The front door was a big mahogany thing with a glass panel, so you could see who was out there ringing the bell. I had five children under seven in the dining-room. I looked through the door and there was Penelope. I thought, 'Oh my God – this is the absolute *end*!' She came in. The place was a mess – cereal all over the floor, children screaming. But she was happy. She said: 'I just wanted to see what an American family's like when they're unprepared.'[65]

Also among the leading families of Cincinnati were the great Jewish dynasties, the Fleishmanns, the Bettmans and the Ransohoffs. The Fleishmanns, arriving in Cincinnati in the 1860s, had made a fortune from a Hungarian process of manufacturing yeast. Julius ('Junkie') Fleishmann was often host to the Betjemans in his 1927 Lutyens-like house in Indian Hill. The Camargo Hunt met in the courtyard of the house and the hounds were from the Fleishmann kennels. It was in this house, in 1953, that Stephen Spender and Irving Kristol had met to discuss plans for a new magazine, *Encounter*; Spender later discovered that the magazine was financed by the CIA through a foundation of Fleishmann's. Gil Bettman described 'Junkie' Fleishmann as 'one of the few people I have known who had an aura of evil'.[66]

Bettman's father, also a Gilbert, had been attorney-general of Ohio.[67] On his mother's side, Gil Bettman's great-grandfather was Isaac Mayer Wise, the founder of Reformed Judaism in the United States. In 1866 Wise built the Plum Street Temple, an Alhambra-style edifice which delighted John. Gil Bettman's mother Iphigene, the former colleague of George Elliston, was of the Ochs family which owned the *New York Times*. But, with all his wealth and powerful connections, Gil Bettman, a quiet, charming, humorous man, was almost as left-wing as his wife. The Cincinnati Establishment regarded him as a 'bleeding heart' judge; a decade later, he was the only elected official in Ohio to speak out against the Vietnam war.

Danny Ransohoff and Gil Bettman sometimes had a friendly argument over whose family had been longer established in Cincinnati. Ransohoff was a fifth-generation Cincinnatian. His grandfather, Dr Joseph Ransohoff, had been a well-known medical doctor and scientist in the city.[68] Ransohoff liked to act as a guide to eminent visitors to the city. He had shown Berryman, Spender and Lowell the sights; he found John Betjeman more receptive than any of them.[69]

Ransohoff always began his tours by taking his guests to Symmes Street, where an exposed cliff showed the compounded strata of fifty million years, with layers of fossilized worms, snails, brachiopods and fish. John exclaimed: 'All of Shakespeare would fit in one hundred thousandth of an inch!'[70] Then Ransohoff would summarize the history of Cincinnati, a city poised between the North and the South; how it had been founded in 1788; how it had grown rich by river trade, 'when Chicago was still a mud hole'; how it had become a centre of the pig market, 'Porkopolis'; how Frances Trollope, the novelist's mother, had been rude about it but Dickens had admired it. He would go on to describe how the spread of railroads had caused a decline in river transport and blighted Cincinnati's hopes of becoming a second capital; how large numbers of German immigrants had arrived after 'the unpleasantness of 1848' (the revolution in Germany); and how Ohio, as a free state bordering a slave state, had been a refuge for runaway black slaves – as Harriet Beecher Stowe (born and married in Cincinnati) told in *Uncle Tom's Cabin*. The visitor also heard how German industries, beer and iron, had flourished in the nineteenth century, and how Procter & Gamble, makers of 'Ivory' soap, had become and still were the biggest industry of the city.

If the guest was staying for any length of time, Ransohoff would give him two tours of the city: one of its architectural showpieces, the other of its slums. John was taken on both. We know which buildings he liked best, from an article he contributed to the *Cincinnati Enquirer* after he returned to England in April. He liked the Taft Museum, the beer barons' mansions, the City Hall, of 'streaky bacon' Gothic brick, and the German domestic architecture of the downtown area known as 'Over the Rhine'. His 'favourite skyscraper' was 'your Union Central Building by Cass Gilbert, architect of the Woolworth Building, which is still New York's handsomest bit of skyline'.[71] John paid tribute to a house designed by Frank Lloyd Wright in 1953 for Cedric Boulter, the Professor of Classics, and his wife Pat.[72] The luxurious suburbia of Walnut Hills and Avondale also appealed to him. But he added that he could not end with a good conscience without mentioning the slums between Third Street and Seventh Street – which he had seen on his second tour.

> I know the London slums, but they are not as bad as these, partly because of bylaws which make windowless rooms illegal and which insist on fire precautions.
>
> I went up black evil-smelling stairs from a front hall studded with mailboxes in houses where there was only one sink and an outside toilet which had to be emptied by a vaultman after use by 40 people. I was amazed at how well kept these waterless, brittle, insanitary rooms proved to be once one was inside them. There was garbage in the streets piled feet high.

What these places must be like in hot weather I dread to think . . . The many kind friends I have made in Cincinnati will not, I hope, feel I am unaware of their generosity to me, their hospitality and their welcome if, remembering the slums so near the padded luxury of the Terrace Hilton, I end with these Victorian lines:

> 'Oh loved Cincinnati, I bid thee farewell,
> Thy heights are perfection. Thy basin is hell.'[73]

On 11 March the *Cincinnati Times-Star* took the Betjemans through the riverside towns of the Ohio Valley. 'Cincinnati has the most beautiful gas-lights in the world,' John told the gratified reporter.[74] The Royal Fine Art Commission, of which he was a member, had been 'looking for something like that for a long time. I must have a picture of it to show the others . . . We just don't have any lights in England as pretty as that.'[75] In the same park, John was photographed, in one of his most punished felt hats, sketching the neo-classical Temple of Love, which he called 'a perfect crown to the hill'. He also revelled in the nearby Scarlet Oaks, a Gothic house erected by one of the immigrant German industrialists of Cincinnati. He realized that Germans who made good in Cincinnati built houses as similar as possible to the castles they remembered on the Rhine.

John later wrote:

Who can forget the ride along Columbia Parkway above the wide sweeps of the Ohio, with the Kentucky hills on the opposite bank and the March skies glittering in the sliding water? I shall always remember standing at sundown in Moscow, Ohio, with a crimson sunset behind the Kentucky hills and the river very still and no wind moving the ivy on the old bricks of the Speke house down by the water. I felt that at any moment a Red Indian might emerge from between the motionless trees.[76]

After Moscow – which in 1957 did not boast the nuclear plant which stands there today – the Betjemans were taken to the birthplace of President Ulysses S. Grant at Mount Pleasant, Ohio. The small clap-boarded house 'reminded Mr and Mrs Betjeman of a cottage in Scotland – before "progress" '.[77] In Ripley, still on the Ohio side of the water, John admired the 'steamboat Gothic' ironwork of the houses – the style had reached the Ohio valley, by river, from New Orleans. He and Penelope squeezed under low timbers to peer down a well in the pre-Civil War Rankin house in Ripley. 'I shall never forget it,' John said diplomatically.[78] In the 1850s and 1860s the house had been a main station on the 'underground railway' which helped runaway slaves to escape from Kentucky. The Rev. John Rankin had raised twelve children in Ripley and, with the aid of a farmer on the Kentucky shore, had brought more than 2,000 slaves to freedom in the north in spite of harassment by US marshals.[79]

John and Penelope were driven over the suspension bridge into Kentucky for the climax of the excursion, the town of Maysville: more steamboat Gothic ironwork, on early-nineteenth-century houses better preserved than most comparable buildings in English towns. The Betjemans were photographed on the steps of Maysville's Mason County Courthouse (1838). John praised its 'noble Doric columns' and 'simple ironwork' but 'was displeased with a "fake antique" lantern'.[80] Where architectural integrity was at stake, John would carry diplomacy only so far; no doubt, too, he was aware that his compliments would seem more plausible, less syrupy, if accompanied by the odd brickbat. Maysville was one of the earliest settlements on the Ohio. Daniel Boone's family had run a small tavern there; John and Penelope were shown where some of them were buried, behind the Maysville Public Library. The Betjemans sampled the transparent pies which are a local speciality. John politely finished one pie. Penelope gobbled two and asked for the recipe.

On 14 March John delivered his second Elliston lecture, on 'Tennyson: Master of Landscape and Sardonic Wit'. It was as well received as the first. Two days later, the *New Yorker* published Brendan Gill's profile of John. As a fillip to his reputation in Cincinnati, it could not have been better timed. Cincinnatians had had two weeks to decide what they thought of him; now they realized that he was not just a British celebrity, he was an international celebrity. John's third lecture, 'Local Poetry and Love of Place', was on 20 March. 'There's an immense field of inspiration for poetry to come from this district,' he told his large audience. He suggested that Cincinnati poets should investigate the possibilities in 'the extraordinary landscape of used car marts'. 'The flashing lights, the brightly coloured cars! They're hideous but surely they could be turned into poetry. It could be either satirical or inspirational.'[81] The previous Sunday, he said, he had stood on the deck of the steamer *Delta Queen*, with its paddle 'taking water out of the Ohio River and putting it back again' and he had looked up at the cobblestone sweep of the Public Landing. 'I suddenly saw the America of the '60s, and had the feeling of pioneers fighting against Indians.' For 'sheer adventure', he recommended going down to the Dixie Terminal, taking a bus to Covington, Kentucky, then hopping on a train back to Union Terminal. 'It was most thrilling,' he said. 'Everyone on the train was tired except me. Cost, 50 cents.'

On 25 March he lectured on 'The Macabre'. This lecture consisted solely of a reading of 'Miss Kilmansegg and her Wooden Leg'. 'As a poetry reader he was good,' George Ford wrote, 'but not great like Dylan Thomas or Berryman. He could recite a narrative poem . . . very effectively. Rather godawful nineteenth-century poems he could present with affection so that they came to life.'[82]

On 27 March 1957 Van Meter Ames took Dieter Dux, UC's Professor of Political Science, to George Ford's house for a meeting of the Jolly Boys, a private literary society. John showed slides of nineteenth-century English churches – 'imitation Gothic and freer use of Gothic, and then some that broke both from Gothic and Renaissance, some with quite comic effects of "Gothic freely treated". Finally, some private houses, a couple of which he thought might have influenced Frank Lloyd Wright.'

Again Betjeman surprised and touched us by his familiarity with houses in and around Cincinnati, and recurred to praise of our City Hall, which no one around here has thought of admiring. Spoke of its Byzantine effect, the hugeness of the blocks of stone, the rhythm of sandy and reddish bands of stone, the fact that it was all three-dimensional, good from any angle [but he] wished it could stand more apart.[83]

After the slide-show, the Jolly Boys lived up to their name with a heavy drinking session. Ames asked John if he would read them a couple of his poems, 'perhaps from those with an architectural theme'.

He said he would be glad to, and he read the one about King's College Chapel at Cambridge, the one about the modernized tavern, and then one he said couldn't be printed, about how Lady —— [Rhondda] had 'sacked' him as literary adviser of the periodical *Time and Tide*. Then we got into a discussion as to what poetry is, when I asked him about his remark of the other evening about insisting that his students in the Poetry Workshop here learn to scan. He admitted that poetry could get away from scansion, as in the Bible and in Whitman. Just thought it was important to be able to hear it and do it.[84]

John's last lecture in Cincinnati, on 28 March, was a triumph. His subject was 'The Nineties'. Van Meter Ames thought the talk was 'the best of all, with so many colorful figures to talk about, some of whom he knew'.[85] John spoke of Oscar Wilde and Ernest Dowson, and told the audience, 'I was the last gasp of the Nineties.' The *UC News Record* reporter wrote that the lecture closed 'amid a storm of applause mingled with a feeling of sadness'.

This middle-aged man with the pixy smile had completely won the hearts of all who attended his lectures and as he left the lecture room there were audible comments from every side which served as sufficient proof that Mr Betjeman will be long remembered.

Dr Clark, head of the Department of English, said afterwards that the attendance at this year's lectures averaged higher than at any time in the past. Mr Betjeman spoke to standing-room-only audiences . . .

Dr Clark compared Mr Betjeman's interest in cities to that of Charles Lamb. 'He wanted to see and know everything about Cincinnati. His curiosity reminded one of a charming small boy who is seeing the world for the first time.'[86]

At the Clarks' party afterwards, Van Meter Ames nerved himself to give John a copy of his book *Out of Iowa*. He wrote in the front:

> For John and Penelope Betjeman
> for love of the local
> and for enhancing love
> of this place, where you
> will always have a place.[87]

Ames had put the book in an envelope. He told John he could mail it to him if it was too much to take along. John took the envelope, felt that there was a book inside, and said, 'How sweet of you.' He started to give Ames a copy of the yellow-jacketed little volume *A Few Late Chrysanthemums*, but Ames reminded him that he had written in his copy the night before. 'His brown-eyed warmth was wonderful,' Ames wrote, 'and his farewells to all of us, as we clustered about at the last, and people took final pictures of him on the steps, lifted us so that the Fords had the Hamishes and us come down for a drink, to sustain the mood a little longer.'[88]

The Clarks also held a small party for John to say goodbye to the members of his workshop. Alvin Greenberg recalled:

Betjeman presented each of us with an inscribed copy of one of his books, which had to have cost him a good bit of money because he surely didn't bring them with him; but, most amazing of all, he gave each of us . . . probably each of us in the class had bought one of his books; he managed to give each of us the *other* book, the one we didn't have. I guess that at one time or another we'd each asked him to sign a copy – and he had paid attention. That was such a generous, thoughtful, kind thing for him to do. In the long run, it would be hard for me to detect Betjeman's influence on the ways I write. But I think what he did show me – which I haven't seen a lot of in other writers that I've known – is that you can be an artist and be a decent human being at the same time.[89]

Penelope left for New York, before John, on 27 March; she was back in England on 1 April. John left on 31 March. Before he went, he recorded an interview which the Ames' daughter, Damaris, heard on the local radio station that evening. In it, he said again that he had never had such a responsive and appreciative audience. He had been afraid they wouldn't understand his 'Limey' accent, but he had enjoyed his audience so much that 'it was a form of self-indulgence'.[90] The less pleasurable aspects of his month in Cincinnati were trenchantly described by Penelope in a letter to Mollie Baring: 'John's lectures are being a great success, but he is so exhausted from the entertaining that he can hardly wait to get home, and the central heating nearly *kills* us.'[91]

On 8 April, back in Wantage with her ponies and the goslings that had hatched while she was away, Penelope wrote happily to Lucien Wulsin and his wife: 'Everything is a month ahead here and our forsythia is OVER! And all our Mayflowering tulips and bluebells are out and wallflowers, it is a crazy spring but very beautiful and there is masses of lush green grass about whereas usually we have to go on feeding hay to ponies living out till the end of April.'[92] She thanked the Wulsins for having given her a mount in the 'lovely hunts' and enclosed an article, 'Hunting with the Camargo Hounds', which Wulsin had promised to send to the editor of *The Chronicle*, an old-established Virginian sporting journal. The article was Penelope's notion of a diplomatically toned-down version of the account she had given of her adventures in the letters to Mollie Baring and Silvia Combe; but it was not toned down enough, and the article was rejected.[93] The strapless evening dress Penelope had bought for Candida – 'the Cincinnati Formal', as it was always known – was a success. It was of mauve taffeta, and daringly off the shoulder.[94] 'My brother was so overcome when he saw her in it', said Dominick Harrod, 'that he had to be put to bed for a *week*.'[95]

Like Penelope, John must have sat down to record his impressions of Cincinnati soon after returning to England, since his article 'To See Oursel's as Ithers See Us' appeared in the *Cincinnati Enquirer* on 14 April.

He kept up with some of his Cincinnati friends. Lucien Wulsin and his wife visited them and were overturned in a ditch in Penelope's governess cart.[96] William and Gladys Clark made a second visit to Wantage in 1962. Penelope had become a vegetarian, Gladys noted; and Candida, just married, was 'off round the world in a van'.[97] Later in 1962 Elizabeth Bettman also came to Wantage and was photographed by John Lehmann at an evening picnic on the downs with the Betjemans and Jock Murray. (Beside the camp-fire, John gave a bombastic performance of Vachell Lindsay's 'Congo', with saucepan *obbligato*.)[98] Penelope, well aware of the *tendresse* that had developed between John and Liz, wrote on the back of Lehmann's photograph of the two of them: ' "LUST" '.

The Laniers continued a 'Christmas card friendship' with the Betjemans for some years. Other Cincinnati friends were dropped. Keith Stewart still felt some resentment about this over thirty years later:

> Our acquaintance did not conclude as cheerily as it had begun. At the time that he was here [in Cincinnati] I was preparing to spend a year in London with my family, working at the British Museum. Betjeman urged me to let him know when we were there. I did so, and he suggested some time in mid-December that my wife and I meet him at St Bartholomew's in the City and he would show us around. We looked forward to that, but it happened that we all came down with the 'flu. I reached him by telephone the day before we were to meet. 'Oh, I'm glad you called because I can't be there,' said he. 'Well,' or something like that, said I in my 'flu-ridden misery, 'have a pleasant Christmas.' 'I shall,' said Betjeman, 'Goodby[e].' That rather put me in my place, and I didn't try to see him again. I still like his poetry and value my copy of *A Few Late Chrysanthemums*, which he inscribed during his stay in Cincinnati with a drawing of an oversize Scottish thistle on the fly-leaf.[99]

Despite the impression he gave, did John in fact 'loathe' Cincinnati, as he later told Stephen Spender? A letter of 12 March 1957 to Candida suggests that he did.

Darling Wibz,
    Mummy has bought you a very pretty pink dress here and the other day I saw in a delicatessen store the following things for sale – broiled octopus, English liquorice allsorts, rattlesnake meat, fried Japanese grasshoppers, fried Mexican worms. I get very tired here, nobody stops talking, the wireless is on everywhere even in the hotel elevators, and sometimes two different programmes in the same room. I can make little contact with the students I have to teach as I have so little in common with them. We are foreigners here. The English are either much liked or not liked at all. The city is a collection of different frictions – Jewish v Christian, Negro v White, RC v Protestant, North v South (for Cincinnati is on the Mason–Dixon line which divides the old southern states who practised

slavery from the ascetic, hard-working, rather egalitarian and self-righteous North). And oh my goodness it *is* ugly though the Arts Museum is good. The nearest main road to this hotel is appropriately called 'Reading Road'. Most roads and towns look like the approach to Didcot from Wallingford and big towns are like the Great West Road. The suburbs in Treeclad Hill alone are pretty.

I long to see you and Wantage again – my goodness, I do. Don't forget Mummy and me. We think of you a lot and envy you *even* at school. It could not be worse than here.

Tons and tons of love from MD [Mad Dadz][100]

Setting down this very English poet in this very American city had almost the character of a chemistry experiment – it was like dropping a piece of sodium into a dish of water and watching it fizz about. The entertainment certainly exhausted John. He was parted from Elizabeth Cavendish and exposed for weeks on end (not just at week-ends) to Penelope at her most horse-mad and cantankerous. Clearly he enjoyed the adulation of the crowds. But he never went back to Cincinnati, or indeed to America.

Part of the trouble may have been the nature of the America to which the Betjemans were exposed. The country was at its most flauntingly materialist. It was also conformist, just emerging from the horrors of McCarthyism. Looking back specifically at the year 1957 in his 1988 novel *The Beautiful Room is Empty*, Edmund White (born in Cincinnati in 1940) wrote – in the person of his protagonist – ' That was a time and place where there was little consumption of culture and no dissent, not in appearance, belief, or behavior . . . It felt, at least to me, like a big gray country of families on drowsy holiday, all stuffed in one oversized car and discussing the mileage they were getting and the next restroom stop they'd be making . . .'[101] In her letter from Cincinnati to Lady Silvia Combe, Penelope recommended 'a simply *excellent* new book on America', *A Surfeit of Honey* by Russell Lynes, editor of *Harper's*. She wanted to get copies sent to the Baring boys and Billa Harrod's undergraduate circle, 'as our boys *must* be warned what it is really like here, in case they think of emigrating'.

Really, what is left of our sort of life in England is *far* nicer and we *must* fight against the over-gadgeting of our houses: the dish-washers don't wash up properly, and waste food disposers under the sinks, instead of leaving the food to be economically disposed of by pigs and chickens, overload the sewage disposal works with sludge: there are new gadgets advertised every day so that everything can be done from your armchair, so why not go right down into your grave now if you are never going to get up again?[102]

To her, the gadgets seemed to encourage 'a philosophy of laziness';
but what she deplored above all was 'the car snobbery . . . perhaps the
most fantastic aspect of American life to us'.

You can go along a darkie slum downtown at night, where the Negro families and lots of 'poor whites' too sleep eight and ten in a room and have
no hot water laid on; and the roads will be lined with *enormous vulgar
high-powered cars*, all beautifully cleaned and polished, belonging to the
slum-dwellers. A lorry-driver here earns circa £1500 pa (more than I have
to run the Mead on!) and it is a snob rule among them to own a Cadillac,
which costs them a whole year's salary. It is really materialism gone mad,
and the title [of Lynes's book] is well chosen from *Henry IV* Part I – 'They,
surfeited with honey, began to loathe the taste of sweetness, Whereof a
little more than a little is by much too much.'[103]

When John returned to his *Spectator* column on 12 April, he was
more indulgent.

I have been for a month in Cincinnati, Ohio, Queen City of the West, lecturing to breathless sophomores, striding round the maple-studded
campus, listening to Louis Armstrong, drinking Bourbon, seeing the old
river towns, those Cheltenhams in white wood, visiting Kentucky, the
home of horse-worship, seeing the houses of millionaires in the generously laid-out suburbs of Cincinnati, suburbs which stretch for miles over
wooded and grassy hills, looking at much really fine modern architecture,
glass and stone interpretations of the teahouses of Japan, hearing about
the Cincinnati house of the Wurlitzers of cinema organ fame, whose
dining-room floor very slowly revolves so that at the beginning of a meal
you are facing a wall and by the end of it you are looking out of the
window to the winding Ohio, visiting too some of the worst slums I have
seen which are mercifully being pulled down – all this I have done on the
eastern borders of the Middle West, and 1860 over there seemed as old to
me as Perpendicular does here, and Red Indians seemed as long ago as
Anglo-Saxons, and what is time anyway?[104]

IN THE LATE 1950s

I'm now fifty-two. Can I last the course? I must.

John Betjeman, letter to Cecil Roberts, 13 February 1959

Although John's liaison with Elizabeth Cavendish did not get into the gossip columns until the 1970s, the couple were not particularly circumspect about it. As early as 1954 Violet Trefusis – the daughter of Edward VII's mistress, Alice Keppel – put their names side by side on a list of people to be invited to a party she and Patrick Kinross were organizing together. The invitations were printed *Please bring your comb*: combined with lavatory paper, the combs were to become primitive kazoos for a concert in which the guests would be the musicians.[1] In 1957 Ann Fleming, perhaps the most malignant gossip in England (she was married to Ian Fleming, the creator of James Bond), sighted the lovers at a much more public gathering. She wrote to Evelyn Waugh on 5 July:

You made a mistake in missing Lady Pamela Berry and Mr Mike Todd's[2] party at the Festival Gardens to aid the Newspaper Benevolent Fund and publicize the film of *Round the World in Eighty Days*. Those of us who wished the maximum pleasure embarked at midnight from Charing Cross pier in a flotilla of river steamers, rain was falling and the cabins and bars were filled with Jewish film producers, publishers and interior decorators. On each deck was a brass band playing 'Rule Britannia' and other appropriate tunes and the remaining available space was occupied by us foolish goys . . . Present Paddy Leigh Fermor, Vivien Leigh, Stephen Spender looked handsome in a black sou'wester, the Warden of All Souls [John Sparrow] was in transparent white plastic, John Betjeman and Elizabeth Cavendish wore identical pale transparent blue . . .[3]

In August, Penelope went to Italy – her reward for having endured the cocktail parties and central heating of Cincinnati. She returned to Wantage, at the end of September, with an idea for revitalizing King

Alfred's Kitchen. In Rome she had seen the up-to-the-minute Gaggia machines for making espresso coffee. She now ordered one and installed it in the 'caff'.[4] 'We had to experiment with it,' said Kathleen Philip, a local historian who helped out at the café. 'Hot milk jumped out and the whole thing fizzed all over the place. It was great fun.'[5] It was the age of the coffee bar. Teenagers, anglicizing the Italian word, called the beverage 'Expresso'. The musical *Expresso Bongo*, scripted by John's *Time and Tide* contributor Wolf Mankowitz, began a West End run in 1958 and was filmed in 1960 with Cliff Richard as the hero, a teenage rock star. Frank Norman referred to 'froffy coffee' in his cockney musical *Fings Ain't What They Used to Be* (1959). The drink was usually served in translucent plastic cups, with the peculiar property of conducting all the heat of the liquid to the handle.

The silvery Gaggia machine, with its one-armed-bandit handle, was a piece of impulse buying which Penelope later regretted. It was true that undergraduates, in their tweed sports jackets and cavalry twills, still drove out to the Kitchen, particularly when there was a chance to see the Betjemans' beautiful daughter, whose looks rivalled those of the most stunning women undergraduates, Anita Auden (a niece of the poet), Grizelda Grimond (daughter of the Liberal leader, Jo Grimond) and Maggie Keswick (daughter of the Hong Kong *Taipan*, Sir John Keswick). But this was also the time of the Teddy boys – teenagers who dressed in an ersatz 'Edwardian' style, with 'DA' (duck's arse) haircuts, bootlace ties, long 'drape' jackets with velvet collars, drainpipe trousers and 'winklepicker' or 'brothel-creeper' shoes, sometimes with flick-knives as accessories. They tended to buy one Expresso and lounge around all morning or afternoon drinking it, frightening off the genteel ladies who used to come in for tea and toasted teacakes.[6] John was increasingly worried about the café's drain on the family finances.

Early in February 1958 he and Elizabeth stayed with the Devonshires at Lismore Castle, their house in Ireland. It was the place to which Lady Caroline Lamb had come in 1812 to try to forget Lord Byron. Expecting romantic desolation in tune with her mood, she had been disappointed by the 'dapper parlours' installed by the 'Bachelor Duke'.[7] Also in the 1958 party were Ann Fleming, Elizabeth's sister Lady Anne Tree and the artist Lucian Freud, whose marriage to the writer Lady Caroline Blackwood, daughter of John's beloved Oxford friend Basil Dufferin, had just ended in divorce. On 9 February John wrote to Candida: 'Today I went by train to the salmon fishing on the River Blackwater at Careysville . . . Lucian Freud drew a salmon in water-colour but he draws so slowly that he had only got as far as the eye when it went bad.'[8] John had privately printed, by the Lismore printer Browne, twenty copies of his poem 'Ireland's Own' or 'The Burial of Thomas Moore', ten on green paper for the Devonshires' children Peregrine Hartington and Emma and Sophia Cavendish, ten on mauve paper for other friends.[9] After leaving Lismore, John, Elizabeth and Princess Margaret attended a concert at the University College of North Staffordshire, Keele, where John's friend George Barnes was now Principal.[10] The Princess had recently become the University's Chancellor. Thanking the Duchess of Devonshire for her hospitality, on 15 April, John wrote:

The visit to Keele was uproariously funny and we all had the giggles on our return just as though we were kiddiz. Little Friend [Princess Margaret] was on her best form. Have you ever heard Hiawatha?[11] The words are dotty enough anyhow.

> Never had our fine tobacco
> Tasted pleasanter and sweeter
> Said the handsome old Nokomis
> O Wa Wa my little owlet!

and that sort of thing – but when it is sung with the London Symphony Orchestra, the chorus of five hundred and Flash Harry [Malcolm Sargent] conducting, it is funnier than ever . . .[12]

Late in April John took Candida on a tour of the Scottish islands. He and Penelope knew the Earl and Countess of Wemyss, whose daughter Elizabeth ('Buffy') Charteris was a schoolfriend of Candida and had stayed at The Mead in 1954.[13] In 1957 John had been the guest of David and Mavis Wemyss at Gosford House, East Lothian, when giving a lecture at Edinburgh University.[14] Wemyss was chairman of the National Trust for Scotland and in 1958 invited John and Candida on an 'experimental tour' of the islands, including Fair Isle and St Kilda, two of the Trust's properties. John wrote an article about their experiences ('Guano and Golden Eagles') in The Spectator of 16 May.

A Norwegian[15] motor ship, the Meteor, of the Bergen Line with Captain Knut Maurer in command, was chartered. With 150 passengers, 'most of them bird-watching lairds and their wives', the ship sailed from Leith on 26 April while a Norwegian orchestra played 'Loch Lomond' and while 'the hills of Fife and East Lothian slid by and goat cheese, smoked salmon and a hundred Scandinavian dishes made us forget we might ever be sick'.[16] They climbed the Bass Rock which stank of guano and would, they were told, be alive with earwigs later in the year. John was surprised to find how large that sandstone fortress was. 'In crawling into a dungeon there I put my hand on a centipede.'[17]

On the Sunday (27 April) they landed at Kirkwall. John was impressed by the 'huge red cruciform cathedral of St Magnus', noting that it was a Norwegian building, for the Orkneys were not ceded to Scotland until 1486 (actually, 1472). 'Why go to Mycenae,' he asked, 'when the walk we took through a tunnel in a green mound in Orkney led us to the tomb chamber of Maeshowe?' – a room of about 1500 BC vaulted with large flat stones.[18] He thought Orkney 'a *cul de sac* of the Stone Age people on their journey from the Mediterranean'.[19] He wondered what the sixty or so flaxen-haired people of Fair Isle, who were mostly called Stout or Wilson, thought of the party's luxurious vessel when they visited it. 'They must live a hard life in that windy, treeless place . . .'[20] A gale brought the Atlantic and the North Sea clashing into mountains of water as they crossed from Fair Isle to St Kilda, passing 'the lonely outline of Rona with its ruined church, and the hoy and mysterious Flannan Isles'.[21] Even the best sailors were pale, John recorded – a euphemistic way of saying that all the passengers and some of the crew were seasick.[22] At sunset the tremendous cliffs and stacks of the St Kilda group came into view. With the sea calm at last, they anchored in Village Bay 'and when we landed found ourselves in Oxford Street'.

The RAF is building on the top of one of the three mountains of Hirta, the main island, a radar station for Duncan Sandys [Sandys, who had been at Magdalen, Oxford, with John, and married a daughter of Winston Churchill, was now Minister of Defence]. The ruined crescent of the village, evacuated in 1930, looks pathetically down at huts and tents and lorries. The noise of lorries and the fumes of petrol spread over the deep semi-circle below the mountains. Kenneth Williamson took some of us to the medieval village of dry-stone hovels above the deserted crescent and simple graveyard and on through the mist to the quieter side of the island, where are the remains of a matriarchal settlement as yet uninvestigated by the archaeologist. Sailing round the island in royal blue water we saw guillemots huddled on unapproachable ledges, shags, shearwaters and cheerful puffins which looked like red-nosed waiters.[23]

That evening, the naturalist Seton Gordon played the 'Farewell to St Kilda' on the pipes as the RAF party sailed back to camp. 'What Celtic gloom was there, my countrymen! What sadness, not just for the deserted island, but for the RAF men stranded on it with only the primitive brown sheep like goats, and the mice for pets, with the wireless on in their creamed-out Nissen hut of a mess, with irregular

letters from home, irregular supplies and those piles of unopened fort-
night-old newspapers looking so trivial in the damp, forbidding
grandeur of the island!'[24]

The *Meteor* returned to the sunlit emerald waters of the Western
Isles, whose variegated rocks reminded John of the background of
Holman Hunt's *Scapegoat*.[25] The passengers landed on Rhum and
saw a golden eagle fly above an Edwardian castle. On Iona they picked
up green pebbles at West Bay and knelt in 'the rugged pink cathedral'.
John ended his account of the trip: 'Why go to the hot south when the
warm north has so much more history and colour?'[26] This was not just
a rhetorical flourish to please Lord Wemyss. Candida later wrote of
her father: 'He loved the Scottish islands more than I can express, and
at Skara Brae on the Orkneys, as though in celebration, there hung
before us, about six feet off the ground, a bright green mist for about
a minute which then faded to nothing in the morning light.'[27]

In May Candida went to stay with a family in France, an experience
she hated.[28] John wrote to her:

> It's very typical here at the Mead. Mummy is telephoning to Sheila
> Birkenhead. Angela Wakeford[29] is here substituting for Mrs Hughes at the
> Caff. Marco is asleep in the scullery and I miss you very much. I went into
> your room and it looked just as though you were there. It was harvest fes-
> tival this morning and it went on for hours and hours. That irritating lady
> in front of us brought in a lot of children who crowded out the pews and
> a family came into where I was sitting and squashed me out and I had to
> sit beside that pair of little old women who cough gently every other
> minute. Glory to God in the highest! I had to concentrate a lot to keep
> charity and God in my heart. Powlie is now at Trinity College, Oxford.
> Mummy and Angela went to his rooms today which are panelled Georgian
> and looking down the gardens to those gates that won't be opened until a
> Stuart ascends the throne. He has joined the Jazz Club and the French
> Club. I am going to see him on Monday evening at the Diocesan Dinner[30]
> which is in Trinity.[31]

Just as John had prescribed, Paul had done his National Service
before going up to Oxford. He served in Lord Chetwode's old regi-
ment, the 19th Hussars (now the 15th/19th). Dick Squires remembered: 'He arrived in Northern Ireland on a motor-bike with a saddle
and a saxophone. Penelope said, "No one will have his own car; there's
a marvellous saddle club, nobody will have his own horse." Paul wrote
back and said, "Everybody's got his own car, or two, and everybody
has a hunter and polo ponies. There's no such thing as a saddle club
and they're all enormously rich." '[32] While he was in the Army,

National Service was abolished for anyone born in 1938 or later; so when he arrived at Oxford many of the undergraduates were at least two years younger than he.

Tall, fair-haired and good-looking, he cut a dash at the University. Both Penelope's father and John's mother had left him some money. He used it to buy a vintage Rolls-Royce – to Penelope's disgust.[33] 'Paul rather fancied himself,' said Squires. 'He went through a stage when he was very dandyish. His tie had to be just right. He had terribly smart luncheon parties. The *Isis* gossip-columnist wrote: "The other day I went down Beaumont Street and passed Paul Betjeman, hand-in-hand with Paul Betjeman." Paul had two saxophones. He was on a gig somewhere, I think at Henley, and he ran over the saxophones in the Rolls in a pub car park.'[34] Paul took a Fourth in geography. The idleness required to obtain a Fourth had to be nicely gauged. (In 1962 the Magdalen poet Colin Alexander got into the newspapers by winning a *double* Fourth – the feat previously achieved by Richard Hughes.)[35]

The Betjemans did not lose touch with their friends in Uffington. In June John and Candida attended the wedding of Candida's first friend, Sally Weaver – Queenie Weaver's daughter. John wrote a poem about the event, later published in the *New Yorker*.[36] John overindulged in drink at the reception in the village hall.[37] On the way back, there was a mysterious incident in the twilight.

> We were driving along the Icknield Way between Kingston Lisle and Sparsholt, under an avenue of tall beeches like a cathedral aisle [Candida writes]. I was at the wheel, and JB suddenly shouted, 'Stop, stop, stop!' Aghast, I stopped the car and asked, 'What's the matter?' He said, 'Just wait and I'll get out and open the gate.' I said, 'What gate?' There was clearly no gate. He said, 'Yes, there is. Across the road.' I told him to shut up and drove on. *Had* there been a toll-gate there? *Had* he seen a ghost?[38]

If so, it would not have been the first time. He told Candida that in the late Forties, when driving his mother from Lincolnshire to London, he had a sensation of the supernatural, and stopped the car. Both he and Bess smelt gunpowder. On looking at the map, they found they were at the site of the Battle of Naseby.[39]

In September, Colonel Kolkhorst died. John contributed an obituary notice to *The Times*, which ended: 'He was kind and gentle to the humble and unknown, and, which is harder, to the famous . . . Though a don, he valued Oxford as a place and way of life rather than an exam. factory and had no tolerance for pedantic research.'[40] He attended the funeral and described it in a letter to Billy Wicklow, who was in hospital in Dublin. 'I very much enjoyed your account of the

Colonel's funeral,' Wicklow replied on 3 October, 'and of Hedley [Hope-Nicholson] saying, "that horrid Mr Bryson, I meant to cut him and I smiled at him." '[41]

In February 1959 John wrote to an old friend, the author Cecil Roberts: 'I dare not drop journalism until my son (now at Oxford and with two years and a bit to go) and daughter (in France and aged sixteen and pretty and clever) are off my hands. Then, by Jove, I will. I'm now fifty-two. Can I last the course? I must. Penelope has a small income and so have I, enough to live on, just – but only just.'[42] Because of the great success of his *Collected Poems*, published in December 1958, his financial situation improved. He was even prepared to be indulgent about King Alfred's Kitchen. Writing to Penelope in May 1959, after she had had to pay for the café's roof to be repaired, he complimented her on the way she was running the business, adding, 'I daresay I had better cough up for the roof out of shares . . . NIL DESPERANDUM things might be much worse.'[43]

In the same month, John wrote to thank the Duchess of Devonshire for another week he and Elizabeth had enjoyed at Lismore Castle in April.

> I find it hard to believe that this time last week Feeble and I were sitting in a bar in Mallow eating our sandwiches and drinking Guinness after testing the mineral water in Mallow Spa, an 1840s building near the gasworks. Those glorious days of Lismore were some of the best and most fruitful I have ever spent in my life as I was able to write verse, talk rubbish to Feeble and you and the kiddiz, play with Andrew and admire the castle and cathedral. The phrase 'play with Andrew' is Feeble's. She said one morning I was to go upstairs and write poetry and 'not go playing about with Andrew' until after I had written it.[44]

He was writing *Summoned by Bells*.[45]

Also in May he went on a second cruise round the Scottish islands, this time with Elizabeth. They met (Sir) John Smith, who later founded the Landmark Trust, turning historic properties into holiday homes. On 6 May he wrote in his diary: 'John Betjeman is one of the party, and while we were sorting ourselves out on board he said, for the benefit of anyone who cared to listen, "My daughter Candida couldn't come, so I've brought Elizabeth Cavendish instead." '[46] At Mingulay, at the southern end of the Outer Hebrides, John went paddling 'in his grey pork-pie hat and carrying his straw fishmonger's bag' – 'making this spot, uninhabited since 1911, feel like Margate . . .'[47] Smith found John wonderful company, 'high-spirited, inventive, and very funny'.[48] In a deserted spot given over to birds, 'he said to our eager naturalist companions, "I'm only interested in what Man has done." '[49]

Had the Betjemans been living together at The Mead full-time, a 'devoted couple', we should know far less about their preoccupations at this time than we do. As it was, letters flew back and forth between Wantage and Cloth Fair or Edensor. John's were full of protestations of his love for Penelope, in Irish-accented babytalk.[50] Now that Paul's immediate future was settled, Candida's became the principal topic of the correspondence. In November 1959 – she was seventeen – the Betjemans were debating whether she should go to Italy, be sent to a crammer's for the spring and summer and forgo the London Season, or start in a job, perhaps as a trainee window-dresser, in January. 'It is not easy to talk to her,' John wrote to Penelope, 'and she is too old to be ordered about & accept what is planned for her. Girls develop earlier than boys.'[51]

While, to some extent, John had played the heavy father with Paul, his instinct with Candida was to allow her considerable freedom. Penelope was less sure that this was a good idea. On 12 November 1959 John wrote to her from Edensor:

> I will promise not to let Wibz be rude to you these hols if I can help it.
>
> I think it much better that she should find a place of her own as she has done. It is to be allowed to stand on her own feet more & more & not have things planned for her.
>
> I wish I were with you to help & comfort you in your arguments about Wibz. I see you in my mind's eye lying in bed & thinking of Wibz in desperate situations, no Tewpie [himself] by you.
>
> But let me tell you this. Wibz is healthily 'reacting' against both of us. She hates Art History in the Courtauld sense because you like it & she probably is bored by Mrs Lestrange (who is now 30 years older than when you knew her) partly because Mrs L. did *not* bore you. She hates looking at churches because I like them. She is not in the least interested in what interests us just because these things interest us.[52]

This was a singularly enlightened attitude for a father to take in the 1950s; though, once again – as he sheepishly admitted – John was leaving Penelope in the front line.

'A REALLY THRILLING MOMENT OF TRIUMPH'

I've never seen anything quite so swish as that red velvet edition [of *Collected Poems*] in its morocco box except that which was in the long, royal fingers on that horrifying occasion.

John Betjeman to John G. Murray, Christmas Day 1958

One of the most complimentary reviewers of *A Few Late Chrysanthemums* was Renée Haynes (Tickell), John's old friend from the British Council. In her notice in *The Tablet* she asked, 'Is it not time for a collected Betjeman? The *Selected Poems* which came out a year or two ago omitted some of the most agreeable pieces of work published in those small early books with grotesque typography which are now unobtainable . . .'[1] On 24 March 1955 Jock Murray wrote to John:

I hope you will approve of a plan of doing a complete edition of your poems in the autumn of 1957. By complete I mean that it should include those poems that you can be persuaded not to feel embarrassed to see in print. It would include the Selected and Chrysanths, about four additional early poems which were left out of Selected and poems written after Chrysanths and it is for consideration whether we try to make arrangements for Poems in the Porch to be included also.[2]

Poems in the Porch – a set of Betjeman poems about churches, with illustrations by John Piper, published by SPCK in 1954 – were eventually excluded from the 'collected' volume. John thought them not up to standard; but some of his admirers regretted that the hilarious 'The Friends of the Cathedral' was not admitted.[3]

Murray's hopes of publishing the *Collected Poems* in the autumn of 1957 proved too optimistic. On 19 November 1957 he wrote a memorandum for his staff: 'Discussed the collected volume with John

Betjeman and it was agreed that the poems should be in chronological order of appearance in book form.'[4] It was also agreed that the page area would be similar to that of *Selected Poems*; that a limited edition would be printed on India paper with a limp binding and that Lord Birkenhead would be shown the collection and should suggest which poems might be deleted and which included.[5] Why Lord Birkenhead? He had been a friend of John's at Oxford and had written an able biography of his father, the great F.E. Smith.[6] But he was not among John's closest friends; and in the past John had relied on Tom Driberg and John Sparrow for advice on his poems. It was probably the influence of Birkenhead's sister, the forceful Lady Pamela Berry, rather than his own merits, that prompted the choice of Birkenhead, who eventually both garnered the poems for inclusion in the volume and introduced them. Lady Pamela was not only a significant figure in the social life of Lady Elizabeth Cavendish and John; she liked, as Osbert Lancaster put it, 'to have a finger in every cultural pie'.[7] She had introduced John to Elizabeth; now her brother would introduce him to the world.

John proposed that the poems should be illustrated by Michael Tree of Mereworth Castle, Kent, who was Elizabeth Cavendish's brother-in-law, having married her sister, Lady Anne. 'John Betjeman mentioned a possible plot for his Collected Poems which might involve you,' Murray wrote to Tree on 19 December 1957. 'Is there any chance that you might be in London and of our meeting, for without seeing them [presumably, Tree's drawings], I'm a little in the dark.'[8]

John next suggested, as a compromise, that Tree should illustrate only the long 'Cornish poem' ('North Coast Recollections', abstracted from John's autobiographical work known as 'The Epic'). Murray was not happy with the idea: he would prefer all the poems to be unillustrated, and said it would look odd to have only one poem with pictures. He counter-proposed that Murray should print a small limited edition of the Cornish poem with Tree illustrations 'as a separate thin volume, dependent on our seeing Michael Tree's work'.[9] In any case, Murray noted on 1 January 1958, after lunching with John, 'JB is keen on the binding of the Collected volume having a design in Ricketts or *art nouveau* style for which Michael Tree might do the design.'[10] (This design was not used. If it had been, it would have anticipated – as had the Gabriel Pippet water-lily design in *Continual Dew* – the Art Nouveau revival of the early 1960s, heralded by exhibitions of Alphonse Mucha and Aubrey Beardsley, by Cecil Beaton's designs for Ascot costumes in the film *My Fair Lady* (1964) and by books by Maurice Rheims, Mario Amaya and Robert Schmutzler – the style that contributed so much to 'psychedelic' art.)[11] Michael Tree came to see Jock Murray on 23 January 1958 but brought no samples of his work. It was agreed that he would do a trial engraving for the Cornish poem. Murray added drily, in a further memo for his staff: 'He was enamoured of a book published in France with engravings but as this is in two volumes and costs about 100 gns it is not altogether relevant.'[12]

On 27 January 1958 John went to tea with Lord Birkenhead to discuss which poems should go into the *Collected* volume. Most had been published in Murray books but some had never appeared in volume form. Birkenhead telephoned Murray on 12 March. He agreed to send the poems in three weeks and his introduction in a month: that would mean an early start could be made on printing the poems.[13]

John needed the money that the poems would bring. On 17 April he sent Jock Murray a *cri de coeur*.

> Will you put in any money that is owing to me to my bank, Brown, Shipley & Company . . . ? I have been faced with an overwhelming demand for income tax for past years. It seems that Percy Popkin [his then accountant] whose health broke down about six months ago, had not been declaring my income right. I have no redress and will have to give up a secretary, clubs and sell some books. If you ever hear of a weekly job for me which will bring in a weekly sum, I shall feel most relieved. This free-lance existence at my age and with my family at its most expensive is becoming unendurable.
>
> I enclose Freddy's selection of my poems.[14]

Murray obliged with a transfer of funds to Brown, Shipley.

The selection of poems was not quite complete. John wanted Birkenhead to consider whether 'Caprice', the poem about his being fired from *Time and Tide* by Lady Rhondda, might be included. On 1 June Birkenhead wrote to him: 'I can't read one word of your bloody artistic writing and therefore cannot riposte. Please send me the poem about being sacked.'[15] It was finally decided that the poem was too 'sensitive' to be published. By 9 June Birkenhead's preface was finished. 'I think it is tremendously flattering,' John told Murray, 'and I like the lonely figure he makes me out to be.'[16] Murray wrote to tell Birkenhead how much he had enjoyed the preface, but suggested that some of the quotations from John's verse should be shortened. A publisher's reader had suggested that 'your comments should stir the reader's curiosity to get into the body of the book without having more than a brief and tempting example and that too much quotation spoils the impact when it comes to reading the poem in its sequence in the book.'[17] Birkenhead agreed, and the quotations were reduced.

On 3 July Murray sent the printers, William Clowes of Beccles, Suffolk, an order for 10,000 copies. Galley proofs were ready on 25 July. Birkenhead returned his set on 4 August. Writing to thank him four days later, Jock Murray added, 'I am trying to get John's proofs out of *him*.'[18] John finally returned them on the 16th. On the same day he wrote to Murray from Elizabeth Cavendish's house, Moor View, in Derbyshire:

> Michael Tree has produced a charming design for the cover which he is now finishing. He is also doing some alternative designs. His and my idea is that the spine and front should be stamped with this design in gold on a cream and white binding and that the dust wrapper should be the same design executed in blue or black ink on white paper. His designs partake of the character of Aubrey Beardsley and are what might be called 1890 Abstract, e.g. rather like the Beardsley cover to Dowson's poems.[19]

There was trouble a week later when John was sent Murray's artist's reworking of Michael Tree's sketch. John sent an angry letter from Moor View to Jane Boulanger of Murray's.

> Mr Lancaster who is staying here and I have carefully considered the designs Miss Simmonds kindly sent to me.
>
> We do not like any of them and I would prefer a perfectly plain cover even to any of those suggested & a plain wrapper too with Baskerville or Modern caps. *Please on no account let any of the designs you sent for wrapper or binding be proceeded with.*
>
> As regards wrapper 1, the effect is of nothing, of no period, & the lettering is out of key with Edwardian typography, while the wreaths and device on the back look like somebody imitating an imitation of Rex Whistler and the same goes for the binding of No. 1.
>
> As to the wrapper of No. 2, the artist has missed the delicacy and proportion of Mr Tree's design . . .[20]

Unfortunately, this letter crossed with an infinitely diplomatic one from Jock Murray, dated 22 August: 'Realising that, although you liked them earlier on, you now disliked the chains [motif], and realising that a publisher is the servant of his author – and realising that an author is nearly always right – I have dropped my chains. We are going ahead on the rope of leaves, using your green as the colour and adopting your idea of lines . . . The wrapper is now *very urgent* and we must not hold up the printing . . .'[21] The dust-wrapper row was still rumbling on in September. John continued to fuss about the colours of the binding and the wrapper ('Michael Tree has an eye for colour which amounts to genius'), though he added, 'I fear I have been very difficult about all this.'[22] Even the equable Jock Murray was losing patience. On 17 September he wrote to John firmly, 'We have settled on a rather sumptuous kind of *sang de boeuf*.'[23]

The book was published on 1 December 1958 – rather late for the Christmas market. Besides the 10,000 ordinary copies, a special edition of one hundred copies was printed, with marbled endpapers and a leather binding on a thin board in the same style as George Borrow's *Bible in Spain*. After all the fuss John had made about the cover, and all the designs that had shuttled back and forth between London and Derbyshire, the ordinary copies were finally issued with the plainest of covers, stamped only with a rule set about half an inch from the book's edges all round. The jacket had simple typography against a pink background. Jock Murray sent Lord Birkenhead an advance copy on 19 November. 'I hope you will approve of its modest elegance,' he wrote. 'As you know, the temptation to make it Art Nouveau in appearance was very great.'[24] A launch party was held on 3 December. The next day, Murray wrote to Birkenhead: 'We are frantically reprinting your edition of Betjeman. One or two misprints got through us all and these are being corrected.'[25] These included, in 'A Subaltern's Love-song', 'important' for 'importunate', which, as the bookseller Heywood Hill pointed out, 'neither scans nor makes sense'.[26] Several readers had pleaded for the inclusion of poems which had been omitted – 'Clay and Spirit', 'Variation on a Theme by C.W. Rolleston', 'The Sandemanian Meeting House in Highbury Quadrant' and 'Suicide on Junction Road Station after Abstention from Evening Communion in North London'. Asked his opinion, Birkenhead relented and said he thought all four should be admitted, but left a final decision to John. 'Clay and Spirit' was excluded; the other three went in.

The runaway sales of *Collected Poems* were the publishing phenomenon of 1958. One week after the initial order of 10,000 copies, a further 8,000 copies were ordered for the second printing. The book was selling at the rate of just under 1,000 copies a day. The printers worked through the night. Hatchard's bookshop received fifty copies one morning and were sold out by lunch-time. The reviews were predominantly good. Raymond Mortimer, in the *Sunday Times*, described himself as 'one of his earliest and still most fervent admirers'. John's book criticisms seemed to him 'sometimes too idiosyncratic, always too insular', but 'in his verse and poetic prose, his peculiarities become bewitching'. Mortimer did not find the poetry insular. 'Cowper, Tennyson, Meredith, Father Prout, Ingoldsby, Hardy and the hymn-writers are the authors by whom he has been most obviously influenced; but in the complexity of his feelings he reminds me of perverse Frenchmen whom he may never have read, Baudelaire, Laforgue and Huysmans.'[27]

Anthony Powell reviewed the book in *Punch*, under the heading 'The Swan of Wantage'. He had particular empathy with John, who could be seen as achieving in verse what Powell was doing in prose – using traditional forms to write about contemporary Britain. Powell wrote:

> Impressions shower down on the reader of this volume, among them – perhaps the most overwhelming – that of the personality of the poet. We feel ourselves in the presence of a man of strong will; indeed, a man of iron. Nowadays the term 'Betjemanesque' may be found even in letters to the daily papers (usually employed to deprecate those who delight in good architectural design in contrast with an urge for concrete lampposts) . . . The interesting thing is that all those kestrels and pylons of the early 'thirties have, in their way, dated more distinctly than Betjeman's pitch-pine and stucco. Crashing his way through the *zeitgeist* to the swelling notes of the church harmonium, John Betjeman has become, perhaps, the poet through whom the vagaries of our age will in the last resort be remembered.[28]

Powell thought John's poetry was 'in the best sense traditional'. He noted that his lines (from 'In the Public Gardens'),

> You so white and frail and pale
> And me so deeply me[29]

immediately recalled:

> Makes thee a gleesome, fleasome
> Thou, and me a wretched Me

of Kipling's *Departmental Ditties*. Powell emphasized that he did not intend such comparisons to be disparaging, 'but on the contrary to show the ancestral descent of a great and legitimate pedigree . . . One of the most absurd facets of contemporary criticism is a tendency to suggest that, because from time to time an author is "like" an earlier writer, there must be something wrong about his own approach. Nothing could be greater rubbish.'[30] Powell ended his review with words that were to appear on countless future editions and printings of John's poems, including those of 2001: 'It would be difficult – in my opinion impossible – to point to a contemporary poet of greater originality or more genuine depth of feeling.'[31]

Frank Kermode praised John in *The Spectator*,[32] Anthony Lejeune in *Time and Tide*.[33] In *The Listener*, W.G. Hoskins, who is credited with inventing the subject of landscape history, claimed the *Collected Poems* was 'beyond question the best book to be published in 1958 about the landscapes and towns of England'.[34] One review that gave John special pleasure was Philip Hobsbaum's in *Gemini*, which compared him with his old Marlborough rival Louis MacNeice, to the latter's detriment.

Two of [Betjeman'] best poems appeared in his last volume, the uneven *Few Late Chrysanthemums*: 'Original Sin on the Sussex Coast', with its changes of viewpoint and tone from nostalgic adult to childhood uncertainties, and the clean-cut and unsentimental 'In Memory of Walter Ramsden'.

Louis MacNeice can also turn out a crisp elegy.

'Damn,' you would say if I were to write the best
Tribute I could to you. 'All clichés'.

('The Casualty')
But since MacNeice has less feeling than Betjeman he deserves less credit for restraining it. Whereas Betjeman is limited in subject-matter but has considerable variety of tone, MacNeice writing about the death of his father (in 'Strand'), a jaded libertine, and the British Museum Reading Room reduces them all to the same crackle of wit.[35]

Even the BBC radio Critics, with one exception, were complimentary. The main speaker was Margaret Lane, who had been at Oxford with John and had married the Earl of Huntingdon. She thought that 'the beauty of this collected edition is that it shows him entire, as far as he has gone . . . true, musical and technically accomplished . . .'[36] She asked the question, which neither she nor the others answered, 'How would it strike us if we knew nothing at all about that very peculiar, much publicized personality?' Murray's still today quote her judgement of John on the jackets of his books: 'A true poet, who extends experience and gives pleasure . . .' Fred Majdalany, also on the programme, said: 'One of the things I particularly like about him is that you can't classify him, you can't hang a label round his neck and say exactly what he is – he's a sort of odd man *in*, possibly a lesser Horace who's worked on the *Manchester Guardian* [*laughter*] . . .' Margaret Lane said she thought it possible to dislike 'a kind of snigger which sometimes rises to the surface' in the poems. Answering her, Philip Hope-Wallace agreed that 'that snigger thing is very strange . . . I can only say I find it a kind of chorus-boy thing – a kind of – when Noël Coward says "That was made by an aunt of mine in Wantage," or something like that, in one of his plays, it has the same effect.' The chairman interrupted: 'When Noël Coward says "That was made by an aunt of mine in Wantage" he doesn't know what his aunt in Wantage would in fact have made. John Betjeman does know exactly what his aunt would have made and in a way loves it and feels . . . in compassion with it.'

The BBC Critic who did not like the poems was the art historian Basil Taylor.

> I found the reading of this book an extraordinarily enervating experience; I'm aware of being a sort of Empire Loyalist in a Conservative Party meeting [*laughter*] on this occasion, but there it is. I think first of all these references to such things as kinds of lemon squash or Clemency the General's daughter, or whatever it may be – first of all, they seem to me to be tacked on to poems to give a kind of picturesque effect and I do find this sniggering quality very constant there. I feel that while he is prepared to sympathize with his own feelings for neo-Perpendicular, when he comes to somebody else's feelings for neo-Tudor in Slough, it is a snigger, a kind of patronizing tone which comes, and that I find very unpleasant.[37]

In the *New Statesman*, the book was reviewed by the magazine's literary editor, Janet Adam Smith, widow of the poet Michael Roberts who had edited *The Faber Book of Modern Verse* in 1936. John was not her sort of poet, but she did her best to be fair.

> Three cheers for Betjeman the celebrator of oil-lit chancels and barge-boarded country stations; two for the recorder of nostalgia in Brentford, lost innocence in Norfolk; not much of a cheer for the Betjeman who looks at the social scene today; and no cheers at all for Lord Birkenhead, who does no service to this excellent writer of light verse by claiming too much for him. I can't think that he is likely to win Mr Betjeman new admirers by remarks like 'one who has always stood aloof and alien among the modern poets upon many of whom the autumnal blight of obscurity seems finally to have settled.' Who is he talking about? Empson or Auden? Larkin or Enright?[38]

Louis Johnson, writing in the *Hawkes Bay Herald-Tribune*, also thought John had been overrated. Disputing Auden's opinion that John used 'the common language to create poetry of the greatest possible depth of feeling', he wrote: 'I would like to concur with Auden, but cannot find myself, ever, deeply moved by Betjeman. Interested, yes. Amused, often. But never picked up and then thrown bodily down in the manner which one concedes to be the ability of the master poet.'[39]

Johnson's was one of several foreign reviews which indicated that the name of John Betjeman was becoming known abroad. Houghton Mifflin in New York ordered 250 unbound copies and bumped up the order to 500 when the book 'took off' in London.[40] John fitted the American stereotype of the Englishman as cultured eccentric. *Time* magazine published a full-page profile by Michael Demarest. ('John Betjeman, 52, is a gentle, witty, rumpled Englishman who has been called "the greatest bad poet now living". It would be in character if he agreed with that estimate, although he can be called "bad" only in the sense that his rhymes sometimes jingle like a song writer's . . .')[41] The *Collected Poems* received long, favourable notices from Orville Prescott in the *New York Times*[42] and Walker Gibson in the *New York Review of Books*. 'He is a very attractive poet,' Gibson wrote, 'and the reader never knows when the most frivolous passages may dissolve into deep and finely controlled feeling.'[43] He noted signs of development in John's poetry. 'In Betjeman's more recent work, the tone has become a good deal more urgent as the speaking voice has come closer to home. Instead of hearing the subaltern sing to his tennis-playing lass while we smile tolerantly on all parties, we are now asked to witness a middle-aged man complaining (however amusingly) about his own ridiculous-pathetic rôle . . .'[44]

In December 1958 there was a new boost to John's fame and sales when Princess Margaret presented him with the Duff Cooper Prize. The judges were Maurice Bowra, Lord David Cecil and Harold Nicolson, all old friends of John. They had seriously considered awarding the prize to General de Gaulle for his memoirs, but after debate decided that he already had honours enough.[45] The ceremony took place on 18 December at the home of Lady Jones (the writer Enid Bagnold) near Churchill's house at Hyde Park Gate.[46] On 11 December Jock Murray wrote to John to tell him the 'drill': 'Bowra will make an introduction, Princess Margaret will make the gestures and you ought to say a few words of thanks, somehow introducing Duff Cooper's name in whose honour the award is given. It may well be that Diana Duff Cooper will also say a word or two.'[47]

On the day of the presentation, the *Evening Standard* reported: 'Poet John Betjeman, 52, whose London home in Cloth Fair was recently swept by fire, was at work today in the house of his neighbour and landlord Lord Mottistone, the architect. Betjeman is sleeping in a room in Rotherhithe lent to him by photographer Tony Armstrong-Jones.'[48]

Lady Diana Cooper was nervous about the ceremony. She wrote to Lord Kinross to try to ensure that Prince Jean de Caraman-Chimay would get some credit in the gossip columns for his generosity in giving 'dozens of champagne' for the party.[49] On the day of the award, there were not too many hitches. Among the guests at Hyde Park Gate were the Duke of Devonshire, Joan Aly Khan, Lord Sheffield, Judy Montagu[50] and Rupert Hart-Davis. The Princess looked like a 'jewelled, silky bower-bird, with a close-fitting, wild duck's preened feather hat, no hair, skin like a tea rose, wonderfully pretty – and she made her funny, faultless speech with art and sophistication,' Lady Diana wrote.[51] Presenting John with a cheque for £150 and a leather-bound copy of Duff Cooper's memoirs, *Old Men Forget*, the Princess said it was a particular pleasure to her that that year's recipient of the prize should be 'a friend of mine'. ('John London' of the *News Chronicle* explained: 'The poet first met the Princess five or six years ago. He has taken her to look at some of the old churches about which he is so enthusiastic.')[52] The Princess continued: 'Anyone who has studied John Betjeman's poems closely will have learned not only all about England's lovely old churches but also how to move in society with confidence.'[53] This drew laughter by its obvious reference to the poem beginning, ''Phone for the fish-knives, Norman . . .' (The *Daily Express* noted: 'Nobody asked the butler where the toilet was. The U-word for this is straightforward.')[54] Diana Cooper recorded that 'Poor Betch was crying and too moved to find an apology for words,'[55] though next day the *Daily Telegraph* reported him as saying, 'I am overwhelmed by getting the prize. Duff Cooper was a friend of mine, and of many of my friends. I served under him for a short while at the Ministry of Information. We exchanged some very funny notes.'[56] The *News Chronicle* man observed that 'The poet clean forgot at the appropriate moment to present the Princess with a copy of the poems bound in red velvet. He slipped it to her later under the table – but then it had to be given back to him again for an inscription.'[57]

Sir Roderick Jones, the head of Reuters news agency and 'the only living man shorter than the Princess', insisted on winding up with an interminable speech about the Empire, 'punctuated by whispers from his wife – half proud, half explanatory – of "You know, he's eighty one!"'[58] He gave some offence to the chairman of the judges by referring to him as 'Sir Horace Bowra'.[59] Whether from this slight or from jealousy at John's success, Maurice Bowra later composed a malicious poem about the occasion. The first of the seven stanzas ran:

> Green with lust and sick with shyness,
> Let me lick your lacquered toes,
> Gosh, O gosh, your Royal Highness,
> Put your finger up my nose,
> Pin my teeth upon your dress,
> Plant my head with watercress.[60]

John received one of the three velvet-bound copies of the *Collected Poems*[61] from Jock Murray for Christmas, with a case of wine. He wrote a thank-you letter on Christmas Day:

I've never seen anything quite so swish as that red velvet edition in its morocco box except that which was in the long, royal fingers on that horrifying occasion. No man ever had a kinder or more considerate publisher than you. All I've had from Collins is a bill for £21 against some extra copies I ordered of Parish Churches. How different is Mr Murray, who sends delicious wine as well as the books, in which we drunk [*sic*] your health at lunch today.

Of course next year there will be the reaction and I shall suffer contempt, neglect & frustration, but I can now always look back to a really thrilling moment of triumph . . .[62]

APPENDIX

The poem Maurice Bowra wrote in 1937 to celebrate the birth of John and Penelope Betjeman's son Paul. *By kind permission of the Warden and Fellows of Wadham College, Oxford.*

Uffington Downs

At Garrard's Farm, under the White Horse Hill,
Lived John and little Yellow, – daughter she
Of some famed general in the Indian Wars,
Who oft led red-coats to the battle-line,
And wore three rows of medals on his chest
For gallant service to our gracious Queen.
But John came from the sturdy middle-class,
Who from the strange intricacies of trade
Had laid a little nest-egg by, well placed
In consols and gilt-edged securities
With annual yield of three per cent. The twain
Lived happily on this, and gave their time
To social service and to daily deeds
Of kindness to the folk of White Horse Hill.
   Among his dog-eared books and coloured prints
Of hunting scenes and ancient monuments
And architectural piles in foreign climes
John would peruse the works of bygone men
And write great tomes of learning lightly borne;
Sunk in the past was he, but not afraid
To grapple with the present's many needs,
To play at cricket on the village green,
To study miracles of gas and steam,
To take the village boys upon his knees
And tell improving stories, or to kiss
Their upturned innocent faces full of love.

But Yellow was more active in her ways,
She physicked horses when they had the thrush,
Or lectured to the Women's Institute,
Or knitted jerseys for the godly poor,
Or taught the middle classes how to cook,
Blanc-mange or rich red jellies or meringues,
Or put the cloves in the apple-tart.
Each Lord's Day, when the Matins' summons rang,
The twain, in Sabbath godliness, would go
To Church, where Dr. Harton spoke of God,
Yellow would lead the trebles in the choir
To chants by Dykes or Stamford or by Monk,
Whilst John, with deep resounding organ tones,
Would read from Numbers or Leviticus.
Nor failed they twice a year to take their share
Of bread and wine, spread neatly on a cloth
Upon an oaken table, whilst kind words
Came from good Dr. Harton's reverent lips.
    So passed they happily from day to day,
Nor found allurement from the thought of sin;
But that mysterious Providence, which guides
Our earthly journey, though it blessed them much,
Denied one blessing; for they had no child.
They loved each other much, and every night
John would implant a kiss on Yellow's brow,
Or put his arms around her swelling bust,
Or play with her small hands, – but still no child.
The village talked of it with sympathy,
But others, in whom riches had half-killed
The love of God, would talk with harsher tongues,
And say the fault lay or with her or John,
Right punishment for early years misspent.
And foremost midst these idle chatterers
Was she who reigned in a great country-house,
Elizabethan-Gothic, full of plate
And aspidistras and mahogany,
The Lady Pakenham, not herself well-born
But married to a wealthy nobleman
And fully conscious of her new-found class.
Her talk would reach the happy pair, and oft
They spent the day in weeping over it,
That their sad want should be a cause for jests
And callous comments from the Upper Class.

One Easter Monday, at the great rich house
Where Viscount Pakenham swayed his wide estate,
A fête was held, with booths and roundabouts,
And Punch and Judy shows and tin toy trains.
To this went John and Yellow, well attired
In broadcloth he, in scarlet satin she,
To taste the simple pleasures of the poor.
Her Ladyship was there in all her pearls,
Clad in her new hand-woven mackintosh,
Surrounded by her company of beaux.
She listened to their airy badinage
And watched the stallions sporting with the mares;
For the rich lord was proud of his great stud
And bred up winners for the Derby Race.
To them came John and Yellow, ignorant
Of nature's simple means to propagate,
And saw the stallions sporting with the mares.
'Look! Look!' cried Yellow in her innocence,
'That horse is riding on the other's back!'
And turning to her Ladyship enquired:
'What are your horses doing over there?'
The Lady laughed and did not make reply,
While Yellow blushed and did not understand.
But John was pensive all the afternoon,
And missed three catches in the cricket-match,
Prey to some new and strange anxiety.
    They came back to their cottage without talk,
And Yellow could not see what irked John so,
But did not like to ask him, for she feared
He might be meditating some high theme
Of Grace or Faith or words of Holy Writ,
Then suddenly John went out of the room,
And came back with some reins and snaffle-bit,
And bearing on his arm a mackintosh.
Mysteriously he addressed his wife:
'Come, let us see if God's will may be done.'
She, always faithful to her loving spouse,
Did just as she was bid, and loathed it not,
But found a new delight in solacing
John's strange new interest in natural things.
    The months rolled by, and with them every day
Made Yellow's waistline show a broader curve,
And villagers with kindly nods would say

That Providence had blessed them after all.
So nine months passed, and then the happy twain
Added a third to their sweet company;
Good Dr. Harton held baptismal rites
And named the infant Paul Sylvester George,
And Lady Pakenham gave a silver cup,
Embossed with scenes of Greek mythology,
And fifteen shillings in the Savings Bank.

ACKNOWLEDGEMENTS

As with the earlier volume, my first and greatest debts of gratitude are to John Betjeman, for authorizing this book and recording some recollections for it, and to Penelope Betjeman, for giving all possible help until her death in 1986; and I make grateful acknowledgement to their Estates.

The Murray family, whom I have known for over forty years, have shown a superhuman patience and trust in me. This volume is dedicated to the memory of Jock Murray, one of the great publishers. I am proud to have been – like John Betjeman – one of his authors and one of his friends. His son, John R. Murray, has been equally loyal and encouraging; and John's wife Virginia has given valuable help in her capacity as Murray's archivist.

I have had constant support from all Murray's directors; in particular, it is difficult to find the right words adequately to thank Grant McIntyre, who took over from Jock the main steering rôle and edited the text with adroitness and tact. I am also very grateful to his assistant Caroline Westmore, not just for her heroic labours at the copying machine, but for her always upbeat tackling of temporary problems – temporary thanks to her.

Again, I could not have been more fortunate in having Peter James as copy-editor: unlike the notorious fact-checkers I encountered during five years in America, he never raised an unnecessary point. Also, he gave in with a good grace when I pointed out to him that 'precellent' *is* a word in the *Oxford English Dictionary*.

My late parents, Jack and Mary Hillier, read many of the chapters and gave wise counsel, as did Alan Bell, late Librarian of the London Library. I am delighted that his predecessor as Librarian, Douglas Matthews, was able to undertake the indexing of this volume, just as he did of the first one.

My sister Mary has sustained me to a degree that can never be calculated. My brother-in-law Nigel Thompson, my niece Amy and my nephew Oliver have also helped, both in practical ways and by their sympathetic interest in my work. Duncan Andrews of New York, who early made available to me his treasured collection of Betjemaniana, has cheered me on. I must add my gratitude to my bank, HSBC – especially to Maxine Greaves and David Farmer – for their understanding approach to my bank balance in the years devoted primarily to this biography.

I have had marvellous help from the staff of the Bodleian Library, the BBC Written Archives at Caversham, near Reading, the Huntington Library, San Marino, California, the London Library, the McPherson Library of the University of Victoria, British Columbia, Canada (where most of Betjeman's papers are lodged), the National Library of Ireland, Dublin, and Trinity College Library, Dublin; individual acknowledgements to some of them appear in the list of names that follows. I have tried to remember everyone who helped me, and beg forgiveness if I have left anyone out.

The late Sir Harold Acton; Mr Nick Adams; the late Mario Amaya; Mrs Betty Ames; Mr Mark Amory; Mr Clive Aslet; the late Eric Asprey; the late Philip Asprey; Ms Margaret Barber; the late Desmond Baring; the late Mollie Baring; Mr Nigel Baring; Mr

Anthony Barnes; Ms Joy Bassett; the late Doris Baum; Professor John Bayley; the late Nicolas Bentley; Mrs June Berliner; Mr Robert Berliner; Mrs Diana Berry; Ms Georgia Berry; the late Elizabeth Bettman; the late Judge Gilbert Bettman; Mr Jerry Bick; Lady Rachel Billington; Mr Harry Blacker; Lady Veronica Blackwood; the late Georgiana Blakiston; the late Noel Blakiston; Sister Mary Bland; the late T.S.R. Boase; Mr John Bodley of Faber & Faber; Mrs Pat Boulter; Mr Richard Bourchier; the late Dallas Bower; Mr Delian Bower; the late Professor John Edward Bowle; Lord and Lady Briggs; the British Council; Mrs Frances Brody; Mr Humphrey Carpenter; Ms Christine Carter; the late Ernestine Carter; the late John Carter; the late Sir Hugh Casson; Mr Manuel Catral; the late Lord David Cecil; Ms Anna-Mei Chadwick; Mrs Ruth Childers; the Cincinnati Historical Society; the University of Cincinnati; the late Alan Clark MP; Mrs Gladys Clark; the late Lord Clark; Lady Mary Clive; Ms Joanna Collihole; Lady Silvia Combe; the late Cyril Connolly; the late Dame Catherine Cookson; Mr John Cooney; the late Lady Diana Cooper; Ms Diana Cox; Dr David Crook; the late Dame Sylvia Crowe; Mr Patrick Cullinan; Mr Anthony Curtis; Mrs Anne Dalgety; Ms Frances Daly; the late Professor Donald Davie; Mr C.S.L. Davies and the Warden and Fellows of Wadham College, Oxford; Mrs Philippa Davies, founder chairman of the Betjeman Society; Mr John Deacon; Lady de Bunsen; Mr Frank Delaney; Lord de Mauley; Serena Belinda, Marchioness of Dufferin and Ava; Ms Katherine Duncan-Jones; the late Lady Mary Dunn; Mr Justin Earl; Mr John Edwards; the late Lady Elton; Ms Julia Elton; the late Rowland Emett; Dr Christine Ferdinand, Fellow Librarian of Magdalen College, Oxford; Lady Fergusson of Kilkerran; the late Peter Fleetwood-Hesketh; Ms Louise Fletcher; Mr John-Paul Flintoff; the late Gill Foot; Mr Michael Foot; Mrs Pat Ford; the late Sir Denis Forman; the late Christina Foyle; Mr Luke Franklin; Professor Sir Christopher Frayling; Mr Mario Galang; Mr Peter Gammond, ex-chairman of the Betjeman Society; Mr Simon Garwood; Mr Howard Gerwing; Sir Martin Gilbert; Mr Anton Gill; the late Sidney Gilliat; Lord Gilmour of Craigmillar; Ms Victoria Glendinning; the Knight of Glin; the late John Gloag; Mr Chandra Gopal; the Duke of Grafton; the late Ian Grant; Ms Ti Green; Professor Alvin Greenberg; Mrs Vivien Greene; the late Tom Greeves; the late Joyce Grenfell; Mr John Gross; Mrs Valerie Grove; the late Wallace Guenther; Professor Richard Guyatt; the late John Hadfield; Mr Martin Haldane; Mrs Petronella Haldane; the late William Hammond; the late P. J. R. Harding; Mr Robert Harling; Councillor George Harratt; Mrs June Harris; Mr David Harrison; Mr Dominick-Harrod; Lady Harrod; the late Sibyl Harton; the late Lord Hartwell; Sir Max Hastings; Lady Selina Hastings; Mr Mark Haworth-Booth; Mr John Heald, chairman of the Betjeman Society; Lord Healey; the late Robert Heber Percy; Dr Winifred Hector; the late David Herbert; Mrs Brenda Herbert; the late Derek Hill; Mr Anthony Hobson; Ms Sue Hodson; the late Diana Holman-Hunt; Mr Michael Holroyd; Dr Michael Hooker; Mr Aaron Howard; Lady Howe; the late Archbishop Trevor Huddleston; the late Cardinal Basil Hume; the Rev. Prebendary Gerard Irvine; the late Walter Ison; Mrs Joan Jackson (the former Miss Joan Hunter Dunn); the late Edward James; the Rev. Canon Eric James; Mr Simon Jenkins; Mr Stephen Jessel; Dr D.P. Johnson, Librarian-in-Charge, the Oxford Union Society; Jenefer, Lady Jones; Mr Girish Karnad; Mrs Saras Karnad; Mr John Keay; Sir Ludovic Kennedy; Mr Benedict Kiely; Mr Francis King; the late Lord Kinross; Mr James Kirkup; Mrs Hester Knight; Mr Hiromichi Kurumada; Mrs Marie-Jaqueline Lancaster; the late Sir Osbert Lancaster; Mr Jack Lane; the late Reginald Langbridge; Mr Walter Langsam; Mr Addison Lanier; Mrs Melissa Lanier; the late Mary Lasker; Ms Kit Lawie; Mr Patrick Lawrence; Mrs Molly Lawrence; Lord Lawson of Blaby; the late James Lees-Milne; Mr Hector Legge; Mr Anthony Lejeune; Mr Peter Lester; Mr Jeremy Lewis; Mr Roger Lewis; the late Professor Karl Leyser; the late Ronald Liddiard; Mr John Linnell; the late Christine, Countess of Longford; Elizabeth, Countess of Longford; the late Earl of Longford; the late Professor Seton Lloyd; Mr Christopher Loyd; the late K.B. McFarlane; Ms Blanche McIntyre; Mr Hugh MacLean; Mrs Janet MacLean; the late Ruari McLean; the late Dr Nicholas Mansergh; Mr Philip Mansergh; Mrs Yvonne

Mansergh; Mrs Mary Matthews; Mr Henry Maxwell; Mr Jack Miles; the late Canon Paul Miller; Mrs Marion Milne and 3BM Television; Mr Robert Milner; Mr William Scudamore Mitchell; Ms Julie Moller; Mrs Ruth-Ellen Moller; Mrs Amanda Morgan; Judge Hugh Marsden Morgan; Ms Patt Morrison; the late Lord Moyne (Bryan Guinness); the late Malcolm Muggeridge; Lord Justice Mummery and Lady Mummery; Mrs Ann Norman-Butler; Mrs Belinda Norman-Butler; Dr Conor Cruise O'Brien; Mrs Máire Cruise O'Brien; Ms Felicity O'Mahony; Mr Robert Opie; Professor Nicholas Orme; Mrs Rona Orme; Ms Verity Orme; Lady Ormrod; Mr Cathal O'Shannon; Mrs Christine Outhwaite; the Rev. Tony Outhwaite, Master of the Hospital of St Cross, Winchester; Oxford City Council; the Oxford Preservation Trust; Mrs Betty Packford; Mr George Packford; Mrs Verily Anderson Paget; Mr George D. Painter; Mr Thomas Pakenham; Mrs Valerie Pakenham; Mr William Palin of Sir John Soane's Museum, London; Mr Michael Parkin; Ms Rosemary Pearce; Ms Jenny Pearson; the late Edmund Penning-Rowsell; the late Lionel Perry; Dr William Peterson; Mr Christopher Petter; Ms Kathleen Philip; Mrs Miriam Phillips; Mr Michael Pick; the late Professor Stuart Piggott; Mr George Pipe; the late John Piper; the late Myfanwy Piper; the late Anthony Powell; the late Lady Violet Powell; Mr Alan Powers; Professor John Press; Dr Judith Priestman; the late Marjorie Proops; the late Alan Pryce-Jones; Mr David Pryce-Jones; the late Sir Peter Quennell; Mr Danny Ransohoff; Mrs Marilyn Ravicz; the late Dr Robert Ravicz; Mr James Reeve; the late Mary Renault; the late Sir James Richards; Mrs Jenny Richardson; Mr John Richardson; Mr Nicholas Richardson; Ms Hilary Rittner; Mrs Magda Rogers; the late Dr A.L. Rowse; the library of the Royal Institute of British Architects; Ms Joan Ryan; Mr John Saumarez-Smith; Mrs Lynn Sayer; Mr Martin Sayer; the late Adrian Secker; Mrs Anthea Secker; Mrs Marcella Seymour; Major Bruce Shand; the late Mrs Jessie Sharley; Ms Veronica Sharley; Mr Robert Shaw; Mr David Sheehy, Diocesan Archivist, Archbishop's House, Drumcondra, Co. Dublin, Ireland; Mr Ned Sherrin; Mr Leslie Sherwood; Miss Nerina Shute (Mrs Howard Marshall); the late Robin Skelton; Mr Peyton Skipwith; Mr Anthony Smith, President of Magdalen College, Oxford; Mr Godfrey Smith; Mr Neil Somerville; Dr Per Sörbom, Cultural Counsellor at the Swedish Embassy, London; the late John Sparrow; the late Sir Stephen Spender; Mr Iain Sproat; Mrs Kirsty Squires; the late Ottilie Squires; Dr Richard Squires; Professor Jon Stallworthy; Dr Gavin Stamp; Ms Jaci Stephen; Mrs Betty Stewart; Mr Keith Stewart; Lady Stirling; the late Bishop Mervyn Stockwood; Ms Janet Street-Porter; the late Sir John Summerson; Dr Leslie Sutton; Mr A.G. Swift; Mr David Synnott; the late Pierce Synnott; Mrs Natasha Talyarkhan; Mr Rishad Talyarkhan; the late A.J.P. Taylor; Mrs Jean Sharley Taylor; Mr Peter Temple; Mr Erreg Thami; Mr Charles Thomson; the late Mari Meredyth Thompson; Mr Gary Thorn of the British Museum; the late Rev. Henry Thorold; Brother Philip Thresher; the late Mrs Renée Tickell; the editorial staff of the *Times Literary Supplement*; the late Elizabeth Tollinton; Mr Ion Trewin; the Victorian Society; Mrs Emily Villiers-Stuart; the late Brother Charles Wagner; Mr Cyril Wallworth; Ms Sarah Waters; Dr Maureen Watry; Ms Barbara Watson; the late Auberon Waugh; Mrs Florence May ('Queenie') Weaver; the late Lord Weinstock; the late Eric Walter White; Eleanor, Countess of Wicklow; Mr Edward Wild; Ms Jocelyn Williams; Mr Jonathan Williams; the late Sir Angus Wilson; the late Edward Wolfe RA; Mrs Ann Wolff; the late Douglas Woodruff; the late Joan Woods (Joan Maude); Mr Christopher Woodward; the Rev. Michael Wright; Mr John Wulsin; Mrs Rosamund Wulsin; the late Lord Wyatt of Weeford; Mrs Carolyn Wylie; Mr Deane Wylie; Mrs Billie Yarbrough; Mr Raymond Yarbrough; and the late Miss Loretta Young.

Acknowledgement is gratefully made to the following for permission to reproduce. Details of text material quoted can be found in the Notes. It has not proved possible to trace all copyright holders, but anyone inadvertently overlooked should contact John Murray Publishers. Associated University Presses: Clive Coultass, *Images for Britain: British Film and the Second World War*. B.T. Batsford: Cecil Beaton, *Ashcombe*. A&C Black: Malcolm Muggeridge, *My Life in Pictures*. André Deutsch: *Gilbert Harding by His*

Friends, ed. Stephen Grenfell; Richard Percival Graves, *Richard Hughes: A Biography*. Doubleday & Co.: W.H. Auden, preface to *Slick But Not Streamlined*. Valerie Eliot. Faber & Faber: W.H. Auden, *Verse Letter to C.S. Lewis*; W.H. Auden and Louis MacNeice, *Letters from Iceland*. Bernard Geis Associates: William Glenton, *Tony's Room: The Secret Love Story of Princess Margaret*. Gill & Macmillan: Tony Gray, *Mr Smyllie, Sir*. HarperCollins: *The Letters of Ann Fleming*, ed. Mark Amory; *Letters to a Friend from Rose Macaulay*, ed. Constance Babington Smith; Malcolm Muggeridge, *Chronicles of Wasted Time*; Nigel Nicolson, *Diaries and Letters 1939–1945*; Brian Nolan (Flann O'Brien) *Further Cuttings from Cruiskeen Lawn*. The Lancaster Estate. Little, Brown: Tony Gray, *The Lost Years: The Emergency in Ireland*. Longman: John Lehmann, *I am My Brother*. John Murray: Kenneth Clark, *The Other Half*; James Lees-Milne, *Diaries 1942–1945: Ancestral Voices and Prophesying Peace*. Orion Group: John-Paul Flintoff, *Comp: A Survivor's Tale*. Penguin Books: R.F. Foster, *Paddy and Mr Punch*; *Hostage to Fortune: the Letters of Joseph P. Kennedy*, ed. Amanda Smith. Random House Group: John Betjeman: *Letters 1926–1951* and *Letters 1951–1984*; Ralph Glasser, *Gorbals Boy at Oxford*; Nancy Mitford, *The Pursuit of Love*; Caroline Moorehead, *Sidney Bernstein*; Nicholas Mosley, *Beyond the Pale, Sir Oswald Mosley and Family*; A.J.P. Taylor, *A Personal History*; Evelyn Waugh, *Scott-King's Modern Europe*; Anthony West, *John Piper*; Derek Wood and Derek Dempster, *The Narrow Margin*. Weidenfeld & Nicolson: C.M. Bowra, *Memories*; Tom Driberg, *The Best of Both Worlds*; *Edith Oliver: From Her Journals 1924–1948*, ed. Penelope Middelboe; Meryle Secrest, *Kenneth Clark*; *Kenneth Tynan Letters*, ed. Kathleen Tynan; *The Diaries of Evelyn Waugh*, ed. Michael Davie; *Letters of Evelyn Waugh*, ed. Mark Amory. We are grateful to the *Evening Standard* and the *Daily Telegraph* for the use of John Betjeman's reviews and to *The Spectator* for the use of his columns. Illustrations in the text are reproduced by kind permission of the following: those on pp. 82 and 430–1, the Estate of Osbert Lancaster; those on pp. 186, 438 and 439, Clarissa Lewis; those on pp. 432 and 433 the Estate of Peter Fleetwood-Hesketh; those on pp. 517 and 518 the Estate of Leonora Ison; and that on p. 526 the Estate of Nicolas Bentley.

NOTES

Abbreviations

BBCWA   BBC Written Archives Centre, Caversham Park, Reading
CLG   Candida Lycett Green
DA   Diocesan Archives, Archbishop's House, Drumcondra, Co. Dublin
Huntington   The Huntington Library, San Marino, California
interview   This denotes a tape-recorded interview with the author, conducted at the stated
      date
JB   John Betjeman
JBP   John Betjeman's papers
OPT archives   Oxford Preservation Trust archives
PB   Penelope Betjeman
Victoria   The McPherson Library of the University of Victoria, British Columbia, Canada
YB   Bevis Hillier, *Young Betjeman*, London 1988
JBLP   Bevis Hillier, *John Betjeman: A Life in Pictures*, London 1984

Chapter 1: Uffington

1 Quoted by A.J.P. Taylor, *English History 1914–1945*, Oxford 1965, p. 351.
2 See *ibid.*, pp. 309–10; also R.J. Minney, *Viscount Southwood*, London 1954, pp. 267–69.
3 Taylor, *op. cit.*, p. 351.
4 W.F. Deedes, '"In 1931 to be a reporter was heaven"', *Daily Telegraph*, 21 July 2001.
5 JB, *Letters*, ed. CLG, i, 134.
6 In 1925 X. Marcel Boulestin opened a subterranean restaurant in Southampton Street,
   London, with murals by Marie Laurençin and J.F. Laboureur. It closed down in 1994.
   Boulestin had formerly been secretary to Henry Gauthier-Villars ('Willy'), husband of the
   writer Colette, who portrayed him as Marcel in her novel, *Claudine in Paris* (1901) and
   acted with him at the Théâtre-Royal, Paris, in 1906.
7 See the letter from JB to Pierce Synnott, 3 October 1927, quoted in *YB*, p. 203.
8 The phrase 'a handy-andy fellow' occurs in a poem JB wrote in 1926 – see *YB*, p. 155.
9 In *S by B* (p. 11), JB quotes Ernest: 'Fourth generation – yes, this is the boy.'
10 JB, *Letters*, ed. CLG, i, 127.
11 *Ibid.*, i, 99.
12 *Ibid.*, p. 100.
13 *Loc. cit.*
14 *Loc. cit.*
15 JB letter to Bryan Guinness, 14 January 1934. JB, *Letters*, ed. CLG, i, 129.
16 JB letter to Bryan Guinness, 20 January 1934. JB, *Letters*, ed. CLG, i, 130.
17 Quoted, JB, *Letters*, ed. CLG, i, 130n.
18 *Loc. cit.*
19 Quoted, JB, *Letters*, ed. CLG, i, 97.

20 *Ibid.*, p. 130n.
21 Ken Freeman, interview, 1989.
22 *Ex inf.* Ron Liddiard, interview, 1989.
23 Jessie Sharley, interview, 1995.
24 'Upper Lambourne', *Collected Poems*, 2001 edn., p. 44.
25 JB, *Letters*, ed. CLG, i, 192.
26 *Loc. cit.*
27 *Loc. cit.*
28 *Loc. cit.*
29 JB gave an account of Garrards Farm in *Archie and the Strict Baptists*, the children's story which, though written years earlier, was published by John Murray in 1977 with illustrations by Phillida Gili.
30 Ron Liddiard, interview, 1989.
31 Sir Osbert Lancaster, interview, 1977.
32 JB, *Letters*, ed. CLG, i, 133.
33 Betty Packford, interview, 1989.
34 *Ibid.*
35 Ron Liddiard, interview, 1989.
36 JB, *Letters*, ed. CLG, i, 133.
37 Ron Liddiard, interview, 1989.
38 Ken Freeman, interview, 1989.
39 *Ibid.*
40 George Packford, interview, 1989.
41 *Collected Poems*, 2001 edn., p. 264.
42 Ken Freeman, interview, 1989.
43 *Ibid.*
44 Ron Liddiard, interview, 1989.
45 *Ex inf.* Sir Osbert Lancaster, interview, 1977.
46 *Murray's Handbook to Berks., Bucks., and Oxfordshire*, 2nd edn. revised, 1872, p. 267, records that Radcot, Oxfordshire is 'a small hamlet; its *Bridge* crosses the Thames into Berks . . . Here De Vere, Earl of Oxford, the minister of Richard II, was defeated and put to flight by the partisans of the Duke of Gloucester (20 December 1387).'
47 Ken Freeman, interview, 1989.
48 *Ibid.*
49 JB knew Noel Blakiston through Cyril Connolly, who had had a great crush on Blakiston at Eton – see *A Romantic Friendship: The Letters of Cyril Connolly to Noel Blakiston*, ed. Noel Blakiston, London 1975. Blakiston's father was rector of the church of Kirkby-on-Bain, Lincolnshire, which inspired JB's poem 'A Lincolnshire Tale'. (See Chapter 19.)
50 *Dai Greatcoat: A Self-Portrait of David Jones in his Letters*, ed. René Hague, London 1980, p. 63.
51 *Love from Nancy: The Letters of Nancy Mitford*, ed. Charlotte Mosley, London 1993, p. 65.
52 A clip from PB's television programme was included in Edward Mirzoeff's television film of 29 December 2001, *John Betjeman: The Last Laugh*.
53 Eleanor Fortescue Brickdale RWS (1871–1945), illustrator, painter and designer. Her works are mostly of sentimental and morally uplifting medieval subjects, in brilliant colours. She designed stained glass for Bristol Cathedral.
54 (Sir) Osbert Lancaster, *All Done from Memory*, London 1967, p. 124.
55 Professor Piggott, interviews, 1989–90.
56 *Ibid.*
57 *Ibid.*
58 *Ibid.*
59 *Ibid.*
60 Ron Liddiard, interview, 1989.
61 JB, *Letters*, ed. CLG, i, 135.
62 Ron Liddiard, interview, 1989.
63 Professor Seton Lloyd, interview, 1990.

64 *Ibid.*
65 *The White Horse Recipe Book*, ed. Sheila Matthews, Wantage 1979, p. 5.
66 PB interview, 1976.
67 Mrs Marcella Seymour, interview, 1989.
68 *Ibid.* I am grateful to Mr Robert Opie for the information that in *Home Chat* magazine in 1926 there appeared an advertisement for GENASPRIN, 'to banish headaches'.
69 *Ibid.*
70 Mrs Jean Rome, interview, 1990. She explained, 'When our generation were at school we used to wear serge woollen knickers under our gym slips. And if you were taken out to tea you used to stuff odd cakes under the elastic.' Mrs Rome was formerly married to Brigadier Geoffrey Kellie, who had been on the staff of PB's father in India in the 1930s.
71 PB interview, 1976. See also Mark Amory, *Lord Berners*, London 1998.
72 Nancy Mitford, *The Pursuit of Love*, London 1945, p. 40.
73 Robert Heber Percy, interview, 1976.
74 *Ex inf.* Edward James, interview, 1980. See also Mark Amory, *op. cit.*, 1999 edn., p. 132.
75 Amory, *op. cit.*, pp. 149–50.
76 Edward James, interview, 1980.
77 Amory, *op. cit.*, p. 41.
78 Edward James, interview, 1980.
79 Nancy Mitford, *op. cit.*, p. 41.
80 *JBP.*
81 Robert Heber Percy, interview, 1976.
82 *Ibid.*
83 The photograph is reproduced in Humphrey Carpenter, *The Brideshead Generation*, London 1989, plate facing p. 350.
84 Quoted Amory, *op. cit.*, p. 152.
85 JB, conversation, 1972; and Amory, *op. cit.*, p. 160.
86 JB, conversation, 1971.
87 JB, 'City and Suburban', *The Spectator*, 25 May 1956.
88 The letter is reproduced in *JBLP*, p. 123.
89 Amory, *op. cit.*, p. 152.
90 See *ibid.*, plate two pages before p. 83, for a reproduction of a photograph of Lady Mary Lygon, Loelia, Duchess of Westminster, JB and Robert Heber Percy.
91 Quoted, *ibid.*, p. 153.
92 Quoted *loc. cit.*
93 Novel by Ellen Wood (Mrs Henry Wood, 1814–87). See Ellen Wood, *East Lynne*, ed. Andrew Maunder, Peterborough, Ontario 2000, p. 9: '*East Lynne* was published in 1861 and gained its author Ellen Wood international success. Within one year of its appearance this sensational story of murder, adultery and divorce had captured the imagination of a world-wide reading public. Of several adaptations for the stage the best known was T.A. Palmer's, which opened in 1874. In it, Lady Isabel cries: 'Oh, Willie, my child, dead dead dead! and he never knew me, never called me mother.'
94 Stuart Piggott, interview, 1989.
95 Amory, *op. cit.*, p. 57.
96 See *ibid.*, pp. 48–51.
97 *Ibid.*, p. 110.
98 Quoted, *ibid.*, p. 111.
99 *Loc. cit.*
100 *Loc. cit.*
101 Quoted, *loc. cit.*
102 Quoted, *loc. cit.*
103 Quoted, *ibid.*, p. 157.
104 *Ibid.*, p. 159.
105 *Ibid.*, p. 194.
106 Sir Harold Nicolson, 10 December 1941. *Harold Nicolson Diaries and Letters 1939–1945*, ed. Nigel Nicolson, London 1967, p. 195.

107 Quoted, Amory, *op. cit.*, p. 194.
108 Mrs Jean Rome, interview, 1990.
109 Ron Liddiard, interview, 1989.
110 Quoted, *ibid.*
111 Farmer Wheeler took a *de haut en bas* attitude towards some of the Uffington shopkeepers. Ken Freeman (interview, 1989) remembered a 'mud-slinging match' he had with Willis the shoemaker, who had a notice 'NO TICK' at the back of his shop and was notorious for being unable to find one's shoes in a great heap, when he had repaired them. At the end of the row, Wheeler stalked out of the shop, with the parthian shot, 'Oi shall have to sharpen moi wits against you, moi man!'
112 'We lived in Vale Cottage in the centre of Uffington,' Ken Freeman recalled (interview, 1989). 'Right behind it was a field called White Horse Orchard. There was a chicken-run by the back fence; Father made a little pop-hole in the fence and chickens were let out into the field: Father's, Alf Joyce's and Walt Thomas's. Anyway, one day this field was rented by Farmer John Wheeler. A few days later, a little chicken-house appeared out in this field. It was padlocked, with some corn inside. There was a nest-box with hay. Once a week Farmer John came round, undid the lock, went in and picked out the eggs. So Father and Alf and Old Walt got Ernie Packford, a little weedy sort of boy. They gave him a penny and he used to wriggle into the field through the pop-hole. He'd reach into the chicken-house, and out would come the eggs.'
113 Ken Freeman, interview, 1989.
114 Rober Heber Percy, interview, 1975.
115 Mrs Peggy Phillips, interview, 1990.
116 *Ibid.*
117 Ron Liddiard, interview, 1989.
118 PB, interview, 1976.
119 Quoted, JB, *Letters*, ed. CLG, i, 193.
120 *Loc. cit.*
121 *Ibid.*, i, 253.
122 *Collected Poems*, 2001 edn., p. 188.
123 *Ibid.*, pp. 236–37.
124 *Murray's Berkshire Architectural Guide*, ed. JB and John Piper, London 1949, p. 147.

Chapter 2: Film Critic

1 For a photograph of PB with H.G. Wells and Baroness Budberg, see *JBLP*, p. 105.
2 *Evening Standard*, 23 March 1935.
3 Quoted, James Lees-Milne, *Harold Nicolson: A Biography*, London 1981, vol. 2: *1930–1968*, 32.
4 Malcolm Muggeridge, *Chronicles of Wasted Time*, London 1973, vol. 2: *The Infernal Grove*, 51.
5 See *YB*, p. 286.
6 On John de Forest, later Count de Bendern, amateur golf champion, see *YB*, p. 285.
7 *The Diaries of Sir Robert Bruce Lockhart*, ed. Kenneth Young, London 1973, 14 July 1931, p. 177.
8 Sir Osbert Lancaster, interview, 1977. On Lord Trimlestown, see *YB*, pp. 312–13 and 348.
9 *Evening Standard*, 19 December 1933.
10 Cudlipp's letter offering JB the post is reproduced in *JBLP*, p. 100.
11 Muggeridge, *op. cit.*, ii, 50.
12 *Loc. cit.*
13 Muggeridge, *op. cit.*, ii, 52.
14 *Loc. cit.*
15 *Loc. cit.*
16 *Evening Standard*, 23 March 1935.
17 Lady Mary Clive, letter to the author, 19 May 1988.

18 Malcolm Muggeridge, *My Life in Pictures*, London 1987, pp. 33–34.

19 JB's prank may have been inspired by an incident recounted to him in his Oxford days by his friend Henry Yorke (the novelist Henry Green) – see *YB*, p. 148. According to John Sparrow (*loc. cit.*), JB had already tried out the 'frothing at the mouth' act as an undergraduate.

20 Douglas Fairbanks, jr, *The Salad Days*, London 1988, pp. 216–17.

21 *Ibid.*, p. 217.

22 *Ibid.*, p. 222.

23 See *YB*, p. 246.

24 JB to Endellion Lycett Green, 22 July 1977, JB, *Letters*, ed. CLG, ii, 527.

25 JB's memory was at fault in recalling the film. He covered *George White's Scandals* in the *Evening Standard* on 31 March 1934 and on 4 April 1934 – in each case, earlier than the day of his father's death.

26 JB to Endellion Lycett Green, 22 July 1977. JB, *Letters*, ed. CLG, ii, 527. JB also told the story to Susan Barnes ('"Betjeman, I bet your racket brings you in a pretty packet"', *Sunday Times Magazine*, 30 January 1972) and to the newspaper editor Sir John Junor, who recalled it in his autobiography, *Listening for a Midnight Tram*, London 1990, p. 217.

27 Alan Pryce-Jones, *The Bonus of Laughter*, London 1987, p. 231. If Pryce-Jones's version is accurate, the 'second family' may indeed have been a shock to JB; but he was already well aware that his father had a mistress or mistresses: see *YB*, pp. 199 and 434, n. 13.

28 See *YB*, p. 290.

29 Will of Ernest Betjemann, signed 2 May 1934, *Victoria*.

30 *Ibid.* I am grateful to Councillor George Harratt of Kilrush, Co. Clare, Ireland, who writes (letter to the author, 13 March 2000):

> One of the residents [of Kilrush] . . . informed me that his father's second wife was a Noreen Kennedy, and that they married in Dublin in 1928.
>   The Ryan family had extensive business interests including milling, import and export shipping . . . The family was involved in a trade dispute with another local family. The workers of both came together at a local pub on Christmas Eve 1931 and whatever bitterness there was spilled over on to the streets. In the ensuing riot one girl was shot in the arm, and some property was burned. The local parish priest had to leave the celebration of Midnight Mass, to intervene. Guards were summoned from Ennis (twenty-seven miles away) and Limerick (fifty miles away), but after they fired shots in the air they too were put to flight. The whole affair made the national dailies' front page headlines.
>   During the dispute Noreen drove a lorry for the Ryan faction, and she was most dangerous at her wheel. From what I have been told she was a formidable woman.

31 William Hammond, interview, 1978.

32 Lord Clonmore to Lionel Perry, 19 August 1940. Quoted, JB, *Letters*, ed. CLG, i, 136.

33 Though JB's poem 'On a Portrait of a Deaf Man' (*Old Lights for New Chancels*, 1940) is ostensibly affectionate, there is a distasteful, gloating quality to the descriptions of mortifications of the flesh. In 'Norfolk' (*A Few Late Chrysanthemums*, 1954) JB looks back wistfully to the days before the rift with his father. Two years before his death, JB wrote of his father to the film-maker Jonathan Stedall (8 March 1982): 'He was a great man, and because he was deaf I feared him.' (JB, *Letters*, ed. CLG, ii, 574.)

34 Nerina Shute (Mrs Howard Marshall), interview, 1989.

35 On Iris Barry and Ezra Pound, see Humphrey Carpenter, *A Serious Character: The Life of Ezra Pound*, London 1988, pp. 206, 250, 262–63, 298–99 and 325.

36 Nerina Shute (Mrs Howard Marshall), interview, 1989.

37 Obituary of Iris Barry, *The Times*, 1 January 1970.

38 Nerina Shute (Mrs Howard Marshall), interview, 1989.

39 In an interview with CLG in 1992, JB's friend Ron Liddiard recalled that JB had Ralph Lynn and Tom Walls to stay in Uffington. 'After church on Sunday morning they went for a walk and called in at the Wentworths who had a smallholding outside the village and made home-made wine. Mrs Betjeman had to get her horse and cart out to pick them up – they were so drunk they couldn't walk.' JB, *Letters*, ed. CLG, i, 134.

40 Nerina Shute (Mrs Howard Marshall), interview, 1989.
41 *Ibid.*
42 *Ibid.*
43 *Ibid.*
44 JB mentioned Howard Marshall in a letter to J.R. Ackerley of 24 January 1933 (JB, *Letters*, ed. CLG, i, 113). Marshall was later best known for his radio commentary on the D-Day landings.
45 See B. Hillier, 'A bisexual made for two', *The Spectator*, 19/26 December 1992, pp. 60–62.
46 Dallas Bower, interview, 1992.
47 *Ibid.*
48 See Chapter 11, 'Minnie'.
49 Lady Mary Clive, letter to the author, 19 May 1988.
50 *Ex inf.* Sidney Gilliat, interview, 1991.
51 *Ibid.*
52 *Evening Standard*, 12 August 1935.
53 *Collected Poems*, 2001 edn., p. 71.
54 See *YB*, pp. 153, 160 and 171.
55 On Anthony Bushell, see Evelyn Waugh, *A Little Learning*, London 1964, pp. 178, 211, 212 and 229. Bushell appeared in the 'talkie' version of *Disraeli* (1929) with George Arliss. JB wrote about Bushell in the *Evening Standard*, 20 June 1934.
56 *Evening Standard*, 13 March 1935.
57 *Ibid.*, 25 August 1934.
58 *Ibid.*, 20 August 1935.
59 *Ibid.*, 25 May 1935.
60 *Ibid.*, 6 March 1935.
61 *Ibid.*, 9 June 1934 and 11 June 1934.
62 *Ibid.*, 2 February 1935.
63 JB, conversation, 1975.
64 *Evening Standard*, 9 February 1935.
65 *Ibid.*, 26 January 1935.
66 *Ibid.*, 9 June 1934.
67 On the popularity of Mickey Mouse, see Arthur Millier, *Los Angeles Times*, 5 November 1933, as quoted in B. Hillier, *Mickey Mouse Memorabilia*, New York 1986, p. 11.
68 *Evening Standard*, 10 December 1934.
69 *Ibid.*, 19 May 1934.
70 *Ibid.*, 19 January 1935.
71 On Shirley Temple, *ibid.*, 9 July 1934; on *David Copperfield*, *ibid.*, 9 March 1935.
72 *Ibid.*, 9 March 1935.
73 Nerina Shute (Mrs Howard Marshall), interview, 1989.
74 On Graham Greene's review of Shirley Temple and the ensuing libel case, see Norman Sherry, *The Life of Graham Greene*, i, 619–24 and 656–58.
75 On the purity campaign, see Philip French, *The Movie Moguls*, London 1969, pp. 77–89.
76 Dame Anna Neagle, BBC television interview, 1989.
77 Loretta Young, interview, 1985.
78 Quoted French, *op. cit.*, p. 82.
79 I am indebted to Mr John Deacon for this information.
80 Cedric Belfrage (1904–90), journalist and author. He wrote the 'faction' book *Promised Land* (1938) about the Hollywood myth. He edited the left-wing periodical *National Guardian* and was expelled from the United States in a McCarthyite purge of 1955. See his obituary in *The Times*, 25 June 1990 and the tribute to him by Professor Roger Sharrock, *ibid.*, 2 July 1990.
81 In the 1930s James Douglas (1867–1940) was a columnist of reactionary views on the *Daily Express*. See *Who Was Who*, iii, 378.
82 The programme is now in the present writer's possession.
83 The record is now in the present writer's possession.
84 *Ibid.*

85 *Evening Standard*, 26 March 1934.
86 *Ibid.*, 4 April 1934.
87 *Ibid.*, 3 August 1935.
88 *Ibid.*, 30 January 1935.
89 Respectively: *ibid.*, 22 May 1934; 15 October 1934; 13 November 1934; and 4 January 1935.
90 *Ibid.*, 4 March 1935.
91 *Ibid.*, 21 June 1935.
92 *Ibid.*, 1 August 1934.
93 Rex Graves to *JB*, 2 August 1934. *Victoria*. Though JB did not agree to help Graves with his film he did write up (*Evening Standard*, 27 February 1935) his plans for a film on John Bunyan.
94 See B. Hillier, *Art Deco of the 20s and 30s*, London 1968, p. 106.
95 *Loc. cit.*
96 *Evening Standard*, 20 August 1935.
97 *The Diaries of Sir Robert Bruce Lockhart*, ed. Kenneth Young, London 1973, i, 307.
98 Simon Jenkins, interview, 1990.
99 The offending article appeared in the *Evening Standard* of 23 October 1934.
100 *Evening Standard*, 20 May 1935.
101 On John Sutro, see Evelyn Waugh, *A Little Learning*, London 1964, pp. 182, 188–90, 192, 193–96, 209, 212–13 and 221.
102 Cecil Beaton, *Ashcombe: The Story of a Fifteen-Year Lease*, London 1949, pp. 63–64.
103 Penelope Middelboe, *Edith Olivier: From her Journals 1924–48*, London 1989, p. 167.
104 *Ibid.*, p. 139.
105 *Loc. cit.*
106 *Ibid.*, p. 151.
107 *Loc. cit.*
108 Beaton, *op. cit.*, p. 64. JB also took a part in another film, *Treason's Bargain*, produced by Osbert Lancaster's mother-in-law, Lady Harris – 'a dramatic and historical Comedy in 5 Acts of 106 Scenes depicting the courage and resource of an elderly aristocrat successfully pitted against the dare-devilry and cunning of a bad man'.
        This film survives and was shown at an exhibition of the works of 'Rognon de la Flèche' (Lady Harris) at the Michael Parkin Gallery, Belgravia, in 1988.
109 Nerina Shute (Mrs Howard Marshall), interview, 1989.
110 *Evening Standard*, 20 August 1935.
111 *Loc. cit.*
112 *Loc. cit.*
113 *Loc. cit.*
114 *Loc. cit.*
115 JB also, in the company of Hilaire Belloc, Cyril Connolly, Ronald Knox and others, contributed to *Press Gang!*, ed. Leonard Russell, London 1937, entertaining parodies of different newspaper film critics.

Chapter 3: The Diarist

1 This and all other extracts from JB's diary of 1935–36 are from the autograph MS at *Victoria*.
2 Although JB was not, like Morris, a Socialist, he had in common with him that he was a poet and an architectural conservationist. (Morris founded the Society for the Protection of Ancient Buildings.)
3 Arthur Mee wrote of Great Coxwell, in *The King's England: Berkshire* (London 1945, p. 98): 'It has a marvel of a barn, two centuries older than the fine Elizabethan farmhouse with which it stands.'
4 William Morris called the barn at Great Coxwell 'as noble as a cathedral'. (Quoted, Nikolaus Pevsner, *Berkshire*, London 1988 edn., p. 147.)

5 George Bernard Shaw's *The Intelligent Woman's Guide to Socialism* was published in 1928.

6 Maurice John George Ponsonby, fourth Baron de Mauley of Canford. Born 7 August 1846. Vicar of Wantage 1903–18. Died 15 March 1945. His principal residence was Langford House, near Lechlade. The present (sixth) Baron de Mauley (b. 1921) is his grandson.

7 Frederick Etchells (1886–1973), English painter, designer and architect. Before the First World War he lived for a time in Paris, where he met Picasso and Braque. Back in London, he collaborated with Duncan Grant on a mural for Virginia Woolf's house in Brunswick Square. Roger Fry included his work in the Second Post-Impressionist Exhibition in 1912. In 1913 Etchells joined the Omega Workshops, but seceded from the group, with Wyndham Lewis, and exhibited with him and other 'vorticists' in Brighton, Sussex in 1913–14. After the war he became an architect and in 1930 designed one of the earliest 'Modern Movement' buildings in England. For this information I am indebted to Richard Cork's entry about Etchells in *The Dictionary of Art*, ed. Jane Turner, London 1996, x, 547.

   See also Etchells's obituary in *The Times*, 18 August 1973; also, JB's obituary of him in *The Architectural Review*, October 1973, pp. 271–72, and *YB*, pp. 4, 266–67, 351, 365, 375, 390 and 397.

   Etchells and his wife Hester lived not far from the Betjemans, at France House, East Hagbourne near Didcot.

8 JB's poem of the 1950s, 'How to Get on in Society', echoes this phrase.

9 See *YB*, p. 349.

10 On *The Dance of Death*, see Humphrey Carpenter, *W.H. Auden: A Biography*, London 1981, pp. 139, 144, 164–68, 190, 204, 330 and 345. The production JB and his friends saw was that of Rupert Doone and Tyrone Guthrie at the Westminster Theatre, London, which opened early in October 1935.

11 In his poem 'On a Portrait of a Deaf Man', clearly about his father, JB wrote:

> But least of all he liked that place
> Which hangs on Highgate Hill
> Of soaked Carrara-covered earth
> For Londoners to fill.

12 See Chapter 1 of the present volume; also, JB, 'Oxford', in *W.H. Auden: A Tribute*, ed. Stephen Spender, London 1975, p. 44 (on JB's and Auden's amusement at Bradford's verse).

13 CLG writes (JB, *Letters*, ed. CLG, i, 257n):

> The Revd E.E. Bradford (1860–1944) wrote very funny poetry about young boys. JB used to read the risqué poems out loud, and make everybody laugh. He visited him in Norfolk. Bradford had been forced to move out of his vicarage when its foundations collapsed after he had attempted to dig a swimming pool too close to it in order that he might watch the village boys swimming from his dining room window. Bradford's books were nearly all novels in verse centring around sentimental friendships between older men and boys. His name appeared in Auden's and MacNeice's *Letters from Iceland*, casually dropped in along with those of the greatest writers.

14 The Rev. S.E. Cottam, another paedophile vicar: on JB's visit to him with Auden, see *YB*, p. 177, and below, in the present chapter.

15 Henry Scott Tuke (1858–1929), artist famous for his paintings of naked boys. See also *YB*, pp. 125 and 427, n. 15.

16 The much reproduced *Princes in the Tower* by the Pre-Raphaelite artist Sir John Everett Millais (1829–96) was painted in 1878 and is now at the University of London, Royal Holloway and Bedford New College, Egham.

17 Sir Arthur Stanley Eddington, OM (1882–1945), author of *Science and the Unseen World* (1929) and *The Expanding Universe* (1933).

18 Sir James Hopwood Jeans, OM (1877–1946), author of *The Mysterious Universe* (1930).

19 JB used this euphemism for 'homosexual' in the title of his poem 'Monody on the Death of a Platonist Bank Clerk', published in *High and Low* (1966).

20 That is, masturbation – from the Biblical character Onan, the second son of Judah and the Canaanite Shua. (See Genesis 38:8 and Deuteronomy 25:6.)

The American writer and wit Dorothy Parker named her canary Onan 'because he spilled his seed upon the ground'. (Marion Meade, *Dorothy Parker: What Fresh Hell is This?*, London 1988, p. 78.)

21 Sir Julian Huxley (1887–1975), zoologist and author.

22 See *YB*, p. 170.

23 *Ibid.*, p. 112.

24 MacNeice's first wife (he married her in 1930) was Giovanna Marie Thérèse Babette (Mary) Ezra, b. 1908.

25 On Clifford Canning, see *YB*, pp. 100 and 119.

26 On Cyril Norwood, see *ibid.*, pp. 92–93, 96, 99, 102–03, 111, 118 and 258.

27 JB's hated classics master. See *ibid.*, pp. 94–96, 99–100, 108, 320 and 405.

28 Anthony Thomas Stewart Currie Richardson (b. 1899) was at Marlborough College from 1913 to 1917. He published a novel, *The Transgressor*, in 1928. He disregarded A.R. Gidney's advice, since in 1942 he published *Because of These: Verses of the RAF.*

29 The future Archbishop Laud was President of St John's College, Oxford, from 1611 to 1621.

30 (Sir) Robert Birley (1903–82) became headmaster of Charterhouse in 1935; held that post until 1947; and from 1949 to 1963 was headmaster of Eton.

31 *Collected Poems*, 2001 edn., p. 1.

32 See Chapter 14, '*Daily Herald*'.

33 See JB, *Letters*, ed. CLG, ii, 24, 29 and 30n.

34 See *YB*, p. 213. As stated there, JB did not formally resign from the Society of Friends, which he had joined in 1931, until March 1937.

35 On the 'King and Country' debate of 1933 (in which Professor C.E.M. Joad, later a friend of JB, was the most telling speaker), see for example F.M. Hardie, 'Pacifism at the Oxford Union', *Political Quarterly*, 1933, vol. 4, pp. 268–73; I am grateful for this information from Dr D.P. Johnson, Librarian-in-Charge, the Oxford Union Society.

Chapter 4: 'That's Shell – That Was!'

1 JB to John Piper, 23 October 1964. *Victoria*.

2 JB did not finally resign until 1967. Richard Ingrams and John Piper write, in *Piper's Places: John Piper in England and Wales*, London 1983, p. 123:

> In the 1950s the Shell Guides continued as before but as the years passed Betjeman's interest began to wane and Piper found himself playing more and more of an active rôle . . . until eventually in 1962 he became joint editor of the Guides along with Betjeman. Then in 1967 Betjeman picked a quarrel with Shell when the company withdrew what they considered a defamatory reference to the Norwich Union Building Society from Juliet Smith's Northamptonshire *Guide*. There was a major public row and Betjeman resigned: 'I remember feeling despondent walking down the embankment and wondering whether it had been worth it, having all those jokes with typography.'

Piper then took over the editing on his own, though JB kept a paternal eye on the Guides, and was very angry in the late 1970s when Piper's son Edward, who had become the Guides' designer, introduced designs which JB thought ugly and unsuitable. This episode led to a temporary rift between JB and the Pipers. 'We were almost not on speakers [on speaking terms],' Piper said (interview, 1978).

3 John Piper, interview, 1978.

4 Mark Haworth-Booth, *E. McKnight Kauffer: A Designer and his Public*, London 1979, p. 70.

5 JB to Jack Beddington, 24 April 1939. *Huntington*.
6 *Ex inf.* William Scudamore Mitchell, interview, 1982.
7 John Piper, interview, 1977.
8 Kenneth Clark, *Another Part of the Wood: A Self Portrait*, London 1974, p. 253.
9 John Piper, interview, 1977.
10 JB, *Letters*, ed. CLG, i, 126n.
11 Richard Guyatt, letter to the author, 17 August 1992.
12 Harry Blacker, interview, 1977.
13 On Clark and Mary Kessell, see Meryle Secrest, *Kenneth Clark: A Biography*, London 1984, pp. 158, 166, 167–72, 173 and 191–92.
14 Haworth-Booth, *op. cit.*, p. 71.
15 Ruari McLean, letter to the author, 13 January 1976.
16 See YB, p. 275.
17 *Victoria.*
18 *Huntington.*
19 John Armstrong (1893–1977), British artist, much influenced by the surrealists. Painter of murals, gouaches, etc., with a pronounced left-wing political content.
20 *Huntington.*
21 *Ibid.*
22 *Ibid.*
23 *Ibid.*
24 *Ibid.*
25 *Ibid.*
26 *Ibid.*
27 *Ibid.*
28 *Ibid.*
29 *Ibid.*
30 *Ibid.*
31 *Ibid.*
32 *Uncollected Poems*, London 1982, pp. 41–2.
33 Peter Temple, letter to the author, 25 February 1979.
34 JB to Jack Beddington, 14 January 1935. *Huntington*.
35 *Ibid.*
36 Sir James Richards, interview, 1979.
37 Arthur Waugh (1866–1943). Father of the novelists Alec and Evelyn Waugh. Contributed to *The Yellow Book* in the 1890s. Was chairman of Chapman and Hall, publishers, 1926–36, in which capacity he had dealings with JB. (See YB, pp. 361–62.)
38 Timothy Mowl, *Stylistic Cold Wars: Betjeman versus Pevsner*, London 2000, pp. 72–73.
39 *Ex inf.* John Piper, interview, 1977.
40 For a photograph of Mitchell, see *JBLP*, p. 109.
41 The autograph manuscript is illustrated, *ibid.*, p. 110.
42 William Scudamore Mitchell, interview, 1982.
43 Harry Blacker, interview, 1977.
44 Peter Jacobsohn. His life prior to meeting JB, his extraordinary further adventures and subsequent career, are described by Peter and Leni Gillman, *'Collar the Lot!': How Britain Interned and Expelled its Wartime Refugees*, London 1980, pp. 47–48. Peter Jacobsohn did not lose contact with JB.
45 A photograph of Jacobsohn is reproduced in *ibid.*, between pp. 144 and 145.
46 William Scudamore Mitchell, interview, 1982.
47 Harry Blacker, interview, 1977.
48 William Scudamore Mitchell, interview, 1982.
49 John Piper, interview, 1977.
50 This was confirmed by Anthony Pegg, a former Shell trainee and staff member, in an interview with Jeremy Treglown (Treglown, *Roald Dahl: A Biography*, London 1994, p. 30).
51 Peter Temple, letter to the author, 25 February 1979.

52 I am indebted to Haworth-Booth, *op. cit.*, for the information on the artist. See also B. Hillier, *Posters*, London 1969, pp. 113, 246, 247 and 264.

53 Ruari McLean, letter to the author, 13 January 1978. On the Dragon weathercock, see *YB*, p. 34.

54 See *YB*, Chapter 15, 'Pakenham Hall'.

55 Anthony Powell, letter to the author, 30 October 1988.

56 Anthony Powell, *Journals 1987–1989*, London 1996, p. 147.

57 Dallas Bower, interview, 1982.

58 Sidney Gilliat, interview, 1982.

59 Ruari McLean, letter to the author, 13 January 1978.

60 *The Times*, 23 April 1959.

Chapter 5: 'To Mr and Mrs John Betjeman, a Son'

1 C.M. Bowra, *Memories, 1898–1939*, London 1966, p. 272.

2 *Loc. cit.*

3 PB, interview, 1977.

4 Bowra, *op. cit.*, p. 272.

5 Alan Pryce-Jones wrote *Pink Danube*, London 1939, under the pseudonym 'Arthur Pumphrey'.

6 Wilfried Blunt, *Married to a Single Life*, London 1983, p. 182.

7 *Loc. cit.*

8 Bowra, *op. cit.*, p. 325.

9 Osbert Lancaster, *With an Eye to the Future*, London 1967, p. 124.

10 Wilfrid Blunt, *Slow on the Feather: Further Autobiography 1935–1959*, London 1986, p. 98.

11 *Loc. cit.*

12 Blunt, *Married to a Single Life*, pp. 184–85.

13 *Loc. cit.* John's Oxford friend Michael Dugdale drove with John and Adrian Bishop to see Lord Alfred in Hove. ('A very horrible old man,' Dugdale wrote in his diary, unpublished, shown to the author by courtesy of Lady Fergusson of Kilkerran.)

14 Professor Seton Lloyd, interview, 1989.

15 JB probably obtained MacKenzie the post through his (JB's) friend Arthur Marshall (later a well-known television personality and humorous writer) who, educated at Oundle, had returned as a master.

16 Professor Seton Lloyd, interview, 1989.

17 Sibyl Harton, interview, 1989.

18 *Ibid.*

19 PB, interview, 1977.

20 *Ex inf.* PB, interview, 1977.

21 *Ibid.*

22 Sibyl Harton, interview, 1989.

23 *Ibid.*

24 Bowra, *op. cit.*, p. 326.

25 Sibyl Harton, interview, 1989.

26 Quoted, Bowra, *op. cit.*, p. 172

27 *Loc. cit.*

28 Sibyl Harton, interview, 1989.

29 *Ibid.*

30 John Sparrow, interview, 1977.

31 We know that Paula was with the Betjemans by 5 July 1934 when Edith Olivier visited Garrards Farm and wrote in her diary: 'I had luncheon with Penelope . . . she has a German maid who cooked a good vegetarian meal. Penelope in scarlet trowsers [*sic*] and bright blue shirt mounted her white arab and rode round the field . . .' *Edith Olivier from her Journals 1924–48* ed. Penelope Middelboe, London 1989, p. 156.

32 Bowra, *op. cit.*, p. 171.
33 Mrs Peggy Phillips, interview, 1989.
34 Ken Freeman, interview, 1989.
35 Brigadier-General Charles Higgins (1879–1961), Oxfordshire Light Infantry; served in the South African War and the First World War.
36 Bowra, *op. cit.*, p. 179.
37 The cartoon is reproduced in colour in *JBLP*, p. 106.
38 Ms Joy Bassett, interview, 1989.
39 PB, interview, 1977.
40 Ken Freeman, interview, 1989.
41 *Ibid.*
42 The fire-engine is now in the Newbury Museum.
43 Named after Leslie Hore-Belisha, Minister of Transport.
44 CLG, who quotes part of this poem (JB, *Letters*, ed. CLG, i, 137–38), describes it (*ibid.*, i, 137) as 'a long and eventually filthy Tennysonian verse, "An Idyll"'. Bowra sent JB a copy of the poem, as we know from a letter of 22 April 1938 from JB to Jack Beddington (*ibid.*, i, 208). 'It is a bit rude,' JB wrote, 'so don't leave it about.'
45 PB, interview, 1977.
46 Sibyl Harton, interview, 1989.
47 Betty Packford, interview, 1989.
48 *Ibid.*
49 *Ibid.*
50 *Ibid.*
51 Graham Sutherland OM (1903–80), painter and designer. Born in the same year as John Piper, he was at Epsom College with him.
52 Mrs Betty Packford, interview, 1989.
53 *Ibid.*
54 Philip Larkin, *Required Writing: Miscellaneous Pieces, 1955–1982*, London 1983, p. 111.
55 Alan Pryce-Jones, interview, 1976.
56 Sibyl Harton, interview, 1989.
57 Mrs Mary Matthews, interview, 1989.
58 Florence May Weaver was called 'Queenie' because she was 'the first baby born in Uffington after Queen Victoria's death in 1901'. JB, *Letters*, ed. CLG, i, 324.
59 Mrs Queenie Weaver, interview, 1989.
60 Captain Kellie is pictured with Field-Marshal Sir Philip (later Lord) Chetwode, Lady Chetwode, Penelope Chetwode (later Betjeman) and members of the Commander-in-Chief's staff in India, in *JBLP*, p. 93.
61 Jean Rome, interview, 1989.
62 Robert Heber Percy, interview, 1976.

Chapter 6: The Pipers

1 John Piper, interview, 1978.
2 Quoted, *ibid.*
3 David Piper, in the symposium *To John Piper on his Eightieth Birthday, 13 December 1983*, ed. Geoffrey Elborn, London 1983, p. 61.
4 John Piper, interview, 1978.
5 *Ibid.*
6 Myfanwy Piper, interview, 1978.
7 John Piper, interview, 1978.
8 (Sir) Thomas Kendrick (1895–1979), director and principal librarian of the British Museum 1950–59. Author of *The Druids*, London 1927, and other books.
9 (Sir) Alfred Clapham (1883–1950), secretary, Royal Commission on Historic Monuments, England, 1933–48; commissioner, 1948. Author of *English Romanesque Art*, London 1930, 1934, and other books.

10 John Piper, interview, 1978.

11 *Ibid.*

12 On the 'tree of knowledge' caption, see *YB*, p. 330.

13 Richard Ingrams and John Piper, *Piper's Places: John Piper in England and Wales*, London 1983, p. 44.

14 John Piper, *Piper at 80*, BBC television, 1983.

15 On JB's being introduced to Arthur Machen's novel *The Secret Glory* (published 1922), see *YB*, p. 122; on the 'Myfanwy' references in that book, see *ibid.*, pp. 320–21.

16 Or 'Goldilegz'.

17 *Collected Poems*, 2001 edn., p. 69.

18 *Ibid.*, pp. 71–72.

19 JB to Myfanwy Piper, 28 January 1938. Shown to the author by John and Myfanwy Piper.

20 Myfanwy Piper recalled the precise date in a 1992 interview with CLG. JB, *Letters*, ed. CLG, i, 195.

21 'We had kebabs of lamb with onion and tomato. I remember being impressed by the broccoli which was tied up in bundles.' Myfanwy Piper in interview with CLG, 1992. *Ibid.*

22 Myfanwy Piper, interview, 1978.

23 *Ibid.*

24 Quoted by John Piper, interview, 1978.

25 *Ibid.*

26 *Ibid.*

27 Derek Verschoyle had been a boy at Arnold House school, Llanddulas, Denbighshire, when Evelyn Waugh was a master. In 1943 Waugh took over a London flat from Verschoyle and found he had 'inherited a feud with the management'. *The Diaries of Evelyn Waugh*, ed. Michael Davie, London 1976, p. 538.

28 See John Piper, interview with B. Hillier, in B. Hillier and Mary Banham, *A Tonic to the Nation*, London 1976, pp. 123–25.

29 Stuart Piggott, in the symposium *To John Piper on his Eightieth Birthday*, p. 33.

30 Myfanwy Piper, interview, 1978.

31 *Ibid.*

32 John Piper, interview, 1978.

33 *Ibid.*

34 *Ibid.*

35 *Ex inf.* John Piper, *ibid.*

36 Osbert Sitwell, 'Mr Piper's Brighton', *The Listener*, 4 January 1940, p. 38.

37 John Piper, interview, 1978.

38 Conversation with the late John G. Murray, 1990; see also Horder's obituary, *The Times*, 7 July 1997.

39 John Piper, interview, 1978.

40 Stuart Piggott, in *To John Piper on his Eightieth Birthday*, p. 34.

41 John Piper, interview, 1978.

42 Ingrams and Piper, *op. cit.*, p. 49.

43 John and Myfanwy Piper, interview, 1978.

44 Ingrams and Piper, *op. cit.*, p. 50.

45 *Ibid.*, p. 47.

46 Quoted, *loc. cit.*

47 Quoted, *loc. cit.*

48 John Piper and John Betjeman, *Shropshire: A Shell Guide*, London 1951, p. 38.

49 *Ibid.*, p. 28.

50 Quoted, Ingrams and Piper, *op. cit.*, p. 50.

51 Anthony West, *John Piper*, London 1979, pp. 93–104.

52 Ingrams and Piper, *op. cit.*, p. 47.

53 Stuart Piggott, in *To John Piper on his Eightieth Birthday*, p. 33.

54 Ingrams and Piper, *op. cit.*, p. 50.

55 This verse was the subject of an article in *The Times* of 18 December 1997. I am grateful to Mr William Palin of Sir John Soane's Museum, London, for this information.

56 Myfanwy Piper, 'The Game of Social Comment', *The Times*, 30 October 1984.
57 *Ibid.*
58 *Ibid.*

Chapter 7: *Continual Dew* and *An Oxford University Chest*

1   See *YB*, pp. 353–56.
2   JB, *Letters*, ed. CLG, i, 142.
3   John G. Murray, interview, 1991.
4   *Ex inf.* John G. Murray, conversation with the author, 1990.
5   Shown to the author by the late John G. Murray.
6   Murray's still have the 'Inigo Jones notebook', though this is in fact only a skilful facsimile of Jones's notebook of 1614. They also possess a number of original sketchbooks attributed to the neo-classical artist John Flaxman, of which one is dated 1809.
7   *John Murray archives.*
8   John G. Murray, interview, 1991.
9   JB to John G. Murray, 6 December 1931. *John Murray archives.*
10 *Ibid.*
11 JB to John G. Murray, 30 May 1932. *John Murray archives.*
12 *The Priest and the Acolyte* (1894) by 'X' (i.e. John F. Bloxam): a novel of 'Uranian' (homosexual) tendencies.
13 JB to John G. Murray, 20 September 1932. *John Murray archives.*
14 *John Murray archives.*
15 JB to John G. Murray, 9 October 1933. *John Murray archives.*
16 John G. Murray, interview, 1991.
17 *Victoria.*
18 *Ibid.*
19 JB to John G. Murray, 28 September 1936. *John Murray archives.* The full text of this letter is given in JB, *Letters*, ed. CLG, i, 159–60.
20 JB to John G. Murray, 18 February 1937. *John Murray archives.*
21 *John Murray archives.*
22 John Hadfield (1907–99) was an editor of J.M. Dent & Sons from 1935 to 1942. Later he became editor of the *Saturday Book*, to which JB contributed.
23 G.M. Ellwood (1875–1955), decorative artist and writer. He was awarded a medal at the Paris Exhibition of 1900.
24 *John Murray archives.*
25 *Ibid.*
26 JB to John G. Murray, 23 October 1937, *John Murray archives.*
27 JB to Edward James, 2 November 1937. *Victoria.*
28 *Night and Day*, 25 November 1937.
29 *New Statesman*, 13 November 1937.
30 *The Listener*, 8 December 1937.
31 *John Murray archives.*
32 The two poems Auden selected for his anthology were 'Westgate-on-Sea' and 'The Death of King George V'.
33 Fergusson wrote an article about his experiences accompanying Moholy-Nagy when the Hungarian photographed Eton. See *The Times*, 27 August 1977.
34 *Ibid.*
35 Lázló Moholy-Nagy (1895–1946). Hungarian-born American painter, sculptor, photographer, designer, film-maker, theorist and teacher. See the entry on Moholy-Nagy by Terence A. Senter in *The Dictionary of Art*, ed. Jane Turner, London 1996, xxi, 792–796.
36 In 1924 Hayden wrote a laudatory introduction to the brochure available on the stand of Betjemann & Sons at the British Empire Exhibition at Wembley, London. *JBP.*
37 JB, *The Times*, 27 August 1977.
38 H.F. Paroissien was later managing director of Penguin Books.

39 JB, *The Times*, 27 August 1977.

40 *Ibid.*

41 *Ibid.*

42 *The Listener*, 29 December 1938.

43 'May-Day Song for North Oxford', *Collected Poems*, 2001 edn., p. 96.

44 Graham Greene, 'Oxford Infelix', *The Spectator*, 16 December 1938.

45 *London Mercury*, February 1939.

46 *The Times*, 13 December 1938.

47 JB, *An Oxford University Chest*, London 1938, p. xvi. On Gynes, see *YB*, p. 133.

48 See James Lees-Milne, *Another Self*, London 1970, p. 94.

49 Maurice Hastings, 'Town and Gown', *The Architectural Review*, May 1939, p. 257.

50 'Gutnish' appears to have been a satirical invention by JB. Professor John Bayley writes (letter to the author, 18 April 2002): 'I have inquired about the fascinating *Gutnish*. I think it was a Betjeman fantasy. He detested C.S. Lewis, didn't he, but liked John Bryson at Balliol. Both were fluent in Gutnish. Old English is meant – vulgarly known as Anglo-Saxon. A surviving friend of John Bryson (W.W. Robson) once told me he was much amused by B[etjeman]'s digs. Lewis, I'm sure, was *not* amused.'

51 *Loc. cit.*

Chapter 8: Decoration

1 W.H. Auden, 'September 1, 1939', *Selected Poems*, ed. Edward Mendelson, London 1979, p. 86.

2 On *Antiquarian Prejudice*, see Chapter 23, 'A Preservationist in the Making'.

3 On A.E. Doyle of *The Architectural Review*, see *YB*, pp. 256–57.

4 Hubert de Cronin Hastings to JB, 28 January 1939. *Victoria*.

5 See JB, *Letters*, ed. CLG, i, 249. Possibly JB was treated by R.A. Howden, of whom he wrote to Alan Pryce-Jones on 29 July 1950, 'RA Howden, an RC Queer psychotherapist, is your man, if you feel too dry to live.' (JB, *Letters*, ed. CLG, i, 519.)

6 Quoted, JB, *Letters*, ed. CLG, i, 138.

7 Geoffrey Grigson to JB, 24 June 1938. *Victoria*.

8 Graham Robertson (1866–1948), aesthete, artist, writer; as a young man, a friend of Oscar Wilde. His portrait by John Singer Sargent is in the Tate Gallery.

9 Thanking JB for his article on 9 June 1938 (*Victoria*), Thomson wrote: '. . . I am still worried about your conscientious scruples. Believe me, all danger of a clash along the lines you fear may be obviated by men of good will aiding our Movement in its struggle. I have no doubt that the grave mistake of the Catholic Church in Germany was in supporting the dictatorship of Doctor Bruening which despite all good-will became the tool of the darkest financial interests against resurgent National Socialism. That the Church would suffer from this alliance when the Nazis came to power was inevitable but to my mind Hitler has already used his influence as far as he can to obviate the worst of the clash.'

10 Osbert Lancaster, *With an Eye to the Future*, London 1967, p. 150.

11 PB, interview, 1976.

12 JB, conversation, 1973.

13 Dorothy Grimes to JB, 27 October 1939. *Victoria*.

14 M. Nettleton to JB, 2 November 1939. *Victoria*.

15 *Victoria*.

16 William Packford, interview, 1989.

17 Cyril Connolly, conversation, 1970.

18 See Michael Shelden, *Friends of Promise: Cyril Connolly and the World of Horizon*, London 1989, pp. 1, 44, 47 and 152–53.

Shelden records that, for the issue of *Horizon* of September 1946, 'Cyril Connolly wanted to know what a comfortable income for a writer was, whether the money could be earned solely from writing. If a second job was necessary, what sort of work was most "suitable"? . . . The most imaginative response came from John Betjeman, who answered, "I can only speak for myself. I would like to be a station master on a small country branch line (single track)." '

19 Eliot asked John to write an article for *The Criterion* on the Bressey Report which the Ministry of Transport had commissioned from Sir Charles Bressey, highway engineer, and Sir Edwin Lutyens, to survey highway developments in the London area designed to keep pace with the expansion of road traffic. John needed several polite reminders about delivering the article.

20 Eliot's letter thanking PB for her hospitality is reproduced in *JBLP*, p. 20.

21 The episode is recounted in JB to John Hayward, 4 July 1938. JB, *Letters*, ed. CLG, i, 211.

22 Michael Sadleir to JB, 23 February 1938. *Victoria*. Michael Sadleir (1888–1957) changed the spelling of his surname to avoid confusion with his father Sir Michael Sadler (1861–1943), Master of University College, Oxford. Sadleir was one of Rupert Brooke's lovers at Rugby; he was later an author and a director of Constable & Co., publishers.

23 José Manser, *Hugh Casson: A Biography*, London 2000, p. 79.

24 *Loc. cit.*

25 Quoted, *ibid.*, p. 81.

26 *Victoria*.

27 *Victoria*.

28 Robert Harling to JB, 29 June 1938. *Victoria*.

29 P. Morton Shand to JB, 27 July 1938, *Major Bruce Shand*.

30 JB and Gloag never hit it off. JB referred to Gloag satirically in his poem 'Before the Lecture', *Collected Poems*, 2001 edn., p. 374.

31 *Victoria*.

32 The burden of JB's letter may be judged from Gloag's reply of 21 November; see the passage referred to in note 33.

33 John Gloag to JB, 21 November 1938. *Victoria*.

34 John Gloag to (Sir) Gordon Russell, 25 November 1938. Copy at *Victoria*.

35 *Victoria*.

36 Alvar Aalto (1898–1976): Finnish architect, designer and environmentalist, influenced by Le Corbusier and the Dutch De Stijl group and a friend of his contemporary László Moholy-Nagy. See Göran Schildt's entry for Aalto in *The Dictionary of Art*, ed. Jane Turner, 1996, i, 7–11.

37 P. Morton Shand to JB, 2 February 1939. *Major Bruce Shand*.

38 P. Morton Shand to JB, 16 February 1939. *Major Bruce Shand*.

39 Robert Harling to James Shand, 20 March 1939. *Victoria*.

40 *Ibid.*

41 James Shand to JB, 4 April 1939. *Victoria*.

42 P. Morton Shand to JB, 11 April 1939. *Major Bruce Shand*.

43 A.J.A. Symons (1900–41), poet, author and gourmet, best known for his book *The Quest for Corvo*, London 1934. On him, see Julian Symons, *A.J.A. Symons: His Life and Speculations*, London 1950.

44 *Victoria*.

45 On Edward Pakenham, sixth Earl of Longford and his wife Christine (*née* Trew), see *YB*, pp. 142, 304–11, 315–16, 317 and 318.

46 Robert Harling to JB, 17 July 1939. *Victoria*.

47 Quoted, JB, *Letters*, ed. CLG, i, 198.

48 On Cathleen Delaney (later O'Dea) see *YB*, p. 308. JB called her 'the Colleen' and her husband John O'Dea 'the Eigenherr' (that is, Engineer). Anthony Powell told CLG (JB, *Letters*, i, 45) that JB 'had a thing about' Cathleen Delaney.

49 The home of Lord Dunsany, the playwright and author, on whom see *YB*, pp. 210 and 314.

50 Cathleen Delaney to JB, 7 February 1938. *Victoria*.

51 A photograph of Loch Derravaragh in the 1930s is reproduced in *JBLP*, p. 84.

52 Cathleen Delaney to JB, 17 January 1939. *Victoria*.

53 JB to T.S. Eliot, 13 July 1938. *Victoria*.

54 Edward, Earl of Longford to JB, 29 September 1938. *Victoria*.
55 JB to Bess Betjeman, 5 October 1938. *Victoria*.
56 Constantia Maxwell to JB, 19 November 1938. *Victoria*.
57 The *Sunday Times* of 19 March 2000 carried a story headlined 'Fight to publish memoir of T.S. Eliot's spurned love'.

> She was T.S. Eliot's closest female companion for two decades [it began]. She helped him to write some of his greatest works, was the inspiration for Julia in *The Cocktail Party* and had some 'doodles' of poems composed for her.
> In 1949, Mary Trevelyan proposed to the poet in a letter. He turned her down. She tried again the following year. Again, Eliot rejected her marriage offer. She was devastated when he later married his secretary, Valerie, in 1957.
> But their love story was eventually written as a memoir by Trevelyan, who first offered it in the late 1960s to Faber and Faber, Eliot's publisher. It has been barred from publication for the past 35 years, partly to protect Eliot's reputation.

The newspaper also recorded that 'Eliot and Trevelyan first met in 1938 at a Christian conference in Derbyshire. This was the same year as his first wife, Vivienne, was put into a hospital because of her "madness".'

58 Michael Roberts (1902–48), poet and editor of *The Faber Book of Modern Verse*, London 1935. Married (1935) the critic Janet Adam Smith.
59 Presumably the Rev. Canon Thomas Cruddas Porteus (1876–1948), president of the Lancashire and Cheshire Antiquarian Society 1940–43 and author of *Memories of an Antiquary*, London 1942.
60 On Joad, see Chapter 3, 'The Diarist', Chapter 8, '*Decoration*', Chapter 13, 'Ireland', Chapter 21, 'On the Air in the Forties', and Chapter 27, '*A Few Late Chrysanthemums*'.
61 T.S. Eliot to JB, 15 July 1938. *JBP*.
62 On JB's relations with his former Oxford tutor C.S. Lewis, see *YB*, pp. 71, 135–38, 140, 169, 183–86, 191–92, 324, 343 and 405. A.N. Wilson (*C.S. Lewis*, London 1990, p. 99) records – giving as his source 'oral tradition' via Charles Monteith:

> On one occasion when [he, then an Oxford undergraduate] had failed to produce an essay for the third week running, Betjeman wandered sheepishly into Lewis's room and threw himself on his knees by the hearth.
> 'What is the matter, Betjeman?' asked Lewis.
> 'I'm hopeless. I've failed to produce an essay yet again. I shall be a failure. I shall have to take Holy Orders, but you see I'm in such an agony of doubt, I can't decide.'
> 'What can't you decide, Betjeman?'
> 'Whether to be a High Church clergyman with a short lacy surplice, or a very Low Church clergyman with long grey moustaches.'

63 JB to Edward and Christine Longford, 31 July 1939. *Lady Mary Clive*.
64 *Victoria*.
65 JB to T.S. Eliot, 9 August 1939. JB, *Letters*, ed. CLG, i, 233–34.
66 JB to James Shand, 20 August 1939. *Victoria*.
67 James Shand to JB, 21 August 1939. *Victoria*.
68 *Victoria*.
69 Richard de la Mare to JB, 30 September 1939. *Victoria*.
70 JB to Richard de la Mare, 4 October 1939. *Victoria*.

Chapter 9: Observer Corps

1 In writing this chapter, the author has been particularly indebted to two books: Derek Wood with Derek Dempster, *The Narrow Margin: The Battle of Britain and the Rise of Air Power*, London 1969 edn., especially pp. 68–77; and Derek Wood, *Attack Warning Red: The Royal Observer Corps and the Defence of Britain 1925 to 1975*, London 1976.

2 See Note 1.
3 Wood and Dempster, *op. cit.*, p. 68.
4 William Heath Robinson (1872–1944), illustrator and cartoonist known for drawing weird and whimsical pieces of machinery.
5 Wood and Dempster, *op. cit.*, p. 69.
6 Ronald Liddiard, interview, 1998.
7 *Ibid.*
8 *Ibid.*
9 El-San: portable lavatory.
10 Ronald Liddiard, interview, 1998.
11 JB to Ronald Liddiard, 5 August 1971. Shown to the author by Mr Liddiard.
12 JB, *Letters*, ed. CLG, i, 241.
13 See Chapter 3, 'The Diarist'.
14 JB's letter and the Ministry reply are at *Victoria*.
15 W.H. Auden, 'Verse-letter to C. Day-Lewis'. Quoted Sean Day-Lewis, *C. Day-Lewis: An English Literary Life*, London 1980, p. 310.
16 Humbert Wolfe to JB, 3 December 1939. *Victoria*. On Wolfe, see Richard Church, *The Voyage Home*, London 1964, pp. 29, 32, 81–84 and 107; also, *YB*, pp. 337–38.
17 JB to Humbert Wolfe, 4 December 1939. Copy at *Victoria*.
18 Sibyl Harton to JB, December 1939. Copy at *Victoria*.
19 *Ibid.*
20 H. Beauchamp to JB, 26 January 1940. Presumably a reference to the psychoanalysis for 'persecution mania' which JB had apparently undergone. See JB to Myfanwy Piper, 23 November 1939. JB, *Letters*, ed. CLG, i, 249 and 249n.
21 Field-Marshal Sir Philip Chetwode to JB; quoted, JB, *Letters*, ed. CLG, i, 194.
22 Sidney Gilliat, interview, 1989.
23 Lord Clark, interview, 1980.
24 See B. Hillier, *Art Deco of the 20s and 30s*, London 1968, pp. 45–46.

Chapter 10: Taking to the Air

1 See *YB*, p. 208.
2 John Bowle, interview, 1976.
3 On Reith's 'passionate friendship' with a youth named Charlie Bowser, see Ian McIntyre, *The Expense of Glory: A Life of John Reith*, London 1993, p. 18 and Chapter 3.
4 On Burgess's Cambridge friendship with Blunt, see Andrew Boyle, *The Climate of Treason*, London 1979, p. 70.
5 Respectively, Lionel Fielden, *The Natural Bent*, London 1960, and J.R. Ackerley, *My Father and Myself*, London 1968.
6 Ackerley, *op. cit.*, p. 142. Ackerley does not identify this *outré* figure as Heard, but Peter Parker does so, in *Ackerley: A Life of J.R. Ackerley*, London 1989, p. 110.
7 See *YB*, p. 208.
8 JB to Malcolm Brereton, 9 January 1929. *BBCWA*.
9 JB to Malcolm Brereton, 12 June 1935. *BBCWA*.
10 Anthony Powell, who was at Balliol with Brereton, recalled (letter to the author, 9 September 1990): 'Brereton's appearance was remarkable. His teeth stuck out like a cowcatcher.'
   In 1973 JB and (Sir) Laurens van der Post both wrote introductions to *Collected Poems* by Sir Ian Horabin, whom JB had first met in 1964 when Horabin was released from prison after serving a sentence for homosexual offences. Horabim was a cousin of Malcolm Brereton.
11 *Oxford University Calendar*, 1925.
12 Malcolm Brereton to JB, 10 January 1929. *BBCWA*.
13 Fielden, *op. cit.*, pp. 106–07.
14 Lance Sieveking, *The Eye of the Beholder*, London 1957, pp. 20, 93 and 275–85.
15 *Ibid.*, pp. 275, 277 and 279.

16 Lance Sieveking, *John Betjeman and Dorset*, Dorset Natural History and Archaeological Society, Dorchester 1963.

17 *Ibid.*

18 JB used this name in his early poem 'Camberley' – 'I wonder whether you would make/A friend of Mrs Kittiwake . . .' (*Collected Poems*, 2001 edn., p. 10).

19 Quoted, Sieveking, *John Betjeman and Dorset*.

20 OTC: Officers' Training Corps.

21 Quoted Sieveking, *John Betjeman and Dorset*.

22 'Puddletrenthide' was a BBC genteelism. On Piddletrenthide, see B. Hillier, *Master Potters of the Industrial Revolution: The Turners of Lane End*, London 1965, p. 55.

23 Quoted, Sieveking, *John Betjeman and Dorset*.

24 BBCWA.

25 JB to JR Ackerley, 18 October 1932. *BBCWA*.

26 Lionel Fielden to J.R. Ackerley, BBC internal memo, n.d. but almost certainly October 1932. *BBCWA*.

27 Howard Percival Marshall (1900–73), broadcaster. He married, as his second wife, Nerina Shute in 1944.

28 Sir (Alfred) Daniel Hall FRS (1864–1945), expert on agriculture and horticulture. Author of *Digressions of a Man of Science* (1932) and *The Pace of Progress* (1935).

29 Lionel Fielden to JB, 6 April 1932. *BBCWA*.

30 The writer Reginald Reynolds recorded of Fielden, in *My Life and Crimes*, London 1956, p. 210: 'I have never met a man who could tell more ludicrous stories of little people in big positions.'

31 Lionel Fielden to J.R. Ackerley, BBC internal memo, n.d. but presumably October 1932. *BBCWA*.

32 JB to Lionel Fielden, 29 March 1934. *BBCWA*.

33 Lionel Fielden to JB, 11 April 1934. *BBCWA*.

34 J.R. Ackerley to JB, 5 July 1934. *BBCWA*.

35 Malcolm Brereton to JB, 11 June 1935. *BBCWA*.

36 JB to Malcolm Brereton, June 1935. *BBCWA*.

37 G.N. Pocock to Malcolm Brereton, BBC internal memo, July 1935. *BBCWA*.

38 The programme went out on *West Country Calendar*, 18 May 1936. *BBCWA*, which also record the payment to JB.

39 JB to Ronald Boswell, 29 April 1938. *BBCWA*.

40 *Ibid.*

41 Guy Burgess to JB, 6 July 1937. *BBCWA*.

42 JB to Guy Burgess, 8 July 1937. *BBCWA*.

43 Guy Burgess to JB, 9 July 1937. *BBCWA*.

44 JB to Guy Burgess, 8 July 1937. *BBCWA*.

45 On JB's interest in Adolphus Cooke, see *YB*, p. 317.

46 JB to Guy Burgess, 29 August 1937. *BBCWA*.

47 Guy Burgess to JB, 17 August 1937. *BBCWA*.

48 Ronald Boswell to Talks Booking Manager, BBC internal memo, March 1946. *BBCWA*.

49 JB, 'Bristol', 12 April 1937. *BBCWA*.

50 JB, 'Plymouth', 28 April 1937. *BBCWA*.

51 *Ibid.*

52 JB, 'Swindon', 8 May 1937. *BBCWA*.

53 Quoted JB, *Letters*, ed. CLG, i, 141.

54 Quoted, *loc. cit.*

55 JB, 'Seaview' (I), 22 April 1938. *BBCWA*.

56 JB, 'Seaview' (II), 27 April 1938. *BBCWA*.

57 BBC Religious Adviser to C. Pennethorne Hughes, BBC internal memo, 3 February 1939. *BBCWA*.

58 C. Pennethorne Hughes to BBC Religious Adviser, BBC internal memo, 4 February 1939. *BBCWA*.

59 On this prank, see *YB*, pp. 255–56; also JB in the *Evening Standard*, London, 22 May 1934.

60 Quoted by R. Maconachie, BBC internal memo to C. Pennethorne Hughes, 14 April 1939. *BBCWA*.

61 *Ibid.*

62 Reading Furse's foreword to Newbolt's *A Perpetual Memory and Other Poems*, London 1939, one can see how JB may have been misled into thinking Newbolt's son was killed in the Great War. Furse quotes Newbolt's lines:

> Who under these all-shattering skies
> Plays not his captain's part
> With the last darkness in his eyes
> And *Domum* in his heart.

He then adds: 'That, it may now be said, was written of his only son.'

63 M.T. Candhi to Head of Talks, BBC internal memo, January 1940. *BBCWA*.

64 Captain Newbolt to W.P. Watt of A.P. Watt, 16 January 1940, forwarded to BBC. *BBCWA*.

65 C. Pennethorne Hughes to Head of Talks, BBC internal memo, February 1940. *BBCWA*.

66 George Barnes to C. Pennethorne Hughes, BBC internal memo, March 1940. *BBCWA*.

67 C. Pennethorne Hughes to George Barnes, BBC internal memo, March 1940. *BBCWA*.

68 C. Pennethorne Hughes to George Barnes, BBC internal memo, March 1940. *BBCWA*.

69 George Barnes, BBC internal memo, 27 March 1940. *BBCWA*.

70 BBC minute, June 1940. *BBCWA*.

71 C. Pennethorne Hughes to George Barnes, BBC internal memo, 10 August 1940. *BBCWA*.

Chapter 11: 'Minnie'

1 *Asprey archives.*

2 Michael Bonavia, *London Before I Forget*, Upton-upon-Severn, 1990, pp. 180–81.

3 *Ibid.*, p. 183.

4 Quoted, Caroline Moorehead, *Sidney Bernstein: A Biography*, London 1984, p. 111.

5 Ian McLaine, *Ministry for Morale: Home Front Morale and the Ministry of Information in World War II*, London 1979, p. 3.

6 *Loc. cit.*

7 *Loc. cit.*

8 Bonavia, *op. cit.*, p. 185.

9 Sir John Reith, diary, 20 February 1940. *The Reith Diaries*, ed. Charles Stuart, London 1975, p. 241.

10 Sidney Gilliat, interview, 1989.

11 Sidney Gilliat, in BBC television programme *Filming for Victory*, presented by Professor (Sir) Christopher Frayling, 1989.

12 Sidney Gilliat, interview, 1989.

13 See Moorehead, *op. cit.*, p. 116.

14 *Loc. cit.*

15 Michael Powell, *A Life in the Movies: An Autobiography*, London 1992 edn., p. 307.

16 This passage, written by Nicolson on 8 November 1940, is quoted by Meryle Secrest, *Kenneth Clark: A Biography*, London 1984, p. 154. Secrest adds: '[This] was the night the building sustained a direct hit.'

17 Moorehead, *op. cit.*, p. 113.

18 *Loc. cit.*

19 *Loc. cit.*

20 Secrest, *op. cit.*, p. 156.

21 Bonavia, *op. cit.*, p. 191.

22 *Ibid.*, p. 183.

23 Rawstock (also known as 'filmstock') was film put in the camera in order to take pictures. After being used it was sent for processing into a negative – then a set of positives for

editing. For this information I am grateful to Mr Anthony Smith, President of Magdalen College, Oxford, and formerly director of the British Film Institute.

24 See B. Hillier, *Fougasse*, London 1977, p. 15 and several of the illustrations.

25 Sidney Gilliat, interview, 1989.

26 Caroline Moorehead (*op. cit.*, p. 119) writes: '. . . John Betjeman . . . had decided that he was entitled to a carpet. One day he walked up the road to Heal's and ordered a white fluffy rug. The administrative officers at the MoI forced him to return it.'

27 *Ibid.*

28 *Ibid.*

29 Clive Coultass, *Images for Battle: British Film and the Second World War*, London 1989, p. 64.

30 See Chapter 2, 'Film Critic'.

31 Dallas Bower, interview, 1989.

32 *Ibid.*

33 On John Sutro, see Chapter 2, 'Film Critic', note 105.

34 Dallas Bower, interview, 1989.

35 *Ibid.*

36 *Ibid.*

37 *Ibid.*

38 Henry Maxwell, interview, 1989.

39 *Ibid.*

40 *Ibid.*

41 Sir Osbert Lancaster, interview, 1977.

42 Bonavia, *op. cit.*, p. 195.

43 Henry Maxwell, interview, 1989. This was not the only time that JB used the technique of discomfiting somebody he disliked, in the lift. Caroline Moorehead writes (*op. cit.*, p. 119):

> Betjeman . . . devised a way of intimidating those of the civil servants he found most pompous: he would wait until there was a lift full of people, then say in a very loud voice, picking on some unfortunate employee, cowering in a corner, 'It's not true, you know, that [X] is a Communist (or German spy, or homosexual, or whatever he felt best suited the occasion).

44 Lord Clark, interview, 1980.

45 Nicolas Bentley, conversation, 1976.

46 Bonavia, *op. cit.*, p. 194.

47 Duff Cooper, *Old Men Forget*, London 1953, p. 288.

48 Moorehead, *op. cit.*, p. 117.

49 Dallas Bower, interview, 1989.

50 Moorehead, *op. cit.*, p. 117.

51 *Loc. cit.*

52 *Ibid.*, p. 125.

53 Quoted, *ibid.*, p. 126.

54 Michael Balcon, *Michael Balcon Presents . . . A Lifetime of Films*, London 1969, p. 150.

55 Dallas Bower, interview, 1989.

56 Sidney Gilliat, interview, 1989. Gilliat wanted 'to get the Ministry more interested in having an organized system – like the Germans. They had two hundred war cameramen when the war broke out; we had a grand total of fourteen, three months after war broke out.' An obvious first step was to try to get hold of some of the propaganda films the Germans were making about the British. The ideas committee's greatest coup was to arrange a viewing of Hans Steinhoff's anti-British film *Ohm Krüger* (Uncle Krüger) about the Boer struggle against the British in South Africa. Beddington managed to have a print smuggled in, for discussion. Peter Ustinov pleaded with the MoI to let the film out on general release. 'It was the best British propaganda ever,' Gilliat said. 'Because they had Winston Churchill as the head of a concentration camp in South Africa and throwing rashers of bacon to a bulldog. Churchill was eating very sloppily and every now and again would throw this rasher and

the bulldog would go, "Tschaw! Tschaw! Tschaw!" It was absolutely absurd. And then Queen Victoria, who was slightly sozzled, was being pushed in her wheelchair by John Brown in his kilt. She would say, "Noch eine whisky!" "Ja, meiner Hochhein."' The film was flown out secretly from one of the Scandinavian countries. It had to be back on the Monday so that it would be in place when the German supervisor came round. Gilliat further recalled:

> Jack Beddington said, 'We're going to send it to Mr Churchill. I'm sure you'll all agree he'd be interested.' Well, when it came to the Monday, the film had to go back, but Beddington said, 'I'm awfully sorry to tell you that Mr Churchill never saw it. He preferred *Hellzapoppin*' [a surreal comedy anticipating Monty Python].

57 Arthur Calder-Marshall (1908–92). Not to be confused with the jolly humorist and television personality Arthur Marshall. He was markedly left-wing.
  JB may have disliked him in the 1940s; but, if so, he came round to him. In 1957 JB wrote to PB (*Letters*, ed. CLG, ii, 130): 'By great luck I've had a book for review by Arthur Calder-Marshall, an old Communist chum of mine [*No Earthly Command*] . . . It really is a marvellous book, very well written and absolutely thrilling to read.'
  The present author spoke with Calder-Marshall on the telephone; but, apart from Lady Elizabeth Cavendish, he was the only person who refused to help in any way with this biography.
58 Rex Warner (1908–86). Author of poems, critical essays and novels, including *The Aerodrome* (1941). On him, see Maurice Bowra, *Memories, 1898–1939*, London 1966, p. 149 and Plate 9.
59 James Fisher (1912–70). Naturalist. His books included *Watching Birds* (1940) and *The Birds of Britain* (1942).
60 (Charles Francis) Christopher Hawkes (1905–92). Archaeologist. Married, 1933, Jacquetta Hopkins (marr. diss. 1953), who married (1953) J.B. Priestley; she died 1996.
61 (Rajani) Palme Dutt (1896–1974). Expelled from Oxford for 'Marxist propaganda', 1917; ed. *Labour Monthly* from 1921; ed. *Daily Worker* 1936–38; author of several books on politics. On him, see JB, introduction to *GGT*, 1970 edn., p. xxiv.
62 'Tinketty-tonk' or 'Tinkerty-tonk' was a slang way of saying 'goodbye' when JB was at Oxford, and for a while afterwards.
63 Godfrey Winn (1908–71). Author and broadcaster. See his autobiography *The Positive Hour*, London 1970.
64 For example, in 'The Planster's Vision' and 'The Town Clerk's Views'.
65 See *YB*, pp. 189–90.
66 See JB, *Letters*, ed. CLG, ii, 317.
67 JB still harboured some dislike of Helen de Moulpied (later Lady Forman) in 1974, when he wrote to her husband, (Sir) Denis Forman (4 April 1974): 'I might have known that your Helen would have taken a Min of Inf Arts Council view of *Coronation Street*. Tell her that what I love in it is that it never plays a false note . . .' (JB, *Letters*, ed. CLG, ii, 476). *Coronation Street* was produced by Granada Television, of which Denis Forman was chairman.
68 JB to Geoffrey Grigson, 26 July 1940. JB, *Letters*, ed. CLG, i, 261.
69 Moorehead, *op. cit.*, pp. 120–21.
70 *Loc. cit.*
71 Sidney Gilliat, interview, 1989.
72 While at the MoI, JB often had lunch with Arthur Elton at the Rising Sun pub in Tottenham Court Road, which had been a favourite haunt of the young Evelyn Waugh and his friends in the 1920s. Also, as a change from the restrictive formality of staying with the Chetwodes in St John's Wood, JB sometimes spent a few nights in Hampstead, in the house Elton shared with his girlfriend, the artist Eve Disher. 'He was having one of his "enthusiasms" for a woman at the time,' Lady Violet recalled (telephone conversation, 2001), '– I think her surname was Benson. Eve Disher did several drawings of them, entangled.' Disher also drew a head-and-shoulders portrait of JB, which he thought made him look like the actor Alastair Sim. (The portrait is reproduced in *JBLP*, p. 124.)

73 Sydney Gilliat, interview, 1989.
74 *Ibid.*
75 *Ibid.*
76 *Ibid.*
77 Dallas Bower, interview, 1989.
78 *Ibid.*
79 *Ibid.*
80 BBC television programme, *Filming for Victory*, presented by Professor (Sir) Christopher Frayling, 1989.
81 Coultass, *op. cit.*, p. 47.
82 Sidney Gilliat, interview, 1989.
83 JB to Sidney Gilliat, 8 November 1940. Shown to the author by the late Mr Gilliat.
84 Sidney Gilliat, interview, 1989.
85 Shown to the author by the late Mr Gilliat.
86 JB to Sidney Gilliat, 10 December 1940. Shown to the author by the late Mr Gilliat.
87 Shown to the author by the late Mr Gilliat.
88 *Ibid.*
89 Bonavia, *op. cit.*, p. 177.
90 Joan Jackson, interview, 1995.
91 *Ibid.*
92 *Ibid.*
93 Peter Crookston, 'Joan Hunter Dunn', *Sunday Times Magazine*, 8 August 1965, p. 18. ('A Subaltern's Love-song' appeared in *Horizon*, vol. III, no. 14, February 1941.)
94 Peter Crookston, 'Joan Hunter Dunn', *Sunday Times Magazine*, 8 August 1965, p. 18.
95 The wedding took place at St Mark's Church, Farnborough, Hampshire, on 20 January 1945. The wedding invitation is reproduced in *JBLP*, p. 118.
96 Joan Jackson, interview, 1995.
97 Quoted by Peter Crookston, 'Joan Hunter Dunn', *Sunday Times Magazine*, 8 August 1965, p. 18.

Chapter 12: Old Lights for New Chancels

1 JB to John G. Murray, 12 October 1939. *John Murray archives.*
2 JB to John G. Murray, 20 October 1939. *John Murray archives.*
3 Mullingar was the small town nearest to Pakenham Hall (now Tullynally), Co. Westmeath. (See *YB*, Chapter 10.)
4 JB to John G. Murray, 20 October 1939. *John Murray archives.*
5 *John Murray archives.* The archives show that *Continual Dew* had not, in fact been outstandingly successful in commercial terms. Only 2,014 copies were printed, in November 1937, and these sold in modest quantities until the edition went out of print towards the end of the war.
6 JB to John G. Murray, 20 October 1939. *John Murray archives.*
7 *Ibid.*
8 *John Murray archives.*
9 *Ibid.*
10 John G. Murray to JB, 4 November 1939. *John Murray archives.*
11 *John Murray archives.*
12 *Ibid.*
13 *Ibid.* .
14 *Ibid.*
15 *Ibid.*
16 JB to John G. Murray, 23 November 1939. *John Murray archives.*
17 Preface to *Old Lights for New Chancels*, London 1940, pp. xvii–xviii.
18 John G. Murray to JB, 24 November 1939. *John Murray archives.*
19 *Ibid.*

20 *John Murray archives.*
21 *Ibid.*
22 JB to John G. Murray, 3 December 1939. *John Murray archives.*
23 *Ibid.*
24 John G. Murray to JB, 6 December 1939. *John Murray archives.*
25 *Ibid.*
26 John G. Murray to JB, 7 December 1939. *John Murray archives.*
27 *John Murray archives.*
28 *Ibid.*
29 *Ibid.*
30 John Carter to John G. Murray, 12 December 1939. *John Murray archives.*
31 *John Murray archives.* Ann Taylor (1782–1866, afterwards Gilbert) and her sister Jane Taylor (1783–1824) wrote *Original Poems for Infant Minds* (1805), *Rhymes for the Nursery* (1814) and *Hymns for Infant Minds* (1818). See *DNB* on both authors and on their brother Isaac Taylor, author of books on 'Enthusiasm'.
32 JB to Sir John Murray, 24 July 1940. *John Murray archives.*
33 L.A.G. Strong to John G. Murray, 15 February 1940. *John Murray archives.*
34 William Plomer to John G. Murray, 19 February 1940. *John Murray archives.*
35 John Sparrow to John G. Murray, 19 February 1940. *John Murray archives.*
36 George Gordon to John G. Murray, 19 February 1940. *John Murray archives.* Gordon (1881–1942) was President of Magdalen College, Oxford, 1928–42, and Professor of Poetry.
37 Edmund Blunden to John G. Murray, 21 February 1940. *John Murray archives.*
38 Geoffrey Grigson to John G. Murray, 21 February 1940. *John Murray archives.*
39 John G. Murray to JB, 12 March 1940. *John Murray archives.*
40 The house of the Chetwodes, JB's parents-in-law, in Avenue Road, St John's Wood, London.
41 JB to John G. Murray, 17 April 1940. *John Murray archives.*
42 *The Listener*, Supplement 49, vii, January–June 1940.
43 *Ibid.*
44 J.R. Ackerley (1896–1967), author and literary editor of *The Listener*. On him, see Peter Parker, *Ackerley: A Life of J.R. Ackerley*, London 1989.
45 and 46 Books by the 'Uranian' poet, the Rev. E.E. Bradford. On him, see Chapter 3 of the present work, 'The Diarist'.
47 JB, *Letters*, ed. CLG, i, 257.
48 *New Statesman*, 30 March 1940.
49 *Ibid.*
50 *The Spectator*, 3 May 1940.
51 *Ibid.* Rees is hinting at Ruskin's partiality for young girls – on which see Timothy Hilton, *John Ruskin: The Early Years 1819–1859*, New Haven, Conn. 1985, pp. 253–54 and 267–68; and his *John Ruskin: The Later Years*, New Haven, Conn. 2000, pp. 1, 8–9, 19–22, 26–31, 38–39, 51–53, 112, 114, 231, 233–39 etc.
52 *Time and Tide*, 13 April 1940.
53 *Times Literary Supplement*, 23 March 1940.

Chapter 13: Ireland

In writing this chapter, I have found specially helpful, for background – and some foreground – to JB's years as Press Attaché in Dublin, the following (here listed in alphabetical order): Robert Cole, ' "Good Relations": Irish Neutrality and the Propaganda of John Betjeman 1941–43', *Éire-Ireland*, vol. 30, no. 4, Winter 1996, pp. 33–46 (referred to in this chapter as 'Cole'); Tim Pat Coogan, *De Valera: Long Fellow, Long Shadow*, London 1993, (referred to as 'Coogan'); Lt-Col. John P. Duggan's unpublished MLitt. thesis, 'Herr Hempel at the German Legation in Dublin 1937–1945' (1979), lodged at Trinity College Library, Dublin (referred to as 'Duggan/"Hempel"'); Robert Fisk, *In*

Time of War: Ireland, Ulster and the Price of Neutrality 1939–45, London 1983 (referred to as 'Fisk'); and transcripts kindly supplied by Marion Milne of 3BM Television, of interviews conducted by that company for the Channel 4 television programme *The Real Betjeman* (2000), which gave me some valuable leads (referred to as '3BM').

1 *Asprey archives.*
2 Tony Gray, *The Lost Years: The Emergency in Ireland 1939–1945*, London 1998 edn., p. 15.
3 Shown to the author by the Rev. Prebendary Gerard Irvine.
4 PB, interview, 1976.
5 Peter Somerville-Large, in *Irish Voices: An Informal History 1916–1966*, London 2000 (p. 218), records that the Hamiltons' house was 'near Lucan'.
6 PB, interview, 1976.
7 *Ibid.*
8 *Ibid.*
9 *Ibid.*
10 *Ibid.*
11 Henry Maxwell, interview, 1978.
12 A.L. Rowse wrote, in *All Souls in my Time*, London 1993, p. 19:

> I was delighted, on my first experience of examining [for All Souls fellowships], to catch a young economist of promise, which he certainly fulfilled. This was Harry Hodson (was he descended from 'Hodson's Horse'? – he had a rather equine appearance). [Lionel] Curtis shortly corralled him for the Round Table [of enthusiasts for Lord Milner's ideas].

13 On Hodson, see his obituary in *The Times*, 29 March 1999.
14 H.V. Hodson in interview with Nicholas Cull (1987), quoted by Cole, p. 34.
15 See *YB*, Chapter 10, 'The Stately Homes of Ireland'.
16 See *YB*, pp. 203–06, 295–96 and 348.
17 Quoted Cole, p. 37.
18 *Loc. cit.*
19 JB, *Letters*, ed. CLG, i, 200.
20 *Ibid.*, i, 200–01.
21 Ruth Childers, interview, 1976. (Mrs Childers, the second wife of the Irish Government Minister Erskine Childers, served at the office of the United Kingdom Representative in Dublin just after JB left it.)
22 Gray, *op. cit.*, p. 14; also, 3BM.
23 Kees van Hoek, *Diplomats in Dublin*, Dublin 1943, p. 57.
24 *Ibid.*, p. 58.
25 As can be seen from the photograph of the two of them together, reproduced in *JBLP*, p. 115.
26 Van Hoek, *op. cit.*, pp. 57–58.
27 Duggan/'Hempel'.
28 *Ibid.* JB mentioned John Addington Symonds (1840–93) as a former Fellow of Magdalen College, Oxford, in *An Oxford University Chest*, London 1938, p. 149.
29 'Eva Hempel [*née* Ahlemann] . . . caused many a staid bureaucratic heart to beat a little faster, such was her striking beauty.' Duggan/'Hempel'.
30 Van Hoek, *op. cit.*, p. 14.
31 Duggan/'Hempel'.
32 *Ibid.*
33 'Petersen . . . had a flair for getting himself into scrapes. Hempel damned him with faint praise and put his shortcomings down to youth and political inexperience abroad.' Duggan/'Hempel'.
    JB wrote to John and Myfanwy Piper about Petersen on 20 April 1941 (JB, *Letters*, ed. CLG, i, 287): 'Martin Travers' daughter Sally who acts over here with a repertory

company is pro-German and sleeps with my opposite number. He is so unpopular here except among politically minded tarts and stockbroking and lawyer place-hunters that he does his cause more harm than good. I am a little sunbeam and very pure in contrast.' (Martin Travers, the neo-Baroque church decorator, is mentioned in JB's poem 'Anglo-Catholic Congresses', *Collected Poems*, 2001 edn., p. 265.)

34 Ruth-Ellen Moller, interview, 2001.

35 JB, *Letters*, ed. CLG, i, 267.

36 Van Hoek, *op. cit.*, p. 44.

37 *Ibid.*, pp. 45–46.

38 John Cooney, *John Charles McQuaid: Ruler of Catholic Ireland*, Dublin 1999, p. 444, n. 29.

39 Van Hoek, *op. cit.*, p. 41.

40 'A Romance': a version with names altered by JB is in *Collected Poems*, London 2001 edn., pp. 366–68; the original version is in JB to Diana Craig, May 1946 [?]. JB, *Letters*, ed. CLG, i, 390–91. In the earlier version the name appears, correctly, as 'Dobrzynski'; in the altered version, as 'Dobrezynski'.

41 Van Hoek, *op. cit.*, p. 110.

42 JB to William Plomer, 24 August 1941. JB, *Letters*, ed. CLG, i, 294.

43 PB, interview, 1976.

44 *Ibid.*

45 See Fisk, Chapter 1, 'The Sentinel Towers'.

46 Quoted, Coogan, p. 116.

47 *Ibid.*, p. 346.

48 Members of a British auxiliary police force used in Ireland against the republicans from July 1920 to July 1921.

49 PRO FO 800/310 Bowen to Dominions Office, 9 November 1940. Quoted by Fisk, p. 356.

50 Duggan/'Hempel'. The phrase had a catchy, poetic assonance when translated into German – 'Englands Verlegenheit ist Irlands Gelegenheit.'

51 Quoted by Fisk, p. 175.

52 Kingsley Martin, *Editor*, London 1968, p. 276.

53 PRO FO 800/310 Bowen to Dominions Office, 9 November 1940. Quoted by Fisk, pp. 355 and 526 n. 14.

54 Fisk, Appendix I, p. 483.

55 Quoted, Duggan/'Hempel'.

56 Quoted, Coogan, p. 539.

57 Duggan/'Hempel'.

58 Nicholas Mansergh, *The Unresolved Question: The Anglo-Irish Settlement and its Undoing 1912–72*, New Haven and London 1991, p. 3.

59 Dr Nicholas Mansergh, interview, 1989.

60 *Ibid.*

61 *Ibid.*

62 *Ibid.*

63 J.H. Thomas when Dominions Secretary, quoted by Fisk, p. 26.

64 Frank Gallagher (1893–1962). Director of the Government Information Bureau and one of the people closest to De Valera: JB saw a lot of him. He was also a journalist and author under the pen-name 'David Hogan'. See D.J. Hickey and J.E. Doherty, *A Dictionary of Irish History since 1800*, Dublin 1980, p. 186.

65 'Maffey told [Lieutenant-Colonel Sir Wilfred] Spender [head of the Northern Ireland civil service] that Seán MacEntee, the Minister for Industry and Commerce, was "a strong Anglophobe". It is amusing to note that Eduard Hempel informed his superiors in Berlin that MacEntee was 'strongly pro-British'. Duggan/'Hempel'.

66 Máire Cruise O'Brien sold the poem at auction, at a time before JB manuscripts had became valuable.

67 Máire Cruise O'Brien, interview, 2001.

68 *Ibid.* '[Joyce] maintained his links with old friends such as Constantine Curran (who wrote his obituary in the *Irish Times*) . . .' Brian Fallon, *An Age of Innocence: Irish Culture 1930–1960*, Dublin 1999, p. 65. JB mentioned Con Curran in a letter of 19 July

1941 to Kenneth Clark (JB, *Letters*, ed. CLG, i, 293). Elizabeth Curran contributed articles on art to *The Bell*, e.g. vol. 2, no. 2, May 1941.

69 Quoted, Máire Cruise O'Brien, letter to the author, 20 November 2001.

70 *Ibid.*

71 *Ibid.*

72 *Ibid.*

73 *Ibid.*

74 *Ibid.*

75 *Ibid.*

76 Ruth-Ellen Moller, interview, 2001.

77 (Hon. Sir Egbert) Udo Udoma (1917–98), president of the Dublin University Philosophical Society, 1942–43; called to the Bar 1945; became Justice, Supreme Court of Nigeria, Lagos, 1969; Chief Justice, 1963–69.

78 Paul Ferris writes of Macnamara in *Caitlin: The Life of Caitlin Thomas*, London 1993, p. 20: 'His rages were well known, and so was a boastful, strutting quality that made him an exhibitionist who could be entertaining as long as he wasn't too embarrassing.'

79 Raymond Edwards (Gram) Swing (1887–1968), foreign correspondent and news correspondent. See *The Dictionary of American Biography*, ed. John A. Garraty and Mark C. Carnes, Supplement Eight, 1966–1970, New York and London 1988, pp. 639–41.

80 Ruth-Ellen Moller, interview, 2001.

81 Joan Haslip (1912–94). See *Who Was Who 1991–95*, London 1996, pp. 238–39.

82 Quoted, Dónal Ó Drisceoil, *Censorship in Ireland 1939–1945: Neutrality, Politics and Society*, Cork, 1996, p. 205.

83 *Ibid.*, p. 231.

84 Tony Gray, *Mr Smyllie, Sir*, Dublin 1991, p. 156.

85 Dr Maurice Craig, 3BM.

86 *Horizon*, January 1942.

87 *Ibid.*

88 The cartoon is reproduced in Peter Costello and Peter van de Kamp, *Flann O'Brien: An Illustrated Biography*, London 1987, pp. 90–91.

89 Tony Gray, *The Lost Years*, pp. 94–96.

90 *The Bell*, vol. 16, no. 1, November 1950, p. 5.

91 JB, *Letters*, ed. CLG, i, 271.

92 *Loc. cit.*

93 *Loc. cit.*

94 Costello and van de Kamp, *op. cit.*, p. 84.

95 *Flann O'Brien at War: Myles na gCopaleen 1940–1945*, ed. John Wyse Jackson, London 1999, p. 28.

96 Myles na gCopaleen (Flann O'Brien), *Further Cuttings from Cruiskeen Lawn*, London 1976, p. 77.

97 JB to John Piper, 10 January 1941. JB, *Letters*, ed. CLG, i, 277.

98 Dr Nicholas Mansergh, interview, 1989.

99 *Ibid.*

100 *Victoria.*

101 *Ibid.*

102 Cole, p. 42.

103 Dr Nicholas Mansergh, interview, 1989.

104 See YB, p. 293.

105 Dr Nicholas Mansergh, interview, 1989.

106 Dr Nicholas Mansergh, interview, 1989.

107 Quoted, *ibid.*

108 *Ibid.*

109 *Ibid.*

110 *Ibid.*

111 *Ibid.*

112 *Ibid.*

113 Oliver Stonor was a novelist who also wrote under the pseudonym 'Morchard Bishop', the name of a village near his home in Exeter. (JB, *Letters*, ed. CLG, i, 172 and 237.)

114 JB to Oliver Stonor, 27 March 1943. JB, *Letters*, ed. CLG, i, 314.

115 JB, *Letters*, ed. CLG, i, 270.

116 John Lehmann, *I Am My Brother*, London 1960, p. 172.

117 *The Bell*, vol. 4, no. 6, September 1942, p. 420.

118 Sean O'Faolain, *Vive Moi!*, ed. Julia O'Faolain, London 1993, p. 311.

119 Christopher Fitz-Simon, *The Boys: A Double Biography*, London 1994, p. 130.

120 *Loc. cit.*

121 *Victoria.*

122 John Cooney, *John Charles McQuaid: Ruler of Catholic Ireland*, Dublin 1999, p. 142. I am grateful to Mr Cooney for an informative telephone conversation with him in 2002.

123 On McQuaid and the 1937 Constitution, see *ibid.*, Chapter 8, 'Co-maker of the Constitution'.

124 Ó Drisceoil, *op. cit.*, p. 224.

125 Fisk, p. 370.

126 See JB's letter to MacManus of 28 April 1933, reproduced in *YB*, Plate 41.

127 On McQuaid's anti-Semitism, see Cooney, *op. cit.*, pp. 44, 53, 238, 240 and 294. On Pius XII's anti-Semitism, see John Cornwell, *Hitler's Pope: The Secret History of Pius XII*. London 1999 edn., in particular pp. 295–97.

128 Duggan/'Hempel'.

129 Quoted, *ibid.* On this encyclical of Pius XI, see also Cornwell, *op. cit.*, pp. 141, 181–84, 205, 280 and 296.

130 Quoted, Duggan/'Hempel'.

131 Cole, p. 41.

132 *Loc. cit.*

133 Ó Drisceoil, *op. cit.*, p. 147.

134 *Loc. cit.*

135 Archbishop McQuaid to Archbishop William Godfrey, 7 June 1941. *Copy in DA*.

136 Archbishop McQuaid to Archbishop William Godfrey, 19 December 1941. *Copy in DA*.

137 The article appeared in the *Catholic Herald*, 12 December 1941. Cutting in *DA*. See also Cooney, *op. cit.*, p. 160.

138 It was named after Désiré-Joseph Mercier (1851–1926), Belgian educator, reviver of the philosophy of St Thomas Aquinas; Archbishop of Malines (1906) and Cardinal (1907).

139 On whom, see León Ó Broin, *Frank Duff*, Dublin 1982.

140 He decided to let the next meeting go ahead as the next speaker was JB's old friend Christopher Hollis, an English Catholic.

141 The paper 'Communism and the Answer' was read on 25 February 1943 by the Rev. R.C. Elliott of Abbey Presbyterian Church. *Minutes of the Mercier Society, DA*.

142 The paper 'The Liturgy' was read on 24 June 1943 by the Rev. Mr Ferrar. *Minutes of the Mercier Society, DA*.

143 Possibly Ossie Dowling, an 'experienced journalist' whom McQuaid put in charge of his press relations office in 1965. See Cooney, *op. cit.*, p. 368.

144 *Minutes of the Mercier Society, DA*.

145 Memorandum to Archbishop McQuaid from his secretary, 27 July 1943. *DA*.

146 *DA*.

147 Cooney, *op. cit.*, p. 459, n. 53.

148 *Loc. cit.*

149 Kavanagh wrote to JB (undated): 'My poems are being considered by T.S. Eliot for Faber's. The one I wrote for Candida I left – not to flatter or please you (which it may not) but because it happens to be a good poem . . .' (JB, *Letters*, ed. CLG, i, 271). The poem was first published in the *Irish Press*, 23 September 1943; see also Patrick Kavanagh, *Collected Poems*, London 1964, p. 80. Kavanagh wrote about his friendship with JB in his magazine *Kavanagh's Weekly*, 12 April 1952.

150 Quoted by PB, interview, 1976.

151 JB, *Letters*, ed. CLG, i, 271.
152 Quoted *ibid.*, 270.
153 Ruth-Ellen Moller, interview, 2001.
154 JB to John Piper, 17 March 1943. JB, *Letters*, ed. CLG, i, 283.
155 JB to John and Myfanwy Piper, 2 March 1941. JB, *Letters*, ed. CLG, i, 280.
156 PB to Myfanwy Piper, 20 May 1941. Quoted, JB, *Letters*, ed. CLG, i, 269.
157 PB, interview, 1976; also JB, *Letters*, ed. CLG, i, 272.
158 Tony Gray, then a young reporter on the *Irish Times*, was sent to interview Beverley Nichols, as he describes in *The Lost Years: The Emergency in Ireland 1939–1945*, London 2000, pp. 199–200.

> In his suite at the Shelbourne Hotel . . . he sat at a baby grand piano, a white silk scarf loosely knotted around his throat, strumming excerpts from compositions of his own, mostly thin imitations of Noël Coward's music, and complaining that he had been invited by the Palace Bar crowd to accompany them on the annual Boyne Walk . . . Having sat waiting for them in the Shelbourne foyer from 10 o'clock in the morning, dressed in a Donegal tweed suit and stout walking shoes, he had then returned after an excellent lunch to continue waiting all afternoon . . . A straggle of them arrived just as it was getting dark . . . one of them explained to him, 'it has taken so much time to get from the Palace Bar to the Shelbourne, that it wouldn't be wise to attempt the Boyne Walk this year.'

159 Kenneth Clark, *The Other Half: A Self-Portrait*, London 1977, p. 35.
160 *Loc. cit.*
161 *Loc. cit.*
162 Harold Nicolson to Vita Sackville-West, 16 March 1942. Harold Nicolson, *Diaries and Letters 1939–1945*, ed. Nigel Nicolson, London 1967, p. 210.
163 Quoted, *ibid.*, pp. 218–19n.
164 Nicolson's diary, 17 March 1942. *Ibid.*, p. 218.
165 Nicolson's diary, 20 March 1942. *Ibid.*, p. 220.
166 Dr Nicholas Mansergh, interview, 1989. See also Tim Carroll, 'The Mystery of Flight 777/A', 'Weekend Telegraph', *Daily Telegraph*, 1 November 1997; and Ronald Howard, *In Search of my Father: A Portrait of Leslie Howard*, London 1981.
167 Dallas Bower, interview, 1989.
168 *Ibid.*
169 John Cottrell, *Laurence Olivier*, London 1975, pp. 192–93.
170 Dallas Bower, interview, 1989.
171 In 1913 de Valera joined the Irish Volunteers who had been organized to resist opposition to Home Rule for Ireland. In the anti-British Easter Rising in Dublin (1916) he commanded an occupied building and was the last commander to surrender. Because he had been born in America he was spared execution but was sentenced to penal servitude.
172 *Ibid.*
173 *Ibid.*
174 PB, interview, 1976.
175 Christine, Countess of Longford, interview, 1976.
176 Elizabeth Bowen, *The Shelbourne*, London 1951, p. 188.
177 *Ibid.*, p. 189.
178 On JB's early friendship with Lord Clonmore (later Earl of Wicklow), see YB, 144, 145, 149–51, 164, 168, 198–99, 200, 201–03, 287, 291–92, 375, 382–83, 385–86, 388, 390 and 392.
179 Eleanor, Countess of Wicklow, interview, 1976.
180 *Ibid.*
181 Francis Johnston (1760–1828), Irish architect. JB was particularly interested in him because he designed Pakenham Hall, Co. Westmeath, 1806, where JB stayed with the Longfords. (See YB, Chapter 15, 'Pakenham Hall'.)
182 At the beginning of the Second World War, Professor Butler, with Lord Rosse and the architect Mannin Robertson, had set up the Architectural Records Committee with the

aim of collecting the drawings for all the public buildings in Dublin. After the Easter Rising of 1916, when such fine buildings as the Custom House, the Four Courts and the Post Office were burned, Butler, through his pressure groups, had helped to have them restored to what they had been, from the original drawings.

When the Architectural Records Committee was set up in 1940, Butler's assistant, a university lecturer, became one secretary, and Eleanor became the recording secretary for the drawings. One day Eleanor Butler told John about all the Johnston drawings in the Institute of Architects in Merrion Square. John knew that she had been cataloguing the other drawings with her father's assistant, but asked if he might sort the Johnston papers with her. 'I'm very interested in Francis Johnston,' he said. Lady Wicklow (interview, 1976) described what happened next.

As Press Attaché, John must have given a statement to the Press about the drawings being 'found'. They weren't 'found', because my father had said exactly where they were. But the *Evening Press* came out with the headline: 'John Betjeman, British Press Attaché, Discovers Unknown Find of Drawings'. Father was furious. He begged me to get John to contradict the story, but my father was by then very ill, and I was too upset. However, for about two years, until John left Ireland, we went on cataloguing the Johnston drawings.

183 *The Pavilion: A Contemporary Collection of British Art & Architecture*, ed. Myfanwy Evans [Piper]. Contributions by Wyndham Lewis, John Betjeman, Edward Bawden, Anthony West, Robert Medley, John Ruskin, Geoffrey Grigson, etc., London 1946.

184 JB to Gerard Irvine, April 1941. Shown to the author by the Rev. Prebendary Gerard Irvine.

185 Eleanor, Countess of Wicklow, interview, 1976.

186 JB, *Letters*, ed. CLG, i, 273.

187 *Loc. cit.*

188 *Loc. cit.*

189 Emily Villiers-Stuart, interview, 1978. Terence Gray contributed an article on ballet to *The Bell*, vol. 2, no. 5, August 1941.

190 Emily Villiers-Stuart, interview, 1978.

191 *Ibid.*

192 On George Martyn's house, Tulira Castle (which George Moore calls Tillyra), see George Moore, *Hail and Farewell*, London 1937, vol. 1: *Ave*, pp. 33 and 180 ff. Tulira was only about four miles from Lady Gregory's Coole, and Yeats was often in both houses.

193 The St George mausoleum is illustrated in Maurice Craig and Michael Craig, *Mausolea Hibernica*, Dublin 1999, p. 103. The St Georges were descendants of Olivia St George and her husband Arthur French. She was the eldest sister of the second Lord St George (1715–75). The French family assumed the name St George.

194 Emily Villiers-Stuart, interview, 1978.

195 PB, interview, 1976.

196 In March 1999 I wrote to my old friend Godfrey Smith, of the *Sunday Times*, for information about a lecture by JB which he had attended as an Oxford undergraduate. Smith rang me with the answer, asked how I was progressing with the Betjeman biography, and enquired whether my next volume would contain any 'revelations'. 'Well,' I said, 'I am thinking of asking whether John Betjeman *might* have been a spy – for the British, of course – during his time in Ireland.' Smith said he would like to fly that kite in his column, and did so. But, at the proof stage, his column was read by the newspaper's editor, who said, 'But this is a major news story! Betjeman a spy!' and aked his arts editor, Richard Brooks, to telephone me. And on 21 March 1999 the story appeared, across six columns, 'Betjeman "a wartime spy in Dublin"'. In talking to Godfrey Smith, I had forgotten that the press is a double-edged sword. The next day, the *Daily Telegraph* carried a story headed: 'Betjeman's family scorn spying claim'. The newspaper also published an amusing editorial in Betjemanesque verse, 'Life of Reilly: A Report from John Betjeman to Military Intelligence, Dublin, 1941'. It began:

Keep your eye on Father Reilly
Who, I'm told, is often seen
Strolling with the German Consul
Arm-in-arm on Stephen's Green.

Seán O'Dowd is reading Nietzsche;
Neil Malone was overheard
Praising Schiller's *Wilhelm Tell* and
Whistling bits from Mahler's *Third*.

Entertaining as this was, it was all 'old news'. The suggestion that JB might have been a British Intelligence agent had been made before. (Peter Gammond and John Heald, in *A Bibliographical Companion to Betjeman*, Guildford and Canterbury 1997, refer to an article of 1988 by John McEntee in the *Sunday Independent*, 'So was Sir John really a spy?') In the present chapter I attempt to answer that question, drawing on all the varied evidence now available.

197 In his admirable unpublished MLitt. thesis, 'Herr Hempel at the German Legation in Dublin 1937–1945', Lt-Col. J.P. Duggan is at pains to explain this distinction.

198 *Ibid.*

199 *Ibid.*

200 *Ibid.*

201 Neutral countries in wartime tend to become nests of spies. Dublin in the Second World War was less notorious than Casablanca or Lisbon, but still there was a belief that it was 'a natural centre for intrigue and spying of every kind'. The 'mystery men with sealed lips and locked brief cases' whom Elizabeth Bowen sighted in the Shelbourne Hotel fitted into this cloak-and-dagger scenario. Some of the spy scares were comic false alarms. (One agitated woman informed the authorities that she had heard men 'talking in Morse Code' in the house next door.) Germany had been deprived of some of its best pre-war spies in Dublin, because at the time Hitler invaded Poland many of them were attending a Nuremberg rally and were unable to return. These included Professor Adolph Mahr, a Nazi Party leader who had risen to be director of the National Museum in Dublin, and whose travels round Ireland in search of antiquities had included a good deal of photographic reconnaissance for the German military. But there were German spies in Ireland – among them, Oscar Carl Pfaus, an adventurer who had been a cowboy and a Chicago policeman; Gunther Schütz, who in April 1941 was arrested dressed as a woman and wearing dark glasses; and Dr Ernst Weber-Drohl, who had fathered two children by an Irish girl before the First World War and had become a wrestler and weight-lifter under the name 'Atlas the Strong' before being recruited by the Abwehr (German military intelligence). These men worried Hempel more than the British. And rumours of a fifth column were much exaggerated. The Anglo-Irishman Sir Charles Tegart, a former chief of the Bombay Police, was convinced that Eire was swarming with hundreds of pro-Nazi Irishmen, infiltrated into Ireland by U-boat in readiness for the takeover of the Government in Dublin and the invasion of Britain.

202 After the war, Goertz (1890–1947) contributed seven articles to the *Irish Times* about his exploits (25 August, 27 August, 1 September, 3 September, 5 September, 8 September and 10 September 1947). I am grateful to Mr Edward Wild for obtaining me photocopies of these articles.

203 Duggan/'Hempel'. On espionage in Ireland during this period, see Carolle J. Carter, *The Shamrock and the Swastika: German Espionage in Ireland in World War II*, Palo Alto, California 1977; Fisk, pp. 75, 112, 118, 121–29, 161, 206, 246, 250, 251, 289, 324–25, 327 and 381; Gray, *The Lost Years*, Chapter 3, 'German Spies in Ireland'; David Stafford, *Secret Agent: The True Story of the Special Operations Executive*, London 2000, p. 205; and Enno Stephan, *Spies in Ireland*, London 1965.

204 John Feeney, 'After a long struggle The Standard dies', *Sunday Independent*, 16 April 1978. I am indebted to Fisk, p. 529 n. 141, for this reference.
Two Irish republican authors, Jack Lane and Brendan Clifford, write in *Elizabeth*

Bowen: 'Notes on Eire' – Espionage Reports to Winston Churchill, 1940–2; With a Review of Irish Neutrality in World War 2, Aubane, Millstreet, Co. Cork 1999, p. 9:

> Elizabeth Bowen's espionage during the War was, of course, not an isolated case. Numerous others in various fields of life were doing similar work, supervised by John Betjeman and Nicholas Mansergh. There is a gap in modern Irish history until the full story of this work is told . . . The official records on these matters have been so pruned and sanitized as to make them of scant use as a source of information on this topic . . .

> When the present author visited Dr Nicholas Mansergh at St John's College, Cambridge, in 1989 to talk about JB, he sternly prefaced the interview with the words: 'I must make it clear that I am not prepared to answer any questions as to whether John Betjeman was or was not a British spy' – though the author had not raised the issue beforehand.

205 Fisk, p. 381. He bases this statement on an interview of 1978 with Frank Ryan, a prominent IRA member.

206 *Ibid.*, p. 381n.

207 John P. Duggan, *Neutral Ireland and the Third Reich*, Dublin and Totowa, New Jersey 1985, pp. 88–89.

208 JB wrote to John Piper on 12 October 1941 (letter concluded 20 December 1941):

> I have been given an assistant. A woman called Miss [Joan] Lynam. Nice enough. She pronounces every foreign word in the language in which it is spelt and she reads Kafka, Rilke, Putsch, Lorca (pronounced Lewerthieer), Stefan Zweig, Houdini, Rimbaud, Colbert, Querido, Borodini; she is left, and has of course read Auden, Spender, MacNeice, Day-Lewis, Maxim Gorki, Karel Čapek, Edward Bono, Edouard Roditi. On the other hand she is Irish and more pro-Irish than any of us and has met Arthur Griffiths, Redmond, Flaherty, O'Higgins, Kevin Collins, Michael Drayton, Michael Collins, Wilkie Collins, Maxim Gorki, Horace Plunkett, Yeats, Hilda Doolittle, Father Finlay; she has of course read Browning, Wordsworth, Byron, Shelley, Cowley, Shakespeare, Spenser, Lyly, Lely, Leland, Lillie, Nash, Naish, Nish, Nice; but for all that she is very nice and efficient, thank God. (JB, *Letters*, ed. CLG, i, 299.)

209 Diarmuid Brennan to JB, 10 December 1967. *Victoria*.

210 'Some of the younger members of the IRA . . . had come to the conclusion that the recent series of setbacks, arrests and internments had not been the result either of carelessness on the part of the IRA or of good police work by the Special Branch, but was due to treachery by old hands within the IRA itself. The blame appeared to devolve on the Chief of Staff, Stephen Hayes, who was arrested at a routine IRA meeting in Dublin on 30 June 1941.' (Gray, *The Lost Years*, p. 167.)

211 Diarmuid Brennan to JB, 10 December 1967. *Victoria*.

212 *Ibid.*

213 *Ibid.*

214 JB to Frank O'Connor, 7 March 1941. JB, *Letters*, ed. CLG, i, 281.

215 Frank Delaney, *Betjeman Country*, London 1983, p. 81.

216 The official records do not help. As Robert Fisk discovered, 'British intelligence activities around Ireland were regarded as particularly sensitive during the war and even today many of the official records that would normally be open to historians are still closed without any time limit upon them.' He further notes that 'A large number of Dominions Office files on Eire have been destroyed. These include, for example, all reports to London from British military attachés in Dublin between 12 December 1940 and 7 June 1941. They are marked "destroyed under statute".'

217 *Victoria*.

218 *Ibid.*

219 Hector Legge, interview, 1976.

220 R.F. Foster, *Paddy and Mr Punch*, London 1993, pp. 112–13.

221 Elizabeth Bowen, *The Heat of the Day*, London 1949, pp. 23–24.

222 Foster, *op. cit.*, p. 115.
223 *Ibid.*, p. 117.
224 Cole, pp. 40-41.
225 On JB's antipathy to fishing, see *YB*, pp. 199-200. However, he does seem to have enjoyed the sport more on the River Blackwater in Ireland in 1958. See JB, *Letters*, ed. CLG, ii, 139.
226 Her father was superintendent of railway police in Madras.
227 David O'Donoghue, *Hitler's Irish Voices: The Story of German Radio's Irish Service*, Belfast 1998, p. 77.
228 *Ibid.*, p. 93.
229 Interview of Edward Sweney by David O'Donoghue, 9 June 1991. O'Donoghue, *op. cit.*, pp. 94 and 97 n.4.
230 O'Donoghue, *op. cit.*, pp. 93-94.
    Susan Hilton was later sacked from German Radio for drunkenly using endearing terms, on the air, to another broadcaster for the Nazis, James Blair, who was sacked too. In 1944 she visited the Turkish Consulate in Vienna, attempting to get a visa to leave the Third Reich. When the Gestapo learned of this, they imprisoned her. At the end of the war, she was brought back to London to face trial for 'assisting the enemy' and in February 1946 was sentenced to eighteen months in Holloway. She was the only wartime broadcaster who managed to be imprisoned by the Nazis *and* MI5 – both considering her an enemy collaborator. (*Ex inf.* Donoghue, *op. cit.*, p. 97.)
231 One wonders whether it was JB's intrepid expedition to Sweney's poultry farm that suggested the title of his poem 'Invasion Exercise on the Poultry Farm', published in his collection *New Bats in Old Belfries*, London 1945.
232 *Victoria*.
233 Constantia Maxwell (1886-1961) was Professor of Economic History at Trinity College, Dublin, 1939-45 and Lecky Professor of Modern History, 1945-51. See her obituary, *The Times*, 7 February 1961.
234 *Victoria*.
235 Foster, *op. cit.*, p. 116.
236 Hector Legge, interview, 1976.
237 Foster, *op. cit.*, p. 113.
238 Lehmann, *op. cit.*, pp. 174-75.
    Others also thought highly of JB's work in Ireland. As early as March 1941 – he had been *en poste* only two months – E. Rawdon Smith of the MoI's Empire Division wrote to him: 'I hear you are immensely popular, but that some folk doubt your sanity. I cannot imagine a better foundation for success.' (Quoted, Cole, p. 39.) A more surprising tribute came from Martin Quigley jr, whose father, Martin Quigley sr, John had attacked in the London *Evening Standard* in 1935 for his part in the Hollywood 'purity' campaign. Quigley junior was hoping to persuade the Irish Government to permit the treaty ports to be used as American bases, in return for a promise by the United States Government to use its influence at the end of the war to bring an end to partition. (Inevitably) thwarted in his mission, he filled in time by writing a booklet, *Great Gaels* (1944), to explain Eire's stance to puzzled and indignant Americans. In a chapter entitled 'Little John of West Britain', he praised Sir John Maffey, adding that 'British prestige in Eire recently was also enhanced considerably by the activities of John Betjeman, press attaché for three years in Dublin . . .'
239 JB to Oliver Stonor, 27 March 1943. JB, *Letters*, ed. CLG, i, 323.
240 This front page is illustrated in *JBLP*, p. 118.
241 JB, *Letters*, ed. CLG, i, 275.
242 JB to Frank Gallagher, 16 June 1943. *Manuscripts Department, Trinity College Library, Dublin*.
243 Ruth-Ellen Moller, interview, 2001.
244 On Terence de Vere White (1912-94), see his obituary in *The Times*, 18 June 1994. In reviewing JB's poetry collection *High and Low* in the *Irish Times*, 5 November 1966, de Vere White wrote:

John Betjeman, when he was in Ireland, did more than anyone to make us open our eyes to the architectural treasure in our midst. His charm and enthusiasm were irresistible . . . He is a man with unaltered enthusiasms and convictions. Nor does he hanker after a comprehensive internationalism. He is of a type we should sympathize with: an English Sinn Feiner.

De Vere White was literary editor of the *Irish Times*, 1961–77, and in 1982 married the biographer Victoria Glendinning.

245 Quoted, JB, *Letters*, ed. CLG, i, 275.
246 Gallagher's rough notes for his farewell speech are in the Manuscripts Department of Trinity College Library, Dublin.
247 James Lees-Milne, 4 January 1944. *Diaries 1942–1945: Ancestral Voices and Prophesying Peace,* London 1995 edn., p. 262.

Chapter 14: Daily Herald

1 JB, *Letters*, ed. CLG, i, 345. CLG adds (*ibid.*, i, 346): 'Mabel Fitzgerald and her husband Desmond were great friends of JB's in Ireland. He had been Minister of Defence and written several plays . . .'
2 Francis Williams, *Nothing So Strange*, London 1970, p. 77.
3 *Loc. cit.*
4 Williams, *op. cit.*, p. 154.
5 *Loc. cit.*
6 Williams, *op. cit.*, p. 131. In the war, Williams, like John, worked at the Ministry of Information; in 1962 he was created a Labour life peer, Lord Francis-Williams.
7 *Daily Herald*, 11 November 1943.
8 *Daily Herald*, 17 November 1943.
9 On A.G. Street (1892–1966), farmer, author and broadcaster, see his obituary in *The Times*, 22 July 1966; also, Pamela Street, *My Father, A.G. Street*, London 1969.
10 *Daily Herald*, 24 November 1943.
11 *Loc. cit.*
12 See JB, *Letters*, ed. CLG, i, 192.
13 *Evening Standard*, 14 April 1970.
14 JB adopted this phrase from Evelyn Waugh. See JB to Evelyn Waugh, 27 May 1945. JB, *Letters*, ed. CLG, i, 354.
15 Michael Foot, interview, 1990.
16 *Ibid.*
17 Hugh Cudlipp (1913–98), brother of Percy Cudlipp. Chairman, Daily Mirror Newspapers and chairman, International Publishing Corporation. Created life peer, 1974.
18 Michael Foot, interview, 1990.
19 JB to William Collins, 10 March 1946. JB, *Letters*, ed. CLG, i, 385.
20 Marjorie Proops, interview, 1990.
21 *Ibid.*
22 Michael Foot, interview, 1990.
23 *Daily Herald*, 24 June 1947.
24 Marjorie Proops, interview, 1990.
25 On 20 November 1946 Kolkhorst's notes to JB included:

A few jottings now on 'Oxford Marmalade' by Paul Harrison. 9/6. Peter Davies Ltd. London.
The author calls it a *farcical novel*. But it is not pure farce, really. It is a mixture. It lacks consistency in this respect. At times it is even *serious*.
It lacks the firm outline and *artistry* of a Max Beerbohm, a Lord Berners, an Evelyn [Waugh].
It is far from being a *master-piece*, like a Max Beerbohm. *Very* far.
It is obviously derivative; but it derives from *various* sources in *different* styles.

It is not in *one key*. And the various keys do not always fit in together. They jar on occasion. Rather badly.

26 A.L. Rowse, letter to the author, 22 July 1990.
27 *Daily Herald*, 9 August 1944.
28 *Daily Herald*, 6 July 1944.
29 In his as yet unpublished memoirs, 'Playback', the late Dallas Bower wrote of his time with JB at the Ministry of Information:

> Betjeman was an admirer of 'Bartimeus' (Captain R. Ricci RN) who was one of the naval liaison officers attached to the MoI. Ricci was to make a broadcast on the Home Service about the function of the small boats pool in the evacuation of Dunkirk. At Betjeman's request Ricci asked me to listen to it. I thought it quite outstanding – so much so, in fact, that I asked one of the Treasury liaison officers, Crossley, if I might have an additional £1,500 over and above my 'five minuter allowance' [that is, money for making five-minute propaganda films]. It was going to cost quite a bit more than the others. I decided to write a scenario based on the broadcast and produce it personally as one of the weekly films. [Anthony] Asquith directed it and I had Gordon Harker, Robert Newton and Peggy Ashcroft and a battalion of Guards (who had actually been at Dunkirk) in the cast. Betjeman, [Sidney] Bernstein and I saw the final cut one morning and Bernstein suggested it should be called *Channel Incident*. Peggy Ashcroft's performance was as superb as one might have expected; her closing line never failed to bring a lump to the throat. I am told Churchill invariably closed his wartime weekend film showings at Chequers with *Channel Incident*.

(Kindly shown to the author by Mr Delian Bower.)

30 *Daily Herald*, 19 September 1945.
31 *Daily Herald*, 13 December 1944.
32 *Daily Herald*, 19 December 1945.
33 *Daily Herald*, 7 February 1946.
34 *Loc. cit.*
35 *Daily Herald*, 1 May 1946.
36 *Daily Herald*, 3 December 1947.
37 *Daily Herald*, 24 June 1947.
38 *Daily Herald*, 29 June 1945.
39 *Daily Herald*, 19 June 1946.
40 *Daily Herald*, 30 August 1944.
41 JB to Evelyn Waugh, 27 May 1945. JB, *Letters*, ed. CLG, i, 354.
42 *Daily Herald*, 6 June 1945.
43 *Daily Herald*, 24 April 1946.
44 *Daily Herald*, 7 October 1947.
45 *Daily Herald*, 24 June 1947.
46 *Daily Herald*, 25 October 1945.
47 JB had written in the *Daily Herald* (17 April 1946):

> When I have provided for my family, why do I want money? For the same reason, I suspect, that you want it.
> Not to live in greater style than my neighbours: not to drink, eat or go to pictures, plays and races several times a week.
> I want to buy myself some TIME to do the work I enjoy doing. Your pleasure in life may be gardening, carpentry, mechanics. Mine is writing books. And, like you, I can't afford the *time*.
> It is a condemnation of our age that so many of us have to earn our living one way when our talents intended us to earn it in another.

48 *Daily Herald*, 31 October 1945.
49 *Loc. cit.*
50 *Daily Herald*, 16 January 1946.

51 *Loc. cit.*

52 *Daily Herald*, 15 January 1947.

53 *Daily Herald*, 28 August 1946.

54 Francis King, letter to the author, 27 August 1990.

55 *Daily Herald*, 9 January 1946.

56 On JB's antagonism towards Pevsner, see the chapter on '"Vic. Soc." and "the Dok"' in the third volume of this work.

57 *Daily Herald*, 25 July 1945.

58 *Daily Herald*, 27 January 1944.

59 *Daily Herald*, 5 March 1945.

60 *Daily Herald*, 6 August 1947.

61 *Daily Herald*, 18 October 1944.

62 *Daily Herald*, 19 December 1945.

63 *Daily Herald*, 27 February 1946.

64 On 11 May 1951, JB wrote to his friend George Barnes of the BBC to recommend Dylan Thomas for employment by the Corporation. (JB, *Letters*, ed. CLG, i, 533.) As a result Thomas gave poetry readings on the Third Programme, but because of his drunkenness he was not offered a staff post.

65 *Daily Herald*, 13 June 1945.

66 *Daily Herald*, 6 August 1947.

67 See *YB*, pp. 41–42.

68 *Daily Herald*, 4 April 1944.

69 *Daily Herald*, 5 November 1947.

70 *Daily Herald*, 13 December 1944.

71 *Daily Herald*, 16 January 1946.

72 *Daily Herald*, 15 October 1947.

73 On Biddesden House, near Andover, the home of JB's friend Bryan Guinness (Lord Moyne), whose first wife was Nancy Mitford's sister Diana, see *YB*, pp. 299–300.

74 Nancy Mitford had caricatured Lord Berners and Edward Sackville-West in *The Pursuit of Love*.

75 JB to Nancy Mitford, 19 December 1945. JB, *Letters*, ed. CLG, i, 378.

76 *Daily Herald*, 17 July 1946; 24 July 1946; 4 April 1946.

77 *Daily Herald*, 7 February 1945.

78 *Daily Herald*, 12 December 1945.

79 *Daily Herald*, 24 July 1946.

80 The words end the Hopkins sonnet which begins 'To seem the stranger lies my lot . . .' *The Poems of Gerard Manley Hopkins*, ed. W.H. Gardner and N.H. Mackenzie, Oxford 1962, p. 101.

81 *Daily Herald*, 26 March 1947. For an obituary of Reid (1875–1947), see *The Times*, 7 January 1947; see also, *DNB*.

82 *Daily Herald*, 7 June 1944.

83 *Loc. cit.*

84 Forrest Reid, *Illustrators of the Sixties*, London 1928.

85 See JB to Siegfried Sassoon, 19 April 1952. JB, *Letters*, ed. CLG, ii, 24. Also, JB to Cecil Beaton, 1 September 1952. *Ibid.*, ii, 29–30; and *ibid.*, 30n.

86 See *YB*, p. 181.

87 *Daily Herald*, 12 December 1945.

88 *Daily Herald*, 25 September 1946.

89 *Daily Herald*, 27 September 1944.

90 *Daily Herald*, 30 January 1944.

91 *Collected Poems*, 2001 edn., p. 264.

92 *Daily Herald*, 9 January 1946.

93 *Loc. cit.*

94 *Daily Herald*, 20 December 1944.

95 *Daily Herald*, 13 December 1944.

96 *Daily Herald*, 23 January 1947.

97 *Daily Herald*, 5 February 1947.
98 *Daily Herald*, 6 June 1946.
99 *Daily Herald*, 26 July 1944.
100 *Daily Herald*, 25 March 1947.
101 *Daily Herald*, 25 September 1946.
102 *Daily Herald*, 27 August 1947.
103 *Daily Herald*, 18 June 1947.
104 *Daily Herald*, 22 October 1947.
105 His daughter writes (JB, *Letters*, ed. CLG, i, 376): 'The job was to become the bane of his life and he never stopped complaining about it to my mother and all and sundry.'
106 JB to Evelyn Waugh, 9 October 1950. JB, *Letters*, ed. CLG, i, 520. When JB was kicked, he always kicked back. In describing his *Herald* review of 1950 as 'jaunty', it is likely that he was pointedly reminding Waugh of how, in *The Month* of January 1949, Waugh had referred to his (JB's) 'jaunty sub-aestheticism of the Third Programme' (JB, *Letters*, ed. CLG, i, 450).
107 See Chapter 16, 'Farnborough'.
108 See Chapter 16, 'Farnborough', note 90.
109 *Daily Herald*, 11 October 1950.
110 *Loc. cit.*
111 *Daily Herald*, 4 April 1944.
112 *Collected Poems*, 2001 edn., p. 232.

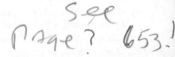

Chapter 15: Admiralty

1 JB, *Letters*, ed. CLG, i, 345. Desmond Fitzgerald, twenty-eighth Knight of Glin, and his wife Mabel were friends of JB's in Ireland. Fitzgerald had been Minister of Defence and was a playwright.
2 JB, *Letters*, ed. CLG, i, 335–36 and 335–36n.
3 *Ibid.*, 335.
4 *Loc. cit.*
5 *Loc. cit.*
6 *Ibid.*, 326.
7 Quoted, *ibid.*, i, 327.
8 See *YB*, p. 106.
9 Richard Percival Graves, *Richard Hughes: A Biography*, London 1994, pp. 15–16, 45, 75, 77, 100–02, 111.
10 *Ibid.*, pp. 58–66, 80–92, 96–97, 161–68, 249–51, 177–82, 186–89, 244–46, 252–54, 261–68, 270–71.
11 *Ibid.*, p. 288.
12 *Ibid.*, p. 290.
13 *Ibid.*, p. 291.
14 *Loc. cit.*
15 Richard Hughes to Harold, 16 August 1940; quoted, *loc. cit.*
16 Richard Hughes to Frances Hughes, 13 September 1940; quoted, Graves, *op. cit.*, pp. 294–95.
17 Richard Hughes to Violet Johnson, 31 July 1940; quoted, *op. cit.*, p. 295.
18 Lance Sieveking, *The Eye of the Beholder*, London 1957, pp. 163–64.
19 *Loc. cit.*
20 Graves, *op. cit.*, p. 306.
21 Richard Hughes to Frances Hughes, 3 February 1943; quoted, *ibid.*, p. 307.
22 J.D. Scott and Richard Hughes, *The Administration of War Production* (History of the Second World War, United Kingdom Civil Series), London 1955, p. 82.
23 *Ibid.*, p. 83.
24 *Ibid.*, pp. 84–85.
25 *Ibid.*, p. 85.
26 Graves, *op.cit.*, p. 293.

27 Sieveking, *op. cit.*, pp. 175–76.

28 *Loc. cit.*

29 Helen Holmes to JB, 28 March 1965. *Victoria.*

30 *The Spectator*, 7 October 1955.

31 Helen Holmes to JB, 28 June 1955. *Victoria.*

32 Helen Holmes thanks JB for helping her to be thus honoured, in an undated letter. *Victoria.*

33 Helen Holmes to JB, 12 January 1949. *Victoria.*

34 Helen Holmes to JB, 5 December 1954. *Victoria.*

35 Helen Holmes to JB, 22 December 1945. *Victoria.*

36 S. (?or G.) Alford to JB, 29 March 1945. *Victoria.*

37 *Loc. cit.*

38 Nikolaus Pevsner, *North Somerset and Bristol*, Harmondsworth 1958, p. 123.

39 Charles Robertson, *Bath: An Architectural Guide*, London 1975, p. 63

40 Cyril Wallworth, interview, 1998.

41 Dawn Macleod, 'Betjeman at War', *The Spectator*, 3 November 1984, p. 15.

42 Graves, *op. cit.*, pp. 296–97 and 308. The statistics regarding Germany's U-boat successes need to be viewed with some caution in the light of recent research by Clay Blair (himself an American wartime combat submariner) in his two magisterial volumes *Hitler's U-boat War: The Hunters 1939–1942* (London 1997) and *Hitler's U-boat War: The Hunted 1942–1945* (London 1999). Blair maintains that 'the U-boat peril has been vastly overblown'.

43 Graves, *op. cit.*, p. 306.

44 *Ibid.*, p. 307.

45 *Ibid.*, p. 308.

46 *Loc. cit.*

47 Graves, *op. cit.*, p. 309.

48 *Ibid.*, p. 310.

49 Richard Hughes to Frances Hughes, following the raid of 25 April 1942; quoted, *ibid.*, p. 299.

50 *Ibid.*, p. 300.

51 *Ibid.*, p. 301.

52 Cyril Wallworth, interview, 1998.

53 JB to Nancy Mitford, 16 May 1944. JB, *Letters*, ed. CLG, i, 344.

54 *Ibid.*, p. 327.

55 *Loc. cit.*

56 Lord Weinstock, interview, 1983.

57 JB, *Letters*, ed. CLG, i, 327.

58 *Loc. cit.*

59 Jenefer, Lady Jones, letter to the author, 4 December 1998.

60 That JB wrote that to Dawn Macleod appears in her letter to him, 5 January 1958. *Victoria.*

61 Dawn Macleod, *Oasis of the North*, London 1958, pp. 216–17.

62 On Sir Francis Younghusband, see Anthony Verrier, *Francis Younghusband and the Great Game*, London 1991, and Patrick French, *Younghusband: The Last Great Imperial Adventurer*, London 1994.

63 Dawn Macleod, 'Betjeman at War', *The Spectator*, 3 November 1984, p. 15. Hughes's biographer R.P. Graves (*op. cit.*, p. 387) records: 'The summer [of 1962] was enlivened by the renewal of Diccon's connection with the Betjeman family, when John's daughter Candida came to be his secretary: she was said by her father to be "*thrilled* at the prospect of working for you"; though when it came to the point, she stayed with him for less than a year.'

64 Dawn Macleod, 'Betjeman at War', *The Spectator*, 3 November 1984, p. 15.

65 *Ibid.*

66 *The Observer*, 15 October 1944.

67 In a letter of 1942 to John Piper JB gloated over a 'fine attack [anonymous] on Batsford'

in the *New Statesman* (JB, *Letters*, ed. CLG, i, 306); and in February 1944, negotiating with Collins over a proposed series of guidebooks, he wrote: 'The text would have to be scholarly and somewhat of the final word on the subject – none of this Batsford business of running up something in the office to justify the re-issue of a haul of old blocks called the "Spirit of this" or the "Heart of that" or the "Magic of something else".' (JB to Mr Foges of Collins, 1 February 1944. JB, *Letters*, ed. CLG, i, 341.)

68 *The Observer*, 15 October 1944.
69 *Loc. cit.*
70 *Loc. cit.*
71 The Great Bed of Ware is now in the Victoria & Albert Museum.
72 Dawn Macleod, 'Betjeman at War', *The Spectator*, 3 November 1984, p. 16.
73 JB, conversation, 1973.
74 JB to Sybil Shand, 2 May 1960. *Lady Stirling*. An obituary of P. Morton Shand in *The Times* of 2 May 1960 commented adversely on his facetiousness and his inexplicable dislike of port. JB replied to these criticisms in a tribute published in *The Times* on 6 May 1960.
75 Lady Stirling, interview, 1998.
76 *Ibid.*
77 Lady Howe (interview, 1998) said: 'There is no doubt at all that John Betjeman had a crush on my sister.'
78 Written by JB on Oxford Preservation Trust stationery, and thus of c. 1946–48.
79 *Collected Poems*, 2001 edn., p. 163.
80 *Ibid.*, p. 95.
81 *Loc. cit.*
82 *Loc. cit.*
83 Lady Stirling, interview, 1998.
84 *Ibid.* Sybil Shand wrote to JB on 27 November 1946: 'Dear John, Mary writes that you are going to Wycombe next Saturday and may call for her then. I am very glad that she will have this chance of an "outing".'
85 On the furniture of Mary Shand, see *Country Life*, 23 September 1993.
86 Lady Stirling, interview, 1998.
87 *Collected Poems*, 2001 edn., p. 105.
88 Keith Brace, *Portrait of Bristol*, London 1971, p. 20.
89 On 21 April 1937 the Dean of Bristol wrote to JB to thank him for his broadcast 'Town Tour' about Bristol on 12 April and for the kind things he had said about the Cathedral. *Victoria*.
90 Graves, *op. cit.*, p. 196.
91 Bishop Stockwood, interview, 1993.
92 Michael De-la-Noy, *Mervyn Stockwood: A Lonely Life*, London 1996, p. 38.
93 The novelist John Stevenson, who was in Stockwood's circle, conversation, 1992.
94 Said by PB to Osbert Lancaster, and repeated by him to the author, interview, 1976.
95 Robert Robinson, *Skip All That: Memoirs*, London 1996, p. 22. Garrett is also described in Paul Vaughan, *Something in Linoleum*, London 1994, pp. 94–187. And De-la-Noy (*op. cit.*, p. 183) writes that Stockwood conducted a 'gay blessing' for Garrett, 'whose partner was an Anglican priest, still alive . . .'.
96 The present author met Wolfe in the early Seventies through Ms Janet Street-Porter, who lived next to Wolfe in Narrow Street.
97 De-la-Noy adds (*loc. cit.*): 'Two out of the three people with whom he was most emotionally involved were schoolboys when he first met them. One was Dick Chapman . . . [with whom] there developed what Dick has described as "a very close and intense relationship".' However, Chapman told De-la-Noy that the friendship remained 'chaste' – 'I think that Mervyn had an aversion to sex. Absolutely nothing happened . . .' (De-la-Noy, *op. cit.*, p. 62.)
98 *Collected Poems*, 2001 edn., p. 58.
99 The church is described, under the heading 'Modern Churches', in J.F. Nicholls and John Taylor, *Bristol Past and Present*, Bristol 1881, ii, 280.
100 A.J.P. Taylor, introduction to Len Deighton, *Fighter: The True Story of the Battle of Britain*, London 1977, pp. 12–13.

101 Bishop Stockwood, interview, 1992.
102 *Ibid.*
103 *Ibid.*
104 *Collected Poems*, 2001 edn., p. 89.
105 For example, Charles (later Sir Charles) Wilson later became Professor of Modern History at Cambridge and Alec Clifton-Taylor won renown as an architectural historian and, after JB's death, as his successor as a television *cicerone*.
106 Macleod, *op. cit.*, p. 14.
107 Richard Hughes to Frances Hughes, 14 March n.d. [but 1942]; quoted, Graves, *op. cit.*, p. 298.
108 JB to Mabel Fitzgerald, 20 August 1944. JB, *Letters*, ed. CLG, i, 345.
109 Pamela Barlow to JB, 31 October 1944. *Victoria.*
110 P. Morton Shand to JB, 4 December 1944. *Victoria.*
111 Helen Holmes to JB, 21 January 1945 [but misdated 1944]. *Victoria.*
112 Helen Holmes to JB, 5 December 1954. *Victoria.*

Chapter 16: Farnborough

1 PB, interview, 1976. CLG writes (JB, *Letters*, ed. CLG, i, 331), 'It was Robert Heber Percy who first found the Old Rectory at Farnborough . . .', as opposed to PB's memory that it was Sir Ralph Glyn who told her and JB about the house. This may well be correct; or possibly both men drew the house to the Betjemans' attention.
2 Victory in Europe Day, 8 May 1945.
3 PB, interview, 1976.
4 *Ibid.*; also, letter from JB to Evelyn Waugh, 27 May 1945. Kindly made available to the author by the late Auberon Waugh.
5 Two former neighbours of the Betjemans commented on this in interviews.
6 *Lilliput*, July 1943.
7 *JBP.*
8 PB, interview, 1976.
9 Ian Yarrow, *Berkshire*, London 1952, p. 305.
10 *Ibid.*, p. 76.
11 Lady Agnes Bertie, daughter of the sixth Earl of Mexborough, married in 1930 Thomas More Eyston (1902–40), High Sheriff of Berkshire in 1936.
12 JB to Evelyn Waugh, 27 May 1945. Kindly made available to the author by the late Auberon Waugh.
13 JB to Geoffrey Taylor, 8 June 1945. JB, *Letters*, ed. CLG, i, 355.
14 On 15 July 1945, after his cyst operation, JB wrote in the *Daily Herald* (and possibly the nurse to whom he referred was Mary Renault): 'I have recently reached the luxurious stage of convalescence after illness, and I said to the Nurse the other day, "Please get me the most old-fashioned novel you can find in the library." She brought *The Clever Woman of the Family*, by Charlotte M Yonge, first published in 1878. An excellent choice, for in that South Devon book there are no fewer than twenty-three clearly-defined characters.'
15 Mary Renault, letter to the author, 18 November 1976.
16 In his autobiography, *Wheels within Wheels: An Unconventional Life* (London 2000, p. 167–68), Lord Montagu of Beaulieu wrote: 'I love John Betjeman's "Youth and Age on Beaulieu River". He wrote it for Clemency Buckland whom I knew well as a child. Her father, Brigadier Buckland, was responsible for Special Operations Executive's training school coming to Beaulieu in 1940.'
17 JB to PB, 22 July 1945. JB, *Letters*, ed. CLG, i, 358.
18 Osbert Lancaster, interview, 1977.
19 JB, 'Oxford', in *W.H. Auden: A Tribute*, ed. Stephen Spender, London 1975, p. 44.
20 JB to John Bryson, Epiphany 1939. JB, *Letters*, ed. CLG, i, 221.
21 JB, *Letters*, ed. CLG, i, 331.

22 Recited to the author by Lady Longford, 1977.
23 Canon Paul Miller, interview, 1981. During the Second World War, when Miller was in a Japanese prisoner-of-war camp, he unexpectedly met Driberg again. The politician was touring the liberated camps with Lord Mountbattten. (See Francis Wheen, *Tom Driberg: His Life and Indiscretions*, London 1990, pp. 216–17.)
24 JB, *Summoned by Bells*, London 1960, p. 97.
25 JB to Alan Pryce-Jones, 24 January 1945. JB, *Letters*, ed. CLG, i, 352.
26 Sent by JB to the Rev. Gerard Irvine, and kindly shown by him to the author.
27 *Ibid.*
28 *Ibid.*
29 JB to Kenneth Clark, 16 November 1949. JB, *Letters*, ed. CLG, i, 498.
30 Alan Clark, letter to the author, 18 March 1999.
31 JB to John Piper, 23 September 1945. JB, *Letters*, ed. CLG, i, 361.
32 JB to Eileen Molony, 3 November 1945. JB, *Letters*, ed. CLG, i, 377.
33 Eileen Molony to JB, 12 November 1945. JB, *Letters*, ed. CLG, i, 377n.
34 Lys Dunlap (later Lubbock, then Connolly, then Koch). On her affair with Cyril Connolly see Clive Fisher, *Cyril Connolly: A Nostalgic Life*, London 1995, pp. 208–10; on her changing her name to Connolly, *ibid.*, p. 262. She aspired to marry Connolly but he did not marry her.
35 JB to Cyril Connolly, 28 December 1945. JB, *Letters*, ed. CLG, i, 380.
36 JB to Tom Driberg, Octave of Epiphany 1946. JB, *Letters*, ed. CLG, i, 380.
37 JB to Kenneth Clark, 28 January 1946. JB, *Letters*, ed. CLG, i, 383.
38 JB to Ninian Comper, 20 March 1946. JB, *Letters*, ed. CLG, i, 387.
39 Evelyn Waugh to Nancy Mitford, 26 August 1946. *The Letters of Evelyn Waugh*, ed. Mark Amory, London 1980, p. 233.
40 *The Diaries of Evelyn Waugh*, ed. Michael Davie, London 1976, p. 660.
41 JB, *Letters*, ed. CLG, i, 365.
42 *Ibid.*, i, 366.
43 *Ibid.*, i, 368.
44 *Ibid.*, i, 367.
45 *Loc. cit.* For the eventually published version, see *Collected Poems*, 2001 edn., p. 279.
46 JB, *Letters*, ed. CLG, i, 367.
47 *Ibid.*, 368.
48 *Loc. cit.*
49 *Ibid.*, 367.
50 E.g. in his poem 'The Interior Decorator', *Collected Poems*, 2001 edn., pp. 344–46.
51 JB, *Letters*, ed. CLG, i, 366.
52 Osbert Lancaster, interview, 1977.
53 JB, *Letters*, ed. CLG, i, 370.
54 *Loc. cit.*
55 During the Second World War, the title was changed to *The Pre-Raphaelite Dream*, as the publishers felt that, in comparison with what people were going through in the war, the Pre-Raphaelites' experiences could not be classed as 'tragedy'.
56 JB, *Letters*, ed. CLG, i, 460.
57 *Ibid.*, 368.
58 On A.E. ('Hum') Lynam, see *YB*, pp. 33–34, 36–38, 72 and 324.
59 JB, *Letters*, ed. CLG, i, 368.
60 *Loc. cit.*
61 *Ibid.*, 369.
62 In letters to CLG, JB often signed himself 'MD', standing for 'Mad Dadz'.
63 CLG, 'Father's praise made me feel safe, just like a security blanket', *The Express* 'Weekend' section, 22 November 1997.
64 JB, *Letters*, ed. CLG, i, 468.
65 *Loc. cit.*
66 CLG, 'Father's praise made me feel safe, just like a security blanket', *The Express* 'Weekend' section, 22 November 1997.

67 *Loc. cit.*
68 Catherine Stott, 'Betjeman, naked on the waves', *Daily Mail*, 7 February 1968.
69 Candida Crewe, 'A Childhood: Candida Lycett Green', *The Times Saturday Review*, 29 June 1991.
70 Catherine Stott, 'Betjeman, naked on the waves', *Daily Mail*, 7 February 1968.
71 Candida Crewe, 'A Childhood: Candida Lycett Green', *The Times Saturday Review*, 29 June 1991.
72 Lady Veronica Blackwood, conversation with the author, 1982.
73 JB, *Letters*, ed. CLG, ii, 54.
74 Betty Packford, interview, 1988.
75 A number of the Betjemans' neighbours recalled this episode.
76 Ronald Liddiard, interview, 1988.
77 Jean Rome, interview, 1989.
78 See *YB*, p. 213.
79 JB to Gerard Irvine, 20 March 1947. Shown to the author by the Rev. Prebendary Irvine.
80 Gerard Irvine to JB, 1 April 1947. Shown to the author by the Rev. Prebendary Irvine.
81 'Penelope, quite independently, after long and varied study, and under no persuasion from anyone else, was received into the Roman Catholic Church in March 1948.' Christopher Sykes, *Evelyn Waugh: A Biography*, London 1975, p. 329. PB told the present author about her vision in Assisi (conversation, 1978).
82 *Oxford and Cambridge*, June 1933, pp. 194–95.
83 Evelyn Waugh to PB, 14 July [1947]. *The Letters of Evelyn Waugh*, ed. Mark Amory, London 1980, p. 256.
84 Evelyn Waugh, *Scott-King's Modern Europe*, London 1947, p. 49.
85 *Ibid.*, pp. 28–29.
86 *Ibid.*, p. 29.
87 *Ibid.*, pp. 56–57.
88 Evelyn Waugh, diary, 14 December 1946. *The Diaries of Evelyn Waugh*, ed. Michael Davie, London 1976, p. 666.
89 Evelyn Waugh, *A Handful of Dust*, London 1934 (1948 edn.), p. 10.
90 In reviewing Martin Stannard's *Evelyn Waugh: The Early Years 1903–1939* in the *Literary Review*, December 1986 (p. 21), Auberon Waugh wrote, quoting from the book (p. 282):

> 'Penelope Betjeman was most alarmed when, both before and after her marriage, Waugh made advances on her. "I remember being very shocked as he was a practising Roman Catholic . . . He never attracted me in the very least." Lady Betjeman proceeded to psychoanalyse this curious behaviour.'
>
> Evelyn Waugh's memory, at any rate in his later years, was different. On one of the last occasions I saw him I happened to ask – *à propos* of something he had said – whether he had ever been to bed with Lady Betjeman. The term I used was coarser and rather more explicit. 'Since you ask,' he said after a pause, 'Yes.'
>
> There is a veiled reference to this episode in Maurice Bowra's autobiography but the two people who could have cleared the matter up are now both dead.

In a letter published in the next issue of the *Literary Review* (January 1987), Richard Ingrams, addressing Auberon Waugh who was the editor of that magazine, wrote:

> When Mark Amory edited Evelyn Waugh's letters he was advised by Lord Weidenfeld's lawyer, Mr Paisner, to delete one libellous passage. Writing to Lady Betjeman from Africa, Evelyn Waugh asked her to do some little favour for him, for which her reward was to be 'a fine fuck when I get back'. I also remember Sir Osbert Lancaster telling me that your Father once confided in him in a moment of bitterness, 'She always laughs when I come.'

91 Evelyn Waugh to JB, 22 December 1946. *The Letters of Evelyn Waugh*, ed. Mark Amory, London 1980, p. 242.
92 *Ibid.*, p. 243.
93 Mrs Ottilie Squires, the widow of JB's doctor, Dr Vaughan Squires, recalled (interview,

1989) that, while at Farnborough, JB needed a medical check for insurance purposes. Dr Squires, who was very busy at the time, asked if he could examine him on a Sunday morning. 'I'm afraid not,' JB replied. 'You see, at Farnborough Church I *am* the congregation.'

94 Evelyn Waugh to JB, 9 January 1947. *The Letters of Evelyn Waugh*, ed. Mark Amory, London 1980, p. 244.

95 *Collected Poems*, 2001 edn., p. 232.

96 JB to Evelyn Waugh, 11 January 1947. Kindly made available to the author by the late Auberon Waugh.

97 Evelyn Waugh to JB, 14 January 1947. *The Letters of Evelyn Waugh*, ed. Mark Amory, London 1980, p. 246.

98 *Loc. cit.*

99 JB to Evelyn Waugh, 23 January 1947. JB, *Letters*, ed. CLG, i, 404.

100 JB to Evelyn Waugh, 3 February 1947. JB, *Letters*, ed. CLG, i, 405.

101 Evelyn Waugh to JB, 2 April 1947. *The Letters of Evelyn Waugh*, ed. Mark Amory, London 1980, p. 248.

102 PB to Evelyn Waugh, April 1947. Quoted, *ibid.*, p. 250n.

103 Evelyn Waugh to JB, May 1947. *The Letters of Evelyn Waugh*, ed. Mark Amory, London 1980, p. 250.

104 JB to Evelyn Waugh, Whitmonday 1947. JB, *Letters*, ed. CLG, i, 411–12.

105 *Ibid.*

106 Evelyn Waugh to JB, 28 May 1947. *The Letters of Evelyn Waugh*, ed. Mark Amory, London 1980, p. 250.

107 Evelyn Waugh to PB, 4 June 1947. *Ibid.*, p. 252.

108 On Woodruff and Hollis, see *YB*, p. 132.

109 JB's Oxford friend William, Lord Clonmore (variously nicknamed 'Crax', 'Cracky', 'Billy' and 'Dotty') succeeded his father as eighth Earl of Wicklow in 1946. See *YB*, pp. 144, 145, 149–51, 164, 168, 198–99, 200, 202–03, 206, 209, 271–72, 280, 287, 291–92, 375, 382–83, 385–86, 388, 390 and 392.

110 PB to Evelyn Waugh, June 1947. *Ibid.*, p. 253n.

111 JB to Evelyn Waugh, 25 July 1947. JB, *Letters*, ed. CLG, i, 418.

112 Evelyn Waugh, diary for 4 August 1947. *The Diaries of Evelyn Waugh*, ed. Michael Davie, London 1976, p. 684.

113 Evelyn Waugh to Nancy Mitford, 6 August 1947. *The Letters of Evelyn Waugh*, ed. Mark Amory, London 1980, p. 256; and Evelyn Waugh to Penelope Betjeman, 8 August 1947. *Ibid.*, p. 257.

114 Evelyn Waugh to Nancy Mitford, 26 December 1947. *Ibid.*, p. 264.

115 Evelyn Waugh to JB, December 1947. *Ibid.*, p. 265.

116 Evelyn Waugh to JB, 26 July 1948. *Ibid.*, p. 280.

117 Evelyn Waugh, diary for 9 January 1948. *The Diaries of Evelyn Waugh*, ed. Michael Davie, London 1976, p. 694.

118 JB to Evelyn Waugh, 17 January 1949. JB, *Letters*, ed. CLG, i, 450.

119 Evelyn Waugh to JB, 18 January 1949. JB, *Letters*, ed. CLG, i, 450n.

120 Evelyn Waugh to PB, 7 January 1950. *The Letters of Evelyn Waugh*, ed. Mark Amory, London 1980, pp. 317–18.

121 Evelyn Waugh to PB, 10 February 1948. *Ibid.*, p. 267.

122 JB to Geoffrey Taylor, 6 March 1948. JB, *Letters*, ed. CLG, i, 439.

123 At one stage the poem was also given the title 'Easter, 1948'.

124 JB, *Letters*, ed. CLG, i, 439–40.

125 Susan Barnes, ' "Betjeman, I bet your racket brings you in a pretty packet" ', *Sunday Times Magazine*, 30 January 1972.

126 Dr Richard Squires, interviews, 1976 and 1989; and JB, *Letters*, ed. CLG, i, 374.

127 JB, *Letters*, ed. CLG, i, 374–75.

128 PB to JB, May 1949. JB, *Letters*, ed. CLG, i, 462n.

129 JB to PB, 2 June 1949. *Ibid.*, p. 460.

130 *Ibid.*, i, 461.

131 Paul Betjeman was accepted by Eton in March 1951. (JB to Patrick Cullinan, 13 March 1951. Kindly made available to the author by Mr Cullinan.)

132 The Rev. Prebendary Gerard Irvine, interview, 1990.

133 JB, *Letters*, ed. CLG, i, 465.

134 See JB to Anne Barnes, 13 November 1947. JB, *Letters*, ed. CLG, i, 421.

135 JB, *Letters*, ed. CLG, i, 465–66.

136 Eve Disher was an artist. See Chapter 10, 'Minnie', of the present book. For her portrait of JB, see *JBLP*, p. 124.

137 Eve Disher to JB, 24 October 1949. JB, *Letters*, ed. CLG, i, 466.

138 JB, *Letters*, ed. CLG, i, 466.

139 JB to Anne Barnes, 16 July 1949. JB, *Letters*, ed. CLG, i, 479–80.

140 JB to Anne Barnes, 19 July 1949. JB, *Letters*, ed. CLG, i, 480–81.

141 JB to Anne Barnes, 9 September 1949. JB, *Letters*, ed. CLG, i, 485.

142 JB to Cyril Connolly, 4 December 1949. JB, *Letters*, ed. CLG, i, 500.

143 JB to Anne Barnes, 25 February 1950. JB, *Letters*, ed. CLG, i, 505.

144 JB to Anne Barnes, 2 November 1950. JB, *Letters*, ed. CLG, i, 523.

145 Edmund Penning-Rowsell, letter to the author, 2 July 1999.

146 JB to Margaret Wintringham, 18 January 1951. Kindly made available to the author by the late Edmund Penning-Rowsell.

147 JB, *Letters*, ed. CLG, ii, 310.

148 Edmund Penning-Rowsell to JB, 12 March 1972. JB, *Letters*, ed. CLG, ii, 374.

149 JB to Edmund Penning-Rowsell, 21 March 1972. *Loc. cit.*

150 JB, *Letters*, ed. CLG, ii, 6.

151 JB to Ruth Webb, May 1951. JB, *Letters*, ed. CLG, i, 534.

152 JB, *Letters*, ed. CLG, i, 466.

153 JB to George Barnes, 3 June 1951. JB, *Letters*, ed. CLG, i, 535–56.

154 Kenneth Tynan to Julian Holland, 4 February 1946. *Kenneth Tynan Letters*, ed. Kathleen Tynan, London 1994, pp. 106–07.

155 Ludovic Kennedy, *On my Way to the Club*, London 1989, pp. 178–79.

156 JB, *Letters*, ed. CLG, i, 469.

157 Nicholas Mosley, *Beyond the Pale*, London 1983, p. 281.

158 'Cullinan Diamond. The world's largest gem diamond, which weighed about 3,106 carats when found in 1905 at the Premier mine in Transvaal, South Africa.' See *Encyclopaedia Britannica*, 1998 edn., Micropedia, ii, 781.

159 JB to Patrick Cullinan, 27 January 1950. Kindly made available to the author by Mr Cullinan.

160 *Ibid.*

161 JB, 'Childhood Days: or Old Friends and Young Bullies', BBC radio talk, 16 July 1950. *BBCWA*.

162 CLG (JB, *Letters*, ed. CLG, i, 502) gives 'poetry', but this is clearly a misreading.

163 JB to Patrick Cullinan, 27 January 1950. Kindly made available to the author by Mr Cullinan.

164 CLG (JB, *Letters*, ed. CLG, i, 472) suggests this letter is undated; but in fact it is dated 'Valentine's Day', i.e. 14 February 1950 (which happened to be PB's fortieth birthday).

165 JB to Patrick Cullinan, 14 February 1950. Kindly made available to the author by Mr Cullinan.

166 Some examples:

JB to Cullinan, 14 April 1950: 'That sonnet, though – I won't pass the sextet yet. I mean if you are using metre & rhyme, you can't dispense with rhyme.'

JB to Cullinan, 4 July 1950: 'Your Petrarchan sonnet shews that nice little conflict between the lusts of the flesh & the desires of the spirit which go on in you so fiercely. One syllable too little in the 4th line. You have established the "you" and "I" theme in it very well. I notice breasts still absorb you – or rather you still absorb them.'

Letters kindly made available to the author by Mr Cullinan.

167 Patrick Cullinan, diary, 1 March 1950. Kindly made available by Mr Cullinan.

168 JB to Patrick Cullinan, 8 March 1950. Kindly made available by Mr Cullinan.
169 Patrick Cullinan, letter to the author, 27 September 1998.
170 *Ibid.*
171 *Ibid.*
172 JB, *Letters*, ed. CLG, i, 472.
173 Patrick Cullinan, letter to CLG, 1993. Copy kindly made available by Mr Cullinan.
174 JB, *Letters*, ed. CLG, i, 472.
175 Patrick Cullinan, letter to CLG, 1973. Copy kindly made available by Mr Cullinan.
176 JB to Patrick Cullinan, 15 July 1950. Kindly made available by Mr Cullinan. Lady Chetwode had died in 1946. See her obituary in *The Times*, 1 July 1946; also an anonymous tribute to her, *ibid.*, 6 July 1946.
177 JB to Patrick Cullinan, 8 August 1950. Kindly made available by Mr Cullinan.
178 JB, *Letters*, ed. CLG, i, 473.
179 Patrick Cullinan, letter to the author, 27 September 1998.
180 JB to Patrick Cullinan, 19 October 1950. Kindly made available by Mr Cullinan.
181 JB to Patrick Cullinan, 13 December 1950. Kindly made available by Mr Cullinan.
182 JB to Patrick Cullinan, 29 December 1950. Kindly made available by Mr Cullinan.
183 JB to Patrick Cullinan, 24 May 1951. Kindly made available by Mr Cullinan.
184 JB to Patrick Cullinan, 29 May 1951. Kindly made available by Mr Cullinan.
185 JB, *Letters*, ed. CLG, i, 473.
186 *Loc. cit.*
187 That is, Edward Burne-Jones, the Pre-Raphaelite artist.
188 That is, Dante Gabriel Rossetti, the Pre-Raphaelite artist and poet.
189 JB to Patrick Cullinan, 2 May 1950. Kindly made available by Mr Cullinan.
190 JB, *Letters*, ed. CLG, i, 474.
191 *Loc. cit.*
192 *The Times*, 16 February 1951.
193 Quoted, Francis Wheen, *Tom Driberg: His Life and Indiscretions*, London 1990, pp. 248–49.
194 Tom Driberg, diary for 30 June 1951. Tom Driberg, *The Best of Both Worlds: A Personal Diary*, London 1953, p. 53.
195 Wheen, *op. cit.*, p. 251.
196 On Seretse Khama and his friendship with Driberg, see *loc. cit.*
197 Shown to the author by the late John G. Murray; and also reprinted, *ibid.*, pp. 253–55.
198 JB to Patrick Cullinan, 9 June 1951. Kindly made available by Mr Cullinan.
199 JB, *Letters*, ed. CLG, i, 536n.
200 *Ibid.*, i, 474.

Chapter 17: New Bats in Old Belfries

1 On 'the Epic', see *YB*, p. xvi.
2 JB to John G. Murray, 20 April 1943. *John Murray archives.*
3 *Ibid.*
4 *Ex inf.* John R. Murray, telephone conversation, 2002.
5 *Ibid.* Noël Carrington was also an author. With Clarke Hulton he wrote *English Popular Art*, London 1945. He also wrote *Life in an English Village*, London 1949, illustrated by Edward Bawden.
6 On her, see Gretchen Gerzina, *Carrington: A Life of Dora Carrington 1893–1932*, London 1989; also, *Carrington: Letters and Extracts from her Diaries*, ed. David Garnett, London 1970. There are many references to her in Michael Holroyd, *Lytton Strachey*, London 1967–68.
7 *John Murray archives.*
8 *Ibid.*
9 *Uncollected Poems*, London 1982, p. 30, where it was printed under the heading 'Cheshire'.
10 *John Murray archives.*
11 *Ibid.*

12 That is, Basil, Marquess of Dufferin and Ava. On JB's feelings for him at Oxford, see *YB*, pp. 174–75 and 181.

13 James Lees-Milne, *Deep Romantic Chasm: Diaries 1979–1981*, ed. Michael Bloch, London 2000, p. 101 (diary entry for 21 July 1980).

14 *Loc. cit.*

15 *John Murray archives.*

16 *The Observer*, 13 March 1983.

17 *Collected Poems*, 2001 edn., p. 119.

18 I am grateful to Dr Per Sörbom, cultural counsellor at the Swedish Embassy, London, for this information.

19 That is, the poem later given the title 'The Irish Unionist's Farewell to Greta Hellstrom in 1922'.

20 That is, the poem 'A Lament for Moira McCavendish' (*Collected Poems*, 2001 edn., pp. 249–50).

21 I am grateful to Mr Jonathan Williams, literary agent, of Dun Laoghaire, Co. Dublin, Ireland, for kindly sending me a photocopy of this cutting, which is undated but must be of between May and December 1984, as it refers to JB as 'the late' and to 1974 as 'ten years ago'.

22 *Collected Poems*, 2001 edn., p. 119.

23 On JB's visits to Lismore Castle with Lady Elizabeth Cavendish in 1958 and 1959, see JB, *Letters*, ed. CLG, ii, 138 and 169.

24 On Strancally Castle, see Mark Bence-Jones, *Burke's Guide to Country Houses*, vol. 1: *Ireland*, London 1978, p. 266.

25 Brian de Breffny, *Castles of Ireland*, London 1977, p. 46.

26 Bence-Jones, *op. cit.*, pp. 27–28, describes Ballysaggartmore as 'on the side of a steep hill overlooking the River Blackwater'.

27 *Ibid.*, p. 108.

28 *Loc. cit.*

29 *Victoria.*

30 Honor Tracy to JB, 11 September 1946. *Victoria.*

31 *Victoria.*

32 When Honor Tracy died in 1989 *The Times* subtitled her obituary 'Humorous delineation of the Irish scene'. For the outline of her life and career which follows, I am particularly indebted to that obituary (*The Times*, 15 June 1989); to Maurice Harmon, *Sean O'Faolain: A Life*, London 1994; and to Peter Conradi, *Iris Murdoch: A Life*, London 2001. I have also spoken with a number of people who knew Tracy.

   Tracy mocked Iris Murdoch for (in her view) wanting to seem more Irish than she in fact was (Conradi, *op. cit.*, p. 22); but that was rich coming from Tracy, who was born in Bury St Edmunds, Suffolk, in 1913. (Murdoch was at least born in Dublin.)

   During the Second World War Honor Tracy worked at the Ministry of Information, where she became a friend of both JB and Osbert Lancaster.

   Letters from Tracy to JB (*Victoria*) show that he tried to obtain her a post at the British Council, but failed; then he gave her an introduction to Sean O'Faolain, who employed her in Dublin after the war. (Harmon, *op. cit.*, p. 148). Then she joined the staff of *The Bell*, in Lower O'Connell Street, Dublin.

   In 1953 Tracy wrote an amusing non-fiction book about the Irish, *Mind You, I've Said Nothing*. Her best-known novel, *The Straight and Narrow Path*, was published in 1956. Ruth-Ellen Moller remembered (interview, 2001): 'One of her books was banned in Ireland because she had a nun leaping over a bonfire with no knickers on.' Tracy was a Roman Catholic, but with a strong strain of anti-clericalism. Moving to a base in rural Ireland, she contributed a light-hearted column to the *Sunday Times*, which led to a notorious pair of legal cases. She also contributed to *The Observer*, the *Manchester Guardian* and the *Daily Telegraph* and wrote travel books about Japan, Spain and the West Indies.

33 See Sean O'Faolain, *Vive Moi!*, ed. Julia O'Faolain, London 1993.

34 Frances Daly, telephone conversation with the author, 2002.

35 Harmon, *op. cit.*, p. 150.

36 Conradi, *op. cit.*, p. 22.
37 Cathal O'Shannon, telephone conversation with the author, 2002.
38 Harmon, *op. cit.*, p. 150.
39 Ruth-Ellen Moller, interview 2002; Cathal O'Shannon, telephone conversation with the author, 2002.
40 Professor John Bayley, letter to the author, n.d. but 11 February 2002.
41 Lady Hemphill to JB, 30 September 1945. *Victoria.*
42 The wedding invitation sent to JB is reproduced in *JBLP*, p. 118.
43 Joan Jackson to JB, 30 September 1945. *Victoria.*
44 He did not use her surname; but 'Clemency the General's daughter', taken in conjunction with the Beaulieu setting, would have been more than enough to identify her.
45 Schoolboy-sure she is this morning;
     Soon her sharpie's rigg'd and free ...
     Collected Poems, 2001 edn., p. 110.
46 Clemency Buckland to JB, 24 September 1945. *Victoria.*
47 *John Murray archives.*
48 On M.J. Tambimuttu (1915–83), see JB, *Letters*, ed. CLG, i, 378; also Peter Conradi, *op. cit.*, pp. 169, 219 and 320; Jane Williams (ed.), *Tambimuttu: Bridge between Two Worlds*, London 1989; Julian Maclaren-Ross, *Memoirs of the Forties*, London 1965; and Gavin Ewart, 'Tambi the Great', *London Magazine*, December 1965. Tambimuttu, who had arrived from Ceylon in 1938 almost penniless, was a protégé of T.S. Eliot and edited the leading poetry magazine of the 1940s, the bi-monthly *Poetry London.*
49 *John Murray archives.*
50 Terence Holliday to John G. Murray, 2 December 1945. *John Murray archives.*
51 John G. Murray to Terence Holliday, 9 December 1945. *John Murray archives.*
52 *New Statesman*, 19 January 1946.
53 *Ibid.*
54 *The Listener*, 14 February 1946.
55 *Ibid.*
56 Pelmanism: a system of mind-training to improve the memory, devised by the Pelman Institute, founded 1898.
57 *The Listener*, 14 February 1946.
58 *The Spectator*, 15 February 1946.
59 *Time and Tide*, 9 February 1946.
60 J. Ashby-Sterry wrote *The Lazy Minstrel*, London 1886.
61 Harry Cholmondeley-Pennell wrote *Puck on Pegasus*, London 1862, and *Pegasus Resaddled*, London 1877. His complete poems were published under the title *From Grave to Gay*, London 1884.
62 *Times Literary Supplement*, 5 January 1946.
63 The first suggestion for a national festival was made in 1943 by the Royal Society of Arts, which proposed a commemoration of the 1851 Great Exhibition. See Mary Banham and Bevis Hillier, *A Tonic to the Nation: The Festival of Britain 1951*, London 1976, pp. 26–27 and 76.

Chapter 18: British Council

1 *British Council archives.*
2 *Ibid.*
3 Brian Kennedy-Cooke to JB, 26 September 1944. *Victoria.*
4 *Ibid.*
5 JB to Brian Kennedy-Cooke, 28 September 1944. *Victoria.*
6 *Ibid.*
7 *Ibid.*
8 JB to Mr Beadle, 5 October 1944. *Victoria.*
9 Lady de Bunsen, interview, 1990.

10 Renée Tickell, interview, 1990.
11 *Appointment with Venus* (United States title, *Island Rescue*) was filmed in 1951; director, Ralph Thomas.

JB knew Jerrard Tickell, as the film producer Betty E. Box records in her autobiography *Lifting the Lid*, Lewes, Sussex 2000, p. 60:

> I often met Jerrard Tickell at Betty's Bar in the Connaught Hotel, where, he said, he met colleagues during his days in Intelligence. He introduced me to his friend John Betjeman; he and Tickell struck me as two very lovable eccentrics as we sat with our drinks, talking about *Appointment with Venus*. Betjeman said: 'History must not be written with bias – both sides must be given, even if there is only one side,' and that's what we tried to do with our movie.

Betty Box describes the story and the making of the film in her Chapter 7 (pp. 57–66). The heroine of the film was a pedigree Jersey cow, known to the crew as the 'Venus de Milko'.

12 Renée Tickell, interview, 1990.
13 Michael Hooker, interview, 1981.
14 *Ibid.* Agag: a king of Amalek who was defeated in battle by King Saul. Saul wanted to spare Agag's life; but the prophet Samuel dealt with him harshly, as reported in 1 Samuel 15: 32–33.
15 Lady de Bunsen, interview, 1990.
16 *Ibid.*
17 Joanna Collihole, interview, 1990.
18 The assistant to whom JB wrote about poetry was Joan Barton. The letter was shown to the author in 1983 by Miss Barbara Watson.
19 Joanna Collihole, interview, 1990.
20 Michael Hooker, interview, 1981.
21 Anne Lush married Roger Ormrod (later the Rt. Hon. Sir Roger Ormrod, a Lord Justice of Appeal) in 1938.
22 Lady Ormrod, interview, 1990.
23 Renée Tickell, interview, 1990. The pun refers, of course, to Daniel 5: 25 – the writing on the wall at Belshazzar's feast, 'MENE, MENE, TEKEL, UPHARSIN'.
24 Michael Hooker, interview, 1981.
25 *British Council archives.*
26 All concerning Mr Milner that follows was sent by him to the author on 24 June 1990.
27 Lady de Bunsen, interview, 1990.
28 *British Council archives.*
29 Lady de Bunsen, interview, 1990.
30 Michael Hooker, interview, 1981.
31 Robert Milner, letter to the author, 24 June 1990.
32 Shown to the author by Miss Barbara Watson, 1983.
33 Barbara Watson, interview, 1983.
34 Lady de Bunsen, interview, 1990.
35 Renée Tickell, interview, 1990.
36 *Ibid.*
37 Lady Ormrod, interview, 1990.
38 *Ex inf.* Barbara Watson, interview, 1983.
39 Lady de Bunsen, interview, 1990.
40 On the Hon. Jane Digby El Mezrab (Lady Ellenborough, Baroness von Venningen, Countess Theotoky) see Lesley Blanch, *The Wilder Shores of Loves*, London 1954 edn.
41 Lady de Bunsen, interview, 1990.
42 Rosemary Pearce, interview, 1990.
43 Lady de Bunsen, interview, 1990.
44 Lady Ormrod, interview, 1990.
45 Margaret Barber, interview, 1990.
46 Ralph Glasser, *Gorbals Boy at Oxford*, London 1988, p. 1.

47 This recollection of Lady de Bunsen (interview, 1990) seems to conflict with JB, *Letters*, ed. CLG, i, 331, where the prize was awarded to 'a girl called Clementina Fisher'. Possibly there were two competitions.

48 Lady de Bunsen, interview, 1990.

49 A.J.P. Taylor, *A Personal History*, London 1983, p. 174.

50 Lady Ormrod, interview, 1990.

51 *Ibid.*

52 For more on Diana Craig (later Peel) and JB's choice of her as his secretary, see JB, *Letters*, ed. CLG, i, 330.

53 Barbara Watson, interview, 1983.

54 For the full original text of this poem, and its inspiration, see JB, *Letters*, ed. CLG, i, 390–91 and 391n.

55 On Ehrsam and the George see *YB*, pp. 133–34.

56 Michael Hooker, interview, 1981.

57 *Ibid.*

58 Powell misspells O'Donnell's Christian name 'Paedar'. On Peadar O'Donnell, see Brian Fallon, *An Age of Innocence: Irish Culture, 1930–1960*, Dublin 1999, pp. 13, 22, 45, 219–20 and 233; Dónal Ó Drisceoil, *Censorship in Ireland, 1939–1945*, Cork 1996, pp. 85 and 237; and Tim Pat Coogan, *De Valera: Long Fellow, Long Shadow*, London 1993, pp. 381–82, 411, 413, 463–64, 466 and 479.

59 Michael Powell, *A Life in Movies*, London 1986, p. 565.

60 See *YB*, Chapter 11, 'H.P.'.

61 Powell, *op. cit.*, p. 565.

62 *Loc. cit.*

63 Powell set out with a glamorous caravanserai, his progress across Ireland reported by the Dublin columnist Patrick Campbell (later Lord Glenavy and a famous stuttering television personality).

64 Powell, *op. cit.*, p. 565.

65 Lady Ormrod, interview, 1990.

66 JB is mentioned not at all in A.J.S. White's *The British Council: The First Twenty-Five Years*, London 1965, and is accorded the merest footnote in Lady Donaldson's *The British Council: The First Fifty Years*, London 1984, as one of a group of well-known writers who had worked for the Council.

As nominal head of the books division at the end of the war, John could perhaps take some reflected credit for approving such imaginative ideas as John Hampden's microfilm scheme. Hampden realized that European scientists were going to need British scientific and medical periodicals, which were not available because wartime runs had been so limited as a result of the paper shortage.

But against whatever credit John might claim for the things that went right must be set his failure effectively to supervise, which allowed some things to go disastrously wrong. After he left in May 1946, Molly Fernald had to be sacked ('Mr Kennedy-Cooke agonized over that for *days*,' Joanna Collihole said) because she had allowed unlimited credit to foreign booksellers and the money could not be recouped (Joanna Collihole, interview, 1990).

67 Shown to the author by Lady de Bunsen.

Chapter 19: A Lincolnshire Tale

1 A.J.P. Taylor, *A Personal History*, London 1983, p. 89.

2 John Innes Mackintosh Stewart (1906–94), Reader in English Literature, Oxford University, 1969–73, and author of detective fiction (as J.I.M. Stewart). He had been an undergraduate at Oriel College with Taylor and Yates.

3 Taylor, *op.cit.*, p. 75.

4 The 'Georgoisie': undergraduates who frequented 'the George' (St George's Café-and-Restaurant) in Oxford – see *YB*, pp. 133–34.

5 On Eric Walter White, later of the Arts Council of Great Britain, see *YB*, pp. 165–66, and Chapter 27 of the present volume, '*A Few Late Chrysanthemums*'.

6 JB's poem 'Sun and Fun: Song of a Night-Club Proprietress' (*Collected Poems*, 2001 edn., pp. 173–74) is about Skindles' Hotel, Maidenhead. JB, conversation, 1973. JB's friend Peter Quennell was sent down from Oxford for having sexual relations with a woman there. (See *YB*, p. 165.)

7 Jack Yates, unpublished autobiography. Shown to the author by the late Gill Foot.

8 One of the Radley stories was about a boy called Holcroft, 'looking like a Greek god, properly unclothed, running from his cubicle to the baths, suddenly confronted by Miss Gibson, the quite hideous but lovable Scots matron. As he hurriedly tried to cover himself with a towel she called in a shortbread accent, "It's all right, Holcroft. I'm here on business, not for pleasure."' Jack Yates, *op. cit.*

9 Lancelot Ridley Phelps (1853–1936), Provost of Oriel, 1914–29. On Phelps (and for a drawing of him) see Osbert Lancaster, *With an Eye to the Future*, London 1967, p. 63. Yates was also amusing about his history tutor, Stanley Cohn, who told him, 'I have been making a will. I have left a sum of money to the City Council to build a public lavatory like the front of Oriel College to get my revenge on those who built the front of Oriel College like a public lavatory.' (Yates, *op. cit.*)

10 Taylor was mistaken. Mansfield College was a Congregationalist foundation.

11 Taylor, *op. cit.*, pp. 89.

12 Yates, *op. cit.*

13 *Ibid.*

14 *Ibid.*

15 Taylor, *op. cit.*, p. 169.

16 Gill Foot, interview, 1989.

17 Yates, *op. cit.*

18 *Ibid.*

19 *Ibid.*

20 Goodwin and his friend did breed bees in Tobago; but the business was ruined by waxmoth and they ended up running a laundry in North Africa. (Yates, *op. cit.*)

21 Yates, *op. cit.*

22 *Ibid.*

23 *Ibid.*

24 *Ibid.*

25 Gill Foot, interview, 1989.

26 The future Cardinal (George) Basil Hume (1923–99) was senior modern language master of Ampleforth, 1952–63, housemaster, 1955–63, and Abbot of Ampleforth, 1963–76.

27 Gill Foot, interview, 1989.

28 Dr David Crook, interview, 1989.

29 Gill Foot, interview, 1989.

30 *Ibid.*

31 JB, speech to the Lincolnshire Association, 1963.

32 *The Letters of Alfred, Lord Tennyson*, ed. Cecil Y. Lang and Edgar F. Shannon, Oxford 1982, i, 317, n. 2.

33 *Collected Poems*, 2001 edn., p. 91.

34 Gill Foot, interview, 1989.

35 JB, speech to the Lincolnshire Association, 1963.

36 *Ibid.*

37 Gill Foot, interview, 1989.

38 (Frederick) Rowland Emett (1906–90), artist and inventor. Best known for improbable inventions and eccentric railway trains, in line and in three dimensions. On him see B. Hillier, introduction to Rowland Emett, *The Early Morning Milk Train*, London 1978.

39 Other jaunts were to Brocklesby Park, seat of the Earls of Yarborough, near Immingham on the Humber, and Great Limber, two miles south of Brocklesby.

40 JB also described Woodhall Spa, in *Ghastly Good Taste*, London 1933, p. 119, as 'that half-timbered Camberley among unexpected fir trees'.

41 *Collected Poems*, 2001 edn., p. 161.

42 Yates, *op. cit.*

43 *Collected Poems*, 2001 edn., p. 168.

44 JB to George Barnes, 18 June 1946. *JBP*.

45 The now redundant church of Goltho, about ten miles east-nor'east from Lincoln, is small and primitive. It is hardly grand enough ever to have had 'high pannelled [*sic*] pew[s]' (line 49 of 'A Lincolnshire Tale'), a 'tenor bell' (26 and 37), which would imply the presence of other bells, a coat of arms looking down 'high from the chancel arch' (53 and 54), a 'forest of woodwork' (45) or 'A three-decker pulpit' (56). As for Horsington Church, the brick building with limestone dressings and quoins was brand new in 1860. It follows that the building would not have been 'Restored with a vengeance' twenty-eight years later (lines 27 and 28 of 'A Lincolnshire Church'); and indeed it was not. So the Piper illustrations are red herrings.

46 The church of Langton-by-Spilsby has no tall tower (line 25 of 'A Lincolnshire Tale'). And it has no chancel arch (53). But in other respects it fits like a glove. Of its six bells, one is a tenor (26 and 27). It has 'clear leaded glass' (40); a 'forest of woodwork' (45); 'candles ensconced on each pannelled [*sic*] pew' (49); 'A sign-painter's beasts in their fight for the Crown' (53) and – the clinching evidence – 'A three-decker pulpit' (56). On top of all these resemblances is the recorded fact that JB visited and admired the Langton church. A pamphlet about it, written in the 1960s and signed by J.S. Thorold, Rector, and J.C.P. Langton and F.W. Walter, churchwardens, quotes JB as describing Langton Church as 'one of the most attractive and interesting churches in Lincolnshire and therefore in England – because Lincolnshire is rich in remarkable churches'.

47 Walking with Langton to the top of a hill in the parish known as the Sheepwalks, Johnson declared he had not had a roll for a long time, emptied his pockets of keys, purse and knife, and 'could not be dissuaded from lying down parallel with the edge of the hill and turning over and over till he came to the bottom'. George Birkbeck Hill, *Dr Johnson, His Friends and His Critics*, London 1878, pp. 268–69.

48 In several respects the church of the poem tallies with Huttoft. It is on 'a gentle eminence' (line 5). John described the tower as 'Silver and brown in the sunlight' (7). The tower is a patchwork of masonry of varying quality. The quoins and dressings are in a light limestone ashlar which may well appear as silver in bright sunlight. Much of the lower wall, especially in the upper reaches, is now quite green, like verdigris on old copper. But through this green may be seen patches of a brownish colour, notably on the west face. Huttoft is but two unprotected miles from the coast and is perpetually battered by sea winds (8). John described the architecture as 'Lincolnshire Middle Pointed' (9): Victorian windows were inserted into the chancel in 1869. The path to the church is 'a grassy mat' (23). The headstones (23 and 24) do slope crazily in all directions, though the grass is now better kept than it would have been shortly after the Second World War. The roof *is* of 'unsuitable slate' (26). John describes the church as 'Restored with a vengeance' in 'About eighteen eighty-eight'. As 'eighty-eight' had to rhyme with 'slate', one cannot rely on the historical accuracy of this; but Huttoft was restored in 1869 and 1897 – not by the abhorred Fowler of Louth, but by the lesser-known James Murgatroyd, so JB was not too far off the median. Huttoft has five altars, including the one in the south aisle mentioned by JB (31).

   JB was not the first to write a poem on Huttoft Church. In 1851 the *Church of England Magazine* published a poem on 'The Parish Church, Huttoft'. It begins with an attack on insensitive restoration, that could pass for Betjeman; like JB, writing almost a century later, the Victorian poet deplores the stripping of the lead roof.

49 The Rev. Theophilus Caleb, deacon 1907, priest 1908, became Vicar of Huttoft in 1943 (*Crockford's Clerical Directory*). The Rev. Michael Wright, sometime Vicar of Louth, wrote about him in 'Betjeman's Lincolnshire Church', an article in *The Betjemanian* (2000–01):

It may well be that the poet and Jack Yates went to Evensong. He quotes words from Psalm 51. And they see the Vicar appear in the chancel. Clergy of the Church of England always fascinated John Betjeman.

> There in the lighted East
> He stood in that lowering sunlight,
> An Indian Christian priest.

The poet would immediately be taken by this devout Indian vicar. He was the Reverend Theophilus Caleb, born in North India about 1878. His father had financed the printing of the first Bible in Hindi. So Theophilus and his brothers clearly came from a Christian family. He took his degree in Persian at the University of Allahabad and then came to London . . . and was called to the Bar.

When his father died he used his legacy to do what he dearly wanted to do and paid for his training for the Ministry of the Church of England at Chichester Theological College. There he gained a Bachelor of Divinity degree and also met his beloved wife, Annie Elizabeth. This is the answer to Betjeman's query:

> And why was he here in Lincolnshire
> I neither asked nor knew . . .

. . . [In 1943] he moved to Huttoft, where he died in 1959, having completed half a century of faithful ministry . . . His spirituality and pastoral care were much valued and appreciated. Times were not easy for him; to have a black man as Vicar in the marshland parish was even more unlikely then than it would be today. He felt deeply the agony of racial hatred on occasions. It hurt him.

The Rev. Mr Wright's article first appeared in *Lincolnshire Past and Present*, no. 40, Summer 2000. In it he expressed his indebtedness, for information, to Mrs M. Reading, daughter of the Rev. Theophilus Caleb.

Further information about Caleb appeared in an article in *The Betjeman Society Newsletter* of April 2001 (no. 45) by Kit Lawie, who wrote:

> In the early 1930s the Reverend Caleb's arrival on the scene constituted a startling event in the hamlet. The locals were almost all directly or indirectly connected to agriculture and were either devout Wesleyan Methodists or regular Church of England attenders.
> After the departure of the Reverend Lawd there descended upon this little community something approaching shock horror – 'the new parson's an Indian'! Word went round 'he looks just like Gandhi'! At this time Mahatma Gandhi was not receiving a good press, with his civil disobedience campaign and subsequent support of the Swaraj movement. Perhaps some degree of prejudice against someone of similar appearance could be forgiven, for in 1930 incomers from as far away as ten miles were regarded as 'furreners'.

50 *Ex inf.* Gill Foot, interview, 1989.
51 In lines 3, 38 and 68.
52 The Rev. Henry Thorold, chaplain, then housemaster, at Lancing College (1949–68), squarson of Marston, Lincolnshire. See his obituary in *The Times*, 8 February 2000. He met Yates in the Louth bookshop one school holiday, and was later introduced to him more formally by Frank Doherty, the headmaster of Lancing, who had taught Yates at Radley. Thorold was also a friend of John Piper, who sent his son Edward to Lancing and designed stained-glass windows for the school.
53 Henry Thorold, interview, 1989. The Rev. Michael Wright (*op. cit.*) was told by Jack Yates himself that the poem was about Huttoft and that it was sent as a collins to Yates's mother. Wright also suggests that the opening lines of the poem ('Greyly tremulous the thunder/Hung over the width of the wold . . .') would have reminded Yates and his mother of the freak thunderstorm which had devastated homes near the River Lud in 1920.
54 A.J.P. Taylor wrote (*op.cit.*, p. 170): 'Labour had refused to accept [Yates's] non-party character. A Labour candidate had run against him and he had lost the seat. "And do you know what they said about me, dear? They said I had used my position on the county

council to get the education committee to buy all its school books through my bookshop. Now wasn't that an unkind thing to say, dear?" I asked, "And did you get the education committee to buy its books through your bookshop?" "Of course, I did, dear." '

55 Henry Thorold, interview, 1989.
56 Yates is buried beside his parents in the churchyard of Keddington Church, Louth.
   Later, a more revealing epitaph on him was written. As a bookseller he had kept in touch with Joan Barton and Barbara Watson, who had worked with JB and himself at the British Council and then set up a bookshop in Marlborough together on leaving the Council at the end of the war. When Joan Barton heard of Yates's death, she wrote a poem about him to which she gave the title 'Gay News'. Its first stanza reads:

> We were fond of him:
> he was such good company, with all
> his innocent snobberies,
> sharp jests, and traveller's tales
> of jaunts with well-heeled friends
> told in that mannered drawl;
> and one who cared
> most tenderly for his mother
> in her long old age.

(Reproduced here by kind permission of Miss Barbara Watson.)
57 JB to Henry Thorold, 22 September 1981. JB, *Letters*, ed. CLG, ii, 572. The Norton Disney entry reads: 'Lost in the willows of the Brant, and surrounded by woods, this romantic village was once dominated by the castle of the Disney family whose name lives on in the creator of Mickey Mouse, a descendant of a junior branch.'
   Henry Thorold went on to write more Shell Guides than anybody else.

Chapter 20: Oxford Preservation Trust

1 John Betjeman, *An Oxford University Chest*, London 1938, p. 11.
2 Sir Michael Sadler (1861–1943), Master of University College, Oxford; not to be confused with his son, Michael Sadleir (see Chapter 8, '*Decoration*', note 22).
3 Betjeman, *op. cit.*, p. 8.
4 *OPT archives.*
5 On Lionel Curtis, see Lionel Curtis, *With Milner in South Africa*, Oxford 1951, and Deborah Lavin, *From Empire to International Commonweath: A Biography of Lionel Curtis*, Oxford 1995. At the beginning of her admirable book, Lavin writes: 'Lionel Curtis was once counted among the great and the good; he has been relegated to the status of an imperial crank on the lunatic fringe' (p. ix).
6 On Lionel Perry's friendship with JB, see *YB*, pp. 147, 149–51, 153–54, 171, 178, 180, 280 and 299, and *JBLP*, pp. 53 and 149.
7 On Milner's 'Kindergarten', young men in training to run the British Empire after the Boer War, see for example Terence H. O'Brien, *Milner*, London 1979.
8 John Sparrow, interview, 1977.
9 A.L. Rowse, *All Souls in my Time*, London 1967, pp. 72, 79, 80, 84–90, 123–34, 135 and 165.
10 Lionel Perry, interview, 1979.
11 On JB's regard for J.M. Thompson, see *YB*, p. 137.
12 *Ibid.*, pp. 266–8.
13 *OPT archives.*
14 *Ibid.*
15 *Ibid.*
16 *Ibid.*
17 *Ibid.*

18 On 29 January 1927 JB had written in the *Cherwell*: 'A VERY BEAUTIFUL NINE-TEENTH-CENTURY SHOP FRONT in the Cornmarket that used to belong to Hookham's has been destroyed in the march of commercialism round Oxford and a probably more useful creation in the Tuscan style has taken its place.' (Quoted, *YB*, p. 156.)

19 For the dubious claim that Shakespeare was Davenant's godfather, or even father, see the *DNB*.

20 Some of the words had become obscured, but the wording seems to have been: [First in thi Rising] And last of thi rest by thou God's servante for that hold I best. In the mornynge earlye serve God devoutlye. Fear God above all thynge and . . . and the Kynge.'

21 Aubrey's *Brief Lives*, ed. Andrew Clarke, Oxford, 1898, i, 204–09.

22 Osbert Lancaster, interview, 1977.

23 *OPT archives.*

24 Sam Smith's obituary in the *Oxford Times* (30 October 1964) recorded that he was 'a tiny man, under five feet'.

25 *OPT archives.*

26 *Ibid.*

27 *Ibid.*

28 See Chapter 3 of the present volume, 'The Diarist', entry for 9 April 1936.

29 *OPT archives.*

30 *Ibid.* On 13 March 1879 Hopkins wrote 'I have been up to Godstow this afternoon – I am sorry to say that the aspens that lined the river are everyone felled.' (*The Correspondence of Gerard Manley Hopkins and Richard Watson Dixon*, ed. Claude Colleer Abbott, Oxford 1935, p. 26.) This observation inspired Hopkins's poem 'Binsey Poplars felled 1879'.

31 *Collected Poems*, 2001 edn., p. 144.

32 *Ibid.*, p. 146.

33 John Edwards, letter to the author, 5 January 1990.

34 *Ibid.*

35 *Ibid.* Edwards also concedes that six further lines of the poem could well be thought to refer to Plowman (*Collected Poems*, 1985 edn., pp. 178–79):

> But as for Dorset's flint and Purbeck stone,
> Its old thatched farms in dips of down alone –
> It should be merged with Hants and made to be
> A self-contained and plann'd community.
> Like Flint and Rutland, it is much too small
> And has no reason to exist at all.

36 *OPT archives.*

37 John Edwards, letter to the author, 5 January 1990.

38 *OPT archives.*

39 *Ibid.*

40 On Schumacher/ffennel see Lavin, *op. cit.*, p. 263. Lionel Curtis mentions him as 'Schoemaker' in *With Milner in South Africa*, Oxford 1951, p. 341; and A.L. Rowse, in *All Souls in my Time*, p. 87, describes the meeting between Curtis and ffennel which led to ffenel's gift to the OPT.

41 *OPT archives.*

42 *Ibid.*

43 *Ibid.* The main reason the Luftwaffe abandoned the 'Baedeker raids' of 1942 was that its losses were too high.

44 *Ibid.*

45 *Ibid.*

46 *Oxford City Council archives.*

47 *Ibid.*

48 *Ibid.*

49 *Ibid.*

50 *Ibid.*
51 *Ibid.*
52 *Ibid.*
53 *Ibid.*
54 *Ibid.*
55 OPT *archives.*
56 *Ibid.*
57 John Edwards, letter to the author, 5 February 1990.
58 OPT *archives.*
59 *Ibid.*
  The South Park affair gives a glimpse of John in action at the OPT; but it was not an issue that deeply engaged his interest. One that did engage it was the proposal to alter the architecture of the Radcliffe Observatory so as to accommodate a hostel for nurses from the Radcliffe Infirmary. Here John's sympathies were divided. On the one hand, he loved the Observatory – it was the building Christopher Sykes remembered his applauding when he passed it as an undergraduate (*JBLP*, p. 62). On the other hand, he had lately been cared for by Oxford nurses, who deserved the best housing that could be devised.
60 John Edwards, letter to the author, 5 February 1990.
61 OPT *archives.*
62 *Ibid.*
63 Cutting of letter, OPT *archives.*
64 *Ibid.*
65 *Ibid.*
66 *Ibid.*
67 *Ibid.*
68 *Ibid.*
69 *Ibid.*
70 John Johnson made a celebrated collection of printed ephemera, now in the Bodleian Library, Oxford.
71 OPT *archives.*
72 *Ibid.*
73 *Ibid.*
74 *Ibid.*
75 *Ibid.*
76 *Ibid.*
77 *Ibid.*
78 *Ibid.*
79 A.L. Rowse, conversation with the author, 1990.

Chapter 21: *On the Air in the Forties*

1 JB, 'Coming Home – or England Revisited', BBC Home Service, 23 February 1943, *BBCWA.*
2 JB to Ronald Boswell, 18 September 1943. *BBCWA.*
3 Geoffrey Grigson to Winifred Salmon (Assistant Director of Talks, London), BBC internal memo, September 1943. *BBCWA.*
4 Winifred Salmon to Geoffrey Grigson, BBC internal memo, September 1943. *BBCWA.*
5 Geoffrey Grigson to Winifred Salmon, BBC internal memo, September 1943. *BBCWA.*
6 JB to Geoffrey Grigson, 19 June 1939. JB, *Letters*, ed. CLG, i, 228.
7 JB, 'Move with the Times', *Under Thirty*, London 1939. Quoted *ibid.*, ii, 228n.
8 Geoffrey Grigson to Godfrey James, BBC internal memo, 23 June 1944. *BBCWA.*
9 Godfrey James to Geoffrey Grigson, BBC internal memo, 26 June 1944. *BBCWA.*
10 JB, 'Books', 15 August 1939. *BBCWA.*
11 *Ibid.*

12 JB, 'Secondhand Books', 4 November 1943. *BBCWA*.
13 JB to Ronald Boswell, 6 December 1946. *BBCWA*. The talk on Waugh was transmitted in *Living Writers*, 14 December 1946.
14 Terence de Vere White to JB, 18 December 1946. Quoted, JB, *Letters*, ed. CLG, i, 370.
15 'John Betjeman gave a "talk" about me on the wireless. We borrowed [F.W.] Deakin's apparatus and listened. Too much of it was quotation. He read a long passage from *Vile Bodies* and succeeded in breathing life in those dry old bones.' *The Diaries of Evelyn Waugh*, ed. Michael Davie, London 1976, p. 666.
16 Ronald Lewin to JB, 2 December 1946. *BBCWA*.
17 JB to Ronald Lewin, 17 December 1946. *BBCWA*.
18 Ronald Lewin to JB, 18 December 1946. *BBCWA*.
19 JB to Ronald Lewin, 21 December 1946. *BBCWA*.
20 Ronald Lewin to JB, 23 December 1946. *BBCWA*.
21 The story was printed in *The Listener*, 9 January 1947.
22 JB, 'Exeter', 1937. *BBCWA*.
23 JB, 'Christmas Nostalgia', 25 December 1947. *BBCWA*. See also p. 306 of this book.
24 *Ibid.*
25 A photograph of him, taken to celebrate that appointment, is reproduced in *JBLP*, p. 119.
26 BBC memo to Anna Kallin from her secretary, 17 March 1947. *BBCWA*. On Anna Kallin, see Humphrey Carpenter, *The Envy of the World: Fifty Years of the BBC Third Programme and Radio 3*, London 1996, pp. 66 and n. 6, 118, 121, 124, 127, 187, 193 and 298.
27 See Basil Taylor, *Stubbs*, London 1975.
28 JB to Basil Taylor, 10 October 1948. *BBCWA*.
29 *The Oxford Book of English Talk*, ed. James Sutherland, Oxford 1953, p. 420.
30 *Ibid.*, pp. 433–35.
31 *Ex inf.* Dr Richard Squires, telephone conversation with the author, 1999.
32 *The Oxford Book of English Talk*, pp. 433–35.
33 *The Spectator*, 13 May 2000. JB had picked up archaic tricks of pronunciation from Penelope. For example when reading 'Indoor Games near Newbury' on a gramophone record, he pronounced 'frosty' as *frorsty*.

Chapter 22: 'The Betje-bus'

1 *John Murray archives.*
2 *Ibid.*
3 *Ibid.*
4 John G. Murray to John Sparrow, 8 July 1946. *John Murray archives.*
5 John Sparrow to John G. Murray, 25 July 1946. *John Murray archives.*
6 John G. Murray to John Sparrow, 26 July 1946. *John Murray archives.*
7 See *YB*, p. 171.
8 *Encounter*, February 1962, pp. 35–43.
9 John G. Murray to JB, 11 August 1946. *John Murray archives.*
10 JB to John G. Murray, 19 August 1946. *John Murray archives.*
11 *John Murray archives.*
12 Martin Secker to John G. Murray, 3 September 1946. *John Murray archives.*
13 John G. Murray to JB, 15 January 1947. *John Murray archives.*
14 'North Coast Recollections', *West Country Magazine*, vol. 2, no. 1, Spring 1947, pp. 18–21.
15 John Sparrow to John G. Murray, 16 September 1947. *John Murray archives.*
16 Richard Ingrams and John Piper write in *Piper's Places: John Piper in England and Wales*, London 1983, pp. 122–23:

    In 1951 the *Shell Guides* were published again, and the Betjeman/Piper *Shropshire* appeared. The Guides had been discontinued during the war and meanwhile Piper and Betjeman had become involved in a new guidebook project with their publishing friend

John Murray. Three guidebooks were produced, *Buckinghamshire* (1948), *Berkshire* (1949), both by Betjeman and Piper, and *Lancashire* (1955) by Peter Fleetwood-Hesketh; but in the difficult post-war period, the books proved too expensive to produce and Murray reluctantly abandoned the scheme.

17 JB, *Letters*, ed. CLG, i, 371.
18 *Victoria*.
19 On Humbert Wolfe, see *YB*, pp. 337–38.
20 W.H. Auden, preface to John Betjeman, *Slick but not Streamlined*, Garden City, New York 1947, pp. 9–10.
21 *Loc. cit.*
22 See *YB*, pp. 266–67.
23 John G. Murray to JB, 21 February 1947. *John Murray archives*.
24 *John Murray archives*.
25 *Ibid.*
26 *Ibid.*
27 John G. Murray to JB, 28 August 1947. *John Murray archives*.
28 *John Murray archives*.
29 John Sparrow to John G. Murray, 21 September 1947. *John Murray archives*.
30 John G. Murray to John Sparrow, 22 September 1947. *John Murray archives*.
31 *John Murray archives*.
32 John G. Murray to John Sparrow, 8 October 1947. *John Murray archives*.
33 John Sparrow to John G. Murray, 6 November 1947. *John Murray archives*.
34 Sir Harold Acton, letter to the author, 4 July 1977.
35 John Sparrow, preface to John Betjeman, *Selected Poems*, London 1948, p. ix.
36 *Ibid.*, pp. xiii–xiv.
37 *Ibid.*, p. xiv.
38 *Ibid.*, p. xxii.
39 *John Murray archives*.
40 *Ibid.*
41 *Ibid.*
42 John G. Murray to JB, 22 December 1947. *John Murray archives*.
43 JB, *Letters*, ed. CLG, i, 427.
44 *John Murray archives*.
45 *Ibid.*
46 Myfanwy Piper to John G. Murray, 27 December 1947. *John Murray archives*.
47 John G. Murray to JB, 5 January 1948. *John Murray archives*.
48 *John Murray archives*.
49 *Ibid.*
50 *Ibid.*
51 *Ibid.*
52 *Ibid.*
53 *Evening News*, 6 October 1948.
54 *Time and Tide*, 6 November 1948.
55 *The Spectator*, 10 December 1948.
56 *The Listener*, 3 February 1949.
57 *New Statesman*, 11 December 1948.
58 *Ibid.*
59 *The Eighteen Nineties: A Period Selection*, ed. Martin Secker, London 1948, p. xii.
60 *The Month*, January 1949, p. 49.
61 JB to Evelyn Waugh, 17 January 1949. JB, *Letters*, ed. CLG, i, 410.
62 Evelyn Waugh to JB, 18 January 1949. JB, *Letters*, ed. CLG, i, 450n.
63 *John Murray archives*.
64 *Ibid.*

Chapter 23: A Preservationist in the Making

1 *The Future of the Past: Attitudes to Conservation 1174–1974*, ed. Jane Fawcett, London 1976, p. 55.
2 *Loc. cit.*
3 I am most grateful to Mr Gary Thorn, assistant archivist of the British Museum, for the following information: The Rev. Richard Garnett (1789–1850) upon his death was assistant keeper of Printed Books, a post he held from 1838. His son Richard Garnett (1835–1906) obtained a post within the same department in 1851. He retired in 1899.
    The younger Garnett died in the year JB was born. Perhaps there was a Widow Garnett or an unmarried Miss Garnett still living in JB's childhood.
4 *The Future of the Past*, ed. Jane Fawcett, London 1976, p. 55.
5 See JB, *Summoned by Bells*, London 1960, p. 19.
6 *The Future of the Past*, ed. Jane Fawcett, pp. 55–56.
7 See 'Norfolk', *Collected Poems*, 2001 edn., p. 168.
8 *The Future of the Past*, ed. Jane Fawcett, p. 56. Apart from a 1960s block on the site of some demolished houses, Glenhurst Road is much as JB knew it.
9 *The Future of the Past*, ed. Jane Fawcett, p. 56.
10 See JB in *My Oxford*, ed. Ann Thwaite, London 1977, p. 63.
11 *The Future of the Past*, ed. Jane Fawcett, p. 56.
12 See *Summoned by Bells*, p. 74.
13 See *YB*, p. 49.
14 *Ibid.*, pp. 114–15.
15 *The Future of the Past*, ed. Jane Fawcett, p. 56.
16 *Loc. cit.*
17 Richardson's book was published in London in 1912.
18 *The Future of the Past*, ed. Jane Fawcett, pp. 56–57.
19 JB, *Ghastly Good Taste*, London 1971 edn., pp. xix–xx.
20 See *YB*, p. 109.
21 Quoted, *ibid.*, p. 202.
22 Quoted, *loc. cit.*
23 Quoted, Lady Harrod, letter to the author, 29 August 1992.
24 On the foundation of the Georgian Group, see *Architectural Journal*, vol. 135, no. 13, 31 March 1982, Georgian Group Special Issue, with contributions from Colin Amery, Gavin Stamp and others.
25 See *YB*, p. 345.
26 J.C. Squire, 'A New Song of the Bishop of London', *Collected Poems*, London 1959, pp. 194–97.
27 *The Times*, 14 December 1932.
28 *Ibid.*
29 See *YB*, p. 148.
30 See, for example, Osbert Sitwell, 'Brass Button', and 'Other Times, Other Climes', *The Collected Poems and Satires of Osbert Sitwell*, London 1931, pp. 186–89; and 'Mr and Mrs Goodbeare', *ibid.*, pp. 231–32.
31 Quoted, *YB*, p. 111.
32 *Ibid.*, p. 108.
33 JB gave a copy of this early poem to John G. Murray, who sent a copy to the author in 1988. JB had told Murray that he wrote the poem at the age of sixteen.
34 *The Future of the Past*, ed. Jane Fawcett, p. 57.
35 See *YB*, pp. 198–99.
36 For a more extended quotation, see *YB*, p. 156.
37 Felicia Dorothea Hemans (1793–1835), English poet, author of such lines as 'The stately homes of England' and 'The boy stood on the burning deck'. Her *Poetical Works* were collected in 1832.

38 JB to Lionel Perry, n.d. (but summer 1926). JB, *Letters*, ed. CLG, i, 39.

39 JB's first letter to *The Times*, signed 'John Betjemann', was published on 15 September 1926. In it he deplored the destruction of church galleries.

40 *The Times*, 12 November 1927.

41 From 1659 to 1954 (when it was given to the National Trust) the Cornish island of St Michael's Mount was owned by the St Aubyn family (thus spelt; after 1887 Lords St Levan). Piers St Aubyn (b. 1815) became an architect; he was elected a Fellow of the Royal Institute of British Architects in 1856. In his introduction to the *Collins Pocket Guide to English Parish Churches* (1958; London 1964, p. 27) JB wrote:

> The practised eye can tell at a glance how severe the restoration has been, and often indeed who has done the damage. For instance almost every other church in Cornwall, besides many farther east, was restored by Mr J.P. St Aubyn late in the last century, and he has left his mark at the church porch in the form of a scraper of his own design, as practical and unattractive as his work.

42 JB to Ward, Lock & Co., Ltd., 11 November 1928. JB, *Letters*, ed. CLG, i, 39.

43 *The Times*, 5 June 1931.

44 *The Times*, 5 March 1932.

45 *The Times*, 22 July 1932.

46 See the epigraph to the present chapter, taken from Kenneth Clark's letter to Michael Sadleir (dated July 1949), which prefaced the second edition of *The Gothic Revival*, London 1950. In the same letter, Clark wrote:

> A generation influenced by the poetical insight of Mr Betjeman will find it hard to believe in the state of feeling towards nineteenth-century architecture which prevailed in 1927 [i.e. when Clark was writing the book published in 1928]. In Oxford it was unanimously believed that Ruskin had built Keble [College], and that it was the ugliest building in the world.

47 Evelyn Waugh, *Labels: A Mediterranean Journey*, London 1930, pp. 173–74.

48 JB, *Ghastly Good Taste*, London 1933, p. 120.

49 JB to Bryan Guinness, 30 January 1934. JB, *Letters*, ed. CLG, i, 130.

50 On the rift over religion, see Chapter 16, 'Farnborough'.

51 See Selina Hastings, *Evelyn Waugh: A Biography*, London 1994, p. 562; Martin Stannard, *Evelyn Waugh: No Abiding City*, London 1992, p. 341 and n. 121; and *The Letters of Evelyn Waugh*, ed. Mark Amory, London 1981, pp. 413, 416, 417 and 632.

52 On Waugh's relationship to William Holman Hunt, see Diana Holman-Hunt, *My Grandfather, his Wives and Loves*, London 1969, p. 2.

53 Evelyn Waugh, *Brideshead Revisited*, London 1946 edn., p. 135.

54 *The Times*, 8 February 1936.

55 On the All Hallows controversy, see *The Times*, 18, 19 and 29 January and 10 February 1937.

56 See *ibid.*

57 *The Times*, 8 February 1937.

58 *The Times*, 5 March 1937.

59 *Loc. cit.*

60 C.R. Ashbee to JB, 7 March 1937. *Victoria.*

61 Quoted by JB, *The Times*, 30 July 1937.

62 *Loc. cit.*

63 JB to John Summerson, 4 November 1937. JB, *Letters*, ed. CLG, i, 181.

64 JB to Bryan Guinness, 17 December 1937. *Ibid.*, i, 183.

65 Osbert Lancaster to JB, 30 November 1936. *Victoria.* JB does not appear to have written a poem about the Crystal Palace; but Bryan Guinness did so, and dedicated it to JB.

66 JB to Sir Giles Gilbert Scott, 16 December 1938. JB, *Letters*, ed. CLG, i, 220.

67 Byron's squib, first published in *The Architectural Review*, May 1937, was subsequently reprinted as a separate pamphlet.

68 JB, *Antiquarian Prejudice*, London 1939, p. 11.

69 Ernest William Tristram (1882–1952). Preserved medieval paintings and monuments; see *Who Was Who*.

70 JB, *Antiquarian Prejudice*, pp. 10–11.

71 *Ibid.*, p. 16. South Africa House (1930) in Trafalgar Square, London, was designed by Sir Herbert Baker. On Sir Reginald Blomfield's New Regent Street, see *YB*, p. 362, and JB's poem attacking it in *The Times*, 14 December 1932 (reprinted in *Collected Poems*, 2001 edn., pp. 363–64).

72 JB, *Antiquarian Prejudice*, p. 16.

73 *Ibid.*, p. 19. JB's parents-in-law lived in St John's Wood, and he often stayed with them there in 1939.

74 *Ibid.*, p. 24.

75 *Ibid.*, p. 26.

76 *Ibid.*, p. 24.

77 *Ibid.*, p. 27.

78 *Ibid.*, pp. 22–23.

79 *The Times*, 19 July 1946.

80 *The Times*, 26 April 1947.

81 I am grateful to Mr Iain Sproat, the former Conservative Minister, for this anecdote.

82 *The Times*, 30 April 1947.

83 *The Times*, 1 May 1947.

84 *The Times*, 6 February 1948.

85 *The Times*, 14 February 1948.

86 *Loc. cit.*

87 *The Times*, 19 February 1948.

88 Quoted, Sir Osbert Lancaster, interview, 1977.

89 *The Times*, 30 October 1948.

90 *Loc. cit.*

91 *Loc. cit.*

92 *The Times*, 24 November 1948.

93 *The Times*, 3 December 1948.

94 *The Times*, 10 October 1949.

Chapter 24: 'Tame and Tade'

1 CLG gives the date of JB's letter to T.S. Eliot as 23 August 1949. (JB, *Letters*, ed. CLG, i, 484.) This date cannot be correct; for the review of Pound which JB commissioned from Wolf Mankowitz when Eliot declined his offer appeared in *Time and Tide* on 30 July 1949 (see note 3).

2 JB to T.S. Eliot (see note 1 on its date).

3 Wolf Mankowitz, 'The Pisan Cantos', *Time and Tide*, 30 July 1949.

4 Anthony Lejeune, letter to the author, 24 September 1988.

5 On the life and career of Lady Rhondda, see for example Shirley M. Eoff, *Viscountess Rhondda: Equalitarian Feminist*, Columbus, Ohio, 1991.

6 A.L. Rowse wrote to the author (28 April 1990): 'Of course I was in on *Time and Tide*, and wrote a lot for it, but through my pupil Veronica Wedgwood. JB's association with it was fairly brief, and not close. For they were all a lot of lesbians. Lady R, an awful woman, "global" indeed, her lover Theodora Bosanquet – I think that's right – Henry James's secretary, to whom he dictated his last books – that's why they are so intolerably long-winded; and of course dear Veronica.'

7 Reginald Langbridge, interview, 1990.

8 Vera Brittain, *Testament of Friendship*, London 1997 edn., p. 267.

9 *Chronicle of Friendship: Vera Brittain's Diary of the Thirties 1932–1939*, ed. Alan Bishop, London 1986, pp. 104 and 138.

10 Reginald Langbridge, interview, 1990.

11 JB, conversation with the author, 1974.

12 Reginald Langbridge, interview, 1990.
13 *DNB*.
14 *Ibid.*
15 *Time and Tide*, 25 March 1950, p. 286.
16 Wolf Mankowitz became better known as the author of the novels *Make Me an Offer* (1952) and *A Kid for Two Farthings* (1953), both of which were turned into films. In 1952 he published *The Portland Vase and the Wedgwood Copies* and in 1957 (with Reginald Haggar) *The Concise Encylopaedia of English Pottery and Porcelain*.
17 Rose Macaulay to Jean Macaulay, 10 June [1954], *Letters to a Sister from Rose Macaulay*, ed. Constance Babington Smith, London 1964, p. 158.
18 See *Parson's Pleasure*, Oxford, 15 October 1958.
19 *Time and Tide*, 26 August 1950.
20 See Mary Banham and Bevis Hillier, *A Tonic to the Nation: The Festival of Britain 1951*, London 1976, pp. 15 and 26–38.
21 His sole contribution appears to have been to have written the captions for a Cotswold Crafts exhibition organized in Cirencester by the architect Oliver Hill. I am grateful to Mr Alan Powers for kindly drawing the catalogue to my attention.
22 See the chapter 'Back to Cloth Fair' in the third volume of the present work.
23 In *Oxford and Cambridge Magazine*. See *JBLP*, p. 68.
24 In 1975 JB wrote, in a Foreword to B. Hillier, *Austerity/Binge: The Decorative Arts of the Forties and Fifties*, that the 1951 Festival of Britain left 'the South Bank swept of wharfs and instead dominated by the Festival Hall whose river front undoubtedly looks like an outsize television set'.
25 *Time and Tide*, 26 April 1952.
26 See *YB*, pp. 40–41.
27 *Ibid.*, p. 288.
28 The poem was written by JB's friend the Rev. Sandys Wason. On him, see Roy Tricker, *Mr Wason . . . I Think*, London 1994; on the 'Anglican Alphabet', see *ibid.*, p. 130.
29 JB, *Summoned by Bells*, London 1960, p. 58.
30 Kirkup's poem was 'The love that dares to speak its name', describing the reactions of a centurion after the crucifixion. The trial of *Gay News* and its editor Denis Lemon for blasphemous libel, instigated by Mrs Mary Whitehouse, began on 4 July 1977 (*The Times*, 4 July 1977). The paper was found guilty (*The Times*, 12 July 1977). It was held that Kirkup's poem portrayed Christ as a practising homosexual.
31 Kirkup's poem 'A City of the North' appeared in his collection *A Correct Compassion and other poems*, Oxford 1952, pp. 6–7.
32 JB wrote to Kirkup on 5 March 1952 (letter shown to the author by Mr Kirkup): 'Dear Mr Kirkup, I am so sorry to have been so long about Leeds. This has been because *We have been changing our printers* & the new ones are so nervous & feeble, they won't undertake the sort of layout I had in mind & that Mr de Saumarez & you worked out on that bit of cardboard. So I shall have to give up the idea. And then will the poem be too long? that is what bothers me. They only print . . . snippets of poems here & if you don't mind waiting, we'll print it in time. But *do* you mind waiting? If you do, I'll return it for you to send to someone else. As for Mr de Saumarez, they must pay him – T & T – I suggest we pay him 6 gns (1 gn a drawing) . . . but will he accept? Please ask him. Send more poems to us. God bless you. I will return the drawings. Yours sincerely, John Betjeman'.
33 The *DNB* records of Seymour Stocker Kirkup (1788–1880):

> In 1840 Kirkup, Bezzi and Henry Wilde, an American, obtained leave to search for the portrait of Dante, painted, according to tradition, by Giotto, in the chapel of the Palazzo del Podestà at Florence. In this they were successful on 21 July 1840. Kirkup was able surreptitiously to make a drawing and a tracing before an ill-conceived restoration in 1841 . . .

34 James Kirkup, letter to the author, 2 August 1988.
35 The poem appears on p. 161 of Driberg's *The Best of Both Worlds: A Personal Diary*, London 1953:

Cycle with Masks

Sovereign and sure as the alluvial downflow
  of the gravid river, the loving
sprang in the swell and verve of the fevered spring.

Summer poised it glistening high-green like a salad
  for our saucy greed: oil on chin,
fleck of chive on skin or freckle on skin, fierce sun of sinning.

The swings hang still, or are strapped up for the winter,
  Wiseacres advise of a fiddle-string snapped,
of a peremptory nip in the air. Adjust your visors before leaving.

Driberg wrote of this poem (*loc. cit.*): 'The sixth line was rather sham-Hopkins, but I wasn't too displeased with the thing as a whole.'

36 See *YB*, p. 167.
37 Driberg, *op. cit.*, p. 161.
38 *Ibid.*, pp. 220–21.
39 JB, *Letters*, ed. CLG, ii, 24.
40 The inscribed photograph is illustrated in *JBLP*, p. 15.
41 JB, *Letters*, ed. CLG, ii, 13.
42 *Loc. cit.*
43 *Victoria.*
44 *Collected Poems*, 2001 edn., p. 182.
45 *Time and Tide*, 2 December 1950.
46 Randolph Churchill to JB, 27 August 1949. *JBP.*
47 Mr Alan Bell suggests that 'HMB' was probably Hugh Murray Baillie, who became a librarian at the National Library of Scotland and a member of the Royal Fine Art Commission.
48 *Letters to a Friend from Rose Macaulay*, ed. Constance Babington Smith, London 1961, p. 274.
49 Nancy Mitford, *The Pursuit of Love*, London 1945, p. 31.
50 *Collected Poems*, 2001 edn., p. 203.
51 *Encounter*, September 1955.
52 JB, *Letters*, ed. CLG, ii, 92n.
53 Anthony Lejeune, letter to the author, 24 September 1988.
54 Interview, 1982. (The sub-editor wished to remain anonymous.)
55 As recorded in the diary of Van Meter Ames. See Chapter 33, 'Cincinnati'.
56 Anthony Lejeune, letter to the author, 1988.
57 *Ibid.*
58 Anthony Lejeune (b. 1928): son of C.A. (Caroline) Lejeune, who reviewed films alongside JB in the 1930s (see Chapter 2, 'Film Critic'); like JB a friend of the novelist Arthur Machen; with C.A. Lejeune, Anthony Lejeune contributed to *Arthur Machen: Essays*, ed. Brocard Sewell, Llandeilo 1960 (mentioning JB, p. 33); and he was on the staff of *Time and Tide* just after JB was sacked.

Chapter 25: Wantage

1 JB, *Letters*, ed. CLG, i, 474.
2 PB, interview, 1976.
3 Douglas Woodruff, interview, 1977. JB was familiar with the poem by Hayman beginning:

There's the quaintest of towns
On the Berkshire Downs

NOTES TO PAGES 450–456

That enjoys a Utopian state;
For the place has possessed
Imperturbable rest
Since the days of King Alfred the Great.

4 JB, *Letters*, ed. CLG, ii, 3.
5 *Ibid.*, 3–4.
6

'It's for Regency now I'm enthusing
   So we've Regency stripes on the wall . . .'
'Winthrop Mackworth Redivivus', *Collected Poems*, 2001 edn., p. 209.

7 JB, *Letters*, ed. CLG, ii, 4.
8 Dr Richard Squires, interview, 1976.
9 *Ibid.*
10 *Ibid.*
11 Mr O'Brien, interview, 1976.
12 *Ibid.*
13 *Ibid.*
14 *Ibid.*
15 Dr Richard Squires, interview, 1976.
16 Ottilie Squires, interview, 1989.
17 Ottilie Squires recalled of her husband (interview, 1989): 'He said Penelope was the only person he ever liked lending his horses to. Vaughan said you could tell when somebody good had been riding your horse: it walked properly. Whereas, if you lent it to most people, you had to train it up again.'
18 Ottilie Squires, interview, 1989.
19 I am indebted to Dr G.E. Smith for this information.
20 Mollie Baring, interview, 1989.
21 'County', *Collected Poems*, 2001 edn., p. 316.
22 Hester Knight, interview, 1989.
23 *Ibid.*
24 Hester Knight, interview, 1976.
25 *Ibid.*
26 Anne Dalgety, Desmond and Mollie Baring's daughter, has published a book about them, *Moll & Dez: A Tribute in Words and Pictures*, Trowbridge, Wiltshire 2001. I am indebted to this work, and to the memorial tribute to Mollie Baring, by CLG, printed in it, for the information in the following note.

Mollie Baring (1912–98) was the daughter of Ben Warner (1899–1974), who was first a successful bookmaker, then a racehorse owner and professional backer. Warner married Margaret Budd, whose father ran a pub and a butcher's shop. Mollie was briefly at RADA, where she played Puck to Vivien Leigh's Titania. In 1937 she met Desmond Baring (1914–91) and they married in 1938.

Desmond Baring's father Nigel Baring devoted much of his time to hunting. His mother, Sybil Roche, was the only child of Lord and Lady Fermoy. The Barings' children, Peter, Nigel and Anne, were born between 1939 and 1944.

Anne Dalgety writes that Desmond was 'genuinely classless' but that Mollie was 'terribly aware of etiquette' and was coached in this by Lady Glyn, at nearby Marndhill, who advised her that 'one should never read a novel before lunch' and (well aware that her husband had a mistress) that 'My dear, it's quite impossible for one woman to satisfy a man.' The Barings lived in some state. They had a 'mad butler' called Sheldrake, who wore full livery and once threatened the children's nanny with a knife. Up to the mid-1950s the Barings also had a cook and two housemaids.

JB first met the Barings about 1949, when he was still living at Farnborough.
27 Mollie Baring, interview, 1989
28 *Ibid.*

29 Dalgety, *op. cit.*, p. 116.
30 *Ibid.*, p. 83.
31 *Ibid.*, p. 122.
32 *Ibid.*, pp. 90–91.
33 *Ibid.*, p. 95
34 Quoted, JB, *Letters*, ed. CLG, ii, 369.
35 Mollie Baring, interview, 1989.
36 *Ibid.*
37 *Ibid.*
38 '*Groundnuts scheme*: notorious development scheme by the Attlee government in 1948–49 to grow groundnuts (peanuts) in Tanganyika (now Tanzania). The scheme proved an almost total failure, incurring heavy losses, because of poor planning and unsuitable agricultural techniques.' (*The History Today Companion to British History*, ed. Juliet Gardiner and Neil Wenborn, London 1995, p. 357.)
39 *Ex inf.* Dr Richard Squires, interview, 1976.
40 Dr Richard Squires, interview, 1976.
41 *Ibid.*
42 JB wrote to his friend Edward Hornby, 'I realise how important all our companies are to each other. Michael [Hornby] came last night to us at Wantage and he and the Pipers and Karen Lancaster and Heck and Guy Knight and the Barings and the children sang popular hits of the twenties until one a.m.' (JB, *Letters*, ed. CLG, ii, 102–03.)
43 See JB's letter to John Piper, 9 November 1952. JB, *Letters*, ed. CLG, ii, 32.
44 See JB's letter to Bess Betjeman, 18 November 1952. JB, *Letters*, ed. CLG, ii, 34.
45 *Ibid.*, 34n.
46 Henrietta Lawrence, interview, 1976.
47 Molly Lawrence, interview, 1976.
48 JB to George Barnes, 6 December 1951. JB, *Letters*, ed. CLG, ii, 19.
49 JB, *Letters*, ed. CLG, ii, 9.
50 Evelyn Waugh wrote in his diary on 24 August 1946: '. . . I went to stay with Pamela Berry in a luxurious ranch-house near Reading.' (The other guests included Randolph Churchill, Seymour Berry and Peter Fleming.) Waugh added: 'John Betjeman came to luncheon and read his erotic poetry aloud.' (*The Diaries of Evelyn Waugh*, ed. Michael Davie, London 1976, pp. 657–58.)
51 See the chapter '*Daily Telegraph*' in the third volume of the present work.
52 'Blunt looked ill at ease, and waffled on to Berlin about the embarrassment of being found surrounded by Conservatives. "I suppose," Berlin mused, ". . . he felt I wasn't to think that he was really a friend of these terrible people."' Miranda Carter, *Anthony Blunt: His Lives*, London 2001, p. 346.
53 Andrew Boyle, *The Climate of Treason: Five Who Spied for Russia*, London 1979, p. 83.
54 Carter, *op. cit.*, p. 341.
55 Lord Hartwell similarly told Miranda Carter (*loc. cit.*) that he had decided not to offer Burgess a job on the *Daily Telegraph* – 'When Berry asked for something of Burgess's to read, Burgess gave him a document marked "Top Secret". "I was appalled when I read it. His writing had certainly gone to seed."'
    The possibility cannot be discounted that Hartwell wished to save himself the embarrassment of admitting that he had been about to employ a Soviet spy.
56 Miranda Carter (*op. cit.*, pp. 344–45) makes clear Rees was proposing to go to the authorities with his suspicions about Burgess.
57 Boyle, *op. cit.*, pp. 385–86.
58 Carter, *op. cit.*, p. 346.
59 *Loc. cit.*
60 Lord Hartwell told Miranda Carter (*loc. cit.*), 'It was said later that when the news of the escape came out, Blunt went to bed for a week.'
61 JB, *Letters*, ed. CLG, ii, 9.
62 Helen Cathcart, *Princess Margaret*, London 1974, p. 128. Cathcart also wrote (*loc. cit.*):

'Lady Elizabeth, tall, delicate of frame, looked what was fine-bred almost to a fault, a Gainsborough lady, yet a Fragonard, too, with her spirited sense of fun.'

63 Major-General Sir Robert Laycock (1907–68), Evelyn Waugh's commanding officer and patron during the Second World War. He is part-model for 'Tommy Backhouse' in the 'Sword of Honour' trilogy. (*The Diaries of Evelyn Waugh*, ed. Michael Davie, London 1976, p. 802n.)

In 1935 Laycock married Angela Clare Louise, daughter of the Rt. Hon. William Dudley Ward PC.

64 Kathleen Kennedy to Joseph P. Kennedy, 17 November 1943. Amanda Smith (ed.), *Hostage to Fortune: The Letters of Joseph P. Kennedy*, New York 2001, pp. 570–71.

65 Quoted, Peter Collier and David Horowitz, *The Kennedys: An American Drama*, New York 1984, p. 144.

66 JB, *Letters*, ed. CLG, ii, 9.

67 *Loc. cit.*

68 Alan Pryce-Jones, interview, 1976.

69 See photograph of JB and Lady Elizabeth with the Barneses in France, Plate 57.

70 JB, *Summoned by Bells*, London 1960, p. 25.

71 For a photograph of Peggy Purey-Cust, see *JBLP*, p. 19; for one of Lady Elizabeth Cavendish shortly after her first meeting with JB, see JB, *Letters*, ed. CLG, ii, Plate 2b.

72 JB to the author, 23 September 1972.

73 See, for example, JB to Sir George Barnes, 25 September 1956. JB, *Letters*, ed. CLG, ii, 113 and 114n. *Little Friend* was the title of a film, directed by Greta Garbo's friend Berthold Viertel, which JB had admired in his days as a film critic. See *YB*, p. 1.

74 Members of the 'Princess Margaret set' (by no means all raffish) included Lord Blandford, Mark Bonham Carter, Rachel Brand, Lady Anne Coke, Lord Dalkeith, Lady Caroline Douglas-Scott, Dominic Elliott, Judy Montagu, Lord Ogilvy, Simon Phipps, Lady Rosemary Spencer-Churchill, Colin Tennant, Michael Tree (who married Lady Elizabeth Cavendish's sister, Lady Anne, and illustrated JB's *Summoned by Bells*) and Billy Wallace, a grandson of JB's old friend Sir Edwin Lutyens.

John Osborne wrote in his autobiographical volume *Almost a Gentleman* (London 1991, p. 117):

The subject matter of [Osborne's 1959 play] *The World of Paul Slickey* was the disagreeable exploits of a newspaper gossip columnist . . . Recently an underclass of mountebanks, including photographers and ballet dancers, American comedians, interior designers and the 'Princess Margaret Set' had proved a new, decidedly 'camp' addition to the Edwardian City and racing fraternity.

75 Edmund Wilson, 12 January 1954. *The Fifties: From Notebooks and Diaries of the Period*, ed. Leon Edel, New York 1986, p. 114.

76 Quoted, JB, *Letters*, ed. CLG, ii, 9.

77 PB, interview, 1976.

78 On 15 May 1947 Evelyn Waugh wrote in his diary: 'Laura's brother Auberon came for the night at his own invitation . . . We made him tell something of his courtship of Elizabeth Cavendish.' (*The Diaries of Evelyn Waugh*, ed. Michael Davie, London 1976, p. 678.)

79 Dame Iris Murdoch and John Bayley, joint letter to the author, 12 August 1989.

80 Dr Richard Squires, interview, 1976.

81 JB, *Letters*, ed. CLG, ii, 108.

82 JB wrote to Patrick Kinross on 21 August 1953: 'When I asked the Dowager Duchess at Hardwick whether she had ever used Chiswick House she said, "Only for breakfasts. But people don't have them now. We went there by a barouche. In those days *everyone* had a villa – there was Syon, Osterley and the Buccleuchs had that place at Richmond."' (JB, *Letters*, ed. CLG, ii, 42.)

83 Evelyn Waugh to Nancy Mitford, 29 October [1951]. *The Letters of Nancy Mitford and Evelyn Waugh*, ed. Charlotte Mosley, London 1996, p. 244.

84 JB to PB, 28 November 1953. *JBP*.

85 Lady Silvia Combe, article describing her visit of August 1953. By kind permission of Lady Silvia Combe.
86 *Ibid.*
87 *Ibid.*
88 *Ibid.*
89 Ottilie Squires, interview, 1989.
90 Dr Richard Squires, interview, 1976.
91 *Ibid.*
92 Mollie Baring, interview, 1989.
93 Ottilie Squires, interview, 1989. When John tried to play his part with the children, it sometimes seemed to Penelope that he was undermining what she was trying to achieve. Mollie Baring remembered (interview, 1989):

> One year, Penelope had a great economy drive. She grew a field of potatoes; and my boys, Peter and Nigel, were detailed with Paul to go in and harvest the potatoes – for nothing. 'I'll give them a jolly good tea afterwards,' she said . . . But John felt so guilty about it that he came out and gave each of them a pound, which was quite a lot in those days. Penelope heard about it . . . of course she was raving mad. She said, 'I might as well have got O'Brien to do it: the idea of having the boys do it was to make them earn their keep a little bit.'

94 JB, *Letters*, ed. CLG, ii, 5.
95 CLG, 'Father's praise made me feel safe, just like a security blanket', *The Express*, 'Weekend' section, 22 November 1997.
96 JB, *Letters*, ed. CLG, ii, 11.
97 *Loc. cit.*
98 JB, *Letters*, ed. CLG, ii, 4–5.
99 CLG, 'Father's praise made me feel safe, just like a security blanket', *The Express*, 'Weekend' section, 22 November 1997.
100 JB wrote to PB on 17 March [year unclear]: 'The Powlie was v embarrassed when I dined with it at the Van Oss's. It came to my recital of my own verse & was more embarrassed still poor little fellow. (*JBP.*)
101 JB, *Letters*, ed. CLG, ii, 5.
102 Dr Richard Squires, interview, 1976.
103 Dr Richard Squires, interview, 1989.
104 *Ibid.*
105 Mollie Baring, interview, 1989.
106 Dr Richard Squires, interview, 1989.
107 Mollie Baring, interview, 1989.
108 JB, *Letters*, ed. CLG, ii, 4.
109 Dr Richard Squires, interview, 1976. See also JB, *Letters*, ed. CLG, ii, 10.
110 Ottilie Squires, interview, 1989.
111 Dr Richard Squires (interview, 1976) remembered that PB was upset that JB was encouraging Paul to be a gourmet, too.
112 For a reproduction of the 1954 price list, see *JBLP*, p. 127.
113 PB, interview, 1978.
114 *Ibid.*
115 *Ibid.*
116 Diana Cox, who helped PB on the duck farm, recalled (interview, 1989): 'When Penelope fed the ducks she used to fetch pigswill by the dustbinful from Chaddleworth. We'd put the dustbins in the back of her car . . . it stank dreadfully. The geese and ducks ate the pigswill mixed with corn. And on one occasion one of these dustbins tipped over. You can imagine, it was absolutely awful. But Penelope said, "I know what we'll do: we'll catch some of the geese and put them in the back of the car, they'll clear up the mess for us. We'll go and have a cup of tea." When we came back, "Oh my God!" she said, "they've cleared up the pigswill and it has all come out the other end." '
117 PB, interview, 1978.

118 *Ibid.*

119 *Ibid.*

120 In 1948 JB's friend C.E.M. Joad was fined for travelling on a British Railways train without a ticket. The scandal destroyed his broadcasting career.

121 PB, interview, 1978.

122 *Ibid.*

123 Archbishop Trevor Huddleston, interview, 1990.

124 Kathleen Philip, interview, 1976.

125 PB, interview, 1978.

126 Christine Carter, interview, 1989.

127 Diana Cox, interview, 1989.

128 Dr Richard Squires, interview, 1989.

129 In 1955 PB went on a 'culture tour' of Italy, taking Paul Betjeman and a friend. In March 1957 PB was in Cincinnati with JB (see Chapter 33, 'Cincinnati'), after which she took Candida to Italy. She went to Paris with Paul and Candida in 1958. In 1961 she was in Spain.

130 Mollie Baring, interview, 1989.

131 JB, *Letters*, ed. CLG, ii, 52.

132 PB, interview, 1978.

133 JB, *Letters*, ed. CLG, ii, 52.

134 Dr Richard Squires, interview, 1976.

135 JB, *Letters*, ed. CLG, ii, 53.

136 Oliver Van Oss to JB, Lent 1955. Quoted in JB, *Letters*, ed. CLG, ii, 53–54.

137 *JBP.*

138 Sylvester Gates (1901–72), banker and long-time British friend of the American critic and novelist Edmund Wilson.

139 *JBP.*

140 *Ibid.*

141 *The Spectator*, 31 August 1956.

142 *Collected Poems*, 2001 edn., p. 350.

Chapter 26: First and Last Loves

1 JB, *Summoned by Bells*, London 1960, p. 105.

2 A.L. Rowse, *A Cornishman at Oxford*, London 1983 edn., pp. 311–12.

3 Lady Ottoline Morrell described Rowse to Bertrand Russell in 1926 as 'a wonderful young man, the son of a stonemason in Cornwall . . .P[hilip] and I were enchanted with him.' Miranda Seymour, *Ottoline Morrell: Life on the Grand Scale*, London 1992, p. 332.

4 During the General Strike of 1926 he went with his friend K.B. McFarlane, the young Magdalen history don, to harangue the car workers at Cowley. (K.B. McFarlane, conversation with the author, 1961.)

5 Rowse, *The Poet Auden: A Personal Memoir*, London 1987, pp. 8–9.

6 See Richard Ollard, *A Man of Contradictions: A Life of A.L. Rowse*, London 2000 edn., pp. 64, 86 and 112.

7 This is a familiar version of the pun; a slightly different one is given by John Lowe in *The Warden: A Portrait of John Sparrow*, London 1998, p. 246.

8 A.L. Rowse, letter to the author, 22 April 1987.

9 *John Murray archives.*

10 John G. Murray to JB, 8 February 1945. *John Murray archives.*

11 *Ibid.*

12 JB to John G. Murray, 2 December 1948. *John Murray archives.*

13 The *Daily Express* sent its list on 5 May 1949. *John Murray archives.*

14 These arrangements were outlined by John G. Murray in a letter to JB, 23 June 1949. *John Murray archives.*

15 *Ibid.*

16 *John Murray Archives.*
17 *Ibid.*
18 *Ibid.*
19 *The Listener*, 9 October 1952.
20 *Daily Telegraph*, 12 September 1952.
21 *John o' London's Weekly*, 26 September 1952.
22 *The Spectator*, 3 October 1952. The previous year, John had published Brooke's 'Silver Age' in *Time and Tide*.
23 *Ibid.*
24 *New Statesman*, 4 October 1952.
25 *Ibid.*
26 *Ibid.*
27 *Ibid.*
28 See the chapter 'Euston Arch' in the third volume of the present work.
29 From Dr William Spooner (1844–1930) is derived 'spoonerism' e.g. 'our queer Dean' for 'our dear Queen'). From W. Banting (1797–1878) is derived 'banting' (weight-reduction by avoiding fat, sugar and starch – which Banting, a London cabinet-maker, urged on the public in 1863).
30 *The Month*, December 1952.
31 *Ibid.*
32 *Ibid.* It is likely that, in lumping JB together with the only members of the MARS Group with foreign names, the anti-Semitic Waugh was implying – what a number of JB's acquaintances believed – that JB was himself Jewish. (John Edward Bowle, who had known JB's father Ernest, was asked in 1976 what he was like. 'A typical old Jew,' he replied.) There is no evidence that this was the case.
33 Transcript of the broadcast in *John Murray archives.*
34 Berger wrote (*Tribune*, 10 October 1952):

> Looking backwards is a favourite game among intellectuals today, now that progress has ceased to be fashionable. How vile are the boring amenities of the welfare state! Oh, for the romantic days of the 18th century, when the lower classes didn't bother about culture – or democracy.
>
> [John Betjeman's] new book of essays . . . gives the game away, right from the start. For he obviously equates 'modern barbarism' with the bad manners of the bar attendant at the Grand Hotel . . . And one notes that in his introduction, after sneering at the efforts of ordinary people to win back some sort of culture, he indulges in self-righteous quotations about Charity from the Book of Common Prayer. This is an aesthete's snob-view of life – with the smugness of social snobbery thrown in too.

35 *World Review*, December 1952.
36 *RIBA Journal*, 6 April 1953.
37 *Sunday Times*, 14 September 1952.
38 *Ibid.*

Chapter 27: A Few Late Chrysanthemums

1 *John Murray archives.*
2 *Ibid.*
3 *Ibid.*
4 *Ibid.*
5 JB, conversation with the author, 1971; and elsewhere. As a Magdalen man, JB would have read the Magdalen novel *Sinister Street* by his friend (Sir) Compton Mackenzie, in which the college servant Venables ('Venner', based on the Magdalen servant Gunstone – 'Gunner') describes (London 1949 edn., p. 508) how some Magdalen men mistakenly climbed into Pembroke College, thinking it was Christ Church.
6 *John Murray archives.*

7 In 1954 Lionel Edgar Salt and Herbert Lionel Drake were Emeritus Fellows of Pembroke College and Frederick Homes Dudden was Master. See John Platt, 'John Betjeman and Pembroke', *The Betjemanian*, vol. 13, 2001/2002, pp. 27–42.

8 Ronald MacCallum (1898–1973) became a Fellow of Pembroke College, Oxford, in 1925, and was Master, 1955–67. He lived near the Betjemans at Letcome Regis, Wantage.

9 *John Murray archives.*

10 *Ibid.*

11 *Ibid.*

12 *Ibid.*

13 *Ibid.*

14 *Ibid.*

15 *Ibid.*

16 *Ibid.*

17 *Ibid.*

18 *Ibid.*

19 The *Oxford English Dictionary* gives this definition of 'Grandsire': 'Bell-ringing: A particular method of ringing the changes on a ring of bells.

20 *John Murray archives.*

21 *Ibid.*

22 *Ibid.*

23 *Ibid.*

24 *Ibid.*

25 *Ibid.*

26 *Ibid.*

27 *Ibid.*

28 *Ibid.*

29 *Ibid.*

30 *Ibid.*

31 *Ibid.*

32 *Ibid.*

33 C.E.M. Joad (1891–1953), author, philosopher, University Reader in Philosophy, Birkbeck College, University of London, 1930–53. On the radio *Brains Trust* he was famous for his recurrent phrase, 'It depends what you mean by . . .'

34 *John Murray archives.*

35 *Ibid.*

36 *Ibid.*

37 *Ibid.*

38 *Ibid.*

39 *Ibid.*

40 *Ibid.*

41 *Time and Tide*, 17 July 1954, p. 971.

42 *Truth*, 10 September 1954.

43 *Sydney Morning Herald*, 2 October 1954.

44 *The Month*, December 1954.

45 *The Isis*, 20 October 1954.

46 *The Listener*, 5 August 1954.

47 Walter Allen (1911–95), novelist and critic; literary editor of the *New Statesman*, 1960–61.

48 E. Arnot Robertson (Lady Turner), d. 1961. Writer, broadcaster and lecturer.

49 Transcript of broadcast, *John Murray archives.*

50 *Loc. cit.*

51 *New Statesman*, 31 July 1954.

52 *Signature*, a West Country Magazine of the Arts, BBC West of England Home Service, 20 April 1955. Transcript of broadcast, *John Murray archives.*

53 *Literary Guide*, December 1954.

54 *Wednesday Book Programme*, BBC, 7 July 1954. Transcript of broadcast, *John Murray archives.*

55 *John o' London's Weekly*, 30 July 1954.

56 *The Sketch*, undated cutting in *John Murray archives*. On JB's friendship with Gladys Bertha ('Peter') Stern, see JB, *Letters*, ed. CLG, ii, 69, 92, 117 and 287. JB wrote to her on 22 August 1954 (*ibid.*, ii, 69): 'Dear Peter, What a sweet and understanding review of my verse in the *Sphere* [*sic*] . . . It is far the most discerning review I have read . . . I'm told by Jock [Murray] that the poems are selling quite well, about three thousand so far, I think. Not bad for poetry . . .'

57 *The Spectator*, 16 July 1954. Arlott wrote:

> Between *Mount Zion* – issued in a limited edition and a firework paper binding in 1931 – and this new book of poems, Mr Betjeman has been 'selected' and collected. He is now a booksellers' 'esteemed author'. Thus, while his first book is now quite remarkably expensive, this one may receive stern treatment for failing to surprise as *Mount Zion* did twenty-three years ago.
>
> In the same period, however, the undergraduate who expressed so originally his refusal to be bound by fashion has, whether he would or not, become a fashion himself.
>
> It is dangerous but easy to confuse the poet with the light versifier . . . Passion is perhaps the chief – and the most frequently overlooked – of John Betjeman's characteristics.

58 *National and English Review*, August 1954.

59 *South Wales Argus*, 8 November 1955.

60 *Church Times*, 6 August 1954.

61 *Reader's Review*, September 1954.

62 *Ibid.*

63 *John Murray archives*.

64 *The Spectator*, 8 October 1954.

65 *Ibid.*

66 *Sunday Times*, 26 December 1954.

67 *John Murray archives*. As was customary at the time, not all the copies were bound straight away.

68 On JB's friendship with and poem about Eric Walter White, at Oxford, see *YB*, pp. 165–66.

69 *Daily Telegraph*, 12 March 1955.

70 *The Bookseller*, 19 March 1955.

71 *Manchester Guardian*, 12 March 1955.

72 *Daily Sketch*, 12 March 1955.

73 *Daily Mail*, 12 March 1955.

74 *Daily Telegraph*, 12 March 1955.

75 David Garnett to Sylvia Townsend Warner, 1 November 1971. *Sylvia and David: The Townsend Warner/Garnett Letters*, ed. Richard Garnett, London 1984, p. 162.

On 'death packets', see Richard Kennedy, *A Boy at the Hogarth Press*, Whittington, Gloucestershire and London 1972, p. 35.

76 *Manchester Guardian*, 12 March 1955.

77 *Birmingham Post*, 12 March 1955.

78 *The Bookseller*, 19 March 1955.

Chapter 28: Cloth Fair and Rotherhithe

1 See *YB*, Chapter 14, 'With the Bright Young People'.

2 Daintrey drew JB in 1960. The pen-and-ink portrait will appear in the third volume of the present work.

On Daintrey, see his autobiography, *I Must Say*, London 1963. Also, Anthony Powell, *To Keep the Ball Rolling*, I, 'Infants of the Spring', London 1976; II, 'Messengers of Day', London 1978; and Anthony Powell, *Journals 1982–1986*, London 1995 and *Journals 1987–1989*, London 1996.

In reply to the question, 'Was Daintrey the part-original of any character in [Anthony Powell's] novels?' Lady Violet Powell wrote (letter to the author, 22 September 2001): 'There are resemblances to Daintrey in *From a View to a Death* (Arthur Zouch) and in *A Dance to the Music of Time* (Ralph Barnby).'

3   Jill Storer (CLG interview, 1994), JB, *Letters*, ed. CLG, ii, 14.

4   *Loc. cit.*

5   *Loc. cit.*

6   JB, *Letters*, ed. CLG, ii, 37n.

7   See JB to Anita Dent, 15 April 1953. JB, *Letters*, ed. CLG, ii, 37 and 37n.

8   JB, *Letters*, ed. CLG, ii, 37n.

9   *Ibid.*, 55.

10 *Ibid.*, 68.

11 *Loc. cit.*

12 JB, *Letters*, ed. CLG, ii, 67–68.

13 *Ibid.*, ii, 68n.

14 Verily Anderson Paget, interview, 1999.

15 *Ibid.*

16 For illustrations of Eltham, see Clive Aslet, 'An Interview with the late Paul Paget 1901–1985', *Thirties Society Journal*, no. 6, 1987, pp. 17–18.

17 Aslet, *op. cit.*, p. 22.

18 JB, *Letters*, ed. CLG, ii, 57.

19 JB to Sir George Barnes, 29 October 1953. JB, *Letters*, ed. CLG, ii, 47.

20 JB, *Letters*, ed. CLG, ii, 64–65 and 65n.

21 According to CLG, *ibid.*, 56.

22 JB, 'The City', *Observer Magazine*, 24 July 1977.

23 *Ibid.*

24 See Sir D'Arcy Power, *A Short History of St Bartholomew's Hospital*, London 1955. JB wrote a poem, 'St Bartholomew's Hospital' (JB, *Church Poems*, London 1981, p. 24).

25 JB, conversation with the author, 1971.

26 *Ex inf.* Dr Winifred Hector, interview, 1998.

27 *Henry VI, Part II*, iv, 7. JB was also told the macabre story of the chef Richard Rose who, accused of poisoning seventeen diners, was boiled alive at Smithfield gallows in 1555. Such stories lost nothing in the telling by the meat porters to whom JB chatted in the Smithfield café where he often took breakfast. One of the porters, the late Charlie Wagner, recalled (interview, 1999): 'We knew he was a poet, but he never gave himself airs. When he asked us about our work, you knew he wasn't just pretending to be interested: he *was* interested.'

28 *A Poem upon the Death of His Late Highness Oliver, Lord Protector of England, Scotland & Ireland, Written by Mr. Dryden*, London, Printed for William Wilson; and is to be sold in Well-Yard, near Little St. Bartholomew's Hospital, 1659.

29 Jenny Uglow, *Hogarth: A Life and a World*, London 1997, p. xi. Dr Uglow writes (*ibid.*, p. 6): 'By the late seventeenth century, the tangled streets east of the market – Cloth Fair, Barley Mow Passage, Cloth Court, Rising Sun Court, Half-moon Court, King Street – the site of an old textile trade – were occupied by small merchants, artisans and shop-keepers . . .'

30 Rena Gardiner, *The Story of Saint Bartholomew the Great*, London 1990, p. 28.

31 JB to John Summerson, November 1949. JB, *Letters*, ed. CLG, ii, 493–94.

The verse riddle was headed, within a fancy cartouche, 'WHO WAS HE? A puzzle addressed to J. Newenham S[ummerson] Esq. O.H. [Old Harrovian] FSA [Fellow of the Society of Antiquaries] ARIBA [Associate of the Royal Institute of British Architects]. JB represented himself as 'J BETJEMAN & SON Rhymes, Jokes and Novelties' (JB, *Letters*, ed. CLG, i, 493–94).

Summerson guessed the answer correctly, as is made clear in a letter to him from JB of 5 November 1949 (JB, *Letters*, ed. CLG, i, 494).

The riddle-poem was published in *The Harlequin* in 1950, with the title 'The Corporation Architect' (JB, *Letters*, ed, CLG, i, 494).

32 Gardiner, *op. cit.*, p. 30.
33 JB, 'The City', *Observer Magazine*, 24 July 1977.
34 JB, *Letters*, ed. CLG, ii, 56–57.
35 Sir Osbert Lancaster, interview, 1977.
36 Aslet, *op. cit.*, p. 22.
37 JB, *Letters*, ed. CLG, ii, 108.
38 *Loc. cit.*
39 Except where otherwise stated, the information which follows, about the late Sister Mary Bland and Sister (now Dr) Winifred Hector, is from interviews with both of them in 1993 and from further meetings with Dr Hector in 1999.
40 Dr Winifred Hector, interview, 1999.
41 JB, *Letters*, ed. CLG, ii, 108.
42 *Loc. cit.*
43 *Loc. cit.*
44 *Loc. cit.*
45 JB, *Letters*, ed. CLG, ii, 124.
46 *Ibid.*, 124–25. There are in fact longer palindromes. In the 1980s Lawrence Levine of St Augustine, Florida, wrote a 31,594-word novel entitled *Dr Awkward and Olson in Oslo*. It was one giant palindrome. (See *Los Angeles Times*, 7 September 1986.)
47 The poem appeared in *London Magazine*, vol. 4, no. 5, May 1957, p. 11.
48 The poem appears as 'The Dresser' in *Poems of Walt Whitman*, selected and ed. by William Michael Rossetti, London 1868, p. 213.
49 See David S. Reynolds, *Walt Whitman's America*, New York 1995, p. 427.
50 *Collected Poems*, 2001 edn., p. 276.
51 JB, *Church Poems*, London 1981, p. 24.
52 JB to the Duchess of Devonshire, 11 October 1957. JB, *Letters*, ed. CLG, ii, 133.
53 Sir Osbert Lancaster, interview, 1977.
54 Lady Oaksey, CLG interview, 1994. JB, *Letters*, ed. CLG, ii, 109.
55 JB, *Letters*, ed. CLG, ii, 100.
56 William Glenton, *Tony's Room: The Secret Love Story of Princess Margaret*, New York 1965, p. 6.
57 *Ibid.*, pp. 13–14.
58 *Ibid.*, p. 16.
59 *Ibid.*, p. 18.
60 *Ibid.*, pp. 23–25.
61 *Ibid.*, p. 23.
62 *Ibid.*, p. 24.
63 *Loc. cit.*
64 *Ibid.*, pp. 28 and 33.
65 *Ibid.*, p. 27.
66 Helen Cathcart, *Princess Margaret*, London 1974, p. 132.
67 *Ibid.*, p. 136.
68 The Highland Light Infantry and the 3rd King's Own Hussars. (*Loc. cit.*)
69 Cathcart, *op. cit.*, pp. 136–37.
70 Glenton, *op. cit.*, pp. 33–34.
71 *Ibid.*, pp. 34–35.
72 Quoted, *ibid.*, p. 35.
73 *Loc. cit.*
74 *Loc. cit.*
75 Glenton, *op. cit.*, p. 36.
76 *Loc. cit.*
77 *Loc. cit.*
78 *Loc. cit.*
79 Glenton, *op. cit.*, pp. 36–37.
80 Quoted, *ibid.*, pp. 37–38.
81 *Ibid.*, p. 39

82 *Loc. cit.*

83 Glenton, *op. cit.*, pp. 39–40.

84 *Ibid.*, p. 40.

85 *Ibid.*, p. 43.

86 *Loc. cit.*

87 *Loc. cit.*

88 *Ibid.*, p. 44.

89 Cathcart, *op. cit.*, pp. 145–46. Glenton's book was published (but only in America) in 1965, five years after Princess Margaret's marriage to Armstrong-Jones.

90 'The commentators on the tourist river steamers pointed out the Room or, more usually, the bay window of the room above it, as if it belonged to romantic history, and no one dreamed that the historic lovers could still be there. One evening, when the spring tides were high and the steamers came closer than usual, the loudspeaker broke in, "Right there, where that young couple is sitting, is the very room", and Margaret and Tony drew back in alarm into the shadows.'
(Cathcart, *op. cit.*, p. 164.)

91 JB to Leonora Ison, 20 September 1963. *The late Walter Ison.*

92 *Ibid.*

93 Glenton (*op. cit.*, p. 166) records how, as a result of Margaret's urging, the then Minister of Works in the Conservative Government, Lord John Hope, came to look at the Rotherhithe house; but, as Glenton writes (*loc. cit.*), there was small chance that Hope could influence the Labour-controlled LCC; neither did he do so.

94 Lord Snowdon wrote to Leonora Ison on 9 October 1963 asking if he might buy the originals of her drawings, which had appeared in the *Daily Telegraph* with JB's article on the previous Monday. On 16 October 1963 he wrote again to her: 'It was a tremendous pleasure and excitement to receive the two drawings of Rotherhithe you so kindly sent me . . .'

Chapter 29: On the Air in the Fifties

1 Sir George Barnes (1904–60). Joined the Talks Department of the BBC in 1930 and became its director in 1941. In 1945 became the first head (later Controller) of the Third Programme and in 1950 director of BBC TV. Knighted 1953. See Humphrey Carpenter, *The Envy of the World: Fifty Years of the BBC Third Programme and Radio 3*, London 1996.

2 George Barnes to JB, 18 March 1944. *BBCWA.*

3 JB to George Barnes, 6 April 1944. *BBCWA.*

4 George Barnes to JB, 11 April 1944. *BBCWA.*

5 George Barnes to JB, 14 April 1944. *BBCWA.*

6 Anthony Barnes, interview, 1995.

7 JB may well have been projecting on to this imaginary character a habit which he and James Lees-Milne deplored in Maurice Hastings, brother of H. de Cronin Hastings, editor of *The Architectural Review*. When living at Rousham, Oxfordshire, Maurice Hastings used to take pot-shots at the genitalia of the statues in the grounds. See *YB*, pp. 248–49.

8 Anthony Barnes, interview, 1995.

9 JB to George Barnes, n.d. but 1948. JB *Letters*, ed. CLG, i, 432.

10 Anthony Barnes, interview, 1995.

11 JB to Anne Barnes, 19 July 1949. JB, *Letters*, ed. CLG, i, 481.

12 On 21 April 1944 JB wrote to George Barnes: 'So long as I live I shall not forget that romantic visit to the Marsh. The first sight of the farm, the LIKEN on the red tiles and the brick, the view over the Richard Wilson hills . . .' JB, *Letters*, ed. CLG, i, 343. As CLG states (*ibid.*, 343n.), the argument over 'lichen' 'was to run and run'. See Chapter 16, 'Farnborough'.

13 JB, 'The Commander', *Collected Poems*, 2001 edn., p. 268.

14 JB, *Letters*, ed. CLG, i, 375.

15 Anthony Barnes, interview, 1995.

16 Sir Percy Elly Bates (1879–1946), fourth Bart, was chairman of the Cunard Line from the 1920s to 1946. His great achievement was to order that two liners should ply the Transatlantic crossing. These were the *Queen Mary* and the *Queen Elizabeth*. He died in 1946 on the eve of the *Queen Elizabeth*'s launching, so never saw his dream realized. I am grateful to Dr Maureen Watry and Mr Peter Lester for kindly supplying this information.

17 Anthony Barnes, interview, 1995.

18 Lady Diana Cooper, late British ambassadress, was now living with her husband at the Château de Saint-Firmin, Chantilly.

19 Anthony Barnes, interview, 1995.

20 *Ibid.*

21 JB to George Barnes, 30 September 1951. JB, *Letters*, ed. CLG, i, 539.

22 Anthony Barnes, interview, 1995.

23 Humphrey Carpenter, *op. cit.*, p. 133.

24 JB to Sir George Barnes, 29 October 1953. JB, *Letters*, ed. CLG, ii, 46.

25 The drawing is reproduced by Carpenter, *op. cit.*, between pp. 146 and 147.

26 Anthony Barnes, interview, 1995.

27 *Ibid.*

28 *Ibid.*

29 JB to Anthony Barnes, 6 October 1949. CLG, *Letters*, i, 487.

30 Anthony Barnes, interview, 1995.

31 JB to Anthony Barnes, 15 October 1949. JB, *Letters*, ed. CLG, i, 488–89.

32 Anthony Barnes, interview, 1995.

33 George Barnes to JB, 9 December 1944. *BBCWA*.

34 George Barnes to JB, 22 October 1945. *BBCWA*. On JB's illnesses, see Chapter 16, 'Farnborough', note 15.

35 George Barnes to JB, 17 January 1947. *BBCWA*.

36 JB to George Barnes, 31 March 1947. *BBCWA*.

37 BBC minute. *BBCWA*.

38 Carpenter, *op. cit.*, p. 65. The full poem, of which JB sent a copy to Anna Kallin in July 1947, is given in JB, *Letters*, ed. CLG, i, 416.

39 JB to Anna Kallin, 2 April 1948. *BBCWA*.

40 Harman Joseph Gerard Grisewood, actor, BBC executive and author (1906–97). See obituaries in *The Times*, 11 January 1997, *The Independent*, 10 January 1997, *The Guardian*, 11 January 1997 and (further contributions) *The Independent*, 20 January 1997.

41 Douglas Cleverdon, publisher and radio producer (1903–87). See obituary in *The Times*, 3 October 1987.

42 Both Grisewood and Cleverdon had been associated with Eric Gill, who carved controversial reliefs on the façade of Broadcasting House, and both were friends – as were JB and PB – of the writer and artist David Jones. See Fiona MacCarthy, *Eric Gill*, London 1999.

43 See *YB*, p. 161. A caricature of Grisewood as he looked when at Oxford with JB is reproduced in *JBLP*, p. 64.

44 See note 40 to the present chapter.

45 See Douglas Cleverdon, *The Growth of Milk Wood: with the textual variants of* Under Milk Wood *by Dylan Thomas*, London 1969.

46 Douglas Cleverdon to JB, 27 December 1945. *BBCWA*.

47 According to BBC records, Cleverdon was in charge when JB and Lancaster rehearsed the programme in the Langham Hotel; it went out on 20 December 1947. *BBCWA*. On the giggles, see JB, *Letters*, ed. CLG, ii, 255.

48 JB to Harman Grisewood, June 1949. *BBCWA*.

49 Harman Grisewood to Ronald Lewin, BBC internal memo, 15 November 1950. *BBCWA*.

50 *Ibid.*

51 Eileen Molony, BBC talks producer who moved from Bristol to London. JB's easy relationship with her is shown by a letter he wrote to her on 3 November 1945 (JB, *Letters*, ed. CLG, i, 377) beginning, 'Ah my darling dark yellow-stockinged Amazon, So you have

come back to me and I cannot even remember what the P.E. looked like for thoughts of your large eyes . . .' Eileen Molony replied on 12 November (JB, *Letters*, ed. CLG, i, 377) that his letter, 'not being marked "Personal", bounced its way merrily from hand to hand through BBC Registry, and eventually ran me to earth in the Talks Department . . . The whole organization is humming with interest and speculation as a result.'

52 Ronald Lewin to Harman Grisewood, BBC internal memo, November 1950. *BBCWA*.

53 Theophilus Julius Henry Marzials (1850–1920), poet, musician and artist. JB's talk, *Theo Marzials*, went out on Christmas Eve 1950. CLG recalls the Betjeman family's singing Marzials's songs at Farnborough (JB, *Letters*, ed. CLG, i, 467).

54 Sir F. Paolo Tosti (1847–1916), composer. 'Good-bye' was one of his best-known compositions. JB mentions it in *Summoned by Bells*.

55 Eileen Molony to JB, January 1951. *BBCWA*.

56 Ronald Lewin to Eileen Molony, BBC internal memo, 5 June 1951. *BBCWA*.

57 JB to Eileen Molony, 13 June 1951. *BBCWA*.

58 Derwent May writes in *Critical Times: The History of the* Times Literary Supplement, London 2001, pp. 365–66:

> The historian A.L. Rowse . . . became very angry with the *Lit. Supp.* for its treatment of him. His book *William Shakespeare* was reviewed in December 1963 by John Crow, a brilliant if eccentric lecturer in English at King's College, London . . .
> Crow had a fine sense of the nature of literature, and was appalled by what he considered the reckless and insensitive way Rowse had simply used Shakespeare's work as evidence for his theories about Shakespeare's life.

A.J.P. Taylor writes in *A Personal History*, London 1983, p. 169:

> John Crow . . . was an enormous figure, over twenty stone, and with a correspondingly enormous zest. One night he and I went to *Casablanca*. At one dramatic moment, when the German secret service were about to arrest a member of the Resistance, Bogart said to the café orchestra, 'Play the Marseillaise'. I burst into tears. Crow did more. He let out a deafening howl and his whole twenty stone rocked with grief. The cinema seats rocked too. Members of the audience fell off right and left. The manager threatened Crow with the police. No good. He continued to howl until the scene was over.

59 Nest Cleverdon, obituary tribute in *The Independent* after Harman Grisewood's death, published on 20 January 1997.

60 The television film *Tennyson: A Beginning and an End*, made with Julian Jebb in 1968 and 1969, is discussed in the third volume of the present work.

61 JB, 'Festival Oddities', 7 May 1951. *BBCWA*. On JB's general attitude to the Festival of Britain, and his minimal involvement in it, see Chapter 24, 'Tame & Tade'.

62 Sir Sydney Cockerell (1867–1962). Secretary to William Morris and to the Kelmscott Press, 1892–98; Director of the Fitzwilliam Museum, Cambridge, 1908–37.

63 Sir Sydney Cockerell to JB, 1952. Quoted, JB, *Letters*, ed. CLG, ii, 11.

64 William Burges (1827–81), English architect and designer. He designed the extravagantly 'medieval' Cardiff Castle (1868–81) for the third Marquess of Bute and the hunting-lodge Castell Coch (1876–81).

65 JB, 'Cardiff Castle', 12 May 1952. *BBCWA*.

66 Elizabeth Rowley, Talks Organizer, Home Service and Light Programme, BBC internal memo, 1 March 1954. *BBCWA*.

67 JB to Elizabeth Rowley, 3 March 1954. *BBCWA*.

68 JB, 'Foreigners', 1954. *BBCWA*.

69 Gilbert Harding (1907–60), broadcaster, journalist and author. JB wrote of him, in *Gilbert Harding by his Friends*, ed. Stephen Grenfell, London 1961, pp. 158–59:

> He was an ardent but insecure sacramentalist . . .
> I remember how in a panel game called 'Who Said That?' we were made to seem more natural by being sat down in a drawing room with four walls and the cameras were hidden behind gauze on which pictures had been painted. Thus we could not see

where the cameras were. Under the hot studio lights the room became very parching and Gilbert kindly concealed, in a vase of flowers and microphones on a low table in the middle of the room, a bottle of whisky for the performers . . .

Nothing shows up falseness like a television camera. The smooth man out for himself, fails. The liar is shown up in his untruth. If what is said is said with honest conviction, even those who do not agree with it will see by television whether the speaker is sincere. The one thing that was patent about Gilbert was his complete honesty. Millions of people felt that they knew him because of this . . .

See also Gilbert Harding, *Along my Line*, London 1953; and Roger Storey, *Gilbert Harding: By his Private Secretary*, London 1961.

70 Kenneth Adam (1908–78). He was Controller of the BBC Light Programme, 1950–55; General Manager, Hulton Press, 1955–57; Controller of Television Programmes, BBC, 1957–61; Director of BBC Television, 1961–68.
71 Archie Gordon to JB, 17 January 1955. *BBCWA*.
72 JB to Pat Dixon, 1 November 1955. *BBCWA*.
73 Frederick Grisewood, *The World Goes By*, London 1950, p. 245.
74 Head of Talks, Television, to Assistant Head of Programme Contracts, BBC internal memo, 25 April 1956. *BBCWA*.
75 BBC to Miss J. LeRoy of Pearn, Pollinger, 30 April 1956. *Copy in BBCWA*.
76 JB to Michael Wharton, 2 May 1956. *BBCWA*. Michael Wharton started the 'Peter Simple' column in the *Daily Telegraph*.
77 JB to Miss Kirwan, 18 May 1956. *BBCWA*.
78 Pat Dixon to JB, 14 February 1958. *BBCWA*.
79 On Mary Chubb's schooldays with JB, see *YB*, pp. 21–23.
80 Archie Gordon to JB, 27 February 1958. *BBCWA*.
81 JB to Robert C. Moore, 14 November 1958. *BBCWA*. Kenneth Grahame was born in 1859.

Chapter 30: 'City and Suburban'

1 On the 1950s taste for whimsy and nostalgia see B. Hillier, *Austerity/Binge: Decorative Arts of the 1940s and 50s*, London 1975.
2 Brian Inglis, *Downstart*, London 1990, p. 201.
3 *Ibid.*, p. 206.
4 (Henry) Wilson Harris (1883–1955) was editor of *The Spectator*, 1932–53.
5 Inglis, *op. cit.*, p. 200.
6 Quoted, *loc. cit.*
7 On Smyllie, see Chapter 13 of the present volume, 'Ireland'.
8 Inglis, *op. cit.*, p. 164.
9 *Ibid.*, pp. 26–27. Like John, Inglis was taught by 'Hum' Lynam and 'Tortoise' Haynes.
10 See *YB*, pp. 35–36, 38–39, 41–43.
11 Inglis, *op. cit.*, p. 219.
12 Quoted, *loc. cit.*
13 JB, *Letters*, ed. CLG, ii, 58.
14 Cyril Ray (conversation with the author, 1990) chose the drinks. Patrick Campbell (Inglis, *op. cit.*, p. 241) feelingly described the hangovers the parties caused.
15 JB, 'Billy Graham', *The Spectator*, 12 March 1954, p. 282.
16 JB, 'A Spectator's Notebook', *The Spectator*, 2 August 1954, p. 383.
17 JB, 'A Spectator's Notebook', *The Spectator*, 27 August 1954, p. 244.
18 C.O. Ellison, letter, *The Spectator*, 3 September 1954, p. 278.
19 *Ibid.*
20 JB, 'Not Necessarily Leeds', *The Spectator*, 1 October 1954, p. 392.
21 JB, 'A Spectator's Notebook', *The Spectator*, 3 September 1954, p. 272.
22 Joyce Cary, 'Horror Comics', *The Spectator*, 18 February 1955, p. 177.
23 JB, 'A Spectator's Notebook', *The Spectator*, 3 September 1954, p. 272.

24 Christopher Sykes (1907–86) was at Oxford with JB and in 1936 married Camilla Russell, to whom JB had been engaged (see *YB*, pp. 292–98 and 303). He wrote Evelyn Waugh's first biography.

25 JB, 'A Spectator's Notebook', *The Spectator*, 3 September 1954, p. 272.

26 JB, 'City and Suburban', *The Spectator*, 15 October 1954, p. 461.

27 JB, 'City and Suburban', *The Spectator*, 3 December 1954, p. 705.

28 JB, 'City and Suburban', *The Spectator*, 10 December 1954, p. 746.

29 JB, 'City and Suburban', *The Spectator*, 4 March 1955, p. 252.

30 *Loc. cit.*

31 JB, 'City and Suburban', *The Spectator*, 27 May 1955, pp. 675–76.

32 JB, 'City and Suburban', *The Spectator*, 24 June 1955, p. 796.

33 JB, 'City and Suburban', *The Spectator*, 12 August 1955, p. 218.

34 JB, 'City and Suburban', *The Spectator*, 22 November 1955, p. 711.

35 JB, 'City and Suburban', *The Spectator*, 20 January 1956, p. 76.

36 JB, 'City and Suburban', *The Spectator*, 2 March 1956, p. 277.

37 JB, 'City and Suburban', *The Spectator*, 9 March 1956, p. 310.

38 JB, 'City and Suburban', *The Spectator*, 7 December 1956, p. 828.

39 JB, 'City and Suburban', *The Spectator*, 28 December 1956, p. 930.

40 *Loc. cit.*

41 JB, 'City and Suburban', *The Spectator*, 25 January 1957, p. 108.

42 JB, 'City and Suburban', *The Spectator*, 9 December 1955, p. 798.

43 General Sir Brian Robertson, later first Baron Robertson of Oakridge (1896–1974), had been Chief Administrative Officer to Field-Marshal Alexander, C-in-C Italy, 1944–45. He was the son of Field-Marshal Sir William Robertson who was Chief of the Imperial General Staff, 1915–18.

44 James Chuter Chuter-Ede (1882–1965). MP for South Shields, 1921–31 and 1935–64. Home Secretary, 1945–51. Leader of the House of Commons, March–October 1951. Became Baron Chuter-Ede, 1964.

45 JB, 'City and Suburban', *The Spectator*, 20 April 1956, p. 524.

46 JB, 'City and Suburban', *The Spectator*, 27 April 1956, p. 573.

47 JB, 'City and Suburban', *The Spectator*, 26 July 1957, p. 131.

48 Reported to the author by Mr A.G. Swift, late of British Rail.

49 JB, 'City and Suburban', *The Spectator*, 6 July 1956, p. 74.

50 On JB's visits to Sezincote in his youth, see *YB*, pp. 151–52, 215, 218, 288, 292–93, 304, 348 and 355.

51 JB, 'City and Suburban', *The Spectator*, 6 July 1956, p. 74.

52 Monsignor Ronald Knox (1888–1957). Received into the Church of Rome, 1917; Catholic Chaplain at Oxford, 1926–39; a Protonotary Apostolic, 1951. Prolific author. See Evelyn Waugh, *The Life of Ronald Knox*, London 1959.

53 Katherine Asquith, sister of Edward Horner of Mells, Somerset, married in 1907 Raymond Asquith (1878–1916), killed in the First World War. On her, see Waugh, *op. cit.*

54 JB, 'City and Suburban', *The Spectator*, 30 August 1957, p. 272.

55 Lady Mary Pakenham, sister of the seventh Earl of Longford, married Meysey Clive, an Army officer. See *YB*, also the present volume, Chapter 2, 'Film Critic'.

56 Anthony Powell, *Journals 1987–1989*, London 1996, p. 119.

57 JB, 'City and Suburban', *The Spectator*, 26 November 1954, p. 669.

58 JB, 'City and Suburban', *The Spectator*, 26 August 1955, p. 274.

59 JB, 'City and Suburban', *The Spectator*, 3 December 1954, p. 704.

60 JB, 'City and Suburban', *The Spectator*, 11 March 1955, p. 280.

61 JB, 'City and Suburban', *The Spectator*, 13 May 1955, p. 612.

62 JB, 'City and Suburban', *The Spectator*, 1 July 1955, p. 12.

63 JB, 'City and Suburban', *The Spectator*, 25 May 1956, p. 726.

64 JB, 'City and Suburban', *The Spectator*, 1 November 1957, p. 573.

65 JB, 'City and Suburban', *The Spectator*, 29 October 1954, p. 516.

66 JB, 'City and Suburban', *The Spectator*, 26 November 1954, p. 669.

67 JB, 'City and Suburban', *The Spectator*, 24 December 1954, p. 805.

68 Teddy boy: in the 1950s some teenagers, mainly of the working class, dressed in long coats ('drapes') with velvet collars, also wore 'drainpipe' trousers, 'bootlace' ties and 'winkle-picker' or 'brothel-creeper' shoes, and combed their greased hair into a 'DA' (duck's arse) style at the back. From the fancied resemblance of their coats to Edwardian frock-coats, they were known as 'Teddy boys' or 'Teds'. JB made several references to Teddy boys in his column (e.g. 20 May 1955, 11 October 1957 and 29 November 1957).

69 JB, 'City and Suburban', *The Spectator*, 15 July 1955, p. 91.

70 JB, 'City and Suburban', *The Spectator*, 29 October 1954, p. 516.

71 JB, 'City and Suburban', *The Spectator*, 2 June 1956, p. 851.

72 JB, 'City and Suburban', *The Spectator*, 28 June 1957, p. 843.

73 Lord Gilmour of Craigmillar, letter to the author, 26 August 1995.

74 JB, 'City and Suburban', *The Spectator*, 29 June 1956, p. 885.

75 JB, 'City and Suburban', *The Spectator*, 28 October 1955, p. 550.

76 JB, 'City and Suburban', *The Spectator*, 29 October 1954, p. 516.

77 JB, 'City and Suburban', *The Spectator*, 5 November 1954, p. 554.

78 *Collected Poems*, 2001 edn., p. 216.

79 JB, 'City and Suburban', *The Spectator*, 12 November 1954, p. 572.

80 *Collected Poems*, 2001 edn., p. 210.

81 JB, 'City and Suburban', *The Spectator*, 10 August 1956, p. 204.

82 *Collected Poems*, 2001 edn., p. 141.

83 JB, 'City and Suburban', *The Spectator*, 30 August 1957, p. 272.

84 *Collected Poems*, 2001 edn., p. 256.

85 JB, 'City and Suburban', *The Spectator*, 31 August 1956, p. 284.

86 JB, 'City and Suburban', *The Spectator*, 9 August 1957, p. 186.

87 *Loc. cit.*

88 *Loc. cit.*

89 JB, 'City and Suburban', *The Spectator*, 27 January 1956, p. 121.

90 Canon Vigo Auguste Demant (1893–1983). JB wrote to Gerard Irvine on 2 January 1944 (JB, *Letters*, ed. CLG, i, 336): 'I fire watch with Canon Demant of St Paul's. Most interesting my evenings are, with him.'

91 JB, 'City and Suburban', *The Spectator*, 21 September 1956, p. 380.

92 Graham Hough, letter, *The Spectator*, 5 October 1956, p. 451.

93 JB, 'City and Suburban', *The Spectator*, 10 January 1958, p. 40.

94 JB, 'City and Suburban', *The Spectator*, 19 April 1957, p. 512.

95 JB, 'City and Suburban', *The Spectator*, 23 November 1956, p. 712.

96 Ian K. McDougall, letter, *The Spectator*, 7 December 1956, p. 831.

97 Francis Schwarzenberger, letter, *The Spectator*, 11 January 1957, p. 50.

98 JB, 'City and Suburban', *The Spectator*, 11 February 1955, p. 152.

99 JB, 'City and Suburban', *The Spectator*, 25 February 1955, p. 215.

100 JB, 'City and Suburban', *The Spectator*, 30 March 1956, p. 405.

101 *Loc. cit.*

102 JB, 'City and Suburban', *The Spectator*, 5 November 1954, p. 544.

103 In 1973 I walked through a public service station (garage) with JB on the way to a restaurant. The proprietor came out and said, rather pointedly, 'Can I help you, sir?' 'No, you *can not*,' JB snapped. It was my first glimpse of the less genial side of his character.

104 JB, 'City and Suburban', *The Spectator*, 4 October 1957, p. 428.

105 *Loc. cit.*

106 JB, 'City and Suburban', *The Spectator*, 17 June 1955, p. 767.

107 JB, 'City and Suburban', *The Spectator*, 20 May 1955, p. 640.

108 JB, 'City and Suburban', *The Spectator*, 14 December 1956, p. 860.

109 Austin Duncan-Jones, letter, *The Spectator*, 21 December 1956, p. 901; David Leggatt, letter, *loc. cit.*

110 R. Lush, letter, *The Spectator*, 21 September 1956, p. 382.

111 Vilma Levy, letter, *The Spectator*, 17 June 1955, p. 769.

112 JB, 'City and Suburban', *The Spectator*, 25 January 1957, p. 108.

113 Jocelyn Brooke, letter, *The Spectator*, 1 February 1957, p. 144.

114 Inglis, *op. cit.*, p. 249.
115 JB, *Letters*, ed. CLG, ii, 110.
116 JB to Michael Berry, 16 October 1957. JB, *Letters*, ed. CLG, ii, 134.
117 JB, 'City and Suburban', *The Spectator*, 10 January 1958, p. 40.
118 'A Spectator's Notebook', *The Spectator*, 10 January 1958, p. 35.

Chapter 31: Television Personality

1 Mary Adams, 'Microscope to Microphone', *Punch*, 18 November 1959.
2 Obituary of Mary Adams, *The Times*, 18 May 1984.
3 Mary Adams, 'Microscope to Microphone', *Punch*, 18 November 1959. Although a feminist and career woman, Mary Adams married Major Vyvyan Adams, a Conservative MP. John was sympathetic when in 1951 he was drowned while bathing at Gunwalloe Church Cove, Cornwall.
4 Obituary of Mary Adams, *The Times*, 18 May 1984.
5 *Ibid.*
6 Mary Adams, 'Microscope to Microphone', *Punch*, 18 November 1959.
7 Mary Adams to JB, 13 July 1937. *BBCWA*.
8 Mary Adams to JB, 13 July 1937. *BBCWA*.
9 JB to Mary Adams, 15 July 1937. *BBCWA*.
10 Edmund Arnold Greening Lamborn (1877–1950), described in *Who Was Who* as 'Schoolmaster, Antiquary and Man of Letters'. The same work states that he was 'educated by books, buildings and the companionship of wild creatures'. He wrote *Architecture in Oxford Stone* and *The English Parish Church* among other books.
11 JB to Mary Adams, 15 July 1937. *BBCWA*.
12 Mary Adams to JB, 25 August 1937. *BBCWA*.
13 JB to Mary Adams, 19 September 1937. *BBCWA*.
14 Mary Adams, internal BBC memo, September 1937. *BBCWA*.
15 Andrew Miller Jones, memo to Mary Adams, 11 August 1939. *BBCWA*.
16 JB to Mary Adams, 21 October 1937. *BBCWA*.
17 [Dame] Gracie Fields (1898–1979), Lancashire-born actress and singer.
18 JB to Mary Adams, 21 May 1971. JB, *Letters*, ed. CLG, ii, 414–15.
19 The photograph is reproduced in *JBLP*, p. 113.
20 JB to George Barnes, 3 June 1951. *BBCWA*.
21 On the Murray Guides, see Chapter 22, 'The Betje-bus'.
22 David Bryson to JB, 7 May 1951. *BBCWA*.
23 David Bryson, internal BBC memo, 28 May 1951. *BBCWA*.
24 Mary Adams to JB, 19 June 1951. *BBCWA*.
25 *Ibid.*
26 JB to Mary Adams, 22 June 1951. *BBCWA*.
27 *Ibid.*
28 Mary Adams to George Barnes, internal BBC memo, 25 June 1951. *BBCWA*.
29 T.H. White (1906–64), novelist. In *T.H. White: A Biography*, London 1967, Sylvia Townsend Warner wrote (p. 249): 'John Betjeman, who, with his family, stayed with White in 1950, recalling "an impression of laughter, high seas, steep cliffs, empty beaches out of the wind, and a sense of home in that house in Connaught Square", particularly remembers how "we all used to enjoy exploring the sinister remains of Nazi occupation – underground forts with German notices in them, and remnants of offices under ground and electric light fittings". The Betjeman visit was a success. Others were not.'
    There is a discrepancy between the date given by Warner (1950) and the date of JB's letter from Alderney to George Barnes (1951). This may either mean that there were two visits in successive years, or that JB, in writing to Warner, misremembered the date.
30 JB to George Barnes, 14 August 1951. *BBCWA*.
31 Pat Stapley to George Barnes, internal BBC memo, 20 August 1951. *BBCWA*.
32 [Sir] Basil Spence (1907–76), Scottish architect. Designed new university buildings,

housing estates, and pavilions for the Festival of Britain (1951). His prize design for the new Coventry Cathedral (1951) was his best known.

33 Peter de Francia to JB, 17 September 1951. JB accepted, 19 September 1951. *BBCWA*.
34 Peter de Francia, internal BBC memo, 12 October 1951. *BBCWA*.
35 Peter de Francia, internal BBC memo, 30 October 1951. On Rooney Pelletier see Humphrey Carpenter, *The Envy of the World: Fifty Years of the BBC Third Programme and Radio 3*, London 1996, pp. 166, 172 and 223.
36 Peter Black, *The Mirror in the Corner*, London 1972, p. 16.
37 Cecil McGivern to Stephen McCormack, internal BBC memo, 14 July 1952. BBCWA.
38 Richard Dimbleby (1913–65), broadcaster and journalist. In 1946 he became a freelance broadcaster, in demand for covering royal occasions.
39 JB to Stephen McCormack, 8 September 1951. *BBCWA*.
40 JB to Stephen McCormack, 17 October 1952. *BBCWA*.
41 *BBC Recordings Archive*.
42 David Attenborough to JB, 1954. *BBCWA*.
43 Sir David Attenborough to CLG, 1992. JB, *Letters*, ed. CLG, ii, 377.
44 Nancy Thomas to JB, 4 November 1955. *BBCWA*.
45 On Mary Adams and the founding and course of *Animal, Vegetable, Mineral?* see Jacquetta Hawkes, *Sir Mortimer Wheeler: Adventurer in Archaeology*, London 1982.
46 *Ibid.*, p. 229.
47 Quoted, *ibid.*, p. 300.
48 JB to Nancy Thomas, 7 November 1955. *BBCWA*.
49 Marie Bingham to JB, 18 November 1955. *BBCWA*.
50 Michael Ayrton (1920–75), English sculptor, painter, book illustrator and art critic.
51 Internal BBC minute, 5 December 1955. *BBCWA*.
52 JB to John Piper, 16 July 1955. JB, *Letters*, ed. CLG, ii, 54.
53 *Ibid.*
54 As CLG recalls, JB, *Letters*, ed. CLG, ii, 55.
55 George Barnes, internal BBC memo, 20 August 1955. *BBCWA*.
56 George Barnes to John Read, 22 February 1956. *BBCWA*.
57 Comments of JB noted down by George Barnes, 14 February 1956. *BBCWA*.
58 JB to Miss D.E. Knight, 16 October 1957. *BBCWA*.
59 *Ibid.*
60 The BBC wrote to Blunt on 26 April 1956. He was away at the time. *BBCWA*.
61 Sir Anthony Blunt to Nancy Thomas, 4 May 1956. *BBCWA*.
62 JB to Nancy Thomas, 17 December 1956. *BBCWA*.

Chapter 32: Preservationist's Progress

1 *The Times*, 16 August 1950.
2 I am grateful to Mr Iain Sproat for this anecdote.
3 Margaret Thatcher, *The Path to Power*, London 1995, pp. 75–76.
4 *The Times*, 12 September 1952.
5 Quoted, *The Times*, 3 February 1953.
6 Both quotations are from John-Paul Flintoff, *Comp: A Survivor's Tale*, London 1999 edn., p. 28.
7 *Ibid.*, pp. 28–29.
8 *The Times*, 29 May 1954.
9 *The Times*, 2 June 1954.
10 *Loc. cit.*
11 The late James Lees-Milne told the present author (interview, 1992) that when he suggested to JB that the sacraments of the Christian religion were much more important than church architecture, JB agreed, 'but I felt his heart was not in the agreement'.
12 *The Times*, 25 October 1954.
13 *The Times*, 28 April 1955.

14 *The Times*, 16 May 1955.
15 The poem was 'Inland Waterway', *Collected Poems*, 2001 edn., p. 338.
16 *The Times*, 21 January 1956.
17 *The Times*, 4 February 1956.
18 *The Times*, 9 February 1956.
19 *The Times*, 27 February 1956.
20 P. Morton Shand to JB, 21 October 1958. *Major Bruce Shand.*
21 *The Times*, 11 May 1957.
22 *The Times*, 3 June 1957.
23 *The Times*, 7 June 1957.
24 *The Times*, 13 June 1957.
25 *The Times*, 15 June 1957.
26 Agatha Christie, *They Do It with Mirrors*, London 1952 edn., p. 24.
27 Quoted, *Times Literary Supplement*, 22 June 1973.
28 *The New Yorker*, June 1956.
29 Christie, *op. cit.*, p. 24.
30 *The Times*, 19 October 1957.
31 *Ibid.*
32 See YB, p. 259.
33 *The Times*, 24 October 1957.
34 *Ibid.*
35 See Woodrow Wyatt, foreword to John Martin Robinson, *The Wyatts: An Architectural Dynasty*, Oxford 1979.
36 Jacob Rothschild called Wyatt 'Toad of Tote Hall', in reference to Wyatt's being chairman of the Tote (Horserace Totalisator Board). See *The Journals of Woodrow Wyatt*, ed. Sarah Curtis, London 1999 edn., i, 211.
37 Sir Peter Parker (1924–2002), chairman, British Rail Board, 1976–83. On his friendship with JB, see the chapter 'His Last Bow' in the third volume of the present work.
38 Gillian, Lady Parker (*née* Rowe-Dutton) was JB's doctor in his later years. See the chapter 'His Last Bow' in the third volume of the present work.
39 Anthony Hobson was a friend of Anthony Powell. See Anthony Powell, *Journals 1982–1986*, London 1995, pp. 33, 77–78, 97–98, 107, 112, 137, 162, 192, 229, 236, 266 and 267; *ibid. 1987–1989*, London 1996, pp. 27, 39, 40, 45, 72, 103, 106, 185 and 187; and *ibid. 1990–1992*, London 1997, pp. 30–31, 34, 49, 57, 58, 65, 66 and 144.
40 On Tanya Hobson, see *ibid. 1982–1986*, pp. 33, 77, 97, 98, 112, 137, 162, 192, 224, 236, 266 and 267; and *ibid. 1987–1989*, pp. 27, 40, 45, 72, 103, 106 and 107–08.
41 JB's friend John Summerson, who in 1958 was Slade Professor of Fine Art, Oxford, had written *John Nash, Architect to George IV*, London 1935.
42 In his diary (31 December 1986), Woodrow Wyatt recorded that he and Richard Dimbleby were founder members of the BBC television news programme *Panorama*. See *The Journals of Woodrow Wyatt*, ed. Sarah Curtis, London 1999 edn., i, 257.
43 *Ibid.* (4 December 1986), 239.
44 Anthony Hobson, letter to the author, 8 June 2002.

Chapter 33: Cincinnati

1 For information on the life and works of George Elliston I am indebted, except where otherwise stated, to the Cincinnati Historical Society.
2 *Ex inf.* Judge Gilbert Bettman, interview, 1989.
3 In the collections of the Cincinnati Historical Society are two group photographs of the editors of the *Harvard Advocate*, both of which include the young Eliot and Wulsin.
4 Quoted by Wulsin's son, John Wulsin, interview, 1989.
5 'The only thing I know about Coffin, besides that he wrote bad poetry,' said Keith Stewart, a Cincinnati English lecturer (interview, 1989) 'is that he painted a picture of Stephen

Foster's Old Kentucky Home above the entrance to the Elliston Room. It has now been obliterated. It's too bad.'

6 Quoted, John Haffenden, *The Life of John Berryman*, Boston and London 1982, p. 225.
7 Quoted, *ibid.*, p. 226.
8 *Ex inf.* Elizabeth Bettman, interview, 1989.
9 *Ibid.* However, Senator Robert Taft allowed Spender to use as a lecture hall the magnificent 'Federal' mansion of the Taft family.
10 Ian Hamilton, *Robert Lowell: A Biography*, London 1983, p. 209.
11 Elizabeth Bettman, interview, 1989.
12 George Ford, quoted Hamilton, *op. cit.*, p. 209.
13 Judge Gilbert Bettman, interview, 1989.
14 *Ibid.*
15 Hamilton, *op. cit.*, p. 213.
16 Quoted, Keith Stewart, interview, 1989.
17 *Ex inf.* Elizabeth Bettman, interview, 1989.
18 Quoted, Keith Stewart, interview, 1989.
19 William Clark had business in Oxford: his book *The Early Irish Stage* was published by the Clarendon Press that year. With difficulty he and his wife found rooms in Faringdon, at the run-down Salutation Hotel. The memorable day which followed made a gala entry for Gladys Clark's journal (extracts kindly supplied to the author by Mrs Clark):

> *Fri. June 24* . . . Isabelle, Penny and I were eating breakfast at 9 when I had a phone call from Mrs Betjeman asking us to come on a picnic, ride horses and see houses (all spoken in one breath) . . . we immediately went across to Faringdon House where Robert [Heber] Percy, nephew of Lord Burners [*sic*] lived. At the house, Mrs Betjeman opened the front door with a sign over the bell 'Mangling done here' . . . We met the lord of the manor – a tall, very good-looking young man in his working clothes. He was most affable, and . . . pointed out the stuffed birds and a pheasant in front of a pretty border of mesembryanthemum.

> Inside, Gladys was shown a Matisse, a Picasso, three Constables and a Guardi. 'There seemed to be curious things set about on the tables, which Mr Percy showed us with delight – an alligator that jumped, a monkey that leaped at you when a rubber ball was punched, and various other prankish animals.'

> We . . . went on to Wantage to the 'Duck Farm', the Betjeman estate. The house was not too attractive outside, but very liveable within . . . We arrived first at the Lloyd [*sic*] grounds of 20,000 acres at Lockinge. Mrs Lloyd was very cordial to us, and when the others came, showed us the beautiful collection of paintings gathered by Lord Wantage (an ancestor) . . . Mr Christopher Lloyd came in to greet us as we were drinking sherry. He is about 30 years old and one of Princess Margaret's friends. Extremely good-looking and friendly, he managed the whole estate.

> . . .

> Carrying our picnic lunch, we walked down a grassy slope, spread a cloth, and waited for John Betjeman to appear from Oxford, on a road we could see from our resting place. We found both of them delightful conversationalists . . . Mrs B. was the Honourable Penelope Chetwode . . . Before she was married she was lady-in-waiting to Queen Elizabeth, but was not interested in society. She now raises horses, ducks and geese to sell. We spread rugs on the grass and had a delicious, but unusual lunch of cold salmon, cucumbers, rolls and ginger beer.

In 1989, aged eighty-eight, Gladys Clark remembered that Penelope had said to her, offhandedly, while pouring the ginger beer, 'I don't know what you Americans like for picnics.'
20 General concurrence among Cincinnati academics, interviews, 1989.
21 JB kept his side of the bargain: in September 1957, six months after the Cincinnati sojourn, PB and Candida were in the Tuscan hill town of Montepulciano.

22 JB, letter to Anne Barnes, 21 June 1956. JB, *Letters*, ed. CLG, ii, 93.
23 *Archives of the University of Cincinnati.*
24 *Cincinnati Enquirer*, 24 February 1957.
25 *Ibid.*
26 For a view of the New York docks in 1957, see the film *The Line-Up* (1958), starring Eli Wallach.
27 Letter kindly shown to the author by Lady Silvia Combe.
28 Brendan Gill, 'Poet on Stopover', *New Yorker*, March 1957.
29 *Ibid.*
30 *Cincinnati Times-Star*, 28 February 1957.
31 *Ibid.*
32 The unpublished journal of Van Meter Ames, kindly shown to the author by his widow, Mrs Betty Ames.
33 *Archives of the University of Cincinnati.*
34 *Ibid.*
35 Keith Stewart, interview, 1989.
36 Professor Alvin Greenberg, interview, 1989.
37 *Ibid.*
38 *Ibid.*
39 Betty Stewart, interview, 1989.
40 Keith Stewart, interview, 1989.
41 John Wulsin, interview, 1989.
42 Elizabeth Bettman, interview, 1989.
43 *Ibid.*
44 This and other details about Elizabeth Bettman's life are, except where otherwise stated, from interviews with her in 1989.
45 Interview, 1989 (name withheld by request).
46 Elizabeth Bettman, interview, 1989.
47 *Ibid.*
48 Alister ('Hamish') Cameron was the author of *The Pythagorean Background of the Theory of Recollection*, Menasha, Wisconsin 1938. Sophocles was his special interest. 'Gil used to call Hamish's book on Sophocles his "Penelope's Web",' said Liz Bettman. 'It took for ever and ever . . . We used to think he undid it at night. John Berryman helped him with it. And they were devoted friends. I think "Puggy" [Cameron's wife] got really jealous of their relationship.' (Interview, 1989.) Hamish Cameron was also a heroic drinker.
49 Extract from poem kindly shown to the author by Van Meter Ames's widow, Betty.
50 PB to Lady Silvia Combe, 19 March 1957. Kindly shown to the author by Lady Silvia Combe.
51 Hugh Maclean, letter to the author, 12 October 1990.
52 Keith Stewart, interview, 1989.
53 George Ford, letter to the author, 17 November 1989.
54 Walter Langsam, interview, 1989.
55 Judge Gilbert Bettman, interview, 1989.
56 JB, letter to Van Meter Ames, 6 April 1957. Kindly shown to the author by Mrs Betty Ames.
57 Sir Osbert Lancaster, interview, 1977.
58 Longfellow had written lines about the sparkling wine produced by the Longworth Wineries, known as Golden Wedding Champagne –

>   the richest and the best
>   Is the wine of the West
>   That grows by the beautiful river . . .

59 Mrs Melissa Lanier, interview, 1989.
60 *Ibid.* Nancy Astor (*née* Langhorne, 1879–1964) was the sister of Irene Langhorne (1873–1956) who married the artist Charles Dana Gibson (1867–1944), creator of the

Gibson Girl. It may have been Nancy Astor or her niece Nancy Lancaster (1897–1994), the interior decorator, who introduced the Betjemans to the Emerys.

On Nancy Astor, Nancy Lancaster and Nora Phipps (later Bennet Flynn), see James Fox, *The Langhorne Sisters*, London 1998.

61 Kindly shown to the author by Mrs Melissa Lanier.

62 President Taft was a Cincinnatian. John met his son, Senator Robert Taft, who tried to talk to him about British politics and denounced the iniquities of British 'socialized medicine'. (Professor John Press, letter to the author, 13 January 1990.)

63 PB to Lady Silvia Combe, 19 March 1957. Kindly shown to the author by Lady Silvia Combe.

64 Mrs Rosamund Wulsin, interview, 1989.

65 *Ibid.*

66 Judge Gilbert Bettman, interview, 1989.

67 Judge Gilbert Bettman's uncle, Alfred Bettman, is known in America as 'the father of city planning', having argued the original zoning-law case, *Euclid* v *Amber Realty*, in the Supreme Court in 1923.

68 In 1987, when the Bellevue Park Overlook was renamed the Daniel J. Ransohoff Overlook in his honour, an editorial in the *Cincinnati Post* (5 December 1987) said: 'He has peddled and pushed the glories of the Queen City to anyone who would listen, for more than 40 years.'

69 Danny Ransohoff, interview, 1989.

70 Quoted, *ibid.*

71 JB, 'To See Oursel's As Ithers See Us', *Cincinnati Enquirer*, 24 April 1957.

72 Cedric Boulter was an expert on Greek vase-painting.

73 JB, 'To See Oursel's As Ithers See Us', *Cincinnati Enquirer*, 24 April 1957.

74 JB and PB were photographed in front of such a gas-lamp: see *JBLP*, p. 135. In the background of the photograph is the Temple of Love, which JB also admired.

75 *Cincinnati Times-Star*, 12 March 1957.

76 JB, 'To See Oursel's As Ithers See us', *Cincinnati Enquirer*, 24 April 1957.

77 *Cincinnati Times-Star*, 12 March 1957.

78 *Ibid.*

79 Rankin's Cincinnati friend, the Rev. Lyman Beecher, visited him often, sometimes with his daughter Harriet – later Harriet Beecher Stowe – who listened to Rankin's tales and, in *Uncle Tom's Cabin*, described how a runaway slave girl, Eliza, escaped her pursuers by leaping from one ice floe to another across the Ohio River, to Ripley and freedom.

80 *Cincinnati Times-Star*, 12 March 1957.

81 *Archives of the University of Cincinnati.*

82 George Ford, letter to the author, 17 November 1989.

83 Unpublished journal of Van Meter Ames, 27 March 1957. The journal was kindly shown to the author by Mrs Betty Ames.

84 *Ibid.*

85 *Ibid.*, 24 March 1957.

86 *Archives of the University of Cincinnati.*

87 Unpublished journal of Van Meter Ames, 28 March 1957.

88 *Ibid.*

89 Professor Alvin Greenberg, interview, 1989.

90 Unpublished journal of Van Meter Ames, 31 March 1957.

91 PB to Mollie Baring, 19 March 1957. Kindly shown to the author by Mrs Baring.

92 PB to Lucien Wulsin, 8 April 1957. Kindly shown to the author by Mr John Wulsin.

93 However, a version of it was later published in *Country Life*.

94 According to Lady Harrod, letter to the author, 23 September 1988.

95 Mr Dominick Harrod, conversation, 1995.

96 *Ex inf.* Mrs Rosamund Wulsin, interview, 1989.

97 Mrs Gladys Clark, letter to the author (drawing on her journal of 1962), 27 August 1989.

98 Lehmann's photograph of this performance is reproduced in *JBLP*, p. 128.

99 Keith Stewart, letter to the author, 23 November 1989.

100 JB to Candida Betjeman, 12 March 1957. JB, *Letters*, ed. CLG, ii, 122.
101 Edmund White, *The Beautiful Room is Empty*, London 1988, p. 7.
102 PB, letter to Lady Silvia Combe, 19 March 1957. Kindly shown to the author by Lady Silvia Combe.
103 *Ibid*.
104 *The Spectator*, 12 April 1957.

Chapter 34: In the Late 1950s

1 Violet Trefusis to Lord Kinross, 11 November 1954. *Huntington*.
2 Mike Todd, film star and third husband of Elizabeth Taylor. Killed in an air crash, 1958.
3 Ann Fleming to Evelyn Waugh, 5 July [1957]. *The Letters of Ann Fleming*, ed. Mark Amory, London 1985, pp. 203-04.
4 JB, *Letters*, ed. CLG, ii, 51.
5 Kathleen Philip, interview, 1976.
6 CLG remembers 'Teddy boys in suede shoes'. JB, *Letters*, ed. CLG, ii, 51.
7 Mark Bence-Jones, *Burke's Guide to Country Houses*, vol. 1: *Ireland*, London 1978, p. 186. See also James Lees-Milne, *The Bachelor Duke*, London 1991.
8 JB, *Letters*, ed. CLG, ii, 159n.
9 *Loc. cit.*
10 *Loc. cit.*
11 The black composer Samuel Coleridge-Taylor (1875-1912) wrote the choral works *Hiawatha's Wedding Feast* (1989), *The Death of Minnehaha* (1899) and *Hiawatha's Departure* (1900).
12 JB, *Letters*, ed. CLG, ii, 138-39.
13 JB wrote to Lord Kinross on 29 June 1954 (JB, *Letters*, ed. CLG, ii, 68): 'Penelope asked the Wemysses to stay my dear without realising from the time they came to the time they went how very grand they were. I've never been through so much embarrassment . . . I have had a sore throat from anxiety ever since.'
14 JB, *Letters*, ed. CLG, ii, 135n.
15 CLG (*ibid.*, 106) writes 'Swedish' but this is not correct.
16 JB, 'Guano and Golden Eagles', *The Spectator*, 16 May 1958, p. 616.
17 *Loc. cit.*
18 *Loc. cit.*
19 *Loc. cit.*
20 *Loc. cit.*
21 *Loc. cit.*
22 *Loc. cit.* Also, JB, *Letters*, ed. CLG, ii, 106.
23 JB, 'Guano and Golden Eagles', p. 617. For a less polite version of what JB thought about the RAF's depredations on St Kilda, see JB to John Summerson, 3 May 1958. JB, *Letters*, ed. CLG, ii, 141.
24 JB, 'Guano and Golden Eagles', p. 617.
25 *Loc. cit.*
26 *Loc. cit.*
27 *Loc. cit.* On 28 April 1958 JB wrote to PB about this experience, from the *Meteor*: 'What was it? No one knew. I shall never forget it' (*JBP*).
28 JB, *Letters*, ed. CLG, ii, 106.
29 Dr Richard Squires recalled (interview, 1976): 'Angela Wakeford was about forty-five to fifty in the late 1950s. She was an old friend of Penelope's, very manic, interested in art and every aspect of Penelope's life. Chattered ceaselessly. She had very good taste in art and all the places she lived in were immaculate . . . Her husband was also immaculate. Perfect tailored suits, waistcoats, bow tie, greying hair and a very precise old-fashioned way of speaking. On occasion he even wore spats – he looked like a character out of Dickens.'
30 JB was a member of the Oxford Diocesan Advisory Committee. JB, *Letters*, ed. CLG, i, 376.

31 JB to CLG, May 1958. JB, *Letters*, ed. CLG, ii, 106.
32 Dr Richard Squires, interview, 1976.
33 JB, *Letters*, ed. CLG, ii, 102. Also, Dr Richard Squires, interviews, 1976 and 1989.
34 Dr Richard Squires, interview, 1976.
35 For Paul Betjeman's Fourth in geography, see *Oxford University Calendar*, Oxford 1964, p. 214.
36 The poem 'Village Wedding', appeared in the *New Yorker* of 11 July 1959 and is reproduced in full in JB, *Letters*, ed. CLG, ii, 106–07.
         The fourth stanza (of seven) runs:

                    Inside the church in every pew
                      Sit old friends, older grown now;
                    Their children whom our children knew
                      Have children of their own now.

37 JB, *Letters*, ed. CLG, ii, 107.
38 *Loc. cit.*
39 *Loc. cit.*
40 *The Times*, 17 November 1958.
41 Lord Wicklow to JB, 3 October 1958. *Victoria.*
42 JB to Cecil Roberts, 13 February 1959. JB, *Letters*, ed. CLG, ii, 167.
43 Quoted, *ibid.*, 157.
44 JB to Deborah, Duchess of Devonshire, 1 May 1959. *Ibid.*, 169.
45 See the chapter '*Summoned by Bells*' in the third volume of the present work.
46 JB, *Letters*, ed. CLG, ii, 156.
47 *Loc. cit.*
48 *Loc. cit.*
49 *Loc. cit.*
50 *JBP.*
51 JB to PB, 6 November 1959. *JBP.*
52 JB to PB, 12 November 1959. *JBP.*

Chapter 35: 'A Really Thrilling Moment of Triumph'

 1 *The Tablet*, 24 July 1954.
 2 *John Murray archives.*
 3 Republished, *Collected Poems*, 2001 edn., pp. 393–94.
 4 *John Murray archives.*
 5 *Ibid.*
 6 The Earl of Birkenhead, *FE: The Life of F.E. Smith, First Earl of Birkenhead*, London 1960.
 7 (Sir) Osbert Lancaster, interview, 1978.
 8 *John Murray archives.*
 9 *Ibid.*
10 *Ibid.*
11 See B. Hillier, *The Style of the Century*, London 1983, pp. 205–10.
12 *John Murray archives.*
13 *Ibid.*
14 *Ibid.*
15 JB, *Letters*, ed. CLG, ii, 110.
16 *John Murray archives.*
17 *Ibid.*
18 *Ibid.*
19 *Ibid.*
20 *Ibid.*

21 *Ibid.*
22 *Ibid.*
23 *Ibid.*
24 *Ibid.*
25 *Ibid.*
26 *Ibid.*
27 One can see something of what Mortimer meant, from a French review of the *Collected Poems* sent to Murray by its cuttings agency. It contained a translation by M. Chiari of John's poem on the death of Basil Dufferin –

> Cessez, ô cloches innombrables, cessez
> De deverser sur les roses et le lierre
> Vos carillons oublieux
> En ce jour vide et non béni de victoire en Europe, –
> Je suis sourd à vos notes, et je gis mort
> A côté du cadavre d'un soldat en Birmanie.

28 *Punch*, 17 December 1958.
29 *Collected Poems*, 2001 edn., p. 234.
30 *Punch*, 17 December 1958.
31 *Ibid.*
32 *The Spectator*, 19 December 1958.
33 *Time and Tide*, 27 December 1958.
34 *The Listener*, 15 January 1959.
35 *Gemini*, Summer 1959.
36 *The Critics*, BBC, 30 November 1958.
37 *Ibid.*
38 *New Statesman*, 6 December 1958.
39 Cutting from the *Hawkes Bay Herald-Times* (date indistinct). *John Murray archives.*
40 *John Murray archives.*
41 *Time*, 2 February 1959.
42 *New York Times*, 13 April 1959.
43 *New York Times Review of Books*, 12 April 1959.
44 *Ibid.* The book's prodigious sales (in the first two and a half months after publication, 33,400 copies were sold) will be treated in the third volume of the present work, as will further reviews of it in 1959.
45 See note 49 to the present chapter.
46 Enid Bagnold (1889–1981), novelist, married 1920 Sir Roderick Jones, for twenty-five years chairman of Reuters. On Jones, see James Lees-Milne, *Another Self*, London 1984 edn., pp. 122–25 and 130–31.
47 *John Murray archives.*
48 *Evening Standard*, 18 December 1958.
49 Lady Diana Cooper to Lord Kinross, 13 December 1958. She also wrote:

> They, the intelligentsia at Oxford, all but gave the prize to de Gaulle! Thank God the idea was scotched, and it's gone to Betj. Please be at the party. I will be in London . . .

50 On Judy Montagu, see Helen Cathcart, *Princess Margaret*, London 1974, pp. 89 and 115; also *The Noël Coward Diaries*, ed. Graham Payn and Sheridan Morley, London 1982, pp. 236, 244 and 438.
51 Quoted, Philip Ziegler, *Diana Cooper*, London 1981, p. 310.
52 *News Chronicle*, 19 December 1958.
53 *Ibid.*
54 *Daily Express*, 19 December 1958.
55 Quoted, Ziegler, *op. cit.*, p. 310.
56 Quoted, *Daily Telegraph*, 19 December 1958.
57 *News Chronicle*, 19 December 1958.

58 Lady Diana Cooper, quoted, Ziegler, *op. cit.*, p. 310.
59 *Loc. cit.*
60 Quoted, Andrew Lycett, *Ian Fleming*, London 1995, p. 231n.
61 'The red velvet edition of *Collected Poems* in its Morocco box was limited to only three: one for JB, one for the Queen and one for J[ock] M[urray]. The cost of binding them up was thirty pounds each.' JB, *Letters*, ed. CLG, ii, 149n. Presumably the copy presented to Princess Margaret on 18 December 1958 was intended for the Queen.
62 JB to John G. Murray, Christmas Day 1958. JB, *Letters*, ed. CLG, ii, 149.

INDEX